T0180650

Lecture Notes in Computer Science   12954

More information about this subseries at http://www.springer.com/series/7407

Osvaldo Gervasi · Beniamino Murgante ·
Sanjay Misra · Chiara Garau ·
Ivan Blečić · David Taniar ·
Bernady O. Apduhan · Ana Maria A. C. Rocha ·
Eufemia Tarantino · Carmelo Maria Torre (Eds.)

Computational Science and Its Applications – ICCSA 2021

21st International Conference
Cagliari, Italy, September 13–16, 2021
Proceedings, Part VI

 Springer

Editors
Osvaldo Gervasi ⓘ
University of Perugia
Perugia, Italy

Beniamino Murgante ⓘ
University of Basilicata
Potenza, Potenza, Italy

Sanjay Misra ⓘ
Covenant University
Ota, Nigeria

Chiara Garau ⓘ
University of Cagliari
Cagliari, Italy

Ivan Blečić ⓘ
University of Cagliari
Cagliari, Italy

David Taniar ⓘ
Monash University
Clayton, VIC, Australia

Bernady O. Apduhan
Kyushu Sangyo University
Fukuoka, Japan

Ana Maria A. C. Rocha ⓘ
University of Minho
Braga, Portugal

Eufemia Tarantino ⓘ
Polytechnic University of Bari
Bari, Italy

Carmelo Maria Torre ⓘ
Polytechnic University of Bari
Bari, Italy

ISSN 0302-9743   ISSN 1611-3349   (electronic)
Lecture Notes in Computer Science
ISBN 978-3-030-86978-6   ISBN 978-3-030-86979-3   (eBook)
https://doi.org/10.1007/978-3-030-86979-3

LNCS Sublibrary: SL1 – Theoretical Computer Science and General Issues

This Springer imprint is published by the registered company Springer Nature Switzerland AG
The registered company address is: Gewerbestrasse 11, 6330 Cham, Switzerland

Preface

These 10 volumes (LNCS volumes 12949–12958) consist of the peer-reviewed papers from the 21st International Conference on Computational Science and Its Applications (ICCSA 2021) which took place during September 13–16, 2021. By virtue of the vaccination campaign conducted in various countries around the world, we decided to try a hybrid conference, with some of the delegates attending in person at the University of Cagliari and others attending in virtual mode, reproducing the infrastructure established last year.

This year's edition was a successful continuation of the ICCSA conference series, which was also held as a virtual event in 2020, and previously held in Saint Petersburg, Russia (2019), Melbourne, Australia (2018), Trieste, Italy (2017), Beijing. China (2016), Banff, Canada (2015), Guimaraes, Portugal (2014), Ho Chi Minh City, Vietnam (2013), Salvador, Brazil (2012), Santander, Spain (2011), Fukuoka, Japan (2010), Suwon, South Korea (2009), Perugia, Italy (2008), Kuala Lumpur, Malaysia (2007), Glasgow, UK (2006), Singapore (2005), Assisi, Italy (2004), Montreal, Canada (2003), and (as ICCS) Amsterdam, The Netherlands (2002) and San Francisco, USA (2001).

Computational science is the main pillar of most of the present research on understanding and solving complex problems. It plays a unique role in exploiting innovative ICT technologies and in the development of industrial and commercial applications. The ICCSA conference series provides a venue for researchers and industry practitioners to discuss new ideas, to share complex problems and their solutions, and to shape new trends in computational science.

Apart from the six main conference tracks, ICCSA 2021 also included 52 workshops in various areas of computational sciences, ranging from computational science technologies to specific areas of computational sciences, such as software engineering, security, machine learning and artificial intelligence, blockchain technologies, and applications in many fields. In total, we accepted 494 papers, giving an acceptance rate of 30%, of which 18 papers were short papers and 6 were published open access. We would like to express our appreciation for the workshop chairs and co-chairs for their hard work and dedication.

The success of the ICCSA conference series in general, and of ICCSA 2021 in particular, vitally depends on the support of many people: authors, presenters, participants, keynote speakers, workshop chairs, session chairs, organizing committee members, student volunteers, Program Committee members, advisory committee members, international liaison chairs, reviewers, and others in various roles. We take this opportunity to wholeheartedly thank them all.

We also wish to thank Springer for publishing the proceedings, for sponsoring some of the best paper awards, and for their kind assistance and cooperation during the editing process.

We cordially invite you to visit the ICCSA website https://iccsa.org where you can find all the relevant information about this interesting and exciting event.

September 2021

Osvaldo Gervasi
Beniamino Murgante
Sanjay Misra

Welcome Message from the Organizers

COVID-19 has continued to alter our plans for organizing the ICCSA 2021 conference, so although vaccination plans are progressing worldwide, the spread of virus variants still forces us into a period of profound uncertainty. Only a very limited number of participants were able to enjoy the beauty of Sardinia and Cagliari in particular, rediscovering the immense pleasure of meeting again, albeit safely spaced out. The social events, in which we rediscovered the ancient values that abound on this wonderful island and in this city, gave us even more strength and hope for the future. For the management of the virtual part of the conference, we consolidated the methods, organization, and infrastructure of ICCSA 2020.

The technological infrastructure was based on open source software, with the addition of the streaming channels on YouTube. In particular, we used Jitsi (jitsi.org) for videoconferencing, Riot (riot.im) together with Matrix (matrix.org) for chat and ansynchronous communication, and Jibri (github.com/jitsi/jibri) for streaming live sessions to YouTube.

Seven Jitsi servers were set up, one for each parallel session. The participants of the sessions were helped and assisted by eight student volunteers (from the universities of Cagliari, Florence, Perugia, and Bari), who provided technical support and ensured smooth running of the conference proceedings.

The implementation of the software infrastructure and the technical coordination of the volunteers were carried out by Damiano Perri and Marco Simonetti.

Our warmest thanks go to all the student volunteers, to the technical coordinators, and to the development communities of Jitsi, Jibri, Riot, and Matrix, who made their terrific platforms available as open source software.

A big thank you goes to all of the 450 speakers, many of whom showed an enormous collaborative spirit, sometimes participating and presenting at almost prohibitive times of the day, given that the participants of this year's conference came from 58 countries scattered over many time zones of the globe.

Finally, we would like to thank Google for letting us stream all the live events via YouTube. In addition to lightening the load of our Jitsi servers, this allowed us to record the event and to be able to review the most exciting moments of the conference.

Ivan Blečić
Chiara Garau

Organization

ICCSA 2021 was organized by the University of Cagliari (Italy), the University of Perugia (Italy), the University of Basilicata (Italy), Monash University (Australia), Kyushu Sangyo University (Japan), and the University of Minho (Portugal).

Honorary General Chairs

Norio Shiratori	Chuo University, Japan
Kenneth C. J. Tan	Sardina Systems, UK
Corrado Zoppi	University of Cagliari, Italy

General Chairs

Osvaldo Gervasi	University of Perugia, Italy
Ivan Blečić	University of Cagliari, Italy
David Taniar	Monash University, Australia

Program Committee Chairs

Beniamino Murgante	University of Basilicata, Italy
Bernady O. Apduhan	Kyushu Sangyo University, Japan
Chiara Garau	University of Cagliari, Italy
Ana Maria A. C. Rocha	University of Minho, Portugal

International Advisory Committee

Jemal Abawajy	Deakin University, Australia
Dharma P. Agarwal	University of Cincinnati, USA
Rajkumar Buyya	University of Melbourne, Australia
Claudia Bauzer Medeiros	University of Campinas, Brazil
Manfred M. Fisher	Vienna University of Economics and Business, Austria
Marina L. Gavrilova	University of Calgary, Canada
Yee Leung	Chinese University of Hong Kong, China

International Liaison Chairs

Giuseppe Borruso	University of Trieste, Italy
Elise De Donker	Western Michigan University, USA
Maria Irene Falcão	University of Minho, Portugal
Robert C. H. Hsu	Chung Hua University, Taiwan
Tai-Hoon Kim	Beijing Jaotong University, China

Vladimir Korkhov   St. Petersburg University, Russia
Sanjay Misra   Covenant University, Nigeria
Takashi Naka   Kyushu Sangyo University, Japan
Rafael D. C. Santos   National Institute for Space Research, Brazil
Maribel Yasmina Santos   University of Minho, Portugal
Elena Stankova   St. Petersburg University, Russia

Workshop and Session Chairs

Beniamino Murgante   University of Basilicata, Italy
Sanjay Misra   Covenant University, Nigeria
Jorge Gustavo Rocha   University of Minho, Portugal

Awards Chair

Wenny Rahayu   La Trobe University, Australia

Publicity Committee Chairs

Elmer Dadios   De La Salle University, Philippines
Nataliia Kulabukhova   St. Petersburg University, Russia
Daisuke Takahashi   Tsukuba University, Japan
Shangwang Wang   Beijing University of Posts and Telecommunications,
                          China

Technology Chairs

Damiano Perri   University of Florence, Italy
Marco Simonetti   University of Florence, Italy

Local Arrangement Chairs

Ivan Blečić   University of Cagliari, Italy
Chiara Garau   University of Cagliari, Italy
Alfonso Annunziata   University of Cagliari, Italy
Ginevra Balletto   University of Cagliari, Italy
Giuseppe Borruso   University of Trieste, Italy
Alessandro Buccini   University of Cagliari, Italy
Michele Campagna   University of Cagliari, Italy
Mauro Coni   University of Cagliari, Italy
Anna Maria Colavitti   University of Cagliari, Italy
Giulia Desogus   University of Cagliari, Italy
Caterina Fenu   University of Cagliari, Italy
Sabrina Lai   University of Cagliari, Italy
Francesca Maltinti   University of Cagliari, Italy
Pasquale Mistretta   University of Cagliari, Italy

Augusto Montisci   University of Cagliari, Italy
Francesco Pinna   University of Cagliari, Italy
Davide Spano   University of Cagliari, Italy
Giuseppe A. Trunfio   University of Sassari, Italy
Corrado Zoppi   University of Cagliari, Italy

Program Committee

Vera Afreixo   University of Aveiro, Portugal
Filipe Alvelos   University of Minho, Portugal
Hartmut Asche   University of Potsdam, Germany
Ginevra Balletto   University of Cagliari, Italy
Michela Bertolotto   University College Dublin, Ireland
Sandro Bimonte   INRAE-TSCF, France
Rod Blais   University of Calgary, Canada
Ivan Blečić   University of Sassari, Italy
Giuseppe Borruso   University of Trieste, Italy
Ana Cristina Braga   University of Minho, Portugal
Massimo Cafaro   University of Salento, Italy
Yves Caniou   University of Lyon, France
José A. Cardoso e Cunha Universidade Nova de Lisboa, Portugal
Rui Cardoso   University of Beira Interior, Portugal
Leocadio G. Casado   University of Almeria, Spain
Carlo Cattani   University of Salerno, Italy
Mete Celik   Erciyes University, Turkey
Maria Cerreta   University of Naples "Federico II", Italy
Hyunseung Choo   Sungkyunkwan University, South Korea
Chien-Sing Lee   Sunway University, Malaysia
Min Young Chung   Sungkyunkwan University, South Korea
Florbela Maria da Cruz Polytechnic Institute of Viana do Castelo, Portugal
   Domingues Correia
Gilberto Corso Pereira Federal University of Bahia, Brazil
Fernanda Costa   University of Minho, Portugal
Alessandro Costantini   INFN, Italy
Carla Dal Sasso Freitas Universidade Federal do Rio Grande do Sul, Brazil
Pradesh Debba   The Council for Scientific and Industrial Research
                           (CSIR), South Africa
Hendrik Decker   Instituto Tecnológico de Informática, Spain
Robertas Damaševičius   Kausan University of Technology, Lithuania
Frank Devai   London South Bank University, UK
Rodolphe Devillers   Memorial University of Newfoundland, Canada
Joana Matos Dias   University of Coimbra, Portugal
Paolino Di Felice   University of L'Aquila, Italy
Prabu Dorairaj   NetApp, India/USA
Noelia Faginas Lago   University of Perugia, Italy
M. Irene Falcao   University of Minho, Portugal

Cherry Liu Fang	Ames Laboratory, USA
Florbela P. Fernandes	Polytechnic Institute of Bragança, Portugal
Jose-Jesus Fernandez	National Centre for Biotechnology, Spain
Paula Odete Fernandes	Polytechnic Institute of Bragança, Portugal
Adelaide de Fátima Baptista Valente Freitas	University of Aveiro, Portugal
Manuel Carlos Figueiredo	University of Minho, Portugal
Maria Celia Furtado Rocha	Universidade Federal da Bahia, Brazil
Chiara Garau	University of Cagliari, Italy
Paulino Jose Garcia Nieto	University of Oviedo, Spain
Jerome Gensel	LSR-IMAG, France
Maria Giaoutzi	National Technical University of Athens, Greece
Arminda Manuela Andrade Pereira Gonçalves	University of Minho, Portugal
Andrzej M. Goscinski	Deakin University, Australia
Eduardo Guerra	Free University of Bozen-Bolzano, Italy
Sevin Gümgüm	Izmir University of Economics, Turkey
Alex Hagen-Zanker	University of Cambridge, UK
Shanmugasundaram Hariharan	B.S. Abdur Rahman University, India
Eligius M. T. Hendrix	University of Malaga, Spain/Wageningen University, The Netherlands
Hisamoto Hiyoshi	Gunma University, Japan
Mustafa Inceoglu	EGE University, Turkey
Peter Jimack	University of Leeds, UK
Qun Jin	Waseda University, Japan
Yeliz Karaca	University of Massachusetts Medical School, USA
Farid Karimipour	Vienna University of Technology, Austria
Baris Kazar	Oracle Corp., USA
Maulana Adhinugraha Kiki	Telkom University, Indonesia
DongSeong Kim	University of Canterbury, New Zealand
Taihoon Kim	Hannam University, South Korea
Ivana Kolingerova	University of West Bohemia, Czech Republic
Nataliia Kulabukhova	St. Petersburg University, Russia
Vladimir Korkhov	St. Petersburg University, Russia
Rosa Lasaponara	National Research Council, Italy
Maurizio Lazzari	National Research Council, Italy
Cheng Siong Lee	Monash University, Australia
Sangyoun Lee	Yonsei University, South Korea
Jongchan Lee	Kunsan National University, South Korea
Chendong Li	University of Connecticut, USA
Gang Li	Deakin University, Australia
Fang Liu	Ames Laboratory, USA
Xin Liu	University of Calgary, Canada
Andrea Lombardi	University of Perugia, Italy
Savino Longo	University of Bari, Italy

Tinghuai Ma	Nanjing University of Information Science and Technology, China
Ernesto Marcheggiani	Katholieke Universiteit Leuven, Belgium
Antonino Marvuglia	Research Centre Henri Tudor, Luxembourg
Nicola Masini	National Research Council, Italy
Ilaria Matteucci	National Research Council, Italy
Eric Medvet	University of Trieste, Italy
Nirvana Meratnia	University of Twente, The Netherlands
Giuseppe Modica	University of Reggio Calabria, Italy
Josè Luis Montaña	University of Cantabria, Spain
Maria Filipa Mourão	Instituto Politécnico de Viana do Castelo, Portugal
Louiza de Macedo Mourelle	State University of Rio de Janeiro, Brazil
Nadia Nedjah	State University of Rio de Janeiro, Brazil
Laszlo Neumann	University of Girona, Spain
Kok-Leong Ong	Deakin University, Australia
Belen Palop	Universidad de Valladolid, Spain
Marcin Paprzycki	Polish Academy of Sciences, Poland
Eric Pardede	La Trobe University, Australia
Kwangjin Park	Wonkwang University, South Korea
Ana Isabel Pereira	Polytechnic Institute of Bragança, Portugal
Massimiliano Pctri	University of Pisa, Italy
Telmo Pinto	University of Coimbra, Portugal
Maurizio Pollino	Italian National Agency for New Technologies, Energy and Sustainable Economic Development, Italy
Alenka Poplin	University of Hamburg, Germany
Vidyasagar Potdar	Curtin University of Technology, Australia
David C. Prosperi	Florida Atlantic University, USA
Wenny Rahayu	La Trobe University, Australia
Jerzy Respondek	Silesian University of Technology Poland
Humberto Rocha	INESC-Coimbra, Portugal
Jon Rokne	University of Calgary, Canada
Octavio Roncero	CSIC, Spain
Maytham Safar	Kuwait University, Kuwait
Francesco Santini	University of Perugia, Italy
Chiara Saracino	A.O. Ospedale Niguarda Ca' Granda, Italy
Haiduke Sarafian	Pennsylvania State University, USA
Marco Paulo Seabra dos Reis	University of Coimbra, Portugal
Jie Shen	University of Michigan, USA
Qi Shi	Liverpool John Moores University, UK
Dale Shires	U.S. Army Research Laboratory, USA
Inês Soares	University of Coimbra, Portugal
Elena Stankova	St. Petersburg University, Russia
Takuo Suganuma	Tohoku University, Japan
Eufemia Tarantino	Polytechnic University of Bari, Italy
Sergio Tasso	University of Perugia, Italy

Ana Paula Teixeira	University of Trás-os-Montes and Alto Douro, Portugal
Senhorinha Teixeira	University of Minho, Portugal
M. Filomena Teodoro	Portuguese Naval Academy/University of Lisbon, Portugal
Parimala Thulasiraman	University of Manitoba, Canada
Carmelo Torre	Polytechnic University of Bari, Italy
Javier Martinez Torres	Centro Universitario de la Defensa Zaragoza, Spain
Giuseppe A. Trunfio	University of Sassari, Italy
Pablo Vanegas	University of Cuenca, Equador
Marco Vizzari	University of Perugia, Italy
Varun Vohra	Merck Inc., USA
Koichi Wada	University of Tsukuba, Japan
Krzysztof Walkowiak	Wroclaw University of Technology, Poland
Zequn Wang	Intelligent Automation Inc, USA
Robert Weibel	University of Zurich, Switzerland
Frank Westad	Norwegian University of Science and Technology, Norway
Roland Wismüller	Universität Siegen, Germany
Mudasser Wyne	National University, USA
Chung-Huang Yang	National Kaohsiung Normal University, Taiwan
Xin-She Yang	National Physical Laboratory, UK
Salim Zabir	National Institute of Technology, Tsuruoka, Japan
Haifeng Zhao	University of California, Davis, USA
Fabiana Zollo	University of Venice "Cà Foscari", Italy
Albert Y. Zomaya	University of Sydney, Australia

Workshop Organizers

Advanced Transport Tools and Methods (A2TM 2021)

Massimiliano Petri	University of Pisa, Italy
Antonio Pratelli	University of Pisa, Italy

Advances in Artificial Intelligence Learning Technologies: Blended Learning, STEM, Computational Thinking and Coding (AAILT 2021)

Alfredo Milani	University of Perugia, Italy
Giulio Biondi	University of Florence, Italy
Sergio Tasso	University of Perugia, Italy

Workshop on Advancements in Applied Machine Learning and Data Analytics (AAMDA 2021)

Alessandro Costantini	INFN, Italy
Davide Salomoni	INFN, Italy
Doina Cristina Duma	INFN, Italy
Daniele Cesini	INFN, Italy

Automatic Landform Classification: Spatial Methods and Applications (ALCSMA 2021)

Maria Danese   ISPC, National Research Council, Italy
Dario Gioia   ISPC, National Research Council, Italy

Application of Numerical Analysis to Imaging Science (ANAIS 2021)

Caterina Fenu   University of Cagliari, Italy
Alessandro Buccini   University of Cagliari, Italy

Advances in Information Systems and Technologies for Emergency Management, Risk Assessment and Mitigation Based on the Resilience Concepts (ASTER 2021)

Maurizio Pollino   ENEA, Italy
Marco Vona   University of Basilicata, Italy
Amedeo Flora   University of Basilicata, Italy
Chiara Iacovino   University of Basilicata, Italy
Beniamino Murgante   University of Basilicata, Italy

Advances in Web Based Learning (AWBL 2021)

Birol Ciloglugil   Ege University, Turkey
Mustafa Murat Inceoglu   Ege University, Turkey

Blockchain and Distributed Ledgers: Technologies and Applications (BDLTA 2021)

Vladimir Korkhov   St. Petersburg University, Russia
Elena Stankova   St. Petersburg University, Russia
Nataliia Kulabukhova   St. Petersburg University, Russia

Bio and Neuro Inspired Computing and Applications (BIONCA 2021)

Nadia Nedjah   State University of Rio de Janeiro, Brazil
Luiza De Macedo Mourelle   State University of Rio de Janeiro, Brazil

Computational and Applied Mathematics (CAM 2021)

Maria Irene Falcão   University of Minho, Portugal
Fernando Miranda   University of Minho, Portugal

Computational and Applied Statistics (CAS 2021)

Ana Cristina Braga   University of Minho, Portugal

Computerized Evaluation of Economic Activities: Urban Spaces (CEEA 2021)

Diego Altafini   Università di Pisa, Italy
Valerio Cutini   Università di Pisa, Italy

Computational Geometry and Applications (CGA 2021)

| Marina Gavrilova | University of Calgary, Canada |

Collaborative Intelligence in Multimodal Applications (CIMA 2021)

| Robertas Damasevicius | Kaunas University of Technology, Lithuania |
| Rytis Maskeliunas | Kaunas University of Technology, Lithuania |

Computational Optimization and Applications (COA 2021)

| Ana Rocha | University of Minho, Portugal |
| Humberto Rocha | University of Coimbra, Portugal |

Computational Astrochemistry (CompAstro 2021)

Marzio Rosi	University of Perugia, Italy
Cecilia Ceccarelli	University of Grenoble, France
Stefano Falcinelli	University of Perugia, Italy
Dimitrios Skouteris	Master-Up, Italy

Computational Science and HPC (CSHPC 2021)

Elise de Doncker	Western Michigan University, USA
Fukuko Yuasa	High Energy Accelerator Research Organization (KEK), Japan
Hideo Matsufuru	High Energy Accelerator Research Organization (KEK), Japan

Cities, Technologies and Planning (CTP 2021)

Malgorzata Hanzl	University of Łódź, Poland
Beniamino Murgante	University of Basilicata, Italy
Ljiljana Zivkovic	Ministry of Construction, Transport and Infrastructure/Institute of Architecture and Urban and Spatial Planning of Serbia, Serbia
Anastasia Stratigea	National Technical University of Athens, Greece
Giuseppe Borruso	University of Trieste, Italy
Ginevra Balletto	University of Cagliari, Italy

Advanced Modeling E-Mobility in Urban Spaces (DEMOS 2021)

Tiziana Campisi	Kore University of Enna, Italy
Socrates Basbas	Aristotle University of Thessaloniki, Greece
Ioannis Politis	Aristotle University of Thessaloniki, Greece
Florin Nemtanu	Polytechnic University of Bucharest, Romania
Giovanna Acampa	Kore University of Enna, Italy
Wolfgang Schulz	Zeppelin University, Germany

Digital Transformation and Smart City (DIGISMART 2021)

Mauro Mazzei — National Research Council, Italy

Econometric and Multidimensional Evaluation in Urban Environment (EMEUE 2021)

Carmelo Maria Torre	Polytechnic University of Bari, Italy
Maria Cerreta	University "Federico II" of Naples, Italy
Pierluigi Morano	Polytechnic University of Bari, Italy
Simona Panaro	University of Portsmouth, UK
Francesco Tajani	Sapienza University of Rome, Italy
Marco Locurcio	Polytechnic University of Bari, Italy

The 11th International Workshop on Future Computing System Technologies and Applications (FiSTA 2021)

Bernady Apduhan	Kyushu Sangyo University, Japan
Rafael Santos	Brazilian National Institute for Space Research, Brazil

Transformational Urban Mobility: Challenges and Opportunities During and Post COVID Era (FURTHER 2021)

Tiziana Campisi	Kore University of Enna, Italy
Socrates Basbas	Aristotle University of Thessaloniki, Greece
Dilum Dissanayake	Newcastle University, UK
Kh Md Nahiduzzaman	University of British Columbia, Canada
Nurten Akgün Tanbay	Bursa Technical University, Turkey
Khaled J. Assi	King Fahd University of Petroleum and Minerals, Saudi Arabia
Giovanni Tesoriere	Kore University of Enna, Italy
Motasem Darwish	Middle East University, Jordan

Geodesign in Decision Making: Meta Planning and Collaborative Design for Sustainable and Inclusive Development (GDM 2021)

Francesco Scorza	University of Basilicata, Italy
Michele Campagna	University of Cagliari, Italy
Ana Clara Mourao Moura	Federal University of Minas Gerais, Brazil

Geomatics in Forestry and Agriculture: New Advances and Perspectives (GeoForAgr 2021)

Maurizio Pollino	ENEA, Italy
Giuseppe Modica	University of Reggio Calabria, Italy
Marco Vizzari	University of Perugia, Italy

Geographical Analysis, Urban Modeling, Spatial Statistics (GEOG-AND-MOD 2021)

Beniamino Murgante	University of Basilicata, Italy
Giuseppe Borruso	University of Trieste, Italy
Hartmut Asche	University of Potsdam, Germany

Geomatics for Resource Monitoring and Management (GRMM 2021)

Eufemia Tarantino	Polytechnic University of Bari, Italy
Enrico Borgogno Mondino	University of Turin, Italy
Alessandra Capolupo	Polytechnic University of Bari, Italy
Mirko Saponaro	Polytechnic University of Bari, Italy

12th International Symposium on Software Quality (ISSQ 2021)

Sanjay Misra	Covenant University, Nigeria

10th International Workshop on Collective, Massive and Evolutionary Systems (IWCES 2021)

Alfredo Milani	University of Perugia, Italy
Rajdeep Niyogi	Indian Institute of Technology, Roorkee, India

Land Use Monitoring for Sustainability (LUMS 2021)

Carmelo Maria Torre	Polytechnic University of Bari, Italy
Maria Cerreta	University "Federico II" of Naples, Italy
Massimiliano Bencardino	University of Salerno, Italy
Alessandro Bonifazi	Polytechnic University of Bari, Italy
Pasquale Balena	Polytechnic University of Bari, Italy
Giuliano Poli	University "Federico II" of Naples, Italy

Machine Learning for Space and Earth Observation Data (MALSEOD 2021)

Rafael Santos	Instituto Nacional de Pesquisas Espaciais, Brazil
Karine Ferreira	Instituto Nacional de Pesquisas Espaciais, Brazil

Building Multi-dimensional Models for Assessing Complex Environmental Systems (MES 2021)

Marta Dell'Ovo	Polytechnic University of Milan, Italy
Vanessa Assumma	Polytechnic University of Turin, Italy
Caterina Caprioli	Polytechnic University of Turin, Italy
Giulia Datola	Polytechnic University of Turin, Italy
Federico dell'Anna	Polytechnic University of Turin, Italy

Ecosystem Services: Nature's Contribution to People in Practice. Assessment Frameworks, Models, Mapping, and Implications (NC2P 2021)

Francesco Scorza   University of Basilicata, Italy
Sabrina Lai   University of Cagliari, Italy
Ana Clara Mourao Moura   Federal University of Minas Gerais, Brazil
Corrado Zoppi   University of Cagliari, Italy
Dani Broitman   Technion, Israel Institute of Technology, Israel

Privacy in the Cloud/Edge/IoT World (PCEIoT 2021)

Michele Mastroianni   University of Campania Luigi Vanvitelli, Italy
Lelio Campanile   University of Campania Luigi Vanvitelli, Italy
Mauro Iacono   University of Campania Luigi Vanvitelli, Italy

Processes, Methods and Tools Towards RESilient Cities and Cultural Heritage Prone to SOD and ROD Disasters (RES 2021)

Elena Cantatore   Polytechnic University of Bari, Italy
Alberico Sonnessa   Polytechnic University of Bari, Italy
Dario Esposito   Polytechnic University of Bari, Italy

Risk, Resilience and Sustainability in the Efficient Management of Water Resources: Approaches, Tools, Methodologies and Multidisciplinary Integrated Applications (RRS 2021)

Maria Macchiaroli   University of Salerno, Italy
Chiara D'Alpaos   Università degli Studi di Padova, Italy
Mirka Mobilia   Università degli Studi di Salerno, Italy
Antonia Longobardi   Università degli Studi di Salerno, Italy
Grazia Fattoruso   ENEA Research Center, Italy
Vincenzo Pellecchia   Ente Idrico Campano, Italy

Scientific Computing Infrastructure (SCI 2021)

Elena Stankova   St. Petersburg University, Russia
Vladimir Korkhov   St. Petersburg University, Russia
Natalia Kulabukhova   St. Petersburg University, Russia

Smart Cities and User Data Management (SCIDAM 2021)

Chiara Garau   University of Cagliari, Italy
Luigi Mundula   University of Cagliari, Italy
Gianni Fenu   University of Cagliari, Italy
Paolo Nesi   University of Florence, Italy
Paola Zamperlin   University of Pisa, Italy

13th International Symposium on Software Engineering Processes and Applications (SEPA 2021)

Sanjay Misra	Covenant University, Nigeria

Ports of the Future - Smartness and Sustainability (SmartPorts 2021)

Patrizia Serra	University of Cagliari, Italy
Gianfranco Fancello	University of Cagliari, Italy
Ginevra Balletto	University of Cagliari, Italy
Luigi Mundula	University of Cagliari, Italy
Marco Mazzarino	University of Venice, Italy
Giuseppe Borruso	University of Trieste, Italy
Maria del Mar Munoz Leonisio	Universidad de Cádiz, Spain

Smart Tourism (SmartTourism 2021)

Giuseppe Borruso	University of Trieste, Italy
Silvia Battino	University of Sassari, Italy
Ginevra Balletto	University of Cagliari, Italy
Maria del Mar Munoz Leonisio	Universidad de Cádiz, Spain
Ainhoa Amaro Garcia	Universidad de Alcalà/Universidad de Las Palmas, Spain
Francesca Krasna	University of Trieste, Italy

Sustainability Performance Assessment: Models, Approaches and Applications toward Interdisciplinary and Integrated Solutions (SPA 2021)

Francesco Scorza	University of Basilicata, Italy
Sabrina Lai	University of Cagliari, Italy
Jolanta Dvarioniene	Kaunas University of Technology, Lithuania
Valentin Grecu	Lucian Blaga University, Romania
Corrado Zoppi	University of Cagliari, Italy
Iole Cerminara	University of Basilicata, Italy

Smart and Sustainable Island Communities (SSIC 2021)

Chiara Garau	University of Cagliari, Italy
Anastasia Stratigea	National Technical University of Athens, Greece
Paola Zamperlin	University of Pisa, Italy
Francesco Scorza	University of Basilicata, Italy

Science, Technologies and Policies to Innovate Spatial Planning (STP4P 2021)

Chiara Garau	University of Cagliari, Italy
Daniele La Rosa	University of Catania, Italy
Francesco Scorza	University of Basilicata, Italy

Anna Maria Colavitti   University of Cagliari, Italy
Beniamino Murgante   University of Basilicata, Italy
Paolo La Greca   University of Catania, Italy

Sustainable Urban Energy Systems (SURENSYS 2021)

Luigi Mundula   University of Cagliari, Italy
Emilio Ghiani   University of Cagliari, Italy

Space Syntax for Cities in Theory and Practice (Syntax_City 2021)

Claudia Yamu   University of Groningen, The Netherlands
Akkelies van Nes   Western Norway University of Applied Sciences, Norway
Chiara Garau   University of Cagliari, Italy

Theoretical and Computational Chemistry and Its Applications (TCCMA 2021)

Noelia Faginas-Lago   University of Perugia, Italy

13th International Workshop on Tools and Techniques in Software Development Process (TTSDP 2021)

Sanjay Misra   Covenant University, Nigeria

Urban Form Studies (UForm 2021)

Malgorzata Hanzl   Łódź University of Technology, Poland
Beniamino Murgante   University of Basilicata, Italy
Eufemia Tarantino   Polytechnic University of Bari, Italy
Irena Itova   University of Westminster, UK

Urban Space Accessibility and Safety (USAS 2021)

Chiara Garau   University of Cagliari, Italy
Francesco Pinna   University of Cagliari, Italy
Claudia Yamu   University of Groningen, The Netherlands
Vincenza Torrisi   University of Catania, Italy
Matteo Ignaccolo   University of Catania, Italy
Michela Tiboni   University of Brescia, Italy
Silvia Rossetti   University of Parma, Italy

Virtual and Augmented Reality and Applications (VRA 2021)

Osvaldo Gervasi   University of Perugia, Italy
Damiano Perri   University of Perugia, Italy
Marco Simonetti   University of Perugia, Italy
Sergio Tasso   University of Perugia, Italy

Workshop on Advanced and Computational Methods for Earth Science Applications (WACM4ES 2021)

Luca Piroddi	University of Cagliari, Italy
Laura Foddis	University of Cagliari, Italy
Augusto Montisci	University of Cagliari, Italy
Sergio Vincenzo Calcina	University of Cagliari, Italy
Sebastiano D'Amico	University of Malta, Malta
Giovanni Martinelli	Istituto Nazionale di Geofisica e Vulcanologia, Italy/Chinese Academy of Sciences, China

Sponsoring Organizations

ICCSA 2021 would not have been possible without the tremendous support of many organizations and institutions, for which all organizers and participants of ICCSA 2021 express their sincere gratitude:

Springer International Publishing AG, Germany (https://www.springer.com)

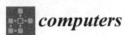

Computers Open Access Journal (https://www.mdpi.com/journal/computers)

IEEE Italy Section, Italy (https://italy.ieeer8.org/)

Centre-North Italy Chapter IEEE GRSS, Italy (https://cispio.diet.uniroma1.it/marzano/ieee-grs/index.html)

Italy Section of the Computer Society, Italy (https://site.ieee.org/italy-cs/)

University of Perugia, Italy (https://www.unipg.it)

University of Cagliari, Italy (https://unica.it/)

University of Basilicata, Italy
(http://www.unibas.it)

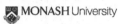

Monash University, Australia
(https://www.monash.edu/)

Kyushu Sangyo University, Japan
(https://www.kyusan-u.ac.jp/)

University of Minho, Portugal
(https://www.uminho.pt/)

Scientific Association Transport Infrastructures,
Italy
(https://www.stradeeautostrade.it/associazioni-e-
organizzazioni/asit-associazione-scientifica-
infrastrutture-trasporto/)

Regione Sardegna, Italy
(https://regione.sardegna.it/)

Comune di Cagliari, Italy
(https://www.comune.cagliari.it/)

Città Metropolitana di Cagliari

Cagliari Accessibility Lab (CAL)
(https://www.unica.it/unica/it/cagliari_
accessibility_lab.page/)

Referees

Nicodemo Abate	IMAA, National Research Council, Italy
Andre Ricardo Abed Grégio	Federal University of Paraná State, Brazil
Nasser Abu Zeid	Università di Ferrara, Italy
Lidia Aceto	Università del Piemonte Orientale, Italy
Nurten Akgün Tanbay	Bursa Technical University, Turkey
Filipe Alvelos	Universidade do Minho, Portugal
Paula Amaral	Universidade Nova de Lisboa, Portugal
Federico Amato	University of Lausanne, Switzerland
Marina Alexandra Pedro Andrade	ISCTE-IUL, Portugal
Debora Anelli	Sapienza University of Rome, Italy
Alfonso Annunziata	University of Cagliari, Italy
Fahim Anzum	University of Calgary, Canada
Tatsumi Aoyama	High Energy Accelerator Research Organization, Japan
Bernady Apduhan	Kyushu Sangyo University, Japan
Jonathan Apeh	Covenant University, Nigeria
Vasilike Argyropoulos	University of West Attica, Greece
Giuseppe Aronica	Università di Messina, Italy
Daniela Ascenzi	Università degli Studi di Trento, Italy
Vanessa Assumma	Politecnico di Torino, Italy
Muhammad Attique Khan	HITEC University Taxila, Pakistan
Vecdi Aytaç	Ege University, Turkey
Alina Elena Baia	University of Perugia, Italy
Ginevra Balletto	University of Cagliari, Italy
Marialaura Bancheri	ISAFOM, National Research Council, Italy
Benedetto Barabino	University of Brescia, Italy
Simona Barbaro	Università degli Studi di Palermo, Italy
Enrico Barbierato	Università Cattolica del Sacro Cuore di Milano, Italy
Jeniffer Barreto	Istituto Superior Técnico, Lisboa, Portugal
Michele Bartalini	TAGES, Italy
Socrates Basbas	Aristotle University of Thessaloniki, Greece
Silvia Battino	University of Sassari, Italy
Marcelo Becerra Rozas	Pontificia Universidad Católica de Valparaíso, Chile
Ranjan Kumar Behera	National Institute of Technology, Rourkela, India
Emanuele Bellini	University of Campania Luigi Vanvitelli, Italy
Massimo Bilancia	University of Bari Aldo Moro, Italy
Giulio Biondi	University of Firenze, Italy
Adriano Bisello	Eurac Research, Italy
Ignacio Blanquer	Universitat Politècnica de València, Spain
Semen Bochkov	Ulyanovsk State Technical University, Russia
Alexander Bogdanov	St. Petersburg University, Russia
Silvia Bonettini	University of Modena and Reggio Emilia, Italy
Enrico Borgogno Mondino	Università di Torino, Italy
Giuseppe Borruso	University of Trieste, Italy

Michele Bottazzi	University of Trento, Italy
Rahma Bouaziz	Taibah University, Saudi Arabia
Ouafik Boulariah	University of Salerno, Italy
Tulin Boyar	Yildiz Technical University, Turkey
Ana Cristina Braga	University of Minho, Portugal
Paolo Bragolusi	University of Padova, Italy
Luca Braidotti	University of Trieste, Italy
Alessandro Buccini	University of Cagliari, Italy
Jorge Buele	Universidad Tecnológica Indoamérica, Ecuador
Andrea Buffoni	TAGES, Italy
Sergio Vincenzo Calcina	University of Cagliari, Italy
Michele Campagna	University of Cagliari, Italy
Lelio Campanile	Università degli Studi della Campania Luigi Vanvitelli, Italy
Tiziana Campisi	Kore University of Enna, Italy
Antonino Canale	Kore University of Enna, Italy
Elena Cantatore	DICATECh, Polytechnic University of Bari, Italy
Pasquale Cantiello	Istituto Nazionale di Geofisica e Vulcanologia, Italy
Alessandra Capolupo	Polytechnic University of Bari, Italy
David Michele Cappelletti	University of Perugia, Italy
Caterina Caprioli	Politecnico di Torino, Italy
Sara Carcangiu	University of Cagliari, Italy
Pedro Carrasqueira	INESC Coimbra, Portugal
Arcangelo Castiglione	University of Salerno, Italy
Giulio Cavana	Politecnico di Torino, Italy
Davide Cerati	Politecnico di Milano, Italy
Maria Cerreta	University of Naples Federico II, Italy
Daniele Cesini	INFN-CNAF, Italy
Jabed Chowdhury	La Trobe University, Australia
Gennaro Ciccarelli	Iuav University of Venice, Italy
Birol Ciloglugil	Ege University, Turkey
Elena Cocuzza	Univesity of Catania, Italy
Anna Maria Colavitt	University of Cagliari, Italy
Cecilia Coletti	Università "G. d'Annunzio" di Chieti-Pescara, Italy
Alberto Collu	Independent Researcher, Italy
Anna Concas	University of Basilicata, Italy
Mauro Coni	University of Cagliari, Italy
Melchiorre Contino	Università di Palermo, Italy
Antonella Cornelio	Università degli Studi di Brescia, Italy
Aldina Correia	Politécnico do Porto, Portugal
Elisete Correia	Universidade de Trás-os-Montes e Alto Douro, Portugal
Florbela Correia	Polytechnic Institute of Viana do Castelo, Portugal
Stefano Corsi	Università degli Studi di Milano, Italy
Alberto Cortez	Polytechnic of University Coimbra, Portugal
Lino Costa	Universidade do Minho, Portugal

Annunziata Esposito Amideo	University College Dublin, Ireland
Dario Esposito	Polytechnic University of Bari, Italy
Claudio Estatico	University of Genova, Italy
Noelia Faginas-Lago	Università di Perugia, Italy
Maria Irene Falcão	University of Minho, Portugal
Stefano Falcinelli	University of Perugia, Italy
Alessandro Farina	University of Pisa, Italy
Grazia Fattoruso	ENEA, Italy
Caterina Fenu	University of Cagliari, Italy
Luisa Fermo	University of Cagliari, Italy
Florbela Fernandes	Instituto Politecnico de Braganca, Portugal
Rosário Fernandes	University of Minho, Portugal
Luis Fernandez-Sanz	University of Alcala, Spain
Alessia Ferrari	Università di Parma, Italy
Luís Ferrás	University of Minho, Portugal
Ângela Ferreira	Instituto Politécnico de Bragança, Portugal
Flora Ferreira	University of Minho, Portugal
Manuel Carlos Figueiredo	University of Minho, Portugal
Ugo Fiore	University of Naples "Parthenope", Italy
Amedeo Flora	University of Basilicata, Italy
Hector Florez	Universidad Distrital Francisco Jose de Caldas, Colombia
Maria Laura Foddis	University of Cagliari, Italy
Valentina Franzoni	Perugia University, Italy
Adelaide Freitas	University of Aveiro, Portugal
Samuel Frimpong	Durban University of Technology, South Africa
Ioannis Fyrogenis	Aristotle University of Thessaloniki, Greece
Marika Gaballo	Politecnico di Torino, Italy
Laura Gabrielli	Iuav University of Venice, Italy
Ivan Gankevich	St. Petersburg University, Russia
Chiara Garau	University of Cagliari, Italy
Ernesto Garcia Para	Universidad del País Vasco, Spain,
Fernando Garrido	Universidad Técnica del Norte, Ecuador
Marina Gavrilova	University of Calgary, Canada
Silvia Gazzola	University of Bath, UK
Georgios Georgiadis	Aristotle University of Thessaloniki, Greece
Osvaldo Gervasi	University of Perugia, Italy
Andrea Gioia	Polytechnic University of Bari, Italy
Dario Gioia	ISPC-CNT, Italy
Raffaele Giordano	IRSS, National Research Council, Italy
Giacomo Giorgi	University of Perugia, Italy
Eleonora Giovene di Girasole	IRISS, National Research Council, Italy
Salvatore Giuffrida	Università di Catania, Italy
Marco Gola	Politecnico di Milano, Italy

A. Manuela Gonçalves	University of Minho, Portugal
Yuriy Gorbachev	Coddan Technologies LLC, Russia
Angela Gorgoglione	Universidad de la República, Uruguay
Yusuke Gotoh	Okayama University, Japan
Anestis Gourgiotis	University of Thessaly, Greece
Valery Grishkin	St. Petersburg University, Russia
Alessandro Grottesi	CINECA, Italy
Eduardo Guerra	Free University of Bozen-Bolzano, Italy
Ayse Giz Gulnerman	Ankara HBV University, Turkey
Sevin Gümgüm	Izmir University of Economics, Turkey
Himanshu Gupta	BITS Pilani, Hyderabad, India
Sandra Haddad	Arab Academy for Science, Egypt
Malgorzata Hanzl	Lodz University of Technology, Poland
Shoji Hashimoto	KEK, Japan
Peter Hegedus	University of Szeged, Hungary
Eligius M. T. Hendrix	Universidad de Málaga, Spain
Edmond Ho	Northumbria University, UK
Guan Yue Hong	Western Michigan University, USA
Vito Iacobellis	Polytechnic University of Bari, Italy
Mauro Iacono	Università degli Studi della Campania, Italy
Chiara Iacovino	University of Basilicata, Italy
Antonino Iannuzzo	ETH Zurich, Switzerland
Ali Idri	University Mohammed V, Morocco
Oana-Ramona Ilovan	Babeş-Bolyai University, Romania
Mustafa Inceoglu	Ege University, Turkey
Tadashi Ishikawa	KEK, Japan
Federica Isola	University of Cagliari, Italy
Irena Itova	University of Westminster, UK
Edgar David de Izeppi	VTTI, USA
Marija Jankovic	CERTH, Greece
Adrian Jaramillo	Universidad Tecnológica Metropolitana, Chile
Monalisa Jena	Fakir Mohan University, India
Dorota Kamrowska-Załuska	Gdansk University of Technology, Poland
Issaku Kanamori	RIKEN Center for Computational Science, Japan
Korhan Karabulut	Yasar University, Turkey
Yeliz Karaca	University of Massachusetts Medical School, USA
Vicky Katsoni	University of West Attica, Greece
Dimitris Kavroudakis	University of the Aegean, Greece
Shuhei Kimura	Okayama University, Japan
Joanna Kolozej	Cracow University of Technology, Poland
Vladimir Korkhov	St. Petersburg University, Russia
Thales Körting	INPE, Brazil
Tomonori Kouya	Shizuoka Institute of Science and Technology, Japan
Sylwia Krzysztofik	Lodz University of Technology, Poland
Nataliia Kulabukhova	St. Petersburg University, Russia
Shrinivas B. Kulkarni	SDM College of Engineering and Technology, India

Pavan Kumar	University of Calgary, Canada
Anisha Kumari	National Institute of Technology, Rourkela, India
Ludovica La Rocca	University of Naples "Federico II", Italy
Daniele La Rosa	University of Catania, Italy
Sabrina Lai	University of Cagliari, Italy
Giuseppe Francesco Cesare Lama	University of Naples "Federico II", Italy
Mariusz Lamprecht	University of Lodz, Poland
Vincenzo Laporta	National Research Council, Italy
Chien-Sing Lee	Sunway University, Malaysia
José Isaac Lemus Romani	Pontifical Catholic University of Valparaíso, Chile
Federica Leone	University of Cagliari, Italy
Alexander H. Levis	George Mason University, USA
Carola Lingua	Polytechnic University of Turin, Italy
Marco Locurcio	Polytechnic University of Bari, Italy
Andrea Lombardi	University of Perugia, Italy
Savino Longo	University of Bari, Italy
Fernando Lopez Gayarre	University of Oviedo, Spain
Yan Lu	Western Michigan University, USA
Maria Macchiaroli	University of Salerno, Italy
Helmuth Malonek	University of Aveiro, Portugal
Francesca Maltinti	University of Cagliari, Italy
Luca Mancini	University of Perugia, Italy
Marcos Mandado	University of Vigo, Spain
Ernesto Marcheggiani	Università Politecnica delle Marche, Italy
Krassimir Markov	University of Telecommunications and Post, Bulgaria
Giovanni Martinelli	INGV, Italy
Alessandro Marucci	University of L'Aquila, Italy
Fiammetta Marulli	University of Campania Luigi Vanvitelli, Italy
Gabriella Maselli	University of Salerno, Italy
Rytis Maskeliunas	Kaunas University of Technology, Lithuania
Michele Mastroianni	University of Campania Luigi Vanvitelli, Italy
Cristian Mateos	Universidad Nacional del Centro de la Provincia de Buenos Aires, Argentina
Hideo Matsufuru	High Energy Accelerator Research Organization (KEK), Japan
D'Apuzzo Mauro	University of Cassino and Southern Lazio, Italy
Chiara Mazzarella	University Federico II, Italy
Marco Mazzarino	University of Venice, Italy
Giovanni Mei	University of Cagliari, Italy
Mário Melo	Federal Institute of Rio Grande do Norte, Brazil
Francesco Mercaldo	University of Molise, Italy
Alfredo Milani	University of Perugia, Italy
Alessandra Milesi	University of Cagliari, Italy
Antonio Minervino	ISPC, National Research Council, Italy
Fernando Miranda	Universidade do Minho, Portugal

B. Mishra	University of Szeged, Hungary
Sanjay Misra	Covenant University, Nigeria
Mirka Mobilia	University of Salerno, Italy
Giuseppe Modica	Università degli Studi di Reggio Calabria, Italy
Mohammadsadegh Mohagheghi	Vali-e-Asr University of Rafsanjan, Iran
Mohamad Molaei Qelichi	University of Tehran, Iran
Mario Molinara	University of Cassino and Southern Lazio, Italy
Augusto Montisci	Università degli Studi di Cagliari, Italy
Pierluigi Morano	Polytechnic University of Bari, Italy
Ricardo Moura	Universidade Nova de Lisboa, Portugal
Ana Clara Mourao Moura	Federal University of Minas Gerais, Brazil
Maria Mourao	Polytechnic Institute of Viana do Castelo, Portugal
Daichi Mukunoki	RIKEN Center for Computational Science, Japan
Beniamino Murgante	University of Basilicata, Italy
Naohito Nakasato	University of Aizu, Japan
Grazia Napoli	Università degli Studi di Palermo, Italy
Isabel Cristina Natário	Universidade Nova de Lisboa, Portugal
Nadia Nedjah	State University of Rio de Janeiro, Brazil
Antonio Nesticò	University of Salerno, Italy
Andreas Nikiforiadis	Aristotle University of Thessaloniki, Greece
Keigo Nitadori	RIKEN Center for Computational Science, Japan
Silvio Nocera	Iuav University of Venice, Italy
Giuseppina Oliva	University of Salerno, Italy
Arogundade Oluwasefunmi	Academy of Mathematics and System Science, China
Ken-ichi Oohara	University of Tokyo, Japan
Tommaso Orusa	University of Turin, Italy
M. Fernanda P. Costa	University of Minho, Portugal
Roberta Padulano	Centro Euro-Mediterraneo sui Cambiamenti Climatici, Italy
Maria Panagiotopoulou	National Technical University of Athens, Greece
Jay Pancham	Durban University of Technology, South Africa
Gianni Pantaleo	University of Florence, Italy
Dimos Pantazis	University of West Attica, Greece
Michela Paolucci	University of Florence, Italy
Eric Pardede	La Trobe University, Australia
Olivier Parisot	Luxembourg Institute of Science and Technology, Luxembourg
Vincenzo Pellecchia	Ente Idrico Campano, Italy
Anna Pelosi	University of Salerno, Italy
Edit Pengő	University of Szeged, Hungary
Marco Pepe	University of Salerno, Italy
Paola Perchinunno	University of Cagliari, Italy
Ana Pereira	Polytechnic Institute of Bragança, Portugal
Mariano Pernetti	University of Campania, Italy
Damiano Perri	University of Perugia, Italy

Federica Pes	University of Cagliari, Italy
Marco Petrelli	Roma Tre University, Italy
Massimiliano Petri	University of Pisa, Italy
Khiem Phan	Duy Tan University, Vietnam
Alberto Ferruccio Piccinni	Polytechnic of Bari, Italy
Angela Pilogallo	University of Basilicata, Italy
Francesco Pinna	University of Cagliari, Italy
Telmo Pinto	University of Coimbra, Portugal
Luca Piroddi	University of Cagliari, Italy
Darius Plonis	Vilnius Gediminas Technical University, Lithuania
Giuliano Poli	University of Naples "Federico II", Italy
Maria João Polidoro	Polytecnic Institute of Porto, Portugal
Ioannis Politis	Aristotle University of Thessaloniki, Greece
Maurizio Pollino	ENEA, Italy
Antonio Pratelli	University of Pisa, Italy
Salvatore Praticò	Mediterranean University of Reggio Calabria, Italy
Marco Prato	University of Modena and Reggio Emilia, Italy
Carlotta Quagliolo	Polytechnic University of Turin, Italy
Emanuela Quaquero	Univesity of Cagliari, Italy
Garrisi Raffaele	Polizia postale e delle Comunicazioni, Italy
Nicoletta Rassu	University of Cagliari, Italy
Hafiz Tayyab Rauf	University of Bradford, UK
Michela Ravanelli	Sapienza University of Rome, Italy
Roberta Ravanelli	Sapienza University of Rome, Italy
Alfredo Reder	Centro Euro-Mediterraneo sui Cambiamenti Climatici, Italy
Stefania Regalbuto	University of Naples "Federico II", Italy
Rommel Regis	Saint Joseph's University, USA
Lothar Reichel	Kent State University, USA
Marco Reis	University of Coimbra, Portugal
Maria Reitano	University of Naples "Federico II", Italy
Jerzy Respondek	Silesian University of Technology, Poland
Elisa Riccietti	École Normale Supérieure de Lyon, France
Albert Rimola	Universitat Autònoma de Barcelona, Spain
Angela Rizzo	University of Bari, Italy
Ana Maria A. C. Rocha	University of Minho, Portugal
Fabio Rocha	Institute of Technology and Research, Brazil
Humberto Rocha	University of Coimbra, Portugal
Maria Clara Rocha	Polytechnic Institute of Coimbra, Portugal
Miguel Rocha	University of Minho, Portugal
Giuseppe Rodriguez	University of Cagliari, Italy
Guillermo Rodriguez	UNICEN, Argentina
Elisabetta Ronchieri	INFN, Italy
Marzio Rosi	University of Perugia, Italy
Silvia Rossetti	University of Parma, Italy
Marco Rossitti	Polytechnic University of Milan, Italy

Sergio Tasso	University of Perugia, Italy
Ana Paula Teixeira	Universidade de Trás-os-Montes e Alto Douro, Portugal
Senhorinha Teixeira	University of Minho, Portugal
Tengku Adil Tengku Izhar	Universiti Teknologi MARA, Malaysia
Maria Filomena Teodoro	University of Lisbon/Portuguese Naval Academy, Portugal
Giovanni Tesoriere	Kore University of Enna, Italy
Yiota Theodora	National Technical Univeristy of Athens, Greece
Graça Tomaz	Polytechnic Institute of Guarda, Portugal
Carmelo Maria Torre	Polytechnic University of Bari, Italy
Francesca Torrieri	University of Naples "Federico II", Italy
Vincenza Torrisi	University of Catania, Italy
Vincenzo Totaro	Polytechnic University of Bari, Italy
Pham Trung	Ho Chi Minh City University of Technology, Vietnam
Dimitrios Tsoukalas	Centre of Research and Technology Hellas (CERTH), Greece
Sanjida Tumpa	University of Calgary, Canada
Iñaki Tuñon	Universidad de Valencia, Spain
Takahiro Ueda	Seikei University, Japan
Piero Ugliengo	University of Turin, Italy
Abdi Usman	Haramaya University, Ethiopia
Ettore Valente	University of Naples "Federico II", Italy
Jordi Vallverdu	Universitat Autònoma de Barcelona, Spain
Cornelis Van Der Mee	University of Cagliari, Italy
José Varela-Aldás	Universidad Tecnológica Indoamérica, Ecuador
Fanny Vazart	University of Grenoble Alpes, France
Franco Vecchiocattivi	University of Perugia, Italy
Laura Verde	University of Campania Luigi Vanvitelli, Italy
Giulia Vergerio	Polytechnic University of Turin, Italy
Jos Vermaseren	Nikhef, The Netherlands
Giacomo Viccione	University of Salerno, Italy
Marco Vizzari	University of Perugia, Italy
Corrado Vizzarri	Polytechnic University of Bari, Italy
Alexander Vodyaho	St. Petersburg State Electrotechnical University "LETI", Russia
Nikolay N. Voit	Ulyanovsk State Technical University, Russia
Marco Vona	University of Basilicata, Italy
Agustinus Borgy Waluyo	Monash University, Australia
Fernando Wanderley	Catholic University of Pernambuco, Brazil
Chao Wang	University of Science and Technology of China, China
Marcin Wozniak	Silesian University of Technology, Poland
Tiang Xian	Nathong University, China
Rekha Yadav	KL University, India
Claudia Yamu	University of Groningen, The Netherlands
Fenghui Yao	Tennessee State University, USA

Contents – Part VI

**International Workshop on Transformational Urban Mobility:
Challenges and Opportunities During and Post COVID
Era (FURTHER 2021)**

**International Workshop on Geodesign in Decision Making:
Meta Planning and Collaborative Design for Sustainable
and Inclusive Development (GDM 2021)**

11th International Workshop on Future Computing System Technologies and Applications (FiSTA 2021)

International Workshop on Geographical Analysis, Urban Modeling, Spatial Statistics (GEOG-AND-MOD 2021)

International Workshop on Digital Transformation and Smart City (DIGISMART 2021)

Analysis of Regional Imbalances in Italy Based on Cluster Analysis

Massimo De Maria[1] , Mauro Mazzei[2] , Oleg V. Bik[1] ,
and Armando L. Palma[2]

[1] Peoples Friendship University of Russia, (RUDN University), 6 Miklukho-Maklaya Street,
Moscow 117198, Russian Federation
{dd-mm,bik-ov}@rudn.ru

[2] National Research Council, Istituto di Analisi dei Sistemi ed Informatica "Antonio Ruberti" -
LabGeoInf, Via dei Taurini, 19, 00185 Rome, Italy
mauro.mazzei@iasi.cnr.it, palma@orazio.it

Abstract. In 2021 ISTAT presented the Report on Equitable and Sustainable
Well-being (BES 2020), consisting of a system of indicators that follow the significant changes that have characterized the Italian society in the last 10 years.
With the integration of new indicators, realized in coherence with the fundamental lines of the Next Generation EU, there has been an enrichment of information
on the country system concerning health aspects, education and training, and economic well-being. The 20 Italian regions, the 2 autonomous provinces of Bolzano
and Trento, the 3 territorial divisions North, Center, South and the total of Italy
constituting a set of 26 territorial units, have been described each with a set of
36 numerical indicators, concerning the areas of Health, Education and Training,
Economic Wellbeing. These areas are the most suitable for highlighting regional
imbalances in Italy. In this paper has been analyzed the input data matrix, made
up of 26 rows, one for each of the territorial units, and of 36 columns, the number of descriptors used for each territorial unit, by means of a factor analysis,
using the principal components method, in order to construct a regional taxonomy
characterized by those of the 36 indicators that are most correlated with each of
the factors that have emerged. Moreover, starting from the coordinates calculated
for each of the 26 territorial units in the factor space, a cluster analysis of the 26
territorial units was carried out, using the connected graph method, in order to
highlight the territorial similarities and differences in Italy.

Keywords: Urban models · Factor analysis · Cluster analysis · Spatial data
analysis · Spatial statistical model

1 Introduction

Equitable and Sustainable well-being indicators (Bes) have been introduced into the
Italian legislative system (Article 14 of Law No. 163/2016 reforming the accounting
law) as an economic planning tool. An ad hoc committee was appointed, chaired by
the Minister of Economy and Finance, to select useful indicators for the assessment

O. Gervasi et al. (Eds.): ICCSA 2021, LNCS 12954, pp. 3–20, 2021.
https://doi.org/10.1007/978-3-030-86979-3_1

of well-being based on the experience gained at national and international level. Ten years after the start of the project, the proposed indicators show that there have been many changes in the profile of well-being in Italy, both in the direction of progress and in the persistence of critical areas. By effect of budget cuts carried out continuously throughout the decade, in our health system there are fewer beds, there are doctors of a higher average age, due to the blocking of turnover, with the result of greater inequality in access to care. There are still too few children enrolled in the nursery and young people who graduate, so the gap with Europe on education continues to widen. At the same time, the number of young people who don't study, don't work and aren't included in professional training programs (NEET) has increased. The quality of work in Italy is objectively critical, and the incidence of absolute poverty in 2019 showed, for the first time, a slight decline and then rose again in 2020. The Bes 2020 Report, presented by ISTAT at the end of 2020, highlights a complex and not merely emergency situation that is at the same time contradictory [3–5]. The extraordinary resources made available by the Next Generation EU Program represent an unprecedented opportunity to intervene substantially for economic recovery. The Bes is therefore a targeted, sensitive and reliable tool to guide decisions and to allow for the evaluation of results of the implemented policies. In this work, 15 variables of the Health area, 13 variables of the Education and Training Area and 8 variables of the Economic Wellbeing Area, as specified below, were assumed as indicators (descriptors) of the 26 territorial units considered.

1.1 Description of the Indicators

Health Area - Description of the 36 indicators of each of the 26 territorial units.

ID	Indicators
1	Life expectancy at birth
2	Healthy life expectancy at birth
3	Mental health index (SF36)
4	Avoidable mortality (0–74 years)
5	Multichronicity and severe limitations (75 years and over)
6	Child mortality
7	Mortality due to road accidents (15–34 years)
8	Mortality from cancer (20–64 years)
9	Mortality due to dementia and diseases of the nervous system
10	Unlimited life expectancy in activities at 65
11	Overweight
12	Smoking
13	Alcohol
14	Sedentary lifestyle
15	Adequate nutrition

Education and Training Area - Description of the 36 indicators of each of the 26 territorial units.

ID	Indicators
16	Attendance in kindergarten
17	People with at least a diploma (25–64 years)
18	Transition to the University
19	Young people who do not work and do not study (NEET)
20	Participation in continuing education
21	Inadequate literacy skills
22	Inadequate numerical competence
23	High digital skills
24	0–2 years old children enrolled in the nursery
25	Graduates in technical-scientific disciplines (STEM)
26	Cultural participation outside the home
27	Reading of books and newspapers
28	Usage of libraries

Economic Wellness Area - Description of the 36 indicators of each of the 26 territorial units.

ID	Indicators
29	Income available
30	Net income inequality (s80 / s20)
31	Risk of poverty
32	Severe material deprivation
33	Severe housing deprivation
34	Great difficulty to get to the end of the month
35	Low labor intensity
36	Overhead of the cost of housing

The corresponding values of the 36 indicators detected by ISTAT during 2020 were associated with each of the 26 territorial units, as listed in Table 1 [1, 2]. Only the data from the areas of health, education and training, economic well-being, of the twelve available, were used, because they were considered more discriminating for the purposes of an analysis of regional imbalances.

Health represents a central element of life and an indispensable condition for individual well-being and the prosperity of populations, as recalled, at European level, by the Lisbon strategy for Development and Work, declared by the European Commission in 2000 in response to the challenges of globalization and aging.

Health has consequences that impact on all dimensions of the life of each individual, being able to modify the living conditions, behaviors, social relationships, opportunities and perspectives of individuals and, often, of their families.

Table 1. .

ID	Territorial units
1	Piemonte
2	Valle d'Aosta/Vallèe d'Aoste
3	Liguria
4	Lombardia
5	Trentino-Alto Adige/Sudtirolo
6	Bolzano/Bozen
7	Trento
8	Veneto
9	Friuli-Venezia Giulia
10	Emilia-Romagna
11	Toscana
12	Umbria
13	Marche
14	Lazio
15	Abruzzo
16	Molise
17	Campania
18	Puglia
19	Basilicata
20	Calabria
21	Sicilia
22	Sardegna
23	Nord
24	Centro
25	Mezzogiorno
26	Italia

Education, training and skill levels influence people's well-being and open up opportunities for social growth that would otherwise be precluded.

Higher educated people have a higher standard of living and have more opportunities to find work, live longer and better, because they have healthier lifestyles and have more opportunities to find work in less risky environments.

Furthermore, a higher level of education usually corresponds to a higher level of access and enjoyment of cultural goods and services, and an active participation in the process of production of culture and creativity. Economic well-being is not considered a goal, but rather as a means by which an individual can have and sustain a certain standard of living.

Variables that contribute to economic well-being include income, wealth, spending on consumer goods, housing conditions, and ownership of durable goods [6–8].

Obviously, the judgment on the level of economic well-being of a society can vary if the same average overall income is equally distributed among citizens or is instead concentrated in the hands of a few wealthy people.

The peculiar characteristic that we call "value" is born in consumer products, a characteristic that can be defined as the ability of a product to excite in the individual the desire to have an exclusive use or at least a use for the total satisfaction of their needs. The 26 territorial units, each described by the 36 numerical variables concerning the three areas mentioned above, were considered as a matrix (input matrix X) of 26 "objects" in a 36-dimensional space [9–12]. We subjected the above matrix to a factor analysis, with the principal components (or Hotelling's) method, in order to obtain a representation of the 26 territorial units projected in a space with only three-four dimensions (factor space) in order to use a simplified description of the 26 territorial units [13, 14]. This synthetic description, obtained from the factorial analysis, allows us to examine the distribution of the 26 territorial units, i.e. their possible mutual proximity in the space of the main components.

Furthermore, the 26 territorial units distributed in the space of the principal components were subjected to a cluster analysis in order to evaluate their similarities or their differences.

Since the factorial model is invariant (equivariance) with respect to changes in scale of the variables contained in the input matrix X, it's possible to standardize the observed variables, in order to examine not the variance and covariance matrix, but the correlation matrix R [15, 16].

Below we briefly illustrate the results obtained with the factor analysis applied to the R correlation matrix of the 36 numerical indicators used for the description of the 26 territorial units.

The eigenvalues and corresponding eigenvectors of this matrix were calculated. The first four eigenvalues explained 77% of the total variance of the system.

Cumulative % of Eigenvalues.

.51	.62	.72	.77

After the rotation of the factor matrix, made up of the four eigenvectors corresponding to the first four eigenvalues, the 4 factor scores (coordinates in the factor space) were calculated for each of the 26 territorial units, with the significant (non-zero) weights (factor loading) of the input variables on each of the 4 factors.

1.2 Factor Analysis

For each factor, the following lists show the number of the variable, the weight of the variable on the factor and the description of each of the variables divided by area. Moreover, for each factor, the coordinates on the factor of the 26 territorial units are listed in an ordered manner. The weights of the variables and the coordinates on each main component are given below (Figs. 1, 2, 3 and 4):

Health Area – Factor loading 1ˢᵗ Main Component.

ID	Weights of variables	Indicators
2	0.57	Healthy life expectancy at birth
4	−0.81	Avoidable mortality (0–74 years)
5	−0.63	Multichronicity and severe limitations (75 years and over)
6	−0.54	Child mortality
8	−0.65	Mortality from cancer (20–64 years)
10	0.80	Unlimited life expectancy in activities at 65
11	−0.80	Overweight
13	0.61	Alcohol
14	−0.84	Sedentary lifestyle
15	0.70	Adequate nutrition

Education And Training Area - Factor loading 1ˢᵗ Main Component.

ID	Weights of variables	Indicators
17	0.90	People with at least a diploma (25–64 years)
19	−0.88	Young people who do not work and do not study (NEET)
20	0.64	Participation in continuing education
21	−0.78	Inadequate literacy skills
22	−0.84	Inadequate numerical competence

Economic Wellness Area - Factor loading 1ˢᵗ Main Component.

ID	Weights of variable	Indicators
29	0.75	Income available
30	−0.88	Net income inequality (s80 / s20)
31	−0.92	Risk of poverty
32	−0.84	Severe material deprivation
34	−0.76	Great difficulty to get to the end of the month
35	−0.91	Low labor intensity
36	−0.82	Overhead of the cost of housing

Coordinates of Territorial Units on the 1st Main Component.

Territorial units	Value
Trento	23.58
Trentino-AltoAdige	23.35
Bolzano/Bozen	17.34
Valle d'Aosta	16.36
Veneto	14.20
Friuli-Venezia Giulia	13.30
Emilia-Romagna	11.09
Toscana	8.81
Marche	7.18
Lombardia	6.94
Umbria	6.81
Piemonte	4.50
Liguria	4.48
Lazio	0.44
Abruzzo	−4.73
Sardegna	−9.43
Molise	−10.96
Basilicata	−12.73
Puglia	−15.53
Calabria	−21.18
Sicilia	−33.70
Campania	−34.87

Health Area – Factor loading 2nd Main Component.

ID	Weights of variables	Indicators
3	0.52	Mental health index (SF36)
7	0.58	Mortality due to road accidents (15–34 years)
12	−0.40	Smoking

Fig. 1. Coordinates of territorial units on the 1st main component

Education and Training Area - Factor loading 2nd Main Component.

ID	Weights of variables	Indicators
18	−0.83	Transition to the University

Coordinates of Territorial Units on the 2nd Main Component.

Territorial units	Value
Bolzano/Bozen	13.49
Trentino-Alto Adige	9.01
Friuli-Venezia Giulia	1.69
Trento	1.68

(continued)

(*continued*)

Territorial units	Value
Veneto	1.66
Lazio	1.02
Puglia	0.74
Calabria	0.55
Sicilia	−0.39
Emilia-Romagna	−0.99
Valle d'Aosta	−1.04
Liguria	−1.17
Abruzzo	−1.41
Umbria	−1.50
Basilicata	−1.58
Lombardia	−1.88
Toscana	−2.10
Campania	−2.14
Sardegna	−2.35
Marche	−3.07
Piemonte	−3.28
Molise	−3.30

Education and Training Area - Factor loading 3rd Main Component.

ID	Weights of variables	Indicators
16	0.94	Attendance in kindergarten
23	0.81	High digital skills
24	0.62	0–2 years old children enrolled in the nursery
26	0.66	Cultural participation outside the home
27	0.66	Reading of books and newspapers.

Coordinates of Territorial Units on the 3rd Main Component.

Territorial units	Value
Trento	8.73
Valle d'Aosta	8.03
Trentino-Alto Adige	5.31
Friuli-Venezia Giulia	4.45

(*continued*)

(*continued*)

Territorial units	Value
Veneto	4.17
Emilia-Romagna	3.92
Bolzano/Bozen	3.89
Toscana	3.63
Lombardia	2.50
Liguria	1.86
Piemonte	1.80
Marche	1.50
Umbria	1.09
Sardegna	0.77
Abruzzo	−1.32
Molise	−2.61
Puglia	−2.77
Basilicata	−3.09
Calabria	−5.10
Sicilia	−9.04
Campania	−9.09
Lazio	−16.81

Health Area – Factor loading 4th Main Component.

ID	Weights of variables	Indicators
1	0.54	Life expectancy at birth
9	−0.72	Mortality due to dementia and diseases of the nervous system

Education and Training Area - Factor loading 4th Main Component.

ID	Weights of variables	Indicators
25	0.64	Graduates in technical-scientific disciplines (STEM)
28	−0.67	Usage of libraries

Economic Wellness Area - Factor loading 4th Main Component.

ID	Weights of variable	Indicators
33	0.51	Severe housing deprivation

Coordinates of Territorial Units on the 4th Main Component.

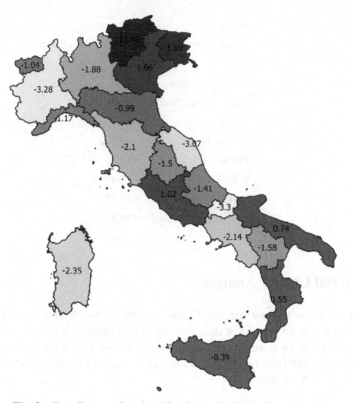

Fig. 2. Coordinates of territorial units on the 2nd main component

Territorial units	Value
Campania	12.84
Calabria	11.62
Sicilia	10.51
Basilicata	8.96
Molise	8.06
Abruzzo	6.76
Puglia	6.68
Lazio	3.40
Umbria	2.60
Sardegna	1.35
Marche	−0.05
Liguria	−2.43
Toscana	−2.76

(*continued*)

(*continued*)

Territorial units	Value
Piemonte	−3.88
Emilia-Romagna	−4.68
Friuli-Venezia Giulia	−4.72
Veneto	−4.80
Lombardia	−4.97
Trento	−10.36
Valle d'Aosta	−12.49
Bolzano/Bozen	−13.82
Trentino-Alto Adige	−14.08

2 Territorial Cluster Analysis

The new coordinates in factor space had been assigned to the 26 territorial units considered, it was possible to search for their proximity (similarity). It seems appropriate to clarify what is meant by similarity between regions. To this end, we introduce a similarity coefficient $S_{i,j}$ between two regions R_i and R_j in such a way that for each pair (i, j), with $i,j = 1, 2,\ldots, N$ we have:

$$0 <= S_{i,j} <= 1.$$

with

$$S_{i,j} = 1.$$

only if (1).

$$R_i = R_j.$$

with.

$$S_{i,j} = S_{j,i}.$$

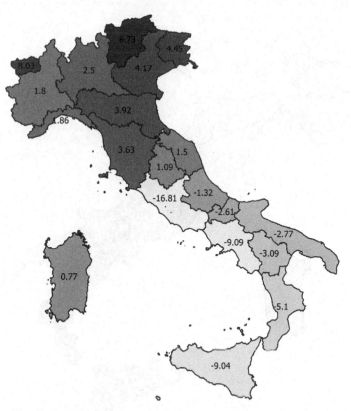

Fig. 3. Coordinates of territorial units on the 3rd main component

(symmetry property). If we denote by Di the modulus of the description vector of the spatial unit Ri where Di, k is the k-th component of the vector Di, the similarity coefficient Si, j can be defined as the addition k of the proportion [18].

$$(D_i, k * D_j, k) / (D_i * D_j)$$

which, as can easily be verified, satisfies the relations given in (1). The square matrix of order N constructed with the coefficients Si,j is called similarity matrix **S**. It is usually transformed into a Boolean matrix B by introducing a threshold t, with $0 < t < 1$, and setting bi,j = 1 if **S**i,j > t and setting bi,j = 0 otherwise [17, 23].

Fig. 4. Coordinates of territorial units on the 4th main component

The similarity matrix S can be interpreted as the adjacency matrix associated with a digraph. Since we are in the presence of a symmetrical matrix, if an arc $S_{i,j}$ exists between any pair (i,j) of nodes, the arc $S_{j,i}$ with the same ends but directed in the opposite direction will also exist [21]. One can then disregard the direction on the arcs and simply consider undirected graphs [20]. The existence of an arc between two nodes indicates that there is a similarity between corresponding regions that exceeds the threshold t adopted. The search for the connected components of a graph can be carried out by introducing the concept of a complete tree associated with each of the components. It is to be noted that a tree is a graph such that between any two nodes of it there is one and only one path; this implies that within a tree there are no cycles and that, if N is the number of nodes, the tree itself consists of exactly N-1 arcs [19, 22].

Considering the problem of the research of homogeneous clusters of our territorial units, having calculated the similarity matrix S, the classes have been identified through an algorithm of research of the connected components of the digraph associated to the Boolean matrix of the adjacencies, as deduced from the similarity matrix S, having imposed the threshold value t = 0.960. The results obtained are shown in the Table 2 below (Fig. 5):

Table 2. .

Cluster	Territorial Units
Cluster 1	Piemonte
Cluster 2	Trentino - Alto Adige
	Bolzano/Bozen
Cluster 3	Valle d'Aosta
	Liguria
	Lombardia
	Trento
	Veneto
	Friuli - Venezia Giulia
	Emilia - Romagna
	Toscana
	Nord Italia
Cluster 4	Umbria
Cluster 5	Lazio
Cluster 6	Abruzzo
Cluster 7	Marche
	Centro Italia
Cluster 8	Molise
	Campania
	Puglia
	Basilicata
	Calabria
	Sicilia
	Sardegna
	Mezzogiorno Italy

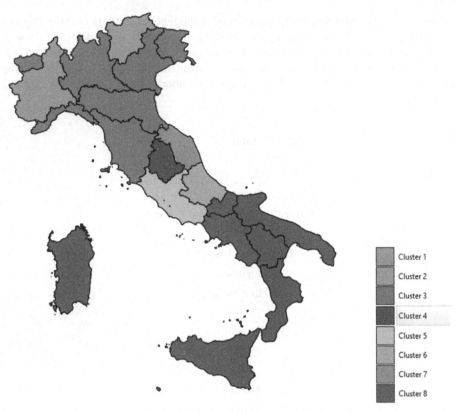

Fig. 5. Cluster of the territorial division

3 Conclusion

From the results obtained, considering the adoption of a highly discriminating value, close to unity, of the t threshold, it can be deduced that Piemonte, as well as Umbria, Lazio, Abruzzo and Marche present specific and peculiar regional profiles, in relation to the 36 descriptive variables used. It should also be noted, however, that the Marche Region has a profile that is most similar to the territorial distribution of Central Italy (cluster n. 7). Cluster n. 2 is formed by the Trentino respectively: the Autonomous Province of Bolzano while the Autonomous Province of Trento, which on the first principal component has assumed the greatest distance (23.58) from the origin of the factorial axes, near which the Lazio region is located, has been included in cluster n. 3 to which all the other regions of the Northern Italy territorial Breakdown also belong.

Finally, a special reflection should be made on cluster no. 8 that includes the seven southern regions, the territorial distribution Mezzogiorno and total Italy. It should be noted that the seven southern regions, Molise, Campania, Puglia, Basilicata, Calabria, Sicilia and Sardegna, described by their respective scores on the four factorial axes, all have negative coordinates on the first and third main components. It is left to the reader to read and easily interpret the weights of the variables on factors I and III, as they emerge from the factor analysis, in order to highlight the shortcomings, and therefore the regional imbalances, in the areas of health, education and training, and economic well-being.

References

1. Bimonte, S., Gensel, J., Bertolotto, M.: Enriching spatial olap with map generalization: a conceptual multidimensional model. In: Proceedings of the 2008 IEEE International Conference on Data MiningWorkshops. ICDMW 2008, Washington, DC, USA, IEEE Computer Society, pp. 332–341 (2008)
2. Bimonte, S., Miquel, M.: When spatial analysis meets olap: multidimensional model and operators. IJDWM **6**(4), 33–60 (2010)
3. Mirco Gamberini, "Data Warehouse – 1a parte: Introduzione e applicazioni nel mondo reale", Mokabyte 154, settembre 2010
4. Golfarelli, M., Rizzi, S.: Data Warehouse: teoria e pratica della progettazione", McGraw-Hill, 2a edizione (2006)
5. Di Martino, S., Bimonte, S., Bertolotto, M., Ferrucci, F.: Integrating Google earth within OLAP tools for multidimensional exploration and analysis of spatial data. In: Filipe, J., Cordeiro, J. (eds.) ICEIS 2009. LNBIP, vol. 24, pp. 940–951. Springer, Heidelberg (2009). https://doi.org/10.1007/978-3-642-01347-8_78
6. Franklin, C.: "An introduction to geographic information systems: linking maps to databases". Journal Database, April, p. 1321 (1992)
7. Malinowski, E., Zimányi, E.: Advanced Data Warehouse Design: From Conventional to Spatial and Temporal Application". Springer, Cham (2008). https://doi.org/10.1007/978-3-540-74405-4
8. Laurini, R., Thompson, D.: Fundamentals of Spatial Information Systems. Academic Press, London (1992)
9. Ahmed, T.O., Miquel, M.: Multidimensional structures dedicated to continuous spatiotemporal phenomena. In: Jackson, M., Nelson, D., Stirk, S. (eds.) BNCOD 2005. LNCS, vol. 3567, pp. 29–40. Springer, Heidelberg (2005). https://doi.org/10.1007/11511854_3
10. Bedard, Y., Merrett, T., Han, J.: Fundamentals of spatial datawarehousing for geographic knowledge discovery. in: geographic data mining and knowledge discovery. Taylor and Francis, pp. 53–73 Research Monographs in GIS series edited by Peter Fisher and Jonathan Raper (2001)
11. Cembalo, A., Pisano, F.M., Romano, G.: Document Warehousing: l'analisi multidimensionale applicata a sorgenti testuali-I parte:panoramica e introduzione", MokaByte 162, maggio (2011)
12. Caranna, V.: "Data Warehouse - III parte: Definiamo un modello progettuale per DWH", MokaByte 158, gennaio (2011)
13. Petrov, D.A., Stankova, E.N.: Integrated information system for verification of the models of convective clouds. In: Gervasi, O., et al. (eds.) ICCSA 2015. LNCS, vol. 9158, pp. 321–330. Springer, Cham (2015). https://doi.org/10.1007/978-3-319-21410-8_25
14. Stankova, E.N., Balakshiy, A.V., Petrov, D.A., Shorov, A.V., Korkhov, V.V.: Using technologies of OLAP and machine learning for validation of the numerical models of convective clouds. In: Gervasi, O., et al. (eds.) ICCSA 2016. LNCS, vol. 9788, pp. 463–472. Springer, Cham (2016). https://doi.org/10.1007/978-3-319-42111-7_36
15. Gankevich, I., et al.: Constructing virtual private supercomputer using virtualization and cloud technologies. In: Murgante, B., et al. (eds.) ICCSA 2014. LNCS, vol. 8584, pp. 341–354. Springer, Cham (2014). https://doi.org/10.1007/978-3-319-09153-2_26

16. Kluge, M., Asche, H.: Validating a smartphone-based pedestrian navigation system proto-type. In: Murgante, B., et al. (eds.) ICCSA 2012. LNCS, vol. 7334, pp. 386–396. Springer, Heidelberg (2012). https://doi.org/10.1007/978-3-642-31075-1_29
17. Mazzei, M., Palma, A.L.: A Decision support system for the analysis of mobility. In: Gervasi, O., et al. (eds.) ICCSA 2015. LNCS, vol. 9157, pp. 390–402. Springer, Cham (2015). https://doi.org/10.1007/978-3-319-21470-2_28
18. Mazzei, M., Palma, A.L.: Spatial statistical models for the evaluation of the landscape. In: Murgante, B., et al. (eds.) ICCSA 2013. LNCS, vol. 7974, pp. 419–432. Springer, Heidelberg (2013). https://doi.org/10.1007/978-3-642-39649-6_30
19. Mazzei, M., Palma, A.L.: Comparative analysis of models of location and spatial interaction. In: Murgante, B., et al. (eds.) ICCSA 2014. LNCS, vol. 8582, pp. 253–267. Springer, Cham (2014). https://doi.org/10.1007/978-3-319-09147-1_19
20. Mazzei, M., Palma, A.L.: Spatial multicriteria analysis approach for evaluation of mobility demand in urban areas. In: Gervasi, O., et al. (eds.) ICCSA 2017. LNCS, vol. 10407, pp. 451–468. Springer, Cham (2017). https://doi.org/10.1007/978-3-319-62401-3_33
21. Mazzei, M.: An unsupervised machine learning approach in remote sensing data. In: Misra, S., et al. (eds.) ICCSA 2019. LNCS, vol. 11621, pp. 435–447. Springer, Cham (2019). https://doi.org/10.1007/978-3-030-24302-9_31
22. Mazzei, M.: Software development for unsupervised approach to identification of a multi temporal spatial analysis model - Proceedings of the 2018 International Conference on Image Processing, Computer Vision, and Pattern Recognition, IPCV 2018, 2018, pp. 85–91 (2018)
23. Mazzei, M.: An unsupervised machine learning approach for medical image analysis. In: Arai, K. (ed.) FICC 2021. AISC, vol. 1364, pp. 813–830. Springer, Cham (2021). https://doi.org/10.1007/978-3-030-73103-8_58

New Smart Mobility Applications: Preliminary Findings on a Pilot Study in the Municipality of Artena

Mauro D'Apuzzo[1] , Azzurra Evangelisti[1] , Daniela Santilli[1]([✉]), Stefano Buzzi[1], Mauro Mazzei[2], and Viviana Bietoni[1]

[1] University of Cassino and Southern Lazio, Via G. Di Biasio 43, 03043 Cassino, Italy
{dapuzzo,daniela.santilli,buzzi}@unicas.it
[2] CNR, Italian National Research Council, Via dei Taurini 19, 00185 Rome, Italy
mauro.mazzei@iasi.cnr.it

Abstract. Whether for work, for leisure or for moving goods necessary for health, people and industry, mobility is a fundamental aspect of economic and social life of each community. Unfortunately, it is not without costs for the society: gas emissions, air, water and noise pollution, road crashes, congestions, are examples which affect health and environment. For these reasons the most severe challenge for the transportation sector is to become more sustainable, resilient and safe. All can be possible only betting on green mobility and cutting-edge digital technologies.

According to this vision, the "Smart Urban Mobility Management" (SUMMa) project has been proposed, with the aim to develop, for the Artena Municipality, new service structures for modernizing and managing transportation systems, by means of digital technologies and 5G communication networks. In particular the proposed digital platform, thanks to enhanced Mobile Broadband, massive Machine Type Communications and Mobile Edge Computing, can support Artificial Intelligence algorithms for recognition image and interpretation of field data, collected by drones or H-D cameras. In real time, Origin-Destination flows, individual trips and environmental data can be update and traffic, congestion and health information can be shared with the citizens.

In this paper, the general architecture of the SUMMa platform has been described and preliminary findings of the pilot project in the Municipality of Artena have been presented.

Keywords: Smart mobility · Smart road · Sustainable mobility · SUMMa project · 5G communication technology · AI technology

1 Introduction

Mobility, today more than ever, is synonymous with freedom, prosperity and health. In fact, comparing the effects suffered by the global economy and by the social and health dynamics, due to the strong reduction or prohibition of free movements (of both people and goods), the COVID-19 pandemic has demonstrated, once again, the crucial

© Springer Nature Switzerland AG 2021
O. Gervasi et al. (Eds.): ICCSA 2021, LNCS 12954, pp. 21–36, 2021.
https://doi.org/10.1007/978-3-030-86979-3_2

function of the transport systems for the modern societies. Rather, the need to extend an efficient supply chains not only within single Nations but in a European or World dimension appears clear [1]. Based on this new impulse, all the projects that invest in modernization, efficiency and digitization of the transport activities become essential for Authorities and Municipalities.

The common vision consists to make transportation systems more sustainable, resilient, intermodal, smart and safe. In this direction, European Commission and National Authorities promoted Guidelines, Plans and Strategies also for targeted investments such as deployment of novel and sustainable technologies in transport, use of drones, unmanned aircraft and cutting-edge tools, deployment of the highest performance of digital infrastructure (as 5G) and employment of Artificial Intelligence (AI) for transport automation and intelligent transport system (ITS) [1–3], in order to achieve *Smart Mobility Systems.*

The term *Smart Mobility* has been intrinsically associated with *Smart Cities* because innovative, green, efficient and connected cities can't be achieved without technological, sustainable, safe and digital transportation infrastructures [4–6]. It requires digital platforms and technical infrastructure able to guarantee optimized, diffused, accessible and intermodal mobility solutions and services [7, 8], preferring, where possible, the safeguard of vulnerable users [9]. Several applications are developing within Europe and World context, and in Italy, thanks to the MIT Decree 70/2018 [10] the on-road testing of connected and automatic driving solutions began. In particular, the *Smart Road* concept was introduced as the "road infrastructure where a digital transformation process is carried out aimed at introducing traffic observation and monitoring platforms, data and information processing models, advanced services to infrastructure managers, public administration and road users, in the framework of the creation of a technological ecosystem favorable to interoperability between infrastructures and new generation vehicles" [10].

The present study is carried out in the framework of the "Smart Urban Mobility Management" (SUMMa) National Project, within the Smarter Italy Project [11], with the aim to valorize new digital technologies such as IoT (Internet of Things), AI, Blockchain and the use of 5G communication networks, to improve the competitiveness of the transportation systems through new services for the management and modernization of both urban and rural mobility systems. The Municipality of Artena hosts the SUMMA pilot project.

1.1 Smart Urban Mobility Management (SUMMa) Project

The "Smart Urban Mobility Management" (SUMMa) Project, promoting the Green Economy and Sustainable Mobility, aims the design and development of a telematic platform, fully-integrated on the 5G platform, for the analysis of mobility.

Through the use of highly innovative tools such as drones, H-D cameras, IoT Sensors on 5G network and AI tools, infrastructures, things and people can be connected one each other for the development of an effective model of Smart Mobility with the implementation of vertical services as: *Smart Parking* - monitoring of parking areas and management of free parking spots to guide the users to the parking stall, optimizing search and stay times in traffic; *Environmental Control* - monitoring of air and water quality in urban environments, and Blockchain certification of the data; *Smart Road Safety* - advanced monitoring of the road arteries for the control of vehicular flows and congestions for the territorial control and *Sustainable Mobility* - provides information to design cycle paths (also useful for a possible subsequent adoption of a bike sharing service) and for the retraining of pedestrian paths. A simplified representation of the SUMMa platform architecture is reported in the Fig. 1.

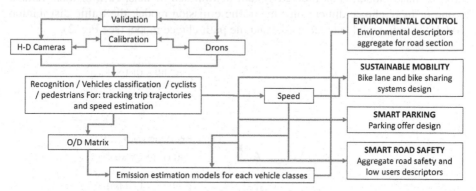

Fig. 1. Simplified SUMMa platform architecture.

These technologies are based on an enhanced and efficient database for collecting and analyzing huge volumes of data (Big data) that the sensors and applied systems make available. For this reason, it will be experimented a simultaneous deployment of enhanced Mobile Broadband (eMBB) connections, massive Machine Type Communications (mMTC) and Ultra-Reliable Low-Latency Communications (URLLC) in a 5G network. The platform, by means of the Blockchain structure which, by the way, guarantees the authenticity of the collected data, will be able to accommodate video analysis services and recognition of critical scenes (i.e. accidents, queues, natural disasters, etc.), integrating video flows from drones and cameras for territorial monitoring. This architecture allows to trace in real time the scenarios relating to the modal distribution of mobility flows in the reference urban context and to monitor the viable arteries to preserve city safety standards.

Therefore, thanks to the real time collected data, within the study area, traffic flows and individual trips will be monitored and, detecting and aggregating the data by time intervals (i.e. peak and off-peak daytime intervals, etc.) and by day types (i.e. working days, holidays, etc.) in real time, update Origin/Destination (O/D) matrices and provide information to authorities and citizens in order to, for example, reduce the time spent on the road by vehicles or to find the parking stall, to optimize the paths favoring the flow of congested areas (also for pedestrians, anti-gatherings, according to policies to combat the spread of Covid 19) and to promote alternative and sustainable mobility modes (as bicycle or walking).

In order to implement statistical models and O/D matrices to adapt the mobility demand to the service offered by the transport system and to optimize the collected traffic data, the mobility in the Artena's territory has to be known, through the development of a Travel Demand Forecasting Model.

2   Travel Demand Forecasting Model

Generally, a travel-demand model can be defined as a mathematical relationship between the travel-demand flows on the one hand, and the transportation network system, on the other hand. The most used traffic prediction model in Transportation Engineering is the Travel Demand Forecasting Model, TDFM [12]. The TDFM, also known as four-step travel demand model, is an ordered system of four sub-models, each of them related to one or more choice dimensions: the traffic emission model, the traffic distribution model, the traffic mode-choice model and the path-choice model (see Fig. 2).

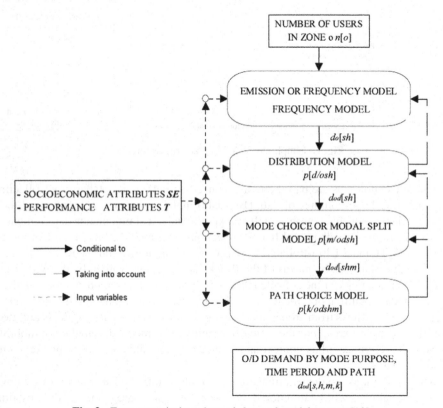

Fig. 2. Four-step trip-based travel-demand model system [12].

It provides, on a specific reference period, all the trips undertaking in a specific analysis area, according to their purpose, time period, origin, destination, path, transport mode, socio-economic role of the user and defining fixed performance attributes (T) of the network system and socio-economic attributes (SE) of the area. The TDFM can be formally expressed by means of the following expression [12]:

$$d_{od}^i[s, h, m, k] = d_o^i[sh](SE, T) \cdot p^i[d/osh](SE, T) \cdot p^i[m/oshd](SE, T) \cdot$$
$$p^i[k/oshdm](SE, T) \tag{1}$$

where:

d^i_{od} [s, h, m, k] is the average number of trips of the class user (cu) i, starting from origin traffic zone o, finishing in the destination traffic zone d, for a specific purpose s, within the time period h, using the transport mode m, and choosing the trip path k;

d_{io} [sh](SE,T) is the average number of trips of the cu i, for purpose s, within the time period h, that starts from o;

p^i (d/osh) is the fraction of trips of the cu i, for purpose s, within the time period h, that starts from o and finishes to d;

p^i (m/oshd) is the fraction of trips of the cu i, for purpose s, within the time period h, that starts from o and finishes to d, by means of the transport mode m;

p^i (k/oshdm) is the fraction of trips of the cu i, for purpose s, within the time period h, with the transport mode m, that starts from o and finishes to d, using the trip path k.

It is worth to be highlighted that, due to specific peculiarities which belong to each activity system and its transportation services and facilities, an ad hoc preliminary evaluation, relating to the identification of relevant spatial dimensions of the transportation network and of spatial characterization of trips, is required.

Generally, it consists into the definition of the study area; the zoning process (subdivision of the defined area into discrete traffic zones with defined socioeconomic characteristics), the identification of the basic network and the development of the O/D matrices [12]. Its application to the Artena's territory has been presented below.

3 Framework of the Study Area

3.1 Framework of the Territory, Infrastructures, Economy and Population of Artena

Artena is an Italian municipality of the metropolitan city of Rome, about 30 km south.

The municipal territory, which extends for about 54.8 km^2, has a morphology characterized by different levels of altitude. The oldest part of Artena, in fact, stands on a hill belonging to the Ernico-Lepino-Ausona ridge and which is between 400 and 600 m above sea level (als). The most recent part, on the other hand, rises on the plain of the Sacco River which stands at altitudes between 200 and 250 m als and surrounds the edge of the ridge on which the ancient part of the city is located.

According to the 15th Census of Population and housing 2011 [13] of the Italian National Institute of Statistics (ISTAT), the Artena's population exceeds 13.660 habitants, considering the resident population 15 years or over, there are: 4913 employed, 825 students, 552 unemployed and 2060 house-workers. Among these, 3642 habitants daily move outside the municipality for work or study reasons.

On the other hand, as far as the economic and productive fabric of the territory of Artena are concerned, according to the 9th Industry, services and non-profit institutions Census 2011 of ISTAT [14], 775 economic units were identified, including private, public and non-profit activities with 2278 employees, 430 volunteers and 33 other-workers categories.

The habited centers, the productive, commercial and services activities are mainly concentrated along the provincial roads, while the remaining part of the territory is mainly characterized by the presence of agricultural plots. It is therefore possible to identify a more densely populated/commercial area within the municipality of Artena (see Fig. 3).

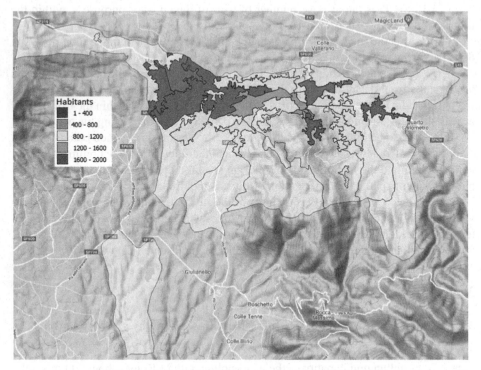

Fig. 3. Population distribution on the territory of Artena [15].

Artena benefits from the presence of several infrastructures, located outside the municipal area, but which strongly affect internal traffic, in fact, to the north is the regional road (SR) 6 Casilina and the A1 Rome-Naples Highway with the "Valmontone" exit about 2 km and the "Colleferro" exit about 8 km from Artena center. To the south is the state road (SS) 7 Appia. The internal penetration network of the Artena territory starting from the municipal border, converges at the foot of the ancient and perched area which is crossed by a single alternating one-way road and is therefore mainly an area intended for pedestrians or two-wheeled vehicles. Finally, the territory of Artena is served to the north, by the Roma Termini - Cassino railway line with the Valmontone and Colleferro stops and to the south by the Roma Termini - Velletri railway line, with relative stop (see Fig. 4).

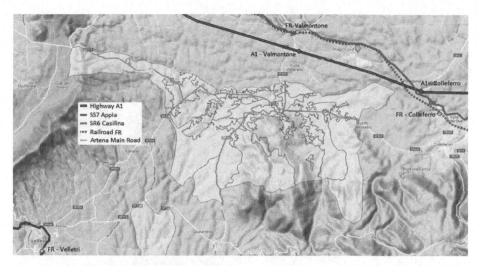

Fig. 4. Main Infrastructures close to the territory of Artena [15].

3.2 Preliminary Traffic Flow Analysis

With the aim to identify an effective zoning, a preliminary analysis of the commuting trips for work and study purposes have been performed, by using the ISTAT open-source database [13]. In particular two different kind of sources data have been used: the *commuting matrix*, which characterizes a generic trip defining Province and Municipality of origin (residence), Gender, Purpose (study or work), Province and Municipality of destination, Mode of transportation, Exit time and Trip duration and *micro-data*, which defines only the geolocation at census-particle level.

According to the well-known Origin/Destination (O/D) matrix structure, the analysis of the commuting trips has been performed for the following groups: internal trips; internal-external exchange trips; external-internal exchange trips and crossing trips.

Artena's Internal Trips: These are all the trips that start and finish within the municipality of Artena, which according to the commuting matrix (municipal level), are 2969 trips per day. Due to the geolocation uncertainty, intrinsic of the micro-data, only 2105 of them can be used for the analysis (equal to 79%, in agreement with 76,57% observed on National scale). In the Fig. 5 a and b, are reported graphical representations of the distribution of emitted trips (census-particle as origin) and attracted (census-particle as destination), respectively.

Artena's Internal-External Exchange Trips: These are all the trips that start from Artena and finish outside the municipal area, which according to the commuting matrix, are 3649 trips per day. In particular, 15 different Provinces attract trips from Artena and more than 98% of the total trips are attracted by the provinces of Rome, Frosinone and Latina. Therefore, taking into account all the municipalities that attract at least 1% of the trips from Artena, 3270 trips per day have been considered (about 89.72%).

In the Fig. 6 is reported the distribution of emitted trips from Artena (census-particle as origin) to the external municipalities.

a)

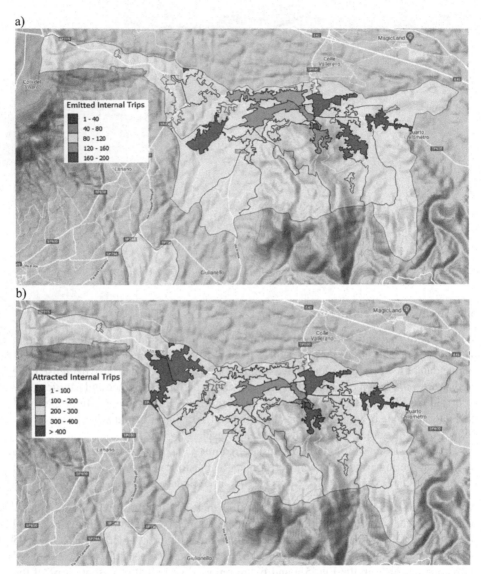

b)

Fig. 5. Distribution of a) Emitted trips (census-particle as origin) and b) Attracted trips (census-particle as destination) [15].

Artena's External-Internal Exchange Trips: These are all the trips that start outside Artena and finish within the municipal area, which according to the commuting matrix, are 946 trips per day. Also in this case more than 99% of the total trips are emitted by the provinces of Rome, Frosinone and Latina. Therefore, taking into account all the municipalities that emit at least 1% of the trips attracted by Artena and summing the geolocation uncertainty, 540 trips per day have been considered (about 57.08%).

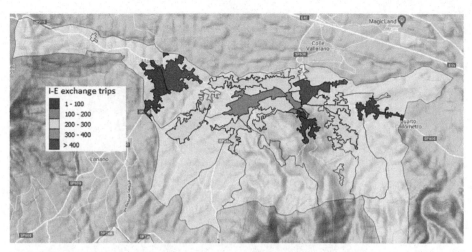

Fig. 6. Distribution of the internal-external exchange trips (census-particle as origin) [15].

In the Fig. 7 is reported the distribution of trips attracted by Artena (census-particle as destination).

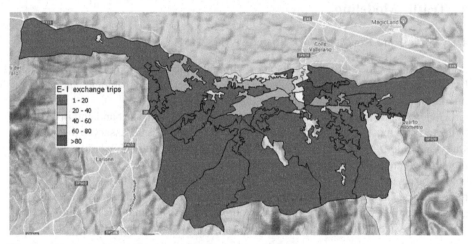

Fig. 7. Distribution of the external-internal exchange trips (census-particle as destination) [15].

Artena's Crossing Trips: These are all the trips that have both their origin and destination external to the Municipal area, but use the transportation system of Artena affecting the internal traffic. In order to describe adequately, albeit approximately, the crossing trips, at least the municipalities adjacent to the territory of Artena have been selected (see Fig. 8) and Rome, Frosinone and Latina as strong attractors within a radius of 50 km area, have been also considered.

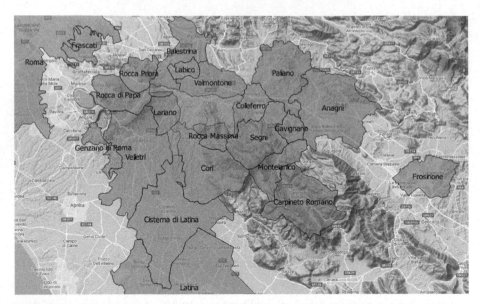

Fig. 8. Position of the Municipalities considered for the crossing trips evaluation [15].

4   Traffic Modeling

4.1   Zoning and Road Network Structure

For this analysis, the study area coincides with the entire municipal territory of Artena. Everything outside the border, called cordon, is external environment and only the interconnections with the study area are taken into account.

Generally, the trips that are carried out in a given area, can start and end in any point of the territory, but to allow the transport system modeling, it is necessary to discretize the study area into traffic zones, characterized by an internal centroid, where it is assumed that all the emitted and attracted trips are located.

As far as the Artena' s territory is concerned, the ISTAT subdivision proposes 38 micro-zones. Taking into account the location of habited zone and productive activities and considering the results obtained by the preliminary trips analysis, a zoning with 11 internal zone and 7 external centroids has been proposed and represented in the Fig. 9.

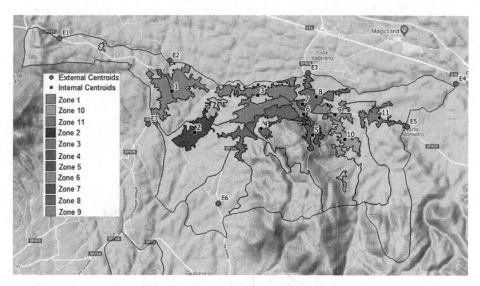

Fig. 9. Proposed zoning of Artena [15].

This simplification is acceptable, in fact, are still considered: 99.7% resident population, 99.8% resident-employed, 92.2% economic activities, 92.5% employees, 92.8% volunteers and 90.9% other-workers category. In the Table 1 the emitted and attracted trips for each traffic zone have been summarized.

Table 1. Emitted, attracted and total trips for each traffic zone.

Zone	Emitted trips	Attracted trips	Total trips
1	499	88	587
2	465	14	479
3	610	213	823
4	652	144	796
5	620	43	663
6	227	234	461
7	358	351	709
8	644	607	1251
9	349	173	522
10	478	31	509
11	2	36	38
%	**99,78**	**88,51**	**96,31**

Finally, the identification of the relevant transportation network of the Artena's territory has been performed and used to model the road network system. Three different level of road category have been identified: State (about 7.5 m of width), municipal (5.5 m) and local roads (3 m) and the representation of the basic network graph can be observed in the Fig. 10.

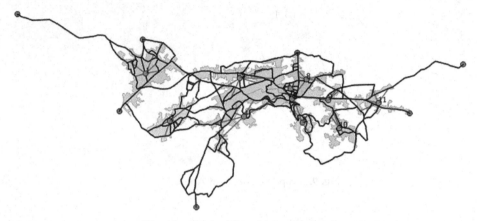

Fig. 10. Graph of Artena's road network.

4.2 O/D Matrix Evaluation

For the evaluation of the O/D matrixes, based on the proposed zoning, the ISTAT commuting matrix has been used to estimate the fractions of trips distinguishing for mode and exit time (ET) interval. By way of example, in the Table 2 have been summarized the coefficients used for splitting up the total trips reported in the micro data database.

In the absence of traffic counts, in order to develop a traffic daily pattern, it has been assumed that: 1) the morning peak hour matrix is the heavier between the four exit time intervals of the ISTAT commuting matrix; 2) the lunch hour matrix is composed of 100% of trips for study purposes and 50% of work trips of public employees (transposed respect to the morning one); 3) the afternoon hour matrix is composed of 50% of work trips of public employees and 100% of work trips of private (transposed respect to the morning one); 4) the off-peak hour matrix is the 0.05 fraction of the morning peak hour. Where:

– for internal trips and external-internal exchange trips the ratios between public and private employees is assumed equal to Artena's reference 88% private workers 12% public workers [14];
– for internal-external exchange trips and crossing trips, the ratios between public and private employees is evaluated with reference to Rome (the external municipality with the most attraction trips 78.5% private workers 21.5% public workers [14].

Table 2. Coefficients of Modal Partition for micro-data internal trips analysis.

Study purpose				
ET interval	<7:15	7:15 ÷ 8:15	8:15 ÷ 9:15	>9:15
	0,04	0,61	0,34	0,00
Car + motorcycle	0,26	0,44	0,57	0,67
Public transportation	0,51	0,40	0,14	0,00
Train	0,12	0,01	0,00	0,33
Bike	0,00	0,00	0,00	0,00
Walking	0,11	0,15	0,29	0,00
Work purpose				
ET interval	<7:15	7:15 ÷ 8:15	8:15 ÷ 9:15	>9:15
	0,49	0,30	0,15	0,07
Car + motorcycle	0,77	0,69	0,67	0,63
Public transportation	0,06	0,02	0,01	0,05
Train	0,01	0,00	0,00	0,00
Bike	0,00	0,00	0,00	0,00
Walking	0,15	0,28	0,32	0,31
Other	0,01	0,00	0,00	0,01

Finally, to take into account the presence of heavy vehicles and other trips purposes, a rate of 10% and of 30%, have been added, respectively.

The data obtained so far, have been used for the preliminary flow evaluation and the results have been reported below.

5 Preliminary Results: Traffic Flows Evaluation

In order to design and apply the better smart traffic strategies for Artena municipality, the development of a complete traffic model of the road network have been performed. Traffic data obtained by the ISTAT open-source database have been used, waiting for more recent and complete traffic count data on the Artena territory, and the traffic assignment has been performed by User Equilibrium method. The preliminary results have been reported below.

By way of example, the traffic flow distribution for the car and motorcycle mode, for both morning and afternoon peak hour matrices have been reported in the Fig. 11a) and b), respectively. As it is possible to see, the internal penetration road infrastructures of Artena (see Fig. 4) are the busiest links of the Municipality, due to the prominent crossing and

a)

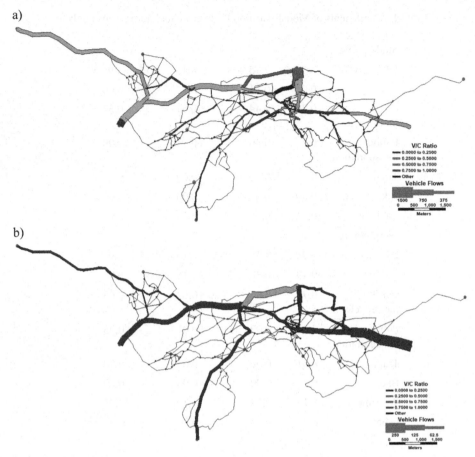

b)

Fig. 11. Car and motorcycle mode traffic flow distribution for a) morning peak hour matrix and b) afternoon hour matrix.

exchange traffic, respect to the internal trips, in fact it is close to an important motorway tollbooth (which connect to main cities like Rome and Frosinone) and to three train stations, for these reasons its territory is therefore also crossed by people who reside in other municipalities, intent to take the motorway or the train.

These preliminary observations have to be validated by the traffic counts and the traffic model have to be calibrated.

6   Conclusion

This paper presents preliminary finding related to the SUMMa Project development, promoted within the Smarter Italy Project. The pilot project took place into Artena Municipality and involved the design and development of a digital platform system for the mobility analysis by means of advanced sensors, drones and cameras that exploit specific AI algorithms and 5G communication infrastructures.

With the aim of optimizing the use of the mobility data that will be made available by the use of the new technologies envisaged by the project, the Travel Demand Forecasting Model of Artena was developed.

The model developed so far, which requires the calibration phase from the traffic counts that will become available, shows that the city of Artena is characterized by a relevant crossing traffic. Instead, the traffic that originates and ends in Artena is lower and would not generate, on its own, reasons for congestion in the area. If these observations will be confirmed by the traffic counts, targeted projects could be design to guarantee traffic fluidification by minimizing crossings and traffic light intersections, and avoiding paths close to downtown activities (schools and offices). The model represents the basis on which the new platform will implement the O/D matrices, updated in real time, and elaborate the best mobility proposal in terms of reducing congestion, emissions and time lost for traveling or searching for parking. The information content will be available to authorities and citizens, to have the best possible experience of smart and sustainable mobility.

As shown in the paper, a depth analysis of the territory and the economy of the study area is needed due to the particularities that characterize each municipality, city or metropolis. It means that the results are specific of the analyzed area and are not applicable without the necessary adaptations. In the same time the presented approach is worldwide suitable because is based on a general and replicable framework and can be used as a guide for the local Authorities intent to design and implement mobility smart applications.

Acknowledgments. The authors wish to acknowledge the contribution by the Italian Ministry of Economic Development (MiSE-DGSCERP) which financed the Smart Urban Mobility Management (SUMMa) project, sponsored by the "Program of support for emerging technologies in the context of 5G", Economical Resources FSC 2014–2020 - CIPE 61/2018.

References

1. European Commission: Sustainable Mobility for Europe: safe, connected, and clean. COM (2018) 293 final (2018)
2. European Commission: Sustainable and Smart Mobility Strategy – putting European transport on track for the future. COM (2020) 789 final (2020)
3. Directive 2010/40/EU of the European Parliament and of the Council on the framework for the deployment of Intelligent Transport Systems in the field of road transport and for interfaces with other modes of transport (2010)
4. Maldonado Silveira Alonso Munhoz, P.A., et al.: Smart mobility: the main drivers for increasing the intelligence of urban mobility. Sustainability 12(24), 10675 (2020). https://doi.org/10.3390/su122410675
5. Pinna, F., Masala, F., Garau, C.: Urban policies and mobility trends in Italian smart cities. Sustainability 9(4), 494 (2017). https://doi.org/10.3390/su9040494
6. Garau, C., Masala, F., Pinna, F.: Cagliari and smart urban mobility: analysis and comparison. Cities 56, 35–46 (2016). https://doi.org/10.1016/j.cities.2016.02.012. ISSN 0264-2751
7. Flügge, B. (ed.): Smart Mobility – Connecting Everyone. Springer, Wiesbaden (2017). https://doi.org/10.1007/978-3-658-15622-0

8. Chow, J.: Informed urban transport systems_ classic and emerging mobility methods toward smart cities. Elsevier (2018). ISBN: 9780128136133
9. D'Apuzzo M., et al.: An exploratory step to evaluate the pedestrian exposure in urban environment. Computational Science and Its Applications – ICCSA 2020 VII, p. pp.645–657. Springer, Cagliari (2020). https://doi.org/10.1007/978-3-030-58820-5_47
10. G.U. 18/04/2018, n. 90. Modalità attuative e strumenti operativi della sperimentazione su strada delle soluzioni di Smart Road e di guida connessa e automatica. D. MIN. INFRAS-TRUTTURE E TRASP. 28/02/2018. English version "Implementation methods and operational tools of road testing of Smart Road solutions and connected and automatic driving" (2018)
11. MITD. https://innovazione.gov.it/argomenti/smarter-italy/. Accessed 07 Mar 2021
12. Cascetta, E.: Transportation Systems Analysis. Models and Applications. 2nd edn., pp. 1–752. Springer, Cham (2009). https://doi.org/10.1007/978-0-387-75857-2
13. ISTAT. https://www.istat.it/en/censuses/population-and-housing. Accessed 07 Mar 2021
14. ISTAT. http://dati-censimentoindustriaeservizi.istat.it/Index.aspx?lang=en&SubSessio nId=286d23f3-7622-4e49-b2e0-e072592a33c3. Accessed 07 Mar 2021
15. QGIS Development Team: QGIS geographic information system. open-source geospatial foundation project (2017). http://qgis.osgeo.org

International Workshop
on Econometrics and Multidimensional
Evaluation in Urban Environment
(EMEUE 2021)

The Benefit Transfer Method for the Economic Evaluation of Urban Forests

Francesco Sica[1](✉) and Antonio Nesticò[2]

[1] Department of Architecture and Design, Sapienza University of Rome, Rome, Italy
francesco.sica@uniroma1.it
[2] Department of Civil Engineering, University of Salerno, Fisciano, SA, Italy
anestico@unisa.it

Abstract. The communities' interest in urban forestry is growing, recently also in order to face the COVID-19 pandemic crisis. Although the multiple benefits (ecosystem services) that forestry provides in cities are recognized by the international community, the issue of economic evaluation of each service in the context of urban renewal processes is still little debated.

This paper describes the Benefit Transfer Method (BTM) as a framework for estimating the total economic value of urban forests. This is done with the aim of outlining an economic model to support decision-making processes. The model is tested on a set of Italian cities. Research perspectives are in the conclusions.

Keywords: Economic evaluation · Ecosystem services · Benefit transfer method

1 Introduction

In the last decades of the twentieth century, contemporary cities are often characterized by uncontrolled urbanization, high air pollution, strong population growth with negative effects on the urban quality levels [1]. Thus, the need to put in place initiatives aimed at defending and preserving the urban ecosystem [2]. These are Nature-Based Solutions (NBS) projects with which to create healthy public spaces for people's well-being [3].

NBS include: *i*) the use and enhancement of existing natural elements (urban forestry); *ii*) the implementation of technologically innovative projects such as green walls or roofs on buildings [4–6]. NBS produce multiple benefits (ecosystem services) with which to mitigate the effects of anthropogenic actions on nature, contribute to the psycho-physical well-being of the population, and promote economic growth [7–9]. In support of NBS, the *Food and Agricultural Organization* (FAO) of the United Nations (UN) and the *Arbor Day Foundation* created the *Tree Cities of the World* program in 2018. This identifies forestry as a key action strategy for eco-sustainable urban development.

Although it is recognized that urban forests contribute significantly to the sustainable development of cities, public decision-makers do not often pay attention to forestry projects. This is due to *i*) the interest in preferring actions with immediate financial

---

This contribution is to be attributed in equal parts to the two authors

© Springer Nature Switzerland AG 2021
O. Gervasi et al. (Eds.): ICCSA 2021, LNCS 12954, pp. 39–49, 2021.
https://doi.org/10.1007/978-3-030-86979-3_3

returns; *ii*) the difficulty in including the economic value of the environmental and social effects of forestry in the economic evaluation of territorial and urban projects [10].

According to the relevant literature, the methods traditionally used for the economic valuation of ecosystem services connected to urban forestry are classified into *stated* and *revealed* preference valuation methods [11–13]. Through *stated* preference methods, the economic value of ecosystem goods and services is expressed in terms of the *Willingness-To-Pay* (WTP) of the community to conserve and/or implement the urban forest [13, 14]. *Revealed* preference methods, on the other hand, are based on the capture of economic prices of economic goods related directly, and not, to the environmental asset. The latter category includes the hedonic price method, commonly used to estimate the market value of the natural components through the marginal prices that determine mercantile valuations.

In addition to stated and revealed preference valuation methods, another assessment strategy is that of the *Benefit Transfer Method* (BTM). With the BTM, the economic values already declared in scientific studies for environmental goods and services can be used as a reference for further analyses conducted in territorial contexts with dissimilar characteristics [15]. The BTM is based on meta-analytical statistical methods in which variables representing the socio-economic and environmental aspects of the place under investigation are included [16]. Research shows that geographic referencing is vital for transferring values for spatially defined goods since location dictates value and this typically decays over increasing distance [17]. In the case of urban forest, the proximity to populations, their density, income levels are crucial drivers of the value provided by the forestation.

2 Work Aim

In relation to the above introductory framework, the research objective is to define an analytical function for estimating the total economic value of urban forests. This function is constructed according to the *Benefit Transfer Method* (BTM) principles.

In the following, *Sect.* 3 (*Materials and Method*) illustrates the set of bibliographical references from which the analysis variables are derived. An explanation on the statistical method based on the *Benefit Transfer Method* is provided. This for the construction of the meta-analytical regression function used to define the economic value of urban forests in the cities. *Section* 4 (*Result*) describes the value function derived from the meta-analysis conducted in literature. The same value function is then applied to a case study. Finally, *Sect.* 5 (*Conclusion*) reports conclusions and research perspectives.

3 Materials and Methods

The Benefit Transfer Method starts from the results of economic analyses relating to areas comparable with the territorial context of study. The method is divided into three steps:

1. literature analysis in which environmental, economic and social data of interest related to territorial contexts similar to the study area are reported (*literature search*);

2. identification and definition of the variables to be used in the statistical model at the base of the Benefit Transfer Method (*meta-analysis variables*);
3. construction of the regression function for estimating the economic, social and environmental value of the analysis asset (*meta-regression model*).

The 3 steps are described below in relation to urban forestry projects.

3.1 Literature Analysis

The analysis of current literature allows to select 13 scientific papers that have as reference Key-Words (KW): (KW1) «*urban forest*», (KW2) «*ecosystem services*», (KW3) «*Willingness-To-Pay*». We make the choice to assume data from the 13 papers as elements of the study meta-sample. Table 1 lists the 13 papers studied.

3.2 Meta-analysis Variables

The economic values of urban forests, expressed in terms of Willingness-To-Pay (WTP), are from the papers in Table 1. In addition to the information on WTP, the drivers that most influence the value of WTP according to each contribution are derived. These are socio-economic variables and morphological-environmental parameters.

Among the socio-economic variables found most frequently in the 13 analysis papers are GDP per capita and population density. Forestry parameters include the canopy cover and the ecosystem services. Ecosystem services are classified into four categories: Provisioning, Regulating, Cultural, and Supporting services [18, 19]. These categories are coded as dummy variables, i.e., variables that assume: unit value when the urban forest provides the i-*th* ecosystem service; zero value otherwise.

Table 2 summarizes the variables, of dependent and non-dependent type, examined for the construction of the meta-analytic value function. The mean value of each variable, calculated from the data collected from the 13 papers, is in the last column (*Mean*) of Table 2.

3.3 Meta-regression Model

Based on the variables in Table 2, the meta analytic function for estimating the economic value of urban forests is constructed.

Two methodological approaches are commonly used for constructing meta-regression models: the least squares method and the multilevel one [17, 20, 21]. The latter is employed for the meta-analytic function at the basis of the present work.

The *Multi-Level Method* (MLM) makes allowances for the variance and heteroscedasticity of the analysis variables [17]. Through the MLM the variance of the error term at each explanatory variable is estimated. This ensures, on the one hand, that the standard errors of the parameters of interest are more accurately calculated; on the other hand, that the coefficients linking the independent variables to the dependent variable are more accurately quantified [20–23].

In the present case, the dependent variable y_i gives the annual monetary value per hectare of the i-*th* urban forest in the investigation area. The explanatory and dummy

Table 1. Overview of valuation studies.

	Document title	Year	Source
1	Public preferences and willingness to pay for invasive forest pest prevention programs in urban areas	2020	Forests
2	Social valuation of regulating and cultural ecosystem services of Arroceros Forest Park: A man-made forest in the city of Manila, Philippines	2019	Journal of Urban Management
3	Economic valuation of the calden (Prosopis caldenia Burkart) forest in the south of Córdoba, Argentina [Valoraci n econ mica del bosque de cald n (Prosopis caldenia Burkart) en el sur de Cordoba	2018	Revista Chapingo, Serie Ciencias Forestales y del Ambiente
4	Value orientation and payment for ecosystem services: Perceived detrimental consequences lead to willingness-to-pay for ecosystem services	2018	Journal of Environmental Management
5	Effect of different personal histories on valuation for forest ecosystem services in urban areas: A case study of Mt. Rokko, Kobe, Japan	2017	Urban Forestry and Urban Greening
6	Atlanta households' willingness to increase urban forests to mitigate climate change	2017	Urban Forestry and Urban Greening
7	Willingness-to-pay for recreation services of urban ecosystem and its value assessment: A case study in the Wenjiang District of Chengdu City, China	2017	Shengtai Xuebao/ Acta Ecologica Sinica
8	Linking Forest to Faucets in a Distant Municipal Area: Public Support for Forest Restoration and Water Security in Albuquerque, New Mexico	2017	Water Economics and Policy

(continued)

Table 1. (*continued*)

	Document title	Year	Source
9	Land use influence on raw surface water quality and treatment costs for drinking supply in São Paulo State (Brazil)	2016	Ecological Engineering
10	Willingness to pay for maintenance of a nature conservation area: A case of Mount Wilhelm, Papua New Guinea	2016	Asian Social Science
11	Individual aesthetic differences evaluation of Yan'an urban forests in the loess plateau China	2014	International Journal of Multimedia and Ubiquitous Engineering
12	Scope for introducing payments for ecosystem services as a strategy to reduce deforestation in the Kilombero wetlands catchment area	2014	Forest Policy and Economics
13	Estimating non-use values of Anzali wetland using contingent valuation method	2010	Journal of Environmental Studies

variables used in the proposed model are processed in vector terms. The vector X_i^S includes the socio-economic characteristics of the reference urban context (*GDP per capita, population density*) and the morphological parameters of the urban forest to be evaluated from an economic point of view (*Canopy Cover*). The vector X_i^{ESS} Involves the dummy values of eco-system services related to forestry.

Each variable in Table 2 is log-transformed. This allows us to define the linear relationship between the dependent and independent variables ensuring a nearly constant degree of elasticity between factors.

The meta-analytic expression assumes the algebraic connotation of the type:

$$y_i = \alpha + \beta_i^S X_i^S + \gamma_i^{ESS} X_i^{ESS} + \mu_i \tag{1}$$

where the term μ_i represents the regression function error.

In logarithmic terms the meta-analytic expression is written:

$$y_i = e^{\alpha + \beta_i^S \ln(X_i^S) + \gamma_i^{ESS} \ln(X_i^{ESS}) + \mu_i} \tag{2}$$

4 Benefit Transfer Function for Urban Forests

The results of the meta-analysis conducted from the items in Table 1 are in Table 3. This reports the regression coefficients for each variable. The estimated coefficients express

Table 2. Variables set.

Variable	Description	Measurement Unit	Mean
Dependent Variable			
Willingness-To-Pay (WTP)	The value of urban forest in US dollars per hectare per year	$/(ha·year)	1,689
Socio-economic and forest variables			
Canopy Cover (CC)	Size of the urban forest in ha	ha	1,465
Gross Domestic Product (GDP) per capita	GDP per capita in US dollars	$	23,130
Population Density (PD)	Population density in number of people per square kilometer	inhab/sqkm	410
Ecosystem Services			
Provisioning (Pro)	1 = ecosystem service is provisioning of food, resources, 0 = otherwise	[0,1]	0.497
Regulating (Reg)	1 = ecosystem service is local climate regulation, 0 = otherwise		0.442
Cultural (Cul)	1 = ecosystem service is preservation of cultural heritage, 0 = otherwise		0.517
Supporting (Supp)	1 = ecosystem service is biodiversity preservation, 0 = otherwise		0.673

the percentage change in the dependent variable (annual $ value of urban forest per hectare) as a function of the percentage point change in the i-*th* explicative variable.

The results obtained illustrate that:

- The regression constant has a significant numerical value. It expresses the economic value of one hectare of urban forest per year provided that the explanatory variables are equal to the mean values (canopy cover = ln (1,465), PIL = ln (23.130) in USD, population density = ln (410) people per square kilometer);
- The coefficient relative to Canopy Cover (CC) is negative and statistically significant. This indicates that larger urban forests have a lower unit economic value than smaller forests, showing decreasing marginal appreciation in relation to the natural area size;
- The income, expressed by Gross Domestic Product (GDP) per capita, is positively and statistically significantly associated with the economic value of the urban forest

Table 3. Meta-regressions results.

Variable	Regression coefficient	
Constant	7.654	(***)
Socio-economic and forest variables		
Canopy Cover (CC)	−1.023	(***)
Gross Domestic Product (GDP) per capita	1.652	(***)
Population Density (PD)	0.356	(*)
Ecosystem Services		
Provisioning (Pro)	−0.319	
Regulating (Reg)	−0.475	
Cultural (Cul)	1.236	(**)
Supporting (Supp)	−0.360	

per hectare. This represents the scenario in which city dwellers with above-average incomes value nature more markedly;
- The population density is positively associated with the dependent variable. This means that in urban areas with higher population density the value per hectare of nature is higher than in areas with lower population density;
- With regard to eco-systemic services, low coefficient values were found for provisioning (Pro), regulating (Reg) and supporting (Sup) services. This is in contrast to services related to the aesthetics and conservation (Cul) of cultural heritage.

Based on the coefficients in Table 3, (2) is written as follows:

$$Value\,of\,urbanforest_i$$
$$= e^{7.654-1.023[\ln(CC)-\ln(1.465)]+1.652[\ln(GDP)-\ln(23.130)]+0.356[\ln(PD)-\ln(410)]_i} \quad (3)$$

4.1 Application of the Transfer Function to a Case-Study

Function (3) is applied for the economic evaluation of urban forests in the cities of Milan, Rome, Naples and Catania. Information on canopy cover and the socio-economic system of the context in which the investigated urban forests are located is from European Urban Nature Atlas database (https://naturvation.eu/atlas; last accessed on 07/05/2021).

Milan, Rome, Naples and Catania have significantly different values of per capita income, population density and canopy cover. The size of the canopy cover in the selected cases varies between 1ha and 27ha.

Table 4 reports the values estimated by means of the proposed value function. Formula (3) returns the annual economic values per hectare of urban forest in relation to the socio-economic characteristics of the locality concerned.

Based on the results of Table 4, the *Ticinello Agrarian Park* of the Milan city records a total economic value per year of $121,625.49 higher than that of the urban forests of

Table 4. Meta-regressions result on urban forests in Italian cities.

	Milan	Rome	Naples	Catania
	Ticinello Agrarian Park	*Flaminio Park*	*Capodimonte Urban Park*	*Cibali Forest*
Socio-economic and forest variables				
Canopy Cover (CC) [ha]	35	27	10	20
Gross Domestic Product (GDP) per capita [$]	31,761	26,215	21,222	19,000
Population Density (PD) [inhab/sqKm]	16,947.74	2,030.12	26,398.74	1,585.32
Economic value per ha per year	$3,475.01	$1,479.48	$1,996.98	$816.57
Total economic value per year	$121,625.49	$39,945.99	$19,969.80	$16,331.37

Rome, Naples and Catania cities. The significant valuation of Milan's natural area from an economic point of view is certainly commensurate with the high values of GDP per capita and population density of the city, as well as the canopy cover of the urban forest. The implementation of (3) also provides a unit economic value of particular significance for the *Capodimonte* park in Naples city (1,996.98 $/ha·y). The numerical data obtained is due to the high population density of the study city context (26,398.74 inhab/sqKm), the highest among those of the four cities examined.

5   Conclusions

The urban forest provides multiple benefits to citizens. Valuation methods for estimating the economic value of ecosystem services are used in multiple case studies in the literature. The application of the *Benefit Transfer Method* is common. This method associates the economic values of urban forests in similar areas with the spatial context of analysis. The value transfer is adjusted by multi-level regression functions [24–27].

In this paper, a meta-analysis of the total economic value of urban forestry is conducted based on recent literature references. From the selected works information on the Willingness-To-Pay of the community to implement and/or preserve urban forests on the territory is found. The research allows to identify the variables that influence the urban forestry economic value: per capita income, housing density, canopy cover, eco-system services.

The meta-analysis conducted on the 13 papers shows the economic value of the urban forest is related to: the size of the natural area through the coefficient −1.023; income per capita and population density through the coefficients + 1.652 and +0.356 respectively. In addition, the economic value of the urban forest depends on the ecosystem services that it is able to generate. The results in Table 3 provide correlation coefficients for recreational, regulatory (local climate control, noise reduction, and flood regulation), biodiversity, and habitat services. Significant correlation occurs with respect to cultural services.

The value transfer function makes it possible to derive in quantitative terms the inter-dependencies between the economic value of forestation and both the socio-economic characteristics of the territory and the ecosystem characteristics of the environmental resource under analysis.

The statistical relationship proposed for the estimation of the total economic value of urban forests (see paragraph 4) is tested on the cities of Milan, Rome, Naples and Catania. In particular, 4 natural areas are examined, one for each of the cities considered. The economic results obtained explain that the total economic value of the i-*th* forest is significantly dependent on canopy cover, GDP per capita and population density. The values obtained also suggest the existence of a proportional relationship between the total economic value and the production of ecosystem services.

Limits of the methodological approach are both in the selection of studied works, both in the parameters of multi-level regression function proposed.

Opportunities of future research developments by the proposed work consist in the definition of a quick evaluation method to assess the total economic value of nature-based elements in urban contexts as that of the urban forests in the cities.

References

1. Eurostat: Urban Europe — statistics on cities, towns and suburbs. Cat. No: KS-01–16–691-EN-N (2016). https://doi.org/10.2785/91120
2. Raymond, C.M., et al.: An impact evaluation framework to support planning and evaluation of nature-based solutions projects. report prepared by the EKLIPSE Expert Working Group on Nature-based Solutions to Promote Climate Resilience in Urban Areas. Centre for Ecology & Hydrology, Wallingford, United Kingdom. 82p (2017)
3. Coscia, C., Lazzari, G., Rubino, I.: Values, memory, and the role of exploratory methods for policy-design processes and the sustainable redevelopment of waterfront contexts: the case of Officine Piaggio. Sustainability - Special Issue "Real Estate Economics, Management and Investments 10(9), 2989, 1–22 (2018). https://doi.org/10.3390/su10092989
4. Elmqvist, T., et al.: Urbanization, Biodiversity and Ecosystem Services: Challenges and Opportunities: A Global Assessment, p. 755. Springer, Cham (2013). https://doi.org/10.1007/978-94-007-7088-1
5. Sutton, P.C., Costanza, R.: Global estimates of market and non-market values derived from nighttime satellite imagery, land cover, and ecosystem service valuation. Ecol. Econ. 41(3), 509–527 (2002)
6. Nesshöver, C., et al.: The science, policy and practice of nature-based solutions: an interdisciplinary perspective. Sci. Total Environ. 579, 1215–1227 (2017)
7. Guarini, M.R., Nesticò, A., Morano, P., Sica, F.: A multicriteria economic analysis model for urban forestry projects. In International Symposium on New Metropolitan Perspectives, pp. 564–571. Springer, Cham (2018). https://doi.org/10.1007/978-3-319-92099-3_63
8. Nesticò, A., Guarini, M.R., Morano, P., Sica, F.: An economic analysis algorithm for urban forestry projects. Sustainability 11(2), 314 (2019). https://doi.org/10.3390/su11020314

9. Guarini, M.R., Morano, P., Sica, F.: Eco-system services and integrated urban planning. a multi-criteria assessment framework for ecosystem urban forestry projects. In Values and Functions for Future Cities, pp. 201–216. Springer, Cham (2020). https://doi.org/10.1007/978-3-030-23786-8_11

10. Naumann, S., et al.: Assessment of the potential of ecosystem-based approaches to climate change adaptation and mitigation in Europe. Final report to the European Commission. Ecologic Institute, Berlin, Germany and Environmental Change Institute, Oxford University Centre for the Environment, Oxford, UK (2011)

11. Dobrovolskienė, N., et al.: Developing a composite sustainability index for real estate projects using multiple criteria decision making. Oper. Res. Int. Journal **19**(3), 617–635 (2017). https://doi.org/10.1007/s12351-017-0365-y

12. Fregonara, E., Coscia, C.: Multi criteria analyses, life cycle approaches and delphi method: A methodological proposal to assess design scenarios | Analisi multi criteria, approcci life cycle e delphi method: Una proposta metodologica per valutare scenari di progetto. Valori e Valutazioni **23**, 107–117 (2019)

13. Champ, P.A., Boyle, K.J., Brown, T.C. (eds.): A Primer on Nonmarket Valuation. TENGR, vol. 13. Springer, Dordrecht (2017). https://doi.org/10.1007/978-94-007-7104-8

14. Nesticò, A., Endreny, T., Guarini, M.R., Sica, F., Anelli, D.: Real estate values, tree cover, and per-capita income: an evaluation of the interdependencies in Buffalo City (NY). In: Gervasi, O., et al. (eds.) ICCSA 2020, vol. 12251, pp. 913–926. Springer, Cham (2020). https://doi.org/10.1007/978-3-030-58808-3_65

15. Bergstrom, J.C., Taylor, L.O.: Using meta-analysis for benefits transfer: Theory and practice. Ecol. Econ. **60**(2), 351–360 (2006)

16. Johnston, R.J., Rolfe, J., Rosenberger, R.S., Brouwer, R. (eds.): Benefit Transfer of Environmental and Resource Values. TENGR, vol. 14. Springer, Dordrecht (2015). https://doi.org/10.1007/978-94-017-9930-0

17. Bateman, I.J., Jones, A.P.: Contrasting conventional with multi-level modeling approaches to meta-analysis: expectation consistency in U.K. Woodland Recreation Values. Land Econ. **79**(2), 235–258 (2003)

18. Millennium ecosystem assessment, M. E. A.: Ecosystems and Human Well-Being, vol. 5. Island Press, Washington, DC (2005)

19. TEEB: The economics of ecosystems and biodiversity: ecological and economic foundations. Kumar P. (ed). Earthscan, London and Washington.Tu, G., Abildtrup, J., Garcia, S. (2016)

20. Brander, L.M., Koetse, M.J.: The value of urban open space: meta-analyses of contingent valuation and hedonic pricing results. J. Environ. Manage. **92**(10), 2763–2773 (2011)

21. Schmidt, F.L., Hunter, J.E.: Methods of meta-analysis corrected error and bias in research findings. J. Am. Statist. Assoc. **20**(7) (2004). https://doi.org/10.2307/2289738

22. Zhou, P., Ang, B.W., Poh, K.L.: A mathematical programming approach to constructing composite indicators. Ecol. Econ. **62**(2), 291–297 (2007)

23. Sardi, A., Sorano, E., Cantino, V., Garengo, P.: Big data and performance measurement research: trends, evolution and future opportunities. Measur. Busin. Excell. (2020)

24. Podvezko, V.: The comparative analysis of MCDA methods SAW and COPRAS. Eng. Econ. **22**(2), 134–146 (2011)

25. Ferreira, F.A., Santos, S.P.: Comparing trade-off adjustments in credit risk analysis of mortgage loans using AHP, Delphi and MACBETH. Int. J. Strateg. Prop. Manag. **20**(1), 44–63 (2016)

26. Cerreta, M., Mazzarella, C., Spiezia, M., Tramontano, M.R.: Regenerativescapes: incremental evaluation for the regeneration of unresolved territories in East Naples. Sustainability **12**(17), 6975 (2020)
27. Morano, P., Tajani, F., Di Liddo, F., Amoruso, P.: The public role for the effectiveness of the territorial enhancement initiatives: a case study on the redevelopment of a building in disuse in an Italian small town. Buildings **11**(3), 1–22 (2021)

The Effects of Covid-19 Pandemic on the Housing Market: A Case Study in Rome (Italy)

Francesco Tajani[1], Pierluigi Morano[2], Felicia Di Liddo[2], Maria Rosaria Guarini[1], and Rossana Ranieri[1(✉)]

[1] Department of Architecture and Design, "Sapienza" University of Rome, 00196 Rome, Italy
rossana.ranieri@uniroma1.it
[2] Department of Civil, Environmental, Land, Building Engineering and Chemistry, Polytechnic University of Bari, 70125 Bari, Italy

Abstract. The present study is part of a wider research line focused on the analysis of the effects caused by the pandemic of the Coronavirus disease (Covid-19) on the Italian residential property market. The paper aims to propose a methodology for the assessment of the effects of this abnormal event on the housing price mechanisms. The research could be an operational support for the Public Administration and private investors in their decision making processes. In particular, with reference to the city of Rome (Italy), two datasets of residential properties have been collected and processed through an econometric technique, in order to identify the variations occurred in terms of market appreciation for specific housing factors. The outputs highlight changes in market demand concerning a preference for outdoor spaces, both condominiums and private (terraces and balconies) and for properties located in peripheral areas of the city.

Keywords: Covid-19 · Pandemic · Housing market · Residential selling prices · Econometric technique

1 Introduction

The acute respiratory syndrome caused by Sars-Cov-2 (Covid-19) has started from China in December 2019, becoming a pandemic within few months with more than 122 million infection cases (March 2021) [27]. With reference to the market variations assessment, the Covid-19 pandemic can be considered an unpredictable anomalous event [1]. As a consequence of this event an economic crisis has emerged worldwide: it is observed that in 2020 the global Gross Domestic Product (GDP) has decreased 3.5% compared to 2019 [26]. In the Eurozone (referred to composition in 27 States) the GDP has dropped by 4.8% in 2020 [7], and it is expected to recover by 4.6% in 2021, as the restrictions have been eased and the impact of monetary and fiscal incentive have been activated [6]. In Italy the GDP decrease in 2020, compared to the previous year, has been equal to 8.9% [12].

© Springer Nature Switzerland AG 2021
O. Gervasi et al. (Eds.): ICCSA 2021, LNCS 12954, pp. 50–62, 2021.
https://doi.org/10.1007/978-3-030-86979-3_4

In addition to economic and financial crisis, the pandemic has globally changed many aspects of daily life, causing effects on both the social dynamics and the mental well-being of the population [3, 4, 8, 11, 13, 25]. Since the end of 2019, collective preventive measures have been taken throughout the world and with several restrictions, such as: social distancing, compulsory confinement, reduction or complete banning of access to public places, interruption of theatre, cinema or concert programmes, and reduction of national and international trade. These preventive measures have forced almost all the world's population to carry out different functions in their homes, i.e. smart working and distance learning activities, or sports and recreational activities, by leading to considerable variation in the ways of using domestic spaces and residential condominium areas. With reference to the labour market, the Italian National Institute of Statistics (ISTAT) reports that in Italy in 2019 were about 570,000 remote workers, and during 2020 the workers involved by this job typology have increased of 16.4% for women and 12.8% for men. Moreover, the number of companies using smart working have enlarged from 28.7% in 2019 to 82.3% in 2020 [2, 5, 10]. Therefore, the health emergency has forced a sudden shift to work to be performed at home in many job sectors. It is likely that this condition, though in smaller numbers, may become a permanent change in the dynamics of the labour market, with consequent modifications in the housing demand [15].

The mandatory confinement phase in the spring 2020 (lockdown) has also determined significant variations in the use of urban spaces. The impossibility of leaving homes and the closure of almost all commercial activities during the emergency phases has suspended city daily life. Since it has not longer been possible to use public areas, intermediate condominium spaces such as courtyards, terraces and gardens for leisure and relaxation or sports activities, have become effective in managing domestic temporary overcrowding [16]. In the post lockdown phase from June 2020 there have also been modifications in the way and frequency of using public and private transport. Due to the fear of contagion, the use of private vehicles and the widespread use of electric micro-mobility, both private and shared, has been favored. In Italy, in 2020 there have been 65,000 shared light vehicles (27,000 scooters and 35,000 bicycles), with 86 services activated in the provincial capitals: 14 in Milan, followed by Rome (11) and Turin (7). In detail, scooter-sharing between December 2019 and September 2020 have increased from 4,900 to 27,150, and in the same period the active mobility companies on the national territory have increased from 12 to 38. In this sense, the scooter sharing, like bike sharing, represents the fastest growing micro-mobility service in the current post-lockdown period [19]. The Covid-19 pandemic has changed (and probably will change) the urban dynamics influencing the whole real estate market, also in terms of the quantity of transactions.

2 Aim

In the present study a methodology that could be a valid reference to define the emerging new framework of residential needs has been developed: the modifications that have arisen during the emergency phase will likely persist, permanently modifying the housing factors' appreciation. The present study is part of a wider line of research aimed to analyze and quantify the effects generated on the property market by the pandemic Covid-19. The analysis focuses on the possible changes in the residential market appreciation of intrinsic factors. In particular, a methodological protocol organized in subsequent phases has been developed to assess the modifications that have occurred in the housing property market in the city of Rome between the second semester of 2019 (Phase I – *ante Covid-19*) and the first semester of 2021 (Phase II – *in itinere Covid-19*). The proposed methodology represents an operational tool to support Public Administrations and private investors in the drafting of planning strategies in the residential segment. In this sense, the analysis of the variations in the market demand is carried out through the comparison of the results of the two phases (Phase I and Phase II), in order to define a framework for the future investment choices of private and public operators and in the design phases related to the individual housing units. In particular, the methodology includes two application phases: the first one (Phase I) with data referring to the second half of 2019, which can be considered free from the influence of the effects of the pandemic; the second one (Phase II) with data referring to the first half of 2021, a period in which the effects of the pandemic on the residential market are already evident and the changes are still underway. The structure of the methodology makes it possible to monitor the effects of the pandemic on the residential market by considering successive evaluation steps *in itinere*. Moreover, the methodology can be used to check the impacts of other types of anomalous events on the territory, such as earthquakes or environmental disasters of various typology.

The paper is structured as follows. Section 3 introduces the case study with reference to the residential market in the city of Rome and introduces the variables chosen to structure the databases. Section 4 illustrates the methodology and the econometric technique adopted. Section 5 describes the implementation of the technique with references to the Phase I and summarizes the results obtained. In Sect. 6 the implementation of the same econometric technique to the data collected in Phase II is carried out. Section 7 explains the comparisons between the outputs of the two phases and, finally, in Sect. 8 the conclusions of the work are reported.

3   Case Study

3.1   The Housing Market of the City of Rome

For the implementation of the proposed methodology, the two datasets, both composed by 165 residential properties, sold in the city of Rome, have been detected. For each property, the main intrinsic positional and technological factors - i.e. internal surface area, floor level, number of bathrooms, presence and consistency of balconies or terraces, presence of green condominium areas, etc. - have been collected. In order to select the variables, for the implementation of the econometric technique, an analysis of the Italian residential segment has carried out.

In Italy, according to data detected by the Italian Revenue Agency [22], in 2019, the volume of residential sales has amounted to 603,541 housing units with an increase of 4.2% year-on-year, continuing a positive trend since 2014. In the second half of 2019, the residential market segment, in the ten largest Italian cities by volume of sales, has shown a preference for the three-room apartments (40.6%), followed by the two-room apartments (23.1%) and the four-room apartments (23.8%) [21]. As regards the province of Rome, in 2019 the volume of houses sold has amounted to 48,809 units, and the highest number of transactions has been recorded in the area of the urban city center (67.1% of the total provincial market), with an overall trend change equal to +3%. With reference to selling prices observed, contrary to the volumes of sales, in 2019, a negative trend (−2.5%) has been found compared to the previous year, due to above all by the overall downward trend of the economic-financial framework of the real estate market, as well as by the difficult access to bank loans. In the context of the municipality of Rome, in the historic center macro-area the highest selling prices have been recorded (5.748 €/m^2), followed by the semi-central macro-areas in detail known as: "Parioli–Flaminio" (5.192 €/m^2), "Prati–Trionfale" (4.157 €/m^2), "Salaria–Trieste–Nomentana" (4.111 €/m^2). In the first two quarter of 2020 in Italy, residential sales volumes have reduced: however, a positive trend has emerged in the third and the fourth quarter, with an increase equal to +8.8%. The national trend of residential sales, compared to 2019, has dropped of 7.7%, with a reduction of approximately 46 thousand units. In the context outlined, the city of Rome represents an exception, with an increase in transactions number of +7.9%. As regards the preferences relating to the size of the residential properties, the highest growth has been recorded for the largest housing units size, between 115 and 145 m^2 (+10.7%) and over 145 m^2 (+14%); however, in the city of Rome, the change is positive in all size classes, and it is less significant for smaller units. Furthermore, referring to the selling prices, on average, in the first three quarters of 2020, compared to the same period in 2019, housing prices has raised by 2.1%. The housing market in the city of Rome is characterized by a strong heterogeneity both in terms of the size of the properties and of the average selling price [23].

Figure 1 shows the municipal trade areas according to the geographical distribution developed by the Real Estate Market Observatory (OMI) of the Italian Revenue Agency [20] and the localization of the residential properties selected for both phases (2019 and 2021).

3.2 Variables of the Model

On the basis of the residential market in the sample city analysis, 13 independent variables (X_n) have been selected (Table 1). These are detected taking into account the indications provided by the local market operators, with reference to the most influencing factors in the negotiation phases for sellers and buyers.

Furthermore, with reference to the aim of the present research the selected factors could be subject to significant variations in terms of market appreciation in the comparison between the Phase I and the Phase II.

In order to implement the econometric technique, the selling price has been chosen as dependent variable (Pr), by considering its natural logarithm ($Y = \ln(Pr)$), in coherence with the results obtained in several studies [14].

The explanatory variables selected have been described in Table 1. The factors considered can be divided into: binary variables, whose assessment could be variable between the score "0" (absence of the characteristic) and "1" (presence of the characteristic); cardinal variables expressed in the reference unit of measurement. For processing

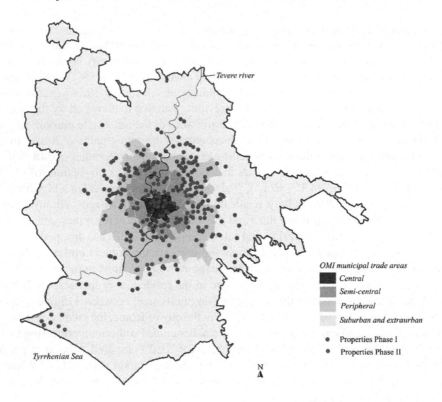

Fig. 1. The localization of residential properties considered for the two phases and the OMI municipal trade areas.

through the econometric technique, all data have been normalized with respect to their maximum value detected.

4   Methodology

The methodology proposed is articulated in two phases. The first one (Phase I) is referred to the second semester of 2019 and it is considered as the condition "*ante* Covid-19" because in this semester the pandemic was not spread worldwide, and the real estate market could be considered as free from the abnormal influences. The second one (Phase II) is referred to the first semester of 2021 and should be considered as a condition "*in itinere*", because the effects of pandemic have already emerged worldwide in the real estate market, but the pandemic is still going on and it is not possible to consider it finished. Both the phases are divided into preparatory and follow-up actions: *i)* data collection and structuring of the database; *ii)* normalization of the collected data and first correlation analyses; *iii)* implementation of the econometric technique and identification of the price function; *iv)* analysis of the outputs in terms of the functional links between the dependent variable (selling price) and the explanatory variables considered.

Table 1. Description of the explanatory variables of the selling price (Pr)

Categories	Acronynim	Denomination	Description	Unite of measure	Variable's type
Surfaces	Si	Internal Surface	Internal surface for the exclusive use of the property	m^2	*Quantitative continous*
	Sb	Surface of the balcony/terrace	Net external area of balconies or terraces directly accessible from the residential unit	m^2	*Quantitative continous*
	Sg	Surface of the private garden	Net external surface area of gardens directly accessible from the residential unit	m^2	*Quantitative continous*
	Se	External condominium area surface	Outdoor areas accessible from the common parts of the building and not for the exclusive use of the residential unit	–	*Binary (1 or 0)*
Maintenance conditions of the property	Me	Excellent	Properties characterized by high aesthetic and structural values with quality finishes great level	–	*Binary (1 or 0)*
	Mg	Good	Houses characterized by good quality finishes that are immediately usable	–	*Binary (1 or 0)*

(continued)

Table 1. (*continued*)

Categories	Acronynim	Denomination	Description	Unite of measure	Variable's type
Property's characteristics	B	Number of bathrooms	Number of bathrooms for the exclusive use of the residential unit	nr.	*Quantitative discrete*
	L	Floor level	Floor level on which the property is located	nr.	*Quantitative discrete*
Building's characteristics	Yc	Construction year	Year of construction of the building in which the residential unit is located (Assessed as the difference between the year 2019 (Phase I) or 2021 (Phase II) and the construction year)	nr.	*Quantitative continous*
OMI's municipal area	C	Central	Municipal trade area in which the property is located	–	*Binary(1 or 0)*
	Sc	Semi-central		–	*Binary(1 or 0)*
	P	Peripheral		–	*Binary(1 or 0)*
OMI's quotation	Vm	Average market value	Average price for the *ante Covid-19* and *in itinere Covid-19* phases	€/m^2	*Quantitative continous*

In particular, the econometric technique used to analyze the data collected is *Evolutionary Polynomial Regression* (EPR). This technique is structured by integrating the characteristics of a numerical regression system with genetic programming techniques [9]; with reference to the real estate sector, EPR has been ordinarily implemented to determine the price function, identifying the most influential factors in the mechanisms of the housing prices formation and analyzing the marginal contribution of each of them on the prices [17, 18, 24].

Having fixed a dependent variable (Y) and n independent variables (X_n), the technique allows to identify the price function (model) whose polynomial expression is a combination of the independent variables and numerical coefficients. The generic mathematical expression of the non-linear model implemented in EPR is summarized by Eq. (1):

$$Y = a_0 + \sum_{i=1}^{n} \left[a_i \cdot (X_i)^{(i,1)} \ldots (X_j)^{(i,j)} \cdot f\left((X_j)^{(i,j+1)} \ldots (X_j)^{(i,2j)}\right) \right] \qquad (1)$$

where a_0 is an optional bias, n is the number of additive terms, the length of the polynomial expression (bias excluded), a_i represents numeric parameters to be identified, X_i are the explanatory variables candidate to be selected by the model, (i, l) - with $l = (1,\ldots, 2j)$ - is the exponent of the l-th input variable within the i-th term, f is a function chosen by the user among a set of possible mathematical expressions.

The outcome function is able to satisfy different conflictual objectives in a Pareto's frontier such as: maximizing the accuracy of the model; minimizing the number of polynomial coefficients; minimizing the number of inputs for each variable [9]. For each model, a series of indicators are calculated to immediately determine the statistical performance of the function and the accuracy of each algebraic expression, i.e. the Coefficient of Determination (CoD) defined in Eq. (2):

$$COD = 1 - \frac{N-1}{N} \cdot \frac{\sum_N (y_{detected} - y_{estimated})^2}{\sum_N (y_{detected} - mean(y_{detected}))^2} \qquad (2)$$

where $y_{estimated}$ are the values of the dependent variable estimated by the methodology, $y_{detected}$ are the collected values of the dependent variable, N is the sample size in analysis. The CoD value varies between 0% and 100%. The closer the CoD value is to 100%, the higher the statistical performance of the model returned by EPR.

Once the model that best satisfies the different objectives described above has been identified, the empirical consistency of the functional links between the independent variables selected by the model and the dependent variable is checked.

With reference to the case study the implementation of EPR has allowed to identify the two models (one for each phase) and to verify the functional correlations between the explanatory variables selected and the selling prices.

5 Phase I: Implementation of the Econometric Technique to the Data Referring to the Second Half of 2019 (*Ante Covid-19*)

The model generated by the application of the econometric technique EPR, and selected as the best in terms of statistical accuracy and mathematical complexity to the reference dataset, assumes the expression in Eq. (3):

$$Y = +2.0813\, Vm^{0.5} + 0.77051\, L^{0.5} B\, Me^{0.5} + 7.5564\, L^{0.5} B^2 Yc$$
$$+ 2833.437\, Sg\, L^2 Mg^{0.5} Vm^2 + 2.6857\, Si^{0.5} + 579.0223\, S^{0.5} Sb^2 L2\, B^{0.5} C^{0.5} Mg^{0.5} + 9.7199 \qquad (3)$$

The CoD is equal to 86.23%, which expresses a high statistical performance and robustness of the chosen model. The selected variables are 8 among the 13 considered. In particular, the variables identified by the model as the most influencing in the selling prices formation mechanism are listed below: for each of them, a synthetic comment about the functional correlation between the specific factor and the selling prices is reported:

- *Internal surface.* The functional link between the selling price and the variable is direct (in average an appreciation of +25% is found).
- *Number of bathrooms.* The correlation between the dependent variable and this factor is direct: in particular, the positive variation is about +15% per bath.
- *Floor level.* The functional relationship is direct, with greater appreciation for the building highest floors and an average appreciation for each floor from the lower floors to the higher ones, equal to +6%. The most significant variations is found in correspondence to the passage from the ground floor to the first floor level (+16%).
- *Construction year of the building.* The functional link is direct and constant at 6%.
- *Maintenance conditions of the property.* The functional correlations are empirically verified. For an excellent conservative state, the positive variation from "good" one is equal to +17%. Furthermore, the variation from "bad" to "good" maintenance property conditions is equal to +10%; this growth increases if the property is located in the OMI central municipal area (+24%).
- *OMI's quotation and municipal area.* The OMI average market values variable shows an increasing functional link, particularly in the variations between € 2,285.00 and € 3,427.50 (+23%). This trend decreases for subsequent values. The significant appreciation is due to the properties located in the OMI central municipal area, for which a positive change of +19% is observed, instead of an average variation of +15%.

6   Phase II: Implementation of the Econometric Technique to Data Referring to the First Half of 2021 (*in Itinere Covid-19*)

With reference to the first half of 2021, 165 properties distributed homogeneously throughout the municipality have been collected (Fig. 1). The model generated by the application of the econometric technique EPR assumes the formulation expressed in Eq. (4):

$$Y = + 2.3773 \, Vm^{0.5} + 0.27166 \, Me - 0.66914 \, Yc^{0.5} \, Me^2 + 9.5008 \, Se \, Yc^2 \, P^2$$
$$+ 1.7449 \, Sb \, L^{0.5} \, B + 3.0846 \, Si^{0.5} + 2.5818 \, Si^{0.5} \, L^{0.5} \, Yc^2 \, Me^2 + 9.402 \qquad (4)$$

The CoD is equal to 89.84%: it confirms that the model selected is the best in terms of statistical accuracy and mathematical complexity for the reference dataset used. The model selects 9 variables among the 13 considered. The variables identified by the model as the most influencing on the selling prices are reported below: moreover, for each of them, a synthetic analysis related to the typology of the functional link between the specific factor and the selling prices is carried out:

- *Internal surface.* The functional link between the selling price and the variable is direct with an average appreciation equal to +23%; the most significant variation is found for property internal surface from 60 m^2 to 90 m^2 (+36%).
- *Surface of the balcony/terrace.* The functional correlation is direct: the variation is positive, equal to about +3%.
- *External condominium area surface.* The functional relationship is direct and, in the situation in which an external area is detected, a growth in selling prices is observed (+19%).
- *Number of bathrooms.* A positive variation in selling prices is recorded equal to about +1%.
- *Floor level.* The functional link is direct, with a constant positive variation passing from the lower floor to higher ones (+1%).
- *Construction year of the building.* The contribution of the present variable is significant if the maintenance conditions of the property is excellent, by attesting a relevant market appreciation for the most recent buildings (+19%).
- *Maintenance conditions of the property.* The functional links are empirically verified: for an excellent conservative state, the positive variation from "good" state is equal to +3%.
- *OMI's quotation and municipal area.* The OMI value variable shows an increasing functional link with selling prices (+15%). This considerable appreciation is due to the properties located in the OMI peripheral municipal area, for which a positive variation of +19% is found.

The analysis of the functional links described above confirms the high representativeness of both models with respect to real existing phenomena.

7   Comparison of the Outcomes of the Two Phases

By comparing the results of the two analyses carried out, significant variations in residential market appreciations have already emerged at the current ongoing (*in itinere*) stage of analysis, able to may identify future new trends in market demand.

The two outcomes related to the Phase I and the Phase II differ both in the selection and in the different appreciation values for the variables selected by models. With reference to the factors identified by model of Eq. (4), in comparison to the Phase I, the Phase II outputs show the relevance of the *surface of the balcony/terrace* and the *external condominium area surface*. It should be pointed out that the significant variation in the appreciation of these factors attests how the changes in the dynamics of daily life caused by the pandemic have affected the need for open spaces, both private and condominium ones, which could be used as recreational spaces during the lockdown period.

Another variable for which a relevant change in the influence on selling prices is found is the property localization in the *peripheral* OMI's *municipal area* rather than in the *central* one: this contingence denotes how the possibility of working remotely for the most of the population and, on the contrary, the impossibility to move daily for work to the more central areas of the city, makes people prefer houses (mainly at the same price, ordinarily larger in surfaces) in less congested and chaotic outer areas. In Table 2 the variables selected by the two models (Phase I and Phase II) are reported.

Table 2. Variables selected by the two models

	Si	Sb	Sg	Se	Me	Mg	B	L	Yc	C	Sc	P	Vm
Phase I	✔			✔	✔	✔	✔	✔	✔				✔
Phase II	✔	✔		✔	✔		✔	✔	✔			✔	✔

A detailed analysis of the results obtained shows considerable differences in each variable contribution in the selling price formation (Fig. 2). In particular, it should be observed that for the *internal surface*, the *OMI's quotation*, the *number of bathrooms* and the *construction year of the building* the contribution in terms of average percentage variation remains similar or with a not very wide gap between the Phase I and the Phase II elaborations; on the other hand, for the *maintenance conditions of the property* - both "good" and "excellent"- the difference in the contribution on the selling prices is more significant. For the Phase II this shows the preference of buyers for properties to be renovated that allow the house to be customized to specific needs. The Covid-19 has already generated a higher attention for the domestic spaces comfort, whereas currently strong differences in the appreciation for the floor level have not yet evident. This situation testifies a scarce perception of the importance related to the acoustic comfort deriving from the properties localization on the highest floors. In Fig. 2 the comparison between the average percentage contributions for the variables for which a relevant variation in the market appreciation has been detected by the analysis is reported.

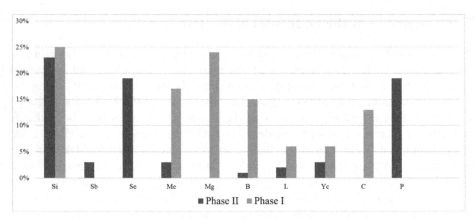

Fig. 2. Comparison between the average percentage contributions found the variables for which greater variation between the Phase I and the Phase II has been found

8 Conclusions

The effects of the Covid-19 pandemic could determine changes in the property market appreciation. The methodology proposed in the present analysis could be useful i) for public subjects, to plan building strategies consistent with the needs of the population and ii) for private investors, to plan investments for which a positive result in the real estate market is expected. This study provides interesting results, defining for the city of Rome a first frame related to the possible variations in the property market appreciation for intrinsic factors. The methodology has been implemented in two phases - *ante* Covid-19 and meanwhile the pandemic is still underway -, in order to identify which are the main effects of the pandemic on the phenomena of housing price formation. The results obtained by the analysis show significant changes in market demand for the city of Rome in the period considered, with a preference for outer areas of the city and a particular emphasis on outdoor surfaces, both private and condominiums. These initial outputs should be monitored, in order to verify whether these variations will persist even after the pandemic or they are a temporary effect linked to the contingent needs of living with it. The proposed methodology is an effective tool for monitoring the effects of pandemic on the real estate market, for this reason consequent developments of the research foresee subsequent applications both *in itinere* and when the pandemic will be concluded. Furthermore, in order to define a framework for the future investment choices of private investors and public operators, after the case pilot proposed in this study, it is planned to proceed with applications at national level.

References

1. Belasen, A.R., Polachek, S.W.: How disasters affect local labor markets: the effects of hurricanes in Florida. J. Human Resour. **44**(1), 251–276 (2009)
2. Del Boca, D., Oggero, N., Profeta, P., Rossi, M.: Women's and men's work, housework and childcare, before and during Covid-19. Rev. Econ. Household **18**(4), 1001–1017 (2020). https://doi.org/10.1007/s11150-020-09502-1
3. Del Giudice, V., De Paola, P., Del Giudice P.F.: COVID-19 infects real estate markets: short and mid-run effects on housing prices in Campania region (Italy). In: Social Science, vol. 9, p. 114 (2020)
4. Della Spina, L., Calabrò, F.: Decision support model for conservation, reuse and valorization of the historic cultural heritage. In: Gervasi, O., et al. (eds.) ICCSA 2018. LNCS, vol. 10962, pp. 3–17. Springer, Cham (2018). https://doi.org/10.1007/978-3-319-95168-3_1
5. Depalo, D., Giorgi F.: Il lavoro da remoto in Italia durante la pandemia: i lavoratori del settore privato, Banca d'Italia, Note Covid-19, gennaio 2021 (2021). https://www.bancaditalia.it/media/notizia/il-lavoro-da-remoto-in-italia-durante-la-pandemia/. Accessed 15 Mar 2021
6. Emea Real estate market outlook, CBRE (2021). www.cbre.com/researchandreports. Accessed 15 Mar 2021
7. Eurostat: Gross domestic product and main components (2021). https://ec.europa.eu/eurostat/databrowser/view/tec00001/default/table?lang=en. Accessed 01 Mar 2021
8. Fardin, M.A.: Covid-19 and anxiety: a review of psychological impacts of infectious disease outbreaks. In: Archives of Clinical Infectious Diseases, vol. 15, no. Covid-19 (2020)
9. Giustolisi, O., Savic, D.: Advances in data-driven analyses and modelling using EPR-MOGA. J. Hydroinf. **11**(3–4), 225–236 (2009)

10. Giuzio, W., Rizzica, L.: Il lavoro da remoto in Italia durante la pandemia: le amministrazioni pubbliche. Banca d'Italia, Note Covid-19, gennaio 2021 (2021). https://www.bancaditalia.it/media/notizia/il-lavoro-da-remoto-in-italia-durante-la-pandemia/. Accessed 15 Mar 2021

11. Inoue, H., Todo, Y.: The propagation of economic impacts through supply chains: the case of a mega-city lockdown to prevent the spread of Covid-19. PLoS ONE **15**(9), 1–10 (2020)

12. Istituto Nazionale di Statistica ISTAT (2021) Gross domestic product and main components. http://dati.istat.it/. Accessed 15 Mar 2021

13. Li, H.Y., Cao, H., Leung, D.Y.P., Mak, Y.W.: The psychological impacts of a Covid-19 outbreak on college students in China: a longitudinal study. Int. J. Environ. Res. Public Health **17**(11), 3933 (2020)

14. Lynch, A.K., Rasmussen, D.W.: Proximity, neighbourhood and the efficacy of exclusion. Urban Stud. **41**(2), 285–298 (2004)

15. Mattiacci, A., Nocenzi, M., Sfodera, F., Sofia, C.: Le conseguenze sull'attività professionale: tra incertezze e opportunità. In: La Società catastrofica, vita e relazioni sociali ai tempi dell'emergenza Covid-19 a cura di Lombardo, C., Mauceri, S., FrancoAngeli, Milano (2020)

16. Mingo, I., Panarese, P., Nobile S.: #Io resto a casa: i mutamenti negli stili di vita e nelle relazioni familiari. In: La Società catastrofica, vita e relazioni sociali ai tempi dell'emergenza Covid-19 a cura di Lombardo, C., Mauceri, S., FrancoAngeli, Milano (2020)

17. Morano, P., Guarini, M.R., Tajani, F., Di Liddo, F., Anelli, D.: Incidence of different types of urban green spaces on property prices. a case study in the Flaminio district of Rome (Italy). In: Misra, S., et al. (eds.) ICCSA 2019. LNCS, vol. 11622, pp. 23–34. Springer, Cham (2019). https://doi.org/10.1007/978-3-030-24305-0_3

18. Morano, P., Rosato, P., Tajani, F., Di Liddo, F.: An analysis of the energy efficiency impacts on the residential property prices in the City of Bari (Italy). In: Mondini, G., Oppio, A., Stanghellini, S., Bottero, M., Abastante, F. (eds.) Values and Functions for Future Cities. GET, pp. 73–88. Springer, Cham (2020). https://doi.org/10.1007/978-3-030-23786-8_5

19. National Report on Sharing Mobility (2020). https://temi.camera.it/leg18/post/OCD15-13722/3-rapporto-nazionale-sulla-sharing-mobility.html. Accessed 15 Jan 2021

20. Osservatorio del Mercato Immobiliare, Agenzia delle entrate (2020). www.agenziaentrate.gov.it. Accessed 15 Mar 2021

21. Osservatorio Residenziale Tecnocasa (2020). https://news.tecnocasagroup.it/ufficio-studi/osservatorio_residenziale/. Accessed 15 Jan 2021

22. Rapporto Immobiliare 2020, Il settore Residenziale, Osservatorio del mercato Immobiliare Agenzia delle entrate (2020). https://www.agenziaentrate.gov.it/portale/documents/20143/263076/RI2020_20200521_Residenziale.pdf/40fee96c-49ad-6edb-e36b-1f54ff623b12

23. Rapporto residenziale IV Trimestre 2020, Osservatorio del mercato Immobiliare Agenzia delle entrate (2021). https://www.agenziaentrate.gov.it/portale/documents/20143/262485/StatisticheOMI_RES_4_2020_20210309.pdf/419be2b6-b6a7-652f-1353-b5ac082b24a1. Accessed 15 Jan 2021

24. Tajani, F., Morano, P., Torre, C.M., Di Liddo, F.: An analysis of the influence of property tax on housing prices in the Apulia region (Italy). Buildings **7**(3), 67 (2017)

25. Wang, C., et al.: Immediate psychological responses and associated factors during the initial stage of the 2019 coronavirus disease (Covid-19) epidemic among the general population in China. Int. J. Environ. Res. Public Health **17**(5), 1729 (2020)

26. World Economic Outlook January 2021, International Monetary Fund. https://www.imf.org/en/Publications/WEO/Issues/2021/01/26/2021-world-economic-outlook-update. Accessed 20 Mar 2021

27. World Health Organization (2021). https://covid19.who.int/. Accessed 15 Mar 2021

The Contribution of the Most Influencing Factors on the Housing Rents: An Analysis in the City of Milan (Italy)

Pierluigi Morano[1], Francesco Tajani[2], Felicia Di Liddo[1], Rossana Ranieri[2(✉)], and Paola Amoruso[3]

[1] Department of Civil, Environmental, Land, Building Engineering and Chemistry, Polytechnic University of Bari, 70125 Bari, Italy
[2] Department of Architecture and Design, "Sapienza" University of Rome, 00196 Rome, Italy
rossana.ranieri@uniroma1.it
[3] Department of Economics and Management, LUM Giuseppe Degennaro University, 70010 Casamassima, BA, Italy

Abstract. With reference to a study sample related to the city of Milan (Northern Italy), the present research intends to identify the impact of the most influencing factors on the residential rents. In particular, in the analysis two hundred and twenty housing properties rented in the second half of 2019 have been collected and the most relevant intrinsic and extrinsic factors in the bargaining phases between the lessors and the potential lessees have been selected. Through the implementation of an econometric technique the investigation of the different functional relationships between the explanatory factors considered and the housing rents has been carried out. The present research could represent a valid reference for the private operators in the investment decisions phases and for the Public Administrations to monitor housing rent dynamics and to provide essential implications for fair housing policies.

Keywords: Rental market · Residential rents · Evolutionary Polynomial Regression · Influencing factors

1 Introduction

In the last years, the housing rental market has been changed. With reference to the previous period to the Covid-19, the demand for rental housing had considerably increased: from 2011 to 2018, in fact, the number of new rental contracts has grown of +18% [25]. Moreover, in addition to the traditional contractual forms, the short-term residential segment has been spread especially in touristic cities and in the urban areas near to the most important historical buildings and/or in the university neighborhoods.

© Springer Nature Switzerland AG 2021
O. Gervasi et al. (Eds.): ICCSA 2021, LNCS 12954, pp. 63–76, 2021.
https://doi.org/10.1007/978-3-030-86979-3_5

Currently, the rental market has a significant dimension: in 2018 the Bank of Italy has reported that about the 20% of the Italian families in 2016 lived in a rented house, whose 38% concerned the youngest people and 46% the poorest community groups [1]. In the first semester of 2020, in the Italian context the number of people that has rented a residential property has increased by 3.3% (74.7% compared to the number of lessees detected in the same period of 2019, when the percentage was 71.4%). In particular, the "classical" residential rental demand represents the 54% of the total housing one and it has increased by +7.8% compared to the 2019, mostly due to the lowered rental values [28].

In the current situation, the spread of COVID-19 pandemic has been determining significant effects on the residential rental market. The use of distance learning and smart working has led many non-resident students (14.8% of the total rental demand, declining by 3.2%) and workers (29.5% of the total rental demand, declining by 3.7%) to leave their rented houses, generating a greater market supply and a lower demand [4].

The greater market supply – mainly related to the return of students and workers to the original houses and to the lower demand of short-term rental for the possibility to journey exclusively for needs related to work or health – has involved the decrease in rental prices equal approximately to −7.5% (−8.0% for the two-room and three-room apartments, −7.2% for four-room apartments). The decrease in residential rents is different according to the geographic context: in the biggest Italian cities a strong reduction has been pointed out (−9.5%), whereas in small and medium-sized cities a lower decrease has been noted (−3.8%) [14].

The variation on the Italian average rents - from 616€/flat in 2019 to 570€/flat in 2020 - determines a return to those charged in 2016 [25]: this situation confirms the higher flexibility of the housing rental market, differently from the stricter residential sales market for which a lower variation in prices has been found.

Finally, in the framework outlined, also for the phenomenon related to the "apartament share" – that represents the 11.6% of the total rental demand – a negative trend has been detected, equal to −2.4% compared to the 2019.

The higher supply related to residential properties is allowing the potential lessees to find the "desired" property, by observing a trend to look for bigger houses with external spaces. In this sense, a variation in rental market demand is expected.

The analysis of the most influencing factors on housing rents has a significant impact for the sustainable urban planning and management: several Authors have highlighted the greater preference of potential housing buyers or homeowners for urban areas in which a high life qualify level is perceived, e.g. characterized by a good accessibility to the green spaces, with healthy air and without acoustic pollution [6, 7, 11, 29]. Other researches have identified the most influencing factors on residential rents, in order to quantify the importance of the physical characteristics in the rental market dynamics [8, 12, 23, 26, 31].

2   Aim

The present analysis concerns the topic outlined. The wok intends to analyze the effects of the most influencing factors on housing rents. With reference to the Italian city of Milan, the paper aims to investigate the functional relationships of residential rents with the main intrinsic and extrinsic characteristics considered by the housing lessors and the potential lessees in the bargaining phases. The analysis is carried out by considering a study sample of two hundred and twenty housing properties rented in the second half of 2019 and located in the city of Milan. The implementation of an econometric technique on the collected sample allows to point out the most significant factors in the rents formation processes and to examine the different functional relationships between the explanatory variables considered and the housing rents.

The results obtained may be a reference for the private owners of properties and investors to identify the most relevant intrinsic and extrinsic factors for potential lessees and, eventually, to adapt the property characteristics according to the tenant requests and to activate renovation interventions able to increase the market rental value. From the Public Administration point of view, the outputs could be used to monitor the housing rent dynamics and to provide essential implications to reach fair housing goals [5].

Furthermore, the paper represents the first step of a wider research focalized on the analysis of housing rental market. In this sense, the work concerns the identification of the most influencing factors on rental values in the ante-Covid period (second half of 2019). The results obtained could be compared with those deriving from the same analysis to be carried out with reference to the post-Covid period, in order to assess likely variations in the rental demand in terms of the most influencing factors considered by potential lessees.

The paper is structured as follows. In Sect. 3 ("Case study") the sample collected and the variables considered have been described. In Sect. 4 ("Method") the econometric technique has been illustrated. In Sect. 5 ("Application of the method to the case study") the interpretation of the results obtained by the implementation of the econometric technique in terms of functional relationships between the explanatory variables considered and the residential rents has been explained. Finally in Sect. 6 ("Conclusions") the findings of the work have been reported.

3   Case Study

With reference to the city of Milan (Northern Italy), a sample of two hundred and twenty residential properties, rented in the second half of 2019, has been collected.

In Fig. 1 the localization of the properties is shown.

It should be observed that the residential units selected are distributed in the three urban areas (central, semi-central, peripheral) of the city of Milan.

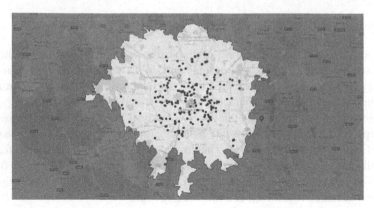

Fig. 1. Localization of the sample of two hundred and twenty residential properties in the city of Milan

3.1 Variables

For each property of the study sample, the rent (dependent variable) and the most influencing intrinsic and extrinsic factors (independent variables) have been detected. As confirmed by the reference local market operators (real estate agents and experts), the factors identified for the analysis represent the main characteristics considered by lessors and lessees in the phases of residential properties negotiation. The two main categories of independent variables are illustrated below.

Intrinsic variables:

- the internal floor surface [Si], expressed in square meters of gross floor area of the property;
- the surface of private external space, i.e. gardens, green areas, courtyards [Sg], expressed in square meters of gross floor area;
- the surface of balcony, terraces and patios [Sb], expressed in square meters of gross floor area;
- the presence of external private condominium areas [Se], assessed as a dummy variables in which the value "zero" indicates the absence of this space, whereas the value "one" indicates the presence;
- the floor on which the property is located [F];
- the number of bathrooms in the property [B];
- the presence of kitchen located in the same living room of the property [K], assessed as a dummy variable for which the value "one" verifies this situation, whereas the value "zero" indicates that the kitchen and the living room are in two different home spaces separated by internal walls and doors.
- the quality of the property maintenance conditions, considered as a qualitative variable and differentiated, through a synthetic evaluation, by the categories "to be restructured" [Mb], "good" [Mg] and "excellent" [Me] as a dummy variable. In particular, for the definition of the quality of the maintenance conditions, the assessment has been carried out by comparing the information obtained from the real estate agents

consulted, surveys carried out by web and on site, i.e. through digital photographs or user comments. Each of the three categories that summarize the three possible states of maintenance denotes different quality and conditions. The "to be restructured" condition (Mp) indicates residential properties for which substantial restructuring interventions are necessary as the conservative state strongly bad, the "good" state (Mg) indicates houses that are immediately usable and in which the maintenance conditions are acceptable, whereas the "excellent" state (Me) refers to properties characterized by high aesthetic and structural values with valuable trimmings and architectural qualities.

- the EPC label, expressed, according with the current regulations, through the denominations from A4 (the highest level) to G (the lowest level). In the present research, the EPC labels from A4 to B are gather into a single explanatory variable [E_ab] and the EPC labels from C to E are gather into a single explanatory variable [E_cde], whereas the EPC labels F and G are not included among the variables selected. The variable is interpreted as a dummy variable, assigning a score equal to "one" to the EPC label of the property and, consequently, the score equal to "zero" to all the others. It is evident that if the property EPC level is F or G both the variables E_ab and E:cde are equal to "zero" score;
- the age of the building in which the residential unit is located [Yc]. This variable is calculated as the difference between the year 2019 and the year of construction of the building.

Extrinsic variables:

- the distance from the nearest subway [Dm], expressed in kilometers it takes to walk to it;
- the distance from the central train station [Ds], expressed in kilometers it takes to walk to it;
- the distance from the nearest university centre [Du], expressed in kilometers it takes to walk to it;
- the distance from the central pole [Dp] of the city, expressed in km it takes to walk to it. In the analysis related to the city of Milan, the central pole is defined as a religious and historical monument located in the centre of the city from which the main arteria roads leading off. In particular, the "Duomo" has been considered;
- the distance from the nearest urban green space [Dg], expressed in km it takes to walk to it;
- the municipal trade area in which the property is located, considering the geographical distribution developed by the Italian Revenue Agency [24], because of the different location characteristics that contribute to the formation of the rental prices. In particular, three trade areas are included in the analysis among those defined by the Italian Revenue Agency: "central" [C], "semi-central" [Sc], "peripheral" [P]. For each property, the score "one" is assigned if the property belong to the specific trade area, whereas the score "zero" is reported for all the remaining locational factors. For the properties located in the suburban area all the variables C, Sc and P are equal to "zero".

4 Method

The econometric technique applied in the present research is the Evolutionary Polynomial Regression (EPR) which integrates the best features of numerical regression [10] with genetic programming [17]. Starting from experimental data, the technique searches for possible models in polynomial form in which each term that appears is composed of the combinations, with a different degree of complexity, of the explanatory variables selected by the user.

A more detailed illustration related to the EPR features and to the advantages of the technique implementation can be found in several contributions of the reference literature [9, 13, 21, 22, 27]. It should be highlighted that the EPR technique has never been implemented for the analysis of the influence of the most influencing factors on the rents. In this sense, the work represent the first applications of the EPR to the rental market sector.

In the present research, a general description about the main aspects of the technique implemented has been illustrated.

To determine the relationship Y = f (Xi), i.e. the price function able to define the functional relationships about the explanatory factors and the property prices, known the dependent variable (Y) and the independent variables (Xi), the generic expression of the non-linear model implemented in EPR is shown in Eq. (1):

$$Y = \sum_{i-n}^{l} \left[a_i \cdot (X_n)^{(i,n)} \ldots (X_j)^{(i,j)} \cdot f((X_n)^{(i,j+n)} \ldots (X_j)^{(i,2j)}) \right] + a_0 \qquad (1)$$

where a_0 is the constant additive term, n is the number of additive terms, i.e., the length of the polynomial expression (constant additive term excluded), a_i represents the numerical parameter to be assessed for each additive term, X_i is the candidate explanatory variables to be selected by the model, (i, l) - with l = (1,..., 2j) - is the exponent of the l-th variable within the i-th additive term, f is a function selected by the user from a set of candidate mathematical expression. The exponents (i, l) are also chosen by the user from a range of candidate real numbers.

The main advantage related to the EPR implementation concerns the ability to simultaneously pursue different objective functions, such as to define an optimal Pareto frontier of the fixed conflictual objectives, that aim at i) the maximization of the model accuracy, through the satisfaction of appropriate statistical indicators; ii) the maximization of the model parsimony, through the minimization of the number of coefficients (ai) of the equation; iii) the reduction of the complexity of the model, through the minimization of the number of explanatory variables (Xi) of the final equation.

In this sense, the application of the econometric technique allows to generate several models characterized by a different statistical accuracy and mathematical structure complexity. In particular, the indicator of the statistical performance is the Coefficient of Determination (CoD), defined in Eq. (2):

$$CoD = 1 - \frac{N-1}{N} \cdot \frac{\sum_{N} (y_e - y_d)^2}{\sum_{N} (y_d - mean(y_d))^2} \qquad (2)$$

where y_e are the values of the dependent variable assessed by the EPR method ($y_{estimated}$), y_d are the collected values of the dependent variable ($y_{detected}$), N is the sample size. The statistic reliability of each model is greater when the CoD is close to the unit value.

5 Application of the Method to the Case Study

With reference to the case study, the EPR technique has been implemented, taking into account the structure of the basic model identified in Eq. (1) without function f selected.

According to the results obtained in several studies [19], the dependent variable Pr (rental price) has been considered in logarithmic form ($Y = \ln(Pr)$).

Furthermore, each price function generated consists of a maximum number of eight terms and each term is the combination of the selected explanatory variables, raised to the appropriate numerical exponents belong to the set (0; 0.5; 1; 2), in order to obtain a wide range of solutions.

The application of the EPR technique has generated several functions. Among them, the model selected as the best is reported in Eq. (3): it is characterized by a very high level of statistical accuracy, as the CoD value is equal to 88.69% and includes most of the explanatory variables considered in the analysis, allowing to determine the contribution of each one in the phenomena of rent price formation.

$$Y = + 0.74039 * C + 0.65355 * B^{0.5} P^{0.5} + 0.85473 * B^{0.5} * Sc^2 + 11.8431* Se^{0.5} * Yc * Dp^{0.5}*Du * Sc^{0.5} + 0.91529 * Sb * F^{0.5} * Me^{0.5} + 3.1017 * Si0.5 - 2.0858 * Si^{0.5} * F^{0.5} * Dp + 2.5784 * Si * F^{0.5} * Me^{0.5} * E\_ab2 + 5.2917$$
(3)

The intrinsic factors selected by the EPR method and included in the model of Eq. (3) as the most influencing ones in rental housing market are:

- Internal floor surface [Si]
- Surface of balconies, terraces and patios [Sb]
- Presence of condominium areas [Se]
- Floor on which the property is located [F]
- Number of bathrooms in the property [B]
- Excellent quality of the property maintenance conditions [Me]
- EPC labels from A4 to B [E_ab]
- Age of the building in which the residential unit is located [Yc]

The extrinsic factors included in the model chosen are:

- Distance from the nearest university centre [Du]
- Distance from the central pole [Dp]
- Property localization in the central municipal trade area [C]
- Property localization in the semi-central municipal trade area [Sc]
- Property localization in the peripheral municipal trade area [P]

Therefore, the variables not included in the model of Eq. (3) are listed below. In particular, with reference to the study sample analyzed for the city of Milan, these factors are not considered among those most influencing in the housing rental prices mechanism.

- Surface of private external space (green areas, gardens, courtyards) [Se]
- Presence of kitchen located in the same living room of the property [K]
- Bad quality of the property maintenance conditions [Mb]
- Good quality of the property maintenance conditions [Mg]
- EPC labels from C to E [E_cde]
- Distance from the nearest subway [Dm]
- Distance from the central train station [Ds]
- Distance from the nearest urban green space [Dg]

5.1 Interpretation of the Results

The empirical coherence of the functional relationships between the input variables and the rental prices has been verified through a mathematical exogenous approach that allows to quantitatively express the influence of each factor selected by the model of Eq. (3) on the housing rental prices. In particular, the variation of the i-th variable in the range of admissible values in the study sample is analyzed by keeping constant the mean values for the quantitative variables (internal floor surface, surface of balconies, terraces and patios, floor on which the property is located, number of bathroom in the property, age of the building in which the residential unit is located, distance from the nearest university centre, distance from the central pole) and by assuming the value 1 for the dummy variables (presence of condominium areas, excellent quality of the property maintenance conditions, EPC labels from A4 to B, property localization in the central municipal trade area, property localization in the semi-central municipal trade area, property localization in the peripheral municipal trade area), paying attention to any alternative situations for the variables belonging to the same category that cannot simultaneously be equal to 1.

In Figs. 2 and 3 the functional relationships between the intrinsic (Fig. 2) and extrinsic (Fig. 3) variables and the housing rental prices are reported.

Firstly, it should be pointed out that the expected functional correlations between the explanatory variables and the rental prices have been confirmed by those generated by the EPR models. With reference to the intrinsic variable related to the internal floor surface of the property [Si], the factor is linked to the rents through a direct relationship, by attesting a higher market appreciation for larger residential properties. Moreover, the positive percentage variation on rents gradually decreases with increasing of property surface, due to the reduction in the market demand – in term of number of potential lessees able to afford higher monetary amounts for the property renting.

In the city of Milan, according to the study sample considered and to the model selected, the surface of balconies, terraces and patios [Sb] has a positive impact on rental prices: in particular, the average percentage contribution is equal to +4%. In the residential rental market in the context of the city of Milan, the presence of these domestic spaces with a surface area equal to 25 m^2 leads to increase the rental values

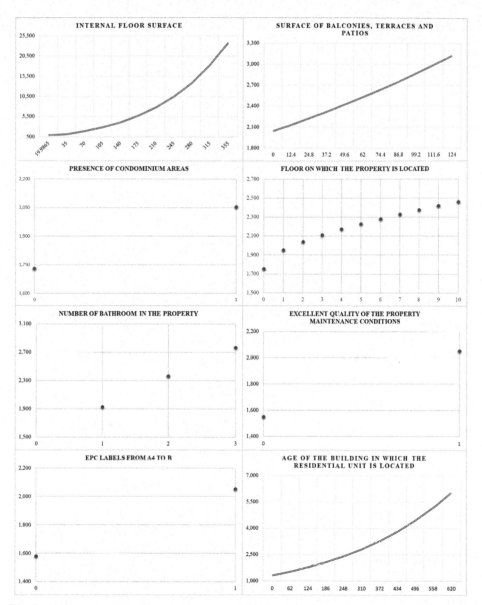

Fig. 2. Functional relationships between the intrinsic factors selected by the model and the housing rental prices

approximately equal to +9% compared to their absence. The contribution of the factor Sb on rental prices decreases progressively as the balconies, terraces and patios surface increases, by denoting a greater importance for these home spaces rather than their dimensions.

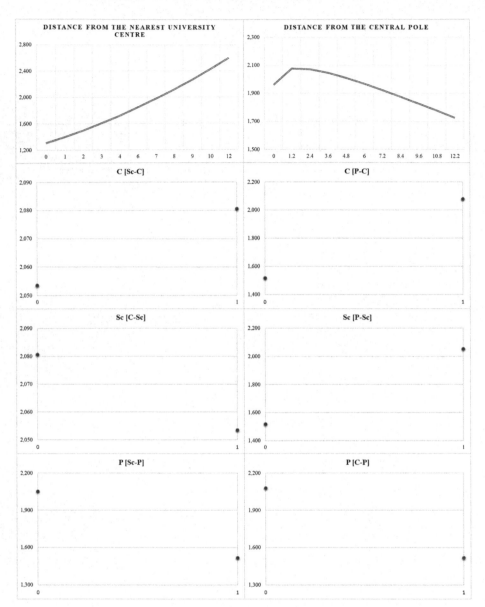

Fig. 3. Functional relationships between the extrinsic factors selected by the model and the housing rental prices

The presence of condominium areas [Se] leads to a growth of residential rents equal to +19%, certifying a relevant influence for the properties characterized by the presence of an area to be used by building residents.

With regards to the intrinsic variable related to the floor level on which the property is located [F], a direct functional relationship has been found (+3%). In particular from the ground floor to the first one the increase of housing rental prices is equal to 11%.

For the number of bathrooms [B], the model generated by EPR for the study sample selected for the analysis is consistent with the expected direct trend, by denoting that an increase of bathrooms number corresponds to high rental values, equal approximately to +26% (from one bathroom to two bathrooms) and to +17% (from two bathrooms to three bathrooms).

A direct functional relationship has been observed also between the dummy variable related to the excellent quality of the property maintenance conditions [Me] and the property rental prices. The average growth observed for this factor is equal to +32%.

The impacts of the energy component in the processes of the housing rental prices formation are relevant: in the model generated by EPR, in fact, the variable for which the variable EPC labels from A to E [E_ab] is included, by demonstrating a direct functional correlation, i.e. an increase in the housing rental prices equal to +30% compared to the residential properties characterized by the lowest energy labels (EPC labels C, D, E, F and G).

With reference to the variable age of the building in which the residential unit is located [Yc] a positive variation in rental prices – approximately equal to +17% - is detected. In this sense, a higher residential rental market appreciation for properties located in historic building compared to those in more recent ones.

An increase in rental prices has been observed at a progressively higher *distance from the nearest university* centre [Du] (on average equal to +7%). The result could be associated to other extrinsic factors that characterize the university districts for which the closeness of university center does not constitute a factor appreciated by potential lessees. Furthermore, it should be noted that the residential properties located in university areas are very often rented to students, by determining the formation of a separate market segment that are usually independent from the general residential rental market. The realization of a University very often gives rise to a phenomenon called "studentification", i.e. the process that leads the residential neighborhoods located close to university centre to become mainly occupied by students. The studentification process often determinates positive impacts on the local real estate market mechanisms, but also it causes negative effects in terms of urban segregation and reduction of housing prices [2, 3, 15, 16, 18, 20, 30].

The model selected points out a parabolic functional relationship between the distance from the central pole [Dp] and the rental prices. In particular, from 0 km to 1.2 km an increase in rental prices is observed (+6%), whereas from 1.2 to 2.4 km a constant trend is detected, beyond which a drop in rental price is found. This confirms a lowest appreciation for the properties facing the central pole, due to other factors that negatively influence the prices (e.g. the chaos for tourist presence, difficulty of finding parking, etc.).

Finally, with reference to the variables related to the municipal trade area in which the property is located, in the model the property position in central municipal trade area [C], in semi-central area [Sc] and in peripheral one [P] are included. In particular, the positive variation on the rental values recorded if the property *ceteris paribus* is located in the central area of the city of Milan is equal to +37% rather than in the peripheral one, and +1% rather than in the semi-central area. A direct correlation (+ 35%) has been found if the property is located in the semi-central area compared to the central one, whereas an inverse link has been detected passing from the property localization in central municipal trade area to the localization in semi-central one. The inverse relationship with the housing rental prices shows a lower appreciation of the market for the property localization in the peripheral municipal trade area compared to those located in semi-central one (−26%) or in central one (−27%).

In the Fig. 4 a summary of the average contributions of the most influencing factors selected by EPR technique on the housing rental prices has been reported.

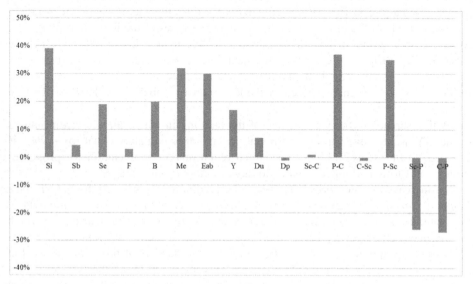

Fig. 4. Average contributions of the most influencing factors selected by the method on the housing rental prices

6   Conclusions

In the present research an analysis aimed to investigate the functional relationships between the intrinsic and extrinsic characteristics and the housing rental prices has been carried out with reference to the Italian city of Milan.

In the current situation related to the Covid-19 the higher market supply – caused by the returning home of non-residential students and workers and by the short-term rental interruption - is allowing a larger quantity of empty residential properties to be rented. In this sense, the potential lessees can choose the property to rent among an increasing number of residential units and in "more accurate" way, e.g. evaluating different factors that so far are not taken into account. Therefore, a variation in housing rental demand in terms of intrinsic and extrinsic characteristics is expected.

The outputs of the present study could represent the first benchmark with which to compare the results deriving from the same analysis to be carried out with reference to the post Covid-19 in order to examine likely different market appreciations related to property factors.

Further insights may concern the implementation of the method used in the present research to different study samples related to Italian or international cities in order to define the most influential factors on the rental prices in other contexts and to provide for a general framework on the rental market appreciation of potential lessees for investors. For example, with reference to different cities located in the Northern Italy, in the Central Italy and in the Southern Italy and Island, the results of the analysis could be aimed to determine the main determinants on rental values in the macro-areas in which the Italian territory is commonly divided, to address the public decisions toward fair housing policies and to support the private investors in the refurbishment intervention choices.

References

1. Banca d'Italia. Indagine sui bilanci delle famiglie italiane nell'anno 2018 (2018). https://www.bancaditalia.it/pubblicazioni/indagine-famiglie/index.html. Accessed 10 Mar 2021
2. Baron, M.G., Diamant, E.R.: Real estate in studentified neighborhoods. In: ERSA Conference Papers (No. ersa16p642). European Regional Science Association (2016)
3. Baron, M.G., Kaplan, S.: The impact of 'studentification' on the rental housing market. In: ERSA Conference Papers (No. ersa10p204). European Regional Science Association (2011)
4. Blog Affitto (2021). https://www.blogaffitto.it/mercato-affitto/. Accessed 10 Mar 2021
5. Calabrò, F., Della Spina, L.: Innovative tools for the effectiveness and efficiency of administrative action of the metropolitan cities: the strategic operational programme. In: Advanced Engineering Forum, vol. 11, pp. 3–10. Trans Tech Publications Ltd. (2014)
6. Cao, X.J., Hough, J.A.: Hedonic value of transit accessibility: an empirical analysis in a small urban area. J. Transp. Res. Forum 47(3), 171–183 (2008)
7. De, U.K., Vupru, V.: Location and neighbourhood conditions for housing choice and its rental value: empirical examination in an urban area of North-East India. Int. J. Hous. Markets Anal. 10(4), 519–538 (2017)
8. Del Giudice, V., De Paola, P.: Spatial analysis of residential real estate rental market with geoadditive models. In: d'Amato, M., Kauko, T. (eds.) Advances in Automated Valuation Modeling. SSDC, vol. 86, pp. 155–162. Springer, Cham (2017). https://doi.org/10.1007/978-3-319-49746-4_8
9. Di Liddo, F., Morano, P., Tajani, F., Torre, C.M.: An innovative methodological approach for the analysis of the effects of urban interventions on property prices [Un approccio metodologico innovativo per l'analisi degli effetti degli interventi di trasformazione urbana sui valori immobiliari]. Valori e Valutazioni 26, 25–49 (2020)
10. Draper, N.R., Smith, H.: Applied Regression Analysis. Wiley, Hoboken (2014)
11. Frew, J., Wilson, B.: Estimating the connection between location and property value. J. Real Estate Pract. Educ. 5(1), 17–22 (2002)
12. Gallin, J.: The long-run relationship between house prices and rents. Real Estate Econ. 36(4), 635–58 (2008)
13. Giustolisi, O., Savic, D.: Advances in data-driven analyses and modelling using EPR-MOGA. J. Hydroinf. 11(3–4), 225–236 (2009)
14. Idealista (2021). www.idealista.it. Accessed 10 Mar 2021
15. Kenna, T.: Studentification in Ireland? Analysing the impacts of students and student accommodation on Cork City. Ir. Geogr. 44(2–3), 191–213 (2011)

16. Kinton, C., Smith, D.P., Harrison, J., Culora, A.: New frontiers of studentification: the commodification of student housing as a driver of urban change. Geogr. J. **184**(3), 242–254 (2018)
17. Koza, J.R.: Genetic Programming: on the Programming of Computers by Means of Natural Selection. MIT Press, Cambridge (1992)
18. Lin, T., Ma, F.: The economic impacts of studentification on local communities-a review of the literature based on cross-strait studies. Acad. J. Humanit. Soc. Sci. **3**(8), 30–40 (2020)
19. Lynch, A.K., Rasmussen, D.W.: Proximity, neighbourhood and the efficacy of exclusion. Urban Stud. **41**(2), 285–298 (2004)
20. Monroy, P., Podmore, J.: Shifting perspectives on studentification: a multi-disciplinary approach. In: Term Research Paper Concordia University, Montreal Quebec (2017)
21. Morano, P., Rosato, P., Tajani, F., Manganelli, B., Di Liddo, F.: Contextualized property market models vs. generalized mass appraisals: an innovative approach. Sustainability **11**(18), 4896 (2019)
22. Morano, P., Tajani, F., Locurcio, M.: Land use, economic welfare and property values: an analysis of the interdependencies of the real-estate market with zonal and socio-economic variables in the municipalities of Apulia region (Italy). Int. J. Agric. Environ. Inf. Syst. (IJAEIS) **6**(4), 16–39 (2015)
23. Oshodi, O.S., Thwala, W.D., Odubiyi, T.B., Abidoye, R.B., Aigbavboa, C.O.: Using neural network model to estimate the rental price of residential properties. J. Financ. Manag. Prop. Constr. **24**(2), 217–230 (2019)
24. Osservatorio del Mercato Immobiliare, Agenzia delle entrate (2020). www.agenziaentrate. gov.it. Accessed 15 Mar 2021
25. Rapporto sul mercato immobiliare della locazione in Italia – 2020 (2020). https://www.agenzi aentrate.gov.it/portale/documents/20143/263076/RI2020_20200521. Accessed 15 Mar 2021
26. Su, Y., Zhu, D., Geng, B.: The spatial structure and affecting factors of the housing rental in Beijing. Econ. Geogr. **34**(4), 64–69 (2014)
27. Tajani, F., Morano, P., Locurcio, M., D'Addabbo, N.: Property valuations in times of crisis: artificial neural networks and evolutionary algorithms in comparison. In: Gervasi, O., et al. (eds.) ICCSA 2015. LNCS, vol. 9157, pp. 194–209. Springer, Cham (2015). https://doi.org/10.1007/978-3-319-21470-2_14
28. Ufficio Studi Solo Affitti (2020). https://www.soloaffitti.it/la-situazione-del-mercato. Accessed 10 Mar 2021
29. Yusuf, A.A., Resosudarmo, B.P.: Does clean air matter in developing countries' megacities? A hedonic price analysis of the Jakarta housing market Indonesia. Ecol. Econ. **68**(5), 1398–1407 (2009)
30. Yuxuan, X., Shenjing, H., Junxi, Q.: An investigation on the emerging housing rental market in a studentified village in Guangzhou: a new institutional economics perspective. Hum. Geogr. **29**(4), 36–43 (2014)
31. Zietz, E.N., Sirmans, G.S.: Determinants of house price: a quantile regression approach. J. Real Estate Financ. Econ. **37**, 317–333 (2008)

The Paradox of Fiscal Inequality in Italy: Exploratory Analyses on Property Tax Rates

Rocco Curto, Alice Barreca, Giorgia Malavasi, and Diana Rolando[✉]

Department of Architecture and Design, Politecnico di Torino, Viale Mattioli 39,
10125 Turin, Italy
{rocco.curto,alice.barreca,giorgia.malavasi,
diana.rolando}@polito.it

Abstract. The Organization for Economic Co-operation and Development (OECD) in the last Going for Growth report (2021) urged the Italian government to redefine the tax on the first home ownership and to review the cadastral rates. This could represent an opportunity to re-discuss the objectives of the property taxation, as a part of the general tax reform announced by the Italian government. The aim of this paper is to perform some preliminary analyses on the fiscal inequality related to luxury properties in six different Italian cities at municipal level. The proposed methodological approach is based on three steps and can be also applied to other urban contexts. A stratified sampling of data from real estate advertisements provide the basis for the calculation of the cadastral values and a set of innovative fiscal inequality indicators. Descriptive statistics and regression analyses are performed to study the relations between property prices, cadastral values and the inequality level expressed by the proposed indicators. Findings show that cadastral values are not related to property prices and that the fiscal inequality level is significant in the analysed cities, even if with some differences that highlight a chaotic fiscal situation. The regression results also highlight the random relationship between tax rates and property prices and thus suggest that redistributive policies are necessary in the Italian context. The outputs of these first exploratory analyses represent a good starting point that deserves to be carried on and developed to test the proposed methodological approach. In particular, further researches could be focused on other housing segments, such as economic properties and tenements, and the analyses could be improved by considering the different urban areas and the related sub-markets.

Keywords: Fiscal inequality · Real estate market · Property taxation · Cadastral values · Property prices · Italy

1 Introduction

In the last decade, the economic crisis has affected the real estate market and has also produced several structural changes. In particular, the process of income polarization, determined by globalization, has amplified social inequalities and has determined the

© Springer Nature Switzerland AG 2021
O. Gervasi et al. (Eds.): ICCSA 2021, LNCS 12954, pp. 77–92, 2021.
https://doi.org/10.1007/978-3-030-86979-3_6

contraction of demand in the urban areas where the population with the lowest creditworthiness lives. Socio-economic characteristics often determine a real territorial polarization between weak urban areas, degraded and with limited services, and prestigious areas of high building and territorial quality. These phenomena, that the Covid-19 pandemic is accentuating, are widely studied in the literature. In this perspective different aspects deserve to be take into account, such as for example social inequality (Atkinson 1970; Bechini 2017), quality of life (Schneider 1976; Diener 1995; Diener and Suh 1997), welfare and well-being (Segre et al. 2011; Andrews and Withey 2012), social vulnerability (Cutter et al. 2000; Schmidtlein et al. 2008; Tate 2013; Lee 2014) and urban vibrancy (Jacobs 1961; Jacobs 1969; Montgomery 1995; Montgomery 1998; Yue et al. 2017).

Recent studies, which analysed social and housing vulnerability and urban vibrancy, identified clear spatial clusters, strictly related to the real estate market dynamics (Barreca et al. 2017; Barreca et al. 2018, Barreca et al. 2020a, Barreca et al. 2020b). The phenomenon highlighted a relation between set of vulnerability and vibrancy indicators and property prices in the city of Turin, but it has an even greater significance if its potentialities are extended to other cities at national level.

In order to reduce territorial and socio-economic inequalities across the urban areas and thus foster territorial welfare, the fiscal inequality and the related property taxation constitute urgent issues to be faced and deeply studied. Coherently with the objectives of the 2030 Agenda for sustainable development, the reform of the property taxation should support local finance and foster processes of territorial redevelopment and urban regeneration.

In particular, in the Italian context the fiscal inequality has currently reached paradoxical levels: often the taxes on luxury properties are lower than taxes on economic buildings or tenements, due to the inaccurate assignment of the cadastral category and relating appraisal rates defined by the Agenzia delle Entrate (a branch of the Italian Ministry of Economy and Finance). The reform of property taxation has been discussed for many years and numerous studies were carried out on different urban contexts at national and international level (Bourassa 1990; Dillinger 1992; Pellegrino et al. 2011; Rosengard 2012; Curto et al. 2014; Yinger et al. 2016; Bordignon et al. 2017; Curto et al. 2017; Elinder and Persson 2017). Nevertheless, in Italy it never started for several reasons. Recently, the Organization for Economic Co-operation and Development (OECD) in the last Going for Growth report (2021) urged the Italian government to institute a tax on the first home ownership and to review the cadastral rates. This could represent an opportunity to re-discuss the objectives of the property taxation, as a part of the general tax reform announced by the Italian government.

To support the reform of property taxation it is fundamental to understand the property tax rates determination process and, in particular, to study the relation between cadastral values (that constitute the tax bases) and property prices. The discrepancy between these values is well-known, but a real quantification of it across different cities is not deeply studied, at least at our knowledge.

The aim of this paper is to perform some preliminary analyses on the fiscal inequality related to luxury properties in six different Italian cities at municipal level (Turin, Milan, Bologna, Florence, Naples and Palermo). In particular, this research aims to create a set of fiscal inequality indicators able to explicit the gap between cadastral values and property prices, as well as to quantify the discrepancy in terms of property taxation.

Findings confirm that redistributive policies are necessary in the Italian context, which is currently characterized by a chaotic fiscal situation. In particular, the results highlight that the reform of property taxation cannot be defined, as requested by the OECD and EU, until the cadastral values are firstly corrected, by taking into account property prices and the real estate market context.

The paper proceeds as follows: the methodological approach is introduced in Sect. 2, while Sect. 3 presents the selected case studies. Results are discussed in Sect. 4 and some concluding remarks are presented in the final section.

2 Methodological Approach

A methodological approach was developed to study the fiscal inequality related to luxury properties. It was based on three main steps that could be applied to analyse and compare different Italian cities: stratified sampling (step 1), Cadastral values and fiscal inequality indicators calculation (step 2) and Regression analyses (step 3).

Step 1 - Stratified Sampling
The first step of the proposed methodological approach is fundamental to a priori establish a series of stratification rules and build comparable data samples across different cities and related databases. Since the aim of this research is to study the housing properties listed on the market with the highest listing prices, the data sampling is not casual and needs to be stratified. As previous studies demonstrated, listing prices can be considered a good proxy of transaction prices (Curto et al. 2012). Thus, even if it represents a key limitation, listing prices can be used, eventually reduced by a certain percentage. It is generally known the absence of transparent information of real estate market in the Italian context; the Ministry of Economy and Finance collects and manages data on transaction prices and cadastral incomes, but unfortunately this important knowledge base is not publically available and accessible. Therefore, stratified samples of luxury houses can be identified by monitoring real estate advertisements published on real estate web platforms and by sorting them by decreasing price. It is worth mentioning that this paper is aimed to present some first exploratory analyses, but further researches may include also housing properties with the lowest prices, in order to perform other analyses to eventually support redistributive policies.

According to the aim of the present research, a set of characteristics has to be preliminary defined to select the listings to be included into the data samples. In the structuring of the data sample and the related database some variables of housing properties listed on the market are defined as mandatory while other as optional. The data related to the price, the apartment size, the cadastral income and the cadastral category are necessary to select the housing properties listed on the market. Other characteristics, such as the apartment floor, the building typology, the building construction period and other intrinsic and extrinsic characteristics, can be observed, even if they do not represent priority features in this first phase of the research. Also, the property address is not a priority feature at this stage: in fact, the selected properties georeferencing are considered at municipal level, due to the fact that the aim is to globally analyse the phenomena in comparison with other cities at national level. Further researches will be addressed to analyse the fiscal inequality by considering also the urban territorial segments and the related real estate sub-markets.

Step 2 - Cadastral Values and Fiscal Inequality Indicators Calculation

To analyze fiscal inequality, the cadastral values of each observation and a set of indicators relating to both the cadastral coefficients and the real estate market values are calculated. The Cadastral Value (CV) of a property does not refer to the market value of an asset, but it is calculated to determine the taxes for the ownership and/or the acquisition of a property. CV is obtained by multiplying the cadastral income revalued by 5% by a certain coefficient established by law based on the cadastral category of the property (in Italy art. 52 of the decree 131/1986 and subsequent amendments and addictions). The cadastral income is calculated on the basis of the size of the property (expressed in cadastral rooms, square meters or cubic meters) and the appraisal rates defined by the Agenzia delle Entrate (a branch of the Italian Ministry of Economy and Finance) which may vary according to the property location and use. The cadastral income is reported in the cadastral certificate, but often it is also indicated in the property listings.

In this research, the calculation of CV is a necessary fundamental step to allow the calculation of the following innovative fiscal inequality indicators.

The first indicator (ΔATP_CV) represents the difference between the property Adjusted Total Price (ATP) and its CV and it is calculated as follows (1):

$$\Delta\text{ATP\_CV} = ATP - CV \tag{1}$$

where ATP is the total listing price reduced by a certain percentage in order to be assimilated to the transaction price and CV is the Cadastral Value. This percentage reduction may vary according to the city and to the specific economic trend of the real estate market.

The second indicator (ATP/CV) represents the ratio between the property Adjusted Total Price (ATP) and its CV, it is calculated as follows (2):

$$ATP/CV = \frac{ATP}{CV} \tag{2}$$

where ATP is the Adjusted Total Price and CV is the Cadastral Value.

The third indicator (ΔIMU) represents the difference between the IMU tax calculated (C_IMU) and the IMU tax effectively paid (P_IMU) as follows (3):

$$\Delta\text{IMU} = C\_IMU - P\_IMU \tag{3}$$

where C_IMU is the property tax calculated on the basis of the property value and the Municipal Rate and P_IMU is the property tax calculated on the basis of the CV and the Municipal Rate.

The fourth indicator (CTR) represents the Calculated Tax Rate, and it is computed as follows (4):

$$\text{CTR} = \frac{P\_IMU}{ATP} 1000 \tag{4}$$

where P_IMU is the property tax paid and ATP is the Adjusted Total Price.

Step 3 - Regression Analyses

In this research a traditional hedonic approach (Rosen 1974) is used to perform preliminary and explorative analyses aimed at investigating whether, how and in what measure there is a relationship between fiscal inequality and the real estate market.

In particular, two Ordinary Least Squares (OLS) models are performed to measure the impact of property prices, assumed as explanatory variable, on cadastral values (first model) and on property tax rates (second model). Both models are tested by means of Jarque-Bera Test (normality of errors) to verify the pertinence of used variables and Breusch-Pagan and Koenker-Bassett tests to verify the absence of heteroskedasticity (Breusch and Pagan 1979). Moreover, a logarithmic transformation of all the considered variables is applied to weaken the collinearity, eliminate heteroscedasticity and reduce the absolute values of the data. Therefore, in the first OLS model the dependent variable is LogCV (Cadastral Value), while in the second model the dependent variable is LogCTR (Calculated Tax Rate). The logarithmic transformation of the ATP (Adjusted Total Price) variable is assumed as explanatory variable in both models.

3   Study Areas and Data Samples

The methodological approach was defined to be applied to different urban contexts. In this phase of the research the following six Italian cities were selected to test some first preliminary results: Milan, Turin, Bologna, Florence, Naples and Palermo.

The selected case studies represent some of the main Italian cities - excluding Rome - characterized by different socio-economic contexts and well distributed throughout the country; for these reasons they can be considered a good starting point for this research in order to compare the results archived after the application of the proposed methodological approach.

The trend of the real estate market in the last 5 years highlights some first principal differences among these six Italian cities. Figure 1 highlights the highest property mean values (>3.600 Euro/m^2) and the highest standardized numbers of property transactions in Milan, which is the only city that presents a clear positive trend for both values. Bologna and Florence present similar property mean values (around 2.800 Euro/m^2) and a slightly decreasing trend; the dynamism of their real estate market is the lowest among the considered cities, aligned with Palermo. The data related to Turin and Naples show a constant trend of the property mean values (in range from 2.100 and 2.200 Euro/m^2), but a considerable difference by analysing the standardized numbers of property transactions, which is higher than 10.000 for Turin and half the size for Naples. Palermo, with the lowest property mean values (around 1.200 Euro/m^2) and a low number of property transactions, presents the weakest real estate market among the considered cities.

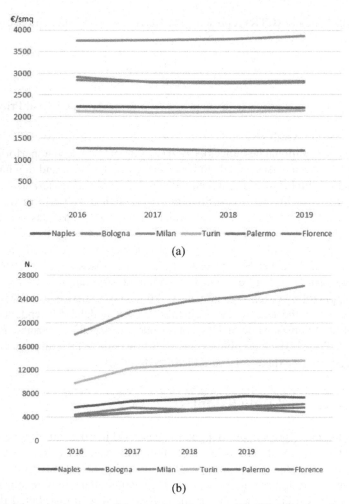

Fig. 1. The real estate market trend in the selected case studies: (a) property values (mean); (b) standardized number of property transactions (Source: Authors' elaboration on OMI - Agenzia delle Entrate data)

For each selected city, the data sampling was carried on according to the abovementioned stratification rules (step 1 of the proposed methodological approach) to obtain six different luxury properties data samples. One of the most relevant Italian real estate web platform (www.immobiliare.it) was assumed as data source to observe property listings published from January to March 2021.

Table 1 shows the summary statistics of the property Adjusted Total Prices (ATP), Adjusted Unitary Prices (AUP) and the Cadastral Incomes (CI) calculated on the data samples consisting of 100 property listings for each considered city. It is worth mentioning that the ATP are calculated by reducing the observed total listing price by 15% in order to be assimilated to transaction prices in 2021. Furthermore, it is important to

Table 1. Summary statistics of the property prices and the cadastral incomes (Source: Authors' elaboration on Immobiliare.it data)

	Freq	ATP (mean)	ATP (st.dev.)	AUP (mean)	AUP (st.dev.)	CI (mean)	CI (st.dev.)	IMU Tax - Municipal Rate 2020
Milan	100	1.758.280	1.212.815	8.571	2.691	2.347	1.665	10,6‰
Florence	100	1.401.850	711.417	4.534	1.515	2.081	1.253	10,6‰
Naples	100	1.200.950	490.116	4.722	1.677	1.901	929	10,6‰
Turin	100	983.760	300.218	3.303	1.001	2.495	1.313	10,6‰
Bologna	100	902.790	333.653	3.386	891	2.169	1.144	10,6‰
Palermo	100	501.390	358.307	1.694	739	784	581	10,6‰

notice that both the mean Adjusted Total Prices and the mean Adjusted Unitary Prices are very high if compared with those showed in Fig. 1, due to the abovementioned stratified sampling aimed at selecting listings of luxury properties. By comparing the summary statistics of the six cities, the high variability of both property prices and cadastral incomes, is evident. In fact, very high values emerge in Milan (with ATP higher than 1.700.000 Euro, AUP around 8.500 Euro/m^2 and CI higher than 2.300), while in Palermo the mean values (ATP around 500.000 Euro, AUP around 1.700 Euro/m^2 and CI lower than 800) are considerably lower. This framework is remarkable, above all considering that this variability among mean values in different Italian cities drastically grows when the range of the minimum and maximum values is analysed.

According to the aim of this research and to the calculation of the above mentioned fiscal inequality indicators, Table 1 also shows the rates that the selected Italian Municipality established in 2020 to determine the taxes for the ownership and/or the acquisition of a property (called IMU tax). It is worth mentioning that currently the IMU tax cannot be applied for first homes ownership, but it is applied for all properties classified in A/1, A/8 and A/9 cadastral categories (stately properties, villas, castles/historical buildings).

Despite the fact that the data samples consist of the property listings with the highest prices, thus representing the luxury housing segment, the descriptive statistics of the "cadastral category" variable in Fig. 2 highlight that most of the properties are classified as "civil properties" (cadastral category A/2), which is probably too generic and so easily associated to several properties. Instead, the rather low number of "stately properties" (cadastral category A/1) highlights the very well-known problem related to the correctness of the cadastral category attribution. For example, by comparing Bologna and Florence, which have similar mean property values, it is surprising that on the one hand in Bologna there are no "stately properties" and on the other in Florence the percentage of the same cadastral category amounts to 20%. These data denote that the fiscal inequality level may be even higher.

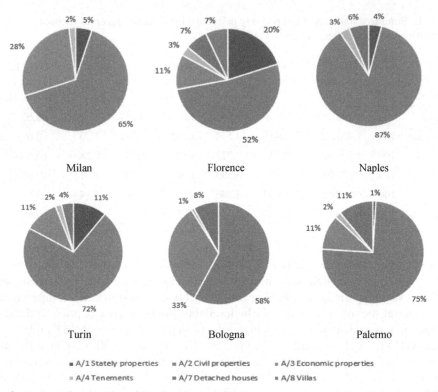

Fig. 2. Cadastral categories of the listed properties (Source: Authors' elaboration on Immobiliare.it data)

4   Results

In accordance with the aim of studying the fiscal inequality related to luxury properties, the proposed methodological approach was applied to analyze the six Italian cities assumed as case studies. Therefore, six different data samples were built following the above mentioned stratification rules and the cadastral values of the selected properties were calculated, as well as a series of fiscal inequality indicators. Finally, regression analyses were performed in order to highlight fiscal inequality issues.

4.1   Cadastral Values and Fiscal Inequality Indicators

The step 2 of the proposed methodological approach was applied to each of the six data samples related to the cities of Milan, Turin, Bologna, Florence, Naples and Palermo.

Figure 3 shows the mean Cadastral Values (CV) calculated from the listed cadastral incomes. The distributions of the CV are not normal in any data sample considered, due to the stratified data sampling that was carried out to select luxury properties. Moreover, each data sample has maximum outliers, which identify properties of exceptional value.

Furthermore, Table 2 shows the minimum and maximum values of the four indicators calculated in order to highlight different ranges in the considered cities.

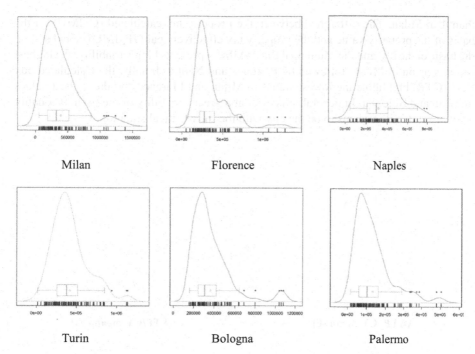

Milan   Florence   Naples

Turin   Bologna   Palermo

Fig. 3. Cadastral value distribution of the listed properties (Source: Authors' elaboration on Immobiliare.it data)

Table 2. Fiscal inequality indicators: minimum and maximum values (Source: Authors' elaboration on Immobiliare.it data)

	ΔATP_CV (€)		ATP/CV (%)		ΔIMU (€)		CTR (%)	
	min	max	min	max	min	max	min	max
Milan	7984	5888472	1,02	16,44	84,6304	62417,8	0,64	10,42834
Florence	−333924	1595008	0,70	80,78	3539,59	16907,08	0,13	15,07767
Naples	−339428	1527260	0,68	6,32	−3597,94	16188,96	1,68	15,57984
Turin	−344972	4204456	0,68	23,35	−3656,7	44567,23	0,45	15,66118
Bologna	−86956	2611440	0,89	14,43	−921,734	27681,26	0,73	11,9065
Palermo	−54304	1854520	0,89	15,36	−575,622	19657,91	0,69	11,95441

The mean values of the four indicators are illustrated in Fig. 4 to compare the fiscal inequality in the six considered cities.

The highest differences between CV and ATP (ΔATP_CV) are in Florence and Milan, both higher than 800.000,00 €. The ratio between ATP and CV (ATP/CV) presents a rather low variability among the six cities, ranging from about 2,3 in Bologna to more than 4 in Milan. The difference between the property tax calculated (C_IMU) on the basis of the property value and the property tax effectively paid (P_IMU) calculated on the basis of the CV and the Municipal Rate (ΔIMU) presents high variability: the highest score is again in Milan, followed by Florence and Naples. Finally, the Calculated Tax Rate (CTR) highlights the lowest values in Milan and Florence and the highest values in Turin and Bologna. In general, it is evident a great variability of the fiscal inequality level, even if Milan seems to be the city with the most critical situation.

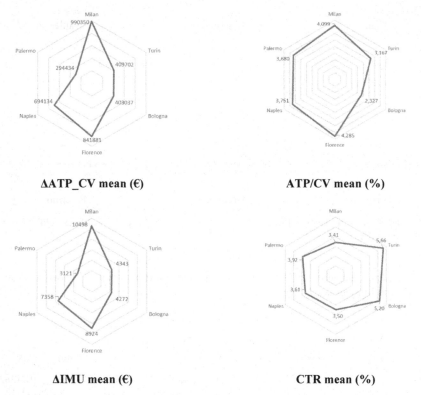

Fig. 4. Fiscal inequality indicators: mean values across the 6 case studies (Source: Authors' elaboration on Immobiliare.it data)

Figure 5 shows the difference between the IMU tax calculated (C_IMU) and the IMU tax effectively paid (P_IMU) related to the properties selected by means of the stratified sampling. Milan presents maximum values higher than 60.000,00 Euro, followed by Florence and Naples with maximum values respectively higher than 40.000 Euro and 25.000,00 Euro: on the contrary, the maximum values in the other cities are significantly lower (on average around 15.000,00 Euro). The fact that in Naples ΔIMU is higher than in Bologna and in Turin deserves to be further investigated, considering that in Naples the number of economic and popular housing properties is certainly higher. These results suggest that in Naples the gap between weak and wealthy urban areas is very high, and it is highlighted by the polarization of property prices, the income distribution and the unemployment level of population.

Therefore, in all the considered cities numerous property owners currently pay lower IMU taxes than they should and this aspect represents one of the key issues that evidently make the reform of property taxation urgent.

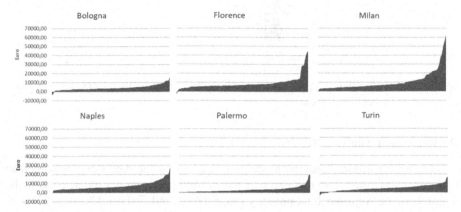

Fig. 5. ΔIMU distribution in the 6 data samples (Source: Authors' elaboration on Immobiliare.it data)

The specific situation in Milan deserves to be further explored by comparing the ATP and the CV of each property: Fig. 6 shows on the right the decreasing ordered ATPs and on the left the related CVs. The graph highlights a random relation between these values. In particular, there are not only several properties with CV higher than ATP, but also properties with CV lower than ATP; it is worth mentioning that in some cases the CV are strongly underestimated, even 300% lower than ATP.

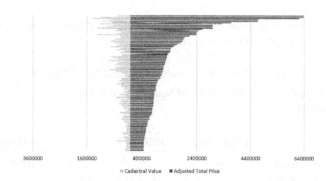

Fig. 6. CVs and ATPs distribution in Milan data sample (Source: Authors' elaboration on Immobiliare.it data)

Finally, it is interesting to analyse the relation between the ATP and the CTR variables. The scatterplot in Fig. 7 highlights a negative relation that means that high property values are generally related to low Calculated Tax Rates.

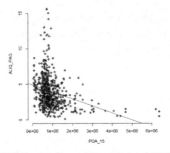

Fig. 7. Calculated Tax Rate (CTR) and Adjusted Total Price (ATP): scatterplot (Source: Authors' elaboration on Immobiliare.it data)

4.2 Regression Analyses Results

A traditional logarithmic hedonic model was applied on the data samples related to the six analysed cities. Two regression analyses were performed in order to study the relation between Adjusted Total property Prices (ATP) and Cadastral Values (CV) - in the first OLS model - and between ATP and Calculated Tax Rates (CTR) - in the second OLS model. On the basis of the normality test of both CV and CTR variables, the logarithmic transformation was preferred: thus, the dependent variable of the first model was LogCV, while the dependent variable of the second model was LogCTR. The ATP variable was also preferred in its logarithmic transformation and assumed as explanatory variable. The results of the first OLS model (Table 3) showed that cadastral values are very weakly related to property prices: in some cities the relation between the dependent and explanatory variables is null (Turin and Florence) or very low (Naples),while in the others is rather weak (R^2 around 30%). Therefore, it is evident that the tax bases, that the cadastral values represent, are independent from the property prices.

Table 3. First OLS model to assess the relationship between Cadastral values (LogCV) and Adjusted Total Prices (LogATP) (Source: Authors' elaboration).

Independent variable: Adjusted Total Price (LogATP)		Dependent variable: Cadastral Value (LogCV)			
		Ordinary Least Squares Model (OLS)			
		Coefficients	Probability		Adjusted R^2
Milan	Intercept	$1.125\,e^1$	$< 2e^{-16}$	***	0.373
	LogATP	$3.601\,e^{-7}$	$8.9e^{-12}$	***	
Turin	Intercept	$1.250\,e^1$	$< 2e^{-16}$	***	0.019
	LogATP	$3.487\,e^{-7}$	0.088		
Bologna	Intercept	$1.213e^1$	$< 2e^{-16}$	***	0.319
	LogATP	$7.499e^{-7}$	$5.25e^{-10}$	***	
Florence	Intercept	$1.248\,e^1$	$< 2e^{-16}$	***	0.016
	LogATP	$1.186e^{-7}$	0.104		

(continued)

Table 3. (*continued*)

		Dependent variable: Cadastral Value (LogCV)			
Independent variable: Adjusted Total Price (LogATP)		Ordinary Least Squares Model (OLS)			
		Coefficients	Probability		Adjusted R^2
Naples	Intercept	$1.211\,e^1$	$< 2e^{-16}$	***	0.160
	LogATP	$4.381e^{-7}$	$2.13e^{-05}$	***	
Palermo	Intercept	$1.104\,e^1$	$< 2e^{-16}$	***	0.333
	LogATP	$1.175e^{-6}$	$1.96e^{-10}$	***	

Signif. codes: $p \leq 0.001$ '***'; $p \leq 0.01$ '**'; $p \leq 0.05$ '*'; $p \leq 0.1$ '.'; $p \leq 1$ ' '.

The results of the second OLS model (Table 4) showed that Calculated Tax Rates are unrelated to property prices since the explanatory power of all the models is very low. Moreover, these results shows the negative sign of the marginal coefficients of LogATP in all the cities, this means that the ratio between the variables, even if low, is in any case inverse, contrary to what it might be expected from a fair tax system.

Table 4. Second OLS model to assess the relationship between Calculated Tax Rates (LogCTR) and Adjusted Total Prices (LogATP) (Source: Authors' elaboration).

		Dependent variable: Calculated Tax Rate (LogCTR)			
Independent variable: Adjusted Total Price (LogATP)		Ordinary Least Squares Model (OLS)			
		Coefficients	Probability		Adjusted R^2
Milan	Intercept	$1.278c + 00$	$< 2e^{-16}$	***	0.073
	LogATP	$-1.237e^{-07}$	0.003	**	
Turin	Intercept	2.187	$< 2e^{-16}$	***	0.115
	LogATP	$-7.28e^{-7}$	$3.23e^{-04}$	***	
Bologna	Intercept	1.804	$< 2e^{-16}$	***	0.060
	LogATP	$-2.89e^{-7}$	0.007	***	
Florence	Intercept	1.606	$< 2e^{-16}$	***	0.266
	LogATP	$-4.29e^{-7}$	2.35e-08	***	
Naples	Intercept	1.541	$< 2e^{-16}$	***	0.120
	LogATP	$-3.64e^{-7}$	$2.32e^{-04}$	***	
Palermo	Intercept	1.512	$< 2e^{-16}$	***	0.180
	LogATP	$-6.77e^{-7}$	$6.33e^{-06}$	***	

Signif. codes: $p \leq 0.001$ '***'; $p \leq 0.01$ '**'; $p \leq 0.05$ '*'; $p \leq 0.1$ '.'; $p \leq 1$ ' '.

5 Conclusion

The proposed methodological approach based on three main steps was applied to analyse and compare the fiscal inequality related to luxury properties in six different Italian cities at municipal level. On the basis of the stratified data samples, exploratory analyses were performed and highlighted interesting preliminary results. The analyses were focused on cadastral categories, cadastral values and on the calculation of four innovative fiscal inequality indicators, proposed to quantify the well-known gap between cadastral values and property prices, as well as to explicit the discrepancy in terms of property taxation.

The descriptive statistics of the "cadastral category" variable highlighted that most of the properties are classified as "civil properties" (cadastral category A/2), although the data samples consist of the property listings with the highest prices of each city and thus represent the luxury housing segment. This results, that suggests that the fiscal inequality level may be very high, is strengthened by the fact that the number of "stately properties" (cadastral category A/1) is rather low. Furthermore, the four fiscal inequality indicators showed that cadastral values are randomly related to property prices and that the fiscal inequality level is significant in the analysed cities, even if with a great variability that denotes a general chaotic fiscal situation. In particular, the ΔIMU indicator explicated the great difference between the IMU tax calculated (C_IMU) and the IMU tax effectively paid (P_IMU), which is particularly evident in the city of Milan. Finally, the regression analyses results also confirmed that redistributive policies are necessary in the Italian context, by highlighting that the cadastral values have to be urgently corrected on the basis of the property prices. Therefore, in order to support the property taxation reform, the first urgent step is to revise the current cadastral rates and consequently the cadastral incomes. However, this chaotic system seems to respond to a single general "rule", according to which the taxes paid are negatively rather than positively correlated to property prices. Therefore the analyses effectively brought out that the cadastral values in Italy are anachronistic and are determined by stochastic components that made that taxes to be randomly paid, regardless of the values and characteristics of the properties. The revision of the cadastral rates can no longer be postponed for two reasons. Firstly, because it represents a crucial point to reduce the territorial and socio-economic inequalities originated by the real economy across the urban areas. Secondly, because it represents the fundamental step to revise the cadastral values, that constitute the tax bases for the IMU tax calculation. In particular, the re-introduction of the tax on the first home ownership, suggested by the OECD and identified as part of the general property taxation reform, could have positive consequences on a social, economic and territorial level, only if, for example, the generated incomes were invested for the redevelopment of the most vulnerable urban areas.

For these purposes, further researches will be addressed in order to analyse the fiscal inequality level by considering the phenomenon not only at municipal level, but also in the urban areas characterized by different real estate submarkets and socio-economic contexts (Whitehead 1999; Watkins 2001; Bourassa 2007). Those analyses will by particularly finalized to support policies to foster the territorial welfare, limit the social injustices caused by the fiscal inequality and tackle tax evasion. Furthermore, these analyses should be also developed by considering all the 8000 Italian municipalities, in order to verify how the property taxation system could really and effectively support redistributive mechanisms across the entire national context between more and less vulnerable areas and people. Moreover, the current analyses, limited to the luxury property segments, are not able to highlight the real impact that the property taxation could produce in social and territorial terms. A further development of this research will be addressed to extend the data sampling and consider also properties with lowest prices and thus representing the economic housing segment. In this way, it could be identified not only the fiscal inequality related to property owners that currently pay lower IMU taxes than they should, but also to those property owners than should pay drastically less.

In conclusion, the property taxation reform should be supported by analyses on both luxury and economic properties, in order to foster fiscal redistributive processes able to balance the current fiscal inequality and social injustice.

References

1. Andrews, F.M., Withey, S.B.: Social Indicators of Well-being: Americans' Perceptions of Life Quality. Springer, Berlin, (2012). https://doi.org/10.1007/978-1-4684-2253-5
2. Atkinson, A.B.: On the measurement of inequality. J. Econ. Theory **2**, 244–263 (1970)
3. Barreca, A., Curto, R., Rolando, D.: Assessing social and territorial vulnerability on real estate submarkets. Buildings **7**(4), 94 (2017). https://doi.org/10.3390/buildings7040094
4. Barreca, A., Curto, R., Rolando, D.: Housing vulnerability and property prices: spatial analyses in the Turin real estate market. Sustainability **10**(9), 3068 (2018). https://doi.org/10.3390/su10093068
5. Barreca, A., Curto, R., Rolando, D.: Urban vibrancy: an emerging factor that spatially influences the real estate market. Sustainability **12**(1), 346 (2020). https://doi.org/10.3390/su12010346
6. Barreca, A., Curto, R., Rolando, D.: Is the real estate market of new housing stock influenced by urban vibrancy? Complexity (2020).https://doi.org/10.1155/2020/1908698
7. Bechini, T.: La disuguaglianza in Italia: Un'analisi multidimensionale per circoscrizioni. EyesReg-Giornale di Scienze Regionali **7**, 64–69 (2017)
8. Breusch, T.S., Pagan, A.R.: A simple test for heteroscedasticity and random coefficient variation. Econom. J. Economy. Soc. 1287–1294 (1979)
9. Bourassa, S.C.: Land value taxation and housing development: effects of the property tax reform in three types of cities. Am. J. Econ. Sociol. **49**(1), 101–111 (1990)
10. Bourassa, S.C., Cantoni, E., Hoesli, M.: Spatial dependence, housing submarkets, and house prices. J. Real Estate Financ. Econ. **35**, 143–160 (2007)
11. Bordignon, M., Grembi, V., Piazza, S.: Who do you blame in local finance? An analysis of municipal financing in Italy. Eur. J. Polit. Econ. **49**, 146–163 (2017)
12. Curto, R., Fregonara, E., Semeraro, P.: Asking prices vs market prices: an empirical analysis. Territorio Italia **1**, 53–72 (2012)
13. Curto, R., Fregonara, E., Semeraro, P.: How can land registry values be made fairer pending a review of valuations? Territorio Italia **1**, 59–82 (2014)
14. Curto, R., Fregonara, E., Semeraro, P.: Market prices and property taxation in Italian real estate: a Turin case study. In: Stanghellini S., Morano P., Bottero M., Oppio A. (eds) Appraisal: From Theory to Practice. Green Energy and Technology. Springer, Cham (2017). https://doi.org/10.1007/978-3-319-49676-4_11

15. Cutter, S.L., Mitchell, J.T., Scott, M.S.: Revealing the vulnerability of people and places: a case study of Georgetown County, South Carolina. Ann. Assoc. Am. Geogr. **90**, 713–737 (2000)
16. Diener, E.A.: A value based index for measuring national quality of life. Soc. Indic. Res. **36**, 107–127 (1995)
17. Diener, E., Suh, E.: Measuring quality of life: economic, social, and subjective indicators. Soc. Ind. Res. **40**, 189–216 (1997)
18. Dillinger, W.: Urban Property Tax Reform Guidelines and Recommendations. The World Bank, Washington, D.C. (1992)
19. Elinder, M., Persson, L.: House price responses to a national property tax reform. J. Econ. Behav. Organ. **144**, 18–39 (2017)
20. Jacobs, J.: The Death and Life of Great American Cities. The Failure of Town Planning. Random House, New York (1961)
21. Jacobs, J.: The Life of Cities. Random House, New York, NY, USA (1969)
22. Lee, Y.J.: Social vulnerability indicators as a sustainable planning tool. Environ. Impact Assess. Rev. **44**, 31–42 (2014)
23. Montgomery, J.: Urban vitality and the culture of cities. Plan. Pract. Res. **10**, 101–110 (1995)
24. Montgomery, J.: Making a city: urbanity, vitality and urban design. J. Urban Des. **3**, 93–116 (1998)
25. OECD: Economic Policy Reforms 2021: going for growth In: OECD Better policies for better lives (2021). https://www.oecd.org/economy/italy-economic-snapshot/. Accessed 07 May 2021
26. Pellegrino, S., Piacenza, M., Turati, G.: Developing a static microsimulation model for the analysis of housing taxation in Italy. Int. J. Microsimul. **4**(2), 73–85 (2011)
27. Rosengard, J.K.: Property Tax Reform in Developing Countries. Springer, New York (2012). https://doi.org/10.1007/978-1-4615-5667-1
28. Rosen, S.: Hedonic prices and explicit markets: production differentiation in pure competition. J. Polit. Econ. **82**(1), 34–55 (1974)
29. Schmidtlein, M.C., Deutsch, R.C., Piegorsch, W.W., Cutter, S.L.: A sensitivity analysis of the social vulnerability index. Risk Anal. **28**, 1099–1114 (2008)
30. Schneider, M.: The "quality of life" and social indicators research. Public Adm. Rev. **36**, 297–305 (1976)
31. Segre, E., Rondinella, T., Mascherini, M.: Well-being in Italian regions. Measures, civil society consultation and evidence. Soc. Ind. Res. **102**, 47–69 (2011)
32. Tate, E.: Uncertainty analysis for a social vulnerability index. Ann. Assoc. Am. Geogr. **103**, 526–543 (2013)
33. Yinger, J., Bloom, H.S., Boersch-Supan, A.: Property taxes and house values: the theory and estimation of intrajurisdictional property tax capitalization. Elsevier (2016)
34. Yue, Y., Zhuang, Y., Yeh, A.G.O., Xie, J.Y., Ma, C.L., Li, Q.Q.: Measurements of POI-based mixed use and their relationships with neighbourhood vibrancy. Int. J. Geogr. Inf. Sci. **31**, 658–675 (2017)
35. Watkins, C.A.: The definition and identification of housing submarkets. Environ. Plan. **33**, 2235–2253 (2001)
36. Whitehead, C.M.E.: Chapter 40 Urban housing markets: theory and policy. In: Handbook of Regional and Urban Economics, vol. 3, pp. 1559–1594. Elsevier, Amsterdam (1999)

The Financial Costs in Energy Efficient District. Alternative Scenarios from the Demo Sites of the CITyFiED Program

Simona Barbaro[✉] and Grazia Napoli[✉]

University of Palermo, viale delle Scienze ed. 14, 90127 Palermo, Italy
{simona.barbaro,grazia.napoli}@unipa.it

Abstract. The European Union's environmental policies actively promote the transition to a low-carbon society and to sustainable energy systems that improve people's quality of life and do not negatively impact the natural environment. To achieve these goals, the European Union funded several programs to pilot energy efficiency measures for buildings and districts and, lately, launched the European Green Deal. The results of these experimentations have shown that often the economic feasibility of retrofitting interventions is not achieved without public grants. This contribution aims to analyze the influence of financial parameters on the profitability of projects of energy efficient districts. The study is based on the data from the demo sites of the CITyFiED program (Soma in Turkey and Laguna de Duero in Spain) that are reworked according to new several alternative scenarios, differentiated by cost financing and amount of public grants.

Keywords: Energy retrofit · Economic feasibility · Energy efficient district · CITyFiED program

1 Introduction

The European Union's (EU) key climate and energy objectives were set out in both the *2020 Climate & Energy Package* and the *2030 Climate & Energy Framework* [1] and since their promulgation, the EU has outlined various strategies to actively promote the transition to a low-carbon society, while creating a sustainable energy sector that improves the quality of life for EU citizens and does not impact the environment. Furthermore, UE has adopted the *17 Sustainable Development Goals* (SDGs), promoted by the United Nations (UN) with the *2030 Agenda for Sustainable Development*, and signed the *Paris Agreement* on climate change.

The attention to the rising needs of sustainability has recently been confirmed by the presentation of the *European Green Deal*, which has strengthened the willingness to support energy efficiency and retrofitting actions at urban and building scales. In fact, the *Renovation Wave Strategy*, published in October 2020, aims to double the rates of renovation in the next ten years to reduce the consumption of energy and resources in buildings [2]. In addition, the EU also intends to update the rules to facilitate the

© Springer Nature Switzerland AG 2021
O. Gervasi et al. (Eds.): ICCSA 2021, LNCS 12954, pp. 93–108, 2021.
https://doi.org/10.1007/978-3-030-86979-3_7

necessary public and private investment in the ongoing green transition, as well as to increase financing opportunities and credit schemes to support the implementation of effective energy retrofit projects. However, to do this it is necessary to conduct adequate evaluations for productively investing the resources made available.

Evaluating the performance of energy retrofitting projects, and any measure of any project, is a complex process, as it requires the simultaneous verification of environmental, social and economic sustainability [3]. In retrofitting projects, the primary objectives are to reduce energy consumption, increase the use of renewable resources and reduce CO_2 emissions. It is usually also included the overall environmental sustainability of the project, which must generate the least possible impact on the environment during the entire life cycle. This latter aspect is assessed through different types of environmental certification (e.g. BREEAM - Building Research Establishment's Environmental Assessment Method, LEED - Leadership in Energy & Environmental Design, etc.).

Social sustainability is also a key factor in achieving energy efficiency results and implies the direct involvement of residents, because they play an active role in the management phase of the intervention and many measures could be ineffective in real implementations without their collaboration [4].

Economic evaluations contribute to defining the performance of an energy retrofitting intervention and play a central role in their implementation since private entrepreneurs and/or owners are willing to invest when they expect the project to be profitable. Moreover, public administrations have the role of providing social welfare, in terms of the comfort of citizens in the short term, and of preserving the environment in the long term. So, they have to manage the allocation of public funds in the environmental sector in order to reconcile effectiveness and efficiency, and to achieve the environmental objectives set by the European Union for 2030 but using the available resources most efficiently [5].

The economic assessment of an investment analyzes the flow of costs and revenues during the economic life of a work and expresses the economic feasibility through a set of indicators, e.g. Net Present Value (NPV), Internal Return Rate (IRR), Payback Period (PB), etc. The values of the indicators depend on numerous technical (type of intervention, building materials, etc.), financial (financing sources, interest rates) and economic (energy price, building cost, etc.) elements and also on the degree of uncertainty associated with the time frame of 20–25 years [6–8].

The topics of economic and financial analysis applied to energy efficiency projects at different scales (building, neighbourhood, city) have been widely studied. These analyses have been diversified to adapt them to the measures that can be implemented and are differentiated by intervention type, building typology, technology and urban context. Some approaches focused on generating and evaluating scenarios on retrofit solutions according to the energy conservation measures adopted [9] or to different climatic conditions [10]. Other studies focused on the evaluation of energy retrofit interventions of different types of existing buildings [11–13], even in highly densified urban [14] or historical-architectural values contexts [15, 16]. Economic-financial analyses often integrate spatial and geo-referenced planning processes [17, 18] or combine financial evaluations with multicriteria evaluations, in order to support the decision-making process [19–21].

This study aims to provide a contribution to the scientific debate on the economic and financial analysis of energy retrofit interventions, meanwhile, the EU is promoting a massive investment plan for the ecological transition through the *European Green Deal*. In particular, some critical issues of economic evaluation that affect the economic feasibility of a project are analysed, concerning the type of financing and public grants. The projects of the European Program CITyFiED [22] were chosen as a case study and a total reworking of the economic evaluation was made. Some alternative scenarios were assumed, each of them corresponds to different funding parameters, in order to evaluate how the main economic indicators NPV and IRR may respond and, consequently, how the decision to implement the project may vary. In fact, even if economic feasibility cannot be considered a strict constraint for this type of projects, since the financial cash flow does not include environmental externalities, nevertheless it is necessary to know the measure of the social and economic price that is paid to achieve greater environmental sustainability.

2   The European Programs of 'My Smart City District'

The European Union has funded numerous programs intending to test the economic and administrative-procedural feasibility promoted within many EU climate and energy initiatives and regulations. Smart cities, which have always been the catalyst for EU policies, have been chosen as testers and promoters of the most interesting initiatives. However, what makes a city smart is not uniquely determined and is still a matter of debate.

According to the Organization of Economic and Cooperation Development (OECD), smart cities are those cities capable of promoting initiatives that use digital and technological innovation to make the provision of urban services more efficient, increase the well-being of citizens and at the same time make living spaces more sustainable and inclusive [23]. The variegated field of application of smart cities programs can be narrowed down to six main domains: Natural Resources and Energy (regarding the wise management of natural resources and the efficient use of energy); Transport and Mobility (referring to the reduction of traffic and polluting emissions); Buildings (related to the efficient management of energy consumption); Living (in terms of quality of life); Governments (referring to the importance of enacted policies); Economy and People (including urban measures that favour an increase in the economic availability of citizens) [24]. Smart cities may also deeply differ in their strategic approaches so, with a spatial reference, four strategic choices can be identified: national versus local strategies; strategies for new versus existing cities; hard versus soft infrastructure-oriented strategies; sector-based versus geographically-based strategies [25]. Furthermore, in the ongoing trends for smart cities of the future, the idea of energy smart cities is the one that is emerging the most [26].

Among the European smart energy cities initiatives, the *My Smart City District* (MSCD) programs have been considered particularly interesting as they have tested neighbourhood-scale energy efficiency strategies and measures in different European socio-economic contexts [22].

These programs are: R2CITIES - *Residential Renovation Towards Nearly Zero Energy Cities*; EU-GUGLE - *European cities serving as Green Urban Gate towards*

Leadership in sustainable Energy; ZenN - *Nearly Zero Energy Neighborhoods*; CITy-FiED - *Replicable and Innovative Future Efficient Districts and Cities*; Sinfonia - *Low Carbon Cities for a better quality of life*; City-Zen - *City Zero (Carbon) Energy*; Celsius Initiative; READY - *Resource Efficient cities implementing ADvanced smart citY solutions* (Fig. 1).

Fig. 1. The European Programs of the *My Smart City District* group.

Each program was granted by the *Seventh Framework Program* (FP7/2007–2013) in order to promote the *Net Zero-Energy District* (NZED), share experiences and know-how, and facilitate large-scale replication of neighbourhood-scale energy efficiency interventions. The projects lasted five years each (the last one was concluded in November 2019) and were developed separately; later they merged into the *My Smart City District* (MSCD) group, in order to strengthen content sharing and increase the synergy of the proposed measures.

For this reason, the programs have significantly different characteristics in terms of coordinating entity, strategic approach, area of intervention, primary energy savings, intended use of the buildings involved, stakeholders, share of European funding and other types of funding. The common elements were, however, the intention to promote an energy renewal strategy for cities and communities that leads to large-scale replicability of successful energy efficiency solutions, as well as the willingness to test these strategies in real case studies. In total, energy efficiency interventions have been completed in 27 neighbourhoods of 25 cities in 13 different European countries.

Although different from each other, the outcomes of the programs within the specific case studies were on average very positive and each of them was able to highlight strengths and weaknesses of the applied technical, economic, social and procedural strategies. A fundamental common element for each program was the European funding, which covered from 54% to 64% of the cost of the measures of all the energy efficiency projects and played a key role in achieving the economic feasibility of the interventions (Fig. 2).

By analysing the MSCD programs, some economic considerations may be made. For example, one of ZenN's goals was to provide a financial plan to support the involvement of community groups, who lack financial resources, in the energy efficiency of their neighbourhood. The study of these plans highlighted that some critical factors can affect the achievement of the economic feasibility of energy retrofitting projects, facilitating or hindering their implementation. The main critical factors are as follows: ownership structure, availability of public incentives or funds, and role of private investors [28].

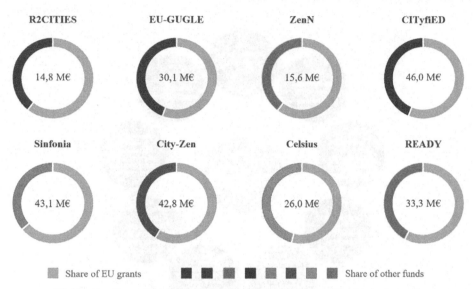

Fig. 2. Funding of European Programs of the *My Smart City District* group.

Instead, CITyfiED, which is the program that required the largest overall investment, is interesting because it focused on business models and financing schemes that would overcome the difficulty of dealing with high initial investment costs.

3 The CITyFiED Program

The CITyFiED (*Replicable and Innovative Future Efficient Districts and Cities*) project was developed from 2014 to March 2019 [22] with the aim of providing a replicable, systemic and integrated strategy to transform the European cities into *Smart Cities*, focusing on the reduction of energy demand and greenhouse gas emissions and increasing the use of renewable energy sources. CITyFiED defined, also, a cost-effective methodology to plan and implement energy efficient retrofitting actions at the neighbourhood scale (Fig. 3).

From a technical and scientific point of view, CITyFiED focused on the development of technologies and solutions that are useful to optimize the redevelopment of residential districts, improve electricity distribution and integrate district heating systems and renewable energy sources. On the other hand, from an economic point of view, CITyFiED drew up business models aimed at supporting the transformation of peculiar urban areas into Net Zero-Energy Districts (NZED).

Three demonstration sites located in different European countries were chosen to test its models within neighbourhood-scale urban renewal scenarios diversified by building types, ownership patterns, technological solutions and socio-economic contexts. The three selected neighbourhoods were: Manisa in Soma (Turkey), Torrelago in Laguna de Duero (Spain) and Linero in Lund (Sweden).

Fig. 3. CITyFiED's objectives.

The demonstration action in the three cities involved the energy efficient retrofitting of 190,462 sq.m of living space and of 2,067 homes, as well as the improvement of the quality of life of more than 5,700 citizens. All the main technological aspects (such as building retrofitting, district heating system and low-voltage distributed generation) were addressed through a systemic approach to achieve significant energy savings, very low energy buildings and minimum CO_2 emissions. At the end of the project, in fact, more than 13,000 MWh per year of final energy savings and over 1,600 t-CO_2-eq per year of emission reductions were achieved (Table 1).

Table 1. Energy performance of the CITyFiED program.

European program	Final energy savings (MWh per years)	Primary energy savings (MWh per years)	CO_2 saving (tCO_2 per years)
CITyFiED	13,261	14,288	1,699

Another key element of the program's strategy was the creation of a *City Cluster* of 11 cities and a *Community of Interest* of 44 other cities in order to maximize the potential replication of the project results by disseminating knowledge about the benefits of energy efficiency in the urban environment and sharing both building energy solutions and business models for urban retrofitting.

CITyFiED required a total investment of more than 46 M€, of which 25,828,319 € are European funds. Approximately 39 M€ was allocated to the three demonstration sites of Soma, Laguna de Duero and Lund and are divided into funds from private or public companies and grants from the European Commission (EC) (Table 2) [22].

Table 2. Funding for the three demonstration sites.

Demonstrative site	Partner	Own funds (M€)	EC grants (M€)	Total investment (M€)
Soma	SEAŞ	2.20	2.30	4.50
	MIR	2.00	2.30	4.30
	Others	1.80	2.40	4.20
	Total	**6.00**	**7.00**	**13.00**
Laguna de Duero	3IA	7.70	7.10	14.80
	VEO	2.20	0.76	3.00
	Others	0.60	0.64	1.20
	Total	**10.50**	**8.50**	**19.00**
Lund	LKF	3.80	2.00	5.80
	Lund	0.23	0.52	0.75
	KEAB	0.32	0.12	0.44
	Total	**4.40**	**2.60**	**7.00**

3.1 Soma (Turkey)

Soma is a medium-sized city in western Turkey. The Manisa demonstration site consists of 82 buildings that were constructed in 1982 (79 residential buildings, 2 guest houses and 1 conference centre). In the district there are one-, two-, three-storey and duplex buildings, with a total of 346 dwellings and 80,980 sq.m of floor area, including 7,037 sq.m of conditioned area. The predominant heating system is coal stoves (70%) as the buildings are only partially heated by boilers.

The owner of the neighbourhood was SEAŞ (SOMA Electricity Generation & Trading Company), a public company that took care of the management of the buildings and also dealt with the rental of houses and the management of the housing and the conference centre. But after the work began, ownership was transferred passed to EÜAŞ (Electricity Generation Company of Turkey).

From a technical point of view, the interventions consist of: the adaptation of the building envelope (installation of thermal insulation for the walls, replacement of windows, etc.); the refurbishment of heating systems (installation of low-temperature radiant heating systems); the implementation of the use of renewable sources (installation of solar thermal systems); the implementation of ICT solutions; the installation of energy management and control systems (installation of a DEMS - District Energy Management System, a BEMS - Building Energy Management System and a HEMS - Home Energy Management System). In addition, other interventions were also planned, such as the installation of a Building Integrated Photovoltaics (BIPV) and a district heating system. However, due to the Turkish administrative processes and some political events, the works were significantly delayed and EÜAŞ decided to stop the works. Obviously, this event affected the business model of the project, making it impossible to definitively achieve the initial goals.

The project was supposed to have 53.16% RES (Renewable Energy Sources) contribution and allow 56.16% energy savings. In fact, the initial investment was to be 13 M€, of which 7 M€ were to be granted by the European Commission, but after the events related to the transfer of ownership of the district the investment decreased significantly.

The main partners of the project were SEAŞ, Manisa Metropolitan Municipality (MAN) and MİR Research and Development Inc (Table 2).

3.2 Laguna de Duero (Spain)

Laguna de Duero is one of the municipalities surrounding the metropolitan area of the city of Valladolid, capital of the province of the same name in the autonomous community of Castile and León. The Torrelago demonstration site consists of 31 private buildings that were constructed between 1977 and 1981 and provided with district heating. The buildings are inhabited by 3,858 people and are all 12 floors with 4 dwellings each, for a total of 1,488 dwellings and 140,000 sq.m of conditioned area.

The main distinguishing feature of this case is the building ownership. In Torrelago, in fact, there is one private owner per dwelling grouped in two legal entities, i.e. two Communities of Owners representing 576 and 912 owners respectively.

From a technical point of view, the interventions concerned: the adaptation of the building envelope (placement of an ETICS - Exterior Thermal Insulation Composite System); the renovation of existing facilities (renovation of the district heating system, partial replacement of gas boilers, etc.); the implementation of Information Communication Technology (ICT) solutions; the establishment of energy management and control systems (installation of DEMS, BEMS and HEMS).

The project was carried out with 57.32% RES contributions and allowed 38.72% energy savings. The total investment was 19 M€, of which 8.5 M€ were granted by the European Commission. The financial scheme was based on a private risk-sharing model between an Energy Service Company (ESCO) and a construction company: the initial investment to pay for the cost of the interventions was supported by the private companies, to be then paid back by the homeowners through monthly fees established by a multi-year contract.

The two main partners in the project were 3IA, responsible for retrofitting the facades, and VEO, responsible for renovating the energy heating system (Table 2).

3.3 Lund, Sweden

Lund is a medium-sized college town where nearly 90% of the heat demand is supplied by district heating. The Linero demonstration site consists of the *Eddan* building block and two buildings in the *Havamal* block, both constructed in the early 1970s, for a total of 28 buildings of three levels each.

The buildings are owned by the public housing corporation Lunds Kommuns Fastighets (LKF) and contain 681 apartments with approximately 2,000 tenants. The CITyFiED project involved only 16 of the 28 buildings, for a total of 379 homes and 40,400 sq.m of conditioned area.

From a technical point of view, the interventions concerned: the adaptation of the building envelope (installation of thermal insulation for the walls, replacement of windows, etc.); the renovation of existing systems (improvement of the ventilation system, restructuring of the district heating system, etc.); the implementation of the use of renewable energy sources in the buildings (installation of photovoltaic systems); the implementation of ICT solutions; the installation of energy management and control systems (installation of DEMS, BEMS and HEMS).

The project was carried out with 70.8% RES contributions and allowed 30.8% energy savings. The total investment was 7 M€, of which 2.6 M€ were granted by the European Commission. The upgrading of the buildings was carried out by LKF under a contract with a construction company; while the renovation of the district heating network was developed by LKF and carried out by Kraftringen AB (KEAB), another public company in Lund.

The main partners in the project were Lund Municipality, LKF and KEAB (Table 2).

4 Scenarios of Economic Feasibility in the Demo Sites of Soma and Laguna de Duero

The investment analysis conducted by CITyFiED aimed to evaluate the economic feasibility of the different energy saving measures (ECMs) that were implemented in the three demonstration sites. The economic analysis was made by applying the most commonly and widely used indicators, namely Net Present Value (NPV), Internal Rate of Return (IRR), Return on Investment (ROI) and Static Payback Period (SPP). There were very different results in the three sites, since two investments were profitable while one was not profitable.

Of course, the values of the indicators depend on: design (choice of retrofitting measures such as building insulation, solar thermal domestic hot water system, control system equipment, lighting control system, etc.), technologic (energy efficiency of the measures), economic (time frame, fuel cost, etc.) and financial factors (discount rate, cost of financing, etc.).

Starting with the data of the CITyFiED reports, a study was conducted to assess how the type of capital and other financial elements may affect the economic indicators NPV and IRR of the interventions, assuming new alternative scenarios. Most of the original data remain unchanged, while the data related to the type of capital invested and other financial parameters vary.

The NPV represents the value of all revenues calculated after costs:

$$NPV = \sum_{t=1}^{n} \frac{(R_t - C_t)}{(1 + r)^t} - C_0 \tag{1}$$

Where: Rt - revenues for the year t; Ct - costs of the year t; r - discount rate; n – period of analysis; C_0 – initial investment.

The IRR is the discount rate that makes the NPV of revenues and costs equal to zero:

$$\sum_{t=1}^{n} \frac{(R_t - C_t)}{(1 + IRR)^t} - C_0 = 0 \tag{2}$$

The feasibility conditions can, therefore, be summarized as follows:

– NPV greater than zero;
– IRR at least equal to the discount rate.

When these conditions are met, the cash flow of the project is sufficient to cover the initial investment and to recover the capital contributed by all parties involved in the investment. Annual costs include operation costs and capital-related costs. Revenues include cost savings, i.e. savings resulting from the increased energy efficiency of the building that implies a reduction in energy demand and bills, and cost avoidance, related to interventions to prevent higher costs in the future.

The projects of the CITyFiED program obtained grants from the European Commission (Table 2), so if the economic analysis of the project is done from the perspective of the investor, the grants are a revenue that reduces the private investment. Whereas if the economic analysis is done with the aim of assessing the cost effectiveness of the intervention, the grants are not included in the cash flow.

Although they were not used in our study, there are other economic indicators of investments such as ROI, SPP and DPP (Dynamic Payback Period). The ROI is a ratio of profit to the investment cost. The SPP is referred to the time required to recover the investment cost and is calculated by dividing the initial investment by the average net cash flow, while the DPP is the numbers of years required to recoup the initial investment based on the discounted cash flow.

4.1 Alternative Scenarios of Economic Analysis in the Demo Site of Soma

The retrofitting interventions in Soma demo site include the following measures: Insulation of buildings, Domestic hot water system, Building Integrated PV system, LED lighting, Low temperature heating system, District heating system and Monitoring.

To evaluate the NPVs and IRRs of each measure, the following original data from the demo site reports are used:

- Total investment (euro);
- Maintenance costs (euro);
- Energy savings (MWh);
- Electricity prices and coal prices (assuming an annual increase of 0.05%);
- Waste heating costs per year;
- Time frame of 15 years (10 and 25 years respectively for LED lighting and Low temperature heating system measures).

As public European and national administrations often give incentives to projects to achieve the reduction of energy consumption and the reduction of greenhouse gases, several new scenarios are defined according to different compositions between risk capital and grants to verify what are the results of the investment of public resources at the district scale. The NPVs are recalculated applying a discount rate that ranges from 0 to 6% under the following scenarios:

- 100% funds - 0 grants;
- 75% funds - 25% grants;
- 50% funds - 50% grants;
- 25% funds - 75% grants.

The results in Fig. 4 show that the NPVs of the measures have very different curves in position and shape and that they are affected to varying degrees by grants. Three measures, namely *Insulation of buildings*, *Domestic hot water* and *LED lighting*, have always positive NPVs both in presence and in absence of grants, so these types of measures are cost-effective and do not need to be supported financially. The other measures are profitable only applying very low rates (from 0 up to 2%) without any grant, but they reach good economic feasibility if the grant covers 25% of the investment cost. The *District heating system measure*, in particular, would benefit greatly from a grant, because the very high initial cost of the intervention would be significantly reduced by a grant of 25% or even more.

The IRRs of the scenarios reflect the same differences between the seven measures that are described above and show the strong influence of a hypothetical increasing share of grants especially towards those measures that need to be supported (Table 3). For instance, if the investment of *Low temperature heating system* is totally covered by a private company (or homeowner) and the IRR is just 1.68%, then this measure is not profitable because the IRR is lower than the discount rate (2%) that was set in the Soma report, whereas it increases up to 8.49% when the grants cover 50% of the investment cost.

4.2 Alternative Scenarios of Economic Analysis in the Demo Site of Laguna de Duero

The economic analysis developed on the demo site of Laguna de Duero differs from that of Soma mainly for the financing of the retrofitting project. In this site, indeed,

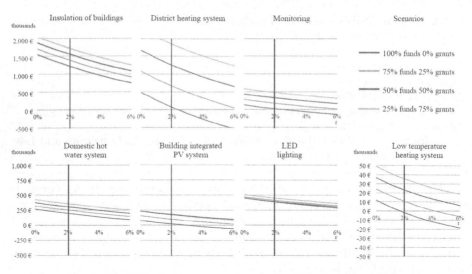

Fig. 4. The NPVs by measures and scenarios in the demo site of Soma.

Table 3. The IRRs by measures and scenarios in the demo site of Soma.

Intervention measures	Scenario 100% funds 0% grants	Scenario 75% funds 25% grants	Scenario 50% funds 50% grants	Scenario 25% funds 75% grants
Insulation of building	20.29%	28.05%	42.73%	85.39%
District heating system	2.37%	6.48%	13.44%	30.76%
Monitoring	2.45%	6.59%	13.06%	31.08%
Domestic hot water system	12.20%	18.12%	28.87%	58.76%
Building integrated PV system	3.03%	7.42%	14.97%	34.31%
LED lighting	68.32%	91.31%	>100%	>100%
Low temperature heating system	1.68%	4.22%	8.49%	19.09%

about 48% of the cost is granted by the European Commission while the remaining costs are covered by an ESCO (Energy Service Company) and other private companies. The community of owners will pay the financing fee to the companies in 20 years.

To evaluate the NPVs and IRRs of the project of Laguna de Duero, the following original data from the demo site are used:

– Private investment (euro);
– Annual cost in the baseline period (before the intervention) (euro);
– Annual cost in the reporting period (after the intervention) (euro);
– Time frame of 25 years;
– EC grant of 50%.

In this case study, the scenarios are diversified by the capital structure, that is a combination of debt and equity, as the amount of a requested loan could be lower than 100% of the investment, like it was set in the contract between the companies and the Community of owner in Laguna de Duero, so that the shared risk will decrease the financing cost.

The NPVs are evaluated applying a discount rate that ranges from 0 to 6% and for a rate of financing cost that varies from 1% to 3%, according to the following new scenarios:

− 100% loan - 0 funds;
− 75% loan - 25% funds;
− 50% loan - 50% funds;
− 25% loan - 75% funds.

The results (Fig. 5) indicate that the elasticity of the NPV with respect to the discount rate varies significantly among the various scenarios according to the distribution of the cost between the present and the future (obviously, NPV is greater for the scenario with the lowest financing share).

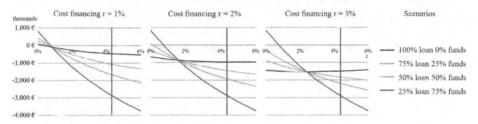

Fig. 5. The NPVs by cost financing and scenarios in the demo site of Laguna de Duero.

However, the intervention does not achieve affordability, as the NPVs are negative as well as all the IRRs are negative or lower than 1% (Table 4). Only if the rate of the financing cost is 1% and the discount rate is close to zero the project reach a very weak profitable, but, since the CITyFiED report applied a discount rate of 4.3%, the private companies can be involved in the project only if the EC grant exceeds 50% of the investment cost.

Table 4. The IRRs by cost financing and scenarios in the demo site of Laguna de Duero.

	Scenario 100% loan 0% funds	Scenario 75% loan 25% funds	Scenario 50% loan 50% funds	Scenario 25% loan 75% funds
Cost financing r = 1%	0.34%	0.58%	0.65%	0.69%
Cost financing r = 2%	−2.54%	−0.67%	0.10%	0.48%
Cost financing r = 3%	−4.81%	−1.90%	−0.48%	0.27%

5 Conclusions

The analysis of the interventions of the CITyFiED program has shown that variability in both characteristics of neighbourhoods and planned measures of energy efficiency may be so great as to generate results at opposite ends in terms of economic feasibility. Indeed, some interventions are very profitable, as in the case of the demo site of Soma, whereas other interventions do not reach the minimum cost-effectiveness, even if the grant covers 50% of the investment cost.

An important issue that may influence the economic feasibility of energy efficiency measures but was not included in this analysis is energy poverty. Energy-poor households do not have energy bills corresponding to their needs, so very low energy bills may cause a mismatch between the ante and post assessments of energy measures and affect the results. A preventive step of analysis of the households' energy bills should be envisaged to verify if they are in line with the satisfaction of basic needs and the attainment of acceptable indoor comfort.

Also, the financial parameters play a central role that condition the involvement of private companies and homeowners. The results of the scenarios defined in this study indicate that the financing cost and risk sharing influence both NPV and IRR, even if they are not able to radically change the economic performance of a project when it is very bad. Instead, the public grants make it possible to appreciate the flow of cost savings and cost avoidance in the medium term by directly reducing the initial investment. This is especially relevant in the case of infrastructural projects at urban scale, e.g. district heating plant, whose initial costs can be very high. Indeed, the NPV graph of the district heating system intervention at the Soma demo site shows that a high incidence of grants contributes greatly to achieving economic feasibility.

The amount of grants to be paid is, however, both a political and an economic issue, as the cash flow does not include all of the negative externalities (pollution, climate impact, etc.) that are avoided by means of the energy efficiency project, nor the change in indoor comfort of the dwellings, potentially resulting in better health of the inhabitants and lower public health expenditure. Therefore, it may be considered fair for the European Commission and/or the national governments to pay a share to reduce such social and environmental damage and invest in the health of citizens.

However, determining what is the maximum price that a community should pay for the reduction of CO_2 emissions and what is a fair distribution of public grants remain both unsolved issues. For example, the original project of Soma had obtained 7 M€ of grant, equal to 50% of the cost of the intervention, but, given the good values of the NPVs (applying a discount rate of 2% as that used in the CITyFiED report), granting 25% of just 4 measures (which is equal to about 835,000 euros) would have been enough to obtain stable economic feasibility of the overall intervention; whereas, it would have been necessary to provide an additional share of grant in the case study of Laguna de Duero.

Therefore, financial and economic evaluations can support the preventive analysis of the performance of a project through the definition of alternative scenarios. This allows to identify the best combination of characteristics and parameters (including the financial ones) and to obtain strong economic feasibility for projects of energy retrofitting of buildings and districts.

References

1. Energy, Climate change, Environment. http://www.ec.europa.eu. Accessed 08 May 21
2. A European Green Deal. https://ec.europa.eu. Accessed 08 May 21
3. Ruggeri, A.G., Gabrielli, L., Scarpa, M.: Energy retrofit in european building portfolios: a review of five key aspects. Sustainability 12(18), 7465 (2020)
4. Bisello, A.: Assessing multiple benefits of housing regeneration and smart city development: The european project Sinfonia. Sustainability 12(19), 8038 (2020)
5. Lindholm, O., Ur Rehman, H., Reda, F.: Positioning positive energy districts in European cities. Buildings 11(1), 19 (2021)
6. Napoli, G., Gabrielli, L., Barbaro, S.: The efficiency of the incentives for the public buildings' energy retrofit. The case of the Italian Regions of the "Objective Convergence". Valori e valutazioni 18, 25–39 (2017)
7. Bottero, M., D'Alpaos, C., Dell'Anna, F.: Boosting investments in buildings energy retrofit: the role of incentives. In: Calabrò, F., Della Spina, L., Bevilacqua, C. (eds.) ISHT 2018. SIST, vol. 101, pp. 593–600. Springer, Cham (2019). https://doi.org/10.1007/978-3-319-92102-0_63
8. Kumbaroğlu, G., Madlener, R.: Evaluation of economically optimal retrofit investment options for energy savings in buildings. Energy Build. 49, 327–334 (2012)
9. De Tommasi, L., Ridouane, H., Giannakis, G., Katsigarakis, K., Lilis, G.N., Rovas, D.: Model-based comparative evaluation of building and district control-oriented energy retrofit scenarios. Buildings 8(7), 91 (2018)
10. Dipasquale, C., Fedrizzi, R., Bellini, A., Gustafsson, M., Ochs, F., Bales, C.: Database of energy, environmental and economic indicators of renovation packages for European residential buildings. Energy Build. 203, 109427 (2019)
11. Barthelmes, V.M., Becchio, C., Bottero, M., Corgnati, S.P.: Cost-optimal analysis for the definition of energy design strategies: the case of a nearly-zero energy building. Valori e valutazioni 21, 61–76 (2016)
12. Gagliano, A., Giuffrida, S., Nocera, F., Detommaso, M.: Energy efficient measure to upgrade a multistory residential in a nZEB. AIMS Energy 5(4), 601–624 (2017)
13. Nocera, F., Giuffrida, S., Trovato, M.R., Gagliano, A.: Energy and new economic approach for nearly zero energy hotels. Entropy 21(7), 639 (2019)
14. Ferrante, A., Fotopoulou, A., Mazzoli, C.: Sustainable urban regeneration through densification strategies: the Kallithea district in Athens as a pilot case study. Sustainability 12(22), 9462 (2020)

15. Napoli, G., Mamì, A., Barbaro, S., Lupo, S.: Scenarios of climatic resilience, economic feasibility and environmental sustainability for the refurbishment of the early 20th century buildings. In: Mondini, G., Oppio, A., Stanghellini, S., Bottero, M., Abastante, F. (eds.) Values and Functions for Future Cities. GET, pp. 89–115. Springer, Cham (2020). https://doi.org/10.1007/978-3-030-23786-8_6

16. Cantatore, E., Fatiguso, F.: An energy-resilient retrofit methodology to climate change for historic districts application in the mediterranean area. Sustainability **13**(3), 1422 (2021)

17. Abastante, F., Lami, I.M., Lombardi, P., Toniolo, J.: District energy choices: more than a monetary problem. A SDSS approach to define urban energy scenarios. Valori e Valutazioni **22**, 109–120 (2019)

18. Acampa, G., García, J.O., Grasso, M., López, C.D.: Project Sustainability: criteria to be introduced in BIM. Valori e Valutazioni **23**, 119–128 (2019)

19. Stanica, D.I., Karasu, A., Brandt, D., Kriegel, M., Brandt, S., Steffan, C.: A methodology to support the decision-making process for energy retrofitting at district scale. Energy Build. **238**, 110842 (2021)

20. Abastante, F., Lami, I.M., Lombardi, P.: An Integrated participative spatial decision support system for smart energy urban scenarios: a financial and economic approach. Buildings **7**(4), 103 (2017)

21. D'Alpaos, C., Bragolusi, P.: Multicriteria prioritization of policy instruments in buildings energy retrofit. Valori e Valutazioni **21**, 15–24 (2018)

22. My Smart City District. http:// http://www.mysmartcitydistrict.eu. Accessed 08 May 21

23. OECD, Smart Cities and Inclusive Growth. http://www.oecd.org. Accessed 16 Jun 21

24. Mori, K., Christodoulou, A.: Review of sustainability indices and indicators: towards a new City Sustainability Index (CSI). Environ. Impact Assess. Rev. **32**(1), 94–106 (2012)

25. Thornbush, M., Golubchikov, O.: Smart energy cities: the evolution of the city-energy-sustainability nexus. Environ. Dev. 10.1016 (2021)

26. Angelidou, M.: Smart city policies: a spatial approach. Cities **41**(1), S3–S11 (2014)

27. De Marco, A., Mangano, G.: Evolutionary trends in smart city initiatives. Sustainable Futures **3**, 100052 (2021)

28. Napoli, G., Barbaro, S., Giuffrida, S., Trovato, M.R.: The European green deal: new challenges for the economic feasibility of energy retrofit at district scale. In: Smart Innovation, Systems and Technologies, pp. 1248–1258 (2021). https://doi.org/10.1007/978-3-030-48279-4_116

Inclusive Strategic Programming: Methodological Aspects of the Case Study of the Jonian Valleys of Peloritani (Sicily, Italy)

Giuseppe Bombino[1], Francesco Calabrò[2(✉)], Giuseppina Cassalia[2], Lidia Errante[3], and Viviana Vinci[4]

[1] Department of Agriculture, Mediterranea University of Reggio Calabria, Reggio Calabria, Italy
giuseppe.bombino@unirc.it
[2] Department of Heritage-Architecture-Urbanism, Mediterranea University of Reggio Calabria, Reggio Calabria, Italy
{francesco.calabro,giuseppina.cassalia}@unirc.it
[3] Department of Architecture, Mediterranea University of Reggio Calabria, Reggio Calabria, Italy
lidia.errante@unirc.it
[4] Department of Law, Economics and Human Sciences, Mediterranea University of Reggio Calabria, Reggio Calabria, Italy
viviana.vinci@unirc.it

Abstract. This paper is the first part of a broader work that illustrates a multidisciplinary research activity carried out as part of an institutional collaboration, between the Mediterranea University of Reggio Calabria and 18 Sicilian municipalities, located in an area called "Jonian Valleys of Peloritani". The collaboration is finalized in order to outline perspectives and strategies for the material and immaterial progress of the area. The research activities are at initial stages, this paper illustrates the methodological aspects.

Keywords: Strategic programming · Stakeholder involvement · Citizenship education · Youth entrepreneurship · Project evaluation

1 Introduction

Stakeholder involvement in the Strategic Development Process (SDP) is inherently complex, because of need to satisfy multiple interests (Richards et al. 2004).

In light of this, the diversity of knowledge and values of the community have to be taken into consideration (Reed 2008); moreover it is necessary to ensure that there is stakeholder participation in decision-making processes (Stringer et al. 2007) and implementation, according to democratic right.

The reciprocal interaction between stakeholders, moreover, improves new relationships (Forester 1999; Leeuwis and Pyburn 2002).

© Springer Nature Switzerland AG 2021
O. Gervasi et al. (Eds.): ICCSA 2021, LNCS 12954, pp. 109–119, 2021.
https://doi.org/10.1007/978-3-030-86979-3_8

Therefore, stakeholders' participation generates a strong sense of ownership over the process and outcomes achieved (Reed 2008).

As SPDs are the means by which government and institutions deliver a range of services to raise awareness, it is important to look at the available best practices in stakeholder participation.

By improving a model to facilitate stakeholders' approaches in SPD, we provide a participative approach as a process where individuals, groups, and organizations choose to take an active role in making decisions that affect them (Wilcox 2003).

To this purpose, an Agreement Framework (AF) between the "Mediterranea" University Reggio Calabria and 18 Municipalities of the entire area of the "Valleys of Peloritani" was developed, in order to outline perspectives and strategies for the material and immaterial progress of the area.

The area is located in the northernmost part of the Sicily region, in front of Calabria region, right in the Strait of Scylla and Charybdis. The four "Valleys of Peloritani" falling down from the homonym mountain of "Peloritani" in the Jonian side (Fig. 1), and develop within as many watersheds covering a total area of about 264 km^2. The relative watercourses have a torrential hydrological regime typical of the Mediterranean semi-arid climate.

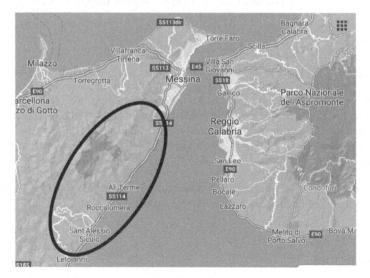

Fig. 1. The study area

More specifically, the AF for SDP of the investigated area aiming to:

– carry out collaborative activities aimed at enhancing the system of villages and the tangible and intangible cultural resources of the geographical area in which they fall;
– encourage the transfer of knowledge from the university to the local communities;
– facilitate the conduct of studies and research specifically aimed at the area of interest;
– exploit and promote the results of the collaboration;

- contribute to the elaboration of Strategic Plans and Programmes for the development of the integrated system of villages;
- encourage the exchange and sharing of good practice and experience in the relevant territory;
- foster, in the strategic programs, processes of active citizenship education and youth entrepreneurship development, by means of participatory paths of research, training and educational networks.

Therefore, the AF has an operational agenda that requires the beneficiary communities to get involved in all the different phases of the project planning and management; in fact, it is generally believed that a process can only be regarded as fully participatory when participants are in direct control of decision making in terms of goal setting, planning, policy making, implementation, and evaluation (Robinson 2002).

After investigating the extent to which the community and stackholders have participated in the planning and management of previous projects.

The AF is managed by a board of Researcher, coordinated by the Rector of the "Mediterranea" University, which is mainly responsible for the project development. The stakeholders that make up the board are the Majors of the 18 Municipalities, representative of the beneficiaries. The board of members have a vested interest in the AF, and hence they contribute personnel to see to their interests in the project.

As the AF, the project should aim at making sure that stakeholders:

- come together to identify common development challenges and a focus that will benefit or lead to the realization of mutually agreed objectives,
- achieve a common understanding of the development challenge,
- integrate the views of the different stakeholders,
- understand the broader context of the challenge,
- state the desired changes that need to occur, and assess the different options that will to achieve the desired changes

On the other side, the AF provide "platform" bringing together the diverse groups of stakeholders, in order to:

- act as a bridge between the public authorities and interest group representatives and actors on the ground;
- support coordination, communication and capacity building among public authorities on all levels;
- help build capacity and develop common positions among actors on the ground and their representative bodies;
- help reach out to and inform a broader concerned audience of the benefits of the policy.

In the following sections, regarding the area of the "Valleys of Peloritani", we illustrate and explain the methodological approach developed for the purpose of surveying, analysis and processing of data relating to the tangible and intangible heritage of the area under study.

Enhancing the large collected data and information, then, are illustrated the main lines to achieve a desirable and sustainable development of the area under study.

Practically all transport models make use of Transport Analysis Zones (TAZ) for aggregate computations on groups of locations and individuals. Larger zones correspond to a greater degree of aggregation and therefore less precision and reduced computational cost.

2 Methods

2.1 Towards an Active Citizenship Education and Youth Entrepreneurship in the Strategic Programs Processes

One of the aims of the protocol of understanding in drawing up the Strategic Programs is to foster processes of active citizenship education and youth entrepreneurship development, by means of participatory paths of research, training and educational networks.

The construct of citizenship points to a complex, polysemic and *interdisciplinary* knowledge, to a dynamic whole of knowledge, mental processes, and decision-making attitudes (Kerr et al. 2009; Ten Dam et al. 2010): this is a rather differentiate dimension, made up of knowledge, skills, attitudes, and values which bring to *effectively and constructively interact with others*, to *act in a socially responsible way* and *in a democratic way* (Eurydice 2012, 2017; UNESCO 2015). This whole of knowledge, skills, attitudes, and values has to be learned not only through a formal curriculum, but also through non-formal and rather informal education, especially through holistic, participatory and whole-school approaches (Eurydice 2017; Perla et al. 2020).

The concept of youth *participation* constitutes the core of both conceptual models, that of *Competences for Democratic Culture*, proposed by the *Council of Europe* (2016), and that of IEA *Civic Education Study* (Schulz et al. 2008). The second one portrays – in an octagonal shape, on the basis of the development theories (Brofenbrenner 1988) and of the situated cognition (Lave and Wenger 1991) – multiple nested settings, in which the citizenship learning and the growth of critical thought by students take place (*family, school, formal community, informal community, peer group*). Young people interact with different but comparable communities, so that they can learn the citizenship not only within one context (family or school), but in any environment in which the opportunities of civic participation, democracy, promotion of the identity, social cohesion, and enhancement of the diversity occur.

The system actions scheduled for the social-economical and cultural development of the area of Peloritans' Ionian Valleys are based on the full participation of young people and on the development of their own *entrepreneurship*.

The *entrepreneurship* has long been considered to be a powerful driver for economic growth, innovation, and social liberation (Gibb 2002; Moreland 2006; CEDEFOP 2011; Blenker et al. 2014). Indeed, it is regarded as a basic form of mind for the development of civic competencies and essential attitudes within social contexts in rapid transformation: creativeness, strategic thinking, spirit of initiative, sense of responsibility, teamwork, decision making, mobilization of human and material resources, effective communication and coping with ambiguity, risk and uncertainty, as well as *ability to transform idea into actions* (EC 2013; Morselli 2019).

These skills are even more important in the contemporary socio-educational context, for the emergency due to COVID-19, because pandemic containment measures – such as the closure of economic, productive, social, cultural and educational activities – have had an impact on material deprivation and educational poverty, with an increase in learning loss, inequalities and school dropout worldwide (Engzell et al. 2020).

In order to educate entrepreneurship, a deep and far-reaching cultural change is needed: in the Communication of the European Commission "Rethinking Education" (EC 2012) the need to renew teaching methods is stressed, enhancing the solution of authentic problems and active and experiential methods.

It is therefore essential for schools and educational institutions to open up to the community and local businesses, especially in rural areas or in geographically isolated areas. It is about breaking down the barriers that separate different learning contexts – formal, non-formal, informal ones –, enhancing their specificities and complementarity at once. The formation of an entrepreneurial mindset can take place not only *within* the school contexts, nor even only *outside* them, but needs an *educational alliance* between school, families, communities, work contexts. Entrepreneurial education needs an openness to outside world, to local communities and to all the learning opportunities that the local environment can offer through activities that enrich community life, which can offer innovative responses to the needs of local businesses and non-professional organizations, while providing real experiences capable of improving the entrepreneurial spirit of students (as occurs, for instance, in the "Service-Learning" proposal, Sigmon 1994; Furco and Billig 2002). This openness is necessary to combat early school leaving and to prevent youth unease, with a positive impact in terms of youth employment and combating depopulation, especially with regard to the so-called "NEET – Not in Education, Employment or Training", i.e. young people who are neither in employment nor in education.

The concept of youth agency (Sarojini Hart et al. 2014; DeJaeghere et al. 2016), closely linked to that of empowerment (Martínez et al. 2016), must be taken within multidimensional learning ecosystems (Schleicher 2016; Vinci 2019, 2020): partnerships and broad educational alliances between schools, educational services and territory, able to avoid isolation, to invest in capital (social, intellectual and professional) and offer young people a range of opportunities and differentiated resources.

Only within learning ecosystems can teachers express their entrepreneurial spirit more fully through the training of *Professional Learning Community* (EC 2018, p. 55), collaborative professional environments within schools, networks of collaboration between teachers, essential for the sharing of professional standards and the co-construction of artifacts functional to the teaching-learning processes (Lisse et al. 2007; Donner et al. 2008).

Teachers play a pivotal role in building school environments where creativity and risk-taking are encouraged and where error is reassessed as an opportunity to learn. For the role of teachers to be truly supportive, it is essential that the entrepreneurial skills of teachers and school managers are also implemented through specific training pathways

(Komárková et al. 2015), and the conditions are created to support entrepreneurship in schools, through the creation of networks of schools and partnerships in the community (UE 2014), in order to reduce the distance between education and the world of work (Draycott et al. 2011).

The importance of rethinking the education system of teachers is particularly felt in European education policies in recent decades (Eurydice 2015; Eurydice 2018; Darling-Hammond et al. 2017; Perla and Martini 2019; Perla 2020), starting with the *Green Paper on Teacher Education in Europe* (Buchberger et al. 2000), which highlighted a number of critical issues in the training courses in force in the Member States, focused on individualistic cultures and considered inadequate to the promotion of professional skills that relate to the complex capacity of mediation and educational transposition of knowledge. In Italy, the so called "Good School" (Law 107/2015) has made mandatory the in-service training: since it has acquired the character of a mandatory, permanent and structural right-obligation, universities, professional associations and educational agencies have been called upon to offer high-level specialist advisory services on the market (Perla et al. 2017; Agrati and Vinci 2020).

The intervention of the Mediterranean University, responding to this request, aims to encourage: the construction of networks of educational institutions, of all levels, engaged in quality improvement and innovation experimentation; educational alliances between universities, schools in network, local authorities, communities and families; the development and enhancement of professional skills of teachers, managers and educators; research activities aimed at improving the quality and effectiveness of schools; knowledge of the most recent school legislation and the opportunities offered at local, ministerial, European level; dissemination of the results of training and research-action experiences, in order to transmit and exchange good practices (including the policies).

The strategic action planned by the Mediterranean University is part of policies to combat the risk of educational poverty in the area and aims at strengthening the link between the university and the world of school, families and the community, ensuring quality training and enhancing geographically isolated, peripheral and at risk of depopulation and marginalization: places of strategic importance, educational communities with a high level of quality and social well-being, memory places, which guard historical, artistic, cultural and environmental heritage, that have not only to be protected through a joint effort of all the institutions of the territory, but whose beauty has also to be conveyed to the new generations in the perspective of enhancing Southern Italy.

2.2 Decision-Making Logics in Strategic Planning: The Role of Evaluations

In the case study of the Jonian Valleys of Peloritani, it is more correct to speak of a path aimed at developing a "Strategic Program", rather than "Strategic Planning" (Gänzle 2016).

The scientific literature identifies, unanimously, some peculiarities that distinguish Programming from Planning, especially in the field of urban and territorial transformations. The first, in fact, as many authors underline, identifies exactly "who" does "what" in "how much time" and with "what resources", thus overcoming the limits of tools too often full of appreciable contents and desirable objectives, which they have rarely translated into real facts in the many experiences carried out (Elbanna 2009). The two essential and peculiar principles, therefore, to which the interventions to be planned must respond are effectiveness and feasibility. The other fundamental principle, sustainability, on the other hand, is also representative of other tools and, obviously, this must permeate programming too: in this case, however, another distinctive trait is the tendency to rebalance the weight of the different dimensions of sustainability, paying the necessary attention also to its economic dimension, alongside the environmental and social dimensions, which often tend to be given greater prominence.

In order for the interventions envisaged by the strategic programs to respect the fundamental principles of effectiveness, feasibility and sustainability, their selection must be made on the basis of careful evaluation (Morano and Tajani 2013; Morano et al. 2021). The ex-ante evaluation of projects, on the other hand, must necessarily be based on a deep knowledge of the dynamics existing in the area in which action is taken: first of all, the main critical issues to be addressed and the resources on which it is possible to focus, but also of what is already been implemented or planned up to now and on the basis of which vision (Nesticò and Maselli 2021).

The territories for which strategic programs are drawn up, in fact, are never at the beginning of a path aimed at promoting their development: over time, interventions have been conceived, proposed and implemented and even if they have not produced the expected results, certainly responded to needs and objectives that must be taken into account, even simply to replace them with others, the important thing is that the choices are made in a conscious way. This is one of the main purposes of project evaluation in the ex-ante phase: to provide the decision maker with information on the effective ability of the hypothesized solutions to provide answers to problems (Nesticò et al. 2021). Due to its nature and given these specific purposes, the evaluation of projects, aimed at selecting the priority interventions, will have a multidimensional character: therefore, different families of techniques will be used, both quantitative and qualitative, monetary and non-monetary (Del Giudice 2021; Nesticò and Galante 2015).

2.3 The Phases of Strategic Programming

Consistently with the above, there are four phases to be developed to design a strategic program of interventions:

1. Knowledge Phase
2. Proposal Phase
3. Evaluation Phase
4. Planning Phase

Phase 1, of a cognitive nature, is in turn divided into two parts:

- 1.a Analysis of the territorial system
- 1.b Listening and territorial animation

In detail, phase "1.a Analysis of the territorial system" has as its object:

– Geomorphology and hydrogeology
– Settlement system
– Infrastructure, accessibility and mobility
– Demographic structure
– Economic-productive system (also historically characterizing activities) and employment dynamics
– Natural and cultural resources – tangible and intangible
– Socio-cultural structure: associations and cultural activities
– Services for the quality of life and social equity
– Planning, governance and express planning tools – funded and unfunded
– Historical Background.

While phase 1.b "Listening and territorial animation" includes:

– Recognition of public and private actors
– Individual meetings with stakeholders and public forum for the needs' analysis and assessment
– Identification of strategic areas.

3 Conclusion

The research is in its first phase; the activities are still in progress, in particular as regards the cognitive aspects. In the continuation of the activities, particular attention will be paid to two aspects: the involvement of citizens and in particular of young people; inter-institutional dialogue and cooperation. At the same time, it will be necessary to refine the techniques to be used for the selection of strategic objectives and projects capable of pursuing them more effectively.

Note: The article is the result of the joint efforts of the authors. However, the following are to be attributed: paragraphs 1 to Giuseppe Bombino; paragraphs 2.2 to Francesco Calabrò; paragraphs 2.3 to Giuseppina Cassalia; paragraphs 2.1 to Viviana Vinci; paragraphs 3 to Lidia Errante.

References

Forester, J.: The deliberative practitioner. MIT Press, Cambridge, MA (1999)
Leeuwis, C., Pyburn, R.: Wheelbarrows full of frogs: social learning in rural resource management. Book Rev. Agric. Syst. **81**, 177–184 (2002)
Reed, M.S.: Stakeholder participation for environmental management: a literature review. Biol. Cons. **141**, 2417–2431 (2008)
Richards, C., Blackstock, K.L., Carter, C.E.: Practical approaches to participation (SERG Policy Brief No. 1). Macauley Land Use Research Institute, Aberdeen, Scotland (2004)
Robinson, L.: Participatory rural appraisal: a brief introduction. Group Facilit.: Res. Appl. J. **4**, 45–51 (2002)

Stringer, L.C., Reed, M.S., Dougill, A.J., Rokitzki, M., Seely, M.: Enhancing participation in the implementation of the United Nations convention to combat desertification. Nat. Res. Forum **31**, 198–211 (2007)

Wilcox, D.: The guide to effective participation (2003). http://www.partnerships.org.uk/guide

Agrati, L.S., Vinci, V.: Training quality teachers. The challenge of design skill. In: Madalińska-Michalak, J. (ed.). Studies on Quality Teachers and Quality Initial Teacher Education. TEPE Network. Teacher Education Policy in Europe, pp. 258–280. FRSE Publications, Warsaw (2020)

Blenker, P., Elmholdt, S.T., Frederiksen, S.H., Korsgaard, S., Wagner, K.: Methods in entrepreneurship education research: a review and integrative framework. Education + Training **56**(8/9), 697–715 (2014)

Brofenbrenner, U.: Interacting systems in human development. In: Bolger, N., Caspi, A., Downey, G., Moorehouse, M. (eds.) Persons in Context: Developmental Processes, pp. 25–50. Cambridge University Press, Cambridge (1988)

Buchberger, F., et al.: Green Paper on Teacher Education in Europe. High Quality Teacher Education for High Quality Education and Training. Thematic Network on Teacher Education in Europe, Umea, Sweden (2000)

Cedefop: Guidance Supporting Europe's Aspiring Entrepreneurs. Guidance Supporting Europe's Aspiring Entrepreneurs. Publications Office of the European Union, Luxembourg, Policy and Practice to Harness Future Potential (2011)

Darling-Hammond, L., Hyler, M.E., Gardner, M.: Effective Teacher Professional Development. Learning Policy Institute, Palo Alto, CA (2017)

DeJaeghere, J., Josić, J., McCleary, K.S. (eds.): Education and Youth Agency. Qualitative Case Studies in Global Contexts. Springer, Cham (2016)

Donner, A., Mandzuk, D., Clifton, R.A.: Stages of collaboration and the realities of professional learning communities. Teach. Teach. Educ. **24**, 564–574 (2008)

Draycott, M.C., Rae, D., Vause, K.: The assessment of enterprise education in the secondary education sector: a new approach? Education + Training **53**(8/9), 673–691 (2011)

EC: Comunicazione della Commissione al Parlamento europeo, al Consiglio, al comitato economico e sociale europeo e al comitato delle regioni. Ripensare l'istruzione: investire nelle abilità in vista di migliori risultati socioeconomici. Strasburgo, 20.11.2012 COM (2012) 669 final (2012).

EC: Comunicazione della Commissione al Parlamento europeo, al Consiglio, al comitato economico e sociale europeo e al comitato delle regioni. Piano d'azione imprenditorialità 2020. Rilanciare lo spirito imprenditoriale in Europa. Bruxelles, 9.1.2013 COM (2012) 795 final (2013)

EC: Boosting Teacher Quality: Pathways to Effective Policies. European Commission, Luxemburg (2018)

Engzell, P., Frey, A., Verhagen, M.D.: Learning Loss Due to School Closures During the COVID-19 Pandemic. SocArXiv, 29 Oct. 2020. https://doi.org/10.31235/osf.io/ve4z7

Euridyce: Citizenship Education in Europe. Education, Audiovisual and Culture Executive Agency, Brussels (2012)

Eurydice: The Teaching Profession in Europe: Practices, Perceptions, and Policies. European Commission, Bruxelles (2015)

Eurydice: Citizenship Education at School in Europe – 2017. Eurydice Report. Publications Office of the European Union, Luxembourg (2017)

Eurydice, E.: Teaching Careers in Europe: Access, Progression and Support. European Commission, Bruxelles (2018)

Furco, A., Billig, S.H.: Service Learning: The Essence of the Pedagogy. IAP, CT (2002)

Gibb, A.: In pursuit of a new 'enterprise' and 'entrepreneurship' paradigm for learning: creative destruction, new values, new ways of doing things and new combinations of knowledge. Int. J. Manag. Rev. **4**(3), 233–269 (2002)

Kerr, D., Keating, A., Ireland, E.: Pupil Assessment in Citizenship Education: Purposes, Practices and Possibilities. Report of a CIDREE Collaborative Project. NFER/CIDREE, Slough (2009)

Komárková, I., Gagliardi, D., Conrads, J., Collado, A.: Entrepreneurship Competence: An Overview of Existing Concepts, Policies and Initiatives. Publications Office of the European Union, Luxembourg (2015)

Lave, J., Wenger, E.: Situated Learning: Legitimate Peripheral Participation. Cambridge University Press, New York (1991)

Lisse, N.L., Swets, L., Zeitlinger, S.L., Louis, K.S.: Professional Learning Communities: Elaborating New Approaches. In: Stoll, L., Louis, K.S. (eds.) Professional Learning Communities: Divergence, Depth, and Dilemmas, pp. 1–14. Open University Press, Berkshire, UK (2007)

Martínez, X.U., Jiménez-Morales, M., Soler Masó, P., Bernet, J.T.: Exploring the conceptualization and research of empowerment in the field of youth. Int. J. Adolesc. Youth 22(4), 405–418 (2016)

Moreland, N.: Entrepreneurship and Higher Education: An Employability Perspective. The Higher Education Academy, York (2006)

Morselli, D.: The Change Laboratory for Teacher Training in Entrepreneurship Education. A New Skills Agenda for Europe. Springer, Cham (2019)

Perla, L.: Testimoni di sapere pratico. Vent'anni di formazione del docente di scuola secondaria. FrancoAngeli, Milano (2020)

Perla, L., Agrati, L.S., Vinci, V.: Vertical curriculum design and evaluation of citizenship skills. In: Andron, D., et al. (Eds.). Education Beyond the Crisis. New Skills, Children's Right and Teaching Context, pp. 48–65. Sense/Brill (2020)

Perla, L., Martini, B.: Professione insegnante. Idee e modelli di formazione. FrancoAngeli, Milano (2019)

Perla, L., Vinci, V., Agrati, L.: The DidaSco Project: a training program for the teachers' professional development. In: Mena, J., García Valcarcel Muñoz Repiso, A., García Peñalvo, F.J., Martín del Pozo, M. (eds.). Search and Research: Teacher Education for Contemporary Contexts, pp. 921–930. Ediciones Universidad de Salamanca, Salamanca (2017)

Sarojini Hart, C., Biggeri, M., Babic, B.: Agency and Participation in Childhood and Youth: International Applications of the Capability Approach in Schools and Beyond. Bloomsbury Academic, London (2014)

Schleicher, A.: Teaching excellence through Professional Learning and Policy Reform: Lessons from Around the World, International Summit on the Teaching Profession. OECD Publishing, Paris (2016)

Schulz, W., et al.: International Civic and Citizenship Education Study Assessment Framework. IEA, Amsterdam, the Netherlands (2008)

Sigmon, R.L.: Linking Service With Learning. Council of Independent Colleges, Washington, DC (1994)

Ten Dam, G.: Measuring young people's citizenship competences. Eur. J. Educ. 46(3), 354–372 (2011)

UE – Unione Europea: Educazione all'imprenditorialità. Una guida per gli insegnanti. Bruxelles: Unità Imprenditorialità 2020, Direzione generale per le Imprese e l'industria (2014)

UNESCO: Global Citizenship Education: Topics and Learning Objectives. UNESCO, Paris (2015)

Vinci, V.: Le competenze progettuali degli insegnanti nella scuola dell'autonomia: analisi dei prototipi di un corso di sviluppo professionale DidaSco. In: Perla, L., Martini, B. (eds.). Professione insegnante. Idee e modelli di formazione, pp. 178–203. FrancoAngeli, Milano (2019)

Vinci, V.: Le competenze imprenditoriali degli insegnanti: sfide per la formazione. Educ. Sci. Soc. 1, 398–425 (2020)

Gänzle, S.: New strategic approaches to territorial cooperation in Europe: from Euro-regions to European groupings for territorial cooperation (EGTCs) and macro-regional strategies. In: Handbook on Cohesion Policy in the EU. Edward Elgar Publishing (2016)

Elbanna, S.: Determinants of strategic planning effectiveness: extension of earlier work. J. Strat. Manage. **2**(2), 175–187 (2009)

Morano, P., Tajani, F.: Break even analysis for the financial verification of urban regeneration projects. In: 2nd International Conference on Civil Engineering, Architecture and Sustainable Infrastructure, ICCEASI 2013; Zhengzhou; China; 13 July 2013 through 15 July 2013; Code 100761, Applied Mechanics and Materials, vol. 438–439, pp. 1830–1835 (2013)

Morano, P., Tajani, F., Guarini, M.R., Di Liddo, F.: An evaluation model for the definition of priority lists in PPP redevelopment initiatives. In: Bevilacqua, C., Calabrò, F., Della Spina, L. (eds.) NMP 2020. SIST, vol. 178, pp. 451–461. Springer, Cham (2021). https://doi.org/10. 1007/978-3-030-48279-4_43

Nesticò, A., Maselli, G.: Cost-benefit analysis and ecological discounting. In: Bevilacqua, C., Calabrò, F., Della Spina, L. (eds.) NMP 2020. SIST, vol. 178, pp. 440–450. Springer, Cham (2021). https://doi.org/10.1007/978-3-030-48279-4_42

Nesticò, A., Sica, F., Endreny, T.: Real estate values and ecosystem services: correlation levels. In: Bevilacqua, C., Calabrò, F., Della Spina, L. (eds.) NMP 2020. SIST, vol. 178, pp. 802–810. Springer, Cham (2021). https://doi.org/10.1007/978-3-030-48279-4_75

Nesticò, A., Galante, M.: An estimate model for the equalisation of real estate tax: a case study. Int. J. Bus. Intell. Data Mining **10**(1), 19–32 (2015). https://doi.org/10.1504/IJBIDM.2015.069038

Del Giudice, V., Massimo, D.E., Salvo, F., De Paola, P., De Ruggiero, M., Musolino, M.: Market Price Premium for Green Buildings: A Review of Empirical Evidence. Case Study. In: Bevilacqua, C., Calabrò, F., Della Spina, L. (eds.) NMP 2020. SIST, vol. 178, pp. 1237–1247. Springer, Cham (2021). https://doi.org/10.1007/978-3-030-48279-4_115

New Housing Preferences in the COVID-19 Era: A Best-to-Worst Scaling Experiment

Marta Bottero[1] , Marina Bravi[1] , Caterina Caprioli[1](✉) , Federico Dell'Anna[1] ,
Marta Dell'Ovo[2] , and Alessandra Oppio[2]

[1] Dipartimento Interateneo di Scienze, Progetto e Politiche del Territorio, Politecnico di Torino,
Viale Mattioli, 39, 10125 Torino, TO, Italy
{marta.bottero,marina.bravi,caterina.caprioli,
federico.dellanna}@polito.it
[2] Department of Architecture and Urban Studies (DAStU), Politecnico di Milano, via Bonardi,
3, 20133 Milano, MI, Italy
{marta.dellovo,alessandra.oppio}@polimi.it

Abstract. The COVID-19 pandemic in Italy, as in many countries around the world, has imposed rigid restrictions on outdoor activities, resulting in forced confinement. The new condition requires an analysis and a rethinking of the way of life and of the new pre- and post-pandemic needs related to the use of domestic spaces, necessary to work, study or carry out other daily activities.

Politecnico di Milano and Politecnico di Torino, with the collaboration of the institute of studies and research Scenari Immobiliari, have launched a survey for exploring the new needs and preferences of residents. These needs, which arose in conjunction with the pandemic, concern not only the desire to readapt their homes, but also to change them. In order to investigate these preferences, a questionnaire was developed using the Best to Worst Scaling (BWS).

The items consider both modifications of the internal distribution and interventions on the efficiency of domestic appliances and systems components. The study aims to highlight how the spread of the pandemic has changed housing needs and how physical space affects people's well-being.

Keywords: COVID-19 · Decision-making processes · Max Difference Analysis (MaxDiff) · Individual preferences · Living spaces · Analytical Best-Worst Score (ABW)

1 Introduction

In February 2020, the World Health Organization (WHO) officially announced the name of the new virus in SARS-COV-2 which causes the infection called COVID-19. In March of the same year, the disease has been recognized as an international public health emergency and as a pandemic [1]. Globally, to date, more than 135 million cases

O. Gervasi et al. (Eds.): ICCSA 2021, LNCS 12954, pp. 120–129, 2021.
https://doi.org/10.1007/978-3-030-86979-3_9

have been confirmed, almost 48 million are in Europe and around 3.7 million in Italy [2]. Countries and governments tried to react by applying place-based approaches to the different instances raised from the unexpected situation both on the health side, by adopting social distance measures, the lockdown and the use of masks, and on the socio-economic side, by providing fiscal support, announcing recovery funds and promoting tax breaks for specific energy efficiency interventions [3].

Rapidly people daily life changed, cities were locked down, schools, offices and all the non-essential professional activities were closed [4], to control the infection. Thus, social isolation and confinement have been adopted by most countries [5]. These restrictions, as widely discussed, have caused negative psychological effects as stress symptoms, anger, insomnia in the longer term [6, 7].

In Italy, the Decree of 9th March 2020[1] officially determined the lockdown for Italians. By focusing on the effects of the pandemic on the real estate market, before the COVID-19 [8], according to the report developed by the Real Estate Market Observatory (Osservatorio del Mercato Immobiliare, OMI), Italy experienced an uptick in sales between 2017 and 2018, and the most dynamic cities have been Milan (Lombardy Region) and Turin (Piedmont Region). Moreover, it emerged how half of Italians were not satisfied with their houses causing an increase of renovation works merely focused on the energetic efficiency and the adoption of sustainable solutions [9, 10].

The situation post-pandemic is still unpredictable, even if it is clear how new needs arose and the perception about the built environment changed [11]. By considering the opinion of urban planners and architects, it is urgent to think about the building density [12], to plan a city where the most important services can be accessed in 15 min (walking distance) [13], to probably modify the concept of offices, and to meet the instance of adaptability and resilience of houses [14].

Within this context, the purpose of the contribution is to understand how housing preferences changed in the inter and post COVID-19 era, with respect to new emerging needs, and in detail if Italians are more willing to readapt their current house or to move to another place. To answer these questions, Politecnico di Milano and Politecnico di Torino, with the collaboration of the institute of studies and research Scenari Immobiliari, have launched a survey specifically devoted to people who live in the metropolitan cities of Milan and Turin, by applying the Best-to-Worst Scaling (BWS) approach. These two areas are the ones most affected by the pandemic in Italy. Preferences of people living in urban areas have been collected since the people living in those contexts perceived strongly the lockdown restrictions and the population density shaped the incidence of COVID-19 cases [7, 15].

The paper is divided into six sections, after a general introduction, in the second part a literature review and a web search are proposed aimed at understanding how scholars and private as well as public institutions carried on analysis on this topic. In the third one, the methodology applied is explained and the questionnaire is further discussed in the fourth section. The preliminary results are then presented in the fifth, while the conclusions try to synthesize the main findings, limits and future perspective of the research.

---

[1] https://www.gazzettaufficiale.it/eli/gu/2020/03/09/62/sg/pdf.

2   The Effects of the Pandemic on the Housing Dimension

During and after the period of the lockdown, several surveys have been developed aimed at understanding how the pandemic affected our habits, our work, the perception of the built and of the natural environment, and more in general our lives. With the purpose of understanding how other studies on this topic have been structured, a literature review together with a web search have been carried. The Scopus database has been consulted and the search developed by using a set of keywords in order to narrow the analysis. Since the aim of this phase is to understand if and how other scholars have investigated the changes in housing preferences, the following keywords have been selected: "questionnaire" or "survey" and "COVID-19" and "housing". A total of 83 paper has been found and 8 have been analyzed in-depth after three phases of screening which contributes to understanding the coherence with the defined purpose. The first limitation was by title (41), the second by abstract (21) and the last one by reading the contribution. Most of the papers have been excluded since mostly related to psychological factors [16–18] and ethnic group disparities [19–21], while the remaining ones address the housing topic by considering different perspectives and identifying a set of questions and items important for the evaluation. The analysis has been developed by detecting the country where the survey has been administered, the aim of the study, the typology of survey structured, the methodology applied and software used for the elaboration of data and/or for its generation, the number of respondents and the main relevant items. Most of the studies (six out of eight) have been developed by European countries and the relation of the effects of the period of lockdown with health and mental health factors is very close. Focusing the attention on main findings related to the built environment, Amerio et al. [7] argued that inadequate indoor spaces with small dimensions, poor quality and without habitable balconies strongly affect the living conditions, since these characteristics influenced the adaptability of the houses to new needs arose during the pandemic [22]. Indeed, families which reported having a sufficient number of home environments are the ones with a shared or private open outdoor spaces, features that positively influenced also physical activity and contrasting sedentary behavior, especially of children [5, 23]. At the same time, teleworking has been influenced by the domestic spaces available and difficulties have been encountered such as the lack of suitable places, lack of support infrastructure and ergonomic conditions [24]. Among all the items detected, those which have been studied and considered important for the general well-being of people, forced to spend time and to work at home, concern the natural light system, the view, the natural ventilation, the acoustic insulation and also the presence of terraces, the number of bathrooms, etc. [25]. As it has been discussed by Marona and Tomal [26], it is not possible to judge if these needs are temporary or permanent and if they are going to affect the market demands and tenants preferences but also different private companies and public institutions working on the real estate sectors launched several surveys in order to understand it. The European Real Estate Society (ERES) administered a questionnaire conducted by the research team from the Manchester Urban Institute, at the University of Manchester, to analyze "Changing housing preferences and use of home due to the Covid-19 Pandemic"[2] and the elaboration of the results is still ongoing. The Global Real

---

[2] https://eres.org/index.php.

Estate Consultants Knight Frank[3] detected the opinion of 700 clients across 44 countries who are willing to change their homes in the next 12 months but in the same location. Furthermore, according to the ING survey[4], 45% of Europeans are thinking of moving home, while for what concerns Italians points of view, they prefer to move to small cities, better if located in rural context (57%) or peripheral areas given the possibility of the smart working (SWG survey[5] and Citrix Systems survey[6]). Given these premises, it is possible to underline how the lockdown changed the perception of the place where we live, both considering intrinsic characteristics as the internal layout, the furniture, the installations, the presence of balconies in addition to the extrinsic ones, as the location in urban, peri-urban context and the proximity to green areas. These results can affect the market demand and the orientation of the building sector and its prediction would be strategic in order to meet real needs.

3 Best Worst Scaling

BWS is supported by the random utility theory (RUT) and was proposed by Finn & Louviere [27]. BWS takes advantage of the fact that collecting "worst" information, similar to "best" information, provides more information than the discrete choice models used in market research. BWS starts from the idea that individuals evaluating a set of three or more objects or elements on a subjective scale, the choice of the upper and lower object should be more reliable than the ranking of the objects, as required, for example, by the ranking method of conjoint analysis which asks you to sort the alternatives by preference. This method has the advantage of requiring less effort and time to identify the best and worst alternative without having to classify those in the middle. The disadvantage, however, is that the information detected is rather limited: in fact, the order of preference between the unselected alternatives and the distance between them are not known.

Among the simple methods for calculating MaxDiff scores, Analytical Best-Worst Score (ABW) proposed by Lipovetsky & Conklin [28] was chosen. ABW is calculated as following Eq. (1):

$$ABW = ln\left(\frac{1 + NBW}{1 - NBW}\right) \tag{1}$$

where NBW is the best-worst score normalized by the unit calculated according to Eq. (2):

$$NBW = \frac{\#Bests - \#Worsts}{Total\ times\ shown} \tag{2}$$

where the difference between $\#Bests$ and $\#Worsts$ (the number of times an item is selected as best and worst respectively) is divided by the number of times the item is

---

[3] https://www.knightfrank.com/research/article/2020-08-05-global-buyer-survey-2020-nor mal-20.

[4] https://think.ing.com/articles/ing-survey-pandemic-or-not-europeans-want-to-move-home.

[5] https://www.swg.it/osservatorio.

[6] https://www.citrix.com/it-it/news/announcements/jan-2021/citrix-and-onepoll-reserch-about-remote-work-it.html.

shown. ABW has a lower error than the Best Minus Worst Scoring for the estimation of latent values of elements proposed by Finn and Louviere [27], and can compare to multinomial logit models while being more computationally efficient [29].

4 Methodological Approach

The Metropolitan cities of Milan and Turin (North-Western Italy) represent the testbed area (Fig. 1) where the new needs and preferences of the citizens are explored. The choice of these two areas is, firstly, related to the higher spreading of COVID-19 compared to other regions in Italy since the beginning of the pandemic and, secondly, the collaboration among Politecnico di Milano, Politecnico di Torino and the Institute of Scenari Immobiliari[7]. In order to investigate these changing preferences, a questionnaire was developed using the Best to Worst Scaling (BWS). The research aims at ordering various attributes, asking the interviewee to select the best and worst options (attributes) within different choice sets built through an orthogonal design.

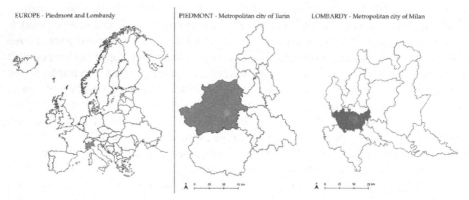

Fig. 1. Localization of the metropolitan cities of Milan and Turin (North-Western Italy) in Europe

Due to the pandemic situation and to collect a great number of answers in a short time, the questionnaire was built in an online format. For the validation and verification of the questionnaire, a first version has been sent to a group of experts and the institute of Scenari Immobiliari. Once obtained their answers, the final version of the questionnaire has been distributed through different social platforms and proper channels of communication (e.g. Facebook, LinkedIn, etc.) to obtain a representative sample of the different socio-demographic profiles. The data collection, for the preliminary analysis, has been undertaken between August and October 2020.

The final version of the questionnaire consists of three sections and an introductory part, called Sect. 0, which contains the motivations and aim of the analysis with a brief description of the broader context of the study. In this section, the sample is also limited to citizens with legal age ($\geq$18 years old) and who reside stably in one of the municipalities within the metropolitan cities of Milan or Turin.

---

[7] https://www.scenari-immobiliari.it/

Section 1 investigates the habits of respondents during the lockdown. With lockdown, we refer to the period between March 9 and May 3 2020, when the Ministerial Decree announced the closure of all activities throughout Italy, except the basic services, and the restriction measures that require staying at home for almost 24 h a day, with the only exceptions related to serious work or health reasons. The interviewee is also asked to describe the characteristics of his/her property and how preferences have changed during the pandemic.

Section 2 contains the experimental part. Using BWS, we ask the interviewee to choose the most relevant action for improving and adapting his/her house/apartment, as well as the least important one, within different choice sets.

Finally, Sect. 3 collects the main socio-economic characteristics of the interviewee, such as age, family members, employment, level of education, income.

The different choice sets (210 in total) contained in Sect. 2 were generated through an experimental design, performed in the SPSS software and characterized by 30 items. The items consider both changes in the internal distribution (i.e. construction of mezzanines, a different internal organization of the spaces), and interventions on the efficiency of domestic appliances and components (i.e. substitution of old windows, wiring, replacement of appliances). These 30 items have been identified after the consultation of various sources, both scientific and grey literature (see Sect. 2).

The survey was built using the Sawtooth – MaxDiff (Maximum Difference Scaling) software and proposes eight combinations of actions/items for each respondent. Each combination contains five actions/items, and, among the five, the respondent selects the most and the least important ones related to the improvement and adaptation of his/her property. Table 1 shows an exemplary combination of choice sets as similar as represented to the respondent.

The respondent chooses the 'most important' and 'least important' item to improve/adapt his/her property in each of the eight sets.

Table 1. Examples of choice sets used in the BTW survey

Most important item	Choice set 1	Least important item
○	30. Purchase of new furniture suitable for the new needs	○
○	25. Purchase of air purification equipment	○
○	23. Replacing the boiler	○
○	22. Installation of a solar-thermal system to produce hot water	○
○	11. Installation of an air conditioning system	○
Most important item	Choice set 2	Least important item
○	21. Installation of a photovoltaic system to produce electricity	○
○	10. Upgrading of the existing Internet connection	○

(continued)

Table 1. (*continued*)

Most important item	Choice set 2	Least important item
O	13. Installation of additional electrical outlets	O
O	12. Refurbishment of the electrical system	O
O	5. Differently organization of spaces for dining	O

Most important item	Choice set 8	Least important item
O	29. Replacement of interior doors	O
O	18. Replacing the old dishwasher with a low-energy one	O
O	2. Acquisition of additional spaces (construction of new spaces, where possible, such as the creation of mezzanines, the recovery of attics, closets, etc.) staying in the same house	O
O	4. Different organization of internal spaces to be used for studying/working	O
O	12. Refurbishment of the electrical system	O

5   Preliminary Results

The ongoing research has allowed to collect and analyze about 450 questionnaires. The sample is balanced between the two metropolitan cities: 52% lives in the metropolitan city of Turin, while 48% in the metropolitan city of Milan. The average age of the sample is 41 years old and 86% of respondents have more than 30 years old. The sample is perfectly in line with the aim to investigate the impacts of the COVID-19 restrictions on the needs related to work-at-home activities. Of the entire sample, 65% of respondents highlight how the lockdown period has affected the use of residential spaces, justifying the idea at the basis of this research. About the properties, 74% of them are apartments and the majority (60%) are located in the two main cities (Milan and Turin). However, despite the difficulties reported, most of the respondents would not change their actual place of residence (i.e. from a city to a town or a village and vice versa), as well as the type of property (92% buying vs. 8% renting). Alternatively, they would be more inclined to change the type of property, in particular to single-family houses. This can be explained by the many hours per day spent within indoor spaces, thus the presence of a private garden or an outdoor space has become increasingly important in the new habits and needs of people.

In the BWS task (second part of the questionnaire), the respondents have to choose the best and worst options in each comparison set. The results shows that the respondents consider as the most urgent the creation of suitable spaces to be used for work (1.05 in the BWS scores) and study (0.89), as well as the presence of an efficient WI-FI connection (1.00). Moreover, the respondents also give importance to the acquisition, where possible, of additional spaces in order to remain in the same property (0.77) or the installation of an air conditioning system (0.77). Conversely, the least urgent actions highlighted by the respondents regard the replacement of interior doors (−1.36) and the installation of a surveillance system (−1.18), even if those aspects are not associated with intense or costly requalification measures. Moreover, the answers have shown low interest in the substitution of existing domestic appliances, such as the oven (−0.80) and dishwasher (−0.98), or extra new electrical outlets (−0.83). This behavior can be interpreted in different ways. Firstly, it could highlight the current presence of high performing appliances in properties. Secondly, it could be associated with a small variation in the electricity costs incurred before and during the pandemic. Thirdly, it can be related to low interest in the negative effects on the environment caused by energy consumptions. The latter is still less likely since many respondents consider as quite important the installation of a photovoltaic system to produce electricity (0.50) or a solar-thermal system to produce hot water (0.47).

6 Conclusions

The unpredictable situation, that we still experience regarding the spread of the COVID-19, requires to examine in-depth and to rethink our way of life. In this context, it is fundamental to analyze the new pre, inter and post-pandemic needs relating to the use of our domestic spaces, that have become, at the same time, the place of working, studying and carrying out all the other daily activities. The study aims to highlight how the spread of the pandemic has changed housing needs and how physical space has influenced people's well-being, despite the digital revolution aiming to completely remove physical barriers and promote efficient interaction.

Considering the metropolitan areas of the cities of Turin and Milan (Northern Italy), the methodological approach proposed in this paper uses the BWS method in order to understand the residents' new habits and preferences and highlight the needs that have emerged during the lockdown period. These new needs could lead people to make different changes in their property, or even to change the type of property or the actual municipality/city of residence. Thus, the further results will provide an overview of the adaptability of the actual living spaces through their modification or, conversely, the need to purchase a new property and/or change the place of living.

Through the preliminary analysis conducted, the results clearly show that the lockdown period had a strong impact on the use of residential spaces for more than half of the population, and many of them have expressed a need for outdoor spaces where to have fun. The most urgent upgrading on the properties, highlighted by the respondents, concerns the re-organization of space for studying or working and a high-efficiency internet connection. Conversely, the least important items regard aesthetic improvements or the installation of a security system, as well as buying more efficient domestic appliances or improving the electrical system.

Future perspectives of this work will provide a greater number of responses to the questionnaire in order to obtain a larger sample. In particular, the data collected will be further analyzed with multinomial statistical methods by even more segmenting the sample. A segmented analysis could investigate the different scores in the items between the two Metropolitan cities; moreover, the sample could be segmented for types of properties (if a single-family house, detached or apartment), place of residence (village, small town or a big city) or it could be possible to show if preferences in the items changing with age, education or income. It would be also of scientific interest to consider the BTW scores for selecting a smaller set of items that could be further explored by means of BTW multicriteria decision-making method [28].

References

1. World Health Organization: Coronavirus disease (COVID-19) pandemic
2. World Health Organization: WHO Coronavirus (COVID-19) Dashboard
3. Allain-Dupré, D., Chatry, I., Michalun, V., Moisio, A.: The territorial impact of COVID-19 : managing the crisis across levels of government. OECD Tackling Coronavirus. 2–44 (2020)
4. Cuerdo-Vilches, T., Navas-Martín, M.Á., Oteiza, I.: A mixed approach on resilience of Spanish dwellings and households during covid-19 lockdown. Sustain. **12**, 1–24 (2020). https://doi.org/10.3390/su122310198
5. Pombo, A., Luz, C., Rodrigues, L.P., Ferreira, C., Cordovil, R.: Correlates of children's physical activity during the COVID-19 confinement in Portugal. Public Health **189**, 14–19 (2020). https://doi.org/10.1016/j.puhe.2020.09.009
6. Brooks, S.K., Webster, R.K., Smith, L.E., et al.: The psychological impact of quarantine and how to reduce it: rapid review of the evidence. Lancet **395**, 912–920 (2020). https://doi.org/10.1016/S0140-6736(20)30460-8
7. Amerio, A., Brambilla, A., Morganti, A., et al.: COVID-19 lockdown : housing built environment's effects on mental health. Int. J. Environ. Res. Public Health **17**(16), 5973 (2020)
8. Canesi, R., Dalpaos, C., Marella, G.: Foreclosed homes market in Italy: bases of value. Int. J. Hous. Sci. Appl. **40**(3), 201–209 (2016)
9. Bottero, M., Bravi, M., Dell'Anna, F., Mondini, G.: Valuing buildings energy efficiency through hedonic prices method: are spatial effects relevant? Valori e Valutazioni (2018)
10. Becchio, C., Bottero, M.C., Corgnati, S.P., Dell'Anna, F.: Evaluating health benefits of urban energy retrofitting: an application for the city of Turin. In: Bisello, A., Vettorato, D., Laconte, P., Costa, S. (eds.) SSPCR 2017. GET, pp. 281–304. Springer, Cham (2018). https://doi.org/10.1007/978-3-319-75774-2_20
11. Oppio, A., Bottero, M., Arcidiacono, A.: Assessing urban quality: a proposal for a MCDA evaluation framework. Ann. Oper. Res. (2018). https://doi.org/10.1007/s10479-017-2738-2
12. Dell'Ovo, M., Oppio, A., Capolongo, S.: Policy Implications. How to Support Decision-Makers in Setting and Solving Complex Problems. In: SpringerBriefs in Applied Sciences and Technology (2020)
13. Caprioli, C., Bottero, M.: Addressing complex challenges in transformations and planning: a fuzzy spatial multicriteria analysis for identifying suitable locations for urban infrastructures. Land Use Policy **102**, 105147 (2021). https://doi.org/10.1016/j.landusepol.2020.105147
14. Giovara, B.: Coronavirus, Boeri: "Via dalle città, nei vecchi borghi c'è il nostro futuro" (2020)
15. Carozzi, F.: Urban Density and Covid-19. IZA Discuss. Pap. No. 13440 (2020)
16. Sordes, F., Guillemot, C., Croiset, A., Cipriani, E.: Psychological distress and feelings of loneliness: what are the impacts of Covid-19 losckdown on the French population? Eur. J. Trauma Dissociation **5**, 100189 (2021). https://doi.org/10.1016/j.ejtd.2020.100189
17. Davidson, B., Schmidt, E., Mallar, C., et al.: Risk and resilience of well-being in caregivers of young children in response to the COVID-19 pandemic. Transl. Behav. Med. **11**, 305–313 (2021). https://doi.org/10.1093/tbm/ibaa124

18. Quílez-Robres, A., Lozano-Blasco, R., Íñiguez-Berrozpe, T., Cortés-Pascual, A.: Social, family, and educational impacts on anxiety and cognitive empathy derived from the COVID-19: study on families with children. Front. Psychol. **12**, 1–11 (2021). https://doi.org/10.3389/fpsyg.2021.562800
19. Bui, C.N., Peng, C., Mutchler, J.E., Burr, J.A.: Race and ethnic group disparities in emotional distress among older adults during the COVID-19 pandemic. Gerontologist **61**, 262–272 (2021). https://doi.org/10.1093/geront/gnaa217
20. Hu, M., Roberts, J.D., Azevedo, G.P., Milner, D.: The role of built and social environmental factors in Covid-19 transmission: a look at America's capital city. Sustain. Cities Soc. **65**, 102580 (2021). https://doi.org/10.1016/j.scs.2020.102580
21. Park, J.: Who is hardest hit by a pandemic? Racial disparities in COVID-19 hardship in the U.S. International Journal of Urban Sciences **25**(2), 149–177 (2021). https://doi.org/10.1080/12265934.2021.1877566
22. Abd Elrahman, A.S.: The fifth-place metamorphosis: the impact of the outbreak of COVID-19 on typologies of places in post-pandemic Cairo. Archnet-IJAR. **15**, 113–130 (2020). https://doi.org/10.1108/ARCH-05-2020-0095
23. Brunelli, A., Silvestrini, G., Palestini, L., et al.: Impatto del lockdown sui bambini e sulle famiglie: un'indagine dei pediatri di famiglia all'interno di una comunità. Recenti Prog. Med. **112**, 207–215 (2021). https://doi.org/10.1701/3565.35460
24. Tavares, F., Santos, E., Diogo, A., Ratten, V.: Teleworking in Portuguese communities during the COVID-19 pandemic. J. Enterprising Communities (2020). https://doi.org/10.1108/JEC-06-2020-0113
25. Zarrabi, M., Yazdanfar, S.-A., Hosseini, S.-B.: COVID-19 and healthy home preferences: The case of apartment residents in Tehran. J. Build. Eng. **35**, 102021 (2021). https://doi.org/10.1016/j.jobe.2020.102021
26. Marona, B., Tomal, M.: The COVID-19 pandemic impact upon housing brokers' workflow and their clients' attitude: Real estate market in Krakow. Entrepr. Bus. Econ. Rev. **8**(4), 221–232 (2020). https://doi.org/10.15678/EBER.2020.080412
27. Finn, A., Louviere, J.J.: Determining the appropriate response to evidence of public concern: the case of food safety. J. Public Policy Mark. **11**, 12–25 (1992). https://doi.org/10.1177/074391569201100202
28. Lipovetsky, S., Conklin, M.: Best-worst scaling in analytical closed-form solution. J. Choice Model. **10**, 60–68 (2014). https://doi.org/10.1016/j.jocm.2014.02.001
29. Marley, A.A.J., Islam, T., Hawkins, G.E.: A formal and empirical comparison of two score measures for best–worst scaling. J. Choice Model. **21**, 15–24 (2016). https://doi.org/10.1016/j.jocm.2016.03.002

An Analysis of the Methods Applied for the Assessment of the Market Value of Residential Properties in Italian Judicial Procedures

Francesco Tajani[1], Felicia Di Liddo[2], Paola Amoruso[3], Francesco Sica[1], and Ivana La Spina[1(✉)]

[1] Department of Architecture and Design, "Sapienza" University of Rome, 00196 Rome, Italy
ivana.laspina@uniroma1.it
[2] Department of Civil, Environmental, Land, Building Engineering and Chemistry, Polytechnic University of Bari, 70125 Bari, Italy
[3] Department of Economics and Management, LUM Giuseppe Degennaro University, 70010 Casamassima, BA, Italy

Abstract. The present research analyzes the main methods implemented for the assessment of the market value of residential properties in Italian judicial procedures. This value represents the reference for the "starting price" in the subsequent property auctions. An Italian study sample of 514 residential properties assessed by technicians in judicial procedures between November 2020 and March 2021 has been collected.

The analysis shows that almost 58% of the studied dataset have used *indirect* sources (e.g. quotations published by public and private entities/operators) for the market value assessment, whereas about 27% do not specify the approach and/or the data elaborated for the evaluation. Only 15.4% have implemented approaches provided by the International Valuation Standards (IVS): in particular, 4.9% have used a market approach method, 1.4% have applied the direct capitalization method, 9.1% have combined different approaches for checking the results obtained through an IVS method or for considering an arithmetical average of the outputs assessed.

Keywords: Property auction · Judicial procedure · Market approach · Income approach · Market value

1 Introduction

In the context of property auctions within judicial procedures, the forced sale indicates circumstances where a seller is under compulsion to sell. The price that could be obtained in these situations will depend upon the nature of the pressure on the seller and the reasons why proper marketing cannot be undertaken [22].

In this sense the forced sale of a property represents a judicial process by which the creditor reach the unpaid credits fulfilment through the allocation of debtor's property [10].

© Springer Nature Switzerland AG 2021
O. Gervasi et al. (Eds.): ICCSA 2021, LNCS 12954, pp. 130–141, 2021.
https://doi.org/10.1007/978-3-030-86979-3_10

In 2020, the Italian property asset involved in auctions within judicial procedures has concerned 95,329 plots – included single property and real estate complex to be sold in block –, for a total number of auctions equal to 117,376, compared to 160,594 plots put up for auction in 2019.

From January to February 2020, a large number of Italian auction processes has been published – 15% more than in the same months of 2019. However, the lockdown period during March and April 2020 – caused by Covid-19 – has led to a decrease equal to 6.6 billion of euro, firstly due to the temporary suspension of auction processes. In particular, 44,191 property auctions have been stopped during the first semester of 2020 – from March to May –, whereas 523 auctions of those scheduled have been postponed in the epidemiological crisis second phase – from October to December 2020. From the analysis of the property asset intended uses, 50.7% has concerned residential functions, 37.8% non-residential ones and 11.5% has been lands [21].

In the existing reference literature, several researches have aimed to investigate the relationship between the auction market and the segment of private negotiation in free market in order to analyse the mechanisms related to the final transaction price. Furthermore, the main causes of discount between list price – i.c. the monetary amount required for a property and determined in the evaluation report – and forced sale value in the real estate auction segment have been explored by numerous Authors [2, 6, 7, 29]. For example, Just et al. [12] have investigated the foreclosure discount for the German residential market from 2008 to 2011, by founding a discount equal to 19% and pointing out that the discounts are linked to specific property factors. Moreover, Singh [24] has estimated a discount of 33% for the pricing of distressed hotels sold at auction compared to non-distressed normal market sales.

It is evident, in fact, that the final price to be defined in the forced sale process – that is a judicial procedure – reflect specific and peculiar circumstances that are different from the free market dynamics [22]. The gap between list price and the forced sale price can generally be considered as a proxy of the ability to gain the highest expected value from an auction. In this context, for example Ong [18] have pointed out how the time to re-auction has a negative impact on the auction price, revealing that sellers use subsequent auctions as a search process for new bidders.

In the auction segment, the selling mechanisms could be significantly different according to the countries legislative or regulatory framework [19].

Most studies that estimate the impact of a forced sale on property prices have quantified the discount amount in excess of 20% [3, 9, 23] – in particular the prevailing discount range is 20 to 25%. In the Reviva report of 2019 [20] the difference between the assessed value and the final selling price has been estimated equal to 29%, whereas in 2020 the gap between the market value and the clearing price has increased up to the national average value of 57%. However, a considerably lower discount in the range of 4–6% has been estimated by Carroll et al. [4] and no statistically significant difference in prices has been assessed by Springer [25].

In the framework outlined, the evaluation report constitutes a fundamental document in which a property detailed description is illustrated and the market value is assessed. In particular, the market valued is "the estimated amount for which an asset or liability should exchange on the valuation date between a willing buyer and a willing seller in an arm's length transaction, after proper marketing and where the parties had each acted knowledgeably, prudently and without compulsion" [22]. The progressive discount on this value should consider it as a reference amount from which one or more downsides are expected. Thus, it should be highlighted the central role played by the market value determined in the evaluation report: the International Valuation Standards (IVS) specifies the mandatory requirements for elaborating a clear, sufficiently detailed and accurate assessment [15, 26]. The relevance of the quality of professional operators in the auction market segment is also a fundamental aspect in foreign contexts [7].

2 Aim

The present research aims to analyse the main methods implemented for the assessment of the market value of residential properties by the technicians in judicial procedures. With reference to the period November 2020 – March 2021 and to the geographical macro-areas in which the Italian territory is commonly divided – Northern Italy, Central Italy and Southern Italy – six regions have been selected for the study: Piedmont and Lombardy for the Northern Italy, Lazio and Tuscany for the Central Italy, Campania and Apulia for the Southern Italy.

For each region analysed, the identification of residential properties sold through auction processes during the period considered has been carried out by consulting an informative database [11]. For each law-court found in the regions selected, the evaluation reports related to the residential properties forced sold have been examined.

In the Fig. 1 a flow chart with the main operational phases carried out in the present research is reported.

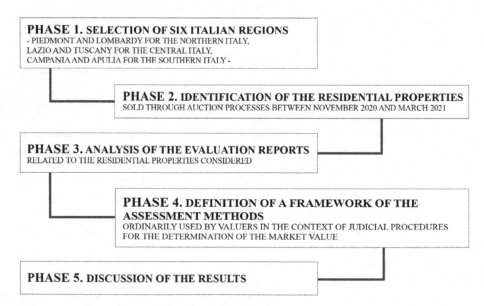

Fig. 1. Flow chart related to the phases implemented in the analysis

The research intends to provide a framework of the assessment methods ordinarily used by valuers in the context of judicial procedures. The summary on the assessment methods studied could be a valid reference for i) national law-courts, ii) investors and iii) credit institutions, in order to verify the congruity between the methods implemented, the explanatory process of the evaluation report and the theoretical standards formalised by the IVS.

The paper is structured as follows: in Sect. 3 the IVS approaches for the determination of the market values – market approach, income approach and cost approach – are recalled. In Sect. 4 the case study is presented: firstly the database collected is described, then the analysis on the data in terms of typologies of assessment methods implemented in each evaluation report is explained. Finally, in Sect. 5 the conclusions of the work are drawn.

3   Assessment Approaches

According to the IVS [1, 5, 13, 1, 22], the approaches aimed at determining the market value can be classified in: i) market approach (MA); ii) income approach (IA); iii) Cost Approach (CA).

The methods involved in the MA can be implemented exclusively if it possible to identify, within an appropriate trade area, similar properties (comparables) recently sold in the reference market. A market approach method should be applied and afforded significant weight under the following circumstances, i.e. the subject asset has recently been sold in a transaction appropriate for consideration under the basis of value, the subject asset or substantially similar assets are actively publicly traded, and/or there are frequent and/or recent observable transactions in substantially similar assets [16, 17]. The MA methods can be classified in mono-parameter ones – if the market comparison is carried out considering only one property factor – and in multi-parameter ones – if the factors considered for the analysis are various. Furthermore, the MA methods require the selection of a sufficiently large number of comparables and the detailed analysis of the main quantitative – assessed through continuous or discrete scale – and qualitative – assessed through a judgment based on score or personal opinions - properties factors.

The IA methods require the presence in the reference trade area of similar properties for which it is possible to collect rents/tariffs that can be used to determine the market value of the subject property to be assessed. The IVS provides three IA methods: i) the direct capitalization method; ii) the yield capitalization method; iii) the Discounted Cash Flow Analysis (DCFA) method. As the most IA method used for the market value assessment of residential properties, the direct capitalization method transforms the property annual rent into its market value through an appropriate discount coefficient, i.e. the capitalization rate.

The CA provides an indication of value using the economic principle that a buyer will pay no more for an asset than the cost to obtain an asset of equal utility, whether by purchase or by construction, unless undue time, inconvenience, risk or other factors are involved [22]. In this sense, the market values is assessed through the current replacement or reproduction cost, by making deductions for physical deterioration and all other relevant forms of obsolescence. It should be highlighted that with reference to the assessment of the market value of residential properties, the CA is not very often applied. Furthermore, according to the European Central Bank [8], in order to "direct" the valuer to avoid using a CA method, even if there are not comparable transactions in the reference market, the assessment should be carried out on the basis of most relevant recent market transactions with appropriate haircuts to account for lack of comparability (discounted replacement cost should not be used).

4   Case Study

The case study concerns the evaluation reports related to residential properties sold within judicial procedures and through auction processes between November 2020–March 2021 in six Italian regions: Piedmont and Lombardy in the Northern Italy, Tuscany and Lazio in Central Italy and Apulia and Campania in Southern Italy.

In Fig. 2 the localization of the Italian regions and the relative law-courts is reported.

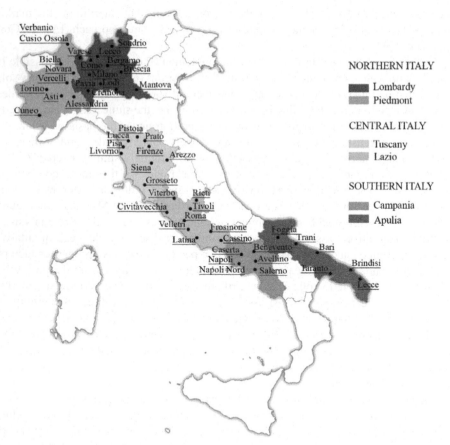

Fig. 2. Localization of the law-courts in the six Italian regions considered in the analysis

In Table 1, for each region and respective law-courts, the number of evaluation reports collected is shown.

Table 1. Number of evaluation reports detected and analysed

NORTHERN ITALY					
REGION	**LAW-COURTS**	**NUMBER OF EVALUATION REPORTS**	**REGION**	**LAW-COURTS**	**NUMBER OF EVALUATION REPORTS**
LOMBARDY	Bergamo	36	PIEDMONT	Alessandria	0
	Brescia	23		Asti	21
	Como	0		Biella	0
	Cremona	0		Cuneo	15
	Lecco	0		Novara	22
	Mantova	18		Turin	23
	Milan	0		Verbano	0
	Pavia	0		Vercelli	10
	Sondrio	0			
	Varese	0			
	TOTAL	**77 (15%)**		**TOTAL**	**91 (17.7%)**

CENTRAL ITALY					
REGION	**LAW-COURTS**	**NUMBER OF EVALUATION REPORTS**	**REGION**	**LAW-COURTS**	**NUMBER OF EVALUATION REPORTS**
TUSCANY	Arezzo	0	LAZIO	Cassino	5
	Florence	3		Civitavecchia	3
	Grosseto	0		Frosinone	3
	Livorno	4		Latina	24
	Lucca	0		Rieti	1
	Massa Carrara	0		Rome	66
	Pisa	35		Tivoli	3
	Pistoia	41		Velletri	19
	Prato	0			
	Siena	0			
	TOTAL	**83 (16.2%)**		**TOTAL**	**124 (24.1%)**

SOUTHERN ITALY					
REGION	**LAW-COURTS**	**NUMBER OF EVALUATION REPORTS**	**REGION**	**LAW-COURTS**	**NUMBER OF EVALUATION REPORTS**
CAMPANIA	Avellino	0	APULIA	Bari	15
	Benevento	0		Brindisi	0
	Caserta	10		Foggia	0
	Naples	53		Lecce	0
	North Naples	11		Taranto	29
	Salerno	12		Trani	9
	TOTAL	**86 (16.7%)**		**TOTAL**	**53 (10.3%)**

TOTAL NUMBER OF EVALUATION REPORTS ANALYZED	514 (100%)

The residential properties identified constitute the population of the study sample.

Each evaluation report includes an explanation of the assessment method implemented. Besides the approach methods provided by the IVS, the analysis shows that several technicians use *indirect* information sources for the assessment of the properties market value, i.e. quotations published by public and private entities/operators.

With reference to the aim of the present research, Table 2 reports for each region the number of evaluation reports consulted and the assessment method typologies used by the technicians.

Table 2. Number of evaluation reports analysed and assessment approaches used

Region	MA		IA	Indirect sources	Unspecified approach	More methods
	MONO*	MULTI**				
Lombardy 77	1 0.2%	3 0.6%	1 0.2%	41 8.0%	30 5.8%	1 0.2%
Piedmont 91	1 0.2%	5 1.0%	0 –	52 10.1%	31 6.0%	2 0,4%
Tuscany 83	3 0.6%	2 0.4%	0 –	48 9.3%	27 5.3%	3 0.6%
Lazio 124	0 –	0 –	2 0.4%	80 15.6%	28 5.4%	14 2.7%
Campania 86	0 –	9 1.7%	2 0.4%	44 8.6%	9 1.8%	22 4.2%
Apulia 53	0 –	1 0.2%	2 0.4%	32 6.2%	13 2.5%	5 1.0%
514 **100%**	**5** 1%	**20** 3.9%	**7** 1.4%	**297** 57.8%	**138** 26.8%	**47** 9.1%

*Mono-parameter.
**Multi-parameter.

Firstly, it should be pointed out that in 9.1% of the cases analysed the market value is assessed implementing more than one method. This situation has been better described in Fig. 3: for each region, the number of evaluation reports that use different assessment approaches – market approach (MA), income approach (IA), indirect sources (IS) – is reported, by pointing out the specific one used. The implementation of various assessment methods is mostly carried out to validate the outputs obtained through the use of a single method: therefore, the "second" method represents a tool for the verification of the market value assessed through the first one. However, in some situations the final output of the assessment is the arithmetic mean of the market values obtained using separately the different methods. In particular, the indirect sources are very often used for the validation of the output deriving from the market or income approach methods, representing a quick reference tool for the valuer.

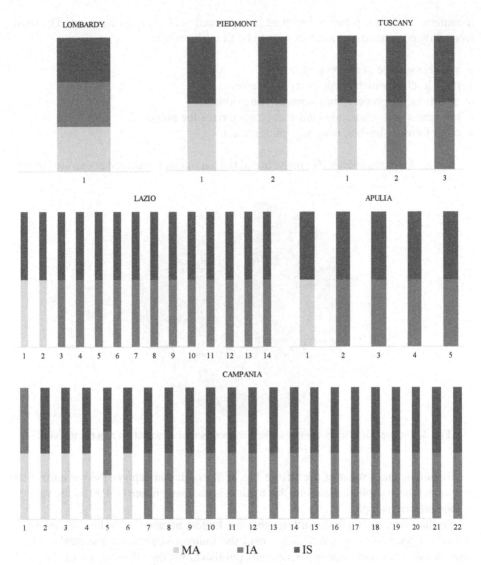

Fig. 3. Number of evaluation reports in which different assessment methods are implemented

In 26.8% of the sample analysed, the assessment method applied for the determination of the market value is not specified: in these situations, the value is assessed by multiplying the saleable floor surface, expressed in square meters of gross floor area of the property, by a unit market value proposed, whose source is not mentioned or explicated.

With reference to the exclusive use of the MA, in 5 evaluation reports a mono-parameter method is implemented, by using the saleable property surface as comparison parameter. The multi-parameter method is performed in 20 evaluation reports. The most frequently comparison parameters chosen by the valuers are:

- saleable surface of the property;
- floor level on which the property is located;
- quality of the property maintenance conditions;
- brightness and panoramic view that characterizes the property;
- other factors (finishes, materials, plants, etc.).

In Fig. 4 the frequencies [%] in the use of the parameters indicated above are shown.

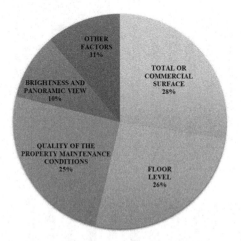

Fig. 4. Frequencies [%] in the use of the parameters in the evaluation reports analysed

Regarding the exclusive use of the IA, in 7 evaluation reports the capitalization method has been applied: therefore, this method is the least chosen (1.4%) by the valuers of the collected sample.

Furthermore, the analysis outlines that the largest number of evaluation reports – 297 of the total 514, i.e. the 57.8% – uses the indirect sources for the market value determination, in particular the quotations published by the Observatory of the Real Estate Market (OMI) of the Italian Revenue Agency, Chambers of Commerce (CC), associations of real estate agencies (AREA).

In Fig. 5 for each region considered the main indirect sources used and the relative frequency in terms of number of evaluation reports that have applied this approach are reported.

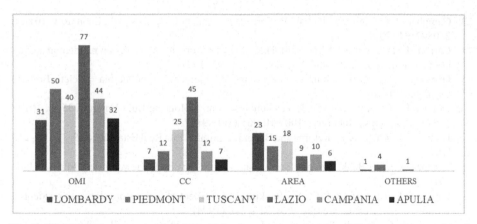

Fig. 5. Main indirect sources used and relative frequency [n.] in the six Italian regions analysed

5 Conclusions

The present research has analysed the main assessment methods applied for the determination of the market value of residential properties involved in judicial procedures. The analysis has concerned six Italian regions equally distributed in the three geographical macro-areas in which the Italian territory is commonly divided – Piedmont and Lombardy for the Northern Italy, Lazio and Tuscany for the Central Italy, Campania and Apulia for the Southern Italy.

The study has pointed out that in a limited number of the sample an IVS approach method has been used, whereas the greatest amount of evaluation reports has applied informative indirect sources, i.e. quotations published by public and private entities/operators: however, this modality constitutes a general and first indication, that is not sufficiently appropriate to express a valid assessment of the market value. It is therefore a reference that could be considered by the valuers in the initial assessment phases, as it does not take into account the subject specific features and conditions.

Furthermore, a consistent number of evaluation reports does not clearly explain the method applied for the market value determination. The IVS claim that the information sources consulted in the assessment path have to be made explicit, in order to verify their robustness and reliability [27]. Taking into account the national context of the analysis, the Italian Property Valuation Standards [28] should be recalled, that promotes the IVS use and define an ethical and deontological code, by pointing out the importance to overcome the expertise approach based on the valuers knowledge, as this can be verified exclusively through the comparison with assessments carried out by other valuers.

References

1. Agenzia del Territorio – Direzione Centrale Osservatorio del Mercato Immobiliare e Servizi Estimativi: Manuale Operativo delle Stime Immobiliari. Franco Angeli (2009)
2. Amoruso, P., Mariani, M., d'Amato, M., Didonato, R.: Italian auction market: features of discounted forced sale price. Real Estate Manag. Valuat. **28**(3), 12–23 (2020)

3. Campbell, J.Y., Giglio, S., Pathak, P.: Forced sales and house prices. Am. Econ. Rev. **101**(5), 2108–2131 (2011)
4. Carroll, T.M., Clauretie, T.M., Neill, H.R.: Effect of foreclosure status on residential selling price: comment. J. Real Estate Res. **13**(1), 95–102 (1997)
5. D'Agostino, A.: Estimo immobiliare urbano ed Elementi di Economia. Società Editrice Esculapio (2008)
6. Donner, H.: Determinants of a foreclosure discount. J. Housing Built Environ. **35**(4), 1079–1097 (2020). https://doi.org/10.1007/s10901-020-09757-1
7. Donner, H.: Foreclosures, Returns and Buyer Intention. J. Eur. Real Estate Res. **39**(2), 189–213 (2017)
8. European Central Bank: Banking Supervision: Asset Quality Review, Phase 2 Manual (June 2018)
9. Forgey, F.A., Rutherford, R.C., VanBuskirk, M.L.: Effect of foreclosure status on residential selling price. J. Real Estate Res. **9**(3), 313–318 (1994)
10. Giacomelli, S., Orlando, T., Rodano, G.: Le procedure esecutive immobiliari: il funzionamento e gli effetti delle recenti riforme (Real Estate Foreclosures: Their Functioning and the Effects of Recent Reforms). Bank of Italy Occasional Paper, 448 (2018)
11. https://www.astegiudiziarie.it/
12. Just, T., Heinrich, M., Maurin, M.A., Schreck, T.: Foreclosure discounts for German housing markets. Int. J. Housing Markets Anal. **13**(2), 143–163 (2019)
13. Medici, G.: Principi di Estimo. Calderini, Bologna (1972)
14. Michieli I., Michieli M.: Trattato Di Estimo. Il Sole 24 ore Ed agricole (2002)
15. Morano, P., Rosato, P., Tajani, F., Manganelli, B., Di Liddo, F.: Contextualized property market models vs. generalized mass appraisals: an innovative approach. Sustainability **11**(18), 4896 (2019)
16. Morano, P., Tajani, F.: Break even analysis for the financial verification of urban regeneration projects. In: Applied Mechanics and Materials, vol. 438, pp. 1830–1835. Trans Tech Publications Ltd. (2013)
17. Morano, P., Tajani, F.: Decision support methods for public-private partnerships: an application to the territorial context of the Apulia Region (Italy). In: Stanghellini, S., Morano, P., Bottero, M., Oppio, A. (eds.) Appraisal: From Theory to Practice. GET, pp. 317–326. Springer, Cham (2017). https://doi.org/10.1007/978-3-319-49676-4_24
18. Ong, S.E.: Price discovery in real estate auctions: the story of unsuccessful attempts. J. Real Estate Res. **28**(1), 39–60 (2006)
19. Pennington-Cross, A.: The value of foreclosed property. J. Real Estate Res. **28**(2), 193–214 (2006)
20. Reviva, Scenario aste immobiliari 2019 (2019). www.scenarioaste.it. Accessed 15 Feb 2021
21. Reviva, Report 'Scenario Aste Immobiliari 2020' (2020). www.scenarioaste.it. Accessed 27 Feb 2021
22. RICS, RICS Valuation – Global Standards. London, United Kingdom (2020). www.rics.org/standards. Accessed 4 Mar 2021
23. Shilling, J.D., Benjamin, J.D., Sirmans, C.: Estimating net realizable value for distressed real estate. J. Real Estate Res. **5**(1), 129–140 (1990)
24. Singh, A.: Estimating the foreclosure discount in financially distressed hotels. Cornell Hosp. Q. (2020). https://doi.org/10.1177/1938965520929652
25. Springer, T.M.: Single-family housing transactions: seller motivations, price, and marketing time. J. Real Estate Financ. Econ. **13**(3), 237–254 (1996)
26. Tajani, F., Morano, P., Locurcio, M., Torre, C.M.: Data-driven techniques for mass appraisals. Applications to the residential market of the city of Bari (Italy). Int. J. Bus. Intell. Data Mining **11**(2), 109 (2016)

27. Tajani, F., Morano, P., Locurcio, M., D'Addabbo, N.: Property valuations in times of crisis: artificial neural networks and evolutionary algorithms in comparison. In: Gervasi, O., Murgante, B., Misra, S., Gavrilova, M.L., Rocha, A.M.A.C., Torre, C., Taniar, D., Apduhan, B.O. (eds.) ICCSA 2015. LNCS, vol. 9157, pp. 194–209. Springer, Cham (2015). https://doi.org/10.1007/978-3-319-21470-2_14

28. Tecnoborsa: Codice delle Valutazioni Immobiliari – Italian Property Valuation Standard, quinta edizione (2018)

29. Wong, W.C., Ng, P.L., Lee, J.Y., Daud, M.N.: Apartment foreclosure discount in Kuala Lumpur. Pac. Rim Prop. Res. J. **21**(2), 127–138 (2015)

Integrated Statistical Data for Planning Social Housing in the City of Taranto

Paola Perchinunno[1] (iD) and Francesco Rotondo[2](✉) (iD)

[1] Aldo Moro University of Bari, Via Camillo Rosalba, 53, 70124 Bari, Italy
paola.perchinunno@uniba.it
[2] Polytechnic University of Marche, Via Brecce Bianche 12, 60131 Ancona, Italy
f.rotondo@univpm.it

Abstract. Housing is often considered a crucial element in determining the level of income and social well-being, in recognition of the ways in which housing shortages, or the use of poor-quality housing, are statistically linked to income levels and can negatively affect on people's well-being (Rolfe et alii, 2020). So, planning social housing isn't just a question of houses, but it claims for a deep understanding of people living conditions, social and economic dynamics. That's why is necessary to integrate different statistical data to develop a model of social and economic living conditions of people to address better and context-based housing policies. The paper analyses methods and tools to integrate appropriate statistical data to guide housing policies in the case of the city of Taranto, selecting those most useful for determining supply and demand to guide urban planning in subsequent participatory and implementation paths. Planning social housing not just to improve physical spaces, but to interpret the needs of living.

Keywords: Housing policies · Statistical integration · Urban planning

1 Introduction

1.1 Contemporary Social Housing Demand

In the first half of the twentieth century, the subject of public buildings played a central role in the construction of the utopia of modernity. The issue of the right to housing was at the center of the programs of most of the national states. With the post-war building expansion, the issue seemed to lose importance in the widespread idea that everyone had free access to the housing market. In Italy, while the share of public intervention in residential construction suffered a substantial collapse that is still significant today, at the same time savings were encouraged for the purpose of buying a home.

The contribution is the result of joint reflections by the authors, with the following contributions attributed to F. Rotondo (paragraphs 1 and 4) and to P. Perchinunno (paragraphs 2 and 3).

According to ISTAT data[1] in Italy in 2011, the incidence of owned homes was 72.5% of the total, in the Puglia Region it was 74.4% and in the Municipality of Taranto at 72.4%. But if the homeowner has certainly contributed to the increase in the level of well-being of the Italian population, it has made the contrast more and more striking with those who are not able to access this market and no longer have available adequate housing policies neither at the national level, nor at a regional level.

The housing problem is a topical issue in the Italian social and political debate due to the emergence of new and more widespread forms of discomfort caused by the difficulty of accessing the residence by a growing and varied number of people, often with characters other than those attributable to those which traditional Public Residential Building was aimed at. It is a complex and not easily delimited concept that includes situations with different characteristics based on intensity and type of discomfort suffered.

The new housing issue is the result of profound changes that have first affected the supply side of housing, which have favored the expansion of home ownership, with the consequent contraction of the rental sector (both social and private) and the significant increase in house prices. On the demand side, housing poverty is the result of demographic and social transformations that are affecting all Western societies, but also the production system, with heavy repercussions on the growth of social vulnerability [1].

The fundamental prerequisite for defining possible strategic lines of intervention for housing policy is to separate the choices relating to public housing, capable of absorbing only a limited part of housing demand, with respect to measures to cope with needs of the so-called gray band. It is necessary to implement innovative interventions, carried out in agreement between the public and private sectors, aiming above all at the normalization of costs and the market, land and housing in ownership and lease [2].

In many cases, housing deprivation is closely linked to conditions of economic poverty. A form of hardship can also be identified in situations that refer mainly to the economic condition, to the title of use of the accommodation and therefore to the trend in rent. In essence, it is a question of considering all those families who at the moment may not even live in a condition of overt hardship, but who risk seeing their situation worsen and falling back into the categories previously examined.

It is a condition that affects the elderly, single parents with children, newly arrived immigrants, single-income families, people with job mobility, young people and university students; people who do not fall within the poverty standards provided for access to public housing but who are unable to deal with the current housing market.

For example, for owner families, the risk is linked to the presence of variable rate mortgages which, in the event of a rise in interest rates, could bring the mortgage payment above the sustainability threshold (30% of income). With regard to rent, the risk can be identified in the difficulty in accessing a rented house if it were required to change residence.

---

[1] ISTAT, 2011, Censimento Popolazioni e abitazioni (www.istat.it). ISTAT is the Italian Institute of Statistics.

For these reasons it was decided to use indicators capable of integrating the housing conditions expressed within the ISTAT Population and Housing Census and those related to the demographic structure.

As will be better illustrated below, a model based on fuzzy logic has been constructed, capable of summarizing the available data on the housing and demographic conditions of the municipality of Taranto to understand the distribution of housing deprivation, integrating it with other data relating to economic and social phenomena.

2 Identifying Indicators of Housing Difficulty

2.1 Introduction

The subject of the case of study arises from the necessity to identify geographical areas characterized by situations of residential deprivation in the city of Taranto (South of Italy). With the aim of analyzing the phenomena of residential poverty on a geographical basis, the work makes use of the data deriving from the most recent Population and Housing Census 2011 carried out by ISTAT; such information allows the geographical analysis in sections according to the census, albeit disadvantaged by the lack of the most recent data. The geographical units of the survey are the 962 census sections for the city of Taranto (of which 915 sections represent all of the data relevant to housing, while the remaining sections are either uninhabitable areas or destined for other uses, for example parks or universities).

With regards to the choice of housing poverty indices there is, therefore, a consideration of various aspects associated to housing conditions along with the quality of housing. The indices were chosen with the aim of identifying the level of residential poverty and were calculated to align elevated levels on the indices with elevated levels of poverty[2]. Connected to the phenomena of residential poverty is the evaluation of the *classification of social and housing status.*

2.2 The Total Fuzzy and Relative Method

At the city level, policies can be addressed by investigating condition of unavailability of housing services and quality, to understand better some peculiar aspect of distribution of housing difficulty.

---

[2] **Index 1** - Incidence of the elderly population: population aged over 70 compared to the total population.**Index 2** - Incidence of the population by educational qualification: population with a qualification below middle school compared to the total population.**Index 3** - Incidence of the illiterate population: illiterate population compared to the total population.**Index 4** - Incidence of empty houses: number of empty houses compared to the total number of houses.**Index 5** - Incidence of period buildings: number of buildings built before 1960 compared to the total number of buildings.**Index 6** - Incidence of residential buildings with poor or poor state of conservation: number of buildings with poor or mediocre state of conservation compared to the total number of buildings.

The approach chosen in order to arrive at the synthesis and measurement of the incidence of relative poverty or residential deprivation in the population in question is the so-called *Total Fuzzy and Relative*, "which utilizes the techniques of the *Fuzzy Set* in order to obtain a measurement of the level of relative poverty within a population, beginning from statistical information gathered from a plurality of indicators" [3].

The TFR approach consists in the definition of the measurement of a degree of membership of an individual to the fuzzy totality of the poor, included in the interval between 0 (not poor) and 1 (poor). Mathematically, such a method consists of the construction of a function of membership to "the fuzzy totality of the poor" which is continuous in nature, and "able to provide a measurement of the degree of poverty present within each unit". Supposing the observation of k indicators of poverty for every family, the function of membership of i-th family to the fuzzy subset of the poor may be defined thus:

$$f(x_i) = \frac{\sum\limits_{j=1}^{k} g(x_{ij})w_j}{\sum\limits_{j=1}^{k} w_j} \quad i = 1, \ldots n \tag{1}$$

For the definition of the function $g(x_{ij})$ please refer to other works [4, 5].

2.3 The TFR Application

The application of the TFR (*Total Fuzzy and Relative*) method begins from the presupposition of synthesizing the five indices elaborated in "*fuzzy*" values which are able to measure the degree of membership of an individual to the totality of the poor (social-housing discomfort), included in the interval between 0 (with an individual not demonstrating clear membership to the totality of the poor) and 1 (with an individual demonstrating clear membership to the totality of the poor). The data arising from various census sections are classified into 5 different typologies of social-housing discomfort in accordance with the resulting fuzzy value:

- Absence of social housing discomfort
- Mild social housing discomfort
- Presence of social housing discomfort
- Significant social housing discomfort
- Relevant social housing discomfort.

According to the set of indicators considered, a differing division of the total 962 census sections for conditions of social and housing discomfort is produced. In relation to the set of indicators of housing and social hardship, 25.8% of the surveyed Sects. (236 sections) showed blurred values representative of the absence of social housing deprivation, 38% had mild social housing deprivation compared to 17.4% of the sections that highlight the presence of social housing deprivation, 12.3% of significant social housing deprivation and only 6.4% with significant social housing deprivation (Fig. 1).

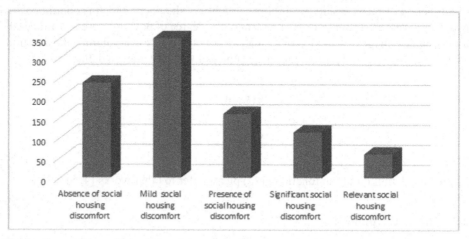

Fig. 1. Composition of absolute values of the census sections of Taranto for socio-housing discomfort.

Analyzing the location of the census sections by "neighbourhood" in terms of percentage composition in the different categories under examination, it is possible to identify areas with lower levels of residential discomfort, such as the quarters named "Lama, Talsano, San Vito" or some parts of the "Borgo".

The neighbourhoods in which a percentage of sections with situations of severe housing problems are detected are, however, "Città vecchia", the historical city centre, Montegranaro, an urban area adjacent to the city centre and Tamburi, the quarter nearest to the big steel plant (Fig. 2).

3   Identification of Cluster of Degraded Areas in the City of Taranto

3.1   The SATScan Model

In order to examine the possibility of applying such methods to regeneration programs it is necessary to introduce a physical reference to urban spaces. In the field of epidemiological studies a range of research groups have developed different typologies of software; these are all based on the same approach, but usually differ from each other in terms of the shape of the window.

Among the various methods of zoning are SaTScan [6] that uses a circular window, FlexScan [7], the Upper Level Scan Statistics [8] and AMOEBA [9].

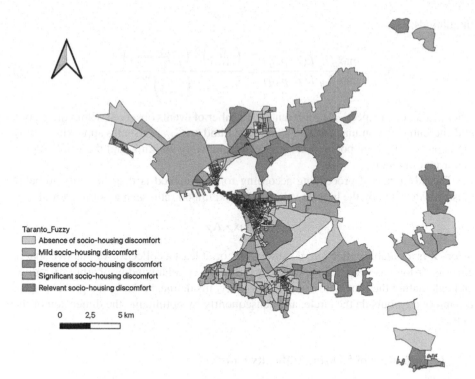

Fig. 2. Composition of percentage values of the census sections of Taranto for socio-housing discomfort in 2011.

SaTScan scans the region of interest with a moving window and compares a smoothing of the intensity inside and outside it: units belonging to contiguous windows with similar intensity are aggregated into a cluster. Multiple different window sizes are used. The window with the maximum likelihood is the most likely cluster, that is, the cluster least likely to be due to chance. A p-value is assigned to this cluster.

In the following description of the SatScan method, it is assumed that the region under investigation can be divided into sub-areas with no common points, along with the existence of precisely one subset Z (constituted by the union of one or more areas) and two independent Poisson processes defined on Z and Z^c, respectively indicated with X_z and $X_z{}^c$ whose intensity functions are:

$$\lambda_Z(x) = p\mu(x) \text{ and } \lambda_{Z^c}(x) = q\mu(x) \tag{2}$$

where p and q describe the individual probability of occurrence, respectively inside and outside the Z zone.

The intensity function of the "background" has a significant digit that varies depending on the particular application considered: for example, in epidemiological investigations, it models the spatial distribution of the population at risk.

The null hypothesis $H_0 : p = q$ that the probability of occurrence within the area considered is not higher than outside, is resolved by the use of the following ratio of likelihoods:

$$\Lambda_Z = \frac{\max_{p>q} L(Z, p, q)}{\max_{p=q} L(Z, p, q)} = \frac{\left(\frac{y_Z}{\mu(Z)}\right)^{y_Z} \left(\frac{y_G - y_Z}{\mu(G) - \mu(Z)}\right)^{y_G - y_Z}}{\left(\frac{y_G}{\mu(G)}\right)^{y_G}} \tag{3}$$

where y_Z and y_G respectively represent the number of events observed within the Z zone and the entire region under study, while $\mu(Z)$ and $\mu(G)$ are usually approximated by the consistency of the population "at risk" respectively within Z and the whole region under investigation.

The advantage of proceeding according to this method is that the most probable cluster is detected by the highest value of the likelihood ratio seen as a function of Z,

$$\Lambda = \max_Z \Lambda_Z \tag{4}$$

where Z is a suitable collection of subset of G, or at least a collection of putative spatial clusters. In this case, SaTScan operates by locating a circular window of arbitrary radius, and calculating the probability of urban poverty, inside the circle, or the probability of urban poverty, outside the circle, and consequently by optimizing the dimension of the radius.

3.2 Identification of Housing Difficulty Clusters

Through the use of the SaTScan model, different clusters of housing demonstrating hardship may be identified, consisting of a number of different sections of a census. The p-value demonstrates the presence of four main clusters. The level of housing hardship identified and defined by the internal average (Fig. 3 and 4).

In the Fig. 3a the quarters named Città Vecchia and Porta Napoli; in the Fig. 3b the quarter named Tamburi. They are the three quarters nearest to the largest steel plant in Europe steel Plant now owned by the company "Arcelor Mittal". The steel plant was identified as the main cause of air pollution by the court of Justice of Taranto in 2012.

In the Fig. 4a the quarter named Montegranaro, the first residential expansion of the modern city. In the Fig. 4b the quarter named Paolo VI, the largest public housing district in the city.

In the Fig. 5 we illustrate photos of some buildings put in evidence by the SaTScan model. This is the oldest quarter of the city built during the Magna Graecia period and always inhabited during all the following centuries. It is the island where the city was born and where the identity of the Taranto community is concentrated despite the abandonment that characterized it after the seventies. It is the objective of a great urban regeneration process financed by the national state which, however, is struggling to start due to the complexity of the restoration interventions to be carried out and the complexity of the bureaucratic machine involved. In the Fig. 5b buildings in via Lisippo in the quarter named Tamburi. These are houses built for a temporary use some decades ago and then remained active until now, with the consequences which can be imagined. In the Fig. 5c, buildings in via Via Lago Varano, in the quarter named Montegranaro, the typical example of the first modernist architecture in the city.

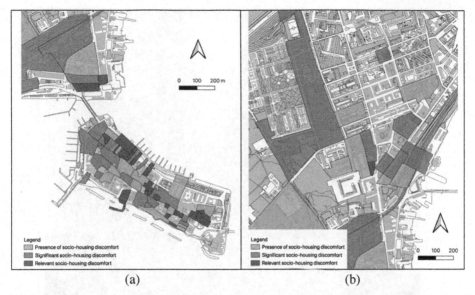

(a)   (b)

Fig. 3. SaTScan model for the identification of cluster of socio-housing discomfort in the city of Taranto.

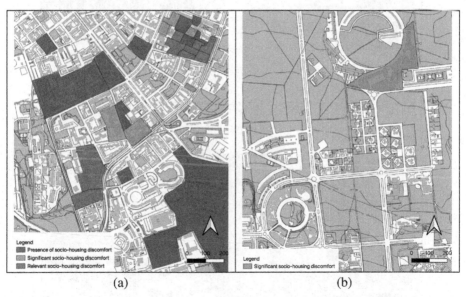

(a)   (b)

Fig. 4. SaTScan model for the identification of cluster of socio-housing discomfort in the city of Taranto.

(a)

(b)

(c)

Fig. 5. Photos of some buildings put in evidence by the SaTScan model. In the figure a via Cava in Città Vecchia (Source Google Street view: https://www.google.it/maps/).

4 Concluding Remarks

As described in the introduction, housing deprivation is a multiple phenomenon strictly related to urban poverty and social and economic disease.

In the case of Taranto, is always important to understand the welfare level, the quality of urban environment, because the city is always characterized by a significant conflict between health and work, due to the presence of the most famous European steel factory [10]. The paper doesn't treat the subject of urban environmental quality, because -even if the topic of steel production and its consequences relevant- we should not forget that anyway the demand of housing services it appropriately still on the desk of local decision makers, just because living, studying, acting socially, working, must go on despite to further questions.

The proposed methodologies identify areas where there is a high disadvantaged index.

As we have noted above, a comparison of the two methods shows that the *Seg*-DBSCAN method is more accurate in identifying the spatial units in which there are housing problems. The future advancement of our work will be to seek a cluster validity index for spatial data, which considers the noise points, that is valid from a statistical point of view and that allows the accurate measurement of the *Seg*- DBSCAN method.

The applications with SaTScan or *Seg-DBSCAN* methodology in order to identify hot spots of housing hardship raises certain considerations for future research in the social field and for urban planning of regeneration areas, particularly relevant to the European Union policy agenda.

Starting from information obtained by the cluster intersection of housing hardship, it could be possible to obtain useful indications for planning urban regeneration policies, making decisional process more transparent and scientifically valid. The preliminary question leading towards the identification of town planning and architectonic solutions to the problem of urban regeneration, in a historical moment characterized by a lack of public resources for investment, focuses on the identification of areas characterized by the highest level of urban poverty to direct the choices of political decision-makers in a transparent, thought-out and objective manner. The model used in this study is able to provide, in the opinion of the authors, relevant data for the identification of such areas.

References

1. Palvarini, P.: Qualità abitativa e vivibilità urbana. Quaderni di Sociologia, p. 52 (2010). http://journals.openedition.org/qds/719. Accessed 30 Nov 2015, 30 July 2021
2. Ferri, G., Pogliani, L., Rizzica, C.: Towards a collaborative way of living – innovating social and affordable housing in Italy. In: Van Bortel, G., Gruis, V., Nieuwenhuijzen, J., Pluijmers, B. (eds.) Affordable Housing Governance and Finance, pp. 59–86. Routledge, Oxford (2018)
3. Cerioli, A., Zani, S.: A fuzzy approach to the measurement of poverty. In: Dugum, C., Zenga, M. (eds.) Income and Wealth Distribution, Inequality and Poverty, pp. 272–284. Springer, Berlin (1990). https://doi.org/10.1007/978-3-642-84250-4_18
4. Cheli, B., Lemmi, A.: A "totally" fuzzy and relative approach to the multidimensional analysis of poverty, economic notes (1995)

5. Lemmi, A., Pannuzi, N., Mazzolli, B., Cheli, B., Betti, G.: Misure di povertà multidimensionali e relative: il caso dell'Italia nella prima metà degli anni '90. In: Quintano, C. (ed.) Scritti di Statistica Economica, 3, Istituto di Statistica e Matematica, Istituto Universitario Navale di Napoli, Quaderni di Discussione, vol. 13, pp. 263–319. Curto, Napoli (1997)
6. Kulldorff, M., Nagarwalla, N.: Spatial disease clusters: detection and inference. Stat. Med. **14**, 799–810 (1995)
7. Takahashi, K., Yokoyama, T., Tango, T.: FleXScan: software for the flexible spatial scan statistic. National Institute of Public Health, Tokyo (2004)
8. Patil, G.P., Taillie, C.: Upper level set scan statistic for detecting arbitrarily shaped hotspots. Environ. Ecol. Stat. **11**, 183–197 (2004)
9. Aldstadt, J., Getis, A.: Using AMOEBA to create spatial weights matrix and identify spatial clusters. Geogr. Anal. **38**, 327–343 (2006)
10. Camarda, D., Rotondo, F., Selicato, F.: Strategies for dealing with urban shrinkage: issues and scenarios in Taranto. Eur. Plan. Stud. **23**(1), 126–146 (2015)

Reconstruction as an Opportunity to Promote Local Self-sustainable Development of Shrinking Territories in Seismic Inner Areas in Central Italy

Luca Domenella[1] , Marco Galasso[2], Giovanni Marinelli[1] ,
and Francesco Rotondo[3]([⊠])

[1] SIMAU, Polytechnic University of Marche, Via Brecce bianche 12, 60131 Ancona, Italy
{l.domenella,g.marinelli}@univpm.it
[2] Via Brecce Bianche 12, 60131 Ancona, Italy
[3] Polytechnic University of Marche, Via Brecce Bianche 12, 60131 Ancona, Italy
f.rotondo@univpm.it

Abstract. The natural disasters that hit the Italian Apennines with increasing frequency, earthquakes, landslides and floods, cause enormous damage to people and things, modifying economies and social contexts, already affected by the scarcity and antiquity of infrastructures and the abandonment of some territories, located in particular in the inner areas of the country. In these territories there is a significant social, historical, economic, environmental and landscape capital of Italy that everyone knows and loves. The need emerges to increase infrastructural resilience, carrying out significant extraordinary maintenance interventions, promoting the technological development of monitoring activities and infrastructures, prevention activities, civil protection and public rescue. Resilience, however, is a broader concept than the physical ability to overcome disasters, as the ongoing pandemic crisis has shown. This includes, for example, the ability of the urban system to respond to unforeseen seismic events or health problems; the solidity of the network of public spaces and services to support communities and their ability to effectively deal with sudden crises. In the event of catastrophic events, it is precisely the peripheral urban contexts of the Inner Areas that are most exposed to "Risks of isolation", as shown by the seismic events of 2016, where the secondary infrastructural network was heavily affected, limiting mobility of residents in an unsustainable way and sentencing them to further forms of isolation. The work explores the experimental methodologies capable of planning substantial changes to the structure of cities and minor urban areas (both with reference to damaged buildings and to the infrastructural network) that reconstruction can allow, making it a unique opportunity to renew and re-organize the territory.

Keywords: Inner areas · Shrinking cities · Urban planning

The paper is the result of a joint work of the authors, also if the paragraph 1 has to be attributed to Francesco Rotondo, the paragraph 2–3 to Giovanni Marinelli, the paragraphs 4 to Luca Domenella, the paragraphs 5 to Marco Galasso, and the paragraph 6 – conclusion, to all the authors.

O. Gervasi et al. (Eds.): ICCSA 2021, LNCS 12954, pp. 153–166, 2021.
https://doi.org/10.1007/978-3-030-86979-3_12

1 Seismic Inner Areas in Central Italy: First Elements of Analysis

A severe earthquake struck Central Italy in 2016, affecting four regions, 10 provinces and 139[1] Municipalities, up to a total of approximately 8,000 km², reaching 6.5 Mw magnitude with the shock recorded on October 30th, which caused the destruction of highly valuable historic centers. The earthquake of 2016 reached a far greater intensity than the previous earthquake that occurred in L'Aquila in 2009, which was regarded as the "fifth most severe disaster in the modern history of Italy", not in terms of the number of victims, but because of the intensity of the earthquake (with the highest peak reaching a 6.3 Mw magnitude) in the affected area.

The Marche Region was the most severely affected region out of the four regions within the area struck by the earthquake, with extensive damage in 86 out of a total of 139 municipalities (3,978 km² of affected regional surface). The toll was very high: with more than 104,000 damaged buildings, 54,000 evacuated buildings and 32,000 displaced people, of whom 28,500 benefited from Autonomous Accommodation contributions (CAS), temporarily accommodating over 8,000 people in Emergency Housing Facilities (SAE) and hosted in accommodation facilities along the Adriatic coast[2].

The majority of population inhabiting areas affected by las seismic events, in spite of the substantial difficulties experienced till now, didn't migrate from their land of origin. The choice of settling temporary shelter modules, SAE – Emergency Housing Solutions – (activity that showed itself as uneconomical and rather complex in this mountainous areas), can find its origin from the very same will not to disperse the local community, composed in the majority of the cases by a predominant + 65 population [14], and to try to contrast in some way the abandonment of the territory as a consequence of the seismic event.

Other than the damage of the built environment and the identarian heritage sites, the earthquake worsened the criticalities already present in this complex environment, regarding minimum standards for dwelling, accessibility and basic services.

Already before 2016 earthquake, with the definition of the SNAI – Inner Areas National Strategy, Italian state put particular attention at the Apennine area (Occupying a vast part of the peninsula), an area that during last decades witnessed a marginalization process and a consequent population shrinkage, resulting in a largely inadequate use and management of the territory.

"Inner Areas" cover a vast part of the Italian territory hosting a population of more than 13.540 million. Around one quarter of Italy's population lives in these areas, divided among more than four thousand municipalities, which cover sixty per cent of the entire national territory [2].

---

[1] On January 1st, 2017 the Municipality of Valfornace was established from the merger of the municipalities of Fiordimonte and Pievebovigliana. The number of municipalities located within the seismic area fell to 139, compared to 140 municipalities set out by decrees Dl 186/2016 and 8/2017.

[2] Variable data surveyed on a monthly basis, source: Osservatorio Sisma (Earthquake Observatory), Marche Region. https://sisma2016.gov.it/.

SNAI emphasised that those marginal areas constitute 53% of Italian municipalities, 23% of the population and 60% of the territory of the nation[3].

This territory possesses a "territorial capital" of exceptional value and diversity, but which is largely unused as a consequence of the long-term demographic decline that began in the 1950s when Italy started its industrial take-off. The Strategy adopted by Italy – now in its experimental phase – has the overall objective of promoting local development by activating unused territorial capital through carefully selected development projects. Improving the quality and quantity of the key welfare services (education, health, transport) in the inner areas is a central pillar of that strategy.

After SNAI evaluation process, 72 pilot areas where selected, identified by a low level of population density, (2001–2011 Census data) and by a population shrinkage of − 4,4% compared to the Italian average of +4,3%. The shrinkage tendency was confirmed by the data of the period 2011–2017, with a further reduction of −3,2% in just 6 years, compared to a +1,9% increase in the national average. This tendency makes even more urgent to increase the dedication and the action to achieve a fast actuation and application of the planned strategies.

In this complex framework, where environmental fragility adds to economic criticalities, becomes central to reflect on the reconstruction planning, projecting in the disaster response the research for new construction and territorial forms, new structural and functional relationships, more sustainable and resilient, to activate substantial development strategies, able to restore better environment and more solid communities to the Central Apennine fragile environment.

2 Infrastructure and Mobility: Evaluation of Accessibility in the Inner Areas of 2016

SNAI approached the transportation topic for the inner areas under 3 big families of needing highlighted in the Guidelines for Inner areas Mobility, namely: "Planning and programming", "Improvement and requalification of infrastructural network" and "Development of transport services (internal and external accessibility)". From the analysis of the documents produced by SNAI (now included in the CIPE report for the year 2018) and now approved, it is clear that in spite of the limited resources, the territories privileged the rethinking of governance for the public transport system, and somehow profited of the increased contractual power when facing the transport providers, given by the support of national level professionals, and by the power a minister has in comparison to a local authority. Among the 138 municipalities affected by the earthquake, 84 fall under one of the 3 categories of Inner area defined by SNAI, also defined by the proximity to an essential service provider.

In total there are 4 project area defined by SNAI (Fig. 1): 2 in Marche (Ascoli Piceno with 15 municipalities and 25.000 inhabitants and Nuovo Maceratese, with 19 municipalities and 18.000 inhabitants), 1 in Umbria (Val Nerina, with 14 municipalities

---

[3] Data source: SNAI annual report, presented to Cipe (Department for the planning and coordination of economic policy of the Italian Government) by the Minister for Territorial Cohesion and the South, December 2016.

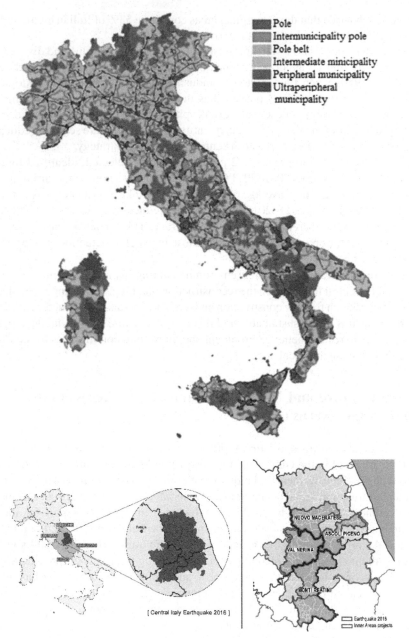

Fig. 1. Central Italy territory affected by earthquake, regions: Abruzzo, Lazio, Marche, Umbria. The inner areas in Italy. UVAL-UVER processing of data from the Ministry of Health, Ministry of Education and FS. The blue area indicates the study area of this work: the inner areas of the Marche region affected by the 2016 earthquake.

and 19.000 inhabitants, and one in Lazio (Monti Reatini, 31 municipalities and 34.000 inhabitants) giving a partial coverage of the examined area.

The topic of connectivity and accessibility to the territory, especially the inner ones hit by the seismic events is a core precondition to local development. SNAI says: "for the peripherality not to transform in marginality it is necessary to improve accessibility to basic services for inner areas, first of all education and health. This can be obtained through 2 modes of action: a) strengthen and rethink the service offering; b) improve mobility, reducing the transport time to access the service hub". It is then clear that accessibility is fundamental, ad basic condition fir the success of all the development intervention.

Till now, the majority of areas that defined the Strategy (around 50) invested resources coming from the rationalization of the system on actions primarily targeting sustainability for the transport network, highlighting a radical shift from traditional service management. This lead not anymore to a generic increase of the services, but rather an increase in efficiency, often using in a more rational way existing resources, and increasing the efficiency. This leads to rather interesting projects, that demand a new governance and more flexible regulations to become widespread examples.

3   Pilot Area Alto Maceratese: A Possible Case Study

For the Marche region, a first pilot case resulted in the definition of the Alto Maceratese Area (17 municipalities, headed by Unione Montana Marca di Camerino), that is related to investments with EAFRD (European Agricultural Fund for Rural Development) and the Italian Stability Law funding, to strengthen local public transportation, with the creation of 3 modal hub and 17 pit-stop micro station to recharge electric vehicle. Hubs are seen as access gates to inner area and to the Monti Sibillini National Park, exchange infrastructure for public infrastructure, for the rental and recharge of electric vehicle, bike-sharing hub and public transport stop, connecting road infrastructure for natural and cultural explorations.

In 2019, with the regional project *"Nuovi Sentieri di Sviluppo per l'Appennino Marchigiano dopo il sisma del 2016"* the 2nd trajectory *"Borghi in rete. Connettività e mobilità sostenibile nelle aree dell'Appennino Marchigiano"*[4] promoted the extension of this strategy to the whole earthquake affected area, imagining an exchange hub network system, connected with natural and cultural heritage exploration paths, connecting national parks, and Rete Natura 2000 areas.

The area explored by the project is characterized by limited connectivity, in terms of digital infrastructure, of road network and of public transport service.

These problems are amplified in in the inner areas, where the combination of "poor digital connectivity + poor physical accessibility" represents one of the greatest limits to development and life quality. From the point of view of physical accessibility, the main criticalities are represented by an imbalance between the offer of services related to local public transport and the potential demand from the territories to be served.

This can be traced back to three main structural characteristics of the territory:

---

[4] https://www.consiglio.marche.it/informazione_e_comunicazione/pubblicazioni/quaderni/pdf/289.pdf.

LOCAL PUBLIC TRANSPORT BY ROAD

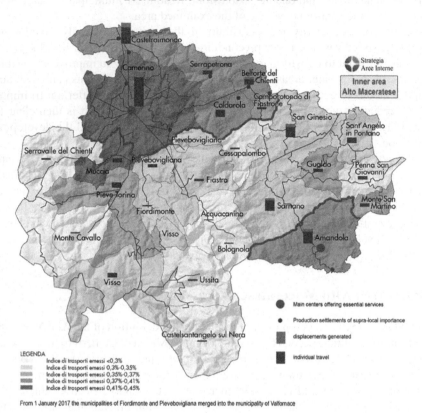

Fig. 2. Alto Macerata Inner Area transport analysis, year 2018.

– the diffusion and fragmentation of the settlement system, consisting of small villages, hamlets and historic centers, with low population density, which necessarily entails, on the one hand, an increase in travel times due to the reduction of travel speed and an increase in the management costs of local public transport services, thus making it uneconomic;

– the morphology of the area, which make it difficult to activate a service suited to the needs of residents and visitors to the area; increased difficulty following seismic events for which, to date, various infrastructures cannot be used, or are only partially, due to damage or due to risk situations induced by landslide slopes or other critical conditions;

– a limited hierarchy of the infrastructural system, due in particular to the lack of supra-local connection infrastructures, able to quickly connect the small internal centers with the surrounding area, both through adequate transversal north-south connections, and through east-west, or coast-inland, connections.

4   Post-earthquake Criticalities in the Marche's Infrastructural Framework: First Assessments and Opportunities

The 2016 earthquake highlighted not only the shortcomings of the existing infrastructural network, but above all its weakness: landslides of roadsides and detachments of road surfaces have worsened the capability to act during the emergency and made it more difficult (in some cases prevented) the operation of rescuers.

Moreover, the presence of collapsed or unsafe buildings at the fringe of some of the access roads to the main cities and villages, compromised even more the accessibility, especially where the road affected was the only way of access. The most recent primary road infrastructure, based on the "Quadrilatero Umbria-Marche" (SS. 76 Vallesina and SS.77 Val di Chienti), Fig. 2, has not suffered substantial damage, with the only exception of the SS.4 Salaria, interrupted due to landslides [7]. Many municipal and provincial roads have suffered a worsening of accessibility, also caused by very little maintenance in recent years due to the scarce financial resources of the managing institutions (Fig. 3). Also due to these criticalities, the Provinces of Marche have returned the management responsibility of the former state-road network to the Regional authorities, which in turn has established a partnership with Anas for the maintenance of the aforementioned road network. This transfer of powers has caused a fragmentation of potential projects (divided between Anas, Provinces and Municipalities, with the Region only responsible as the owner for the ex-Anas viability), with the result that in the "Piano Operativo del Fondo Sviluppo e Coesione Infrastrutture 2014–2020", approved with Resolution CIPE 25/2016, in the Marche's territory no road project has been funded.

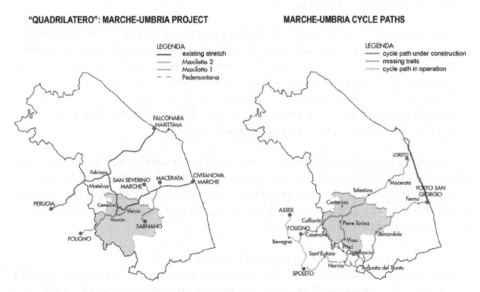

Fig. 3. Marche Region Inner area Alto Maceratese. Primary infrastructure network

Despite the infrastructural network of the Marche crater has shown all its vulnerability, on the other hand it has shown undoubted positive aspects, especially regarding hillside and mountain tourism: the deficiency of the road network is balanced by the substantial environmental integrity of the landscape, with very few exceptions.

Up to now, the mountain has also been protected regarding the settlement of ski resorts and the maintenance of unobstructed views of the cultivated hills and promontories, which in themselves represent a natural resource to be preserved and enhanced.

For these reasons, the need for intervention on the infrastructural network of the Marche territory mitigating local and territorial vulnerability, cannot ignore the protection of the delicate balance between infrastructures and landscape composed by various landscape matrices [17, 18], in line with the development of local economic activities (especially artisanal and agricultural), and of services related to tourism, which do not require new large and fast infrastructures, but rather a complete and safe network with constant maintenance.

4.1 Development Goals for the Secondary Road Network

It is evident that the reconstruction cannot ignore the reorganization of the infrastructural system and the sustainable development of the territory, through a renewed accessibility to the cities at the foothills and "Inner Areas", which allows to live in an effective condition of resilience to cope with future seismic events.

The reconstruction offers the opportunity to make substantial changes to the layout of villages and minor urban areas affected by the earthquake (regarding both the damaged buildings and the infrastructural network), giving a unique and unrepeatable opportunity for innovation and organic rearrangement of the territory [12, 13]. Pursuing this goal means first and foremost ensuring that:

1. The Minimum Urban Structures (SUM) provided for by the O.C. 39 (ordinance governing the Reconstruction Implementation Plans), should have access infrastructures from with a low degree of vulnerability, achieved by a suitable road and building project (junctions, roundabouts, setbacks and localised voids, etc.);
2. Road layouts (regional, provincial and municipal) are made safe from landslides, through containment works, tunnels, reduction of tortuosity and what is necessary to ensure full accessibility even in emergency conditions.

A complex but lasting intervention, which must not consist on new roads, but on the substantial improvement of the existing network and its accessibility, with the goal to make all the cities of the crater that are going to be rebuilt easily accessible, in any weather condition and in any circumstance [8]. An intervention with strong of environmental sustainability qualities, which will require:

– the access to a subsidized and multi-year financial source;
– a singular implementing authority throughout the crater, or at least for each territorial area, through a design and consequent implementation in strict contact with local authorities, with the urban planning decision of each territory;

the improvement of the transversal valley network (e.g. Val d'Aso, Val Tenna, etc.) connecting the area of the crater to the coastal road system, with regional and/or state funding (Fig. 4).

Fig. 4. Marche Region, Visso (MC), Damage to infrastructure caused by the 2016 Central Italy earthquake.

4.2 Development Goals for the Primary Road Network

The road infrastructure of the crater area, in spite of the resiliency shown in 2016, require a development project (since long scheduled by ANAS, the Italian Society for highways) such as the foothill network Fabriano-Muccia (already designed) and Sforzacosta-Sarnano, that even if already part of the Quadrilatero network after 1997 seismic event still demand for a rapid completion.

The road network has to be completed, improving the existing system to facilitate the development of the area exploiting tourism and the rich productive landscape [1].

Finally, it is important to consider the problematic north-south regional connection, rethinking the primary road infrastructure, starting from the missing of the third highway lane in the region, source of limitations especially in emergency situations.

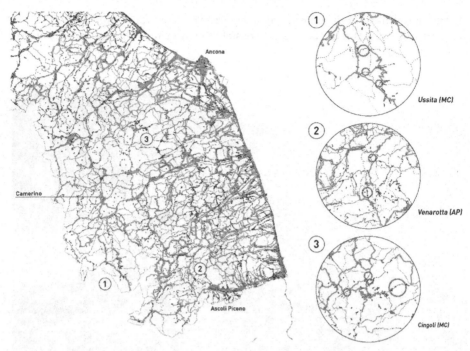

Fig. 5. Regional Mosaic for Emergency Limit Condition (CLE). In orange connective and accessibility infra-structure included in CLE; in red the gaps between CLE regarding neighbouring municipalities.

5   Resilience Infrastructures and Lifelines for a Territorial Safety Project

The seismic events of Central Italy 2016–17 highlighted the vulnerability of the local infrastructural system, so that the sequence of natural events affects the functionality of road infrastructures of local interest and connecting the Adriatic coast to the Tyrrhenian one, often not providing an alternative route. The vulnerability of the territory is linked to the particular morphology of a mountainous area, which is composed by roads through witch is not easy to reach small villages and inhabited centers scattered throughout the territory [3, 4]. The main disruptions of the road infrastructures concern the opening of cracks in the road surface, subsidence and horizontal deformations. These effects are associated with the instability phenomena that involved landslide slopes and support structures. The damage caused to the road infrastructure by the Central Italy sequence is documented in detail in GEER [9, 10], Durante [6] and Lanzo [11].

In the Marche region (the one hit the hardest by the 2016 events) the "safety project" consists almost exclusively of the Emergency Limit Condition (CLE), a tool that by definition represents the "Condition of the urban system under which, following the occurrence of a seismic event, even in conjunction with the occurrence of physical and functional damages, resulting in the interruption of almost all the urban activities including the housing, the urban area still allows, as a whole, the operation of most of the strategic emergency activities, their accessibility and connection with the urban network" [16]. Even if the CLE evaluation is configured as a tool for verifying the instruments of the emergency management system on a municipal scale (strategic buildings, safe areas, accessibility infrastructures), small-medium municipalities erroneously attribute to this the role of a "project", neglecting the constituent components of a project: definition of actions/interventions and their implementation [15].

The analysis and application action of this tool is limited within the municipal boundary, limiting the seismic vulnerability assessments to individual centers and neglecting the territorial criticalities that may emerge following a calamitous event (Fig. 5). This paradigm, limited to the municipal administrative borders, gives rise to a fragmentation in the territorial safety project, in which the connection with the infrastructural systems on a regional scale is not always guaranteed. The peripheral urban systems are exposed to the "risk of isolation" in the event of a calamitous event, a condition found in 2016 following the earthquake, in which the secondary road infrastructures went into crisis, with many inconveniences for those living in the areas.

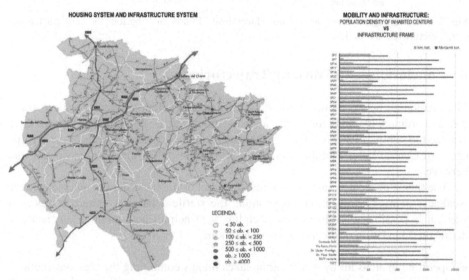

Fig. 6. Marche region Inner area Alto Maceratese, secondary road network and population distribution related to road segments. Analysis of population risk exposure. Secondary road length related to population resident in proximity to each road sector.

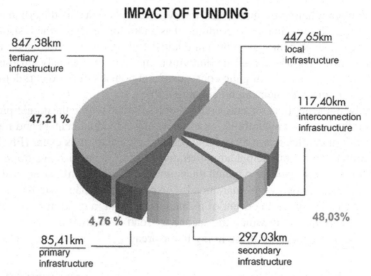

IMPACT OF FUNDING

847,38km
tertiary
infrastructure

447,65km
local
infrastructure

47,21 %

117,40km
interconnection
infrastructure

4,76 %

48,03%

85,41km
primary
infrastructure

297,03km
secondary
infrastructure

Fig. 7. Marche region Inner area Alto Maceratese. Funds distribution for post-earthquake infrastructure reconstruction.

6   Conclusions and Working Trajectories

The integration between prevention tools, territorial development/revitalization strategies and ordinary planning for territorial management can no longer be postponed, there is a need to rethink new urban-territorial balances in the fragile territories of the seismic crater of Central Italy, with the goal of preserving the Italian historical environmental heritage.

The theme of scenario-assessment/management of post-disaster put on evidence the weakness points of prevention. Overcoming the sterile debate on "where it was as it was", it is possible to outline cross-disciplinary principles and common elements, to define the foundation of the reconstruction actions:

- Operating in areas hit by recent earthquakes means combining the "re-construction" plan with a "re-housing" project based on innovative tools and strategies in which prevention, urban quality and safety take on a complementary role for the regeneration of territories in crisis.
- Accepting the risk and seismogenetics of the territory as a permanent factor to deal with is a prerequisite to undertake the technical-cultural leap at the base of the process of reconstruction in Central Italy.
- Highlight the gap, in temporal and economic terms, between the goals and desires of the citizens, and their possible fulfilment [5] and define concrete operational responses.
- Develop a systemic risk prevention project, integrated into reconstruction plans and activate general planning for permanent preparedness of the fragile territories of the Central Apennines.

It is clear that the topic of safety should be addressed together with a multi-risk approach, focusing on places and communities, analysing the various components that can affect the level of safety (Figs. 6–7). It is necessary to overcome the approach linked to homogeneous and undifferentiated policies on the national territory, in favour of targeted policies, defining specific action for each specific risk situation embedded in the site, taking into consideration the living conditions and customs of the communities that live in the area.

It's relevant to enphasize the "unterestimated conflict planning-prevention" and to underline that it can be reduced by providing for future planning, the use of criteria arising from the study ex ante scenarios related to the past events.

As with all policies for inner areas, it should be noted that the entire system of interventions in transport that can be activated with SNAI would greatly benefit from greater attention in national sector policies. Today these policies are unbalanced on the centrality assigned to large urban areas and on efficiency regulations that are "blind" to the territorial diversity of our country. Without reasonable criteria of flexibility, the planning and reorganization efforts that the territories are putting in place risk to penalise transport services in inland areas.

The reactivation of the areas of the earthquake depends on a process of restitution and generation of value in territories that have been compromised by a sequence of events and crises that have conditioned the capacity to generate value. Nonetheless these territories can recover this capacity with combined systemic actions, capable of fostering the recovery and eco-sustainable regeneration, based on the qualities present in the different geographical areas. The idea that moves the PNRR program is that the overall positive result and use in Italy of the Recovery Plan related funding is only possible if it is first of all able to restore vitality and industriousness to those local communities that have been hit by the effects of a crisis that is now more than ten years old, removing the shortcomings in terms of infrastructures and determining real benefits for those who want to live and invest in these places, through the promotion of services and infrastructures capable of overcoming diseconomies and difficulties that have occurred in the recent years, which have reduced the population and the intensity regarding economic activity and social relations.

References

1. Antonelli, G., Viganò, E.: Agricoltura e paesaggio nella regione Marche. Franco Angeli, Milano (2007)
2. Agency for Social Cohesion: Schede regionali, Analisi socio-economica del territorio italiano e delle risorse per le politiche di coesione. http://www.agenziacoesione.gov.it (2017). Accessed 21 Mar 2020
3. Boni, M.P., Menoni, S., Pergalani, F.: Gli effetti domino e a cascata in eventi e contesti complessi. In: 37° Convegno Nazionale del Gruppo Nazionale di Geofisica della Terra Solida, pp. 224–227 (2018)
4. Boni, M.P., Menoni, S., Pergalani, F.: Domino and cascading effects in complex events and territorial contexts. Bollettino di Geofisica Teorica ed Applicata (2020)
5. Bronzini, F., Bedini, M.A., Marinelli, G.: "L'esperienza terremoto nell'Italia dal grande cuore e dalla assoluta assenza di prevenzione e protezione dai rischi dei territori in crisi", in AA.

Planum Publisher, Roma-Milano, VV. Urbanistica è/e azione pubblica. La responsabilità della proposta (2017)

6. Durante, M.G., Di Sarno, L., Zimmaro, P., Stewart, J.P.: Damage to roadway infrastructure from 2016 Central Italy earthquake sequence. Earthq. Spectra **34**(4), 1721–1737 (2018)

7. Farabollini, P., Angelini, S., Fazzini, M., Lugeri, F.R., Scalella, G.: La sequenza sismica dell'Italia centrale del 24 agosto e successive: contributi alla conoscenza e la banca dati degli effetti di superficie. Rend. Online Soc. Geol. It. **46**, 9–15 (2018)

8. Farabollini, P.: La sequenza sismica del centro Italia iniziata il 24 agosto 2016. L'alfabeto della ricostruzione. In: PRISMA Economia – Società – Lavoro, n.3/2018, pp. 59–80 (2018)

9. GEER: Engineering Reconnaissance of the 24 August 2016 Central Italy Earthquake. Version 2. In: Zimmaro, P., Stewart, J.P. (eds.), GEER Association Report No. GEER-050B (2016), https://doi.org/10.18118/G61S3Z

10. GEER: Engineering Reconnaissance following the October 2016 Central Italy Earthquakes. Version 2. In: Zimmaro, P., Stewart, J.P. (eds.), GEER Association Report No. GEER-050D (2017), https://doi.org/10.18118/G6HS39

11. Lanzo, G., et al.: Reconnaissance of geotechnical aspects of the 2016 Central Italy earthquakes. Bull. Earthq. Eng. **17**(10), 5495–5532 (2019)

12. Marinelli, G., Galuzzi, P., Vitillo, P., Domenella, L.: "Dall'emergenza alla ricostruzione dei territori fragili". In: EyesReg – AISRe, Vol. 10, N. 3, Maggio, pp. 1–9 (2020)

13. Marinelli, G.: "Sisma 2016, dall'emergenza alla ricostruzione. Strategie e strumenti per riabitare i territori in crisi". In: Moccia, F.D e Sepe, M. (a cura di), Interruzioni, Intersezioni, Condivisioni, Sovrapposizioni. Nuove prospettive per il territorio, Urbanistica Informazioni, n.278, Inu Edizioni. Roma, pp. 332–338 (2018)

14. Nomisma: Ripartire dopo il sisma del centro Italia. https://www.nomisma.it/ripartire-dopo-il-sisma-del-centro-italia-report/ (2019). Accessed 21 Mar 2020

15. Olivieri, M.: "Regione Umbria. Vulnerabilità urbana e prevenzione urbanistica degli effetti del sisma: il caso di Nocera Umbra". In: Olivieri M. (a cura di) Urbanistica Quaderni, pp. 1–156 (2013)

16. OPCM-Ordinanza Presidente del Consiglio dei Ministri n. 4007, "Contributi per gli interventi di prevenzione del rischio sismico" (2012)

17. Sargolini, M.: "Ricostruzione post-terremoto e post-catastrofe. Introduzione" in Urbanistica Informazioni, n.272, pp 132–133 (2017)

18. Sargolini, M.: Eventi sismici: non ci facciamo più cogliere di sorpresa. Agriregionieuropa, anno 13 n°51 (2017)

Urban Regeneration Processes and Social Impact: A Literature Review to Explore the Role of Evaluation

Maria Cerreta[✉] and Ludovica La Rocca

Department of Architecture, University of Naples Federico II, via Toledo 402, 80134 Naples, Italy
{maria.cerreta,ludovica.larocca}@unina.it

Abstract. From urban regeneration to social regeneration up to culture-led regeneration, the concept of urban regeneration evolves from the idea of the physical transformation of cities to a more complex vision of changing able to improve the inhabitants' quality of life. At the same time, the social dimension of the recognised impacts, from a factor juxtaposed to the regenerative processes, becomes central to build new models of "impact economy" with long-term sustainable effects. In this change of perspective, the driver is the repositioning of culture, the community's centrality and involvement, and the reuse of abandoned cultural heritage spaces. In urban regeneration processes, evaluation has thus assumed a decisive role in guiding strategic choices, empowering the communities involved, supporting decision-makers and attracting new funding. Starting from the keywords "urban regeneration" and "social impact", the paper integrates the literature review with bibliometric maps through the VOSviewer tool to investigate the role of evaluation in a broader framework to feed the contemporary debate on the impacts of urban regeneration.

Keywords: Urban regeneration · Social impact · Literature review · Complex values · Evaluation · VOSviewer

1 Introduction

Faced with the vastness of the subject matter and the complexity of the issues, the concept of "regeneration" has perhaps not yet found a precise codification as well as the actions to be taken to give it substance. Evans and Shaw [1] define urban regeneration as "the infusion of new vitality into declining communities, industries and places, bringing long-term sustainable improvements in economic, social and environmental dimensions." This definition holds together some of the main characteristics that identify the regenerative processes that we intend to analyse: the spatial dimension investigated by the reuse and that of the community, protagonist and beneficiary of the multiple impacts that urban transformations can generate. If historically ample attention has been given to the economic and environmental dimensions of impacts, in recent years, the interest in the social dimension has increased to the point of being, today, a fundamental part

© Springer Nature Switzerland AG 2021
O. Gervasi et al. (Eds.): ICCSA 2021, LNCS 12954, pp. 167–182, 2021.
https://doi.org/10.1007/978-3-030-86979-3_13

of a business interested in long-term prospects. While most definitions consider social impact as a positive social change [2], other authors describe it as reducing negative effects [3], confirming the divergence of views that define the complexity of social impact. Generally, social impact refers to change "capable of affecting lifestyle, culture, communities, political systems, the environment, health and well-being, personal and property rights, and even fears and aspirations" [4]. The concept of social impact has emerged over time, with multifaceted meanings and only more recently integrated into the goals of urban regeneration processes.

In the post-war period, the need to rebuild cities and their economies, together with progressive de-industrialisation, have left a social void that, despite the advent of large-scale regeneration projects, in many cases has not been filled [5]. From the 1940s onwards, there was a bold attempt to merge the physical and economic developments of "urban regeneration" with the social aspects, such that "social regeneration" [6, 7] became central to the political agenda of the 1960s. The emphasis that is placed on community involvement in urban transformation processes [8] is mainly reflected in "social housing" plans [9] and employment training measures.

At the end of the 1980s, in a competitive period in which cities rediscovered themselves as central to regional and national economic performance [10], there was full awareness of the profound changes induced in societies affected by the urban transformation. The advent of the New Economy has led to a redesign of the urban landscape that, if on the one hand, has stimulated the reuse of urban heritage generating new jobs, on the other hand, has contributed to the gentrification phenomena. In the new "urban renaissance", the theme of adaptive reuse is experimented with in brownfields and abandoned cultural assets. At the same time, culture-driven regeneration strategies are developed [11] through mega cultural and sporting events [12] and the showcase of the "European City/Capital of Culture" [13]. Contextually, new reflections on social innovation and sustainability pave the way for the "impact economy" [14]. In light of the crisis of the welfare state, "social impact investing" [15,16] tries to overcome the clear separation between social and business, giving new ethical value, but also economic, to private philanthropy interested in urban regeneration.

Over time, the evaluation theme represents the thermometer of the strategic directions taken by urban regeneration processes. It is clear that the evaluation of impacts, especially social impacts, is complex because place-based projects have different characteristics and are difficult to standardise; monitoring and evaluation require human and financial resources, while social impacts occur in the long term. In addition, the different objectives of the assessment, the related approaches (monetary, quantitative, qualitative) and the methods chosen (procedural, multi-criteria, synthetic), as well as the nature of the projects, have an impact [15].

The current research aims to reconstruct the scientific landscape on urban regeneration and its impacts through the lens of evaluation. Therefore, the purpose is to capture the assessment's challenges over time and its role within these processes. Starting from a bibliographic survey conducted through the Scopus online database, the scientific landscape was defined through the VOSviewer tool to build and visualise the bibliometric networks related to the identified articles.

The article is organised according to the following sections: the first one describes the methodology elaborated for the literature review and the functional tools for bibliometric analysis; the next section presents the results of the research, including a literature review integrated with the analysis of bibliometric maps of the scientific landscape; finally, the last section offers a discussion of the results and the conclusions.

2 Material and Methods

The scientific landscape has been constructed through the following steps: 1. Data collection; 2. Literature review construction; 3. Bibliometric maps generation.

2.1 Data Collection

The data collection process took place between April and May 2021, using a bibliometric approach from metadata extracted from Scopus, a database for scientific publications created in 2004 by the publisher Elsevier. A search was carried out in the Scopus collection using the keywords urban regeneration and social impact to analyse the documents interested in the implications and the role of evaluation in urban regeneration processes. This generic research has allowed obtaining an interesting number of publications, for a total of 527 documents, to draw an overview of the urban regeneration theme evolution and transversally understand the role of evaluation through impacts and, specifically, social impact. The database was filtered to refine the result obtained and exclude the relevant documents for the literature review. From the 478 papers thus filtered, we proceeded with the selection, one by one, of the most pertinent articles for the topic of study, eliminating all those with inconsistent titles and abstracts. This resulted in a sample of 253 analysed articles: the oldest dated 1987 and the most recent published by June 2021.

2.2 Literature Review Construction

A histogram has been generated to facilitate the literature review. It is characterised by the years of publication (on the ordinates) and by the number of publications (on the abscissas) to understand the trend of publications on the topic of interest during the years (Fig. 1).

The analysis of the articles was carried out following a subdivision into four time frames corresponding broadly to ten years and the most significant changes of pace in the frequency of publications on the subject. In addition, to reconstruct a literary picture, texts that did not directly emerge from this first research are also analysed but were cited within the publications that occurred or were particularly significant to contextualise better the publications collected.

Moreover, the main keywords were analysed to obtain a general overview of the main issues discussed in the scientific debate concerning the single time frames.

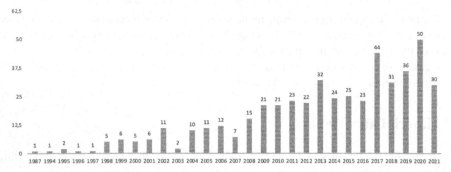

Fig. 1. Histogram of articles published from 1989 to 2021 on the topics of urban regeneration and social impact

2.3 Bibliometric Maps Generation

All 478 papers were exported in CSV format from Scopus with their specific data, including the number of times that the article, author, source, country, and references were cited, in addition to the title, abstract, and keywords. This information was necessary to produce and analyse bibliometric maps to provide opportunities to compare or integrate the literature review conducted.

The maps were generated with VOSviewer version 1.6.16 (0) [17]: software to create maps based on network data and to be able to visualise and explore them. Furthermore, the software manual [18] clarifies how the maps are made up of elements and links: network elements are the objects of interest with which we intend to characterise the maps, i.e. publications, researchers, or terms present within the papers, while relations are the links between two elements, for co-authorship, co-occurrence, citation, bibliographic coupling or co-citation links, represented by a line of variable thickness as the strength of the connection varies. The elements, finally, can be grouped into clusters identifiable by different colours dedicated to them.

The software also offers ways of visualising the maps that emerge: network visuali-sation, i.e., the representation of a map in which the proximity or lack of proximity of the elements expresses the relationship between them and their size expresses their weight; overlay visualisation, in which the variation of default colours indicates the transition from the elements historically less recent, represented by the colour blue, to the most recent ones, identified by the colour yellow; density visualisation, which can be queried to obtain a density map of both elements and clusters.

For the current research, maps of the scientific landscape were generated from bib-liographic data and network data extracted from the Scopus database. In detail, the following analyses were performed through VOSviewer:

1. Co-citation analysis, in which the co-citation connection links two items both cited from the same document. In particular, the links between the cited references were analysed to better investigate the relationships between the references cited within the papers in the database;
2. Network data analysis to build a network of co-occurrence links between terms.

3   Results

This section has been articulated into two main outputs considered complementary for defining the scholarly landscape on the topic at hand: literature review and bibliometric maps.

3.1   Literature Review

The search for scientific literature in Scopus using the keywords "urban regeneration" and "social impact" shows that the number of articles published on the subject has increased, especially in recent years. Most of the publications have the European field of exploration, especially that of the United Kingdom. In general, the articles analysed take on the issue of urban regeneration and its impacts from different points of view: housing as a response to the problems of social exclusion that follows major urban transformations; social regeneration, for a long time, an alternative to urban renewal; the community-based participatory approach to build collaborative decision-making processes; the cultural dimension, superimposed and/or integrated into regenerative strategies, typical of culture-led regeneration. In addition, other authors have approached the issue by analysing the impacts of "major events" and tourism, the mechanisms of public-private and community partnerships and the theme of reuse.

The articles have been divided into four periods: 1987 to 1997, 1998 to 2007, 2008 to 2016, and 2017 to 2021.

The period "1987–1997". The smallest number of articles extracted from the Scopus database was published during this period. Considering that it is between 1998 and 1997, a certain constancy in publications on the subject is acquired. Although the Audit Commission in 1989 [19] encourages an urban regeneration capable of addressing economic and social issues, these are still far from being integrated. In particular, urban dynamics in the post-war reconstruction of cities are studied [20, 21] and the physical and economic impacts of modifying the urban landscape. Part of the scientific debate investigates the evaluation of the environmental implications of these transformations [20] using quantitative indicators [22]. At the same time, the social dimension, aggravated by the de-industrialisation [23], is mainly addressed through housing-oriented programs [20].

"Urban renewal" turns out in these years to be the most shared keyword about the physical transformations taking place in cities. Yet, at the same time, "regeneration" is mainly used in an economic sense, in an era in which effectiveness in implementing public policies counts, and evaluation methodology is a crucial tool to ensure value for money.

The research excludes some publications, cited from those that emerged, that are of particular interest. Thus, for example, between 1994 and 1995, the Centre for Local Economic Strategies (CLES), the Association of Metropolitan Authorities (AMA) and the Commission on Social Justice (CSJ) appeared, emphasising the importance of increasing the involvement of local communities in regeneration processes [24]. In particular, the CSJ takes a radical line by advocating the need for "people-led regeneration" [25] and strategies aimed at building social capital [26] to elicit a social as well as a physical dimension of neighbourhood renewal.

The period "1998–2007". A more significant number of papers are published in the decade ushering in the 21st century. In general, there is growing attention to the quality of life impacts of urban regeneration, with great interest in housing [27, 28]. The social dimension, often mentioned in the "social and economic regeneration" processes [29–31], begins to have a certain weight in urban policies, introducing the concept of "social impact" as a possible consequence of urban transformations and the "new economy" [32], but also, more timidly, capable of generating economic impacts. The European Commission promote various initiatives, from the URBAN project to the MEANS program (Means for Evaluating Actions of a Structural Nature) to measuring the impacts of structural funds in the socio-economic sphere, comparing different evaluation traditions: from the British "value for money" approach to pluralistic Scandinavian models [30]. At the same time, it is significant the publication of the Sustainable Communities Plan [33] and, even earlier, of the New Deal for Communities [34]. For the first time, this one considers mini-good practices capable of generating real impacts through informal, place-based and community-led actions, not only focused on physical regeneration.

Wide attention in these years is also dedicated to the cultural dimension of transformation processes, thanks to some studies that established the theme [35–37] and the many opportunities for reusing brownfield land. While Richard Florida promotes the "creative cities" [38] and Evans and Shaw [1] outline the "culture-led regeneration" approach, different publications try to define the concrete impacts on the territory considering the risks: "…is culture simply a superficial froth that may make people feel better, but has a little tangible impact on the social and economic of places in the twenty-first century? [39].

In this framework appears a "new orthodoxy" towards public/private and local partnerships [40] to facilitate plans implementation and support urban transformation processes. Entrepreneurship and community also find a shared space for reflection within regenerative processes under the umbrella of "Community entrepreneurship" [41]: communities seeking to use the process of entrepreneurship as a force for economic development by providing shared resources and assets.

This result has made it necessary to explore new and increasingly complex ways of measuring, monitoring and evaluating that require indicators other than the quantitative ones usually used, to capture the intangible elements of social and cultural impacts and going beyond the usual economic terms (the growth in the number of tourists, business relocation and inward investment) [13]. Monitoring, in particular, is considered a moment of learning by and for communities [42] whose opinions become necessary to understand the concrete effects of transformation programs [43].

The period "2008–2016". In the years affected by the Great Recession, the scientific debate relates to the effects of an era in which the growth of global cities, also called "urban renaissance" [44] coincided with a rapid economic and urban development, but also with an extreme social polarisation and an alarming growth of inequalities [45]. In this decade, the clear distinction between urban renewal and social regeneration is overcome, trying to integrate into the more shared "urban regeneration" the physical and social dimensions of the impacts, explicitly recognising in the literature the "social impact" [46, 47].

Following international guidelines [48], historic heritage begins to be understood as a common good capable of generating new sustainable processes [49], and its reuse becomes a key factor in improving the quality of life and empower community action and involvement [50]. In particular, "adaptive reuse" emerges as a powerful strategy to manage the changing status of buildings and reduce the environmental, social, and economic costs of the continued expansion of cities [51, 52]. Meanwhile, suppose significant creative activities, cultural and sporting events become part of broader re-branding and place-marketing campaigns of cities [53, 54]. In that case, there is a growing awareness about how culture can intercede in the social and relational dimension fostering the development of social capital in communities [53] in a sustainable perspective.

Similarly, around the issue of sustainability, the language innovates by placing alongside economic and environmental sustainability, "social sustainability" [54] and "sustainable communities" [55], characterised by interaction and participation capable of stimulating multi-dimensional improvements by attracting new investments and opportunities. But, on the other hand, the chance to include communities to improve the process and empowerment of citizens through paths of active citizenship [56] also conceals the risk that participation may become more than symbolism [57, 58].

This context strongly orients the role of evaluation and its approaches since the multitude of variables and actors involved and the "long-term" nature of urban regeneration processes expose the evaluation process to a high degree of uncertainty. Thus, integrated and negotiated decisions are required, and the issue becomes a complex and multi-objective evaluation problem [59]. Furthermore, although it is an emerging concept, traditional evaluation methods integrate with the concepts of happiness, social mixing, social inclusion, community integration, shared values [60, 61] and sense of place, which are definitely less easy to measure [62, 63]. Therefore, new approaches and tools of assessment come into use to better structure decision support environments, such as fuzzy inference systems (FIS) [64], and to measure, among others, social impacts (SIA) [63]. Social Impact Assessment (SIA), specifically, focuses on impacts on people and their daily lives, defining a process during which community involvement and the definition of appropriate sets of criteria and quanti-qualitative indicators become central [65]. In addition, present and future baseline conditions, geographic scale of impacts, cumulative and residual impacts, and impact management during the process are also considered [63]. Thus, adaptive [66] and multi-criteria assessment of socio-economic factors, if previously neglected, becomes the scientific field in which the game is played to overcome the limitations of many of the activated urban regeneration processes.

The period "2017–2021". In the last five years, the most productive from a literary point of view, great emphasis was on the cultural heritage, the chosen for the European year 2018. In an increasingly shared way, cultural heritage is recognised as the "glue" between the different dimensions of sustainable development [55, 67, 68] as capable of improving the economic, social and environmental productivity of the city [69, 70]. For this, Dalmas et al. [71] highlight how the notion of heritage is "inseparable from its multi-dimensional nature" [72], highlighting the need to measure its impacts already previously emerged with the Historic Urban Landscape [73] and the operational tool of the Heritage Impact Assessment [74].

The adaptive reuse of heritage thus becomes a practice of sustainable urban regeneration [75] capable of producing innovation in allowing inhabitants to manage resources as commons [76, 77], through tools that connect local governments with active citizenship and stimulate social innovation in new forms of entrepreneurship. In these collective goods [78], new social enterprises are developed, capable of hybridising profit and non-profit, private and public volunteering by focusing on local communities and facilitating local development [79, 80].

In this sense, urban regeneration is perceived as "interventionist", like a way to mobilise communities to invest in the acquisition of new skills and capabilities [81]. The result is a positive impact both in terms of human capital (access to educational, recreational and cultural activities) and social capital (civic participation; density of horizontal relational networks) [82].

The complexity faced by evaluation in this context is interpreted through various tools, techniques and methods. They include the Community Impact Evaluation (CIE) [83] and the Social Return of the Investment (SROI) [84] to assess social impact and map its change considering social, environmental and economic costs and benefits; and the Multicriteria Decision Analysis (MCDA) [85], or a combination of economic and multi-criteria evaluations. Multicriteria analyses, specifically, allow understanding experts' opinions on how the city should develop [86] by defining in a common framework both quantified and non-quantifiable criteria of project actions, outcomes and impacts [87].

3.2 Bibliometric Maps

3.2.1 Co-Citation Analysis

Co-citation analysis defines the frequency with which pairs of scientific papers were co-cited in the selected articles, thus outlining the intellectual structure of the main issues related to the research field. Specifically, a map was generated in VOSviewer based on bibliographic data extracted from the Scopus database, choosing the "Co-citation" analysis, the "Full Counting" as counting method and the "Cited references" as a unit of analysis. To build the bibliographic map, 3 citations of a cited reference was established as the minimum number, thus obtaining 71 items from the initial 24375 citations. Table 1 shows the 10 items that were cited the most times.

The largest of the most cited articles were published between 2000 and 2005, all concerned with the controversial culture-led regeneration debate. In particular, the most cited paper review by B. Garcìa highlights how the high investments to produce cultural events and related infrastructures were not supported by paths of evaluation of long-term impacts, nor included in broader strategies capable of ensuring a balanced distribution, both spatial and social, of benefits. So, the vagueness of the assessment terms for cultural and social impacts motivates policy-makers to rely on projections based on assessing economic and physical impacts. The result, according to Garcìa, is the creation of "virtually unquestioned 'myths' about the value of hosting the title, which cover up the lack of serious attempts to learn lessons from experience and establish replicable models of successful and, most importantly, sustainable culture-led regeneration" [88]. Regarding the bibliometric map generated (Fig. 2), the connections between the different nodes indicate the presence of co-citations. In contrast, the nodes represent the references

Table 1. Classification of co-cited references

Author	Title	Year	Citation	Total link
B. Garcia	Cultural Policy and Urban Regeneration in Western European Cities: Lessons from Experience, Prospects for the Future	2004	13	41
J. Peck	Struggling with the Creative Class	2005	9	24
S. Miles	The Rise and Rise of Culture-Led Urban Regeneration	2005	7	22
M. Miles	Interruptions: Testing the Rhetoric of Culturally Led Urban Development	2005	5	17
S. Zukin	The Cultures of Cities	1995	5	17
G. Evans	Measure for Measure: Evaluating the Evidence of Culture's Contribution to Regeneration	2005	6	16
B. Garcia	Deconstructing the City of Culture: The Long-Term Cultural Legacies of Glasgow 1990	2005	6	16
A. J. Scott	The cultural economy of cities	2000	6	16
F. Bianchini & M. Parkinson	Cultural policy and urban regeneration: the West-European experience	1993	4	15
R. Paddison	City Marketing, Image Reconstruction and Urban Regeneration	1993	3	15

and their size the number of citations per document. These are divided into 5 clusters represented by 5 different colours.

3.2.2 Network Data Analysis

A network data analysis was generated in VOSviewer to know and visualise the distribution and the relationship between the terms mainly recurring in the analysed articles. The "Overlay" visualisation of this map (Fig. 3) allows us to observe, in addition to the most recurrent terms and their thematic connections, when they were introduced in the debate, thanks to a chromatic gradation that marks the transition from 2010 (blue) to 2018 (yellow).

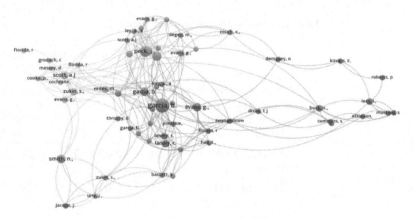

Fig. 2. VOSviewer network visualisation of the cited references bibliometric map

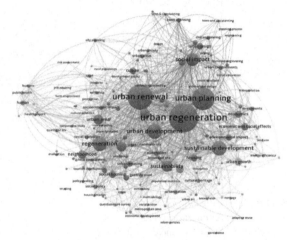

Fig. 3. VOSviewer network visualisation of the network data map's overlay (Color figure online)

In 2010 the terms "social impact", "economic regeneration", and "social exclusion" were already quite widespread. About five years later, the concept of "urban renewal" seems outdated in favour of "urban regeneration". In these years, the literature becomes particularly sensitive to the issue of sustainability, as shown by the sharing of the terms "sustainability" and "sustainable development", but also "quality of life" and "well-being". Between 2016 and 2017, the debate explores the field of "decision making" processes, related to "economic and social effects", but also to the terms "evaluation", "local participation", and "cultural heritage". In yellow colour appear all the terms more shared between 2017 and 2018. The presence in this cluster of "questionnaire survey", along with "methodology" and "assessment method", suggests that the search for qualitative-quantitative evaluation tools and techniques are at the centre of attention in recent years.

4   Discussion and Conclusion

For over thirty years, urban regeneration, with its many forms, has been central to the international and European debate as a practice of transforming cities, capable of affecting their physical and economic development and generating social inequalities and gentrification phenomena. Yet, at the same time, if social objectives were for a long time secondary, consecutive or juxtaposed to the actions of urban regeneration, the social impact has more recently become its motive and engine. This trend reversal is driven by the need to involve communities in decision-making processes and reuse abandoned spaces. The reuse of abandoned cultural heritage, in particular, has generated places of opportunity in which the community can express itself through collaborative processes designed to build social cohesion, produce social innovation and trigger new impact economies.

All of this requires structuring new paradigms. On the one hand, regenerative models' global and replicable perspective has given way to a local place-based, site-specific and community-led vision. On the other hand, identifying new forms of cooperative governance and impact investment has become necessary to generate new value chains. However, although evaluation has played a leading role in the evolution of regenerative strategies, few methodologies can combine multiple approaches to assess social impact with economic, physical and environmental effects. The literature has been enriched with criteria and indicators to accommodate the complexities of the processes and tools. The related impacts evaluation method (SROI, SIA, etc.) has increased and improved in different scientific fields. Nevertheless, these are still difficult to adapt to the singularity of the cases, poorly interconnected and not yet able to assess the creation of value about the processes themselves. Only a smaller strand of literature has been interested in the value of the process, evaluating its ability to build active and sustainable communities and enable them in decision-making processes by developing their capabilities and empowerment. Ultimately, shifting the focus from the outcome of the project evaluation to evaluating the process by which it is implemented.

The reconstruction of the scientific landscape around the fundamental concepts of "urban regeneration" and "social impact", integrating the literature review with analysis of bibliometric maps, aimed to define a general framework to explore the role of evaluation over time grasp the future challenges. From this framework, the research intends to investigate the opportunities of social impact investing about the reuse of abandoned assets as "collective goods" in urban regeneration processes. The intent will be to recognise new hybrid economic models, new forms of social entrepreneurship and new models of social impact measurement.

Author Contributions. Conceptualization, M.C. and L.L.R.; methodology, M.C. and L.L.R.; validation, M.C.; formal analysis, L.L.R.; investigation, L.L.R.; writing—original draft preparation, L.L.R.; writing—review and editing, M.C. and L.L.R.; visualization, L.L.R.; supervision, M.C. All authors have read and agreed to the published version of the manuscript.

References

1. Evans, G., Shaw, P.: The contribution of culture to regeneration in the UK: a review of evidence: a report to the Department for Culture Media and Sport (2004)
2. Santos, F.M.: A positive theory of social entrepreneurship. J. Bus. Ethics **111**(3), 335–351 (2012). https://doi.org/10.1007/S10551-012-1413-4
3. Bartling, B., Weber, R., Yao, L.: -T. Q. J. of and undefined 2015, Do markets erode social responsibility?, *academic.oup.com*, https://doi.org/10.5167/uzh-85623
4. Vanclay, F.: International principles for social impact assessment: their evolution. Impact Assess. Proj. Apprais. **21**(1), 3–4 (2003). https://doi.org/10.3152/147154603781766464
5. Doucet, B.: Global flagships, local impacts. Proc. Inst. Civ. Eng. Des. Plan. **162**(3), 101–107 (2009)
6. Ginsburg, N.: Putting the social into urban regeneration policy. Local Econ. **14**(1), 55–71 (1999)
7. Scott, G., Campbell, J., Brown, U.: The contribution of childcare to local employment: poor work or work for the poor? Local Econ. **16**(3), 187–197 (2001)
8. Lawless, P., Else, P., Farnell, R., Furbey, R., Lund, S., Wishart, B.: Community based initiative and state urban policy: the Church Urban Fund. Reg. Stud. **32**(2), 161–174 (1998)
9. Taylor, M.: Combating the social exclusion of housing estates. Hous. Stud. **13**(6), 819–832 (1998)
10. Rodriguez, A., Martinez, E., Guenaga, G.: Uneven redevelopment: new urban policies and socio-spatial fragmentation in metropolitan Bilbao. Eur. Urban Reg. Stud. **8**(2), 161–178 (2001)
11. Evans, G.: Cultural Planning: An Urban Renaissance? Routledge, London (2002)
12. Carlsen, J., Millan, A.: The links between mega events and urban renewal: the case of the Manchester 2002 Commonwealth Games (2002)
13. Garcia, B.: Deconstructing the city of culture: the long-term cultural legacies of Glasgow 1990. Urban Stud. **42**(5–6), 841–868 (2005)
14. Calderini, M., Chiodo, V., Michelucci, F.V.: The social impact investment race: toward an interpretative framework. Eur. Bus. Rev. **30**(1), 66–81 (2018). https://doi.org/10.1108/EBR-10-2016-0134
15. Coscia, C., Rubino, I.: Fostering New Value Chains and Social Impact-Oriented Strategies in Urban Regeneration Processes: What Challenges for the Evaluation Discipline? In: Bevilacqua, C., Calabrò, F., Della Spina, L. (eds.) NMP 2020. SIST, vol. 178, pp. 983–992. Springer, Cham (2021). https://doi.org/10.1007/978-3-030-48279-4_92
16. Alijani, S., Karyotis, C.: I. B. and Finance, and undefined 2019, Coping with impact investing antagonistic objectives: A multistakeholder approach, Elsevier. Accessed 14 Jul 2021. https://www.sciencedirect.com/science/article/pii/S0275531917306281
17. van Eck, N.J., Waltman, L.: Software survey: VOSviewer, a computer program for bibliometric mapping. Scientometrics **84**(2), 523–538 (2010). https://doi.org/10.1007/s11192-009-0146-3
18. Van Eck, N.J., Waltman, L.: VOSviewer Manual. Univeristeit Leiden, Leiden, Vol. 1, no. 1, pp. 1–53 (2013)
19. Audit Commission for Local Authorities in England: Urban Regeneration and Economic Development: The Local Government Dimension. HM Stationery Office (1989)
20. Ofori, S.C.: Urban policy and environmental regeneration in two Scottish peripheral housing estates. Environmentalist **14**(4), 283–295 (1994)
21. Hubbard, P.: Re-imaging the city: the transformation of Birmingham's urban landscape, *Geography* 26–36 (1996)

22. Skelcher, C., McCabe, A., Lowndes, V., Joseph Rowntree Foundation: Community Networks in Urban Regeneration: 'ItAll Depends Who You Know. Policy Press, United Kingdom, York (1996)
23. Garside, P.L.: The significance of post-war London reconstruction plans for east end industry. Plan. Perspect. 12(1), 19–36 (1997). https://doi.org/10.1080/026654397364762
24. Nevin, B., Shiner, P.: Community regeneration and empowerment: a new approach to partnership. Local Econ. 9(4), 308–322 (1995)
25. Commission on Social Justice: Social Justice: Strategies for National Renewal. Vintage, Report of the Commission on Social Justice. London (1994)
26. Putnam, R.D., Leonardi, R., Nanetti, R.Y.: Making Democracy Work. Princeton University Press (1994)
27. Hoatson, L., Grace, M.: Public housing redevelopment: opportunity for community regeneration? Urban Policy Res. 20(4), 429–441 (2002)
28. Stollberg-Barkley, D.: The impact of socio-economic changes on the housing estate Leipzig-Grunau, Germany. Int. J. Hous. Its Appl. 31(1), 43–54 (2007)
29. Parkin, S.: Sustainable development: the concept and the practical challenge. Proc. Inst. Civil Eng.-Civil Eng. 138(6), 3–8 (2000)
30. McKay, S., Murtagh, B.: Evaluating the social effects of the EU URBAN Community initiative programme. Eur. Plan. Stud. 11(2), 193–211 (2003)
31. Sairinen, R., Kumpulainen, S.: Assessing social impacts in urban waterfront regeneration. Environ. Impact Assess. Rev. 26(1), 120–135 (2006)
32. Hutton, T.A.: The new economy of the inner city. Cities 21(2), 89–108 (2004)
33. Office of the Deputy Prime Minister: Sustainable Communities: Building for the Future. London (2003)
34. SEU: Bringing national strategy for neighbourhood renewal. Social Exclusion Unit, HMSO, London (1998)
35. Scott, A.J.: The Cultural Economy of Cities: Essays on the Geography of Image-Producing Industries. Sage (2000)
36. Byrne, D.: Industrial culture in a post-industrial world: the case of the North East of England. City 6(3), 279–289 (2002)
37. Florida, R.: The Rise of the Creative Class (2004 Paperback ed.) (2002)
38. Florida, R.: Cities and the Creative Class. Routledge, New York (2004)
39. Robson, B.: Culture and the city: a view from the "Athens of the North." Built Environ. 30(3), 246–255 (2004). https://doi.org/10.2148/benv.30.3.246.54298
40. Geddes, M.: Tackling social exclusion in the European Union? The limits to the new orthodoxy of local partnership. Int. J. Urban Reg. Res. 24(4), 782–800 (2000)
41. Haugh, H.M., Pardy, W.: Community entrepreneurship in north east Scotland, Int. J. Entrep. Behav. Res. (1999)
42. Hamdi, N., Goethert, R.: Action Planning for Cities: A Guide to Community Practice. John Wiley & Sons, New York, USA (1997)
43. Taylor, M.: Unleashing the Potential: Bringing Residents to the Centre of Regeneration. Joseph Rowntree Foundation, York (1995)
44. Barber, A., Hall, S.: Birmingham: whose urban renaissance? Regeneration as a response to economic restructuring. Policy Stud. 29(3), 281–292 (2008)
45. Raco, M., Henderson, S.: Flagship regeneration in a global city: the re-making of Paddington Basin. Urban Policy Res. 27(3), 301–314 (2009)
46. Darchen, S., Ladouceur, E.: Social sustainability in urban regeneration practice: a case study of the Fortitude Valley Renewal Plan in Brisbane. Aust. Plan. 50(4), 340–350 (2013). https://doi.org/10.1080/07293682.2013.764909
47. Domšic, L.: Attitudes and perceptions of young local residents about the social impacts of the Špancirfest festival in Varaždin. Informatologia 48(3–4), 185–197 (2015)

48. UNESCO: The UNESCO Recommendation on the Historic Urban Landscape, 2011. http://unesdoc.unesco.org/images/0021/002150/215084e.pdf#page=52. Accessed 20 Jun 2021
49. Council of Europe: Council of Europe Framework Convention on the Value of Cultural Heritage for Society. Faro, Portugal (2005)
50. Bullen, P.A., Love, P.E.D.: Adaptive reuse of heritage buildings. Struct. Surv. **29**, 411–421 (2011)
51. Reed, R.G., Wilkinson, S.J.: The business case for incorporating sustainability in office buildings: the adaptive reuse of existing buildings. In: PRRES 2008: Investing in Sustainable Real Estate Environment: Proceedings of the 14th Annual Conference of the Pacific Rim Real Estate Society, pp. 1–18 (2008)
52. Bullen, P.A., Love, P.E.D.: Residential regeneration and adaptive reuse: learning from the experiences of Los Angeles, Struct. Surv. (2009)
53. Paiola, M.: Cultural events as potential drivers of urban regeneration: an empirical illustration. Ind. Innov. **15**(5), 513–529 (2008)
54. Colantonio, A.: Social sustainability: an exploratory analysis of its definition, assessment methods metrics and tools (2007)
55. UN General Assembly: Transforming our world: The 2030 agenda for sustainable development. https://www.refworld.org/docid/57b6e3e44.html. Accessed 7 Feb 2021
56. Fung, A., Wright, E.O.: Deepening Democracy: Institutional Innovations in Empowered Participatory Governance, vol. 4. Verso (2003)
57. Cleaver, F.: Paradoxes of participation: questioning participatory approaches to development, https://doi.org/10.1002/(SICI)1099-1328(199906)11:4
58. Pollock, V.L., Sharp, J.: Real participation or the tyranny of participatory practice? Public art and community involvement in the regeneration of the Raploch, Scotland. Urban Stud. **49**(14), 3063–3079 (2012). https://doi.org/10.1177/0042098012439112
59. Cerreta, M.: Thinking through complex values. In: Making Strategies in Spatial Planning. Springer, pp. 381–404 (2010)
60. Kenter, J.O., et al.: Shared values and deliberative valuation: future directions. Ecosyst. Serv. **21**, 358–371 (2016). https://doi.org/10.1016/j.ecoser.2016.10.006
61. Cerreta, M., Panaro, S.: From perceived values to shared values: a multi-stakeholder spatial decision analysis (M-SSDA) for resilient landscapes. Sustainability **9**(7), 1113 (2017)
62. Colantonio, A.: Urban social sustainability themes and assessment methods. Proc. Inst. Civ. Eng. Urban Des. Plan. **163**(2), 79–88 (2010). https://doi.org/10.1680/udap.2010.163.2.79
63. Glasson, J., Wood, G.: Urban regeneration and impact assessment for social sustainability. Impact Assess. Proj. Apprais. **27**(4), 283–290 (2009)
64. Yusuf, S.A., Georgakis, P., Nwagboso, C.: Fuzzy logic based built environment impact assessment for urban regeneration simulation. In: 2009 Second International Conference in Visualisation, pp. 90–95 (2009)
65. Ferilli, G., Sacco, P.L., Tavano Blessi, G.: Cities as creative hubs: From instrumental to functional values of culture-led local development, Sustain. City Creat. Farnham Ashgate, 245–270 (2012)
66. Boston, J.: The challenge of evaluating systemic change: the case of public management reform. Int. public Manag. J. **3**(1), 23–46 (2000)
67. United Nations: Draft Outcome Document of the United Nations Conference on Housing and Sustainable Urban Development (Habitat III), New York, USA (2016)
68. Srakar, A., Vecco, M.: Culture as a Fourth Dimension of Sustainable Development? A Statistical Analysis (2016)
69. Fusco Girard, L.: Toward a smart sustainable development of port cities/areas: the role of the 'historic urban landscape' approach, Sustain **5**(10), pp. 4329–4348 (2013), https://doi.org/10.3390/SU5104329

70. Nocca, F., Fusco Girard, L.: Towards an integrated evaluation approach for cultural urban landscape conservation/regeneration, Region **5**(1), 33–51 (2018)
71. Dalmas, L., Geronimi, V., Noël, J.-F., Sang, J.T.K.: Economic evaluation of urban heritage: an inclusive approach under a sustainability perspective. J. Cult. Herit. **16**(5), 681–687 (2015). https://doi.org/10.1016/j.culher.2015.01.009
72. Cerreta, M., Poli, G., Regalbuto, S., Mazzarella, C.: A Multi-dimensional Decision-Making Process for Regenerative Landscapes: A New Harbour for Naples (Italy). In: Misra, S., et al. (eds.) ICCSA 2019. LNCS, vol. 11622, pp. 156–170. Springer, Cham (2019). https://doi.org/10.1007/978-3-030-24305-0_13
73. Cerreta, M., De Toro, P.: A multi-dimensional evaluation model for the historic urban landscape (HUL). In: ICOMOS International Conference Heritage and Landscape as Human Values. Conference Proceedings. Florence (Italy), pp. 302–306 (2014)
74. ICOMOS: Guidance on Heritage Impact Assessments for Cultural World Heritage properties, Paris (2011)
75. Cerreta, M., Elefante, A., La Rocca, L.: A creative living lab for the adaptive reuse of the Morticelli Church: the SSMOLL project. Sustainability **12**(24), 10561 (2020). https://doi.org/10.3390/su122410561
76. Ostrom, E.: Governing the commons: the evolution of institutions for collective action, Resour. J. **32** (1990). https://books.google.it/books?hl=it&lr=&id=4xg6oUobMz4C&oi=fnd&pg=PR11&dq=elinor+ostrom&ots=aP5uBGlIWj&sig=T9o2yvZRGdgcuqoKZwmal AEfPYw. Accessed 18 Jul 2021
77. Mangialardo, A., Micelli, E.: Social capital and public policies for commons: bottom-up processes in public real estate property valorisation. Elsevier **223**, 175–180 (2016). https://doi.org/10.1016/j.sbspro.2016.05.343
78. Putnam, R.D., Cartocci, R.: Capitale sociale e individualismo: crisi e rinascita della cultura civica in America. il Mulino (2004)
79. Roberts, D., Woods, C.: Changing the World on a Shoestring: The Concept of Social Entrepreneurship," Univ. Auckl. Bus. Rev. **7**(1), 45–51 (2005). https://www.researchgate.net/publication/242320433_Changing_the_World_on_a_Shoestring_The_Concept_of_Social_Entrepreneurship. Accessed 18 Jul 2021
80. Venturi, P., Zandonai, F.: Imprese ibride: Modelli d'innovazione sociale per rigenerare valori. EGEA spa (2016)
81. Duarte Alonso, A., Kok, S. K., O'Brien, S., O'Shea, M.: The significance of grassroots and inclusive innovation in harnessing social entrepreneurship and urban regeneration, Eur. Bus. Rev. **32**(4), 667–686 (2020), https://doi.org/10.1108/EBR-05-2019-0102
82. Ferilli, G., Sacco, P.L., Tavano Blessi, G., Forbici, S.: Power to the people: when culture works as a social catalyst in urban regeneration processes (and when it does not). Eur. Plan. Stud. **25**(2), 241–258 (2017)
83. Lichfield, N.: Community impact evaluation: principles and practice (2005). https://books.google.com/books?hl=it&lr=&id=mfaNAgAAQBAJ&oi=fnd&pg=PP1&ots=9nJvqxP7-O&sig=zR3VAhhQAQd4mt8oXmmcu4amfYg. Accessed 18 Jul 2021
84. de Jonge, G., Sprij, A.: 10. In: 36 zieke kinderen, pp. 39–42. Bohn Stafleu van Loghum, Houten (2012). https://doi.org/10.1007/978-90-313-8424-2_10
85. Figueira, J., Greco, S., Ehrgott, M.: Multiple criteria decision analysis: state of the art surveys (2005). https://books.google.com/books?hl=it&lr=&id=YqmvlTiMNqYC&oi=fnd&pg=PR13&dq=Figueira,+J.,+Greco,+S.,+%26+Ehrgott,+M.+(2005).+Multiple+criteria+decision+analysis:+State+of+the+art+surveys.+Boston,+Dordrecht,+London:+Springer+Verlag.&ots=34EX15mb1p&sig=77kCs. Accessed 18 Jul 2021
86. Bielinskas, V., Burinskienė, M., Podviezko, A.: Choice of abandoned territories conversion scenario according to MCDA methods. J. Civ. Eng. Manag. **24**(1), 79–92 (2018). https://doi.org/10.3846/JCEM.2018.303

87. Lee, J.: Spatial ethics as an evaluation tool for the long-term impacts of mega urban projects: an application of spatial ethics multi-criteria assessment to canning town regeneration projects, London. Int. J. Sustain. Dev. Plan. **13**(4), 541–555 (2018). https://doi.org/10.2495/SDP-V13-N4-541-555

88. García, B.: Cultural policy and urban regeneration in western European cities: lessons from experience, prospects for the future. Local Econ. **19**(4), 312–326 (2004). https://doi.org/10.1080/0269094042000286828

Using Artificial Neural Networks to Uncover Real Estate Market Transparency: The Market Value

Laura Gabrielli$^{(\boxtimes)}$ ⓘ, Aurora Greta Ruggeri ⓘ, and Massimiliano Scarpa ⓘ

University IUAV of Venice, Dorsoduro 2206, 30123 Venice, Italy
`laura.gabrielli@iuav.it`

Abstract. In real estate property valuation, the availability of **comparables** is crucial. The reliability of the valuation of the **market value** depends on the number and on the accuracy of data that a professional can rely on. International standards suggest using historical prices as comparable since they are real transactions of sale/rent of a property that actually happened in a specific market. However, in the Italian real estate market, historical transaction prices are not available for professionals, and they have to base their valuations, primarily, on the **asking prices** enclosed in the **selling advertisements**. Asking prices can change in the future as they are subject to negotiation. Besides, sell ads always contain incomplete data or even wrong information. In this research, we employ Artificial Neural Networks to estimate how much offer prices and selling advertisements are misleading in property valuation in Italy. We, in a way, assess the opacity of the Italian real estate market, and we designate the major sources of error. The present work is a first step towards developing a model fitted for estimating data accuracy used generally in real estate estimates, namely, asking prices.

Keywords: Market value · Asking prices · Market transparency · Artificial neural networks

1 Introduction and Background

1.1 Comparison

Real estate valuation methods are based on comparison [1]. Comparison is one of the Italian five valuation principles, and it covers all the estimation approaches recognised by international standards [2]. Comparison, nonetheless, is the principal method sustaining the Market Approach aimed at identifying the market value of a property. Therefore, the only basis for estimating market value is a comparison between the property being valued and other similar properties with known price, cost, or income [3]. As far as the real estate market is concerned, the term "comparable" is often used in every language, both colloquially and within professional standards, in order to restrictively refer to a property, which is located in the same area and which is at similar maintenance level than the subject of the valuation, and whose sale/rental transaction has taken place recently [4].

© Springer Nature Switzerland AG 2021
O. Gervasi et al. (Eds.): ICCSA 2021, LNCS 12954, pp. 183–192, 2021.
https://doi.org/10.1007/978-3-030-86979-3_14

However, a comparable is not only the evidence of a transaction that has taken place in the past but rather any data that real estate professionals employ to formulate an appraisal judgement. Therefore, comparable can refer to historical transactions and asking prices, surveys, market quotations or land registry data, and evaluations made by other professionals. Not all these data provide the same level of information, and their reliability may strongly vary depending on the data source. In this context, a recent report by TEGOVA [5] aims to identify the role of comparables (and therefore their availability) in the quality of property valuation.

1.2 Market Transparency

Market transparency is a concept that belongs to the scientific literature and the theory of real estate valuation about the quality and the reliability of available data sources in a given market [6–11]. A very transparent market would ensure access to all the necessary comparables to be used in a property valuation. Instead, such data is either not available in an opaque market, not it can be purchased with high expenditures, and professionals must therefore refer to other sources of information [12]. A professional who is operating in an opaque market is, in a way, obliged to rely on information that another professional operating in a transparent market would classify as inadequate quality information. This does not depend on the expertise of the professional himself but rather on the natural constraints and limitations of the market in which the properties are valued [13].

The very same kind of data source that is judged as unsuitable for valuations purposes in a transparent market can be used appropriately in valuations, feasibility assessments or real estate market analyses in an opaque market. Each market is confronted with its data availability, and professionals rely on different data sources depending on the market in which they operate.

1.3 The Italian Real Estate Market

Market transparency is a huge problem in the Italian real estate market. Researchers struggle to collect data to build a large, statistically robust, transparent database. In the Italian real estate market, transactions data about sales/rent of properties are rarely available for professionals. So they must rely mainly on the asking prices included in the selling advertisements. Besides, real estate ads lack information. They are very inaccurate and, usually, they also contain inaccurate data, such as, to name a few, wrong localization, untrue energy class or false maintenance conditions. This may cause significant problems when developing forecasting models to predict the market value as a function of its building and neighborhood characteristics. They rely on data that contain themselves wrong information. However, the development of market value assessment tools is one of the major objectives in real estate appraisal and valuation. Reliable forecasting models should be created for this purpose. Accurate databases should consequently be produced and constantly updated. Several factors influence the market value of a property, and the contribution of each of them should also be precisely taken into account during the market value estimation.

1.4 Aim of the Research

This paper aims to investigate the transparency of offer prices data in the Italian real estate market. The aim is to investigate if the lack of knowledge of the historic transaction price is the only problem or whether the use of offer prices leads to other issues that increase the opacity of these data and the property valuations.

We carried out this study to estimate the error produced over the market value valuation when relying on offer prices only. Besides, we also pointed out the significant sources of error, identifying which variables influence the market value the most while containing misinformation or incorrect data.

2 Method

In the first step of this research, we have developed automated crawling software to automatically download the offer prices and the corresponding characteristics of a set of real estate properties on sale from specific selling websites.

We have defined the web search domain and let the web crawler download the required information from the online sell advertisements. This process allowed us to collect thousands of information about the offer prices and the characteristics of the properties in the chosen real estate market.

This process has led to limited knowledge of the given market since it is based only on selling ads. As stated in Sect. 1.3, the use of selling ads hides many other problems besides the intrinsic inaccuracy of the offer price. Selling ads contain, in fact, wrong information, incomplete data and even false statements.

In order to verify how much this inaccuracy influences the correct estimation of the market value, we collected, in a second step, a smaller number of samples of properties on sale exact in the same market but, this time, manually. "Manually collected data" means collecting data one by one and checking the level of maintenance and their precise location via Google Street View, or Earth, where this was possible. Therefore, we verified the correctness of all the collected information, such as the localisation of the premise or its maintenance conditions. Furthermore, we excluded from the database all the samples whose data could not be verified, and we corrected the wrong information declared in the ads.

Afterwards, we developed an Artificial Neural Network (ANN) based on the database collected by the automatic crawler. The ANN is an algorithm that, in this case, can predict the market value of a building as a function of some chosen building characteristics. The input neurons of the network contain the descriptive data of the premises, while the output neuron is the forecasted offer price.

We then used the same ANN to predict the market value of the database collected manually: the building's correct characteristics collected manually constituted the input neurons, while the output neurons were the "forecasted market values". We compared the "forecasted marked values" to the "expected market values", where the "expected market values" were the prices manually collected.

Comparing a forecast value against its expected value gives a measure of the error produced by the inaccuracy contained in advertisements online. Besides, we could determine which information was having the highest error on the forecast, identifying the significant sources of error due to "opacity" in the Italian real estate market.

3 Creating the Web Crawler

First, we defined the selection criteria to identify a web searching domain. We limited the online search to residential properties on sale (not rent) in Padua. As far as the localisation is concerned, we considered all the fourteen areas the Municipality of Padua is divided into.

We included both new constructions and existing buildings for the building typology, comprising apartments, townhouses, detached and semi-detached houses, lofts and penthouses. This online search has led to 4,167 sale adverts. We have considered the most popular and acknowledged property selling websites in Italy, which we do not specify for privacy reasons.

In order to extract the necessary information with the web crawler from each sale advertisement, it was essential to know their corresponding web address. In fact, each one of the 4,167 results could have been identified through its Uniform Resource Locator (URL) in the form of an "https://..." web address.

All the sale adverts listed on the search-result page have an URL given from the combination of the URL of the search-result page and the serial adverts number.

For this reason, the web crawler we have developed in Python is able to read the URL of the search-result page, which is written in HTML language, extract all the serial numbers of the announces, and consequently build the URL of each data.

Afterwards, we implemented in Python the library "*Beautiful Soup*" to read the HTML pages of every sale advertisement. Beautiful Soup is a Python package explicitly used to parse HTML documents developed by Leonard Richardson. Since it creates a parse tree for all the parsed pages, this library can easily be used to extract data from HTML texts.

After, we have defined a class of objects and functions that produce the set of information extracted from each advertisement. The class is illustrated in Table 1.

Table 1. The class of objects and functions

Class Element	Units	Class Element	Units	Class Element	Units	Class Element	Units
Web URL	text	Construction year	number	Private garden area	sqm	Central heating	yes/no
Id	number	Status	text	Common garden	yes/no	Air Conditioning	yes/no
Zone	text	n. bathrooms	number	Garage	yes/no	Optical Fiber	yes/no
Address	text	n. rooms	number	Garage area	sqm	Building automation	yes/no
Latitude	coordinate	n. floor	number	Car box	yes/no	Photovoltaics	yes/no
Longitude	coordinate	n. of internal floors	number	Car box area	sqm	Solar panels	yes/no
Typology	text	Penthouse	yes/no	Cellar	yes/no	MCV	yes/no
Price	€	Lift	yes/no	Cellar area	sqm	Heat Pump	yes/no
Floor area	sqm	Energy Class	A/B/C/D/E/F/G	Terrace	yes/no	Alarm	yes/no
Price/sqm	€/sqm	Private Garden	yes/no	Terrace area	sqm	Fireplace	yes/no

Finally, we have applied in Python the data analysis library "Pandas" (developed by Wes McKinney) to extract a.xls file from the web crawling and organize data in the form of a table. Each row of the table represents an advertisement, while the columns show the class elements (i.e. property information).

4   Developing a Neural Network

We suggest employing Artificial Neural Networks to elaborate a forecasting tool to predict the market value of a property as a function of its intrinsic and extrinsic characteristics. Neural networks can be considered a computational system that acts out like human brains during learning biological processes. ANNs are basically constituted of artificial neurons, the computational units, and artificial synapsis, the connections between neurons.

ANNs are organized into multiple separated layers of neurons. The input layer contains the input neurons, while the output layer contains the output neurons. Between the input and the output layers, there is (are) one (or more) hidden layer(s). In this study, the input neurons are the intrinsic and extrinsic characteristics of the properties, whereas the output neuron is its corresponding market value.

The set of input neurons is represented as a column vector named [Xr], where $1 \leq r \leq R$, and the set of output neurons can be seen as a column vector called [Yp_forecast], in which $1 \leq p \leq P$. Yp_forecast is a function of vector Xr, so that [Yp_forecast] = f([Xr]).

4.1   Training of the Network

Through the training process, ANNs are able to "learn" how input neurons are related to their corresponding outputs.

Neural networks, in fact, analyse any input-output database and iteratively assess the free parameters of the network, i.e. the weighs (w) and the biases (b), until the best forecasting model is defined.

In order to understand this process, it is necessary to understand how information flow at the single-neuron level. Each zth neuron receives one or more numerical inputs named $x_{z,u}$, $1 \leq u \leq U$, in which U is the total number of inputs/connections entering the zth neuron. The information is combined inside the neuron, and a numerical output is consequently produced. Information is combined through the weight function ($w_{z,u}$) and the bias function (b_z), giving the output Y_z. Specifically, an activation function (φ_z) converts the neuron value into a response value as in Eq. 1:

$$\forall \text{ zth neuron, } Y_z = \varphi z \left(\sum_{u=1}^{U} [(w_{z,u} * x_{z,u}) + b_z] \right) \tag{1}$$

During the training process, the weights ($w_{z,u}$) and biases (b_z) of the network are varied until the most reliable forecast is achieved so that vector Yp_forecast becomes the closest as possible to vector Yp_expected. In other words, weights and biases are iteratively adjusted with the aim of minimizing the error signal (err$_p$). The error could be assessed as follow:

$$err_p = Y_{p\_expected} - Y_{p\_forecast}. \tag{2}$$

In Eq. 2 err$_p$ is the error, Yp_expected is the target value, while Yp_forecast is the forecast value.

The total error on the forecasts is represented by a cost function as a way to estimate how wrong the forecasts are in comparison to the expected values contained in the dataset. For this reason, training the network means minimizing the cost function.

4.2   ANN as a Forecasting Tool

The database obtained through the web crawling was made of 4167 instances. However, this number had to be decreased by the 31.15% before training the ANN since we had to exclude the incomplete advertisements. In Table 2 we represent the percentage of incomplete announces per each class element.

Table 2. Percentage of incomplete announces per each class elements

Class Element	%	Class Element	%
Latitude	0.52%	Status	4.92%
Longitude	0.52%	n. bathrooms	3.39%
Price	3.15%	n. rooms	3.12%
Floor area	5.88%	Lift	0.15%
Price/sqm	8.56%	Energy Class	16.58%
Construction year	31.68%		

The number of training instances had to be further decreased down to 2,840 to eliminate the unlikely values from the dataset. At this stage, in fact, we could already exclude those advertisements that contained obvious outliers (such as 0 € as selling price, or 0 sqm as floor area). Besides, we had to exclude the construction year as a variable from the database since too much data were missing.

In Table 3, the progressive number of excluded outliers present in the corresponding number of advertisement is represented.

Table 3. Number of errors and outliers per number of respective ads.

N. ads	Errors and outliers per number of respective ads
2840	0
733	1
362	2
93	3
27	4
8	5
3	6
0	7

We could now define the training set to train the network by randomly selecting 60% of these 2,840 instances. Another 20% of the instances is randomly taken to define the selection set, and the remaining 20% forms the testing set. The training set is used to build several NN models. These different models are afterwards applied to the selection instances so that the one model that performs best on the selection set is chosen and then tested on the testing instances.

As a result, the ANN trained is based on the collected database shows 6 layers: 1 input layer, 4 hidden layers, 1 output layer. The input layer has 37 input neurons, while the output layer shows only 1 output neuron, i.e. the forecasted market value of the property (€/sqm), which is shown in Table 4. Conversely, the hidden layers present 32 hidden neurons each. The activation function employed is the hyperbolic tangent. The mean squared error function is the training strategy chosen, while the data scaling and unscaling process are based on a mean standard deviation scalarization.

4.3 Testing the Neural Network

The second database we collected manually to test the reliability of the ANN is constituted of 1,065 instances.

Again, we defined the same selection criteria to identify the web searching domain. The online search was limited to residential properties on sale in Padua. We decided to focus on the areas of Duomo, Forcellini, Santa Rita, Prato della Valle, Sacro Cuore, and Chiesanuova. Due to the higher availability of data, it was easier to check the correctness of the information contained in the advertisements. Moreover, those areas represent the Centre (Duomo and Prato della Valle), Semi-centre (Santa Rita and Forcellini), suburbs (Sacro Cuore, Chiesanuova).

As far as the building typology is concerned, we have included detached and semi-detached houses, apartments, townhouses, lofts and penthouses.

However, this time we did not simply transcribe the available data online. Instead, we verified the correctness of all the information. We excluded from the database those properties whose information could not have been verified. We added data when it was

Table 4. ANN input variables and output (target) variable.

n.	Variable	Use	n.	Variable	Use
1	Latitude	Input	20	AirConditioning	Input
2	Longitude	Input	21	OpticalFiber	Input
3	Floor_Area	Input	22	Fireplace	Input
4	Type_Villa unifamiliare	Input	23	Type_Apartment	Input
5	ns_Bathroom	Input	24	Type_Apartment in villa	Input
6	ns_Room	Input	25	Type_Attic	Input
7	Penthouse	Input	26	Type_Farm house	Input
8	Lift	Input	27	Type_Hamlet	Input
9	Energy_Classification	Input	28	Type_Loft	Input
10	Status	Input	29	Type_Portion of attic	Input
11	Garden_Private	Input	30	Type_Unfinished building	Input
12	Garage	Input	31	Type_Building	Input
13	ParkingSpace	Input	32	Type_Building for single family	Input
14	Cellar	Input	33	Type_Office	Input
15	Terrace	Input	34	Type_Single house	Input
16	BuildingAutomation	Input	35	Type_Terraced house	Input
17	CentralHeating	Input	36	Type_Semi-detached house	Input
18	Photovoltaics	Input	37	Type_Multifamily villa	Input
19	MCV	Input	38	Value_m2	Target

possible to find more specific details. For sure, this way of collecting data turned out to be a very long and time-consuming process. Nevertheless, still, it was the only way to produce a sort of litmus test to check the market transparency and the data correctness and the availability of information.

5 Results, Discussion and Conclusion

The ANN developed is now employed on the database collected manually so that the correct characteristics of the properties constitute the input neurons. In contrast, the output neuron forecasts the corresponding marked value. We, therefore, name this prediction as "forecasted market value". Conversely, the "expected market value" is the real asking prices we had collected manually.

Let's compare the "expected market value" against the "forecasted market value". It is possible to notice an average of 32.96% error in the forecasts (43.93% as the maximum error, 10.99% as the minimum error). These errors are enormous, and the problem mainly stands in the wrong information contained in the sell advertisements.

Finally, it is possible to determine which parameter is producing the highest impact on the forecast by analysing the correlation chart of the ANN, which is shown in Fig. 1.

This means that if a piece of wrong information in the ads regards the most impactful data (such as the status or the energy class), a considerable error will be made in the market value forecast.

In conclusion, it is possible to state that using artificial neural networks in combination with a web crawler helped estimate the level of opacity of the Italian real estate

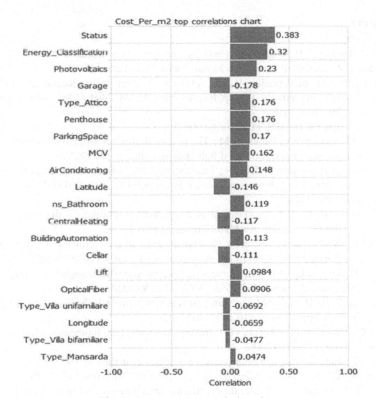

Fig. 1. Input-output correlation chart

market. Among the most significant achievements of this research, the automated web crawler made it possible to rapidly collect a huge amount of data and have a complete overview of all the properties on sale in Padua. Moreover, it is easy to perform this very same kind of analysis on other markets because the web crawler can be immediately applied to different contexts.

The major limitation of this approach is that it is based on offer prices and not on historical transactions. Clearly, the reason is that this is one of the primary sources of opacity in the Italian real estate market, however, as a further development of this research, the authors would like to compare offer prices results against historical transactions to analyse this other significant source of error in market value assessments.

For sure, the authors suggest that selling ads would become more rigorous in the displacement of information, in the correctness of the illustrated data and completeness. Some predefined layout should be slavishly followed by the sellers when composing advertisements, at least to provide complete and accurate information of the property on sale (which would also help potential buyers).

References

1. Forte, C., De Rossi, B.: Principi di economia ed estimo, Etas, Milan (1974)
2. Simonotti, M.: Metodi di stima immobiliare, Dario Flac, Palermo (2006)
3. Pagourtzi, E., Assimakopoulos, V., Hatzichristos, T., French, N.: Real estate appraisal: a review of valuation methods. J. Prop. Invest Finan. **21**, 383–401 (2003). https://doi.org/10.1108/14635780310483656
4. Orefice, M.: Estimo civile. UTET, Torino (1995)
5. Loberto, M., Luciani, A., Pangallo, M.: The potential of big housing data: an application to the Italian real-estate market. Banca d'Italia Eurosistema, p. 117 (2018)
6. Eichholtz, P.M.A., Gugler, N., Kok, N.: Transparency, integration, and the cost of international real estate investments. J. Real Estate Finan. Econ. **43**, 152–173 (2011). https://doi.org/10.1007/s11146-010-9244-5
7. Luo, Y., Chau, K.W.: The impact of real estate market transparency on the linkages between indirect and direct real estate. An MPhil Thesis 27 (2013)
8. Schulte, K.-W., Rottke, N., Pitschke, C.: Transparency in the German real estate market. J. Prop. Invest Finan. **23**, 90–108 (2005). https://doi.org/10.1108/14635780510575111
9. Cellmer, R., Trojanek, R.: Towards increasing residential market transparency: mapping local housing prices and dynamics. ISPRS Int. J. Geo-Inf. **9** (2020)
10. Bloomfield, R., O'Hara, M.: Market transparency: who wins and who loses? Rev. Finan. Stud. **12**, 5–35 (1999). https://doi.org/10.1093/rfs/12.1.5
11. Seidel, C.: Valuation of real estates in Germany. Methods, Development and Current Aspects of Research, pp. 213–220 (2006)
12. Newell, G.: The changing real estate market transparency in the European real estate markets. J. Prop. Invest Finan. **34**, 407–420 (2016). https://doi.org/10.1108/JPIF-07-2015-0053
13. Sadayuki, T., Harano, K., Yamazaki, F.: Market transparency and international real estate investment. J. Prop. Invest Finan. **37**, 503–518 (2019). https://doi.org/10.1108/JPIF-04-2019-0043

Creative Ecosystem Services: Valuing Benefits of Innovative Cultural Networks

Giuliano Poli[1]($\boxtimes$) and Gaia Daldanise[2]

[1] Department of Architecture, University of Naples Federico II, via Toledo 402, Naples, Italy
giuliano.poli@unina.com

[2] Institute of Research on Innovation and Services for Development (IRISS), National Research Council of Italy (CNR), Naples, Italy
g.daldanise@iriss.cnr.it

Abstract. The Ecosystem Services provided by food encompass a vast amount of material and immaterial benefits to human beings and shared values linked to creativity, self-fulfilment, recreation, sociality, culture, and mutual learning, which are at the basis of a modern and eco-instructed community. In Italy, agri-food no-profit sector or small-medium enterprises can empower a community to cope with resource depletion, waste production, biodiversity loss, and climate change by sparking sustainable urban and rural practices preserving the current ecosystem services and generating new ones. Within the ecological economics, the integrated assessments' contribution becomes relevant when the potentials of sustainable agri-food practices and values – which local communities assign to the related Ecosystem Services – have to be estimated to better inform Decision Makers in empowering policy and planning fostering maintenance and regulation of these services in rural and urban contexts. The contribution's purpose was to propose a methodological approach for assessing creative ecosystem services within an agri-food cultural value chain with the Fuzzy Analytic Hierarchy Process (F-AHP) multi-criteria method. The overall results have allowed obtaining a global ranking of the preferable scenarios linked to a Cultural Creative Enterprise (CCE) located in Foggia, Apulia (Italy). The research follow-up addresses the co-creation of creative ecosystem services in synergy with local stakeholders and beneficiaries, generating new job opportunities, awareness and innovation through an advanced form of shared responsibility.

Keywords: Ecosystem services · Creativity · Integrated evaluation · F-AHP

1 Introduction

The United Nations' Millennium Ecosystem Assessment (MA) framework [1] adopted the Ecosystem Services (ES) paradigm, which has emerged as a systematic methodology to define and categorize the relationship between ecosystems and society [2], and it is generally accepted within the international environmental science, policy communities [3] and academia [4]. Despite Cultural Ecosystem Services (CES) – as "the non-material benefits people derive from ecosystems through spiritual enrichment, cognitive growth,

© Springer Nature Switzerland AG 2021
O. Gervasi et al. (Eds.): ICCSA 2021, LNCS 12954, pp. 193–209, 2021.
https://doi.org/10.1007/978-3-030-86979-3_15

reflection, leisure, and aesthetic experience" [5] – have been recognised as crucial, they are not yet totally integrated into the MA's ES framework considering the difficulty of non-material services to be assessed.

As a specification of the MA definition, the Economics of Ecosystem and Biodiversity (TEEB) has defined ES as "the direct and indirect contributions of ecosystems to human well-being regenerating human, social, produced, and natural capitals" [6].

The initiative established by the European Environment Agency to create a Common International Classification of Ecosystem Services (CICES) has undertaken several consultation exercises to develop a more standard approach to describing ecosystem services (http://cices.eu). The 2012 revision work on CICES highlighted that cultural services encompass all non-material and typically non-consumptive outputs of ecosystems that affect people's physical and mental well-being [7].

Implementing the four ES capital stocks aids to investigate an agri-food cultural value chain in terms of material/immaterial flows, ranging from production to processing, distribution, consumption, and assessment. Therefore, linking the creative capital [8] to capital stocks means continuously innovating resources, expertise, knowledge and co-evaluating immaterial values using qualitative and quantitative indicators [9]. Indeed, the creative capital can be defined as an innovation catalyst in which Technology, Talent, and Tolerance (3T) [10] become critical issues for assessing significant impacts on local productivity and attractiveness.

Cultural Creative Enterprises (CCEs) emphasize talents and convergent interests of individuals, private organizations, and public institutions to turn them into original goods and services, sparking a synergic and symbiotic partnership between society, industry, and landscape [11]. Meanwhile, CCEs' creativity, quality, and innovation are crucial for the sustainable competitive advantage of urban-rural systems [12] and generate a new value chain of resources in which tangible and intangible assets join shared values [13].

Some authors have identified multidimensional evaluation models recognising the need to use multi-criteria decision analysis (MCDA) for monitoring local regeneration practices by engaging multiple Stakeholders, weighting site-specific criteria, and choosing best-fit scenarios [14–20].

Despite its popularity and ease of use, the Analytic Hierarchy Process (AHP) is frequently chastised for its failure to deal with the uncertainty of a decision maker's preferences. The judgments in traditional AHP are expressed by exact values on a scale of 1–9 [21]. However, in many real-world circumstances, linguistic assessments of human judgments are often ambiguous, and representing them with precise values is unrealistic. Fuzzy AHP (F-AHP) was created to address these shortcomings accounting for uncertainty and imprecision. It is essentially a hybrid of two techniques: fuzzy set theory and AHP [22].

This contribution constitutes a proof of concept addressed to perform a preliminary framework using creative ecosystem services to evaluate an agri-food cultural value chain. It aims to expand an approach previously tested by the authors [23] to study the benefits of co-creation in terms of cultural networks and social innovation on sustainable development at a local scale.

2   Materials and Methods

The research's purpose was to propose a methodological approach for assessing creative ecosystem services within an agri-food cultural value chain. The adopted case study focuses on a CCE promoting social innovation in agri-food products and co-creation activities and providing different material and immaterial services, i.e. performing arts, networking events, storytelling, food professional consultancy, theatre school, communication, and local agri-food products promotion, packaging design.

The selected CCE – denominated *Vàzapp'* – is in Foggia, Apulia (Italy) (http://www.vazapp.it/). It constitutes an excellent case study for identifying, eliciting and assessing material and immaterial ES and their beneficiaries, which is one of the objectives the authors address to target. *Vàzapp'* provides services and events that promote the exchange of skills and information, as well as the sharing of ideas and problems related to agri-food activities, among local supply chain actors [24].

The proposed model, revised from Cerreta et al. (2020) [23], identifies the agri-food cultural value chain linked to this CCE and includes (Fig. 1):

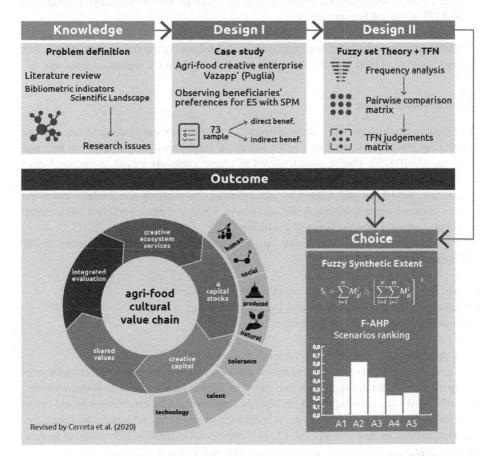

Fig. 1. The methodological workflow for assessing an agri-food value chain

- Creative ecosystem services based on innovative ecosystem solutions;
- Four capital stocks for socio-cultural ES in terms of human, social, produced, and natural benefits;
- Creative capital identified as the fifth capital stock and characterised by 3 T (tolerance, talent, and technology);
- Shared values resulting from the co-creation process generated by the creative capital;
- Integrated assessment approaches for co-evaluating creative ecosystem services.

As shown in Fig. 1, the methodology in four steps addressed to:

1. Explore the scientific literature linking natural, social, and cultural ecosystems in order to highlight primary issues and research pathways (Knowledge phase);
2. Assess direct and indirect users' preferences through a non-monetary Stated Preference Method (SPM) (Design phase I);
3. Aggregate the survey results using Triangular Fuzzy Numbers (TFN) and the fuzzy set theory (Design phase II);
4. Score creative ecosystem services criteria and rank preferable scenarios through the F-AHP (Choice/Outcome phase).

The four steps and related outcome – structured following the framework of Decision Support Systems (DSS) [25, 26] – are described in-depth in the following sections.

2.1 Knowledge Phase

The research issues have been derived from a literature review structured through the quantitative bibliometric approach of the scientific landscapes provided by van Eck and Waltman (2010) [27]. This approach allows to graph a network based on the number of keywords co-occurrences in the articles' title and abstracts within scientific databases. In our case, keywords and related logical operators to perform the analysis from the Scopus database were: (cultural AND ecosystem AND services) AND (art OR culture) AND (assessment OR valuation OR evaluation).

The analysis has allowed three strongly interrelated thematic clusters to be highlighted (Fig. 2):

- Cluster 1: Ecosystems, Culture, and Creative Ecosystems;
- Cluster 2: Ecosystem Services and Decision Making;
- Cluster 3: Ecosystems and Sustainability

A description of critical issues for each cluster follows.

Cluster 1 highlights that CES in urban settings foster more equitable communities by creating or maintaining spaces that provide immaterial services to human beings. However, to do so, consistent and reliable indicators must be established based on an epistemic knowledge of urban contexts for which there are no references and data frequently [28]. According to Rall et al. (2017) [29], social-oriented CES related to leisure, sociality, and cultural heritage are more concentrated in the inner city.

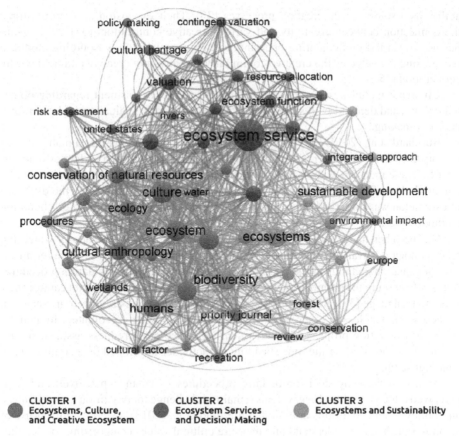

CLUSTER 1
Ecosystems, Culture,
and Creative Ecosystem

CLUSTER 2
Ecosystem Services
and Decision Making

CLUSTER 3
Ecosystems and Sustainability

Fig. 2. The scientific landscape

A recent literature review on these issues [30] has highlighted significant publications 'growth related to CES in urban settings since 2012. The authors pointed out that CES evaluation was primarily ignored in the scientific literature and limited to monetary services like leisure and ecotourism. However, Artmann and Sartison (2018) [31] detected that the most frequently mentioned ecosystem services given by urban and peri-urban agriculture are the cultural services. They found 111 citations in 59 of 166 papers. Their findings show that: tourism prospects play a minor role (0.9% of total citations), compared to the most cited CES, which include nature experience (17%), education and learning (27%), and recreation, mental, and physical health (33%).

In 2017, the European Commission proposed a preliminary version of the Cultural and Creative Cities Monitor – a tool developed to benchmark European cities by gathering 29 descriptive indicators from nine different dimensions – including the ecological or structural essence of creative cultural activities in the urban contexts [32].

Creative industries have been referred to as those industries where creativity is at the core of all economic processes. These globally recognised industries include architecture, film production, fashion, design, video games, and other fields that require creative ability as a source of co-creation processes [33]. Their expansion aims to reinforce the connection between creativity and various creative contributors [34]. As a result, businesses started implementing open innovation, especially crowdsourcing modules, recognising the value of the creative community and ensuring creative and trustworthy cooperation [35].

Cluster 2 includes research issues related to the ES assessment regarding potentials, flows, and demand with spatial analysis and quantitative valuation tools to inform decision-making.

Burkhard et al. (2014) [36] presented a spatial methodology based on matrices connecting CORINE land cover types to potential, flows, demands, and budget estimations for ES. These matrices demonstrated that landscapes have different ecosystem service potentials from flows, particularly in provisioning services. About CES, the difficulty of estimation was remarked upon since their immaterial nature and complex elicitation methodologies.

On the other hand, Jacobs et al. (2016) highlighted the importance of triggering methodological advancements based on practice-oriented perspectives to target mixed uses of valuation methods investigating local cases. Indeed, single-valuation procedures frequently obscure the opinions of certain actors since the tool used does not capture their valuation language [37]. Although these same actors can demonstrate their appreciation for ecosystem services in other ways, such as their willingness to volunteer for conservation or restoration projects [38], their sense of place or sacredness associated with specific locations [39], or the time spending for activities developed by a community in a natural setting.

At last, developing decision-making procedures to balance perceived and non-perceived effects of cultural ecosystems remains a challenge for practitioners, specialists, and policymakers. With this ambition, Satterfield et al. (2013) fostered a mixed-use of valuation methods to understand and measure cultural values categorising four elicitation procedures: 1. Articulation; 2. Classification; 3. Importance; 4. Spatial relevance [40].

Cluster 3 includes articles linking sustainability to ecosystems and exploring the nature-culture nexus.

Diaz et al. (2018) have identified a twofold perspective in agri-food co-production in high-diversity agriculture as, on the one hand, a process that combines a collection of biological and technological inputs aimed at optimizing biodiversity, and, on the other hand, as a "practice of care" by social relationships and association with immaterial values [41].

According to Arowolo et al. (2018), land-use/land-cover (LULC) dynamics have had a significant impact on providing ecosystem services for human existence, livelihood, and well-being [42]. The recent conversion of these natural ecosystems into croplands, tree plantations, and urban areas has resulted in massive food production, fiber, lumber, housing, and other items worldwide [43]. Unfortunately, the gains of these transformations were accompanied by a deterioration in the provision of several ecosystem services, with nearly 60% of ecosystem services degrading in the last five decades [44].

2.2 Design (I)

The Design phase was divided into two sub-steps. The first step (Design I) was addressed to observe beneficiaries' preferences for ES through a Stated Preference Method (SPM). The second step (Design II) has allowed performing an integrated assessment to elicit shared values using Triangular Fuzzy Number (TFN) and Fuzzy Synthetic Extent. The problem modelling in the design phases has allowed creative ecosystem services to be evaluated based on the agri-food cultural value chain.

Within the Design I phase, the study has used the Stated Preference method (SPM)n results obtained by the "*Vàzapp'* survey" (https://bit.ly/2O55BEG) for assessing creative ecosystem services in Cerreta et al. (2020) [23].

The overall number of respondents are 75 people, among which 46,6% (35 persons) include direct beneficiaries of *Vàzapp'*, while 53,4% (40 persons) refers to people that never heard about this practice; nevertheless, they can be considered as potential beneficiaries. They have been sampled according to their interest to be involved in rural experiences, urban resilience strategies and cultural activities linked to agri-food chain discovery and knowledge. The representative sample, indeed, is composed of people with a high education level (45,2% hold a master-degree, while 41,1% are involved in Post-doc) and with job positions as employee (39,7%) and freelance (26,0%).

The survey's objectives were addressed to score the six ES according to preferences expressed on a 5-point Likert scale. Following questions have assessed how much time a person is willing to participate within creative experiences and identified shared values among involved stakeholders (e.g., working partnerships, consultancy, sponsorships).

According to the goals of *Vàzapp'*, the following six ecosystem services have been chosen: Good Job Opportunity, Nutrient Food, Cooperation and Community, and Disintermediation, Natural Ecosystem Enhancement, and Environmental Education. The following are the conditions for choosing the six ES: Exploring Good Job Opportunities entails learning how *Vàzapp'* or a similar practice may help create an enabling environment that encourages jobs through funding and formal/informal collaboration. Nutrient Food has been chosen as the foundation of a cultural agri-food value chain. Cooperation and Community is in line with the goal of these practices, which is to improve the collaboration among stakeholders. Furthermore, this practice ensures Disintermediation as the most appropriate service for reducing steps within a supply chain. Natural Ecosystem Enhancement and Environmental Education have been chosen because cultural activities concentrate on preserving local practices and bequeathed agricultural techniques and the education of new generations in respecting nature.

2.3 Design (II)

The second step of the Design phase has aimed to elicit shared values in terms of priorities using Triangular Fuzzy Numbers (TFN) [45] by arranging data for multi-criteria modelling. The purpose is to define creative ecosystem services based on the agri-food cultural value chain enabling relationships within the local community and boosting innovative services. Among survey respondents, the authors have selected the forty potential beneficiaries' preferences related to site-specific creative scenarios to be replicated in other contexts.

Experts have employed fuzzy logic for a long time to facilitate decision making in many investigation fields when complete and exact information is lacking. TFN have allowed the uncertainty – linked to the priority's assessment of criteria and alternatives – to be included in the decision making problem.

In this application, the authors adopted the mathematical approach by Lyu et al. (2019) [46] changing the frequency range of priorities – observed in the aggregated results of the survey's respondents – into TFN.

The operative steps producing TFN are the following:

- Each criterion's scores are summed up, including the total number of scores allocated and the number of times the survey's respondents assigned a score. Each score becomes an interval number, with the lowest and highest values given to each factor (criterion/alternative), as shown in Tables 1, 2.
- The pairwise comparison of two elements results in forming a judgment matrix in which each coefficient may be characterised as a ratio of the two factors' interval values (Table 3).
- A crisp number replaces the previous interval ratio, which may generally meet the judgement matrix's consistency criterion. A triangular fuzzy number returns the equivalent crisp value in the judgement matrix, and a judgement matrix composed entirely of TFN is established (Table 4).

Table 1. Criteria preferences range.

Alternatives (scenarios)	Preference range					Number interval
	1	2	3	4	5	
C1 - Good job opportunities			10	8	22	3-5
C2 - Sustainable food			1	16	23	3-5
C3 - Cooperation and community activities			3	8	29	3-5
C4 - Disintermediation of agri-food products		1	5	22	12	2-5
C5 - Natural ecosystems enhancement			1	13	26	3-5
C6 - Environmental education			2	9	29	3-5

Table 2. Scenarios preferences range.

Alternatives (scenarios)	Preference range					Number interval
	1	2	3	4	5	
A1 - Social dinner for agri-food professionals	11	13	10	6		1-4
A2 - Celebration days for local products	11	9	14	4	2	1-5
A3 - Performing arts in rural settings	7	14	12	2	5	1-5
A4 - Performing media storytelling agri-food	14	11	9	3	3	1-5
A5 - Other	23	3	9	9		1-4

Frequencies attributed by respondents based on the 5-points Likert scale and related to the most scored among the six ecosystem services have been grouped into preferences ranges, as shown in Table 1.

The same procedure has been applied for the preferable scenarios, which have been scored in terms of willingness to spend time for activities linked to the agri-food cultural value chain. The unit of measure has been changed from hours/month to 5-points Likert following this rule: the more the donated time, the more the scored value (Table 5).

Interval numbers referred to alternatives range 1–5 for three up to five scenarios, while scenarios A1 and A5 range 1–4.

Table 3. Judgment matrix with the ratios of criteria's interval values.

1	3–5/3–5	3–5/3–5	3–5/2–5	3–5/3–5	3–5/3–5
3–5/3–5	1	3–5/3–5	3–5/2–5	3–5/3–5	3–5/3–5
3–5/3–5	3–5/3–5	1	3–5/2–5	3–5/3–5	3–5/3–5
2–5/3–5	2–5/3–5	2–5/3–5	1	2–5/3–5	2–5/3–5
3–5/3–5	3–5/3–5	3–5/3–5	3–5/2–5	1	3–5/3–5
3–5/3–5	3–5/3–5	3–5/3–5	3–5/2–5	3–5/3–5	1

Table 4. TFN judgments matrix for criteria.

1	1	1	1	1	1
1/1*	1/1*	1/1*	1/1*	1/1*	1/1*
1/1*	1/1*	1/1*	1/1*	1/1*	1/1*
2*	2*	2*	2*	2*	2*
1/1*	1/1*	1/1*	1/1*	1/1*	1/1*
1/1*	1/1*	1/1*	1/1*	1/1*	1/1*

Table 5. Transformation from Hours/month to 5-points Likert

Hours/month	Likert value
≤ 1	1
$1 < x \leq 2$	2
$2 < x \leq 6$	3
$6 < x \leq 8$	4
$8 < x \leq 10$	5

The preparatory steps in the Design II phase have allowed returning the AHP comparisons matrices avoiding the pairwise comparison procedures, which are limitations related to the standard AHP procedure.

2.4 Choice Phase

The choice phase has been addressed to rank beneficiaries' preferences for ES with F-AHP to determine how creative ecosystem services can support innovative cultural networks scenarios in the agri-food value chain. The proposed model has aimed to provide recommendations to Decision Makers in terms of creative activities to be pursued.

The decision problem has assessed five scenarios for innovative cultural networks: A1 – Social dinner for agri-food professionals, A2 – Celebration days for local products, A3 – Performing arts in rural settings, A4 – Performing media storytelling for agri-food, A5 – Other. Meanwhile, the decision variables corresponding to the criteria within the hierarchical structure (Fig. 3) have included the six selected ecosystem services.

In this study, the authors adopted linguistic variables and the related triangular fuzzy conversion scale by Chang (1996) [47] since it allows highlighting a difference when identical elements are compared (Just equal) or different ones achieve the same importance (Equally important).

Fuzzy pairwise comparisons matrices – obtained in the design II phase – were processed to derive the weights at criteria and alternatives levels. The fuzzy synthetic extent by Chang (2008) has allowed TFN sum and multiplication – identified with the symbol $\circledast$ – within the matrices' rows and columns following the Eq. (1):

$$S_i = \sum_{j=1}^{m} M_{gi}^{j} \circledast \left[\sum_{i=1}^{n} \sum_{j=1}^{m} M_{gi}^{j} \right]^{-1} \tag{1}$$

Where M_{gi}^{j} represents the (l,m,u) values that describe a fuzzy event for each TFN and is equal to the Eq. (2):

$$\sum_{j=1}^{m} M_{gi}^{j} = \left(\sum_{j=1}^{m} l_j, \sum_{j=1}^{m} m_j, \sum_{j=1}^{m} u_j \right) \tag{2}$$

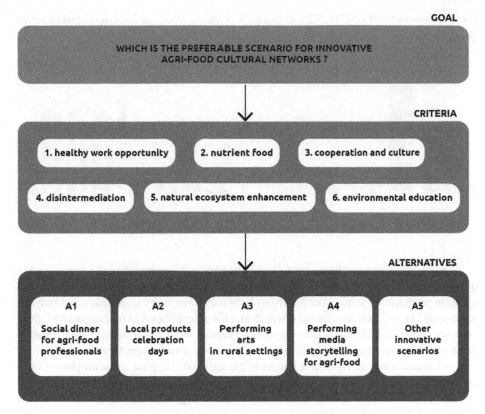

Fig. 3. The AHP hierarchical structure

Where: l_j is the smallest possible value; m_j is the most promising value; u_j is the largest possible value. After some fuzzy operations, an equations system has been solved respecting conditions in the Eq. (3):

$$\mu_{M_2}(d) = \begin{cases} 1 & \text{if } M_2 \geq M_1 \\ 0 & \text{if } l_1 \geq u_2 \\ \frac{l_1 - u_2}{(m_2 - u_2) - (m_1 - l_1)} & \text{otherwise} \end{cases} \quad (3)$$

Finally, the results of the equations system have returned the priorities for criteria and, thus, the ranking of alternatives.

3   Results

The Knowledge phase has allowed the problem definition to emerge from the literature about the three clusters referring to as: 1. Ecosystems, Culture, and Creative Ecosystems; 2. Ecosystem Services and Decision Making; 3. Ecosystems and Sustainability. The number of examined papers amounts to 156, subdivided into 122 articles, 17 review articles, 7 conference papers, 9 book chapters, and 1 note. A growing interest of authors for these issues from 2000 to 2021, with a pick of publications in 2014, has been detected (Fig. 4).

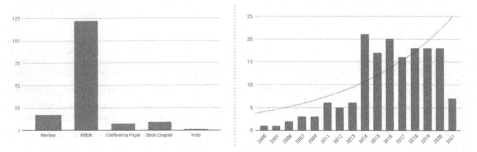

Fig. 4. Article's typology (on the left) and number of publications 2000–2021 (on the right)

The literature survey allowed us to highlight and go in depth to the following research questions: how does creative capital implement the four capital stocks to boost co-creation processes in terms of connections between community knowledge and individual talents? How practice-oriented research at a local scale helps to investigate and, thus, produce shared values linked to ecosystem services? What about the integrated evaluations' role in incorporating both perceived and non-perceived values for the assessment of ES? What innovative ecosystem solutions in the agri-food co-production aim to optimize biodiversity and, concurrently, strengthen social innovation as a "practice of care"?

In response to these questions the 4-step methodology to study the agri-food cultural value chain has been implemented.

In particular, four capital stocks for socio-cultural ES to be analysed regarding human, social, natural, and produced benefits emerged. Within these capital stocks, the six ecosystem services referring to the case study have been prioritised and assessed together with the innovative cultural agri-food activities towards creative ecosystem services.

The Design phase results concerning the indirect beneficiaries' preferences are presented below.

The first question relates to the priorities of six ecosystem services which *Vazapp'* or similar practices can spark. *Cooperation and community* and *Environmental Education* score at the top of the ranking with 29 respondents which attributed maximum Likert value to these services. 74,4% of potential beneficiaries attribute extreme importance to *Cooperation and Community*.

The second observation aims to understand how much time a person could spend enjoying the creative activities provided by agri-food cultural value chain. The overall time amounts to 474 h per month which 40 people are willing to spend to be directly engaged in these activities. Art performances and acting schools emerge as the most interesting activities in which people have declared to spend more time (10 h per month and more).

The results of fuzzy extent analysis - calculated for criteria and alternatives of the decision problem – have allowed to obtain the global ranking (Fig. 5).

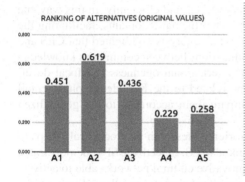 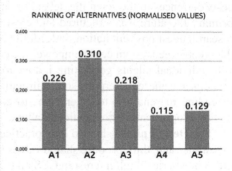

Fig. 5. Final ranking of the alternatives

Following the AHP method, local weights of criteria were multiplied for alternatives 'weights with the Eq. (1) to derive the global alternatives 'priorities. The results in Fig. 5 show that A2 scores high with 31% of preferences. At the second position, A1 and A3 emerge with similar scoring. Finally, A4 and A5 place the last position in the ranking with a short deviation. It means that potential beneficiaries of CES prefer local food events for leisure and the exchange of information related to techniques and procedures for sustainable agriculture.

4 Discussion and Conclusions

The research results allow preliminary reflections about the definition of creative ecosystem services for overcoming critical issues concerning cultural, economic, environmental, and social conflicts that generally affect the southern Italian communities. Pursuing objectives of effectiveness, efficiency, productivity, and sustainability-related to CCEs enabling key-factors that refer to creative capital, shared value, and innovative cultural networks can contribute to solving structural problems at the foundations of agri-food value chains, e.g., the agri-food products quality reduction, low management skills of producers, the deprivation of agri-food producers in socio-economic terms.

The proposed approach aims to implement the current scientific debate on CES for regional regeneration from a systemic and transdisciplinary point of view, where multi-criteria evaluations are combined with creative services and social innovation tools from a multi-stakeholder perspective. In addition, analysed ES assessment studies foster combining objective and subjective evaluations and including tangible and intangible values. In this perspective, the co-creation transforms these values into shared values boosting innovation in cultural services and social cohesion towards a sustainable development.

Each research step has attempted to respond to different questions highlighted from the scientific landscape analysis.

The **Knowledge phase** highlighted that the creative capital implements the four capital stocks of CES thanks to a creative ecosystem aimed to gain a competitive advantage by introducing innovation, inter-industry and individuals' cooperation, which is a prerequisite for ecosystem development. Furthermore, the scientific landscape methodology was a potential of this study since it allowed the most relevant issues in terms of co-occurrences in the scientific debate to emerge faster and efficiently. In this way, the primary literature was structured and clustered into thematic domains, facilitating the research questions' elicitation. Indeed, the literature analysis highlighted that CES and the creative ecosystem could empower the connections between community knowledge and individual talents generating innovation, international openness and local development. On the counterpart, some limitations related to the Knowledge phase entail extending the analysis to other cases to compare them according to the generalized methodological structure mentioned above.

The **Design phase** showed how practice-oriented research at a local scale helps to investigate and, thus, produce shared values linked to ES. Indeed, the SPM demonstrated the beneficiaries' high interest in CES and innovative cultural networks able to activate creative ecosystem services. Moreover, the fuzzy set theory has allowed uncertainty to be included in the decision-making problem incorporating both perceived and non-perceived values in terms of evaluation criteria. The first potential of this phase concerns using a mixed survey including both subjective and objective evaluation in a holistic perspective. Limitations are related to a low number of respondents and a limited sample regarding beneficiaries' typologies and their localisation. The main gain of the Design phase is also related to the simplification of questionnaires for the AHP since it allows avoiding the pairwise comparison that can be troublesome to human thinking. Nevertheless, simplifying the evaluation interface through questionnaires means increasing mathematical procedures for data aggregation, which is time-consuming.

The **Choice phase** has demonstrated what innovative ecosystem solutions in the agri-food co-production aim to optimize biodiversity and, concurrently, strengthen social innovation as a "practice of care". Indeed, ranking scenarios for innovative cultural networks showed that recognising the critical role of community, cooperation, and immaterial values implements the stakeholders' awareness of ES and the creative capital as sustainable development and local competitive advantage.

The choice phase limitations are linked to the scenario's generation, which should be obtained by a co-evaluation process merging potential and direct beneficiaries of CES.

The overall research weak point concerns the time consuming of such a value chain building process and the scarcity of local economic resources, especially in Southern Italy. Continuous and capillary action of trust and awareness-building of the cultural agri-food value chain is necessary, accompanying social and local physical transformations. The main difficulty lies in making people and institutions understand that investing time and money in the intangible values co-creation greatly helps transform tangible assets towards long-term sustainable development.

In this perspective, the research follow-up addresses the co-creation of creative ecosystem services in synergy with local stakeholders and beneficiaries, generating new job opportunities, awareness and innovation through an advanced form of shared responsibility. The creativity embedded in innovative cultural networks contributes to shape creative clusters in the agri-food value chain as the driving force of sustainable projects.

References

1. Millennium Ecosystem Assessment: Ecosystems and Human Well-being: Synthesis. Island Press, Washington, DC (2005)

2. Mooney, H.A., Ehrlich, P.R., Daily, G.: Ecosystem services: a fragmentary history. Nature's Services: Societal Dependence on Natural Ecosystems. Island Press, Washington, DC, pp. 11–19 (1997)
3. Daniel, T.C., et al.: Contributions of cultural services to the ecosystem services agenda. Proc. Natl. Acad. Sci. **109**, 8812 (2012)
4. Neuteleers, S., Hugé, J.: Value pluralism in ecosystem services assessments: Closing the gap between academia and conservation practitioners. Ecosystem Services 49, 101293 (2021)
5. Leemans, R., De Groot, R.: Millennium Ecosystem Assessment: Ecosystems and human well-being: a framework for assessment. Island Press, Washington, DC (2003)
6. TEEB: Mainstreaming the Economics of Nature: A Synthesis of the Approach, Conclusions and Recommendations of TEEB (2010), http://teebweb.org/publications/teeb-for/synthesis/
7. Haines-Young, R., Potschin, M.: Common international classification of ecosystem services (CICES, Version 4.1). Eur. Environ. Agency **33**, 107 (2012)
8. Carta, M.: Creative city. Dynamics, innovations, actions. List (2007)
9. Cerreta, M., Diappi, L.: Adaptive evaluations in complex contexts: Introduction 2014. Italian J. Reg. Sci. **13**(1), 5–22 (2014)
10. Carta, M.: Culture, communication and cooperation: the three Cs for a proactive creative city. Int. J. Sustain. Dev. **12**, 124–133 (2009)
11. Pratt, A.C., Jeffcutt, P.: Creativity, innovation and the cultural economy. Routledge, New York (2009)
12. Troilo, G.: Marketing nei settori creativi. Generare valore per il cliente tramite l'esperienza della creatività. Milano, Pearson Italia Spa, Milano (2014)
13. Kramer, M.R., Porter, M.: Creating shared value. Springer, Dordrecht (2011)
14. Selicato, M., Torre, C.M., La Trofa, G.: Prospect of integrate monitoring: A multidimensional approach, Lecture Notes in Computer Science (including subseries Lecture Notes in Artificial Intelligence and Lecture Notes in Bioinformatics), 7334 LNCS(PART 2), 144–156 (2012)
15. Torre, C.M., Selicato, M.: The support of multidimensional approaches in integrate monitoring for SEA: A case of study. Earth Syst. Dyn. **4**(1), 51–61 (2013)
16. Cerreta, M., Daldanise, G.: Community branding (Co-bra): A collaborative decision making process for urban regeneration, Lecture Notes in Computer Science (including subseries Lecture Notes in Artificial Intelligence and Lecture Notes in Bioinformatics), 10406 LNCS, 730–746 (2017).
17. Cerreta, M., Daldanise, G., Sposito, S.: Culture-led regeneration for urban spaces Monitoring complex values networks in action. Urbani Izziv **29**, 9–28 (2018)
18. Cerreta, M., Panaro, S.: Deliberative spatial multi-criteria evaluation (DSM-CE): Forming shared cultural values. In: Gervasi, O., Murgante, B., Misra, S., Borruso, G., Torre, C.M., Ana Maria, A.C., Rocha, D.T., Apduhan, B.O., Stankova, E., Cuzzocrea, A. (eds.) ICCSA 2017. LNCS, vol. 10406, pp. 747–763. Springer, Cham (2017). https://doi.org/10.1007/978-3-319-62398-6_53
19. Cerreta, M., Panaro, S., Poli, G.: A spatial decision support system for multifunctional landscape assessment: a transformative resilience perspective for vulnerable inland areas. Sustainability **13**(5), 2748 (2021)
20. Anelli, D., Sica, F.: The Financial Feasibility Analysis of Urban Transformation Projects: An Application of a Quick Assessment Model. In: Bevilacqua, C., Calabrò, F., Della Spina, L. (eds.) NMP 2020. SIST, vol. 178, pp. 462–474. Springer, Cham (2021). https://doi.org/10.1007/978-3-030-48279-4_44
21. Saaty, T.L.: Deriving the AHP 1–9 scale from first principles. In: *Proceedings 6th ISAHP.* Berna, Suiza, pp. 397–402 (2001)
22. Ishizaka, A., Nguyen, N.H.: Calibrated fuzzy AHP for current bank account selection. Expert Syst. Appl. **40**, 3775–3783 (2013)

23. Cerreta, M., Clemente, M., Daldanise, G., Poli, G.: Creative ecosystem services for new urban-rural communities: The "VàZapp" Experience. Creative Food Cycles-Book **1**, 69–81 (2020)
24. Lombardi, M., et al.: Network impact of social innovation initiatives in marginalised rural communities. Soc. Networks **63**, 11–20 (2020)
25. Cerreta, M., Panaro, S., Poli, G.: A knowledge-based approach for the implementation of a SDSS in the Partenio Regional Park (Italy). In: Gervasi, O., Murgante, B., Misra, S., Ana Maria, A.C., Rocha, M.A.C., Torre, C.M.M., Taniar, D., Apduhan, B.O.O., Stankova, E., Wang, S. (eds.) ICCSA 2016. LNCS, vol. 9789, pp. 111–124. Springer, Cham (2016). https://doi.org/10.1007/978-3-319-42089-9_8
26. Simon, H.A.: The New Science of Management Decision. Prentice Hall PTR (1977)
27. van Eck, N.J., Waltman, L.: Software survey: VOSviewer, a computer program for bibliometric mapping. Scientometrics **84**, 523–538 (2010)
28. United Nation: Indicators and a Monitoring Framework for the Sustainable Development Goals. Launching a data revolution for the SDGs. A report by the Leadership Council of the Sustainable Development Solutions Network (2015)
29. Rall, E.L., Haase, D.: Creative intervention in a dynamic city: a sustainability assessment of an interim use strategy for brownfields in Leipzig Germany. Landsc. Urban Plan. **100**(3), 189–354 (2017)
30. Abualhagag, A., Valánszki, I.: Mapping indicators of cultural ecosystem services: review and relevance to urban context. J. Landsc. Ecol. **13**(1), 4–24 (2020)
31. Artmann, M., Sartison, K.: The role of urban agriculture as a nature-based solution: a review for developing a systemic assessment framework. Sustainability **10**, 1937 (2018)
32. Montalto, V., et al.: The Cultural and Creative Cities Monitor, 2019th edn. Publications Office of the European Union, Luxembourg (2019)
33. Rill, B.R., Hämäläinen, M.M.: The Art of Co-creation: A Guidebook for Practitioners, 1st edn. Palgrave Macmillan, California (2018)
34. Bujor, A., Avasilcai, S.: Creative entrepreneurship in Europe: a framework of analysis. Ann. Oradea Univ. Fascicle Manag. Technol. Eng. **23**, 151–156 (2014)
35. Avram, E., Hutu, C.A., Bujor, A.: Toward a Creative Dynamic Capabilities Creation Framework: The Evidence from Creative Business Ecosystems. In: Prostean, G., Lavios Villahoz, J.J., Brancu, L., Bakacsi, G. (eds.) SIM 2019. SPBE, pp. 567–574. Springer, Cham (2020). https://doi.org/10.1007/978-3-030-44711-3_42
36. Burkhard, B., et al.: Ecosystem service potentials, flows and demands-concepts for spatial localisation, indication and quantification. Landsc. Online **34**, 1–32 (2014)
37. Jacobs, S., et al.: A new valuation school: Integrating diverse values of nature in resource and land use decisions. Ecosystem Services **22**(B), 213–220 (2016)
38. García-Llorente, M.: The value of time in biological conservation and supplied ecosystem services: a willingness to give up time exercise. J. Arid Environ. **124**, 13–21 (2016)
39. Klain, S.C.: What matters and why? Ecosystem services and their bundled qualities. Ecol. Econ. **107**, 310–320 (2014)
40. Satterfield, T.R.: Culture, intangibles and metrics in environmental management. J. Environ. Manage. **117**, 103–114 (2013)
41. Díaz, S., et al.: Assessing nature's contributions to people. Science **359**(6373), 270–272 (2018)
42. Arowolo, A.O., et al.: Assessing changes in the value of ecosystem services in response to land-use/land-cover dynamics in Nigeria. Sci. Total Environ. **636**, 597–609 (2018)
43. de Groot, R., et al.: Global estimates of the value of ecosystems and their services in monetary units. Ecosyst. Serv. **1**(1), 50–61 (2012)
44. Millennium Ecosystem Assessment: Ecosystems and Human Well-being: A Framework for Assessment. Island Press, Washington, DC (2005)

45. Chang, C.W., Wu, C.R., Lin, H.L.: Applying fuzzy hierarchy multiple attributes to construct an expert decision making process. Expert Syst. Appl. **36**(4), 7363–7368 (2009)
46. Lyu, H.M., et al.: Risk assessment using a new consulting process in fuzzy AHP. J. Constr. Eng. Manag. **146**(3), 04019112 (2020)
47. Chang, D.Y.: Applications of the extent analysis method on fuzzy AHP. Eur. J. Oper. Res. **95**(3), 649–655 (1996)

Ecosystem Services and Land Take. A Composite Indicator for the Assessment of Sustainable Urban Projects

Pierluigi Morano[1] , Maria Rosaria Guarini[2(✉)] , Francesco Sica[2] , and Debora Anelli[2]

[1] Department of Sciences of Civil Engineering and Architecture, Polytechnic University of Bari, 70125 Bari, Italy
pierluigi.morano@poliba.it
[2] Department of Architecture and Design, Sapienza University of Rome, 00196 Rome, Italy
{mariarosaria.guarini,francesco.sica,debora.anelli}@uniroma1.it

Abstract. The worrying levels of land take and insufficient ecosystem services related to phenomena of uncontrolled urban expansion in the cities force many countries far away from achieving Sustainable Development Goals of Agenda 2030. It is necessary to promote strategies which lead to effective and efficient measures in the perspective of sustainable development.

The work aim is to propose an evaluation protocol useful to support public and private subjects for sustainable practices in urban contexts. Depending on the types of use and land cover envisaged, the implementation of the proposed methodological framework allows for the definition of a Composite Indicator (CI) to measure the urban environmental and economic sustainability level. The proposed CI expresses qualitatively and quantitatively the socio-economic and environmental impact (*trade-off*) that single initiative generates in the reference context in terms of ecosystem services as a function of the land use change between *ex-ante* and *ex-post* phases of the urban transformation process.

Multi-parameter methodological approach by a sequence of logical-operational phases that lead to the definition of the CI is proposed. Steps of the proposed method are characterized by the algebraic structures typical of the Benefit of Doubt Approach (BDA) and Goal programming principles. Testing of the proposed protocol for CI construction is in progress.

Keywords: SDG · Ecosystem services · Land take · Composite indicator · Operational research · Sustainability assessment

1 Introduction

The 2030 Agenda of the United Nations (UN) (2015) is a programmatic reference for Member States at international level in the definition of practices to achieve shared sustainable development objectives by 2030 [1] through the pursuit of minimum target levels referred to 17 Sustainable Development Goals (SDGs).

© Springer Nature Switzerland AG 2021
O. Gervasi et al. (Eds.): ICCSA 2021, LNCS 12954, pp. 210–225, 2021.
https://doi.org/10.1007/978-3-030-86979-3_16

Among the SDGs proposed by the UN, some are intended, in general but also in particular in cities [2], to improve the living conditions (health and well-being) of people (SDG 3); to ensure the economic-productive development of the territory (SDG 8); to create inclusive, safe, resilient and sustainable cities and human settlements (SDG 11); to foster the protection of existing natural resources against climate change (SDG 13) and to reduce the consumption of available land (SDG 15). Others can be refereed also to the finance field where the increasing trend of the Green Bond investments make the sustainability performance criterion to be considered in the economic evaluations for urban transformation projects. [3]. According to the Sustainable Finance Disclosure Regulation, environmentally sustainable economic aspects must be an essential part of the investment workflow at multiple territorial administrative [4].

Annually, the Sustainable Development Goals Report provided by United Nations Organization (UNO) screens the target level for each SDG at local and international level [5, 6]. The 2020 Report highlights how the Pan-Europeanisation of COVID-19 has triggered an unprecedented crisis, causing further disruption to progress towards the 2030 SDGs. This in the face of uneven efforts and progress where significant imbalances remain due to the deterioration of the natural environment, persistent and pervasive social, economic and environmental inequalities [7].

The monitoring of the SDG achievements is conducted on the basis of appropriate sustainability performance indicators. The 17 SDGs are categorized into 169 targets, which in turn are expressed through 231 indicators [8]. The measurement of the SDGs and the use of specific performance indicators is a function of the spatial dimensions, as well as the economic, social, environmental and building features of reference context of urban and territorial type.

Furthermore, part of the debate that has been going on for some time at international level on overcoming Gross Domestic Product (GDP), as the only economic indicator capable of expressing the wellbeing level of a territory [9]. Following the *Istanbul Declaration* of 2007 and the *Global Project on the Measurement of the Progress of Societies* by the OECD, a growing number of countries have introduced methodological and political initiatives on how to go "Beyond GDP" to measure well-being and sustainable development. There is a growing sense that the benchmark against which the progress of a society cannot be based only on the market value of all the final goods and services produced in a country over a given time period but should be complemented through the use of composite sustainability indicators that also consider the fundamental social and environmental dimensions of well-being, accompanied by measures of inequality and sustainability that escape GDP accounting.

In particular, at European level, in August 2009, the European Commission published the communication: "Not only GDP. Measuring progress in a changing world" [10]. In September 2009, the Commission on the Measurement of Economic Performance and Social Progress (Stiglitz-Sen-Fitoussi Commission) published a report with 12 recommendations for the measurement of social well-being in all its dimensions, reaffirming the need for policy choices to be based on indicators capable of representing different aspects of the current progress and future sustainability of a society. In 2010 the European Statistical System Committee (ESSC) mandated a "Sponsorship Group on Measuring Progress, Well-being and Sustainable Development" to translate the recommendations of the Stiglitz-Sen-Fitoussi Commission report and the European Commission Communication into actions to be undertaken to update the European Statistical System (ESS) to the changing needs for new information by improving existing statistics. This in order to promote and provide more appropriate indicators [11].

Despite large overlaps between the SDGs and "Beyond GDP", it should be kept in mind that the conceptual framework within which the SDGs were produced puts sustainability first and must address all countries around the world with different levels of well-being and development. Since this means that some of the indicators identified by the UN are not relevant in some more developed national contexts, individual countries are free to supplement the list of indicators defined at supranational level. This is also in order to take into account criteria, indicators and relationships closely linked to the different levels of political, programmatic and operational action related to spatial planning [12].

In Italy, the National Institute of Statistics (ISTAT) plays an active coordinating role in the measurement, elaboration and monitoring of indicators related to the SDGs at the national and existing urban level. The production of these indicators has been integrated with the development of a project (proposed and carried out since 2010) aimed at defining indicators to measure "Equitable and Sustainable Well-being" (ESW) at the national level, integrating traditional economic indicators, first the GDP, with measures on the quality of people's lives and the environment. The ESW project has placed Italy at the forefront of the international panorama in terms of developing indicators on the state of country health that go beyond GDP. This activating a process that takes the multidimensionality of wellbeing as its starting point and, through the analysis of a broad set of indicators describing all the aspects that contribute to the citizens' life quality. In fact, the ESW is configured as a dynamic system and its information base is subject to progress revision thanks to the contribution of experts in order to improve its timeliness and representativeness. Periodically, ISTAT presents and publishes an update on the breakdowns of the indicators useful for measuring sustainable development and monitoring its objectives.

The two sets of indicators are partially overlapping, and complementary (see the framework of ESW indicators included in the SDGs framework: https://www4.istat.it/it/files/2016/12/figuraBES-SDGS.jpg). Among the indicators by ISTAT, some relate to the 231 indicators of sustainability; others, instead, to specific parameters that make it possible to measure the structural and functional organization of the reference context.

From the analysis of the results of the last monitoring of the SDGs promoted by ISTAT in collaboration with the Italian Alliance for Sustainable Development (ASviS) in May 2020, it emerges that the overall pre-covid situation in Italy is positive for most of the SDGs, with the exception of SDGs: 9 (Resilient infrastructures, innovation and fair, responsible and sustainable industrialization), 11 (Inclusive, safe, resilient and sustainable cities and human settlements), 14 (Oceans, seas and marine resources for sustainable development), 15 (Sustainable use of natural resources) [13, 14]. In particular for SDG 11, land consumption resulting from the sealing of natural surfaces due to actions of: *i*) urbanization, *ii*) infrastructure and *iii*) industrialization of cities rises among the main causes for the difficult pursuit of the SDGs in highly urbanized contexts. This with obvious repercussions, above all, on existing natural ecosystems and their intrinsic capacity to produce goods and services (*ecosystem services*) to the population [15, 16]. Green spaces in urban areas, in fact, provide several vital ecosystem services that contribute to the wellbeing and health of inhabitants [17]. These includes basic resources of: *i*) support, *ii*) regulation, *iii*) supply, and *iv*) cultural recreation [18].

The production of ecosystem services depends by multiple features of reference urban context. In detailed terms, to morphological-urban characteristics, specificities of economic, social and environmental type regarding the analysis territory, and to its resilient capacity to adapt at sudden shocks of different nature, like pandemic crisis [19].

In the light of this scenario, it seems especially advisable to adopt strategies aimed at reducing the consumption of natural soil in cities. This is done by encouraging the implementation of initiatives designed to address the multiple effects (eco-systemic services) that natural resources produce on the social and economic life of a place according to a logic of contamination and integration between functionally independent subsystems [19–21].

In order to deal with the complexity of a project process implemented according to some integrated and complementary modus operandi with a view to the SDGs, it is essential to use suitable tools capable of leading decision-makers in the decisional phases, guaranteeing the achievement of results that are easily measurable, quantifiable, and openly usable [22]. In recent years, Composite Indicators (CI) have been widely adopted as systems for monitoring performance, determining specific benchmarks and measuring the level of the sustainable urban mobility, the community disaster resilience and the landscape fragmentation within the built environment to the applications for addressing the corporate social responsibility of firms or analyzing the business cycles and the financial stress and economic dynamics related to several enterprises [23–25]. In particular, with the spread of big data, specific methodologies and analytical tools have become necessary to extract and relate a considerable amount of heterogeneous data in order to investigate the links between different phenomena with the ultimate aim of establishing specific strategies to manage them in the most appropriate way [26]. At a local scale, the diffusion of the use of composite indicators in the evaluation of environmental, social and economic-financial aspects of urban transformation projects has had a rapid growth in the 21st century due to the awareness that an efficient control of all the parameters of the project process allows reducing the negative impacts on the built and natural environment by enhancing the positive ones [27–29]. Dobrovolskiene et al. [30] developed a composite sustainability indicator for real estate projects using multi-criteria decision methods (MCDM). The weighted sum method (WSM) is the most applied MCDM within composite indicator creation for urban projects assessment [31]. By comparing the WSM with the COmplex PRoportional ASsessment (COPRAS), Pod-vezko [32] concluded that if all indicators must be maximized, the calculation results are similar. According to Ferreira et al. [33] there is no absolute best MCDM and the choice of the method should always depend on the decisional context of analysis. Their ability to be a quick communication tools able to support the spread of increasing awareness of specific issues in society, depends greatly on the aggregation and weighting schemes of each indicator considered in the system [34]. Attardi et al. propose a multi-criteria approach to the construction of non-compensatory composite indicators. These for the evaluation of environmental and social performances of urban and regional planning policies. The authors suggest the Land-Use Policy Efficiency Index (LUPEI) to apply on municipal scale [35].

For this reason, the integration of MCDM techniques with goal programming algorithms are applied in the academic and professional field in order to reduce the uncertainties and black-boxes that rise up in the different phases of CI construction.

2 Work Aim

In the above context the aim of the work consists in an evaluation protocol which, based on a theoretical and methodological framework, represents a reference document for guiding private and public subjects to create a CI that is able to assess the economic and environmental sustainability level of urban transformation projects at multiple analysis scales (territorial, city, neighborhoods, plot, street).

The theoretical and methodological framework on which the evaluation protocol is based consists of the following main steps: *i)* data collection of the morphological structure *ex ante* intervention of the urban plot subject to a transformation project *ii)* assessment of eco-systemic qualitative impacts in the surrounding intervention area *ex-post* project; *iii)* implementation of the BoD approach for the construction of the Composite Environmental Indicator (CEI); *iv)* benchmark weighting phase; *v)* definition of the final Composite Environmental-Economic Indicator (CEEI).

The relationship between land use type and environmental-socio-economic feature of the surrounding urban context is expressed with the ecosystem services logic. From a computational point of view, in the present work specific tools are proposed to support the theoretical framework and steps above cited. In particular, the BoD approach is applied to determine the CEI proposed by setting the related optimal benchmark through a goal programming algorithm under adequate constraints. The mathematical programming environment used for writing the regression system is A Mathematical Programming Language (AMPL). It is a simple and intuitive tool used for structuring mathematical programming problems. Resolutions can be developed through specific software. Some examples are CPLEX, FortMP, MINOS and KNITRO.

In this way, public and private subject can be able to take into account the environmental and economic features of urban project that produce positive and/or negative impacts at different analysis contexts in order to *i)* identify the most sustainable alternative; *ii)* improve the morphological composition of a project that is related to a poor CEEI level; *iii)* avoid spending (limited) public and private financial resources on urban projects that do not perform well according to the new sustainability features required by world policy documents provided on a European and global scale.

The paper is structured as follows: Sect. 3 consists in the introduction of the existing main tools and indicator systems designed to achieve the sustainability goal in the literature. Section 4 describes the theoretical and methodology framework of the evaluation protocol proposed. Section 5 provides future developments of the work in order to support an easier achievement of the SDGs.

3 Indicator Systems for Assessing Sustainability

The concept of sustainability born in the early 1970s after the first evidence on the industrial progress damages on health and quality of life [28, 36, 37]. Successively, after the Brundtland Report and the World Summit on Sustainable Development in Rio de Janeiro, in 1992, the sustainability debate has been translated into specific target with the establishment of the Kyoto Protocol in 1997, the Paris Agreement in 2015 and later the Agenda 2030 SDGs.

Since then, different public and private stakeholders ranging from the local to the global importance, have been discussing on tools to assess the sustainability. A lot of quantitative and qualitative data-based decision support tools have been developed in the last decades in order to give a contribution on the topic [38, 39]. Recently, the emerging trends focused attention on the index theory due to its suitability to address a complex issue, such as the sustainability one, which is composed by different and correlated dimensions (social, environmental, economic and politic ones) that can't be assessed individually.

However, there are many questions that need to be carefully analyzed for defining, selecting, measuring and assessing an adequate sample of indicators in order to return a composite indicator that contains all the issues addressed. This gives importance to standardized frameworks of urban indicators. Actually, there are three organizations that produce international standardization studies worldwide: *i)* International Organization for Standardization (ISO), *ii)* the International Telecommunication Union (ITU) and *iii)* the European Telecommunication Standards Institute (ETSI). The European Committee for Electrotechnical Standardization (ECES) and the European Committee for the standardization (ECS), instead, are responsible for ensuring that standards are consistent with European legislation [40].

The standard ISO:37120_2019 (Sustainable cities and communities – Indicators for city services and quality of life) [41] describes indicators system as quantitative, qualitative and descriptive measures that provide information, such as long-term trends or short-term changes, of a complex urban environment system. For these reasons, the indicator systems are mostly applied as decision support tool that are able to clearly highlight the strength and weaknesses of a city [42]. In this way, it can be easier to set priorities and identify the most critical or best performing areas within urban and environmental priorities [43].

In the existing literature, indicator systems that work well for specific criteria, but less well as a comprehensive measure of sustainability can be found [44, 45]. Other studies, instead, in order to assess all the related issues, provide a multi-hierarchy structure such as the Pressure-State-Response model, the three-component model or the Analytic Hierarchy Process [46]. The most important phase of the process and, at the same time, the most critical one, is the selection of indicators for the possible subjectivity attitude. There are some quantitative tools that are implemented for an objective identification of indicators and to determine which indicators account for most of the observed issues, but often, still now, they appear restricted to those have advanced technical skills [47]. Indicators can also be selected after the application of participative or questionnaire-based techniques by using the Contingent Valuation or the Delphi method [48]. More generally, each indicator considered must be scientifically robust, must have a target level (benchmark) with which to compare it and a social and political resonance. At the same time, is important that *i)* reflects the stakeholders' interests, *ii)* is easily comprehensible to decision-makers and *iii)* is replicable by the final users [49–51].

The often subjective interference in the weight's determination process is a critical instance. In order to overcome such limits, the so-called Benefit of the Doubt (BoD) approach has been widespread applied after the study carried out by Melyn and Moesen [52] on the macroeconomic performance evaluation, especially by researchers in Europe [53]. It directly derives from the Data Envelopment Analysis (DEA) which is a linear mathematical programming technique that performs an objective development able to avoid the above cited issues. It has been used to provide different weighting systems for the Human and the Sustainable Development Indexes [54]. In particular, the BoD approach derives the set of optimal weights for each indicator considered from the observed sub-indicator values themselves and by integrating a goal programming algorithm [55]. Several extensions of the BoD approach have been proposed in the literature for its suitability into different research context representing one of the most efficient methodologies for creating a robust composite indicator [56, 57].

In the present work an integration between BoD approach with linear mathematical programming technique is proposed. In the specific terms the linear principles of the Goal Programming are referred. Through these one set of optimal weights can be measured in optimal manner than other analysis and computational methodologies (e.g. Analytic Hierarchic Process, and not only). The description of evaluation protocol for Composite Indicator construction is described in the following Sect. 4.

4   Evaluation Protocol for a Composite Environmental-Economic Indicator Construction

In order to detect the logical-functional dependencies between study variables representative land use types and ecosystem services a multi-parametric optimization analysis is implemented. This allows both to identify the relationships between the parameters, and to establish the terms useful for the creation of environmental and economic composite indicator.

The proposed evaluation protocol consists of the following steps:

1. Data collection *ex-ante* intervention on urban area considered;
2. Assessment of eco-systemic qualitative impacts in the area of intervention *ex-post* renewal project;
3. Implementation of the BoD approach for the construction of the CEI;
4. Optimal benchmark weighting with Goal Programming Model;
5. Definition of the CEEI.

The Figure 1 illustrates the methodological framework on the basis of the evaluation protocol proposed. Subsequently each part of evaluation protocol proposed is described.

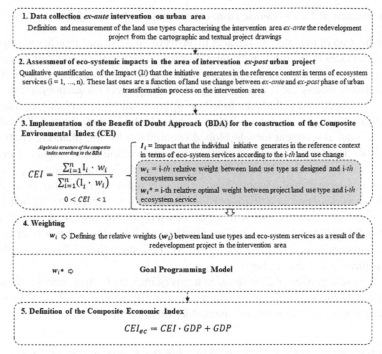

Fig. 1. Methodological framework

4.1 Data Collection *Ex-ante* Intervention on Urban Area

To define an evaluation index under environmental-economic point of view according to the socio-economic and environmental features of territory, the data set is constructed with the values of the variables considered: land use and ecosystem services type. This concerns the *ex-ante status* at the time of implementation of the project in the site of interest.

The values of the variables can be collected using different information systems geo-referenced and not. Among these, e.g. not exhaustive, the best well-known are: *i-Tree Landscape Tool* that gives information on tree cover, land use and basic demographic characteristics of the census areas in United States of America; *Urban Atlas* provides Pan-European comparable land cover and land use data for Functional Urban Areas. These are mainly geo-referenced information layers that give information on social, economic and environmental features of intervention plot. In relation to each land use type ecosystem services are estimated. This through specific performance indicators.

The information on land use type qualifies the survey area according to its capacity to produce goods and services to the community. In addition, it allows to estimate the trade-off between *ex-ante* and *ex-post* urban project implementation in terms of impacts on the ecosystem services production by the land use changes.

4.2   Assessment of Eco-systemic Impacts *Ex-post* Urban Project

The classification of the intervention area in terms of land use and capacity to implement ecosystem services in the reference context is preliminary to the estimation of the trade-off concerning the impact of the project initiative on the urban ecosystem. In order to quantitatively assess the ecosystem impact of the project on territory, multi-criteria evaluation methods and techniques based on operational tools currently in use can be implemented. Among these, for example, it is notable the Natural Capital Planning Tool (NCPT). It is an assessment tool developed specifically for the planning context. The NCPT allows the indicative but systematic assessment of the likely impact of proposed plans and developments on Natural Capital and the ecosystem services it provides to people such as recreational opportunities, air quality regulation and climate regulation. The NCPT was designed as a fit-for-purpose Excel tool which can be applied by non-specialists and in a short period of time; acknowledging the time, resource constrains planners and developers face in everyday practice. NCPT helps planners to create more sustainable places for people and wildlife, whilst at the same time delivering the housing and infrastructure the country needs.

With the use, e.g. of NCPT, *trade-off* in terms of impact (I) on the ecosystem services production regarding specific intervention features are estimated. The I values are on the basis of environmental-economic indicator construction.

4.3   Implementation of the BoD Approach for the Construction of the Composite Indicator

The construction of the environmental-economic indicator to support the evaluation of urban initiatives in ecosystemic key will take place by implementing multi-criteria/multi-objective techniques with the help of goal programming algorithms and advanced techniques for the management and big data use, such as the BoD approach, in charge of a composite indicator definition.

The need to solve complex decision-making processes, characterized by high uncertainties and conflicting goals, has led to the identification of goal programming as one of the most widely used multi-criteria decision-making techniques most of all – but not limited to – within the issues of environmental, financial, social and political assessment [58–62].

The DEA employs linear programming tools to estimate an efficiency frontier that would be used as a benchmark to measure the relative performance of unit elements of different type. This requires construction of a benchmark (the *frontier*), and the measurement of the distance between unit elements in a multi-dimensional framework. The application of DEA to the field of composite indicators is known as the BoD approach, and it was originally proposed to evaluate the macro-economic performance of specific territorial context. In the BoD approach, the Composite Environmental Indicator (CEI) is defined as the ratio of the actual performance to its benchmark reference:

$$CEI = \frac{\sum_{i=1}^{M} I_q \cdot w_q}{\sum_{i=1}^{M} I^* \cdot w_q^*} \tag{1}$$

where I_q is the normalized score of q_{th} individual indicator ($q = 1, ..., Q$) for project's performance p ($p = 1, ..., M$), and w_q the corresponding weights. The last ones can be drawn on the basis of the matrix for the assessment of the different land cover types' capacities to provide selected ecosystem goods and services by Burkhard et al. [63].

Cherchye et al. [64] suggested obtaining the benchmark as the solution of a maximization problem. I* is the score of the hypothetical element unit (Project) that maximizes the overall performance (defined as the WeiGhTed average, WGT), given the (unknown) weights set (WGT) of i-*th* element w. The $CI_{environmental}$ value is in [0–1] range.

4.4 Weighting

The w referred to I* can be solved by using the programming algorithms of Operational Research, capable of solving systems of linear equations in order to maximize and/or minimize an objective function. In this case, Linear Programming algorithms are used.

The AMPL software is used to structure the model. In practice, the use of the AMPL programming environment allows to write the regression problem through the following steps:

1. identification of the problem elements as SETs;
2. specification of the parameters (PARAM) to be included in the system to be solved;
3. definition of the variables' value (VAR);
4. structuring of the objective function, of maximization (MAXIMIZE) or minimization (MINIMIZE), as a linear algebraic expression.

These steps define the structure of a model in parametric form (.mod file) to which the problem data are associated with a separately written.dat file.

The model written in the AMPL programming environment is in Table 1.

The analysis units (set WGT) are described according to three factors (set PARAMETERS): weights and services. The parameters weights are referred to the ordinary values w it is possible to define in corresponding of each ecosystem services type. They are found in the scientific reference literature.

The unknowns (x) are continuous. The objective function is:

maximize *objective*: sum {i in WGT} x[i]*services[i];

The MINOS optimization program is used as a solver implementing algorithm for the linear problem considered in the respect of the CONSTRAINTS.

4.5 Environmental-Economic Composite Indicator

To achieve sustainable development, there is a pressing need to move beyond conventional economic measures like GDP. In fact, it is able to summarizes a vast amount of economic information in a single monetary metric that is widely used by decision makers at different urban planning and design levels. However, GDP fails to capture fully the contributions of nature to economic activity and human well-being. To address

Table 1. The model written in A Mathematical Programming Language (AMPL) software (.mod file).

Model
SETS
set WGT;
PARAMETERS
param weights{WGT};
param services{WGT};
VARIABLES
var x{i **in** WGT} >= 0;
OBJECTIVE FUNCTION
maximize objective: sum{i in WGT} x[i]*services[i];
CONSTRAINTS
s.t.vinc_1: sum{i in WGT} x[i] >= 0;
s.t.vinc_2: sum{i in WGT} x[i] - sum{i in WGT} weights[i] >= 0;
s.t.vinc_3{i in WGT}: x[i] − weights[1] >= 0;
s.t.vinc_4: sum{i in WGT} x[i]*services[i] >= 0;
s.t.vinc_5: {i in WGT}: (x[i] + 1)*services[1] <= TARGET [i];

this critical omission, we develop a measure of (*CEEI*): a measure that summarizes the value of the contributions of nature to economic activity that summarizes the value of ecosystem services in a single monetary metric.

To this regard, Sautton, P. and Costanza, R. [65] express the level of urban economic productivity of an urban area by means of the Subtotal ecological-economic Product (SEP):

$$SEP = GDP + ES \tag{2}$$

i.e. the sum of GDP as thepressure on the level of economic productivity of a territory) and ES, or rather Ecosystem Services due to the existing and/or new natural component, as percentage of GDP value.

According to the (2), the composite environmental-economic indicator (*CEEI_{en}*) proposed is structured as follow:

$$CEEI = CEI \cdot GDP + GDP$$

where *CEI* is obtained by BoD approach in conjunction whit Goal Programming model implementation (see Table 1).

5   Conclusions

The correlation between the urbanization and industrialization processes and the deterioration of the available natural capital with effects on global warming has made the need to overcome social, economic and quality of life disparities of a territory. This has led to the need to pursue sustainable development in economic, social and environmental terms, including through the establishment of specific international agreements that incentivize participating countries to implement effective strategies to mitigate and control the damage caused by human activities to the natural environment and people's life quality. These include the SDGs promoted by the 2030 Agenda.

The current statistical monitoring system used, in an integrated (and complementary) manner, at the global level (UN and OECD), European level (EUROSTAT) and in the various States through the Central Statistical Institutes (in Italy, ISTAT) to determine the achievement of each SDG is based on a system composed of specific social, economic and environmental indicators capable of representing in a simple and effective manner the different reference frameworks for the use of composite sustainable indicators. The importance of synergistic actions promoted at national and local field emerges as part of the different choices to be made at multiple decision-making systems, not least in urban planning and economic-financial evaluation of investments for territorial growth.

The work aim is to propose an evaluation protocol for the definition of a composite indicator able to determine the environmental and economic performance level generated by urban transformation projects. To this end, technical specifications have been implemented in relation to the objectives of each phase of the proposed protocol.

Future insights may concern the application of the proposed protocol and operational framework to real urban transformation interventions in order to test the corresponding effectiveness and limitation. The inclusion of additional environmental variables and the identification of social criteria will allow for the creation of a composite indicator able to synthesize all aspects of sustainability associated with urban transformation projects and the reciprocal relationships of functional dependence.

References

1. United Nations: The Sustainable Development Goals Report (2020)
2. Kovacs, E., Hoaghia, M.A., Senila, L., Scurtu, D.A., Dumitras, D.E., Roman, C.: Sustainability problematization and modeling opportunities. Sustainability **12**(23), 10046 (2020)
3. Banga, J.: The green bond market: a potential source of climate finance for developing countries. J. Sustain. Finan. Invest. **9**(1), 17–32 (2019)
4. Park, S.K.: Investors as regulators: Green bonds and the governance challenges of the sustainable finance revolution. Stanford J. Int. Law **54**, 1 (2018)
5. UNEP, I.: Preventing the Next Pandemic: Zoonotic Diseases and How to Break the Chain of Transmission, p. 82. United Nations Environment Programme (UNEP) and International Livestock Research Institute (ILRI), Nairobi, Kenya (2020)
6. IPBES: Global Assessment Report on Biodiversity and Ecosystem Services (2019)
7. Rubino, I., Coscia, C., Curto, R.: Identifying spatial relationships between built heritage resources and short-term rentals before the Covid-19 pandemic: exploratory perspectives on sustainability issues. Sustainability (Switzerland) **12**(11), 4533 (2020)

8. OECD: Measuring Distance to the SDG Targets 2019: An Assessment of Where OECD Countries Stand. OECD Publishing, Paris (2019)
9. Coscia, C., Curto, R.: Valorising in the absence of public resources and weak markets: the case of "Ivrea, the 20th century industrial city." Green Energy Technol. **9783319496757**, 79–99 (2017)
10. European Commission: Non solo Pil. Misurare il progresso in un mondo in cambiamento. *Comunicazione della Commissione al Consiglio e al Parlamento europeo*. Available: https:// eur-lex.europa.eu/legal-content/EN/TXT/?uri=CELEX%3A52009DC0433 (2009). Ultimo accesso: 27 March 2021
11. European Statistical System Committee: Sponsorship Group on Measuring Progress, Well-being and Sustainable Development. Final Report. Adopted by the European Statistical System Committee November 2011. Available: https://ec.europa.eu/eurostat/documents/733 0775/7339383/SpG-Final-report-Progress-wellbeing-and-sustainabl%20deve/428899a4-9b8d-450c-a511-ae7ae35587cb (2011)
12. Coscia, C., Chiaravalloti, T.: Vuoti urbani e patrimonio del demanio storico-artistico: una road map per l'ex Carlo Alberto di Acqui Terme (ITA). Urban voids and public historical-artistic heritage: a road map for the Carlo Alberto complex of Acqui Terme. Territorio **84**, 128–142 (2018). https://doi.org/10.3280/TR2018-084019
13. ASviS, L.: l'Italia e gli Obiettivi di sviluppo sostenibile (2020)
14. Istat, R.S.: informazioni statistiche per l'Agenda 2030 in Italia (2020)
15. Guarini, M., Nesticò, A., Morano, P., Sica, F.: A multicriteria economic analysis model for urban forestry projects. In: Calabrò, F., Spina, L.D., Bevilacqua, C. (eds.) New Metropolitan Perspectives: Local Knowledge and Innovation Dynamics Towards Territory Attractiveness Through the Implementation of Horizon/E2020/Agenda2030 – Volume 1, pp. 564–571. Springer International Publishing, Cham (2019). https://doi.org/10.1007/978-3-319-92099-3_63
16. Coscia, C., Lazzari, G., Rubino, I.: Values, memory, and the role of exploratory methods for policy-design processes and the sustainable redevelopment of waterfront contexts: the case of Officine Piaggio (Italy). Sustainability **10**(9), 2989 (2018). https://doi.org/10.3390/su1009 2989
17. Elmqvist, T., et al.: Urbanization, Biodiversity and Ecosystem Services: Challenges and Opportunities: A Global Assessment, p. 755. Springer Nature (2013)
18. Millennium ecosystem assessment, M.E.A.: Ecosystems and Human Well-being, vol. 5. Island Press, Washington, DC (2005)
19. Cerreta, M., Panaro, S., Poli, G.: A spatial decision support system for multifunctional landscape assessment: a transformative resilience perspective for vulnerable inland areas. Sustainability **13**(5), 2748 (2021)
20. Coscia, C., Rubino, I.: Fostering new value chains and social impact-oriented strategies in urban regeneration processes: what challenges for the evaluation discipline? Smart Innov. Syst. Technol. **178 SIST**, 983–992 (2021)
21. Guarini, M., Morano, P., Sica, F.: Eco-system Services and Integrated Urban Planning. A Multi-criteria Assessment Framework for Ecosystem Urban Forestry Projects. In: Mondini, G., Oppio, A., Stanghellini, S., Bottero, M., Abastante, F. (eds.) Values and Functions for Future Cities. GET, pp. 201–216. Springer, Cham (2020). https://doi.org/10.1007/978-3-030-23786-8_11
22. De Filippi, F., Coscia, C., Guido, R.: From smart-cities to smart-communities: how can we evaluate the impacts of innovation and inclusive processes in urban context? Int. J. E-Plan Res. **8**(2), 24–44 (2019)
23. El Gibari, S., Gómez, T., Ruiz, F.: Building composite indicators using multicriteria methods: a review. J. Bus. Econ. **89**(1), 1–24 (2018). https://doi.org/10.1007/s11573-018-0902-z

24. Danielis, R., Rotaris, L., Monte, A.: Composite indicators of sustainable urban mobility: estimating the rankings frequency distribution combining multiple methodologies. Int. J. Sustain. Transp. **12**(5), 380–395 (2018)
25. Asadzadeh, A., Kötter, T., Salehi, P., Birkmann, J.: Operationalizing a concept: the systematic review of composite indicator building for measuring community disaster resilience. Int. J. Disaster Risk Reduct. **25**, 147–162 (2017)
26. Aparicio, J., Kapelko, M., Monge, J.F.: A well-defined composite indicator: an application to corporate social responsibility. J. Optim. Theory Appl. **186**(1), 299–323 (2020). https://doi.org/10.1007/s10957-020-01701-1
27. Sardi, A., Sorano, E., Cantino, V., Garengo, P.: Big data and performance measurement research: Trends, evolution and future opportunities. Meas. Bus. Excell. (2020)
28. Morano, P., Guarini, M., Tajani, F., Anelli, D.: Sustainable Redevelopment: The Cost-Revenue Analysis to Support the Urban Planning Decisions. In: Gervasi, O., Murgante, B., Misra, S., Garau, C., Blečić, I., Taniar, D., Apduhan, B.O., Ana, M.A., Rocha, C., Tarantino, E., Torre, C.M., Karaca, Y. (eds.) Computational Science and Its Applications – ICCSA 2020: 20th International Conference, Cagliari, Italy, July 1–4, 2020, Proceedings, Part III, pp. 968–980. Springer International Publishing, Cham (2020). https://doi.org/10.1007/978-3-030-58808-3_69
29. Guarini, M.R., D'Addabbo, N., Morano, P., Tajani, F.: Multi-criteria analysis in compound decision processes: the AHP and the architectural competition for the chamber of deputies in Rome (Italy). Buildings **7**(2), 38 (2017). https://doi.org/10.3390/buildings7020038
30. Tajani, F., Morano, P., Locurcio, M., D'Addabbo, N.: Property valuations in times of crisis: artificial neural networks and evolutionary algorithms in comparison. In: Gervasi, O., Murgante, B., Misra, S., Gavrilova, M.L., Rocha, A.M.A.C., Torre, C., Taniar, D., Apduhan, B.O. (eds.) Computational Science and Its Applications – ICCSA 2015, pp. 194–209. Springer International Publishing, Cham (2015). https://doi.org/10.1007/978-3-319-21470-2_14
31. Dobrovolskienė, N., et al.: Developing a composite sustainability index for real estate projects using multiple criteria decision making. Oper. Res. Int. J. **19**(3), 617–635 (2017). https://doi.org/10.1007/s12351-017-0365-y
32. Fregonara, E., Coscia, C.: Multi criteria analyses, life cycle approaches and Delphi method: a methodological proposal to assess design scenarios | Analisi multi criteria, approcci life cycle e delphi method: Una proposta metodologica per valutare scenari di progetto. Valori Valutazioni **23**, 107–117 (2019)
33. Podvezko, V.: The comparative analysis of MCDA methods SAW and COPRAS. Eng. Econ. **22**(2), 134–146 (2011)
34. Ferreira, F.A., Santos, S.P.: Comparing trade-off adjustments in credit risk analysis of mortgage loans using AHP, Delphi and MACBETH. Int. J. Strateg. Prop. Manag. **20**(1), 44–63 (2016)
35. Attardi, R., Cerreta, M., Sannicandro, V., Torre, C.M.: Non-compensatory composite indicators for the evaluation of urban planning policy: the land-use policy efficiency index (LUPEI). Eur. J. Oper. Res. **264**(2), 491–507 (2018)
36. Zhou, P., Ang, B.W., Poh, K.L.: A mathematical programming approach to constructing composite indicators. Ecol. Econ. **62**(2), 291–297 (2007)
37. Morano, P., Tajani, F., Anelli, D.: Urban planning decisions: an evaluation support model for natural soil surface saving policies and the enhancement of properties in disuse. Property Manag. **38**(5), 699–723 (2020). https://doi.org/10.1108/PM-04-2020-0025

38. Nesticò, A., Endreny, T., Guarini, M., Sica, F., Anelli, D.: Real Estate Values, Tree Cover, and Per-Capita Income: An Evaluation of the Interdependencies in Buffalo City (NY). In: Gervasi, O., Murgante, B., Misra, S., Garau, C., Blečić, I., Taniar, D., Apduhan, B.O., Ana, M.A., Rocha, C., Tarantino, E., Torre, C.M., Karaca, Y. (eds.) Computational Science and Its Applications – ICCSA 2020: 20th International Conference, Cagliari, Italy, July 1–4, 2020, Proceedings, Part III, pp. 913–926. Springer International Publishing, Cham (2020). https://doi.org/10.1007/978-3-030-58808-3_65

39. Morano, P., Tajani, F.: Break Even Analysis for the financial verification of urban regeneration projects. Appl. Mech. Mater. **438–439**, 1830–1835 (2013). https://doi.org/10.4028/www.scientific.net/AMM.438-439.1830

40. D'Amico, G., Taddeo, R., Shi, L., Yigitcanlar, T., Ioppolo, G.: Ecological indicators of smart urban metabolism: a review of the literature on international standards. Ecol. Indic. **118**, 106808 (2020)

41. ISO 37120_2019: Sustainable Cities and Communities — Indicators for City Services and Quality of Life

42. Purnomo, F., Prabowo, H.: Smart city indicators: a systematic literature review. J. Telecommun. Electron. Comput. Eng. **8**(3), 161–164 (2016)

43. Yu, W., Xu, C.: Developing smart cities in China: an empirical analysis. Int. J. Public Admin. Digital Age **5**(3), 76–91 (2018)

44. Shi, Y., et al.: An integrated indicator system and evaluation model for regional sustainable development. Sustainability **11**(7), 2183 (2019)

45. Moghadam, S., Genta, C., Pignatelli, M., Lombardi, P.: Supporting sustainable urban planning process based on scenarios development. IOP Conf. Ser.: Earth Environ. Sci. **588**, 042022 (2020). https://doi.org/10.1088/1755-1315/588/4/042022

46. Satyro, W.C., Sacomano, J.B., Contador, J.C., Almeida, C.M., Giannetti, B.F.: Process of strategy formulation for sustainable environmental development: basic model. J. Clean. Prod. **166**, 1295–1304 (2017)

47. Andrews, S.S., Carroll, C.R.: Designing a soil quality assessment tool for sustainable agroecosystem management. Ecol. Appl. **11**(6), 1573–1585 (2001)

48. Pérez, V., et al.: Measuring the sustainability of Cuban tourism destinations considering stakeholders' perceptions. Int. J. Tour. Res. **19**(3), 318–328 (2017). https://doi.org/10.1002/jtr.2114

49. Blancas, F.J., Caballero, R., González, M., Lozano-Oyola, M., Pérez, F.: Goal programming synthetic indicators: an application for sustainable tourism in Andalusian coastal counties. Ecol. Econ. **69**(11), 2158–2172 (2010)

50. Bernini, C., Guizzardi, A., Angelini, G.: DEA-like model and common weights approach for the construction of a subjective community well-being indicator. Soc. Indic. Res. **114**(2), 405–424 (2013)

51. Salvati, L., Carlucci, M.: A composite index of sustainable development at the local scale: Italy as a case study. Ecol. Indic. **43**, 162–171 (2014)

52. Melyn, W., Moesen, W.: Towards a synthetic indicator of macroeconomic performance: unequal weighting when limited information is available. Public Econ. Res. Pap. 1–24 (1991)

53. Shwartz, M., Burgess, J.F., Berlowitz, D.: Benefit-of-the-doubt approaches for calculating a composite measure of quality. Health Serv. Outcomes Res. Method **9**(4), 234–251 (2009)

54. Despotis, D.K.: A reassessment of the human development index via data envelopment analysis. J. Oper. Res. Soc. **56**(8), 969–980 (2005)

55. Cherchye, L., Moesen, W., Rogge, N., Van Puyenbroeck, T.: An introduction to 'benefit of the doubt' composite indicators. Soc. Indic. Res. **82**(1), 111–145 (2007)

56. Savić, G., Martić, M.: Composite indicators construction by data envelopment analysis: Methodological background. In: Jeremic, V., Radojicic, Z., Dobrota, M. (eds.) Emerging

Trends in the Development and Application of Composite Indicators, pp. 98–126. IGI Global (2017). https://doi.org/10.4018/978-1-5225-0714-7.ch005

57. Puyenbroeck, T.: On the output orientation of the benefit-of-the-doubt-model. Soc. Indic. Res. **139**(2), 415–431 (2017). https://doi.org/10.1007/s11205-017-1734-x

58. Guijarro, F., Poyatos, J.A.: Designing a sustainable development goal index through a goal programming model: the case of EU-28 countries. Sustainability **10**(9), 3167 (2018)

59. Morano, P., Tajani, F.: The transfer of development rights for the regeneration of brownfield sites. Appl. Mech. Mater. **409–410**, 971–978 (2013). https://doi.org/10.4028/www.scientific.net/AMM.409-410.971

60. Nesticò, A., Guarini, M.R., Morano, P., Sica, F.: An economic analysis algorithm for urban forestry projects. Sustainability **11**(2), 314 (2019). https://doi.org/10.3390/su11020314

61. Guarini, M.R., Morano, P., Sica, F.: Integrated ecosystem design: an evaluation model to support the choice of eco-compatible technological solutions for residential building. Energies **12**(14), 2659 (2019). https://doi.org/10.3390/en12142659

62. Caballero, R., Gómez, T., Ruiz, F.: Goal programming: realistic targets for the near future. J. Multi-Criteria Decis. Anal. **16**(3–4), 79–110 (2009)

63. Burkhard, B., Kroll, F., Müller, F., Windhorst, W.: Landscapes' capacities to provide ecosystem services—a concept for land-cover based assessments. Landsc. Online **15**, 1–22 (2009)

64. Cherchye, L., Kuosmanen, T.: *Benchmarking sustainable development: a synthetic meta-index approach* (No. 2004/28). WIDER Research Paper (2004)

65. Sutton, P.C., Costanza, R.: Global estimates of market and non-market values derived from nighttime satellite imagery, land cover, and ecosystem service valuation. Ecol. Econ. **41**(3), 509–527 (2002)

Building Industry and Energy Efficiency: A Review of Three Major Issues at Stake

Sergio Copiello$^{(\boxtimes)}$ ⓘ, Laura Gabrielli ⓘ, and Ezio Micelli ⓘ

Department of Architecture and Arts, University IUAV of Venice, Santa Croce 191,
30135 Venezia, Italy
{sergio.copiello,laura.gabrielli,ezio.micelli}@iuav.it

Abstract. During the last two decades, the European Union regulation has paid more and more attention to the issue of energy efficiency, especially as far as the building sector is concerned. Lately, the adoption of the European Green Deal (EGD) has further fueled interest in the topic. The building industry is expected to step forward towards decarbonization, as well as to mobilize towards a clean and circular economy, so supporting the pursuit of climate neutrality. In this position paper, we aim to discuss three major issues at stake, which are crucial to increase the renovation rate of the building stock and, hence, to the success of the EGD. The first key issue is whether a cost premium has to be expected due to retrofit projects. The second key issue is whether or not the large swing currently experienced in the price premium for building energy efficiency undermines stakeholders' confidence. The third key issue is whether we need tailored evaluation methodologies for energy-efficient building portfolios.

Keywords: Building energy efficiency · Cost premium · Price premium · Construction industry · Real estate market · Spatial econometrics

1 Introduction

Energy-saving, first, starting from the seventies, and energy efficiency, later, from the nineties, have attracted growing attention among policy-makers and have established themselves as prolific research strands, especially as far as the building industry is concerned. In Europe, the first national regulations on energy-saving in buildings date back to the mid-seventies, mostly in the wake of the oil shocks of the time. Remarkable examples are the thermal insulation rules and other codes and standards meant to improve the energy use in residential buildings adopted in France (1974) [1], UK (1975), Italy (1976) [2], Germany (1976–1978) [3, 4], Denmark (1979) [5], and Sweden (1979) [6]. However, as time passed, the regulation focus changed to energy efficiency in buildings as an essential strategy to pursue the long-term sustainability goals [7, 8]. The evolution is clearly noticeable as objectives shifted: no more the mere energy-saving (and money-saving) per se but mostly environmental preservation and climate change adaptation [9]. Also, an evolutionary trend affects the policies, leading to the substitution of command-and-control tools with incentive schemes [10, 11].

© Springer Nature Switzerland AG 2021
O. Gervasi et al. (Eds.): ICCSA 2021, LNCS 12954, pp. 226–240, 2021.
https://doi.org/10.1007/978-3-030-86979-3_17

Starting from the early 2000s, the effort to improve building energy efficiency escalated thanks to the Energy Performance of Buildings Directive (EPBD, Directive 2002/91/EC), with a recast in the early 2010s (Directive 2010/31/EU). The recent adoption of the European Green Deal (EGD) [12] has further fueled interest in building energy efficiency. This action plan meant to protect and improve health and wellbeing of citizens [13] has introduced new keywords into the common lexicon of the related research fields. Due to growing concerns for the human footprint on the environment [14–16], among the pillars of the EGD is climate neutrality, to be achieved by 2050. The decarbonization of the energy system is a critical step to that end. Accordingly, the building industry is asked and expected to mobilize, along with manufacturing and transportation industries, towards a clean and circular economy. Specifically, the construction industry is required to at least double the yearly renovation rate of the building stock [17], involving both private and public buildings and bringing together a variety of stakeholders to address the known barriers to renovation.

In this position paper, we aim to discuss three major issues at stake concerning energy efficiency in the building industry and the real estate market. Addressing these issues is, in our view, crucial to increase the renovation rate of the building stock and, hence, to the success of the EGD. The first key issue is whether or not the large swing currently experienced in the price premium for building energy efficiency undermines stakeholders' confidence. Namely, does the evidence support the assumption that energy-efficient buildings command a price premium and rent premium over conventional ones? And also, is there still too much uncertainty in the estimated magnitude of that price and rent premium, which reflects in a gap between the expected and actual interest of the stakcholders? The second key issue is whether a cost premium has to be expected due to retrofit projects. Namely, should we expect the refurbished, energy-efficient buildings to cost more than those reflecting baseline building standards? And if that is the case, what the anticipated magnitude of the cost premium is? The other key issue can be summarized as follows: do we need tailored evaluation methodologies for energy-cfficient building portfolios? Namely, when shifting the focus from an individual building to a whole building portfolio, can we envision innovative evaluation tools that outperform the usual ones? The discussion here benefits from reviewing the most recent literature, especially the studies modeling construction costs and real estate prices employing spatial econometric methods.

2 Three Major Issues at Stake

2.1 Does the Large Swing in Price Premiums for Building Energy Efficiency Undermine Stakeholders' Confidence?

The recast of the EU Energy Performance of Buildings Directive (2010/31/EU) identifies the energy performance certificate (EPC) as a cornerstone of its strategy. The same act makes it mandatory to hand over the EPC "to the buyer or new tenant" each time "buildings or building units are constructed, sold or rented out" (art. 12, 2nd clause). Although its effectiveness has been questioned [18, 19], the EPC scheme has been interpreted as a useful tool to mitigate the energy efficiency gap - namely, to reduce the information asymmetries characterizing the real estate markets - and increase investments in energy-efficient buildings [20, 21]. Despite several flaws and issues are ascribed to the energy performance certification [22–25], with problems especially credited to misassessment [26, 27], EPCs have been implemented by national regulations and turned into practice in the real estate markets.

Although early analyses on the topic can be traced back to the late eighties [28, 29], the growing availability of EPCs for properties for sale or rent has made it possible to analyze whether a relationship occurs between the property price or rent and the energy performance of the building unit, as summarized by the energy performance index or the energy rating band [8, 30, 31]. The properties characterized by higher energy performance are likely to be sold at a premium, and the same is expected to hold in the case of a tenancy.

So far, to the best of our knowledge, only two studies find huge price premiums in residential properties, far higher than 50% in the comparison between A and G, namely, the best and the worst energy rating band. The first study [32] focuses on the German residential market. A price premium up to 114.3% characterizes the B-labeled properties compared to the G-rated ones. The second study [33] presents an analysis of a medium-size city and a town in Southern Italy. At its maximum, the price gap between high-performance and low-performing dwellings is found to vary in the range of 45.5–84.0%.

However, when comparing the most efficient residential units (energy rating bands B, A, A+, and A1 to A4) to the mid-tier performance ones (energy rating band D), double-digit percentage premiums are usually reported. For instance, a price advantage between 20% and 30% is found in the analysis of housing prices in Belfast, Northern Ireland [34], Wales [35], Helsinki, Finland [36], and Portugal [37]. Furthermore, a price premium of about 10% or more is found concerning the housing markets in the Netherlands [38], Denmark [39], and Northern Ireland [40]. Evidence supporting the occurrence of significant premiums is also identified in several contemporary studies [41–44].

Depending on the estimation methodology, and especially on the functional form used to model the relationship between the energy consumption and property prices, a few other works shift the focus to the elasticity of housing price to energy performance. There, a double-logarithmic (log-log) function is used instead of the common semi-logarithmic (semi-log or log-linear) one. Again, the findings point to the fact that higher performance is rewarded with larger prices. The price change is estimated to be quite small in two early studies: from 0.09% for a percent change in consumption concerning homes in Dublin, Ireland [45], to 0.40% for a percent change in consumption as far as the Swedish private housing market is concerned [46]. Much larger – up to 9.0% – is the price effect of energy efficiency found in another study of single-family homes in Sweden [47] but the sign of the relationship is different than expected since the property prices grow as the energy consumption increases. Also worth noting are the results of an analysis on nine thousand properties located in the Alicante province, Southern Spain [48]. The latter study, which controls for different climate regimes in the analyzed area, tests the hypothesis of the existence of a green premium by assessing the sensitivity of the (asking) price to changes in either the level of energy consumption or the amount of carbon dioxide emissions and find an effect up to 3.10%.

Almost all of the above-referenced studies focus on the European EPC scheme and the housing market. Nonetheless, confirmations of the assumption that energy efficiency commands a price premium are found elsewhere [49–52], which also means according to different energy rating schemes [53–59], and concerning commercial properties too [60–68]. Notably, a growing number of studies focus on rating schemes other than those in place in the Western Countries, signally on the Green Mark labels as adopted in Singapore [69–74]. They all converge towards the occurrence of a price premium, though its magnitude is highly uncertain: from 1% to 9% as far as certified buildings are concerned, 2–40% for the Gold rating, 8–17% for the Platinum rating.

The results above in their own way and, in wider terms, the findings summarized earlier make it clear the issue at stake is about ambiguity and vagueness. To date, uncertainty is an inherent feature of the assessments on building energy efficiency [75], and estimating the price premium makes no exception. Incidentally, uncertainty is further magnified by the finding that the price premium is likely to be non-stationary over time [37, 57, 76]. Aside from that, the large swings experienced in the available studies can be partly explained by the differences in the methodological setting, sample size, climate area, building typology, market features, socioeconomic background, and so forth. Still, they are too wide to answer the stakeholders' demand for sound and viable investment opportunities [2, 77–79]. The econometric research in building energy efficiency is thus asked to go to the roots of this issue. The forthcoming studies are expected to narrow down the uncertainty range and unequivocally identify the reasons behind it. Lately, a great step forward has been taken thanks to the adoption of spatial dynamic models, especially those in the classes of Geographically Weighted Regression (GWR) [80], Spatial Autoregressive (SAR) [81–83], and Spatial Error Models (SEM) [74, 84]. Further research into robust space-time modeling is welcome and should commit to delivering robust estimates.

2.2 Building Industry and Retrofit: Should We Worry About a Cost Premium?

The evaluation of the profitability of green real estate investments must not be confined to a mere estimate of a premium price in terms of market and income values. The eligibility criteria for green investments on traditional ones must take into consideration the possibility of experiencing an increase in the costs due to the use of more expensive materials and processes.

Since the first decade of this century, several researchers have been dealing with the cost rate involved in projects aiming at higher levels of coherence than the targets of sustainability. A first overview of this issue deals with the general perception of sustainable buildings held by market operators: Ekung et al. [85] highlighted how often operators tend to tie up such products with consistent increases in the final cost, still referring to a few significant cases. Green architecture is always judged as more expensive, which indeed represents an obstacle to the application of new technologies [86].

Despite that, empirical research has pointed out that there is no differential cost between certified buildings and traditional buildings. According to the studies conducted by Kats [87], the Morrison Hershfield report [88] and Berry [89], the variation in their costs is quite low, if not even absent at all. Matthiessen and Morris [90] make a comparison between 138 buildings not provided by certification and 83 certified ones: as a conclusion, there is no significant variation between their production costs.

Other researches highlight a possible differential cost rate in LEED constructions and traditional interventions, yet statistically not relevant [91]. Likewise, Bartlett and Howard [92] underline that there is no empirical proof for the common evaluation of a premium cost between 5 and 15%. These scenarios are in fact diverse and some researches might end up in different resolutions. Consistent differentiations in the final value have been detected by other studies in the form of a 5-to-10% deviation, with increasing values compared to the LEED certification levels of the cases in analysis [93]. Along the same lines, some researchers argue that marginal costs are quite irrelevant in lesser value LEED certifications, whereas they grow exponentially in the sight of higher quality standards [94], that is to say, gold and platinum. However, there is a substantial lack in collecting data on operating costs in buildings claimed as sustainable: as a result, it becomes difficult to make long-term comparisons both among them and to the Life Cycle Assessment analysis [95].

By comparing costs and benefits, some studies aim at taking stock by evaluating the overall profitability in support of green real estate investments [96] rather than determining their proper differential costs. As a matter of fact, this cost-analysis scenario reveals itself as wide and concerning. It in fact highlights a particular issue – that is the increasing cost rate in green investments – that finds no systemic consistency in the field of empirical studies. Similarly, profitability measures that bring together benefits and additional costs are still quite vague and therefore potentially subjected to useful insights both in theoretical and in empirical fields of application [97].

2.3 Do We Need Tailored Evaluation Methodologies for Energy-Efficient Building Portfolios?

In the last period, we are witnessing a new paradigm and a new change of mentality: improving the energy efficiency of real estate assets of public administrations, insurance companies, banks, social security institutions, real estate, and non-real estate funds has become a crucial element in the investors' agenda.

Maintenance and energy efficiency measures need to be carefully planned, considering existing and renewal leases and budget and time constraints. In addition to the problems related to the technical design of interventions, there is also the need to plan efficient actions over time and not make a large part of the portfolio involved in the interventions unproductive. Therefore, the energy efficiency of large property portfolios is bound by budgetary, technical, financial and regulatory constraints and requires a careful assessment of the many aspects that need to be considered simultaneously.

The evaluation must necessarily be able to deal with complexity, long-term issues, multiple actors and different points of view. Managing a plethora of edifices simultaneously, comparing numerous alternative design scenarios to achieve the optimal result, needs innovative solutions, complex evaluation techniques, and a multidisciplinary approach.

An extensive literature review on the methodological steps of real estate portfolio energy efficiency has been conducted in [98]. The methodology around which an intervention strategy is developed might involve several steps:

- Database construction: in this phase, the information provided by the client is collected and integrated with original data obtained from surveys and others created through simulation using specific software for energy modelling of buildings;
- Scenario and strategy mapping: possible scenarios are defined concerning the strategy of efficiency improvement, regeneration and adding value processes of the building stock, according to the goals that the investor intends to achieve;
- The assessment of economic and environmental impact: the feasibility of the retrofit actions is verified at the building level, considering the structural and technological aspects, but also at a portfolio level, considering all constraint and different criteria employed to value the best option when considering a plethora of buildings;
- Finally, the last phase of the process concerns optimization.

Concerning the data construction, research and case studies have also shown that handling a real estate portfolio faces a time-and money-consuming analysis. Surveys cannot be carried out for every single building, so a "reference building" (or "sample building") approach is adopted. The reference building is an existing building representative of a particular portion of the stock (cluster) [99–103]. A dataset of information about reference building's materials, geometry, technologies, facilities, users' behaviour and occupation, as well as climate zone, is collected. The results are then extended to all buildings that belong to the same cluster. European authorities have promoted the procedure of "reference building" when acting on different and several categories of buildings [104]. Rather than a real sample building, a building archetype artificially constructed to represent a specific class of building in the stock is also possible [105].

The mapping of scenarios and strategies for a portfolio is most similar to designing interventions conducted for individual buildings. Starting from a set of energy retrofit solutions, combinations can be assumed to achieve different energy consumption outcomes. Energy retrofit measures can be clustered into three groups [106], which concerns the use of renewable energy in buildings, i.e. solar and photovoltaic panels, wind and geothermal energy [107, 108]; the reduction of energy demand by introducing new and more efficient technologies, passive strategies, heating/cooling system upgrade, thermal insulation, windows and shading solutions, natural ventilation [109, 110]; and the change in energy consumption through different user behaviour, occupancy schedule, temperature settings, automation systems [111].

The third step regards the analysis of the economic, ecological, and social impacts. Reducing energy consumption or CO_2 emission is the most common indicator employed in supporting the decision-making process for planning retrofit actions. Nevertheless, the economic approaches are the most used indicators to quantify the efficiency of each retrofit option, allowing the evaluation of the economic and financial impact of the measures. Among the economic assessment techniques, there are Life Cycle Cost (LCC) analysis [100, 112–114] and Discounted Cash Flow [115–117].

Cultural/social criteria have rarely been used to evaluate the energy retrofit measure on buildings and portfolio. However, indicators regarding user/occupant health and indoor comfort are more frequently used among the qualitative indicators.

Few attempts have been made to introduce sustainability indicators in the evaluation, bringing the assessment of retrofits measures to a multi-criteria dimension, even if only the environmental criteria have been used in the techniques, ignoring the social issues [102, 118], as their assessment may seem less straightforward to implement. Multi-criteria evaluation techniques have been used mainly to prioritize different options [119] instead of valuing the retrofit options in all their aspects.

A fourth step rarely addressed in literature and practice is the optimization process, which helps to identify the best solution from the range of possible alternatives. It is an essential and crucial step if an investor wants to deal with energy efficiency at a portfolio level, both for the public and the private sector. At a portfolio level, the complexity of considering the budget restriction, the timetable, the architectural limitations and other constraints leads to optimization functions, where several dependent and independent variables and goals have to be analyzed simultaneously. Usually, multiple objectives are identified, including economic, environmental, cultural or social, and all of these are subject to financial and technical constraints. Reliable and flexible decision support models need to be implemented to help investors and owners of large portfolios increase the value of their properties by optimizing cash flows without excluding environmental, cultural and social objectives. In most of the cases studied in the literature, the optimization process is structured as a "cost-optimal analysis", which is performed by comparing, for each energy retrofit hypothesis, the total costs with the corresponding energy consumption. The cost-optimal methodology is required by the European Directive 2010/31/EU [104], and a methodological framework for cost-optimal estimation in the context of building retrofit has been set up [120].

However, this approach still does not reach the goal of pursuing multiple alternatives under multiple constraints. To this end, multi-attribute or multi-objective procedures can come to the aid of managing a multiplicity of criteria at the same time. In this sense, an important step has been taken in [121–123], where multiple objectives of sustainability, energy efficiency, indoor comfort, thus environmental and financial point of view are considered. In [122], a combination of LCC and LCA has been used to pursue an environmental and financial analysis.

An interdisciplinary approach should connect statistical techniques for the accurate prediction of energy consumption, economic evaluation methodologies, multi-attribute analysis, computer programming and optimisation algorithms, producing an integrated and unified decision-making model. Such a model was proposed by [124]: multiple aspects, architectural, economic, technical, energy, were placed in an optimisation function, including a risk analysis to assess the reliability of the results obtained with the alternative scenario evaluation process.

Such valuation techniques should leap scale and be adapted to real estate stocks belonging to a neighbourhood, a city, or a nation that intends to pursue energy efficiency, monetary savings, improvement of the inhabitants' living conditions, and citizens' health status. On a larger scale, policies and programmes must pay attention to long-term actions. This will improve portfolio management and resource planning and facilitate energy efficiency as a long-term resource, achieving benefits for society.

On the other hand, long-term measures provide long-term value, which is essential for resource planning and can better support non-energy benefits, such as improved health and safety of citizens. These models can be used on many scales, be it at the urban or national level. Their results can be used to identify actions, risk, and possible performances to be achieved. Those methods contribute to decision making in two ways:

- by helping designers of individual buildings to understand how their n choices might influence – or be influenced by – the overall performance of the stock;
- by providing planners and policymakers at various scales (from local to national) with a more robust database on building costs, energy and resource use, environmental effects, and risk management.

3 Conclusions

Consistently with the reasonings above, we expect the growing trend of studies on building energy efficiency is bound to continue over the next years. We also expect new insights into the three issues we discuss here:

- the actual magnitude of the price premium for high-performance building units;
- the potential occurrence of a cost premium for energy-efficient buildings;
- the opportunity to use tailored evaluation methodologies when shifting the focus from an individual residential or commercial property to a building portfolio.

Each of them shapes a specific, prolific research strand. Most importantly, they are closely interconnected with each other, which is why we also expect to see them jointly addressed in forthcoming studies.

References

1. Gauzin-Müller, D.: Sustainable Architecture and Urbanism. Birkhäuser, Basel (2002)
2. Copiello, S.: Leveraging energy efficiency to finance public-private social housing projects. Energy Policy **96**, 217–230 (2016). https://doi.org/10.1016/j.enpol.2016.06.003
3. Schimschar, S.: Policy Instruments: The Case of Germany. In: Torgal, F.P., Mistretta, M., Kaklauskas, A., Granqvist, C.G., Cabeza, L.F. (eds.) Nearly Zero Energy Building Refurbishment, pp. 15–60. Springer London, London (2013). https://doi.org/10.1007/978-1-4471-5523-2_2
4. Weißenberger, M., Jensch, W., Lang, W.: The convergence of life cycle assessment and nearly zero-energy buildings: the case of Germany. Energy Build. **76**, 551–557 (2014). https://doi.org/10.1016/j.enbuild.2014.03.028
5. Tommerup, H., Svendsen, S.: Energy savings in Danish residential building stock. Energy Build. **38**, 618–626 (2006). https://doi.org/10.1016/j.enbuild.2005.08.017
6. Nässén, J., Holmberg, J.: Energy efficiency—a forgotten goal in the Swedish building sector? Energy Policy **33**, 1037–1051 (2005). https://doi.org/10.1016/j.enpol.2003.11.004

7. Economidou, M., Todeschi, V., Bertoldi, P., D'Agostino, D., Zangheri, P., Castellazzi, L.: Review of 50 years of EU energy efficiency policies for buildings. Energy Build. **225**, 110322 (2020). https://doi.org/10.1016/j.enbuild.2020.110322

8. Copiello, S.: Building energy efficiency: a research branch made of paradoxes. Renew. Sustain. Energy Rev. **69**, 1064–1076 (2017). https://doi.org/10.1016/j.rser.2016.09.094

9. Kerr, N., Gouldson, A., Barrett, J.: The rationale for energy efficiency policy: assessing the recognition of the multiple benefits of energy efficiency retrofit policy. Energy Policy **106**, 212–221 (2017). https://doi.org/10.1016/j.enpol.2017.03.053

10. Ramos, A., Gago, A., Labandeira, X., Linares, P.: The role of information for energy efficiency in the residential sector. Energy Econ. **52**, S17–S29 (2015). https://doi.org/10.1016/j.eneco.2015.08.022

11. Bonifaci, P., Copiello, S.: Incentive Policies for Residential Buildings Energy Retrofit: An Analysis of Tax Rebate Programs in Italy. In: Bisello, A., Vettorato, D., Laconte, P., Costa, S. (eds.) SSPCR 2017. GET, pp. 267–279. Springer, Cham (2018). https://doi.org/10.1007/978-3-319-75774-2_19

12. European Commission: The European Green Deal. Brussels (2019)

13. Haines, A., Scheelbeek, P.: European green deal: a major opportunity for health improvement. Lancet **395**, 1327–1329 (2020). https://doi.org/10.1016/S0140-6736(20)30109-4

14. European Commission: A Clean Planet for all. A European long-term strategic vision for a prosperous, modern, competitive and climate neutral economy. Brussels (2018)

15. Trippel, E.: How green is green enough? The changing landscape of financing a sustainable European economy. ERA Forum **21**(2), 155–170 (2020). https://doi.org/10.1007/s12027-020-00611-z

16. Copiello, S., Grillenzoni, C.: Economic development and climate change. Which is the cause and which the effect? Energy Rep. **6**, 49–59 (2020). https://doi.org/10.1016/j.egyr.2020.08.024

17. Pohoryles, D.A., Maduta, C., Bournas, D.A., Kouris, L.A.: Energy performance of existing residential buildings in Europe: a novel approach combining energy with seismic retrofitting. Energy Build. **223**, 110024 (2020). https://doi.org/10.1016/j.enbuild.2020.110024

18. Fleckinger, P., Glachant, M., Tamokoué Kamga, P.H.: Energy performance certificates and investments in building energy efficiency: a theoretical analysis. Energy Econ. **84**, 104604 (2019). https://doi.org/10.1016/j.eneco.2019.104604

19. Broberg, T., Egüez, A., Kažukauskas, A.: Effects of energy performance certificates on investment: a quasi-natural experiment approach. Energy Econ. **84** (2019). https://doi.org/10.1016/j.eneco.2019.104480

20. Aydin, E., Correa, S.B., Brounen, D.: Energy performance certification and time on the market. J. Environ. Econ. Manage. **98**, 102270 (2019). https://doi.org/10.1016/j.jeem.2019.102270

21. Comerford, D.A., Lange, I., Moro, M.: Proof of concept that requiring energy labels for dwellings can induce retrofitting. Energy Econ. **69**, 204–212 (2018). https://doi.org/10.1016/j.eneco.2017.11.013

22. Gonzalez-Caceres, A., Lassen, A.K., Nielsen, T.R.: Barriers and challenges of the recommendation list of measures under the EPBD scheme: a critical review. Energy Build. **223**, 110065 (2020). https://doi.org/10.1016/j.enbuild.2020.110065

23. Hardy, A., Glew, D.: An analysis of errors in the energy performance certificate database. Energy Policy **129**, 1168–1178 (2019). https://doi.org/10.1016/j.enpol.2019.03.022

24. Organ, S.: Minimum energy efficiency – is the energy performance certificate a suitable foundation? Int. J. Build. Pathol. Adapt. ahead-of-print (2020). https://doi.org/10.1108/ijbpa-03-2020-0016.

25. Li, Y., Kubicki, S., Guerriero, A., Rezgui, Y.: Review of building energy performance certification schemes towards future improvement. Renew. Sustain. Energy Rev. **113**, 109244 (2019). https://doi.org/10.1016/j.rser.2019.109244

26. Ahern, C., Norton, B.: Energy performance certification: misassessment due to assuming default heat losses. Energy Build. **224**, 110229 (2020). https://doi.org/10.1016/j.enbuild. 2020.110229

27. Tronchin, L., Fabbri, K.: Energy performance certificate of building and confidence interval in assessment: an Italian case study. Energy Policy **48**, 176–184 (2012). https://doi.org/10. 1016/j.enpol.2012.05.011

28. Gilmer, R.W.: Energy labels and economic search. Energy Econ. **11**, 213–218 (1989). https:// doi.org/10.1016/0140-9883(89)90026-1

29. Dinan, T.M., Miranowski, J.A.: Estimating the implicit price of energy efficiency improvements in the residential housing market: a hedonic approach. J. Urban Econ. **25**, 52–67 (1989). https://doi.org/10.1016/0094-1190(89)90043-0

30. Bio Intelligence Service, Lyons, R., IEEP: Energy performance certificates in buildings and their impact on transaction prices and rents in selected EU countries. Final report prepared for European Commission (DG Energy) (2013).

31. Bonifaci, P., Copiello, S.: Real estate market and building energy performance: data for a mass appraisal approach. Data Brief **5**, 1060–1065 (2015). https://doi.org/10.1016/j.dib. 2015.11.027

32. Cajias, M., Piazolo, D.: Green performs better: energy efficiency and financial return on buildings. J. Corp. Real Estate **15**, 53–72 (2013). https://doi.org/10.1108/JCRE-12-2012-0031

33. Manganelli, B., Morano, P., Tajani, F., Salvo, F.: Affordability assessment of energy-efficient building construction in Italy. Sustainability. **11**, 249 (2019). https://doi.org/10.3390/su1101 0249

34. Davis, P.T., McCord, J., McCord, M.J., Haran, M.: Modelling the effect of energy performance certificate rating on property value in the Belfast housing market. Int. J. Hous. Mark. Anal. **8**, 292–317 (2015). https://doi.org/10.1108/JEIM-07-2014-0077

35. Fuerst, F., McAllister, P., Nanda, A., Wyatt, P.: Energy performance ratings and house prices in Wales: an empirical study. Energy Policy **92**, 20–33 (2016). https://doi.org/10.1016/j. enpol.2016.01.024

36. Fuerst, F., Oikarinen, E., Harjunen, O.: Green signalling effects in the market for energy-efficient residential buildings. Appl. Energy. **180**, 560–571 (2016). https://doi.org/10.1016/ j.apenergy.2016.07.076

37. Evangelista, R., Ramalho, E., Andrade, J., e Silva, : On the use of hedonic regression models to measure the effect of energy efficiency on residential property transaction prices: evidence for Portugal and selected data issues. Energy Econ. **86**, 104699 (2020). https://doi.org/10. 1016/j.eneco.2020.104699

38. Brounen, D., Kok, N.: On the economics of energy labels in the housing market. J. Environ. Econ. Manage. **62**, 166–179 (2011). https://doi.org/10.1016/j.jeem.2010.11.006

39. Jensen, O.M., Hansen, A.R., Kragh, J.: Market response to the public display of energy performance rating at property sales. Energy Policy **93**, 229–235 (2016). https://doi.org/10. 1016/j.enpol.2016.02.029

40. McCord, M., Haran, M., Davis, P., McCord, J.: Energy performance certificates and house prices: a quantile regression approach. J. Eur. Real Estate Res. **13**, 409–434 (2020). https:// doi.org/10.1108/JERER-06-2020-0033

41. Bonifaci, P., Copiello, S.: Price premium for buildings energy efficiency: empirical findings from a hedonic model. Valori e Valutazioni **14**, 5–15 (2015)

42. Hyland, M., Lyons, R.C., Lyons, S.: The value of domestic building energy efficiency—evidence from Ireland. Energy Econ. **40**, 943–952 (2013). https://doi.org/10.1016/j.eneco.2013.07.020

43. Fuerst, F., Oikarinen, E., Shimizu, C., Szumilo, N.: Measuring "Green Value": An International Perspective. London (2014)

44. Fuerst, F., McAllister, P., Nanda, A., Wyatt, P.: Does energy efficiency matter to homebuyers? An investigation of EPC ratings and transaction prices in England. Energy Econ. **48**, 145–156 (2015). https://doi.org/10.1016/j.eneco.2014.12.012

45. Stanley, S., Lyons, R.C., Lyons, S.: The price effect of building energy ratings in the Dublin residential market. Energ. Effic. **9**(4), 875–885 (2015). https://doi.org/10.1007/s12053-015-9396-5

46. Cerin, P., Hassel, L.G., Semenova, N.: Energy performance and housing prices. Sustain. Dev. **22**, 404–419 (2014). https://doi.org/10.1002/sd.1566

47. Wahlström, M.H.: Doing good but not that well? A dilemma for energy conserving homeowners. Energy Econ. **60**, 197–205 (2016). https://doi.org/10.1016/j.eneco.2016.09.025

48. Taltavull de La Paz, P., Perez-Sanchez, V., Mora-Garcia, R.-T., Perez-Sanchez, J.-C.: Green premium evidence from climatic areas: a case in Southern Europe, Alicante (Spain). Sustainability **11**, 686 (2019). https://doi.org/10.3390/su11030686

49. Fuerst, F., Shimizu, C.: Green luxury goods? The economics of eco-labels in the Japanese housing market. J. Jpn. Int. Econ. **39**, 108–122 (2016). https://doi.org/10.1016/j.jjie.2016.01.003

50. Zheng, S., Wu, J., Kahn, M.E., Deng, Y.: The nascent market for "green" real estate in Beijing. Eur. Econ. Rev. **56**, 974–984 (2012). https://doi.org/10.1016/j.euroecorev.2012.02.012

51. Soriano, F.: Energy efficiency rating and house prices in the ACT – Modelling the relationship of energy efficiency attributes to house price: the case of detached houses sold in the Australian Capital Territory in 2005 and 2006. Department of the Environment, Water, Heritage and the Arts, Canberra (2008)

52. Pride, D., Little, J., Mueller-Stoffels, M.: The value of residential energy efficiency in interior Alaska: a hedonic pricing analysis. Energy Policy **123**, 450–460 (2018). https://doi.org/10.1016/j.enpol.2018.09.017

53. Bloom, B., Nobe, M.C., Nobe, M.D.: Valuing green home designs: a study of ENERGY STAR homes. J. Sustain. Real Estate. **3**, 109–126 (2011). https://doi.org/10.1080/10835547.2011.12091818

54. Mesthrige Jayantha, W., Sze Man, W.: Effect of green labelling on residential property price: a case study in Hong Kong. J. Facil. Manag. **11**, 31–51 (2013). https://doi.org/10.1108/14725961311301457

55. Kahn, M.E., Kok, N.: The capitalization of green labels in the California housing market. Reg. Sci. Urban Econ. **47**, 25–34 (2014). https://doi.org/10.1016/j.regsciurbeco.2013.07.001

56. Bruegge, C., Carrión-Flores, C., Pope, J.C.: Does the housing market value energy efficient homes? Evidence from the energy star program. Reg. Sci. Urban Econ. **57**, 63–76 (2016). https://doi.org/10.1016/j.regsciurbeco.2015.12.001

57. Aroul, R.R., Rodriguez, M.: The increasing value of green for residential real estate. J. Sustain. Real Estate **9**, 112–130 (2017). https://doi.org/10.1080/10835547.2017.12091894

58. Fuerst, F., Warren-Myers, G.: Does voluntary disclosure create a green lemon problem? Energy-efficiency ratings and house prices. Energy Econ. **74**, 1–12 (2018). https://doi.org/10.1016/j.eneco.2018.04.041

59. Mangialardo, A., Micelli, E., Saccani, F.: Does sustainability affect real estate market values? Empirical Evidence from the office buildings market in Milan (Italy). Sustainability **11**, 12 (2018). https://doi.org/10.3390/su11010012

60. Eichholtz, P., Kok, N., Quigley, J.M.: Doing well by doing good? Green office buildings. Am. Econ. Rev. **100**, 2492–2509 (2010). https://doi.org/10.1257/aer.100.5.2492
61. Fuerst, F., McAllister, P.: The impact of energy performance certificates on the rental and capital values of commercial property assets. Energy Policy **39**, 6608–6614 (2011). https://doi.org/10.1016/j.enpol.2011.08.005
62. Das, P., Wiley, J.A.: Determinants of premia for energy-efficient design in the office market. J. Prop. Res. **31**, 64–86 (2014). https://doi.org/10.1080/09599916.2013.788543
63. Kok, N., Jennen, M.: The impact of energy labels and accessibility on office rents. Energy Policy **46**, 489–497 (2012). https://doi.org/10.1016/j.enpol.2012.04.015
64. Reichardt, A., Fuerst, F., Rottke, N.B., Zietz, J.: Sustainable building certification and the rent premium: a panel data approach. J. Real Estate Res. **34**, 99–126 (2012)
65. Eichholtz, P., Kok, N., Quigley, J.M.: The economics of green building. Rev. Econ. Stat. **95**, 50–63 (2013). https://doi.org/10.1162/REST_a_00291
66. Chegut, A., Eichholtz, P., Kok, N.: Supply, demand and the value of green buildings. Urban Stud. **51**, 22–43 (2014). https://doi.org/10.1177/0042098013484526
67. Devine, A., Kok, N.: Green certification and building performance: implications for tangibles and intangibles. J. Portf. Manag. **41**, 151–163 (2015)
68. Fuerst, F., McAllister, P.: Green noise or green value? Measuring the effects of environmental certification on office values. Real Estate Econ. **39**, 45–69 (2011). https://doi.org/10.1111/j.1540-6229.2010.00286.x
69. Deng, Y., Wu, J.: Economic returns to residential green building investment: the developers' perspective. Reg. Sci. Urban Econ. **47**, 35–44 (2014). https://doi.org/10.1016/j.regsciurbeco.2013.09.015
70. Heinzle, S., Yip, A., Xing, M.: The influence of green building certification schemes on real estate investor behaviour: evidence from Singapore. Urban Stud. **50**(10), 1970–1987 (2013). https://doi.org/10.1177/0042098013477693
71. Addae-Dapaah, K., Chieh, S.J.: Green mark certification: does the market understand ? J. Sustain. Real Estate **3**, 162–191 (2011)
72. Deng, Y., Li, Z., Quigley, J.M.: Economic returns to energy-efficient investments in the housing market: evidence from Singapore. Reg. Sci. Urban Econ. **42**, 506–515 (2012). https://doi.org/10.1016/j.regsciurbeco.2011.04.004
73. Fesselmeyer, E.: The value of green certification in the Singapore housing market. Econ. Lett. **163**, 36–39 (2018). https://doi.org/10.1016/j.econlet.2017.11.033
74. Dell'Anna, F., Bottero, M.: Green premium in buildings: evidence from the real estate market of Singapore. J. Clean. Prod. **286**, 125327 (2020). https://doi.org/10.1016/j.jclepro.2020.125327
75. Copiello, S., Gabrielli, L., Bonifaci, P.: Evaluation of energy retrofit in buildings under conditions of uncertainty: the prominence of the discount rate. Energy **137**, 104–117 (2017). https://doi.org/10.1016/j.energy.2017.06.159
76. McGreal, S., Taltavull de La Paz, P.: Implicit house prices: variation over time and space in Spain. Urban Stud. **50**(10), 2024–2043 (2013). https://doi.org/10.1177/0042098012471978
77. Copiello, S.: Achieving affordable housing through energy efficiency strategy. Energy Policy **85**, 288–298 (2015). https://doi.org/10.1016/j.enpol.2015.06.017
78. Copiello, S., Bonifaci, P.: Green housing: toward a new energy efficiency paradox? Cities **49**, 76–87 (2015). https://doi.org/10.1016/j.cities.2015.07.006
79. Copiello, S.: Economic viability of building energy efficiency measures: a review on the discount rate. AIMS Energy **9**, 257–285 (2021). https://doi.org/10.3934/energy.2021014
80. McCord, M., Lo, D., Davis, P.T., Hemphill, L., McCord, J., Haran, M.: A spatial analysis of EPCs in the Belfast metropolitan area housing market. J. Prop. Res. **37**, 25–61 (2020). https://doi.org/10.1080/09599916.2019.1697345

81. Walls, M., Gerarden, T., Palmer, K., Bak, X.F.: Is energy efficiency capitalized into home prices? Evidence from three US cities. J. Environ. Econ. Manage. **82**, 104–124 (2017). https://doi.org/10.1016/j.jeem.2016.11.006
82. Bisello, A., Antoniucci, V., Marella, G.: Measuring the price premium of energy efficiency: a two-step analysis in the Italian housing market. Energy Build. **208**, 109670 (2020). https://doi.org/10.1016/j.enbuild.2019.109670
83. Copiello, S.: Spatial dependence of housing values in Northeastern Italy. Cities **96**, 102444 (2020). https://doi.org/10.1016/j.cities.2019.102444
84. Dell'Anna, F., Bravi, M., Marmolejo-Duarte, C., Bottero, M.C., Chen, A.: EPC green premium in two different European climate zones: a comparative study between Barcelona and Turin. Sustainability **11**, 5605 (2019). https://doi.org/10.3390/su11205605
85. Ekung, S., Odesola, I., Oladokun, M.: Dimensions of cost misperceptions obstructing the adoption of sustainable buildings. Smart Sustain. Built Environ. ahead-of-print (2021). https://doi.org/10.1108/SASBE-10-2020-0160
86. Dwaikat, L.N., Ali, K.N.: Green buildings cost premium: a review of empirical evidence. Energy Build. **110**, 396–403 (2016). https://doi.org/10.1016/j.enbuild.2015.11.021
87. Kats, G.: The Costs and Financial Benefits of Green Buildings – A Report to California's Sustainable Building Task Force. Washington, DC (2003)
88. Lucuik, M., Trusty, W., Larsson, N., Charette, R.: A Business Case for Green Building in Canada. Toronto (2005)
89. Berry, T.: Towards a Green Building and Infrastructure Investment Fund: A Review of Challenges and Opportunities. Compass Resource Management, Vancouver (2007)
90. Matthiessen, L., Morris, P.: Costing Green: A Comprehensive Cost Database and Budgeting Methodology. Davis Langdon, London (2004)
91. Rehm, M., Ade, R.: Construction costs comparison between 'green' and conventional office buildings. Build. Res. Inform. **41**, 198–208 (2013). https://doi.org/10.1080/09613218.2013.769145
92. Bartlett, E., Howard, N.: Informing the decision makers on the cost and value of green building. Build. Res. Inform. **28**, 315–324 (2000). https://doi.org/10.1080/096132100418474
93. Uğur, L.O., Leblebici, N.: An examination of the LEED green building certification system in terms of construction costs. Renew. Sustain. Energy Rev. **81**, 1476–1483 (2018). https://doi.org/10.1016/j.rser.2017.05.210
94. Taemthong, W., Chaisaard, N.: An analysis of green building costs using a minimum cost concept. J. Green Build. **14**, 53–78 (2019). https://doi.org/10.3992/1943-4618.14.1.53
95. Rajagopalan, N., Bilec, M.M., Landis, A.E.: Life cycle assessment evaluation of green product labeling systems for residential construction. Int. J. Life Cycle Assess. **17**, 753–763 (2012). https://doi.org/10.1007/s11367-012-0416-9
96. Miller, N., Spivey, J., Florance, A.: Does Green Pay Off? San Diego (2008)
97. Mangialardo, A., Micelli, E.: Off-site Retrofit to Regenerate Multi-family Homes: Evidence from Some European Experiences. In: Calabrò, F., Della Spina, L., Bevilacqua, C. (eds.) ISHT 2018. SIST, vol. 101, pp. 629–636. Springer, Cham (2019). https://doi.org/10.1007/978-3-319-92102-0_68
98. Ruggeri, A.G., Gabrielli, L., Scarpa, M.: Energy retrofit in European building portfolios: A review of five key aspects. Sustainability **12** (2020). https://doi.org/10.3390/SU12187465
99. Mata, É., Sasic Kalagasidis, A., Johnsson, F.: Building-stock aggregation through archetype buildings: France, Germany, Spain and the UK. Build. Environ. **81**, 270–282 (2014). https://doi.org/10.1016/j.buildenv.2014.06.013
100. Luddeni, G., Krarti, M., Pernigotto, G., Gasparella, A.: An analysis methodology for large-scale deep energy retrofits of existing building stocks: case study of the Italian office building. Sustain. Cities Soc. **41**, 296–311 (2018). https://doi.org/10.1016/j.scs.2018.05.038

101. Guardigli, L., Bragadin, M.A., Della Fornace, F., Mazzoli, C., Prati, D.: Energy retrofit alternatives and cost-optimal analysis for large public housing stocks. Energy Build. **166**, 48–59 (2018). https://doi.org/10.1016/j.enbuild.2018.02.003

102. Ascione, F., Bianco, N., Stasio, C., Mauro, G., Vanoli, G.: Addressing large-scale energy retrofit of a building stock via representative building samples: Public and private perspectives. Sustainability **9**(6), 940 (2017). https://doi.org/10.3390/su9060940

103. Nägeli, C., Jakob, M., Sunarjo, B., Catenazzi, G.: A building specific, economic building stock model to evaluate energy efficiency and renewable energy. Cisbat **2015**, 877–882 (2015). https://doi.org/10.1299/jsmeb.45.638

104. European Commission: Directive 2010/31/EU of the European Parliament and of the Council of 19 May 2010 on the energy performance of buildings (recast), pp. 13–35. Off. J. Eur. Union (2010). https://doi.org/10.3000/17252555.L_2010.153.eng

105. Swan, L.G., Ugursal, V.I.: Modeling of end-use energy consumption in the residential sector: a review of modeling techniques. Renew. Sustain. Energy Rev. **13**, 1819–1835 (2009). https://doi.org/10.1016/j.rser.2008.09.033

106. Ma, Z., Cooper, P., Daly, D., Ledo, L.: Existing building retrofits: methodology and state-of-the-art. Energy Build. **55**, 889–902 (2012). https://doi.org/10.1016/j.enbuild.2012.08.018

107. Fathabadi, H.: Increasing energy efficiency of PV-converter-battery section of standalone building integrated photovoltaic systems. Energy Build. **101**, 1–11 (2015). https://doi.org/10.1016/j.enbuild.2015.04.024

108. Hu, B., Sun, W.P.: Research on green residential buildings based on energy efficiency and renewable energy. Appl. Mech. Mater. **361–363**, 331–334 (2013). https://doi.org/10.4028/AMM.361-363.331

109. Pukhkal, V., Vatin, N., Murgul, V.: Central ventilation system with heat recovery as one of the measures to upgrade energy efficiency of historic buildings. Appl. Mech. Mater. **633**, 1077–1081 (2014). https://doi.org/10.4028/AMM.633-634.1077

110. Gabor, T., Dan, V., Badila, I.-N., Tiuc, A.-E., Sur, I.M.: Improving the energy efficiency of residential buildings by using a drain water heat recovery system. Environ. Eng. Manag. J. **16**, 1631–1636 (2017)

111. Wang, Y., Shao, L.: Understanding occupancy pattern and improving building energy efficiency through Wi-Fi based indoor positioning. Build. Environ. **114**, 106–117 (2017). https://doi.org/10.1016/j.buildenv.2016.12.015

112. Pallis, P., et al.: Cost effectiveness assessment and beyond: a study on energy efficiency interventions in Greek residential building stock. Energy Build. **182**, 1–18 (2019). https://doi.org/10.1016/j.enbuild.2018.10.024

113. Yılmaz, Y., Koçlar Oral, G.: An approach for an educational building stock energy retrofits through life-cycle cost optimization. Archit. Sci. Rev. **61**, 122–132 (2018). https://doi.org/10.1080/00038628.2018.1447438

114. Barthelmes, V.M., Becchio, C., Bottero, M., Corgnati, S.P.: Cost-optimal analysis for the definition of energy design strategies: the case of a nearly-zero energy building. Valori Valutazioni **16**, 57–70 (2016)

115. Amstalden, R.W., Kost, M., Nathani, C., Imboden, D.M.: Economic potential of energy-efficient retrofitting in the Swiss residential building sector: the effects of policy instruments and energy price expectations. Energy Policy **35**, 1819–1829 (2007). https://doi.org/10.1016/j.enpol.2006.05.018

116. Kumbaroğlu, G., Madlener, R.: Evaluation of economically optimal retrofit investment options for energy savings in buildings. Energy Build. **49**, 327–334 (2012). https://doi.org/10.1016/j.enbuild.2012.02.022

117. Brotman, B.A.: Green office construction: a discounted after-tax cash flow analysis. J. Prop. Invest. Financ. **32**, 474–484 (2014). https://doi.org/10.1108/JPIF-01-2014-0007

118. Gaglia, A.G., Balaras, C.A., Mirasgedis, S., Georgopoulou, E., Sarafidis, Y., Lalas, D.P.: Empirical assessment of the Hellenic non-residential building stock, energy consumption, emissions and potential energy savings. Energy Convers. Manag. **48**, 1160–1175 (2007). https://doi.org/10.1016/j.enconman.2006.10.008

119. Espen, L.: Use of multicriteria decision analysis methods for energy planning problems. Renew. Sustain. Energy Rev. **11**, 1584–1595 (2007). https://doi.org/10.1016/j.rser.2005.11.005

120. European Commission: Guidelines accompanying Commission Delegated Regulation (EU) No 244/2012 of 16 January 2012 supplementing Directive 2010/31/EU of the European Parliament and of the Council on the energy performance of buildings by establishing a comparative methodology framework for calculating cost-optimal levels, vol.. 55, pp. 1–28. Off. J. Eur. Union (2012). https://doi.org/10.3000/1977091X.C_2012.115.eng

121. Carli, R., Dotoli, M., Pellegrino, R., Ranieri, L.: A decision making technique to optimize a buildings' stock energy efficiency. IEEE Trans. Syst. Man Cybern.: Syst. **47**(5), 794–807 (2017). https://doi.org/10.1109/TSMC.2016.2521836

122. Pombo, O., Allacker, K., Rivela, B., Neila, J.: Sustainability assessment of energy saving measures: A multi-criteria approach for residential buildings retrofitting – a case study of the Spanish housing stock. Energy Build. **116**, 384–394 (2016). https://doi.org/10.1016/j.enbuild.2016.01.019

123. Vimmr, T., Enseling, A., Lützkendorf, T., Behr, I., Vache, M., Beer, A.: Decision support tools for economically viable energy efficiency retrofitting in the European rental housing stock. In: K., S., J., T., A., L., P., H. (eds.) Central Europe Towards Sustainable Building 2016: Innovations for Sustainable Future, CESB 2016, pp. 1518–1525. Grada Publishing, STU-K, a.s., Praha, Czech Republic (2016)

124. Gabrielli, L., Ruggeri, A.: Developing a model for energy retrofit in large building portfolios: energy assessment, optimization and uncertainty. Energy Build. **202**, 109356 (2019). https://doi.org/10.1016/j.enbuild.2019.109356

An Evaluation Model for the Optimization of Property Sales in Auction Markets

Francesco Tajani[1](✉), Pierluigi Morano[2], Marco Locurcio[2], Paola Amoruso[3], and Carmelo Maria Torre[2]

[1] Department of Architecture and Design, "Sapienza" University of Rome, 00196 Rome, Italy
francesco.tajani@uniroma1.it
[2] Department of Civil, Environmental, Land, Building Engineering and Chemistry, Polytechnic University of Bari, 70125 Bari, Italy
[3] Department of Economics and Management, LUM University, Casamassima, 70010 Bari, Italy

Abstract. This paper proposes a logical-deductive model for the estimate of forced sale value, in support of individuals involved in real estate auctions. This value is estimated by starting from market value, considering an appropriate discount/premium coefficient which, due to obtainable yields and associated risk, guarantees transaction admissibility for the investor in terms of convenience. The model borrows from Ellwood logic as applied to the real estate sector, integrated through the evaluation approach of investment risk inherent in Real Options Analysis. Applying this model to one hundred and forty cities in which the Italian courts are based allowed for comparison of the discount/premium coefficients determined by the model with those determined by sector operators. The results of this application underlined the speculative behavior of market operators, who mainly focus on obtaining better discounts than those admissible, while at the same time supplying useful indications on the territorial contexts where the difference between hammer price and admissible value can be maximized.

Keywords: Forced sale value · Auction market · Real options analysis · Ellwood · Market value

1 Introduction

The real estate market has undergone widespread global transformations as a result of the Covid 19 pandemic. At the same time, however, the real estate market in the first half of 2020 recorded transactions totalling € 8bn, € 2bn more than the same period in 2019. There has been a net growth in the NPLs market over the past five years, with non performing exposure stock in the H1 – 2020 amounting to € 130bn [25]. The extraordinary conditions [1, 2] that characterize the market for judicial auctions contribute to the formation of a sale price that is generally (and not infrequently it is worth noting) lower than the market value estimated by the technical consultant. In this context, the Consolidated Banking Act [5] and the Circular 285 of the Bank of Italy [3] have specified that the appropriate value basis for the estimate of real estate guarantees

© Springer Nature Switzerland AG 2021
O. Gervasi et al. (Eds.): ICCSA 2021, LNCS 12954, pp. 241–252, 2021.
https://doi.org/10.1007/978-3-030-86979-3_18

is the market value, i.e. *"the estimated amount at which the property would be sold at the valuation date in a transaction carried out between a seller and a buyer who are aware of normal market conditions after adequate commercial promotion, in the context of which both parties have acted in full knowledge of the facts, prudently and without being subject to constraints"*.

In principle, the aim of ownership transfer in judicial proceedings is to bring the transfer price as near as possible to market value. Since the elements that characterize the definition of market value in these situations are unlikely to be fully satisfied, the appropriateness of referring to the conditions that influence the methods of transferring the property is evident: the result is accordingly a market value based on assumptions, since ownership transfer of property occurs in conditions which are not fully compliant with the set definition.

Indeed, in the event of a judicial sale, one or more of these conditions provided for by the definition of market value cannot be met, specifically:

- the estimated amount must be determined in accordance with normal market conditions while the case in question necessarily takes into account the fact that it is at times impossible to view the property with due attention by the potential buyer, thereby making it impossible to ascertain the state of the property;
- real estate advertising effectiveness is notably reduced as the auction market presents clear barriers to access;
- the seller/debtor does not appear in a situation in which he or she is consenting, as would be the case under normal market conditions;
- property valuation is carried out by the expert on a date that may be well in advance of that of the property sale or transfer procedure;
- there is a temporal uncertainty in regards to maintaining possession of the property by the debtor;
- the debtor, tenant of the property, for the above, is often an obstacle to the property sale.

It comes as no surprise that in this particular market segment RICS [16, 27] defines a specific value – the forced sale value – specifying that it does not constitute an independent basis of value, but rather a market value in specific situations, determined within the premise of the evaluation report through appropriate special assumptions.

The uncertainty related to the economic discrepancy between market value estimated in the appraisal and final hammer price is a binding issue, affecting as it does the overall timing and efficiency of auction procedures.

In order to reduce procedural time and encourage an increase in adjudication prices, Italian legislation has promoted several relevant initiatives between 2005 and 2018 [22]. The Public Sales Portal (pvp.giustizia.it/pvp) was launched by the Ministry of Justice to favour advertising of sales of the assets and of executive and competitive procedures in general, while similar initiatives have been promoted by private facilitators (www.astegi udiziarie.it, www.asteannunci.it, www.astetelematiche.it, www.astagiudiziaria.com).

Despite these various interventions, statistical surveys show that auctions in Italy continue to lack dynamism and tend to be repeated several times, resulting in a significant reduction in the auction price. Lots up for auction totalled 95,329 during 2020, generating a total of 117,376 auctions, which means that each lot went to auction on average 1.23 times. In the same year, real estate auctions suffered significantly as a result of the Covid-19 pandemic: the lockdown made property viewing impossible, while blocks on court activity and suspension through to 31/10/2020 of executive procedures relating to the "first house" led to a 40.6% drop in the number of lots on auction and a 53.9% drop in the number of auctions held [26]. This block had highly significant economic repercussions: we need only consider that 30,815 auctions were postponed during the first lockdown for a value of €3 billion 669 million [10].

Geographically speaking, 16.5% of the lots are concentrated in Lombardy, followed by Sicily (9.7%), while the regions of Veneto, Emilia Romagna, Piedmont, Tuscany, Marche and Lazio have percentages varying between 6.5% and 7.7%, and Puglia and Campania account for 5.5% and 5.3% respectively. The other regions account for less than 5%, with Basilicata, Molise and Valle d'Aosta closing off the ranking with percentages of less than 1%.

2 Aim

The years of economic crisis that hit Italian businesses and families have seen an increase in the number and amount of bad loans [2]. Furthermore, the lengthiness of judicial debt recovery procedures can have significant repercussions on the economic and financial system.

The lengthy duration of the judicial credit recovery procedures is one of the factors responsible for the accumulation of impaired loans, which in recent years have affected bank balance sheets. Indeed, the poor performance of the judicial recovery mechanisms, both in terms of timing and values, has had a negative impact on their management. Shortening recovery procedure times is thus essential in order to favour the disposal of stock of non-performing loans, and – in the same context – avoid the possible negative repercussions of introducing in prudential regulation the concept of calendar provisioning (i.e. the practice of progressively writing off impaired loans over time, regardless of recovery expectations) [4].

This study fits into the framework outlined, aimed as it is at the definition and experimentation of a logical-deductive model for the estimate of forced sale value, determined by starting from market value and, based on the risks of the context under analysis, applying an appropriate reduction (or incremental) coefficient. When implemented in the one hundred and forty cities where the Italian courts are based, this model made comparison possible between the discount/premium coefficient determined by the model and that detected by operators in the sector. With regards to auction procedures, the model allows us to determine the price of the property to be sold which, due to obtainable yields and transaction risks, is admissible for the investor in terms of convenience. The basic assumption here is that the price at which the property will be sold depends *i)* on sales times characterizing the procedure, and *ii)* on the risk inherent in an auction market.

This study is structured as follows. Section 3 describes the proposed model. Section 4 develops an application to the Italian context, comparing the discount/premium coefficients obtained with those found both on a regional basis and in nine Italian cities. Finally, conclusions of the study are drawn, envisaging possible future developments of the research.

3 The Model

Starting from the premise that defining forced sale value starts from market value, by borrowing concepts of financial mathematics, we are able to determine the former (V_{fs}) by means of an appropriate "discount" of the latter (V_m), taking into consideration that the value of the forced sale will take place after a time n (>0), which is the time span between completion of the appraisal and sale of the property. In specific terms, the estimated discount coefficient (i) will constitute a proxy of the risk inherent in the forced sale mechanism.

Translated into formulas, since the market value estimate is carried out at a time "t" while the sale will take place at a time "$t + n$", we can state that:

$$V_{fs} = \frac{V_m}{(1 + i)^n} \tag{1}$$

In order to determine the discount rate i, the model we propose uses Ellwood financial balance [6, 9, 12, 14], simplifying its implementation by introducing suitable hypotheses. Specifically, the proposed model incorporates a number of logical principles underlying the methodology developed by Manganelli et al. [20] to estimate the capitalization rate in the income approach, reworking the algorithm in the present case, as related to determination of the discount coefficient for the estimate of forced sale value.

On the basis of these assumptions, Ellwood's financial statements for real estate investment following an auction sale can be written up as in Eq. (2) below, which, at the first term, indicates revenues deriving from the investment, consisting i) of the financial sum of constant and deferred annual market rents (R), accrued between the year of the sale (n) and the 'exit time, i.e., the moment in which "it is convenient" to dispose of the investment (m), and discounted at the time of the valuation (year zero), and ii) by the allotment price (V_{fs}) revalued/devalued with the coefficient i' for the $m - n$ years of possession. The discounting of items at the first term is carried out using an appropriate rate (i''). The second term is determined by initial investment costs (C), which include the award price of the property, costs associated with the transfer of ownership and due diligence.

$$\frac{R}{(1 + i'')^n} \cdot \left[\frac{(1 + i'')^{m-n} - 1}{i'' \cdot (1 + i'')^{m-n}} \right] + V_{fs} \cdot \frac{(1 + i')^{m-n}}{(1 + i'')^{m-n}} = C \tag{2}$$

Recalling Eq. (1), if we assume that costs for property purchase amount to 10% of the sale price and transferring the costs to the first term, we obtain Eq. (3):

$$\frac{R}{(1 + i'')^n} \cdot \left[\frac{(1 + i'')^{m-n} - 1}{i'' \cdot (1 + i'')^{m-n}} \right] + \frac{V_m}{(1 + i)^n} \cdot \frac{(1 + i')^{m-n}}{(1 + i'')^{m-n}} - 1.10 \cdot \frac{V_m}{(1 + i)^n} = 0 \tag{3}$$

Note that, although they could coincide in value, the discount rate i'' and the discount rate i (the unknown of the model), are conceptually different parameters in terms of risk. The former is in fact related to factors [8] that refer to the yield of a real estate investment in the period of "full and free" availability – context risk (city rank, suitability of the location for the intended use, real estate market trends, etc.), property risk (size, building and maintenance type/quality of the property, fungibility, etc.) and tenant risk (number of current/potential tenants, vacancy, solvency, etc.). The discount rate i, on the other hand, is closely connected to risk factors pertaining to a specific condition, such as that of the auction, in which the probable temporal distance (n) between the moment of property evaluation and that of sale requires analysis of the benefits generated by the possible evolution of the reference market and thus of the tolerable discount for the purposes of financial sustainability of the transaction.

For the estimate of exit time (m), needed for implementation of Eq. (3), investment risk analysis is borrowed as the first step in the Real Options Analysis (ROA). ROA is an investment evaluation technique used to manage the uncertainty related to possible scenario evolutions [23] and to assign a value to the various project solutions, referred to as options [7, 24].

Volatility (σ) – a fundamental parameter for ROA risk analysis – is determined by considering the change in revaluation/devaluation rates of the half-yearly quotations published by the Real Estate Market Observatory (OMI) of the Revenue Agency for the macrozone, the city and the intended use analyzed [29], and by using the exponentially-weighted moving average (EWMA) method [18, 19, 28, 30]. Once volatility has been obtained, the tree of scenarios can be constructed based on the binomial approach, considering as the evolutionary variable the change in the present value of cash flows of the investment (Y), equal to the total of discounted rents received in the period of possession of the property ($m - n$) and any real estate revaluation/devaluation expected from the investment. Since i constitutes the unknown of the problem, it is hypothesized, for the sole purpose of constructing the evolutionary trend of the value Y, that the discount rate i coincides with the discount rate i''. This condition leads us to Eq. (4).

$$Y = R \cdot \left[\frac{(1 + i'')^{m-n} - 1}{i'' \cdot (1 + i'')^m} \right] + V_m \cdot \frac{(1 + i')^{m-n} - 1}{(1 + i'')^m} \tag{4}$$

With the exception of exit time (m), all the parameters in Eq. (4) are assumed to be known. On this condition it is demonstrable that, since the sale will be carried out in the year in which this option is economically at its most convenient, there is a unique relationship between investment value volatility (σ) and exit time (m) [21].

In particular, the model we have developed sees the ideal exit time for the investor (m) as estimated by means of a function of maximization of the evolution of the present value of investment cash flows, taking into account the most pessimistic situation (i.e. $d = e^{-\sigma}$, according to the binomial formulation of the ROA). Accordingly, by using h to indicate the h-th year of evolution of cash flows values ($h > n$), Eq. (5) may be stated as:

$$m = \max\left(d^h \cdot Y \right) \tag{5}$$

Furthermore, as volatility increases, the ideal exit time for the investor decreases: as risk increases, it is worth holding onto the investment for fewer years.

Table 1 shows the equations of the proposed model for estimating the discount/premium coefficient (Δ).

Table 1. Model.

$i = \sqrt[n]{V_m \cdot \left[1.10 - \frac{(1+i')^{m-n}}{(1+i'')^{m-n}}\right] \cdot \frac{i'' \cdot (1+i'')^m}{R \cdot [(1+i'')^{m-n}-1]}} - 1$	Discount rate (variable model)
$Y = R \cdot \left[\frac{(1+i'')^{m-n}-1}{i'' \cdot (1+i'')^m}\right] + V_m \cdot \frac{(1+i')^{m-n}-1}{(1+i'')^m}$	Present value of investment cash flows (rents + capital gains)
$d = e^{-\sigma}$	Pessimistic evolution coefficient of investment value
$m = max\left(d^h \cdot Y\right) \quad h > n$	Ideal investor exit time
$\Delta = \frac{1}{(1+i)^n}$	Discount/premium coefficient for determining forced sales value

4 Application of the Model

The validity of the proposed model was tested by applying it to the Italian context, allowing us to determine the regional average discount coefficients along with those related to nine large Italian cities.

In particular, implementation takes into account sales times (n) – from delivery of the appraisal by the technical consultant to awarding of the asset in the auction phase – as recorded for the one hundred and forty Italian courts in 2019.

With n obtained for each court, the data necessary for implementation of the model was acquired by starting from the OMI quotations published by the Revenue Agency, with reference to residential destination and "central" (OMI band "B"), "semi-central" (OMI band "C") and "peripheral" (OMI band "D") macro-areas. The analysis was carried out on the one hundred and forty cities in which the courts are based.

Annual market rent (R) and market value (V_m) are relative to average OMI prices at the second half of 2019 for city, band and destination under consideration.

The discount rate (i'') is set as equal to the average OMI capitalization rate at the second half of 2019, or the ratio between annual market rent (R) and market value (V_m).

The revaluation rate i' is set as equal to the average of the historical series of revaluation/devaluation rates of purchase and sale prices processed by the OMI during the final three years under analysis (period I semester 2017 – II semester 2019).

Our reference period (T) for estimating volatility (σ) of the historical series of changes in revaluation/devaluation rates of real estate prices runs from the first half of 2005 to the second half of 2019, i.e., the period in which the Revenue Agency made economic data needed for application of the proposed model available.

Results obtained from the application of the developed model were compared to those found by the Immobiliare.it Research Department [15].

The model supplies an average discount coefficient of 36% on the regional level (see Fig. 1), with maximum and minimum values set respectively at 46% (Sicily) and 23% (Trentino Alto Adige and Valle d'Aosta). The area of Italy in which the highest percentage of discounts are expected is Central Italy (41%) followed by the Islands

(37%) and Southern Italy (35%); minor, although significant, discounts are expected to appear in Northern Italy (30%).

Fig. 1. Regional average of discount coefficient obtained from implementation of the model

Examining the data found (see Fig. 2), we see that Veneto and Trentino-Alto Adige compete for the podium with a detected discount of 61%, while Marche's 33% detected discount closes the ranking. North-East Italy offered the largest discounts (57%) followed by the North-West (50%), South Italy (49%) and Central Italy (57%), closing off with the Islands (44%).

By simultaneously analyzing the discount/premium coefficients of the model and those found (see Fig. 3), we observed that the discount detected is nearly always larger when compared to the model, thus indicating that buyers of residential property through the auction mechanism expect an "extra discount" compared to that deriving from analysis of the financial statement described above. The Marche and Sicily are the only regions in which the discount of the model is higher than the one recorded. In the case of the Marche, this unique position is most likely linked to the expectation of a real estate market revival supported by a widespread productive fabric and high savings for families, while in Sicily, on the other hand, the difference between model and recorded discounts is negligible at 5%. The regions where the model performs best, with resulting differences in discounts of less than 10%, are Lazio, Umbria, Puglia, Abruzzo, Calabria and Molise; in contrast, regions showing a difference between discounts of more than 25% are Veneto, Trentino Alto Adige, Lombardy, Campania and Basilicata.

Similar considerations emerge if nine Italian cities are compared (see Fig. 4) in terms of the discount coefficient elaborated by the model and that detected: in all cases except Palermo the model elaborates a higher discount coefficient than that found, with variations ranging from 8% in Rome to 42% in Torino.

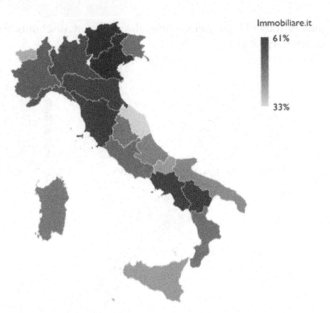

Fig. 2. Regional average of discount coefficient recorded by Immobiliare.it

Fig. 3. Regional difference between discount coefficient detected and that elaborated by the model

These differences are most likely due to a different mindset of buyers in relation to specific contexts: a buyer could thus also "settle" for lower discounts in the regions of Northern Italy or in the main Italian cities, where the real estate market is more dynamic

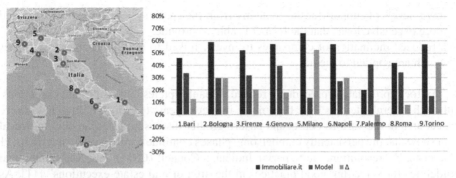

Fig. 4. Comparison for nine Italian cities between discount coefficient detected and that elaborated by the model

and operators do not perceive a decrease in risk, aiming in any case for more sizeable discounts for high discounts due to the uncertainties associated with auction procedures.

This comparison is especially useful in attempting to identify territorial contexts in which the difference between the discount coefficient detected and the admissible discount can be maximized, i.e. Italian regions and cities where it is more convenient to purchase property through auction procedures. Specifically, there are recognized and admissible discounts of 61% and 23% respectively in Trentino Alto Adige, assuring a difference between the detected and admissible discount of 38%. However, this figure is in direct contrast to a relatively small number of lots at auction (1.20% of the national total). Matching the number of lots at auction with the difference between detected and admissible discounts indicates that the most attractive region for a hypothetical investor is Lombardy, followed by Veneto and Campania. Moving on to analysis of the main Italian cities, Milan, the capital of Lombardy, is the city that displays the greatest difference between detected and the admissible discounts, confirming what has already been found on the regional level.

5 Conclusions

A recent report by the International Monetary Fund highlighted that the slowness and excessive bureaucratization of the Italian judicial system are among the main causes of investment reticence by foreign companies (www.esteri.it). This supports the findings of the World Bank Doing Business – Enforcing Contracts 2016, based on parameters of the global duration of enforcement proceedings, real costs incurred by the creditor compared to the amount of credit claimed and the quality of the judicial system in the process as a whole. The attractiveness of Italy is impacted negatively by this, since the lengthiness of the procedures results in:

– increased costs of both funding and risk for credit institutions [17] caused by the closely connected need for higher levels of capital endowment;
– competitive disadvantage of credit institutions when compared to their counterparts in other countries;

– lower levels of support for the economy from the credit system caused by lower and more expensive loans that the former is able to provide;
– a reduced inclination of companies to invest, linked to the higher investment rates which are applied to them.

As for expropriation procedures related to bankruptcies and real estate executions, although several attempts have been made in recent years to reduce timing, harmonize procedures in the various courts and ensure greater disclosure transparency, statistical data show that the persistently cumbersome phases continue to affect efficiency. In its 11 October 2017 resolution, the Superior Judiciary Council (CSM) approved "functional guidelines for spreading good practices in the area of real estate executions" [11]. As a means of monitoring the extent of application, the Permanent Observatory for the efficiency of executive procedures and the implementation of "good practices" was put in place at the Seventh Commission. The CSM then promoted drafting of guidelines established on the basis of the best practices in the field of real estate executions, within the context of complex judicial realities, in which they already tested positively. To ensure liquidation of debtor assets and obtain maximum returns, to be allocated to creditors and, residually, to the debtor in the shortest possible time, forced execution for expropriation must necessarily take place according to criteria of efficiency, effectiveness and speed. In this light, the two-year period from 2015 to 2016 witnessed the launching of two legislative measures containing a wide range of measures focused on favoring more effective management of impaired loans. These include:

– interventions to reduce the time of individual and insolvency enforcement procedures (forced expropriation and bankruptcies);
– interventions to encourage the use of management tools for companies in crisis (restructuring agreements and arrangements with creditors);
– introduction of out-of-court credit recovery mechanisms and the creation of infrastructures aimed at supporting operation of procedures and management of impaired loans (the sales portal and the register of enforcement and insolvency procedures and crisis management tools).

With a view to mapping court performance, the CSM Observatory has determined the turnover index yielded by the percentage ratio between the number of cases defined and the amount of cases that have arisen, i.e. the number of extinguished cases every 100 cases forfeited. This index showed a +38.24% efficiency increase in 2018, with a turnover index that rose from a national average of 102 in 2017 to 141 in 2018.

The logical-deductive model developed and tested in this work aims to provide scientific and practical support for the estimate of forced sale value, starting from the market value along with indication of the most appealing territorial contexts for an investor, i.e. where the difference between admissible and recognized discount coefficients is greatest.

The implementation of this model underlines the extent to which uncertainty about the timing and convenience of operations ultimately leads to speculative behavior by operators interested in buying property packages at highly affordable prices compared to real market values [13], and thus with a discount, compared to appraisal value, which is higher than the discount coefficient returned by the model.

References

1. Agenzia del Territorio: Glossario delle definizioni tecniche in uso nel settore Economico. Immobiliare (2008)
2. Associazione Bancaria Italiana (ABI): Linee guida per la valutazione degli immobili in garanzia delle esposizioni creditizie, gennaio 2018 (2018)
3. Banca d'Italia: Disposizioni di vigilanza per le bance. Circolare n.285 del 17 dicembre 2013 (2013)
4. Banca d'Italia: Le procedure esecutive immobiliari: il funzionamento e gli effetti delle recenti riforme. Questioni di Economia e Finanza, paper 448, luglio 2018 (2018)
5. Banca d'Italia: Testo Unico Bancario. Decreto legislativo 1° settembre 1993, n. 385. Testo unico delle leggi in materia bancaria e creditizia. Versione aggiornata al decreto legislativo 26 ottobre 2020, n. 147 (2020)
6. Born, W., Pyhrr, S.: Real estate valuation: the effect of market and property cycles. J. Real Estate Res. 9(4), 455–485 (1994)
7. Bulan, L., Mayer, C., Tsuriel, S.C.: Irreversible investment, real options, and competition: evidence from real estate development. J. Urban Econ. 65, 237–251 (2009)
8. Cacciamani, C.: Il rischio immobiliare: una soluzione di rating dell'investimento immobiliare. EGEA, Milano (2003)
9. Colwell, P.F.: Tweaking the DiPasquale-wheaton model. J. Hous. Econ. 11(1), 24–39 (2002)
10. Comitato Scientifico dell'Associazione T.S.E.I. – Tavolo di Studio sulle Esecuzioni Italiane: Quarta edizione dello "Studio dei tempi dei tribunali italiani in materia di procedure esecutive individuali", settembre 2020 (2020)
11. Consiglio Superiore della Magistratura (CSM): Buone prassi nel settore delle esecuzioni immobiliari – linee guida. Delibera 11 ottobre 2017 (2017)
12. Del Giudice, V., Passeri, A., De Paola, P., Torrieri, F.: Estimation of risk-return for real estate investments by applying Ellwood's model and real options analysis: an application to the residential real estate market of Naples. Appl. Mech. Mater. 651, 1570–1575 (2014)
13. Donner, H.: Foreclosures, returns and buyer intention. J. Eur. Real Estate Res. 39(2), 189–213 (2017)
14. Ellwood, L.W.: Ellwood Tables for Real Estate Appraising and Financing. Ballinger (1970)
15. Immobiliare.it: Osservatorio annuale di Immobiliare.it (2020)
16. International Valuation Standards Council: International Valuation Standards 2020 (2020)
17. Locurcio, M., Tajani, F., Morano, P., Anelli, D.: A multi-criteria decision analysis for the assessment of the real estate credit risks. In: Morano, P., Oppio, A., Rosato, P., Sdino, L., Tajani, F. (eds.) Appraisal and Valuation. GET, pp. 327–337. Springer, Cham (2021). https://doi.org/10.1007/978-3-030-49579-4_22
18. Lowry, C.A., Woodall, W.H., Champ, C.W., Rigdon, S.E.: A multivariate exponentially weighted moving average control chart. Technometrics 34(1), 46–53 (1992)
19. Lucas, J.M., Saccucci, M.S.: Exponentially weighted moving average control schemes: properties and enhancements. Technometrics 32(1), 1–12 (1990)
20. Manganelli, B., Morano, P., Tajani, F.: La valutazione del rischio nell'analisi finanziaria di Ellwood per la stima indiretta di immobili urbani. Aestimum 55, 19–41 (2009)
21. Manganelli, B., Morano, P., Tajani, F.: Risk assessment in estimating the capitalization rate. WSEAS Trans. Bus. Econ. 11(1), 197–206 (2014)

22. Marcucci, M., Pischedda, A., Profeta, V.: Notes on Financial Stability and Supervision: The Changes of the Italian Insolvency and Foreclosure Regulation Adopted in 2015. Banca D'Italia Eurosistema (2015)
23. Miller, K.D., Waller, H.G.: Scenarios, real options and integrated risk management. Long Range Plan. **36**(1), 93–107 (2003)
24. Morano, P., Tajani, F., Manganelli, B.: An application of real option analysis for the assessment of operative flexibility in the urban redevelopment. WSEAS Trans. Bus. Econ. **11**(1), 476–487 (2014)
25. PWC: The Italian NPL market, December 2020 (2020)
26. Reviva: Scenario aste immobiliari (2020)
27. RICS: RICS Valuation – Professional Standards, London, UK (2019)
28. Tajani, F., Morano, P., Salvo, F., De Ruggiero, M.: An evaluation model for an effective risk assessment in the rent to buy property market. Prop. Manag. **38**(1), 124–141 (2019)
29. Tajani, F., Morano, P.: An empirical-deductive model for the assessment of the mortgage lending value of properties as securities for credit exposures. J. Eur. Real Estate Res. **11**(1), 44–70 (2018)
30. Winters, P.R.: Forecasting sales by exponentially weighted moving averages. Manage. Sci. **6**(3), 324–342 (1960)

Urban Transformation Interventions: A Decision Support Model for a Fair *Rent Gap* Recapture

Pierluigi Morano[1] (ID), Francesco Tajani[2] (ID), Vincenzo del Giudice[3] (ID), Pierfrancesco De Paola[3] (ID), and Debora Anelli[2(✉)] (ID)

[1] Department of Civil, Environmental, Land, Building Engineering and Chemistry, Polytechnic University of Bari, Via Orabona 4, 70125 Bari, Italy
pierluigi.morano@poliba.it
[2] Department of Architecture and Design, "La Sapienza" University of Rome, 00196 Rome, Italy
{francesco.tajani,debora.anelli}@uniroma1.it
[3] Department of Industrial Engineering, University of Naples "Federico II", Naples, Italy
{vincenzo.delgiudice,pierfrancesco.depaola}@unina.it

Abstract. The second post world-war period has been widely characterized by urbanization phenomena related to the urban rent formation dynamics. The scarcity of public financial resources and the growing privatization of the benefits generated by several territorial initiatives have highlighted the need for negotiation tools capable of ensuring a fair redistribution of the rent gap deriving from urban transformation interventions. For this reason, the institution of the "extraordinary urbanization contribution" in the 2014 in Italy represents a significant regulatory support, that legitimizes public administrations in acquiring a share of the private extra-profit. The implementation of this national legislative provision has not been yet sufficiently applied at the local level, due to the lack of a univocal and codified methodology. The aim of this work consists in defining a decision support model that can be adopted in the negotiation phases between public and private subjects, in order to determine the most convenient financial conditions that ensure the law provisions. In particular, by applying the computational logic of Operational Research, the model is able to determine the amount of the main urban planning parameters that affect the balance sheets of the public-private initiatives.

Keywords: Urban rent · Rent gap theory · Public-private partnership · Decision support model · Operational research

1 Introduction

In the second half of the Nineteenth century, the urban rent phenomenon has compromised the sustainable development of European cities. In the 1970s, the spread of industrial centers to the rural outskirts of cities led to a decline in central urban areas, favoring the growth in demand for infrastructure and services in peripheral areas originally intended for agricultural activities. This condition has led to the attribution of new building potentials to the land located on the urban edges, generating an increase in the

© Springer Nature Switzerland AG 2021
O. Gervasi et al. (Eds.): ICCSA 2021, LNCS 12954, pp. 253–264, 2021.
https://doi.org/10.1007/978-3-030-86979-3_19

value of them and the ruin of al lot of central areas [1]. Afterward a turnaround occurred: in the last decades of the twentieth century, the main capital cities have been involved in the urban gentrification phenomenon, a spontaneous process of recovery and redevelopment of degraded central neighborhoods with a population turnover of middle-upper classes, which affected the real estate market dynamics [2, 3]. Relying on systematic observations of urban ground rent variations due to the gentrification conditions, [4] provided an explanatory model - named the *rent gap theory* - based on three pillars: housing value, capitalized land rent and potential land rent. In the long run, urban land rent may increase or decrease due to the continuous changing of the real estate demand for new highest and best uses. The model stated by Smith has been considered a relevant contribution into the urban rent field of research, because it set the conditions to develop a supply side view of the rent's mechanism which arise into the urbanization dynamics. Therefore, the greater the gap between the potential land rent and the capitalized ground rent in a place, the more attractive it is to invest capital for development/redevelopment interventions [5]. In this way, it establishes the role of the urban rent as a synthetic indicator for public and private investment choices for maximizing the expected capital gains [6].

Several researchers have tried to verify the existence of the rent gap theory at the scale of individual properties worldwide [7–9]. As argued by [10], the rent gap is also extremely related to processes operating on different spatial scales within the cities. [11], by considering the metropolitan scale of New York, highlights that, while the urban city center emerging as the target for real estate investment, areas located farther away from the central ones suffer from a process of disinvestment and decline. These interrelated processes of investment and divestment of the suburbs closely link to the city center are the basis of the observable social and demographic changes occurring throughout the entire metropolitan area [12].

Other researchers, taking into account the main typologies of endogenous factors of urban development that affect the rent gap formation mechanism [13, 14], have recently improved the Smith's theory: social [15], tourism [16], sustainable planning [17–19] and taxation issues [20–22] are the main addressed point of view.

In the Italian context, the scarcity of financial resources of the public administration (PA) has raised the need to adopt negotiation instruments in collaboration with the private sector, capable of recovering, through a redistributive approach, a share of the urban rent achievable as a result of urban transformation interventions. Recent regulatory provisions on urban planning - at national and local level - have helped to support the spread of public-private partnership (PPP) models aimed at regulating and managing private capital gains [23]. In this regard, the models based on the principles of non-financial compensation have made a significant contribution to the regulation of the dynamics of profit privatization [24]. However, the current socio-economic conditions resulting from the 2007 economic crisis and aggravated by the Covid-19 health emergency, confirm the growing need for decision support tools that allow the PA to allocate more financial resources for the community [25–27].

2   Aim of the Work

The Italian urban planning legislation has been recently improved with the institution of the "extraordinary urbanization contribution" (Law no. 164/2014 and Law no. 76/2020) – that granted to the PA the chance to limit the privatization of the urban rent gap that derives from *"interventions on areas or buildings in urban planning variant or in derogation"*, by acquiring a share (at least 50%) of the private extra profit generated, to be used for public purposes. The regulatory State requirements, however, avoid an efficient implementation due to the lack of a codified methodology that the PA could adopt to determine the amount of the extraprofit that can be acquired to ensure the minimum financial conditions of both the parties involved.

The present research is part of the framework outlined. In particular it is aimed at developing a decision support model that can be adopted by public and private subjects involved into urban planning variants process, taking into account those concerning the revision of the building parameters provided by the regulatory instruments in force, in order to identify the most convenient financial conditions. Based on the computational logic of the Operational Research (OR), the model determines the combination and the amount of the most important parameters involved in the negotiation phases that can affect the urban rent gap formation, by considering physical, financial and urban planning constraints that characterize two scenarios: in the first one (named *ante variant*) all the urban parameters and indexes are established by the local disposition and therefore are known; in the second scenario (named *post variant*) it is necessary to determine the amount of the parameters that define the balance sheet of both the parties involved and ensure the acquisition of the extraordinary urbanization contribution, that is the prerogative of the PA.

The model is elaborated from a public point of view: the target variables considered translate into mathematical terms the purposes of preserving the natural environment, by promoting affordable housing and reducing the soil sealing into the *post variant* scenario. In this way, the proposed model supports the urban planning decisions that need an efficient methodology for assessing *i)* the financial feasibility of the PPP initiative, *ii)* the extra-profit for the private entrepreneur (i.e. the urban rent achievable), *iii)* the possibility for the PA to make further requests (in addition to those mandatory, according to the law) to the private entrepreneur, ensuring the conditions of minimum financial convenience.

The PA can use the proposed model from the earliest negotiation phases for clearly identifying the financial convenience margins, in terms of urban rent gap generated by the *post variant* scenario, such as to be able to allocate the share allowed by the urban planning legislation for public purposes, thus avoiding a complete privatization of it. The private entrepreneur, instead, can adopt the proposed model in order to verify his personal financial sheet and the convenience that derives from the initiative.

The paper is structured as follows: in Sect. 3 an overview of the main PPP tools currently adopted to avoid the privatization of the urban rent gap generated by transformation interventions is carried out. In Sect. 4 the model is explained, by describing the variables, the constraints and the objective function of the algorithm. In Sect. 5 the potentialities of the proposed model and future insights of the research are discussed.

3 Negotiating Tools Aimed at a Fair Urban Rent Recapture for Financing the Public City

As part of the management tools for the implementation of urban plans, the "integrated programs" represent one of the most significant innovations introduced in the 90's in Italy. In particular, in the execution plans that allow a variation in the intended use and private volumes, the national legislator has recognized a fundamental role in the PPP for the achievement of high levels of efficiency and effectiveness. The perimeter within which the public and private subjects operate concerns the extra-profit generated by the modifications to the parameters provided by the current regulatory plan. In other words, the variation in the urban rent of buildings intended for PPP transformation is the characterizing aspect of the integrated programs. The negotiation activity of the PA, therefore, becomes the path through which recover part of the extra-profit determined by the choices of the plan for public purposes. Furthermore, the ability to mobilize private resources that allow public ones to exploit an important leverage effect is not to be underestimated [28].

The characteristics of the privatization process of urban rent suggest that its regulation must take place by creating conditions of higher equity in its distribution. The need for *win-win* solutions that take into account this trend has led to the spread of innovative instruments that involve non-financial compensation, in order to overcome the limits of traditional instruments of expropriation [29]. The non-financial compensation, properly, consists in the concession by the PA of building rights that the private subject can either use or sold [30].

Recent developments in Italian planning practice concerns new development rights that are used by local planning authorities for community facilities and services by capturing some betterment value. Over time the use of these tools has increased constantly [31]. Moreover, the introduction of a betterment value tax has the potential to support efficient planning through a more reasonable distribution of the costs and benefits of urban transformation interventions. Those who benefit most from the urban rent generated, therefore, also contribute to the costs incurred. A betterment value tax is also able to regulate land speculation by acquiring resources to contribute to the planning system. In India, for example, about $ 17.5 billion have been invested in infrastructure, and the government has also decided to implement a land value tax to capture the increase in land value that could result from this public investment [32].

According to [33], different approaches to urban rent capture can be distinguished: *i)* negotiation solutions; *ii)* information and persuasion; *iii)* fiscal interventions and *iv)* regulation. In all of these cases, the basic principles often refer to the theory developed by [34], called *"Windfalls for wipeouts"*, for justifying this recapturing of extra-profits. The public subjects which release regulations that cause a reduction in property value should compensate landowners for such "wipeouts". However, at the same time, public activities that increase property values should allow the recapture of it by the government: thus, it recaptures the *"windfalls"* that it creates.

4   The Model

The proposed model is structured on the computational logic of goal programming, a branch of OR, that focuses on the application of analytical methods for problem solving and decision-making uncertain conditions [35]. The usefulness of OR in providing a systematic and scientific resolution to government, military, manufacturing, service but also in several business problems is widely recognized in the scientific literature [36]. OR is often utilized in uncertain urban planning decision-making contexts, which are characterized by scarce financial resources and different possible alternative solutions subject to different constraints [37, 38].

In the present research, the urban planning problem to be solved consists in the determination of the amount of the gross floor surface (GFS), for the intended uses considered, to be built and sold in the *post variant* scenario. In particular, the costs and the revenues that take place in this scenario must be such as to:

- cover the higher transformation costs incurred by the private entrepreneur compared to the project planned before the transformation scenario (*ante variant* scenario),
- repay the share of the extraordinary urbanization contribution foreseen and finally guarantee the financial convenience of both the parties involved in the initiative.

For these reasons, the variables of the model are four and represent the most influencing urban planning parameters on which is focused the early stage of the negotiation between the PA and the private entrepreneur:

i.   the gross floor area of the properties that the private entrepreneur has to build and sell on the real estate market with the current prices (GFS_f);
ii. the gross floor area intended for social housing units (GFS_{sh});
iii. the share of the private surface where the entrepreneur has to build the properties (S_{bv});
iv. the share of the private surface where the entrepreneur has to build the private green spaces (S_{gs}).

The percentage share of the extraordinary urbanization contribution (c_{su}) constitutes an exogenous variable. It can be fixed by the PA due to the needs for the local community. It should be highlighted that the S_{bv} and S_{gs} surfaces are variables that directly refer to the GFS to be built. Therefore, the amount of the quantity of GFS_f and GFS_{sh} constitute the main variables of the problem, whereas the S_{bv} and S_{gs} contribute to the definition of the intervention constraints.

The constraints of the model are of two different typologies: *i)* physical-urban planning and *ii)* financial. The first ones derive by taking into account the ordinary division of the total land plot (S_t) into the public surface (S_{pa}) - intended for infrastructure and public buildings -, and the private one (S_{pe}) - where the entrepreneur will have to realize the building volumes (S_{bv}) granted by the PA and allowed by the urban planning buildable index (I_e) -. In particular, in order to include the needs of the growing demand for social housing units that the PA must face, the total gross floor surface (GFS_t) to be realized consists of two shares: *i)* the one that the private entrepreneur has to build and sell on the local real estate market at current market prices (GFS$_f$); *ii)* the one intended for social housing units (GFS$_{sh}$), to be sold at low-price in the local real estate market.

The intended uses allowed are supposed to be known and are established as a percentage of GFS$_f$ fixed by projectual purposes, therefore, three different coefficients that represent each extent are introduced:

- α for the gross floor surface of residential units (GFS$_h$),
- β for the gross floor surface of commercial units (GFS$_c$),
- γ for the gross floor surface of office units (GFS$_o$).

The minimum bounder of the surface intended for public buildings (S$_{pa}$) is determined due to projectual purposes as a share δ of the total land plot (S$_{pa} \geq \delta \cdot$ S$_{t.}$). The upper bounder of the surface for the private building volumes (S$_{bv}$), instead, is established according to the urban parameter of the coverage ratio (R$_c$) of the total land plot and the minimum bounder of the floors number is equal to the ratio between the GFS$_t$ and the S$_{bv}$ surface. Two coefficients – a and b – are introduced to determining the extent of the private green spaces (S$_{gs}$) and the public roads (S$_r$) that respectively depend on the S$_{pe}$ and S$_t$ surfaces. The minimum size of the private surface S$_{pe}$ for parking (S$_{parking}$) is established by total building volumes (Vol$_{tot}$), i.e. with reference to Italian Law No. 122/1989, for which 1 m^2 of parking per each 10 m^3 of new building is to be realized, by supposing that each floor of new buildings has an average height of 3 m.

Table 1. Physical and urban planning constraints.

$S_t = S_{pe} + S_{pa}$	(1)
$S_{pe} = S_{bv} + S_{gs} + S_{parking}$	(2)
$GFS_t = I_e \cdot S_t$	(3)
$GFS_t = GFS_f + GFS_{sh}$	(4)
$GFS_f = GFS_h + GFS_c + GFS_o$ $GFS_h = \alpha \cdot GFS_f$ $GFS_c = \beta \cdot GFS_f$ $GFS_o = \gamma \cdot GFS_f$	(5)
$S_{pa} \geq \delta \cdot S_t$	(6)
$S_{bv} \leq R_c \cdot S_t$	(7)
$N_{f,max} \geq GFS_t/S_{bv}$	(8)
$S_{gs} \geq a \cdot S_{pe}$	(9)
$S_r = b \cdot S_t$	(10)
$S_{pe} = Vol_{tot}/10 = (GFS_t \cdot 3)/10$	(11)

The balance sheet of the financial advantages of the PA and the private entrepreneur is assessed taking into account the cost and revenue items generated by the *post variant* scenario compared to those of the *ante variant* one. The items considered are described in Table 2 and the existing interdependencies among them are explicated in Table 3, such as to allow the definition of the financial constraints of the model.

Table 2. Cost and revenues items considered.

Construction cost (K_c)	Parametric construction cost ($€/m^2$) determined according to the different allowed intended uses (Eq. 12 of Table 3)
Parking ($K_{parking}$) and green private spaces (K_{gs}) construction cost	Costs for the construction of parking plots (Eq. 13 of Table 3) and private green areas (Eq. 14 of Table 3) calculated on the basis of the unit costs ($€/m^2$) of construction established in the price list drawn up by the Order of Architects and Engineers of Milan in 2019 for the Civil Engineering Typography [39]
Urbanization fees (K_{ou})	Primary and secondary urbanization fees are calculated in accordance with the provisions of Art. 3 of Law no. 10/1977, i.e. applying the unit values ($€/m^2$) reported in the appropriate municipal tables according to the intended use and the type of intervention to be carried out. Construction fees are, instead, calculated for each intended use as a percentage of the individual construction cost. The items are summarized in Eq. 15 of Table 3 by applying an average parametric cost that refers to the GFS_{pe}
Technical expenses (K_{te})	The expenses for the commitments of planning, construction management, and the other operations required by the initiative, are calculated as a percentage - equal to 5% - of the total construction cost (Eq. 16 of Table 3)
General expenses (K_{sg})	The expenses deriving from the management of the entire initiative are calculated as a percentage - equal to 4% - of the total construction cost (Eq. 17 of Table 3)
Commercialization fees (K_{cf})	The amounts necessary for the advertising and marketing of the building products of the intervention are assumed to be equal to 2% of the market value of the products (V_{mt}) obtainable from the *post variant* scenario (Eq. 18 of Table 3)

(*continued*)

Table 2. (*continued*)

Financial fees (K_{ff})	The price of use of the bank loan of the private entrepreneur for the implementation of the initiative is calculated as a percentage of incidence - equal to be 6% - of the total transformation cost items (Eq. 19 of Table 3)
Transformation revenues	The revenues from the sale of the realizable surfaces are obtained by multiplying the unit asking prices (€/m^2) of each intended use, indicated respectively with r_h, r_c, r_o, r_{sh} and $r_{parking}$ - by the corresponding gross floor surfaces (Eq. 20 of Table 3)

Table 3. Existing interdependencies among the cost and revenue items.

$K_c = c_{cu,h} \cdot GFS_h + c_{cu,c} \cdot GFS_c + c_{cu,o} \cdot GFS_o + c_{cu,sh} \cdot GFS_{sh}$	(12)
$K_{parking} = c_{parking} \cdot S_{parking}$	(13)
$K_{gs} = c_{gs} \cdot S_{gs}$	(14)
$K_{urb} = c_{urb} \cdot GFS_{pe}$	(15)
$K_{te} = 5\% \cdot (K_c + K_{parking} + K_{gs})$	(16)
$K_{sg} = 4\% \cdot (K_c + K_{parking} + K_{gs})$	(17)
$K_{cf} = 2\% \cdot V_{mt}$	(18)
$K_{ff} = 6\% \cdot (K_c + K_{parking} + K_{gs} + K_{urb} + K_{te} + K_{sg} + K_{cf})$	(19)
$V_{mt} = r_h \cdot GFS_h + r_c \cdot GFS_c + r_o \cdot GFS_o + r_{sh} \cdot GFS_{sh} + r_{parking} \cdot S_{parking}$	(20)

It should be emphasized that the profit of the private entrepreneur is not included within the cost items: in fact, the absence of the theoretical conditions of perfect competition and long-term equilibrium allows to take into account the normal profit expected by the investor in the market value which is assessed in the transformation of the area [40].

Once the cost and revenue items of the initiative have been defined, the conditions of financial convenience for the private investor and the PA are determined.

In the case of the private investor, the transformation value in the *post variant* scenario (Vt_{post}), function of the variables of the model, must be higher than the transformation value in the *ante variant* scenario (Vt_{ante}):

$$Vt_{post}(GFS_f, GFS_{sh}, S_{bv}, S_{gs}) > Vt_{ante}$$

For the PA, on the other hand, the urbanization fees (ΔO_{urb}) and the extraordinary urbanization contribution ($c_{su} \cdot (Vt_{post} - Vt_{ante})$) in the *post variant* scenario must be higher than the loss of value (ΔS_{st}) related to the reduction of surface to be allocated according to urban planning standards:

$$\Delta O_{urb} + c_{su} \cdot (Vt_{post} - Vt_{ante}) > \Delta S_{st}$$

In this case, given the plurality of aspects to be taken into account simultaneously, the objective function is of a complex type and, in mathematical terms, it can be translated into the following expression:

$$Max!(w_f \cdot GFS_f + w_{sh} \cdot GFS_{sh} + w_{gs} \cdot S_{gs})$$

The inclusion of the weights w_i, where i indicates the i-th variable of the objective function, allows to take into account the importance of each variable in pursuing the goal. In Table 4 the algorithm of the model is reported.

Table 4. Algorithm of the model.

Variables	GFS_f, GFS_{sh}, S_{bv}, S_{gs}, c_{su}
Objective function	$Max!(w_f \cdot GFS_f + w_{sh} \cdot GFS_{sh} + w_{gs} \cdot S_{gs})$
Constraints	Vt_{post} (GFS_f, GFS_{sh}, S_{bv}, S_{gs}) > Vt_{ante}
	$\Delta O_{urb} + c_{su} \cdot (Vt_{post} - Vt_{ante}) > \Delta S_{st}$
	Table 1

5 Conclusions

The urbanization phenomena that occurred after World War II were closely linked to the influences of the process of the urban rent formation. The analysis of the factors that contributed to the formation of the rent gap highlighted the role of urban rent as a synthetic indicator of the expected profitability of investments in the different urban areas. Starting from the model of the "rent gap theory" formulated by Smith (1979), there have been numerous contributions by Authors for analyzing the factors that affect the urban rent formation process on both local and metropolitan scale. In recent years, the studies have focused on the increase in land and property value generated by public investment and privatized by directly linked owners. The scarcity of public resources, however, have highlighted the need for negotiation tools and decision support models capable of fairly regulating urban rent with the aim of allocating greater resources for the local community.

The institution of the extraordinary urbanization contribution in Italy in the 2014 have outlined the legitimization of the PA to acquire a share of the surplus value generated by the urban variant interventions carried out in PPP forms. However, the absence of a codified methodology has affected the implementation of the regulatory provisions at the local level.

This research, therefore, is part of the framework outlined. The aim has been to define a decision support model that can be useful in the negotiation phases between the PA and private entrepreneur in the context of interventions that provide for a revision in the building parameters established by the current regulatory instruments.

The proposed model, structured by applying the computational logic of Operational Research, has the potentialities to identify the conditions of higher convenience for the parties involved, by determining the amount of the urban planning parameters to be negotiated. Furthermore, by guaranteeing the conditions of minimum financial convenience and the payment by the private entrepreneur of the minimum value of the extraordinary urbanization contribution required by the national law, the proposed model can be applied by public and private subjects to ensure a fair redistribution of the extra-profit generated by the urban variant interventions.

Future insights may concern the application of the proposed model to a real case study to verify its effectiveness. In particular, some limitations concerning the lack of the importance attributed to each variable can be overcome with the inclusion of appropriate weights and with the variation of the percentage of extraordinary contribution in a given range (e.g. between 50% and 100%). In this way, it would be possible to determine the Pareto front of the objective function considered, by determining the amount of the urban planning parameters negotiated by varying the percentage share of the extraordinary urbanization contribution that the private entrepreneur must transfer to the PA.

References

1. Salzano, E.: Fondamenti di urbanistica. Laterza, Bari (2003)
2. Slater, T.: Planetary rent gaps. Antipode 49(S1), 114–137 (2017)
3. Krijnen, M.: Beirut and the creation of the rent gap. Urban Geogr. 39(7), 1041–1059 (2018)
4. Smith, N.: Toward a theory of gentrification: a back to the city movement by capital, not people. J. Am. Plann. Assoc. 45(4), 538–548 (1979)
5. Liu, G., Chen, S., Gu, J.: Urban renewal simulation with spatial, economic and policy dynamics: the rent-gap theory-based model and the case study of Chongqing. Land Use Policy 86, 238–252 (2019)
6. Diappi, L., Bolchi, P.: Smith's rent gap theory and local real estate dynamics: a multiagent model. Comput. Environ. Urban Syst. 32(1), 6–18 (2008)
7. Clark, E.: The rent gap and transformation of the built environment: case studies in Malmö, 1860–1985. Geografiska Annaler Ser. B 70, 241–254 (1978)
8. Badcock, B.: An Australian view of the rent gap hypothesis. Ann. Assoc. Am. Geogr. 79, 125–145 (1989)
9. Yung, C., King, R.: Some tests for rent gap theory. Environ. Plan. A 30, 523–542 (1998)
10. Hammel, D.: Re-establishing the rent gap: an alternative view of capitalised land rent. Urban Stud. 36, 1283–1293 (1999)
11. Porter, M.: The rent gap at the metropolitan scale: New York City's land-value valleys, 1990–2006. Urban Geogr. 31(3), 385–405 (2010)
12. Hackworth, J.: Inner-city real estate investment, gentrification, and economic recession in New York City. Environ. Plan. A 33, 863–880 (2001)
13. Teresa, B.F.: New dynamics of rent gap formation in New York City rent-regulated housing: privatization, financialization, and uneven development. Urban Geogr. 40(10), 1399–1421 (2019)

14. López-Morales, E., Sanhueza, C., Espinoza, S., Ordenes, F., Orozco, H.: Rent gap formation due to public infrastructure and planning policies: an analysis of Greater Santiago, Chile, 2008–2011. Environ. Plan. A: Econ. Space **51**(7), 1536–1557 (2019)
15. Pizzo, B.: La rendita urbana come questione sociale. Le politiche di welfare sulle diseguaglianze **2030**, 112 (2020)
16. Amore, A., de Bernardi, C., Arvanitis, P.: The impacts of Airbnb in Athens, Lisbon and Milan: a rent gap theory perspective. Current Issues in Tourism, pp. 1–14 (2020)
17. Camagni, R., Capello, R.: Una valutazione dei benefici collettivi di un grande progetto urbano attraverso un indicatore sintetico: la rendita urbana. Scienze Regionali (2005)
18. Agnoletti, C., Bocci, C.: Gli effetti economici e distributivi degli interventi di riqualificazione urbana. In: XVII Congresso nazionale Associazione Italiana di Valutazione–AIV, Napoli, pp. 10–11 (2014)
19. Colli, F.: Principio di agglomerazione: le determinanti della dimensione urbana nelle province della Val Padana (2015)
20. Boca, A., Falco, E.: Il recupero della rendita immobiliare tra strumenti fiscali, oneri, e accordi negoziali: quale futuro per l'Italia? Scienze regionali (2016)
21. Foldvary, F.E., Minola, L.A.: The taxation of land value as the means towards optimal urban development and the extirpation of excessive economic inequality. Land Use Policy **69**, 331–337 (2017)
22. Hu, Y., Lu, B., Wu, J.: Value capture in industrial land renewal under the public leasehold system: a policy comparison in China. Land Use Policy **84**, 59–69 (2019)
23. Falco, E.: Equalization and compensation in Italy: empirical evidence for a new national planning act. Plan. Pract. Res. **26**(1), 59–69 (2011)
24. Nespolo, L.: Rigenerazione urbana e recupero del plusvalore fondiario. IRPET Regione Toscana (2012)
25. Anelli, D., Sica, F.: The financial feasibility analysis of urban transformation projects: an application of a quick assessment model. In: Bevilacqua, C., Calabrò, F., Della Spina, L. (eds.) NMP 2020. SIST, vol. 178, pp. 462–474. Springer, Cham (2021). https://doi.org/10.1007/978-3-030-48279-4_44
26. Della Spina, L., Calabrò, F., Rugolo, A.: Social housing: an appraisal model of the economic benefits in urban regeneration programs. Sustainability **12**(2), 609 (2020)
27. Del Giudice, V., Massimo, D.E., De Paola, P., Del Giudice, F.P., Musolino, M.: Green buildings for post carbon city: determining market premium using spline smoothing semiparametric method. In: Bevilacqua, C., Calabrò, F., Della Spina, L. (eds.) NMP 2020. SIST, vol. 178, pp. 1227–1236. Springer, Cham (2021). https://doi.org/10.1007/978-3-030-48279-4_114
28. Colavitti, A.M., Serra, S.: Non financial compensation for the redevelopment of the historic urban landscape: the case study of Villasor in Sardinia (Italy). City Territory Architect. **7**(1), 1–15 (2020). https://doi.org/10.1186/s40410-020-00124-9
29. Van der Veen, M., Spaans, M., Janssen-Jansen, L.: Using compensation instruments as a vehicle to improve spatial planning: challenges and opportunities. Land Use Policy **27**(4), 1010–1017 (2010)
30. Spaans, M., Van der Veen, M., Janssen-Jansen, L.: The concept of non-financial compensation in spatial planning. In: Janssen-Jansen, L., Spaans, M., Van der Veen, M. (eds.) New Instruments in Spatial Planning: An International Perspective on NonFinancial Planning, pp. 121–139. IOS Press, Amsterdam (2008)
31. Janssen-Jansen, L., Spaans, M.V., der Veen, M.: New Instruments in Spatial Planning: An International Perspective on Non-financial Compensation, vol. 23. IOS Press, Amsterdam (2008)
32. Brown-Luthango, M.: Capturing land value increment to finance infrastructure investment—possibilities for South Africa. Urban Forum **22**(1), 37–52 (2011)

33. Webster, C.J., Lai, L.W.: Property Rights, Planning and Markets, Cheltenham, Edward, Elgar (2003)
34. Hagman, D.G., Misczynski, D.J.: Windfalls for Wipeouts, American Society of Planning Officials Chicago (1978)
35. Wagner, M., de Vries, W.T.: Comparative review of methods supporting decisionmaking in urban development and land management. Land **8**(8), 123 (2019)
36. Blumenfeld, D.E., Elkins, D.A., Alden, J.M.: Mathematics and operations research in industry. Focus **24**, 10–12 (2004)
37. Morano, P., Tajani, F., Anelli, D.: Urban planning decisions: an evaluation support model for natural soil surface saving policies and the enhancement of properties in disuse. Property Manag. **38**(5), 699–723 (2020). https://doi.org/10.1108/PM-04-2020-0025
38. Nesticò, A., Endreny, T., Guarini, M.R., Sica, F., Anelli, D.: Real estate values, tree cover, and per-capita income: an evaluation of the interdependencies in Buffalo City (NY). In: Gervasi, O., et al. (eds.) ICCSA 2020. LNCS, vol. 12251, pp. 913–926. Springer, Cham (2020). https://doi.org/10.1007/978-3-030-58808-3_65
39. Collegio degli ingegneri e architetti di Milano, Prezzi Tipologie Edilizie, DEI-Tipografia del Genio Civile, Roma (2019)
40. Forte, C.: Elementi di Estimo urbano, Etas Kompass (1973)

An Optimization Model for Supporting the Property Asset Allocation Decision-Making Process

Francesco Tajani[1] ⓘ, Marco Locurcio[2] ⓘ, Pierluigi Morano[2] ⓘ, and Debora Anelli[1(✉)] ⓘ

[1] Department of Architecture and Design, "La Sapienza" University of Rome, 00196 Rome, Italy
{francesco.tajani,debora.anelli}@uniroma1.it

[2] Department of Civil, Environmental, Land, Building Engineering and Chemistry, Polytechnic University of Bari, Via Orabona 4, 70125 Bari, Italy
{marco.locurcio,pierluigi.morano}@poliba.it

Abstract. The establishment of real estate funds has made it possible to attract greater local and foreign capital in the context of the enhancement and reuse of the Italian public real estate assets. The process of optimal allocation of the financial resources available in a real estate portfolio, however, is often opaque and linked to multiple factors. The aim of this research is to define an asset allocation model capable of supporting the decision-making processes of public and private investors in the context of the creation of optimized property portfolios. By adopting the logic and principles of goal programming, the model is able to identify the best combination of properties in the portfolio by optimally managing the available financial resources of a generic institutional investor. The ability of the proposed model to be flexible and implementable in any geographical context constitutes one of the main advantages for public and private investors.

Keywords: Real estate investment · Optimization model · Asset allocation strategy · Goal programming · Real estate funds

1 Introduction

In 2019, the Italian public real estate assets surveyed by the State Property Agency was made up of more than 42,000 properties for a total value of € 61 billions [1]. However, the presence of public properties that are underutilized or unused as a result of the post-war industrialization and urbanization processes has encouraged the development of strategies aimed at their recovery and reuse [2, 3]. The enhancement of public assets is, in fact, an essential measure of the government's strategy for the country's economic development. Coverage of operating expenses, debt reduction, improved efficiency in terms of asset management and economic, social and cultural growth of the territories, are only some of the positive effects on public finance and community [4]. In a climate of uncertainty generated by the economic crisis of 2007 and exacerbated by the Covid-19

© Springer Nature Switzerland AG 2021
O. Gervasi et al. (Eds.): ICCSA 2021, LNCS 12954, pp. 265–276, 2021.
https://doi.org/10.1007/978-3-030-86979-3_20

health emergency, the involvement of investors from the private sphere to reduce the weight of these operations on the already limited public finances has represented the driver of many initiatives of urban enhancement and regeneration, that have contributed to the improvement of the livability and quality level of urban areas [5, 6].

Indeed, for national and international investors, Italian public properties are one of the most attractive asset class. In particular, a higher appreciation is shown by foreign capital which, according to the studies conducted by the IPI group, stands at 46% of capital invested in Italy in the third quarter of 2020, confirming the recent trend in the Italian market [7].

About privatization and enhancement of public real estate assets, the main regulatory reference is represented by Law no. 410/2001, which is the starting point for the spread of different operational tools aimed at the management of public asset enhancement processes [8]. Among all, real estate investment funds are designed as indivisible assets owned by different investors who, by subscribing the shares of the fund, entrust the investment and management activity to a Savings Management Company. The development of real estate funds is a significant reality in the Italian outlook, and the tax concessions issued over the years by the national legislator have contributed to its diffusion and growth [9]. At the end of 2020, the Italian real estate fund sector has € 95 billions of directly owned assets and growth in the residential and logistics sectors. The office sector is prevailing with 64% of assets under management, despite a slight decrease in the last quarter of 2020 [10].

There are different types of real estate funds, which can be classified on the basis of the way the fund was established and the type of investors participating [11]. From an economic point of view, however, the structure of a real estate fund depends on the costs and revenues relating to the real estate portfolios held. In particular, the revenues vary according to the type of strategy conducted for: i) income-producing properties, ii) splitting and divestment of portfolios or iii) property development initiatives. Similarly, costs directly depend on the management of the real estate portfolio, as well as on the amount of financial charges on any bank loan [12].

The establishment of real estate portfolios in which the relationship between the risk assumed by the investor is adequately commensurate with the expected returns is, therefore, a complex issue which, if inadequately conducted, can affect the final performance of the fund [13]. According to the majority of studies in the reference literature [14–16], the main factors that directly affect the decisions to allocate financial resources for the construction of the portfolio are:

- Correlation between the types of assets and the geographical location of the properties;
- Investment period;
- Volatility, dynamism and stability of the reference markets;
- Investor profile, in terms of risk appetite and target.

The correct weighting of these factors is able to create real estate portfolios optimized for the specific risk/return profile of the investor. For this reason, the need for methodologies and models capable of adequately managing the process of composing an optimal portfolio, guaranteeing the highest achievable performance and lower risks deriving from the opacity of the process, has emerged. In this way, public and private investors will be able to contribute efficiently to the implementation of initiatives to enhance public real estate assets [17–19].

2 Aim of the Work

This research fits into the framework outlined. The goal is to define an asset allocation model for the definition of optimized real estate portfolios, i.e. capable of maximizing the expected return and minimizing the risk incurred. In particular, the proposed model refers to the hypothesis of a generic institutional investor who intends to allocate his available financial resources in a portfolio consisting of rented properties. The computational logic implemented is the lexicographic goal programming, a widely used mathematical approach in portfolio optimization decision making contexts. The algorithm is able to translate into mathematical terms the main risk factors that affect the performance of a real estate portfolio: geographical location, intended use, size, yield, volatility, dynamism and stability of the real estate market considered. The identification of the best combination of properties capable of ensuring an initial yield that is higher than that obtainable with reference to the municipal trade area of each property (DPR no. 138/1998), takes place taking into account the importance - in terms of weight - that the market value of each property has in the construction of the portfolio. The aspect of diversification, essential for minimizing global risk, is addressed by pursuing the minimization of the correlation among the properties of the portfolio, evaluated in terms of standard deviation of returns.

The use of the model by public and private investors would make it possible to support the decision-making process that takes place in the investment phases in the real estate market - through indirect vehicles (e.g. Real estate investment trusts, hedge funds etc.) - of available financial resources. Furthermore, the ability of the model to be flexible and implementable in any geographic context is a further advantage for operators in the sector.

The paper is structured as follows: Sect. 3 provides a brief overview on the share allocated to real estate over the years and most widely used approaches for the asset allocation problems. Section 4 describes the main features of the model. Section 5, finally, reports the conclusion of the research, in terms of potentialities, limits and possible future insights.

3 Background

The main reason for investing in the real estate sector is related to the security about the protection of the invested capital due to the fluctuation of real estate values according to the local market cycles. This condition guarantees the real value of the capital invested [20]. Due to their attractiveness, several studies have observed the optimal allocation to real estate practiced in a mixed-asset portfolio over the years [21]. In order to examine the variation of the optimal range within which, according to the Authors and the specific factors, the presence of the real estate can generate significant improvements in the overall portfolio performance, a literature analysis on a sample of twenty-one scientific papers written from 1984 to 2019 has been carried out (Fig. 1).

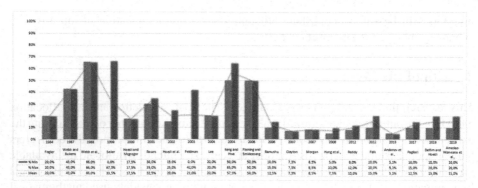

Fig. 1. Maximum and minimum percentage of the optimal real estate allocation in a mixed asset portfolio according to the survey.

The results shown in Fig. 1 highlight a wide variation of the optimal allocation range for the real estate. In particular, several Authors – [22–29] - identify the exact percentage of real estate that would be optimal to consider for investors within a mixed-asset portfolio. Other Scholars – [30–40] - establish a range within which to vary the optimal real estate allocation according to different factors, such as investors' risk aversion, investment period and asset returns.

The trend of the maximum and the minimum level percentage for the optimal real estate allocation, has undergone significant variations over the years of analysis considered. In particular, it is possible to note that starting from 2007 the percentage has significantly dropped, settling in a range that never exceeds 20%. The reason of this episode is linked to the global financial crisis triggered by the subprime mortgages, after which real estate performed poorly across different property types and locations in many countries [41, 42].

Over the years, in order to face the changing market conditions, several approaches for real estate decision making on a portfolio level have been addressed. The use of multi-criteria decision analysis and the multi-objective models for focusing the asset allocation problems has received increased attention in recent years. These methods have been suitable tools for complex asset allocation problems characterized by multiple influencing factors, uncertainties and the participation of multiple stakeholders along the process [43]. [44] perform two fuzzy mathematical programming models to overcome the drawbacks of traditional asset allocation models by including expert adjustment with vague data. [45] have treated the issue of portfolio selection by using fuzzy interactive approach, multiple goals and constraints. [46] attempts to examine whether the home asset bias in a portfolio holding is associated with higher political instability risk, and to what extent international diversification among stocks, in the presence of such risk, outperforms domestic stock portfolios by using a multi-objective approach. [47] provide for a robust multiobjective portfolio optimization with a minimum regret approach in order to incorporate future returns scenarios in the investment decision process. Some Authors choose to calculate the best efficient solutions, but many others address the efficient frontier, which is done with evolutionary or exact algorithms [48]. Approximation of the Pareto frontier and the research in the regions of investors' interests are suggested by [49]. [50], instead, try to solve multi-objective portfolio optimization problems with three or more quadratic objective functions, focusing on convex programs.

As regard to the portfolio selection process with the application of network theory, [51] establish a bridge between the modern portfolio theory framework and network theory, showing a negative relationship between optimal portfolio weights and the significance of assets in the financial market. [52] propose three different methods in order to extract the dependence structure among assets in a network context for then formulate and sort out the asset allocation problem.

4 The Model

From a computational point of view, the model consists in the resolution of an optimal allocation problem regarding the financial resources of a generic institutional investor who is interested in the construction of a real estate portfolio. In particular, the risk-return profile of the generic investor considered is represented by the core and core plus strategies, characterized by high yields and contained risks. In this case, therefore, the goal programming backpack problem ca be translated into:

- the resources available in limited quantities, i.e. the financial budget of the generic institutional investor;
- the alternative uses consisting of the various properties that can be within the real estate portfolio;
- the constraints represented by the mathematical equations and inequalities that identify the trade-offs decisions for the investor's convenience;
- the objective function, i.e. the identification of the best performing real estate portfolio with reference to the risk-return profile considered.

The identification of properties able to be included in the optimal real estate portfolio is structured on the initial yield, the riskiness and dynamism of each property by considering the municipal trade area to which they belong. *Soft* constraints and *hard* constraints are defined depending on the risk parameter considered and their importance in the construction of the real estate portfolio.

4.1 Soft Constraint

The initial yield relating to each property eligible for the optimal portfolio is assessed with reference to the property values defined by the Real Estate Market Observatory (REMO) of the Italian Revenue Agency for each municipal trade area where are placed. According to the D.P.R. no. 138/1998, indeed, the perimeter of an urban area where the real estate market is affected in a similar way by the existing extrinsic factors is called "municipal trade area". If the purchase price of each property is lower (or equal) to the average market value detected for the municipal trade area to which it belongs and the passing rent is higher (or equal) to the average rent charged, the probability for the generic investor to acquire a high capital gain at the time of the sale is higher. For this reason, defined with ΔVm and ΔCm respectively the average variation of the market value and the rent of the i-th property compared to the REMO values detected, the following Eqs. (1) and (2) are obtained:

$$\Delta Vm = (Vm_i - Vm_{REMO})/Vm_{REMO} = (Vm_i/Vm_{REMO}) - 1 \tag{1}$$

$$\Delta Cm = (Cm_i - Cm_{REMO})/Cm_{REMO} = (Cm_i/Cm_{REMO}) - 1 \tag{2}$$

with:

- Vm_i is the market value of the i-th property;
- Vm_{REMO} indicates the average market value detected by the REMO in the municipal trade area considered;
- Cm_i refers to the passing rent of the i-th property;
- Cm_{REMO} is the average rent recorded by the REMO in the municipal trade area considered.

For the optimal construction of a real estate portfolio, therefore, the best condition is represented by the simultaneous minimization of the ΔVm and maximization of the ΔCm. In order to achieve this aim, it is useful to introduce two financial indicators capable of providing information about the profitability and the immediate potential yield deriving from each property: the going-in cap rate ($GICR$) and the initial yield (IY). Considering the incremental ratio between $\Delta GICR$ and ΔIY it is possible to write Eq. (3) relating to the variation of the initial yield:

$$\Delta IY = (IY - GICR)/GICR \tag{3}$$

The $GICR$ is calculated with the ratio of the average rent (ΔCm_{REMO}) and the market value (Vm_{REMO}) detected by the REMO in the municipal trade area considered. The IY is, instead, represented by the ratio between the passing rent (Cm_i) and the market value (Vm_i) of the i-th property under analysis. Through the replacement of these algebraic function in Eq. (3) it's possible to define Eq. (4), relating to the maximization of the variation in the initial yield (ΔIY) of the i-th property related to the market of the municipal trade area considered:

$$\Delta IY = [(\Delta Cm + 1)/(\Delta Vm + 1)] - 1 \tag{4}$$

The risk borne by the generic investor must be as low as possible: it will therefore be necessary to identify dynamic markets with a low volatility of rents and market values. For this reason, the gross annual yield (Y_{ga}) per year t is introduced:

$$Y_{ga} = [(VmR_{EMO}(t) + Cm_{REMO}(t - 1))/Vm_{REMO}(t - 1)] - 1 \tag{5}$$

The gross annual yield of the property is calculated by considering the ratio of the sum of the hypothetical market value at the time of the sale, i.e. after one year ($Vm_{REMO}(t)$), and the rent received in the previous year ($Cm_{REMO}(t - 1)$), with the purchase price $Vm_{REMO}(t - 1)$. The hypothesis admits that the generic institutional investor purchases the i-th property at a price equal to the average market value in the municipal trade area considered in the year $t - 1$ ($Vm_{REMO}(t - 1)$), and acquires - for a period of one year from its purchase - a rent equal to the average one charged in the municipal trade area considered ($Cm_{REMO}(t - 1)$). At the end of this period, the i-th property is sold with a price that corresponds to the average market value of the municipal trade area currently practiced in the year t ($Vm_{REMO}(t)$). This assumption makes it possible to consider the real estate investment under analysis as a generic one. In other words, it is possible to avoid including in the evaluation the costs for notary fees, agency fees, ordinary maintenance etc. borne by the owner. In this way, considering that a stable market is characterized by a limited dispersion of gross annual returns, the generic institutional investor will aim to minimize the standard deviation of returns over the semesters (s) considered in the period t. At the same time, it will be necessary to maximize the average gross annual yield (Y_{aga}) achievable, therefore:

$$\sigma = \sqrt{\frac{1}{s-1} \sum_{t=1}^{s} \left[Y_{ga}(t) - Y_{aga}\right]^2} = \text{MIN} \tag{6}$$

$$Y_{aga} = \text{MAX} \tag{7}$$

The dynamism (D) of the reference market for each i-th property is evaluated through the number of transactions (NT_i) registered by the REMO for the related intended use and in the city in which is located. It is appropriate to carry out a normalization according to the resident population (RP_i) in each city in order to take into account the largest number of transactions that can take place in the most populated municipalities. Furthermore, in Eq. (8) this ratio is multiplied by 10,000, in order to obtain an easy reading and use of the data.

$$D = (NT_i/RP_i) \cdot 10,000 \tag{8}$$

The considerations addressed so far refer to the single property included in the real estate portfolio that is intended to be optimized for the generic institutional investor considered. Therefore, by indicating with p_n ($1 \leq p_n \leq n$, with n equal to the potential number of properties) the number of properties that will be within the portfolio and with p_{en} the maximum extent that it would be better to have by considering the available budget of the generic institutional investor, Eq. (9) is obtained:

$$|p_n - p_{en}| = \text{MIN} \tag{9}$$

Each property, however, depending on its market value can be attractive or not for the investor and, therefore, influencing their choices. To take into account the weight that the i-th property can determine in the decision-making process and, consequently, on the expected absolute yields, Eq. (10) is introduced. It defines the importance (or weight) w_i of the i-th property as the ratio between its market value MV_i and the sum of all the market values of the individual properties that constitute the real estate portfolio $\sum_{i=1}^{pn} MV_i$.

$$w_i = \frac{MV_i}{\sum_{i=1}^{pn} MV_i} \tag{10}$$

The algebraic functions previously defined in relation to the yield and risk for the individual property can be applied to the entire real estate portfolio with Eq. (11) as follows:

$$
\begin{cases}
\sum_{i=1}^{pn} \Delta IY_i \cdot w_i = MAX \\
\sum_{i=1}^{pn} \sigma_i \cdot w_i = MIN \\
\sum_{i=1}^{pn} Y_{aga,i} \cdot w_i = MAX
\end{cases}
\tag{11}
$$

A similar operation can be performed with regard to dynamism D_i and the volatility σ with low standard deviations of D_i:

$$
\begin{cases}
\sum_{i=1}^{pn} \sigma_{D,i} \cdot w_i = MIN \\
\sum_{i=1}^{pn} D_{a,i} \cdot w_i = MAX
\end{cases}
\tag{12}
$$

With D_{ai} is D_i average in the time period considered, whereas $\sigma_{D,i}$ indicates the standard deviation and w_i is the weight of the i-th property.

The last *soft* constraint of the model is represented starting from the introduction of the linear correlation coefficient of Bravais-Pearson (I_c), which allows to express any correlation among the properties in the real estate portfolio ($c_{i,}$). The lower the correlation among them, the lower the portfolio risk.

$$
I_c = \sum_{i,j=1}^{pn} |c_{i,j}| \cdot w_i \cdot w_j = MIN
\tag{13}
$$

4.2 Hard Constraint

The main *hard* constraint of the model is constituted by the financial budget (FR_a) which determines the essential condition for the generic institutional investor considered. Equation (13) shows the translation of this condition into mathematical terms:

$$
FR_a - \sum_{i=1}^{pn} MV_i \geq 0
\tag{14}
$$

The generic investor, in fact, will benefit most from the condition of equivalence (or at most a majority) between the available financial resources and the sum of the market values of the individual properties.

The last hard constraint of the model is, instead, represented by the non-negativity of the solutions and translated into algebraic terms in Eq. (15):

$$
v_i \in I_0^+ = \{z \in \mathbb{R} \ni' 0 \leq z \leq \varepsilon\}
\tag{15}
$$

4.3 Algorithm of the Model

The binary variable x represents the i-th property and assumes a value of "1" if the property is admitted to the portfolio, on the other hand it assumes a value of "0" if the property is not included in the portfolio. The asset allocation model algorithm is summarized in Table 1.

Table 1. Algorithm of the proposed asset allocation model

Type	Mathematical function	Description
Variable	$x_i = \{0; 1\}$	Binary variable
Goal	$\sum_i \Delta IY_i \cdot w_i \cdot x_i = MAX$	Maximization of the variation in the initial yield of the i-th property with respect to the average value of the municipal trade area
Hard constraints	$FRa - \sum_i MV_i \cdot x_i \geq 0$	Budget optimization
	$v_i \in I_0^+ = \{z \in \mathbb{R} \ni' \ 0 \leq z \leq \varepsilon\}$	Non-negativity of the solutions
Soft constraints	$|p_n - p_{ne}| \geq 0$	Optimization of the number of properties in the portfolio
	$\left|\sum_i \sigma_i \cdot w_i \cdot x_i - MIN\{\sigma_i\}\right| \geq 0$	Preference for stable yielding real estate markets
	$\left|\sum_i Y_{aga,i} \cdot w_i \cdot x_i - MAX\{Y_{aga}\}\right| \geq 0$	Maximization of the average return
	$\sum_{i,j} |c_{i,j}| \cdot w_i \cdot w_j \cdot x_i \cdot x_j \geq 0$	Preference of properties belonging to poorly correlated real estate markets
	$\left|\sum_i \sigma_{D,i} \cdot w_i \cdot x_i - MIN\{\sigma_{D,i}\}\right| \geq 0$	Preference of low volatile real estate markets
	$\left|\sum_i D_{a,i} \cdot w_i \cdot x_i - MAX\{D_{a,i}\}\right| \geq 0$	Preference of dynamic real estate markets

5   Conclusions

Italian real estate assets attract local and foreign capital, often conveyed in indirect investment instruments such as real estate funds. However, the identification of the most appropriate asset classes, in terms of risk and target return depending on the investor profile, is a complex issue. From an economic point of view, in fact, the structure of real estate funds gets revenues from the investment strategies adopted. The composition of an optimal real estate portfolio, therefore, allows the implementation of performance of both the portfolio and the real estate fund that owns it.

This research is part of the framework outlined by defining an asset allocation model capable of maximizing the expected return and minimizing the risks incurred by a generic institutional investor interested in core and core plus investments for the available financial resources. The application of the computational logic of goal programming made it possible to develop a decision support model that the investor will have to face when identifying the optimal combination of different types of properties in the real estate portfolio. The translation into soft and hard mathematical constraints of the main risk factors influencing the optimal performance of the portfolio provided transparency and objectivity to the process. The potentialities of the proposed model is the flexibility of being applied for different size of the sample of potential properties in the available portfolio and in any geographical context represents an advantage for public and private investors.

Future insights may concern the efficacy test of the model by applying the algorithm in a real case study. In particular, the lack of georeferenced system can be improved by including GIS tools for modelling the spatial dynamics which affect the decisions of both public and private investors can be an interesting and useful development.

References

1. Agenzia del Demanio Open Data. https://dati.agenziademanio.it/#/consistenzaevalore. Accessed 4 Dec 2020
2. Morano, P., Tajani, F., Anelli, D.: Urban planning decisions: an evaluation support model for natural soil surface saving policies and the enhancement of properties in disuse. Property Manag. (2020)
3. Locurcio, M., Tajani, F., Morano, P., Anelli, D.: A multi-criteria decision analysis for the assessment of the real estate credit risks. In: Morano, P., Oppio, A., Rosato, P., Sdino, L., Tajani, F. (eds.) Appraisal and Valuation. GET, pp. 327–337. Springer, Cham (2021). https://doi.org/10.1007/978-3-030-49579-4_22
4. Novara, A.: La valorizzazione dei beni pubblici: nuove forme di concessione e strumenti per la valorizzazione. Doctoral dissertation, Politecnico di Torino (2015)
5. Calabrò, F., Della Spina, L.: The public-private partnership for the enhancement of unused public buildings: an experimental model of economic feasibility project. Sustainability 11(20), 5662 (2019)
6. Morano, P., Guarini, M.R., Tajani, F., Anelli, D.: Sustainable redevelopment: the cost-revenue analysis to support the urban planning decisions. In: Gervasi, O., et al. (eds.) ICCSA 2020. LNCS, vol. 12251, pp. 968–980. Springer, Cham (2020). https://doi.org/10.1007/978-3-030-58808-3_69
7. Ital Papini Investimenti, Report Investimenti Q3 (2020)
8. Capilupi, S.: I fondi immobiliari. La leva fiscale per far ripartire il mercato immobiliare, I quaderni dell'Osservatorio dell'Agenzia delle Entrate (2014)
9. Gabrielli, L., Giuffrida, S., Trovato, M.R.: Functions and perspectives of public real estate in the urban policies: the sustainable development plan of Syracuse. In: Gervasi, O., et al. (eds.) ICCSA 2016. LNCS, vol. 9789, pp. 13–28. Springer, Cham (2016). https://doi.org/10.1007/978-3-319-42089-9_2
10. Scenari Immobiliari, Aggiornamento Rapporto 2020- I fondi immobiliari in Italia e all'estero, 3 December 2020
11. Gupta, A., Newell, G.: A real estate portfolio management risk assessment framework for nonlisted real estate funds in India. Property Manag. (2020)
12. Hoesli, M.E.R., Morri, G.: Investimento immobiliare: mercato, valutazione, rischio e portafogli. Ulrico Hoepli (2010)
13. Darst, D.M.: The Art of Asset Allocation: Asset Allocation Principles and Investment Strategies for Any Market. McGraw Hill Professional (2003)

14. Manganelli, B.: Real Estate Investing: Market Analysis, Valuation Techniques, and Risk Management. Springer, Heidelberg (2014)
15. Detemple, J.: Portfolio selection: a review. J. Optim. Theory Appl. **161**(1), 1–21 (2014)
16. Braga, M.D.: Methods and tools for portfolio selection. In: Basile, I., Ferrari, P. (eds.) Asset Management and Institutional Investors, pp. 173–201. Springer, Cham (2016). https://doi.org/10.1007/978-3-319-32796-9_5
17. McIntosh, W., Fitzgerald, M., Kirk, J.: Non-traditional property types: part of a diversified real estate portfolio? J. Portfolio Manag. **43**(6), 62–72 (2017)
18. Akbar, R.: The optimal allocation for capital preservation: an evidence australian portfolio. DeReMa (Dev. Res. Manag.): Jurnal Manajemen **13**(1), 110 (2018)
19. Ekemode, B.G., Olaleye, A.: Asset allocation decision-making practices of institutional real estate funds in a developing economy. Property Manag. (2019)
20. Manganelli, B., Tajani, F.: Come le variabili macroeconomiche influenzano il mercato immobiliare italiano. Rivista del Consulente Tecnico **3**, 21–37 (2010)
21. Candelon, B., Fuerst, F., Hasse, J.B.: Diversification Potential in Real estate portfolios, Working Paper Series No. 2020-5, University of Cambridge, Real Estate Research Centre (2020)
22. Fogler, H.R.: 20% in real estate: can theory justify it? J. Portfolio Manag. Winter 6–13 (1984)
23. Webb, J.R., Rubens, J.H.: How much in real estate? A surprising answer. J. Portfolio Manag. **13**(3), 10–14 (1987)
24. Webb, J.R., Curcio, R.J., Rubens, J.H.: Diversification gains from including real estate in mixed-asset portfolios. Decis. Sci. **19**(2), 434–452 (1988)
25. Hoesli, M., MacGregor, B.D.: Property Investment. Longman, Harlow (2000)
26. Lee, S.L.: When does direct real estate improve portfolio performance? Working Papers in Real Estate & Planning No. 17-03. University of Reading, Reading, October (2004)
27. Clayton, J.: PREA Plan Sponsor Research Report. Pension Real Estate Association, Hartford (2007)
28. Morgan, J.P.: The Alternative Asset Survey 2007. JPMorgan Asset Management, Luxembourg (2007)
29. Andonov, A., Kok, N., Eichholtz, P.: A global perspective on pension fund investments in real estate. J. Portf. Manag. **39**, 32–42 (2013)
30. Seiler, M.J., Webb, J.R., Myer, F.C.N.: Diversification issues in real estate investment. J. Real Estate Lit. **7**, 163–179 (1999)
31. Hoesli, M., Lekander, J., Witkiewicz, W.: International evidence on real estate as a portfolio diversifier, working paper. University of Massachusetts, Boston (2002)
32. Rosen, K.T.: Real estate investment trusts: a safe haven in volatile financial markets, Lend Lease Rosen Real Estate Securities. LLC, Berkeley (2001)
33. Feldman, B.: Investment Policy for Securitized and Direct Real Estate. Ibbotson Associates, Chicago (2003)
34. Keng, T.Y.: The role of international property trusts in Australian mixed-asset portfolios. In: Proceedings of Tenth Annual Conference of Pacific Rim Real Estate Society, Bangkok, Thailand (2004)
35. Ramushu, H.T.: The investigation of the role of real estate in a mixed-asset portfolio within the South African pension fund industry (2006). http://hdl.handle.net/10539/1668. Accessed 13 Feb 2020
36. Reddy, W.: Determining the current optimal allocation to property: a study of Australian fund managers. In: 18th Annual Pacific-Rim Real Estate Society (PRRES) Conference, Adelaide, Australia (2012)
37. Falk, J.: Direct and indirect real estate in a mixed-asset portfolio - is direct or indirect preferable? M.Sc. research thesis submitted to the Department of Real Estate and Construction Management, Stockholm, Sweden (2012)

38. Pagliari, J.L.: Another take on real estate's role in mixed-asset portfolio allocations. Real Estate Econ. **45**, 75–132 (2017)
39. Delfim, J.C., Hoesli, M.: Real estate in mixed-asset portfolios for various investment horizons. J. Portfolio Manag. **45**(7), 141–158 (2019)
40. Amédée-Manesme, C.O., Baroni, M., Barthélémy, F., Des Rosiers, F.: Market heterogeneity, investment risk and portfolio allocation. Int. J. Housing Markets Anal. (2019)
41. Lizieri, C.: After the fall: real estate in the mixed-asset portfolio in the aftermath of the global financial crisis. J. Portfolio Manag. **39**(5), 43–59 (2013)
42. Morri, G., Parri, E.: US REITs capital structure determinants and financial economic crisis effects. J. Property Investment Finan. (2017)
43. Kandakoglu, M., Walther, G., Amor, S.B.: The use of multi-criteria decision-making methods in project portfolio selection: a literature review and future research directions (2020)
44. Man Hui, E.C., Fai Lau, O.M., Lo, K.K.: A fuzzy decision-making approach for portfolio management with direct real estate investment. Int. J. Strateg. Prop. Manag. **13**(2), 191–204 (2009)
45. Deep, K., Singh, K.P., Kansal, M.L., Mohan, C.: A fuzzy interactive approach for optimal portfolio management. Opsearch **46**(1), 69–88 (2009)
46. Smimou, K.: International portfolio choice and political instability risk: a multi-objective approach. Eur. J. Oper. Res. **234**(2), 546–560 (2014)
47. Xidonas, P., Mavrotas, G.: Multiobjective portfolio optimization with non-convex policy constraints: evidence from the Eurostoxx 50. Eur. J. Finan. **20**(11), 957–977 (2014)
48. Metaxiotis, K., Liagkouras, K.: Multiobjective evolutionary algorithms for portfolio management: a comprehensive literature review. Expert Syst. Appl. **39**(14), 11685–11698 (2012)
49. Juszczuk, P., Kaliszewski, I., Miroforidis, J.: Trade-off guided search for approximate Pareto optimal portfolios. Multiple Criteria Decis. Making **12**, 49–59 (2017)
50. Jayasekara, P.L., Adelgren, N., Wiecek, M.M.: On convex multiobjective programs with application to portfolio optimization. J. Multi-criteria Decis. Anal. **27**(3–4), 189–202 (2020)
51. Peralta, G., Zareei, A.: A network approach to portfolio selection. J. Empir. Finan. **38**, 157–180 (2016)
52. Clemente, G.P., Grassi, R., Hitaj, A.: Asset allocation: new evidence through network approaches. Ann. Oper. Res. **299**(1–2), 61–80 (2019). https://doi.org/10.1007/s10479-019-03136-y

The Risks Assessment in the Project Financing Initiative for the Cemetery Expansion Intervention in a Small Town in Southern Italy

Marco Locurcio[1], Pierluigi Morano[1], Francesco Tajani[2], Felicia Di Liddo[1]([✉]), and Carmelo Maria Torre[1]

[1] Department of Civil, Environmental, Land, Building Engineering and Chemistry, Polytechnic University of Bari, 70126 Bari, Italy
felicia.diliddo@poliba.it

[2] Department of Architecture and Design, "Sapienza" University of Rome, 00196 Rome, Italy

Abstract. In the present research the risks matrix related to a transformation intervention to be carried out through the Project Financing (PF) operational tool, has been developed. With reference to the expansion and management of the cemetery of a small town located in Southern Italy, the identification and allocation of the risks among the parties involved – private investor and Public Administration – have been implemented. Furthermore, the verification of the feasibility by the Public Administration in the use of the PF operational tool has been performed, by analyzing the results obtained by the project *proposer subject* in financial terms. The risk assessment constitutes a support tool for the public Administration in the decision-making processes aimed to evaluate the PF proposals by the *proposer subject* in order to ensure an appropriate and detailed investigation on the Public Private Partnerships mechanism and to avoid complications and contingencies that could lead to initiative failure. In this sense, the present analysis allows to evaluate the advantages for public and private subjects to use the PF mechanism in bridging the existing gulf between the scarce public resources and the investment demand of expansion and/or redevelopment of urban cemeteries.

Keywords: Public-Private Partnership · Project Financing · Expansion intervention · Municipal cemeteries · New realization project · Small town · Risks matrix · Business plan

1 Introduction

In the context of the Public Private Partnerships (PPP), the Project Financing (PF) constitutes an increasingly being used operational tool for regions and municipalities able to bridge the gap between the available financial resources and the investment needs for the realization and/or redevelopment of infrastructures and collective services [1–3, 11]. Moreover, the PF allows to channel the efficiency and the qualitative standard of the private sector in the renovation of public interest properties and abandoned areas located on urban territory.

© Springer Nature Switzerland AG 2021
O. Gervasi et al. (Eds.): ICCSA 2021, LNCS 12954, pp. 277–292, 2021.
https://doi.org/10.1007/978-3-030-86979-3_21

In general terms, the PF represents a complex procedure in which different fields are involved – legislative, economic and financial –. The Public Administration may use it in order to carry out projects with great technical difficulties and high capital requirement. The PF, in fact, is a contractual tool intended to ensure the cooperation between public entities and private investors in the context of initiative for the territorial development [16].

The satisfaction of the public interest deriving from the realization of the infrastructure is verified without direct public financial burdens. Thus, the central feature of the PF mechanism concerns the financial backing of the planned investments by the private investor, i.e. the design phase and the realization, in exchange for the project direct or indirect management.

Therefore, the financing procedure is not adaptable to all initiatives that require high investments, but only to those able of generating profits, in order to ensure the positive financial balance for the private investor in terms of profit deriving from the cash flows related to the intervention higher than the zero value.

In general, in PPP procedures the public subject has to assess not exclusively the public interest related to the proposal, but to verify its financial feasibility to include the project in the interventions to be realized planning [14].

In the context of the cemetery construction, the PF has over time become a procedural tool implemented by Public Administration for realization and management of cemetery areas, especially due to the convenience in financial and risks terms [8, 17].

The progressive involvement of private sector in projects related to cemetery spaces attests the growing interest in the PF able to allow also the small towns' public entities, unable to bear the required costs for the renovate or expansion of cemeteries, to outsource the redevelopment and management of these.

In the Italian context, the dimensions reached by PF market in the cemetery sector in terms of number of started interventions and activated investments are significant - i.e. among the most relevant are mentioned the projects realized in the cities of Foligno (2003), Avellino (2005), Taranto (2004), Castel Maggiore (2005), Sassari (2007), Pescara (2007), Messina (2008), Latina (2007), Potenza (2009), Venosa (2009), etc. [5].

Through the PF contractual mechanism, the public subjects could obtain a savings in economic and administrative terms. During the concession period, in fact, the Public Administration monitors the agreement performance, as it does not be directly concerned with the niches construction and management. Furthermore, the long-term duration of the public private cooperation allows the Public Administration to avoid the congestion risk of cemeteries and, consequently, to prevent sanitary criticality associated to it. From the private point of view, the interest in PF projects regards the low construction and management costs, the certainty of market demand stability, the competitor absence, operating in a monopoly regime with no other economic operators.

2   Aim

The present research concerns the framework outlined. The paper concerns the application of the PF procedure to a case study related to the expansion of the municipal cemetery of a small town located in Southern Italy.

The work aims to analyze the procedure for the identification and allocation of the risks associated to the realization and management of PF project among the parties involved – Public Administration and private investor. Furthermore, with reference to the mentioned transformation project, the work intends to verify the feasibility by the Public Administration in the use of the PF operational tool by analyzing the assessment carried out by the *proposer subject*. The present study has been developed by the authors and commissioned by Public Administration for assessing the effectiveness in the use of PF procedure for the initiative considered.

In this sense, the results of the research could be a support tool for the Public Administration in the decision-making processes aimed to evaluate the PF proposal by the *proposer subject* in order to ensure an appropriate and detailed investigation on the PPP mechanism. An effective study on the construction, profitability and demand risks of the initiative and a proper description of the economic and financial balance risk represent central phases in the PF convenience assessment.

The paper is structured as follows. In Sect. 3 the different risk typologies connected to a PPP realization and/or renovation project according to Italian legislative references have been illustrated. In Sect. 4 the case study, related to the expansion and the management of the cemetery of a small town located in Southern Italy to be carried out through the PF procedure, has been described. In Sect. 5, the matrix of the main risks associated to the project realization and management considered has been developed to validate the PF initiative. Finally in Sect. 6 the conclusions of the work have been reported.

3   The Risks Assessment

In the existing literature concerning the PPP operational tools for urban redevelopment interventions analysis, several contributions are aimed to define the risks for the parties involved in the transformation initiative – public subjects and private investors [4, 9, 12]. In the Italian context of the PPP operational tools, the National Anti-Corruption Authority (ANAC) Guidelines No. 9 indicate the distribution and allocation of initiative risks between the parties involved on the basis of their respective risk management competences [15]. In particular, the ANAC Guidelines No. 9 point out that the contracting authorities have to identify and assess the specific construction and management risks by allocating them to the subjects with the highest control capacities of them. This is confirmed in the reference literature aimed at analyzing the risks components of a PPP projects: for example, Iyer and Sagheer [10] have pointed out that the initiative success depends on the efficient risks transfer to the sector that can best manage them or Grimsey and Lewis [7] have analyzed the risks of PPP arrangements from the perspectives of the various parties, by explaining the contractual relations between the subjects in infrastructure projects and the most performing mechanisms of distributing risks during different phases of the project.

Furthermore, in order to assess the subject ability to manage each risk, the verification of the possibility to adopt suitable measures for the reduction of likely negative effects, i.e. insurance policies, shall be carried out.

The Guidelines include the risks matrix among the PPP contract documents, aimed at regulating ex-ante modalities and limits for the project financial economic conditions review.

The risks analysis provides to the public administrations a greater awareness of the critical issues that could be arise during the concession period and helps to strengthen the bargaining among the subjects involved – private and public –. In this sense, the risks matrix is part of the made up of contest documents for the tenders evaluation aimed to support the decision processes for the transformation investment implementation. Furthermore, during the execution phase, this document allows the public subject for an adequate monitor on the risks transfer and retention.

In the Italian legislative context, the arts. 3 par. 1 and 180 par. 3 of Legislative Decree No. 50/2016 [13] highlight that in PPP contracts the risk transfer to the private sector implies the allocation to this subject to the *construction, availability* and *demand* risks for the entire procedure period. These risk typologies are included in *operative* risk, i.e. associated to the management of works or services from the demand or the supply side or both points of view.

Moreover, the *construction* risk, as defined in art. 3 par. 1 of Legislative Decree No. 50/16, is related to delay in delivery times, non-compliance with project standards, increased costs, technical problems and failure to finish the planned work. With regards to this risk category, the ANAC Guidelines No. 9 include the specific risks connected to *i)* the design phase, for the occurrence of necessary project variations, resulting from design errors or omissions, such as to significantly affect the time and costs of carrying out the work; *ii)* an project execution that does not conform to the initial project, linked to failure to comply with the fixed standards; *iii)* an increase in the cost of production factors or inadequacy or unavailability of those planned in the project; *iv)* a wrong costs and construction times assessment; *v)* the contractual breaches by suppliers and subcontractors; *vi)* the unreliability and inadequacy of the technology used.

The *availability* risk, as defined in art. 3 par. 1 of Legislative Decree No. 50/16, is associated to the ability, on the part of the concessionaire, to provide the agreed contractual services, both in terms of volume and expected quality standards. The ANAC Guidelines include the risk items related to *i)* an extraordinary and not foreseen maintenance, deriving from inadequate design or construction, with a consequent increase in costs; *ii)* a non-compliance with the performance indicators of the structure or the services provided; *iii)* the total or partial unavailability of the asset and/or of the services to be provided.

In cases of profitable activities, the risk of *demand* for the services provided for, is associated to the lack of users and, therefore, of cash flows to be obtained in operational phase. The specific risks included in this risks typology concerns *i)* the contraction in market demand in terms of a reduction in overall demand for this service; *ii)* the contraction in specific demand, linked to the occurrence in the reference market of a competitive supply from other operators that negatively affects the current demand.

The attainment of the *economic-financial balance* (arts. 180, par. 7 and 165 pars. 3, 4, 5 of Legislative Decree 50/2016) represents the fundamental condition for the correct allocation of construction, availability and demand risks in PPP procures. Defined as the simultaneous presence of economic convenience and financial sustainability conditions - art. 3, par. 1 of Legislative Decree 50/2016 -, the economic-financial balance allows to ensure the project capacity to create value during the contract period and to generate an adequate profitability level for the invested capital (economic convenience) and to generate sufficient cash flows to guarantee the initial capital repayment (financial sustainability).

The ANAC Guidelines report the main performance indicators for the verification of the economic-financial balance of the initiative - Net Present Value (NPV), Internal Rate of Return (IRR), Revenues and Costs Ratio (R/C), Debt Service Cover Ratio (DSCR) and Long Life Cover Ratio (LLCR).

The initiative bankability strongly affects the risks connected to an economic-financial imbalance: the resources availability to cover costs on the financial market in fixed time, the sustainability of these resources and the reasonable return on invested capital constitute the *funding risk*.

With reference to the *financial risk*, i.e. the risk of an increase in interest rates and/or failure to repay one or more loan installments, with a consequent costs rise or the impossibility of continuing the operation, the analysis of this risk component provides for the assumption of different progressively increasing interest rates to assess effects the main on the economic-financial balance, in terms of performance indicators results.

The whole PPP intervention risks assessment includes the risks connected to the obtaining permits (opinions, licenses, authorizations, etc.) from public and private entities. In this risk category, the *commissioning risk* is the likelihood that the work will not have approval, from other public subjects or from the community (stakeholders with regard to the intervention to be carried out), with consequent *i)* delays in the realization, *ii)* occurrence of controversies, or in extreme cases, *iii)* failure of the of the awarding or the entire PPP procedure.

The *administrative risk* is connected to the considerable delay or refusal in the granting of authorizations by competent public and private entities, or also to the granting of authorizations with additional requirements, by causing delays in the realization phases.

Furthermore, the *expropriation risk* concerns delays deriving from expropriation operations or higher costs of expropriation due to wrong planning and/or estimation.

In the same risk category, the *environmental and/or archaeological risk* is linked to the soil characteristics, to the possible reclamation due to soil contamination and to archaeological finds, thereby delays in the project realization and increases in costs for environmental remediation or archaeological protection. Finally, the *legislative-political-regulatory risk* derives from variations in the normative framework and from programmatic policy decisions that cannot be contractually foreseen, by causing increase in costs for adaptation.

The summary of the risks system related to the transformation and management projects carried out through the PF operation tool is rounded off by the *default risk* – i.e. the likelihood that users are unable to pay the price of the services offered -, the *residual value risk* – associated to the return of the asset characterized by a lower market value compared to that expected at the end of contractual relationship -, the *technical obsoleteness risk* – i.e. linked to the faster obsoleteness of plants, by determining higher maintenance costs -, the *above and below service interference risk* – connected to the different typologies services in the part interested by the intervention (electricity, cables, fiber optics, etc.).

In Table 1 a synthetic overview of the main risk categories illustrated is reported.

Table 1. The main risk categories in PPP projects

Operative risk	
Construction risk	Design risk
	Risk of project execution
	Risk of increase in production factors cost
	Risk of wrong costs and construction times assessment
	Risk of contractual breaches by suppliers and subcontractors
	Risk of unreliability and inadequacy of the technology used
Availability risk	Risk of extraordinary and not foreseen maintenance
	Performance risk
	Risks of the asset total or partial unavailability
Risk of *demand*	Risk of contraction in market demand
	Risk of contraction in specific demand
Risk of economic-financial imbalance	
Funding risk	
Financial risk	
Residual value risk	
Commissioning risk	
Administrative risk	
Expropriation risk	
Environmental and/or archaeological risk	
Legislative-political-regulatory risk	
Default risk	
Technical obsoleteness risk	
Interference risk	

4   Case Study

The case study concerns a hypothesis of project financing for the construction of niches and the management for a period of twenty years of the municipal cemetery of a small town located in Southern Italy. The town covers an area of about 40 km², with a population just over 25,000 inhabitants.

4.1   Description of the Cemetery Expansion and Management Project

The project proposed provides for the construction of cemetery niches in the area established for the expansion of the municipal cemetery and their subsequent management. The initiative plays a strategic role for the small town due to the current needs, equal to

476 niches, and to the centrality of this service for the community, as confirmed by the inclusion of the intervention in the Municipal 2017–2019 public works Programming Document.

In particular, the project concerns the realization of 3,968 niches divided into five lots – lot A composed by 812 niches to be built in the first year of the management period, lot B of 2,176 in the second year of the management period, lot C of 140 niches in the fourteenth year of the management period, lot D1 constituted by 448 niches to be realized in the fifteenth year of the entire period considered equal to twenty years and lot D2 of 392 niches in the seventeenth year.

The niches will be built with reinforced concrete walls on a continuous foundation consisting of a reinforced concrete slab. The external shell and the tombstones will be built by using of local materials and the roof will be protected by two layers of water-proofing membrane. The project also provides for the modernization of the pedestrian viability through a paving in pressed bricks, such as to those already existing in other cemetery areas. The trees in the area intended to the niches in lot D will be explanted and replanted in a suitable cemetery spaces.

The project envisages different measures aimed at optimizing management costs, such as the inclusion of votive LED lights, and at allowing the accessibility to the people with low modality, thanks to the absence of architectural barriers and to the presence of an electric vehicle to facilitate the users' movement.

4.2 The PF Procedure

The hypothesis assumed is that the Public Administration and a private investor conclude an onerous and written agreement for a fixed time period - equal to twenty years -, in order to expand and manage the municipal cemetery. The PF procedure provides that the new construction interventions are carried out by the private investor, in exchange for the temporary use of the new portion of cemetery for the fixed time period. In particular, under this assumption the private investor bears the realization costs and manages the new cemetery portion for the entire twenty-year concession period. The revenue items for the private investor will derive from the niches concession, whereas for the Public Administration a royalty equal to 250 € for each niche has been defined to be paid.

The verification of the effective use of PF in terms of financial feasibility from the private investor point of view related to intervention is carried out through the cash flows analysis.

With reference to the case study analyzed, the cash flow analysis has been developed by *proposer subject* and it shall be validated by the authors to verify the outputs obtained in terms of intervention profitability and risks. Starting from the market demand description, by considering the resident population trend and the National Institute of Statistics (ISTAT) mortality and birth rates [18] (Fig. 1), in the cash flows analysis, for each concession year, the costs (investment and management) and the revenues have been assessed and the performance indicators have been determined.

Finally, for the assessment of the risk linked to the economic-financial balance, a cash flows analysis, named new analysis, has been developed. It should be observed that some hypothesis have been borrowed from the *proposer subject* analysis, as considered valid: if a different hypothesis has been introduced in the Manuscript it is highlighted.

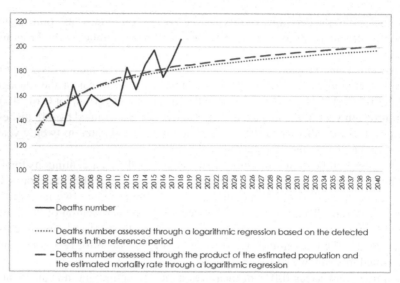

Fig. 1. Number of deaths detected and estimated

Thus, with reference to the case study, the main assumptions of the new analysis can be summarized as follows:

- the period of the analysis is equal to twenty years;
- the construction costs are assessed by considering the unitary costs reported in Regional Price List of Public Works of the year 2019. In the absence of the unitary price, the new realization costs are assessed by price lists of public and private works, currently used in the Region and by the data reported in the "Building typology prices" list [6], and are validated by consulting local operators and construction companies. Moreover, the unitary construction cost related to the case study cemetery project niches is consistent with the parametric unitary costs related to other similar Italian cemetery projects, recently built. In the *proposer subject* cash flows analysis the total construction cost was assessed equal to 3,500,000 €, whereas in the new cash flows analysis the total construction cost assessed is 3,700,000 €, by determining a percentage variation equal to ±6%. In particular, in the new analysis the estimated amounts for the different project components are higher compared those calculated by the *proposer subject*, with increases that vary from +4% to +14%, by depending on the lots (Fig. 2). This variation is in line with the difference in spending capacity between an ordinary investor, i.e. the cost assessment related to the reference price lists, and the specific investor, i.e. the *proposer subject*.

- the 36% of the investment costs related to the niches realizations intervention are borrowed from a credit institution, through a 20-year mortgage to be returned through constant annual down payments with an interest rate equal to 5.00%;

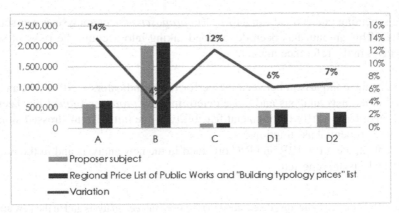

Fig. 2. Comparison between costs estimated by the proposer subject and costs assessed through the price lists

- the technical costs – for the definitive plan, a draft convention, the economic-financial plan, the specification of the service characteristic and of the management – are assessed equal to 60,000 €;
- the general expanses – including the fees for specialized technicians and professionals, the costs of the insurance for the construction phase, etc. – are assessed equal to 100,000 €;
- the management costs include the expenses for equipment, the ordinary mainte- nance costs, the personnel and insurance costs, the expenses for utilities. These costs are assessed by considering those currently borne by Public Administration for the existing cemetery portion;
- the revenue items concern the niches concession and the services as burial, bones- washing, votive lights, etc. The revenues are determined following the demand curve assessed. The market demand depends on two main factors: *i)* the number of deaths expected during the concession period, by deducting the burials, cremations or dead to be placed in private chapels *ii)* the previous market demand (476 niches). Therefore, on the basis of the estimations carried out, the annual deaths number has been estimated equal to 162, i.e. the annual expected average deaths number - equal to 190 – reduced by 15% by considering the potential cremations, burials and dead to be placed in private chapels. The amount estimated is different from the *proposer subject* analysis (180 niches/year) and represents a prudential initial data for the cash flow assessment. With regards to the tariffs implemented by the *proposer subject* in his analysis for the niches concession and for installation of slabs and accessories are equal to 2,500 – 2,600 €/niche. This amount is consistent with the current ordinarily tariffs charged in the specific reference context by Public Administration and, therefore, they are retained in the new analysis;
- for each niche, a royalty equal to 250 € has been defined to be paid to the Public Administration: this monetary amount is include in the tariff paid for the niches concession;

- the discounting rate is fixed equal to 7% (in *proposer subject* analysis it was set equal to 5%). This amount has been determined taking into account the risks of similar initiatives in the reference market.

Finally, the comparison between the performance indicators – NPV, IRR and R/C-assessed in the new analysis and those determined by *proposer subject* has been performed, in order to verify the financial feasibility of the initiative in stressed situations (with more prudential assumptions).

In Table 2, the NPV, IRR and R/C obtained in the new analysis and in the *proposer subject* analysis are reported.

Table 2. Performance indicators determined in *proposer subject* analysis and in the new analysis.

Indicator	*Proposer subject* analysis	New analysis
NPV (€)	2,100,000	1,200,000
IRR	36.2%	32.4%
R/C	1.5	1.2

It should be observed that the economic-financial balance is ensure in the stressed situation assumed in the new analysis. However, the likelihood that the economic-financial balance is not ensured is high, by considering a possible variation of the taxes and duties system, of regulatory framework, the longer time for the granting of authorizations and unforeseen geological or geotechnical characteristics.

5   The Risks Matrix

In order to assess the different risk categories related to the expansion and management project of the cemetery considered in the present analysis, the matrix risks has been developed.

The Table 3 reports a framework of the main risk typologies connected to the project. The investigation allows to carry out an exhaustive analysis of the risks transfer to the various subjects involved in the initiative – private and public sectors -, by explaining the likely root causes, the specific strategic measures aimed at avoiding or, at least, at reducing the effects of negative phenomenon. With reference to each risk item illustrated in Sect. 3 of the present paper, in the Table 2 a qualitative indication of the likelihood that it occurs, the economic effects deriving from its occurrence and the subject to whom the risk is transferred are shown. In particular, the likelihood of each risk occurring has been evaluated by using a verbal scale, as such indicated by ANAC Guidelines No. 9 – nil, minimum, low, medium and high. The assessment process by which the likelihood of risk has been measured, is included in the Table through a synthetic description of the specific aspect of the intervention: thus, the each intervention critical issue and weakness is explored in order to identify and manage the most complex and risky elements of the PF initiative considered.

Table 3. Risks matrix related to the cemetery expansion and management project.

Risk typology	Likelihood of risk occurring	Economic effects assessed	Subject to whom the risk is transferred
Project design and execution risks	**Low** The standardized building typology, associated to specific construction indications, makes it unlikely dissimilarities between the project planned and the work completed	+8% of the construction costs	Private
Risk of increase in production factors cost and risk of wrong costs and construction times assessment	**Medium-low** The technical specifications of the project detect a low level of technical-realization complexity. However, in a concession period of twenty years a costs increase is plausible	+6% of the assessed costs	Private
Risk of the contractual breaches by suppliers and sub-contractors	**Not estimated**		Private
Risks of unreliability and inadequacy of the technology used	**Nil** The construction technologies are easy to implement and the plant component is limited, consolidated and widespread		
Risk of an extraordinary and not foreseen maintenance	**High** In the PF proposal carried out by *proposer subject* there is no explicit reference to extraordinary maintenance. However, in the ordinary maintenance, to be borne by the private investor, only the interventions aimed at contrasting the ordinary usury of structures and plant, the equipment and cleaning materials costs are included	+1% of the assessed costs	Public
Performance and asset total or partial unavailability risks	**Low** The construction complexity is limited and the *proposer subject* is suitable for the project realization both in terms of quantity and expected quality standards. The management model is consistent with similar activities carried out in nearby towns by the *proposer subject*		Private

(continued)

Table 3. (*continued*)

Risk typology	Likelihood of risk occurring	Economic effects assessed	Subject to whom the risk is transferred
Risk of contraction in market demand	**Medium-low** As a precaution, in the assessment the widespread phenomenon of requesting a concession for niches before actual use has not been considered	In the *proposer subject* analysis (180 niches/year) at the last concession period 414 unallocated niches will be, i.e. a foregone revenues of about 870,000 € for the private investor and a loss of royalty of about 100,000 € for the Public Administration	Private and public
Risk of contraction in specific demand	**Nil** There are no possible competitors: the regime provided is unilateral monopoly characterized by a single supplier (i.e. the Public Administration through the private investor) and numerous applicants (i.e. the relatives of the deceaseds)		
Risk of economic-financial imbalance	**High** The likelihood that the economic-financial balance is not determined is high, by considering a possible variation of the taxes and duties system, of regulatory framework, the longer time for the granting of authorisations and unforeseen geological or geotechnical characteristics	NPV: −1 million € TIR: −4%	Public
Funding risk	**Medium** The credit institution shall declare its interest and availability to finance the initiative, by specifying the monetary amount	+1.4 million €	Private
Financial risk	**Low** The possibility related to an increase of interest taxes is remote, as it is connected to macroeconomic conditions variations	+100,000 € of interests for increasing of interest rate of 50 bps	Private

(*continued*)

Table 3. (*continued*)

Risk typology	Likelihood of risk occurring	Economic effects assessed	Subject to whom the risk is transferred
Residual value risk	**Medium-low** Assuming *i)*162 niches/year granted, *ii)* 500 €/niches for the tariff for the renewal of the concession contract after the period of 99 years, *iii)* 7% for the discounting rate fixed, at the end of the concession the residual value is equal about to 4,795 €, to which correspond a present value of 1,240 (1 January 2021). At the end of concession period, the management and maintenence costs will not bear to Public Administration but they will bear to another private subject. In the residual value assessment, possible niches not granted for which the full concession tariffs, in addition to the royalty equal to 250 € for the Public Administration, have not been considered	At the end of the concession, the *proposer subject* assumes that all niches will be granted. The residual value is constituted exclusively by the discounted value deriving from the renewal of the concession for a further 99 years, in compliance with the provisions of Presidential Decree 285/1990	
Commissioning risk	**Low** There are no public entities that can hinder the project implementation and the community has informally expressed a positive opinion on the initiative, given the existing unsatisfied demand		Public
Administrative risk	**Low** The intended use of the property laid down in land-use plan is consistent with the function planned in the intervention		Public
Expropriation risk	**Almost nil** It is not necessary to proceed to expropriation since the area is already intended to municipal cemetery		Public

(*continued*)

Table 3. (*continued*)

Risk typology	Likelihood of risk occurring	Economic effects assessed	Subject to whom the risk is transferred
Environmental and/or archaeological risk	**Low** There are no environmental constraints and, given the intended use and location of the intervention area, there is no incompatibility between the project and the land use		Public
Legislative-political-regulatory risk	**Almost nil** The unsatisfied need to expand the municipal cemetery and the absence of costs to be borne by public subject make nil this risk typology		Public
Default risk	**Medium-high** Although the proposed tariffs are consistent with those current applied by Public Administration for the niches concession, the tariffs review mechanism defined by *proposer subject* afford to uncontrollably increase them		Public
Technical obsoleteness risk	**Low** The planned plants will built with consolidated construction technologies: there is no risk of technical obsolescence, especially by considering effective maintenance interventions measures		Public
Interference risk	**Almost nil** In the area intervention, the presence of various services (electricity, cables, fiber optics, etc.) is confirmed by official documents		Public

6   Conclusions

In the PPP context, the PF operational tool represents an effective procedure to carry out cemetery expansion, new realization and/or redevelopment interventions in Italian cities. The risks matrix constitutes a fundamental document among those place made up of contest, as it is relevant for the proposal/proposals assessment. The identification of the risks associated to the project and the explanation of the each risk occurring likelihood allows to analyze in a detailed manner the initiative and to allocate the different risks typology between the subjects involved – Public Administration and private investor. Furthermore, the risks matrix helps a constant monitoring of risks retention during the construction and management phases in order to avoid or, at least, to reduce the effects of negative occurrences that could led to the initiative failure, i.e. increase in costs or construction time or, in extreme case, interruption of the works.

The case study considered in the present research has concerned a hypothesis of project financing for the construction of niches and the management for a period of twenty years of the municipal cemetery of a small town located in Southern Italy. For each risk category, as regulated by Italian legislative references (Legislative Decree No. 50/2016 and ANAC Guidelines No. 9) the likelihood of its occurring has been assessed by using a verbal scale, in order i) to provide for an exhaustive framework of the different project components, ii) to give specific indications to the Public Administration and the private investor about the respective risk items that should check and iii) to support the risk management phase. The research has pointed out the relevance of risks assessment from the preliminary design stages able to identify likely critical issues of the project and to define the PPP agreement terms for parties involved. In particular, it should be highlighted that the low risk of the intervention – due to the absence of demand risk, to the constructive simplicity, etc. - allows the PF to be a useful tool for the construction and management of cemetery projects, as confirmed by the numerous situations in which it has been applied. Further insights of the research may concern the development of a more detailed Cost-Benefit analysis for the social impacts investigation of the initiative. As the case study shows, the main limitations of the risk matrix concern: i) the use of verbal sentences which could be inadequately interpreted; ii) the absence of a summary indicator of the various risk typologies. To overcome these limits an improvement of risks matrix could be carried out, for example by assessing the likelihood of risks occurring through quantitative measures and indicators and by aggregating the results through a multi-criteria approach, in order to compare different project proposals too.

References

1. Aziz, A.M.A.: Successful delivery of public private partnerships for infrastructure development. J. Constr. Eng. Manag. **133**(12), 918–931 (2007)
2. Calabrò, F., Della Spina, L.: La fattibilità economica dei progetti nella pianificazione strategica, nella progettazione integrata, nel cultural planning, nei piani di gestione. Un modello sperimentale per la valorizzazione di immobili pubblici in Partenariato Pubblico Privato. LaborEst 16 (2018)
3. Calabrò, F., Della Spina, L.: The public–private partnership for the enhancement of unused public buildings: an experimental model of economic feasibility project. Sustainability **11**(20), 5662 (2019)
4. Chen, H., Zhang, L., Wu, X.: Performance risk assessment in public–private partnership projects based on adaptive fuzzy cognitive map. Appl. Soft Comput. **93**, 106413 (2020)
5. Edili, A.N.C.: Il Project Financing in Italia - L'indagine ANCE sulla realizzazione delle opere (2012). Accessed 23 June 2014
6. Engineers and Architects Register of Milan: Prezzi Tipologie Edilizie. DEI Tipografia del Genio Civile. Quine Business Publisher (2019)
7. Grimsey, D., Lewis, M.K.: Evaluating the risks of public private partnerships for infrastructure projects. Int. J. Proj. Manag. **20**(2), 107–118 (2002)
8. Heravi, G., Hajihosseini, Z.: Risk allocation in public-private partnership infrastructure projects in developing countries: case study of the Tehran-Chalus Toll Road. J. Infrastruct. Syst. **18**(3), 210–217 (2012)

9. Iqbal, S., Choudhry, R.M., Holschemacher, K., Ali, A., Tamošaitienė, J.: Risk management in construction projects. Technol. Econ. Dev. Econ. **21**(1), 65–78 (2015)
10. Iyer, K.C., Sagheer, M.: Hierarchical structuring of PPP risks using interpretative structural modeling. J. Constr. Eng. Manag. **136**(2), 151–159 (2010)
11. Jefferies, M., McGeorge, W.D.: Using public-private partnerships (PPPs) to procure social infrastructure in Australia. Eng. Constr. Archit. Manag. **16**(5), 415–437 (2009)
12. Keçi, J.: Public private partnership for infrastructure projects: mapping the key risks. Int. J. Soc. Behav. Educ. Econ. Bus. Ind. Eng. **9**(9), 3141–3151 (2015)
13. Legislative Decree No. 50/2016
14. Morano, P., Tajani, F., Guarini, M. R., Di Liddo, F.: An evaluation model for the definition of priority lists in PPP redevelopment initiatives. In: Bevilacqua, C., Calabrò, F., Spina, L.D. (eds.) New Metropolitan Perspectives, vol. 178, pp. 451–461. Springer, Cham (2020). https://doi.org/10.1007/978-3-030-48279-4_43
15. National Anti-Corruption Authority (ANAC): Guidelines No. 9 - Monitoring of contracting administrations on the economic operator activities in public-private partnership contracts (2018)
16. Scano, D.: Project financing: società e impresa, p. 288. Giuffrè Editore (2006)
17. Shen, L.Y., Platten, A., Deng, X.P.: Role of public private partnerships to manage risks in public sector projects in Hong Kong. Int. J. Proj. Manag. **24**(7), 587–594 (2006)
18. www.istat.it

A Citizen-Led Spatial Information System for Collaborative (Post-)pandemic Urban Strategies: The Ponticelli Experience, Naples (Italy)

Maria Cerreta[✉], Luigi Liccardi, and Maria Reitano

Department of Architecture, University of Naples Federico II, via Toledo 402, 80134 Naples, Italy

{maria.cerreta,luigi.liccardi2,maria.reitano}@unina.it

Abstract. The strong socio-spatial implications of the covid-19 pandemic and the physical distancing measures have emphasised the fundamental role played by socio-digital networks in sharing and urbanising information. Worldwide, the emergence of shared survival needs led to the self-organisation of local communities in care infrastructures for mutual aid, psychological support, sharing experiences and storytelling, often based on crowd-sourcing and crowd-mapping platforms. From the (post-)pandemic urban planning perspective, the growth of this phenomenon has implied the call for spatial research to reconsider ICTs and collaborative spatial information systems as strategic tools to support vulnerable communities and public engagement in collective matters. This contribution aims to define an open-source database to be used and implemented by citizens and social operators to provision territorial care systems and mutual aid initiatives. The adopted methodological approach proposes a citizen-led spatial information system, where updated information, perceptions and preferences can be spatialised and collected, building a crowd-sourced and sharable system of territorial knowledge, useful for collective actions and the development of sustainable and effective strategies in emergency conditions. The obtained results refer to data about mutualism in public space, collected during the pandemic period in the Ponticelli district, the eastern periphery of Naples, Italy. They are to be framed within the broader on-going European HERA research project "PuSH: Public Space in European Social Housing".

Keywords: Mutualism · Public space · (Post-)pandemic city · Citizen-led spatial information system · Crowdsourcing · VGI

1 Introduction

1.1 Mutualism and the (Post-)pandemic City

Mutual aid, shared resources, local democracy, and an open network are the components that redesign relationships, public spaces, and city life [1]. Mutualism is a movement

© Springer Nature Switzerland AG 2021
O. Gervasi et al. (Eds.): ICCSA 2021, LNCS 12954, pp. 293–306, 2021.
https://doi.org/10.1007/978-3-030-86979-3_22

born around the second half of the nineteenth century, in Europe, as one of the first forms of spontaneous association of the working classes [2]. Since the outbreak of the covid-19 pandemic, mutual aid has worldwide produced new systems of care and addressed the need for transformative changes to take place in terms of scaled-up solidarity practices connecting self-organised social movements and building their power [3]. Spade [3], insisting on the fundamental distinction between solidarity and charity, defines mutual aid as a *collective coordination* based on solidarity projects that aim to meet each other's needs and solve problems through collective action in collective space. During the first Italian lock-down period determined by the pandemic, March-April 2020, mutual aid practices [4] created networks of spaces, both physical and digital, and informal supply chains [5], providing people with basic survival services, as well as with psychological, spiritual and cultural support [6] and overcoming, in many cases, the deficiencies caused by the privatisation of the public care services [7]. The socio-digital phenomenon defined as neo-mutualism [8] refers to these recent experiences of collaboration, which, answering to new needs, integrate the realm of social relationships and cooperation with that of the network society [9].

As in this difficult time, solidarity can represent a response to the crisis [10], catalysing emancipatory changes starting from social action and addressed towards the transformation of society [11]. According to this perspective, rather than a compassionate gesture, it should be considered as a bond of reciprocity that is established between those who provide a good or service and those who receive it. Beyond the good, solidarity is achieved through the sharing of a value that allows us to pass from a compassionate logic to a bond of fraternity, in which happiness is not expressed in terms of the individual but of community and therefore of public happiness [12]. The solidarity economy represents the core around which various forms of economies revolve, in particular the social economy [13]. The term *social economy* [14] appeared, for the first time, in France during the first third of the 19th century, and has evolved in meaning over the years. The social economy is, first of all, a collective response to common challenges [15]. It deals with issues and realities related to economic, social and cultural poverty [13]. It does not only deal with the procurement of material goods such as food, clothes, medicines but carries out a process of self-determination. In fact, it aims at the autonomy of individuals through culture and work [14]. It is based on principles of democracy, cooperation and reciprocity, re-distribution, social and cultural emancipation, and it operates by turning criticalities into opportunities [14]. Social actors and citizens can activate forms of social economy, through cooperation processes, that define a continuous dialogue between individuals and society and generate common and community values [16]. Moreover, the social economy is driven by actors belonging to the Third Sector [14]. Institutions of the Third Sector are voluntary organisations, associations, social enterprises, mutual aid societies, foundations that pursue civic, solidarity and social utility purposes by carrying out one or more activities of general interest without the purpose of profit [17]. In recent years, and in particular, with the Covid-19 emergency, we have witnessed the overcoming of the concept that saw this sector as a reality that would make up for the shortcomings due to the State and the Market, to the other two economic systems as well as to the social one [18].

1.2 Socio-Technical Systems, ICTs and Crowd-Sourcing

The covid-19 pandemic implications can be referred to territorial systems as well as social ones. Indeed, the paradigmatic urban geographies of places, services and uses undoubtedly changed, implying the need for urban studies to rethink the (post-)pandemic city [19, 20] as a complex socio-technical system, based on different network infrastructures of hybrid digital and physical spaces, diverse social actors, and interdependent relationships [21]. The socio-technical system perspective considers technology and ICTs as the connective interphase linking the material and the social [22], addressing two related fields of enquiry. On the one hand, the reciprocal influence of social processes and technology use refers to both innovation and opportunities for new social practices [23, 24]. On the other, the strong connection existing between this approach and the socio-ecological system literature emerges, since both engage with properties of complexity, multi-scalarity and adaptation [25]. In particular, it is worth noticing how the definition of cities as complex systems is shifted by the biological world and by urban ecology [26], which identifies in the system's ability to self-produce - or autopoiesis [27] - its intrinsic characteristic, that is responsible for the organisation of the network structure of mutual interactions among the sub-systems and the elements that compose the system. Considering also physical and urban systems as capable to self-produce [28, 29], social ecology [30] stresses how this ability is due to the social diversity, mutual interdependence and connectivity of the social ecosystems or eco-communities [31], which are aspects differently detectable in the socio-technical system dynamics as well [32]. Three types of socio-technical systems can be distinguished in reference to the smart urban realm and, in particular, to the pandemic period [33]: corporate-led forms of platform urbanism; state-led platforms for service management and provision; citizen-led initiatives. This contribution analyses the latter as an alternative to the first and useful application of systems of crowd-sourcing and interactive mapping [34] for collective purposes.

If, during the last year, the spontaneous growth of mutual aid infrastructures determined a shift towards the rethinking of the collective and political meaning of caring city [35], an analysis of the digital instruments, which were used to realise those socio-spatial infrastructures, could, as well, lead to a strategical reconsideration of participatory mapping and crowd-sourcing of spatial data [36] as instruments for co-learning and collective empowerment. Participatory mapping methods involve collaborative spatial surveys, differently referred to as participatory GIS (PGIS) [37], public participation GIS (PPGIS) [38], or volunteered geographic information systems (VGI) [39]. These methods, enabling a framework of knowledge-building shared among all the involved actors, can be used to report specific criticalities and opportunities related to a place, as well as to analyse different perceived aspects of urban life, such as wellbeing [40] or cultural ecosystem services (CES) [41]. Participatory GIS has been used in governmental policy development and collaborative planning to engage with the public and guarantee transparency of the decision-making processes [42]. Furthermore, these methods were recently used in bottom-up strategies and community empowerment projects, in which the same processes of data collection, map creation and information co-production came into being strategic tools for self-determination and self-organisation [43, 44]. VGI can be instead considered as deriving from expert-mediated spatialisation of geographic data voluntarily provided by individuals [45]. Finally, crowd-sourcing, not only entails a collaborative online activity, but constitutes an open call addressed to a broad and heterogeneous public, undertaking a task by bringing their work, experience, knowledge and receiving back a benefit, in terms of services, collective need satisfaction, or social recognition [46].

1.3 Research Questions

This research, learning from the experience of collecting qualitative data about social resilience and mutual aid initiatives during the first Italian lock-down period, through ICTs instruments within the district of Ponticelli, eastern periphery of Naples, Italy, has been driven by the following main questions:

1. How can strategic planning systems support vulnerable communities under social crises and fit the new needs of the (post-)pandemic urban society?
2. How are ICTs and crowd-sourcing to be used for community engagement, ensuring social justice and preventing form the exacerbation of existing disparities?
3. How should spatial decision support systems (SDSS) be implemented in order to enable much broader accessible information on socio-spatial systems?

This contribution aims to propose the activation of an open source and citizen-led decision support system, to be used by citizens and social operators in the development of mutual aid socio-spatial infrastructure and territorial care systems, as well as in the implementation of an always-in-the-making, collaboratively produced and shareable system of territorial knowledge.

The proposed approach is to be conceived within the framework of an on-going research about mutualism in public space, with specific reference to the pandemic period, and in this paper, the results of a first phase of the research will be discussed. In particular, in Sect. 2, the methodological approach is explained; in Sect. 3, the case study is presented, focusing on issues of social vulnerability and isolation; in Sect. 4, the obtained preliminary outcomes of the research are discussed; in Sect. 5, pros and cons of the methodology are investigated.

2 Materials and Methods

To build an interactive spatial database that can be useful for citizens and public administrators to monitor and participate in mutual aid initiatives and care systems, as well as to propose activities, ask for a service and report stories and events, the adopted approach is based on the possibility to involve communities through the methodological steps, and is developed through the following phases (Fig. 1):

1. Collection of data and crowd-sourcing;
2. Processing of crowd-sourced data;
3. Database / volunteered geographic information system (VGI) building.

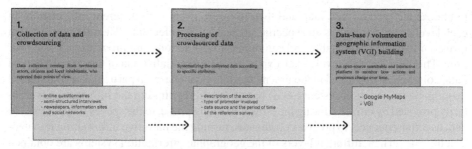

Fig. 1. Methodological framework and steps.

The first step concerns the identification and collection of soft data through different tools such as online questionnaires, semi-structured interviews and searches in newspapers, information sites and social networks. During the lock-down period, March-May 2021, questionnaires were sent online through the main social networks with the aim of collecting data on: 1. The use of physical and digital spaces during Covid, the type of relationship between people, closed in their homes, and physical-digital spaces; 2. The solidarity initiatives developed within the district, investigating the spaces, the social actors and the ways in which they took place; 3. The value attributed to spaces and activities before and during Covid, in particular the perception, the use, the social and cultural dynamics that characterise these spaces. This method involved the crowd-sourcing of information, thus allowing to collect data coming from territorial actors, citizens and local inhabitants, who reported their points of view, preferences and perceptions about the three mentioned themes. The semi-structured interviews were addressed to ten significant operators, who described the initiatives undertaken before the Covid emergency and during the lock-down. The interviews were carried out between May and June 2020, and described the spaces of mutualism, each with its characteristics and the type of urban rhythm that characterised them.

The second step involves systematising the collected data according to specific attributes. The mutual aid initiatives have been classified according to the description of the action, the type of promoter involved, the data source and the period of time of the reference survey. Furthermore, a particular focus was dedicated to the informal and self-organised initiatives, promoted by both NGOs and citizens, and strictly related to the health emergency. These specific initiatives have been detected according to the categories of health and sanitary kits provisioning, educational support, mutual aid and care provisioning, psychological support. As regards the spaces for sociality, mutual aid and care, where the above-mentioned initiatives differently took place, they have been analysed through the categories of planned public spaces and facilities, places for collective use, places for community use, and have been classified according to the type of spaces, the description obtained from the interview or questionnaire, the categories of place functions, people's activities according to the use of space, place perception, the data source and the period of the survey.

The database has been created through Google MyMaps, an open-source platform of Google, which allows to create searchable and interactive maps, accessible to anyone and with the possibility to modify and update information over time. The platform allows to choose the type of base map and then to insert levels with different information. In each level it is possible to assign specific attributes to the elements. Therefore, the system turns out to be implementable and can monitor how actions and processes change over time. This third step has involved an expert-mediated spatialisation of the crowd-sourced data, collected as explained in the first methodological phase. In particular, a volunteered geographic information system (VGI) has been built by linking the information, voluntarily provided by citizens during the crowd-sourcing phase, to the spaces they referred to and, as a consequence, to precise coordinates, turning the narrative information into geographic ones. Then, different layers of the geographic information systems are obtained systematising the situated knowledge, gained by engaging in processes of storytelling [47] and narrative mapping and spatialisation of qualitative information.

3   The Case-Study

The analysed area is the district of Ponticelli, in the easter region of Naples, a hinge with the Vesuvian villages. Until 1925 the district was an autonomous municipality, but with the Great Naples Project, designed by Mussolini, it lost this status. The name of the district is due to the presence of the numerous "bridges" – Italian "ponte" - that crossed the Sebeto River, one of the main rivers present in the eastern area of Naples, of which very few traces remain today. Therefore, the district's origins are mainly linked to the fertility of the land, up to the Industrial Revolution, in which we are witnessing development of the city that sees its peak with the inauguration of the Circumvesuviana station in 1891. After 1925, the district began to host the first groups of social housing complexes, expanding in the 1980s following the earthquake and leading to the formation of different typologies of social housing building. This has led to a series of social, cultural and urban phenomena, ranging from the abandonment of public spaces to the proliferation of forms of organised crime, to the use of spaces as drug consumption areas, to the perception of the district as urban periphery.

In contrast to the district's cultural, economic and social poverty, since recent years and, particularly during the Covid-19 emergency, initiatives of mutual aid, psychological and spiritual support, and accessibility to digital tools for culture have been put in place operators active in the district. In fact, the district, in relation to the Naples and the 6th Municipality to which it belongs, presents, from a socio-demographic point of view, a high rate of school dropout, only 5,8% of the population of the district is in the status of student (over 15 years old) and a high rate of unemployed people (61,3%) compared to people of age and working condition (Fig. 2).

Another relevant aspect concerns unused public spaces and regenerated ones. In the district, there are two large green areas, the Fratelli De Filippo park and the De Simone park. The first is partly usable for free time and thanks to the presence of a community garden created by associations, while a part is in a state of neglection as well as the entire De Simone park. Many spaces within the district are abandoned, and in condition of decay, some of these are reused and regenerated through bottom-up processes, and therefore for initiatives by groups of citizens, associations and other social actors such as parishes, hospitals, committees. The goal of these initiatives is the re-appropriation of these spaces to give them back to the community.

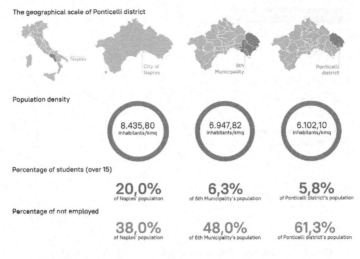

Fig. 2. Case-study district and statistical information.

The self-organised activities also involved the emergency period, in fact, material aid initiatives such as the delivery of food packages were accompanied by support actions through digital spaces. These spaces made it possible to translate what happened in the physical space, stopped and paused during the lock-down, in the digital one and allow to break down physical barriers such as the CoroNauti initiative organised by the non profit organisation "Maestri di Strada" which has allowed many young people to get together and continue the activities undertaken during the year. All this is based on the concept of a network, between different categories of social actors, physical and digital space, and between space, social actors and citizens.

4   Results

The collected soft data have been processed into spatial site-specific indicators of publicness, resulting in a growing open-source map articulated in three main categories: formal/informal spaces of mutualism; solidarity networks of stakeholders and initiatives; solidarity initiatives during COVID-19 crisis. The map has been realised with a google mymaps base and it is accessible at: https://www.google.com/maps/d/edit?mid=1-ZM0 Dat8oDpT6kcH01NDyOWdhvlq2Uz&usp=sharing. It is composed of seven levels: 1. Administrative borders; 2. Planned public spaces and facilities; 3. Places for collective use; 4. Places for community use; 5. Solidarity associations and operators; 6. Solidarity network of cooperation activities; 7. Solidarity initiatives during COVID-19 crisis (Fig. 3).

In the database, the formal and informal spaces of mutualism, recognised by the interviewees, have been mapped in the district and divided into the following three types (Fig. 4). 1. Place for public use: according to [48], public spaces are open places, accessible to all, where people carry out individual or group activities. These spaces can be

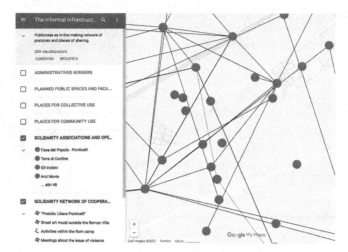

Fig. 3. Screenshot of the spatial database (Google MyMaps).

planned or discovered by chance and identified as public spaces by the community itself.
2. Place for collective use: according to [49], collective spaces are intermediate places
in the city, between the private dimension and the public dimension. They are places
where it is the collective use that makes the space collective. 3. Place for community use:
according to [50], they are socially produced spaces that respond to the community's
needs, ideas, and visions.

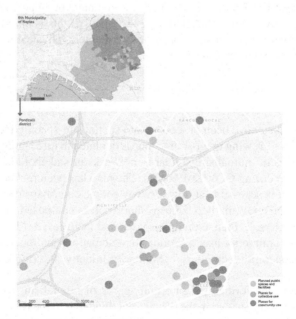

Fig. 4. Screenshot of the spatial database, formal and informal spaces of mutualism.

Then, local social actors have been mapped (Fig. 5). They are recognised by the interviewees as active operators in the complex social context of Ponticelli, promoting cultural and educational initiatives and events. The connections between them represent solidarity and cooperative activities and initiatives supported by the network of actors. The network of relationships gives us back the social vivacity of the district from the point of view of the present actors and the relationships that are created between them in terms of manifestations, events, activities and initiatives.

The mapping of the main solidarity initiatives developed during the Covid-19 was carried out by identifying four types of fields of action: activities related to people's health (32%), psychological and spiritual support (27%), mutual aid through the delivery of basic necessities (23%), collaborative processes related to culture and leisure (18%) (Fig. 6).

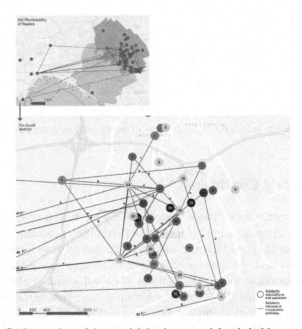

Fig. 5. Screenshot of the spatial database, spatial stakeholder network.

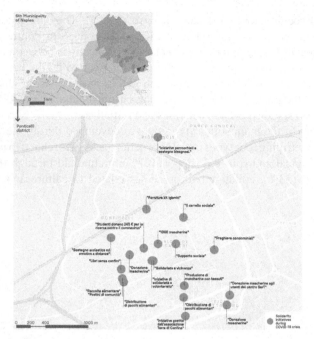

Fig. 6. Screenshot of the spatial database, solidarity initiatives during the first Italian lock-down period.

5   Discussion and Conclusions

The strong socio-spatial implications determined by the health crisis [51] and by the measures of physical distancing [52] have underlined the significant role assumed by the digital networks [53] and their capacity to share and urbanise information [54]. In fact, it is interesting noticing how the shared need to reappropriate the local collective dimension has determined the rapid definition of crowd-sourcing platforms, aimed at mutual aid and support and the collective recognition in a new sense of place identity [55]. This result was achieved through practices and experiences of storytelling and community resilience [56], which are progressively defining new social dynamics and hybrid local communities [57]. Then, in the definition of these processes, the digital, when equally accessible to all [58], plays an important role in shortening physical distances and promoting forms of inclusion and collaboration [59]. Moreover, during the recent health crisis, ICTs, spatial information systems and co-mapping instruments were widely used, not only by citizens but by experts and researchers as well, for qualitative data collection [60]. During this specific period, qualitative researchers faced the challenge of doing fieldwork while adopting social distancing measurement and without recurring face-to-face investigations [61]. The challenge became an opportunity, and many different technology-enabled tools, internet-based surveys, platforms for sharing information and for online questionnaires and interviews soon became new resources for qualitative data collection, aiming to grasp the lived experience of individuals during this difficult time.

The proposed contribution presents on-going research, started few months before the pandemic outbreak, which continuously had to adapt to the uncertainties of the period, using different and integrated investigation methods and instruments, in order to report a constantly updated frame of the very mutable analysed territorial context, everyday solidarity practices and changed use of space according to the health security policy. The collected data refer to a relatively short period of time, corresponding to the first Italian lock-down period. The need to extend this temporal frame to obtain a broader picture about the analysed social phenomena during the year 2020 is currently driving the research towards the definition of a more comprehensive database, collaboratively implementing the spatial information system. Further expected results involve the processing of indicators of mutualism and socio-urban resilience during the pandemic, through which addressing the measurement of intangible and cultural values [62, 63] of the urban solidarity spaces and the related tech-enabled initiatives.

Finally, since the last historical period drastically changed socio-spatial geographies of proximity and the system of use of urban space, the interpretation of the city as an adaptive complex system seems to be fundamental to consider its network structure, through which interdependent, tangible and intangible relationships between social actors and hybrid urban spaces are continuously re-established, in search of new dynamic balances. Then, the democratic relevance recently gained by ICTs, crowd-sourcing and crowdmapping for public engagement in collective matters [64], social self-organisation, and supporting vulnerable communities, made evident the need for strategic urban planning to conceptualise them as fundamental tools to grow co-produced knowledge about territories and, in particular, to develop sustainable and effective planning approaches in emergency conditions.

Acknowledgements. The obtained results of this research synthesise data collected within two scientific frameworks: A. "HousingPonticelliProjectPublicness - HP3". Laboratory of Urban Design, professors O. Fatigato, M. Cerreta, tutors Phd M. Prisco, arch. F. P. Milione, arch. M. Reitano, academic year 2019/2020, University of Naples, Federico II, Department of Architecture; B. "From zero to infinity. Actions and processes for an integrated assessment of publicness in Lotto Zero", Master's Degree Thesis in Evaluation and Urban Planning on Ponticelli and Lotto O, candidate L. Liccardi, tutor prof. M. Cerreta, co-tutors prof. G. Poli, prof. G. Berruti, academic year 2020/2021, University of Naples, Federico II, Department of Architecture (DiARC).

Author Contributions. Conceptualization, M.C., L.L., M.R.; methodology, M.C. and M.R.; validation, M.C.; formal analysis, L.L. and M.R.; investigation, L.L.; writing-original draft preparation, L.L. and M.R.; writing-review and editing, M.C., L.L., M.R.; visualization, L.L. and M.R.; supervision, M.C. All authors have read and agreed to the published version of the manuscript.

References

1. Mogollón, L. D., Eisele, O., Paschou, M.: Applied solidarity in times of crisis: exploring the contexts of civil society activities in Greece and Germany. Acta Politica **56**, 1–22 (2020)
2. Luciano, A.: Dalle Società Di Mutuo Soccorso Alla Mutualità: Risposte Alla Crisi Del Welfare (From Mutual Aid Societies to Mutuality: Responses to the Welfare Crisis) Euricse Working Papers No. 32/12 (2012). https://ssrn.com/abstract=2038203. https://doi.org/10.2139/ssrn.2038203. Accessed 05 May 2021

3. Spade, D.: Mutual Aid: Building Solidarity During this Crisis (and the Next). Verso, London/New York (2020)
4. Springer, S.: Caring geographies: the COVID-19 interregnum and a return to mutual aid. Dialogues in Human Geography **10**(2), 112–115 (2020)
5. Travlou, P.: Kropotkin-19: a mutual aid response to COVID-19 in Athens. Des. Cult. **13**(1), 65–78 (2020)
6. Bavel, J.J., et al.: Using social and behavioural science to support COVID-19 pandemic response. Nat. Hum. Behav. **4**(5), 460–471 (2020)
7. Armocida, B., Formenti, B., Ussai, S., Palestra, F., Missoni, E.: The Italian health system and the COVID-19 challenge. Lancet Public Health **5**(5), e253 (2020)
8. Venturi, P.: Neo-mutualismo tra sociale e digitale. Il Sole 24 Ore (2020). https://www.aiccon.it/neo-mutualismo-sociale-digitale/. Accessed 06 May 2021
9. Castells, M.: The Rise of the Network Society. Wiley, Hoboken (2011)
10. Zamagni, S.: La solidarietà come autentica risposta alla crisi. Arcidiocesi di Bari, Bitonto, Luogotenenza per l'Italia Meridionale Adriatica dell'Ordine Equestre del Santo Sepolcro di Gerusalemme (2014)
11. Venturi, P.: L'impresa sociale nel perimetro del Terzo Settore. Università di Roma LUMSA (2019)
12. Zamagni, S.: La lezione e il monito della pandemia da Covid-19. In: Caporale, C., Pirni, A. (eds.) Pandemia e resilienza. Persona, comunità e modelli di sviluppo dopo la Covid-19. Consulta Scientifica del Cortile dei Gentili. CNR Edizioni, Roma (2020)
13. Lewis, M., Swinney, D.: Social Economy? Solidaridy Economy? Exploring the Implications of Conceptual Nuance for actino in a Volatile World. In: Congreso Mundial sobre Economia Social en Victoria, Canadá. MONZON, JL (2006): Economía Social y conceptos afines: fronteras borrosas y ambigüedades conceptuales del tercer sector. CIRIEC-España, pp. 9–24 (2007)
14. Moulaert, F., Ailenei, O.: Social economy, third sector and solidarity relations: a conceptual synthesis from history to present. Urban Stud. **42**(11), 2037–2053 (2005)
15. Chantier de l'economie sociale. Document de positionnement stratègique, pp. 4–27 (2001)
16. Raymond, C.M., et al.: Mapping community values for natural capital and ecosystem services. Ecol. Econ. **68**(5), 1301–1315 (2009)
17. Ministero della Giustizia. Codice del Terzo Settore. DECRETO LEGISLATIVO 3 luglio 2017, n. 117 (2017)
18. Venturi, P., Villani, R.: Nuovo Welfare e valore aggiunto dell'economia sociale. Aiccon (2016). http://www.ilmondounito.com/19%20nuovo_welfare.pdf. Accessed 06 May 2021
19. Parnell, S.: The enabling conditions of post-pandemic city government. Environ. Plan. B: Urban Anal. City Sci. **47**(7), 1143–1145 (2020)
20. Batty, M.: The Coronavirus crisis: what will the post-pandemic city look like? Environ. Plan. B: Urban Anal. City Sci. **47**(4), 547–552 (2020)
21. Hillier, B.: The city as a socio-technical system a spatial reformulation. In: Conference on Spatial Information Theory (2009)
22. Smith, A., Stirling, A.: Social-ecological resilience and socio-technical transitions: critical issues for sustainability governance. STEPS Working Paper 8. STEPS Centre, Brighton (2008)
23. Russel, S., Williams, R.: Social shaping of technology: frameworks, findings and implications for policy. Shaping Technology, Guiding Policy: Concepts, Spaces & Tools. Edward Elgar, Cheltenham (2002)
24. Cerreta, M., Daldanise, G., Di Lauro, P., La Rocca, L: Collaborative decision-making processes for cultural heritage enhancement: the Play ReCH Platform. In: Nguyen, T.M. (ed.) Systems of Systems-Engineering, Modeling, Simulation and Analysis (MS&A), Gaming and Decision Support. IntechOpen (2021)

25. Voss, J.-P., Newig, J., Kastens, B., Monstadt, J., Nölting, B.: Steering for sustainable development: a typology of problems and strategies with respect to ambivalence, uncertainty anddistributed power. J. Environ. Plan. Policy Manag. **9**(3–4), 193–212 (2007)
26. Douglas, I.: Urban ecology. In: International Encyclopedia of Geography: People, the Earth, Environment and Technology, pp. 1–13 (2016)
27. Varela, F.G., Maturana, H.R., Uribe, R.: Autopoiesis: the organisation of living systems, its characterisation and a model. Biosystems **5**(4), 187–196 (1974)
28. Luhmann, N.: The autopoiesis of social systems. Sociocybernetic Paradoxes **6**(2), 172–192 (1986)
29. Seidl, D.: Luhmann's Theory of Autopoietic Social Systems. Münchner betriebswirtschaftliche Beiträge, 2 (2004)
30. Bookchin, M.: Philosophy of Social Ecology. Black Rose Books, Montreal (2017)
31. Bookchin, M.: Urbanisation Without Cities. The Rise and Decline of Citizenship. Black Rose, Montreal (1992)
32. Borge-Holthoefer, J., Banos, R.A., González-Bailón, S., Moreno, Y.: Cascading behaviour in complex socio-technical networks. J. Complex Netw. **1**(1), 3–24 (2013)
33. Söderström, O.: The three modes of existence of the pandemic smart city. Urban Geogr. **42**, 399–407 (2020)
34. McCullagh, M., Jackson, M.: Crowd-sourced mapping–letting amateurs into the temple? ISPRS-Int. Arch. Photogramm. Remote Sens. Spat. Inf. Sci. **1**(1), 399–432 (2013)
35. Power, E.R., Williams, M.J.: Cities of care: a platform for urban geographical care research. Geogr. Compass **14**(1), e12474 (2020)
36. See, L., et al.: Crowdsourcing, citizen science or volunteered geographic information? The current state of crowd-sourced geographic information. ISPRS Int. J. Geo Inf. **5**(5), 55 (2016)
37. Dunn, C.E.: Participatory GIS—a people's GIS? Prog. Hum. Geogr. **31**(5), 616–637 (2007)
38. Elwood, S., Ghose, R.: PPGIS in community development planning: Framing the organisational context. Cartogr.: Int. J. Geogr. Inf. Geovisualization **38**(3–4), 19–33 (2001)
39. Sui, D., Elwood, S., Goodchild, M. (eds.): Crowd-Sourcing Geographic Knowledge: Volunteered Geographic Information (VGI) in Theory and Practice. Springer Science & Business Media, Dordrecht (2012). https://doi.org/10.1007/978-94-007-4587-2
40. Bijker, R.A., Sijtsma, F.J.: A portfolio of natural places: using a participatory GIS tool to compare the appreciation and use of green spaces inside and outside urban areas by urban residents. Landsc. Urban Plan. **158**, 155–165 (2017)
41. Rall, E., Bieling, C., Zytynska, S., Haase, D.: Exploring city-wide patterns of cultural ecosystem service perceptions and use. Ecol. Ind. **77**, 80–95 (2017)
42. Sieber, R.: Public participation geographic information systems: a literature review and framework. Ann. Assoc. Am. Geogr. **96**(3), 491–507 (2006)
43. Talen, E.: Bottom-up GIS: a new tool for individual and group expression in participatory planning. J. Am. Plann. Assoc. **66**(3), 279–294 (2000)
44. Saadallah, D.M.: Utilising participatory mapping and PPGIS to examine the activities of local communities. Alex. Eng. J. **59**(1), 263–274 (2020)
45. Elwood, S., Goodchild, M.F., Sui, D.Z.: Researching volunteered geographic information: Spatial data, geographic research, and new social practice. Ann. Assoc. Am. Geogr. **102**(3), 571–590 (2012)
46. Estellés-Arolas, E., González-Ladrón-de-Guevara, F.: Towards an integrated crowdsourcing definition. J. Inf. Sci. **38**(2), 189–200 (2012)
47. Goldstein, B.E., Wessells, A.T., Lejano, R., Butler, W.: Narrating resilience: transforming urban systems through collaborative storytelling. Urban Stud. **52**(7), 1285–1303 (2015)
48. Carr, S., Francis, M., Rivlin, L.G., Stone, A.M.: Public Space. Cambridge University Press, Cambridge (1992)

49. Bauman, Z.: Fiducia e paura nella città. Bruno Mondadori, Milano (2007)
50. Lefebvre, H.: The Production of Space. Blackwell Publishing, Oxford (1974)
51. Salama, A.M.: Coronavirus questions that will not go away: interrogating urban and sociospatial implications of COVID-19 measures. Emerald Open Res. **2**, 14 (2020)
52. Alfonzo, M.: Open Letter to Citymakers: 10 key Implications of the COVID-19. newcities.org (2020). https://newcities.org/the-big-picture-open-letter-to-citymakers-10-key-implications-of-the-covid-19/. Accessed 06 May 2021
53. Söderström, O.: The three modes of existence of the pandemic smart city. Urban Geogr. **42**, 1–9 (2020)
54. Sassen, S.: Urbanising technology. In: Citizen's Right to the Digital City: Urban Interfaces, Activism, and Placemaking, pp. 253–256 (2015)
55. Chattopadhyay, S., Wood, L., Cox, L.: Organising amidst COVID-19. Interface: J. About Soc. Mov. **12**(1), 1–9 (2020)
56. Schneider, N.: Digital Community Organizing (AfterCorona #1). urbanpolitical.podigee.io (2020). https://urbanpolitical.podigee.io/17-digital_community_organizing. Accessed 06 May 2021
57. Manzini, E.: Cosa sono le comunità ibride di luogo, un nuovo modello di resilienza sociale. che-fare.com (2020). https://www.che-fare.com/cosa-sono-le-comunita-ibride-di-luogo-un-nuovo-modello-di-resilienza-sociale/. Accessed 06 May 2021
58. De Filippi, F., Coscia, C., Cocina, G.G.: Digital participatory platforms for urban regeneration: a survey of Italian case studies. Int. J.E-Plan. Res. (IJEPR) **9**(3), 47–67 (2020)
59. Van Dijk, J.: The Digital Divide. Wiley, Hoboken (2020)
60. Santana, F.N., et al.: A path forward for qualitative research on sustainability in the COVID-19 pandemic. Sustain. Sci. **16**(3), 1061–1067 (2021). https://doi.org/10.1007/s11625-020-00894-8
61. Lupton, D. (ed.): Doing Fieldwork in a Pandemic (Crowd-Sourced Document). https://docs.google.com/document/d/1clGjGABB2h2qbduTgfqribHmog9B6P0NvMgVuiHZCl8/edit?ts=5e88ae0a. Accessed 06 May 2021
62. Cerreta, M.: Thinking through complex values. In: Cerreta, M., Concilio, G., Monno, V. (eds.) Making Strategies in Spatial Planning. Knowledge and Values. Urban and Landscape Perspectives, vol. 9, pp. 381–404. Springer, Dordrecht (2010). https://doi.org/10.1007/978-90-481-3106-8_21
63. Cerreta, M., Daldanise, G., Sposito, S.: Culture-led regeneration for urban spaces: monitoring complex values networks in action. Urbani Izziv **29**, 9–28 (2018)
64. Haltofova, B.: Using crowd-sourcing to support civic engagement in strategic urban development planning: a case study of Ostrava Czech Republic. J. Competitiveness **10**(1), 85–103 (2018)

The Knowledge Phase of the Strategic Programming: The Case Study of the Jonian Valleys of Peloritani (Sicily, Italy)

Giuseppe Bombino[1], Francesco Calabrò[2(✉)], Giuseppina Cassalia[2], Lidia Errante[3], and Viviana Vinci[4]

[1] Department of Agriculture, Mediterranea University of Reggio Calabria, Reggio Calabria, Italy
giuseppe.bombino@unirc.it

[2] Department of Heritage-Architecture-Urbanism, Mediterranea University of Reggio Calabria, Reggio Calabria, Italy
{francesco.calabro,giuseppina.cassalia}@unirc.it

[3] Department of Architecture, Mediterranea University of Reggio Calabria, Reggio Calabria, Italy
lidia.errante@unirc.it

[4] Department of Law, Economics and Human Sciences, Mediterranea University of Reggio Calabria, Reggio Calabria, Italy
viviana.vinci@unirc.it

Abstract. This paper presents the follow-up phase of a broader work that illustrates a multidisciplinary research activity carried out as part of an institutional collaboration between the Mediterranea University of Reggio Calabria and 18 Sicilian municipalities, located in an area called "Jonian Valleys of Peloritani", Italy. The collaboration is finalized in order to outline perspectives and strategies for the material and immaterial progress of the area. The research activities are at initial stages, this paper illustrates the first results of the cognitive phase relating to the case study.

Keywords: Strategic programming · Stakeholder involvement · Citizenship education · Youth entrepreneurship · Project evaluation

1 Introduction

As explained more fully in the first part of the work, the cognitive activity, preparatory to programmatic choices, it is aimed at acquiring information related to the territorial system. More specifically, there are four phases to be developed to design a strategic program of interventions:

1. Knowledge Phase
2. Proposal Phase
3. Evaluation Phase

© Springer Nature Switzerland AG 2021
O. Gervasi et al. (Eds.): ICCSA 2021, LNCS 12954, pp. 307–320, 2021.
https://doi.org/10.1007/978-3-030-86979-3_23

4. Planning Phase

Phase 1, of a cognitive nature, is in turn divided into two parts:

- 1.a Analysis of the territorial system
- 1.b Listening and territorial animation

In detail, phase "1.a Analysis of the territorial system" has as its object:

- Geomorphology and hydrogeology
- Settlement system
- Infrastructure, accessibility and mobility
- Demographic structure
- Economic-productive system (also historically characterizing activities) and employment dynamics
- Natural and cultural resources - tangible and intangible
- Socio-cultural structure: associations and cultural activities
- Services for the quality of life and social equity
- Planning, governance and express planning tools - funded and unfunded
- Historical Background.

While phase 1.b "Listening and territorial animation" includes:

- Recognition of public and private actors
- Individual meetings with stakeholders and public forum for the needs' analysis and assessment
- Identification of strategic areas.

2 The Territorial System

The Geographical District, the object of the present study, is located in the north-eastern part of the metropolitan area of Messina, Sicily. Bounded upstream by the Peloritani mountains, it is crossed by four rivers: the D'Agrò, Savoca, Dinarini and Nisi streams, within whose valleys fall the 18 municipalities involved in this study. In general, the Geographical District is marked by the presence of the potentialities and criticalities that can be found in the entire South of Italy. On the one hand, the resources offered by the rich historical, cultural and natural heritage in its tangible and intangible features. On the other hand, the worrying employment issue, about the youngest segments of the population. Also, can be outlined issues related to the hydrogeological structure of the territory and its widespread accessibility by the primary and secondary road network. From a morphological and infrastructural point of view, the area tends to be homogeneous, although some socio-economic and historical-cultural emergencies are still evident. The analysis aims at identifying these peculiarities, intending to enhance their value as a system, with particular reference to the valleys. Finally, the single thematic in-depth studies, necessary to produce a rich and exhaustive territorial framework, will always refer to the enhancement of the whole area.

2.1 Overview of the Area

The area's overview starts from a territorial, morphological and infrastructural description. These considerations are relevant to understand the complexity of the territorial system before going into its peculiarities.

The Geographical District has a mild, Mediterranean climate, with average annual temperatures between 18–20 °C and relatively low rainfall (ISPRA 2020) which has favoured the tourist and agricultural-forestry vocation over time. On the other hand, global warming and the decrease in rainfall put the area at risk of desertification (IRSSAT 2020). The high hydrogeological risk of landslides and coastal erosion can be detected due to damming works and inert material withdrawals along the riverbeds, reducing the contribution of solid material to the beaches and causing their retreat (PAI).

The main transport infrastructures are the A18 motorway Messina-Catania, the State Highway 114 Orientale Sicula, the Catania-Messina railway line and the waterfront promenade which extends along the entire coastline interrupted only by the estuaries of the rivers. The railway infrastructure is also the main obstacle between the urban settlements, partially developed close to the coastline and the shoreline. The transversal accessibility, parallel to the development of the watercourses and perpendicular to the valleys, connects the inland municipalities through provincial roads. In this sense, the mobility pattern (Fig. 1) is common to all the territorial units constituted by the valleys.

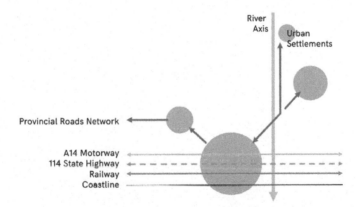

Fig. 1. The mobility pattern of the valley units.

The city settlements are closely related to the morphology and the infrastructure of the Geographical District, which have determined the urban development. The coastal cities are developed between the coastline and the railway line and are the most populated. The inland municipalities are, on the other hand, for the most part closely related to the valley system, with a less compact and more distributed urban development. This aspect is to be considered to the agro-forestry vocation of these towns, often articulated in satellite districts and villages related to the main urban centre.

2.2 Socio-Economic Profiling

The study area covers a total extension of 264.186 km^2, about a tenth of the province of Messina. The municipality with the largest territorial area is Antillo, 43.6 km^2, the innermost municipality in the area; whereas the municipality with the smallest territorial area is Roccafiorita (1.17 km^2) (Table 1) (ASC). At the time of the ISTAT census of 2019, there is a total population of 36,965 inhabitants, about 6% of the province. In this panorama the costal municipality of Santa Teresa di Riva is affirmed for number of inhabitants (9394 units), with a number of inhabitants more than double the number of the second municipality, Roccalumera (4119 units); while Roccafiorita (186 units) is the least populated.

The average density of the entire area is 223.70 people/km^2. In detail, the centers with a higher population concentration are those in the coast side (Santa Teresa di Riva, Roccalumera, Alì Terme and Scaletta Zanclea), while the centers with a lower concentration of inhabitants by surface area are the innermost (Antillo, Casalvecchio Siculo, Mandanici and Ali). Finally, analyzing the variation of population 2019–2011, it is observed that most municipalities recorded a significant depopulation in 2019, with a total of 1419 units less (Praticò 2021; Filippone 2021). The municipalities most affected were those of Scaletta Zanclea, Fiumedinisi, Limina and Casalvecchio Siculo; while the municipalities with a more marked positive variation are the municipality of Santa Teresa di Riva and Sant'Alessio Siculo.

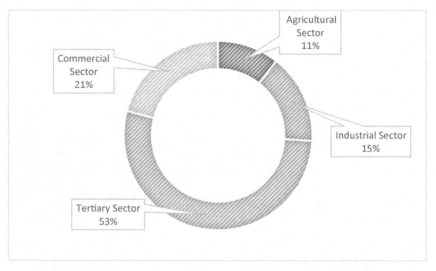

Fig. 2. Employment sectors case study - ISTAT 2011 (8milaCensus)

Looking at the Economic activities and employment dynamics, the analysis show that the average employment rate in the area is 36%, about one percentage point lower than the provincial data (37.2%), which in turn is almost 8 points lower than the national one. It exceeds 40% in the municipalities of Sant'Alessio and Furci Siculo, it stands at 25% in the municipality of Limina (Table 2) (Istat8milacensus). The unemployment rate (about 18%) is lower than the provincial average (about 20%) with a range of about 12% of Fiumedinisi to almost 25% of Forza d'Agrò. The difficulty of young people entering the world of work is highlighted by the lack of employment between generations: the figure of 45-year-old and over is on average over 3 times higher than that of 15–29, in line with the provincial figure. The highest difference is found in the municipality of Limina (5 times higher), the lowest in the municipalities of Antillo and Alì (230%).

Regarding the structure of employment, in 2011 the professions with medium-high level of competence and specialization represent on average 26.47% (provincial figure 30.6%); the weight of the craft or agricultural professions is 15% as in the province of Messina, while the low-level professions are at 25.35% (20.8% provincial data). Figure 2 shows the employment distribution in the four sectors identified by ISTAT: The extra-commercial tertiary sector, which also includes the public sector, covers 53%, follows the commercial sector with 21%, the industrial sector at 15% and the agricultural sector at 11%.

Observing the housing and potential use issue, the study highlighted that in 2011 the living space available to each occupant reaches about 38 m^2 as in the province, about 2 m^2 less than the national data. The incidence of residences in property stands at about 70%, in line with the regional and national data.

The proportion of unused buildings in 2011 was 5.1% in Italy, 7.6% in Sicily. It reaches 12.4% in the province and 15.38% in the case study. In detail, Fig. 3 shows the incidence of unused housing in the centre and periphery per municipality, highlighting differences by category and territory. While the average potential for residential use in the core and scattered houses in the case study is in line with the national figure (37.27% and 37.5%) the potential for residential use in the center in the case study is 41%, 20 percentage points higher than the national average. It is not surprising that the highest incidence of unused housing is found in the more internal areas such as Antillo, Limina, Sant'Alessio Siculo and Pagliara. More particular is the data of Roccafiorita and Roccalumera, municipalities in which there are no unused housing.

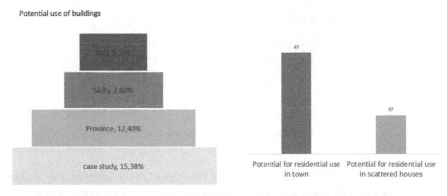

Fig. 3. Potential use of buildings - Istat 2011 (8milaCensus)

Table 3 summarizes the main data relating to the size of the housing stock and in particular: the size of the historical dwellings occupied given by the percentage ratio of dwellings occupied before 1919 to the total of dwellings occupied; given about two percentage points higher than the regional average, but still lower than the national one (case study 7.80%, Sicily 5.3%, Italy 10.2%). To highlight the case of Limina 0% and Alì Terme 0.5% and the case of Alì and Fiumedinisi 40% and 35%. The average state of conservation of the buildings is less good than the national one. Forza d'Agrò, Nizza di Sicilia and Alì Terme are the municipalities with buildings in a better state of conservation, Antillo and Roccafiorita those with the highest incidence of buildings in a bad state of conservation. Finally, the age of the recent housing stock reflects the regional and national average.

Studying the Welfare and social vulnerability matter, the average percentage of families who are in a situation of potential hardship in the care of the elderly coincides with the national and provincial percentage of families who are in a situation of potential hardship in the care of the elderly, around 3%. Higher than the national and provincial data is the share of young people outside the labor market and training (case study 18.20%, province 16.2%, Italy 12.3%).

In 2014, Istat took over the Social and Educational Services for Early Childhood in the area for a total of 80 users with a total expenditure of approximately 750 thousand euro. The only municipalities in which these services have been identified are the municipality of Santa Teresa di Riva, Furci Siculo, Nizza di Sicilia and Scaletta Zanclea.

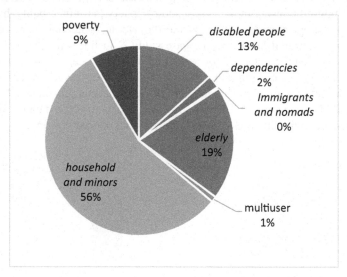

Fig. 4. Municipal social interventions and services

Finally, in terms of interventions and social services of municipalities, Fig. 4 shows the percentage of public expenditure committed by municipalities in the area in 2014: more than half of the funds were used for household and child care services, about 20% for the elderly, 13% for the disabled and about 10% for the fight against poverty and for services aimed at adult and homeless hardship.

2.3   Atlas of Natural and Cultural Resources[1]

The survey of cultural heritage resources, both tangible and intangible, required a taxonomic effort to reconstruct the anthropic development of the places under consideration. The evolution of the communities living there contributes to the rich and complex natural, cultural and productive landscape. According to this complexity, the analytical tool of the atlas accounts for the variety of features that shape such a heterogeneous heritage. The ancient origins can be traced back to the Sicans, the Phoenicians and the Greeks and can still be seen today in the location of the current hillside settlements. For defensive reasons, the urban settlements 'slide' along the valleys, moving from the coast to the hills, while the coastal villages are more recent. The material and immaterial heritage of the Peloritani valleys can be seen in the rich religious, civil and military architecture legacy as well as in the cultural and identity features.

The religious heritage ranges from Christian and Orthodox places of worship, strongly linked to local traditions and rituals, with evidence of Judaic and Islamic worship. Numerous examples of historical and archaeological value can be found among the military architecture, with the numerous fortifications, ruins of watchtowers and castles on the coastline. Oral traditions and expressions, performing arts, social customs, folkloristic events, knowledge related to agriculture and craft production, represent a social tool for teaching and sharing that respects the balance between man and nature. The shared identity, religious, historical, cultural and folkloristic values testify to the strong link between the villages according to their common origins and the historical events they have witnessed. In the light of these considerations, the economy of the valleys, historically based on agricultural activities, is gradually turning to cultural and environmental tourism. The territory is rich in environmental and landscape resources of great value. The valleys are home to several sites of Community interest: the municipality of Antillo is part of the ITA030019 SCI called 'Tratto montano del bacino della fiumara d'Agrò'; the municipality of Roccafiorita is part of the ITA030004 SCI 'Bacino del Torrente Letojanni'.

Origins of the territory

The origins of the first settlements date back to the Neolithic period, with the presence of the ancient peoples of Sicani and Siculi. From the 9th century B.C. onwards, the valleys began to be frequented by the Phoenicians, whose main town Phoinix is identified with the present-day Santa Teresa di Riva. This evidence confirms the strategic importance of the area for trade between Sicily, Greece and the East even during the Imperial period. The Valleys were the field of a battle during the First Punic War between the Carthaginians and the Romans, which took place near the town of Limina.

During the Byzantine period, the valleys were at the centre of the political and religious scene: the town of Sant'Alessio presumably owes its name to Alexis I Comnenus, Emperor of Constantinople, who was a guest in the castle around which the town centre later developed. Numerous traces from that period testify to the presence of the Basilian community and the Greek Orthodox cult. In the Middle Ages, the Arab Emirate of Sicily was succeeded by the Normans, the Swabians, the Angevins and the Aragonese dominations. In this period, given the high exposure to Saracen raids, the fortified coastal

---

[1] All information on the tangible and intangible cultural heritage of the municipalities under study was gathered by consulting the institutional websites of the municipalities.

settlements remained less populated in favour of the hillside villages, where activities linked to trade and agriculture flourished. The culture and traditions of the Valleys and their communities are strongly related to the Spanish domination, which lasted from around 1400 until 1860 and the unification of Italy with the siege of Messina. The communities of the Valleys also actively participated in the events of the Risorgimento, narrated in the museum in Nizza di Sicilia.

Cultural heritage: material and immaterial features

The cultural heritage, both tangible and intangible, reflect the origins and history of the places (Fig. 5).

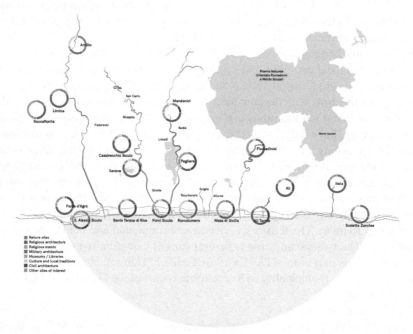

Fig. 5. The density of tangible and intangible cultural resources among the different municipalities.

Religious architecture is the most appreciable due to the high concentration of churches, mainly dating between 1300 and 1700, which host many ancient pieces of art, sculptures, paintings and frescoes. There are also examples of buildings from the early Middle Ages, such as the Monastery of S.S. Pietro e Paolo d'Agrò (in Forza d'Agrò) dating back to 1172. The military architecture, mostly dating from the 16th century, narrates the system of fortifications by the sea with castles and towers. There are also examples of fortified churches and bell towers converted from watchtowers. The civil architecture echoes the richness and elegance of the towns, with noble palaces from the 17th, 18th and 19th centuries. Towns such as Forza d'Agrò, are distinguished by their urban layout in which the houses, huddled together, overlook small internal courtyards. The typical balconies of the civic buildings are made of wrought iron with potholders for basil plant for good fortune. The predominant building materials are sand and local stone, such as sandstone. The use of these materials forms a chromatic continuum within the surrounding landscape. All the dominations that have succeeded one another in the valleys have left their traces and influences on customs, toponymy and architecture. Civil architecture, in particular, reflects the Spanish influence in the decoration of 17th-century buildings and a minor Art Nouveau style in the bourgeois and working-class buildings of the 1900s. Of particular note is the Durazzesco Arch in Catalan Gothic style in Forza d'Agrò, dating from the 15th century. The lime kilns, the ancient spinning and oil mills, and mining quarries that can still be seen today witness to old knowledge and production activities, now almost completely abandoned, still alive in the memory and identity of the places and communities.

Equally rich is the intangible cultural heritage. Numerous festivals in honour of the Patron Saints and processions, festivals, cultural and folkloristic activities animate the months of March and April, around Easter, and the summer period around Santa Maria del Carmelo (16 July) and the first half of September. Another strong religious cult is linked to Saints Alfio, Filadelfo and Cirino, three brothers martyred in 253 AD in Sicily during the Christian persecutions by the Romans. The festivities in honour of the patron saints are important opportunities to recreate local traditions or religious events by using statuary ensembles (the "varette") or actual staged events. Among the many, the Via Crucis and the so-called "Cerca" of Casalvecchio Siculo, the people's search for Jesus Christ to free themselves from their sins and invoke divine forgiveness. These festivities are often associated with the production of typical dishes, such as the Easter 'Collure', loaves of bread handmade by the inhabitants and offered during the processions. Another widespread and recurring activity is that of the 'infiorata', which involves the involvement and participation of the entire community in the creation of floral installations in the main street of the town.

Literary and film culture also play a particularly important role in recognising the area on the international scene. Salvatore Quasimodo, the Nobel Prize winner for Literature, was born here, hence the literary park in Roccalumera. Numerous scenes from Francis Ford Coppola's The Godfather were filmed in the municipalities of Forza D'Agrò and Savoca. The scenery of the famous film is included in a tourist route that retraces its places. The subject of the filming was the church of San Nicolò, the streets of the old town centre and Palazzo Trimarchi, where Bar Vitelli, mentioned in Mario Puzo's novel and whose sign still stands, was reproduced. Some views of Casalvecchio Siculo were the setting for Michelangelo Antonioni's film 'L'Avventura'. There is no shortage of minor cultural events focusing on the dissemination of vernacular poetry and prose. The evolution of communities, in close contact with the development of local places and traditions, are reproduced thanks to the recent establishment of the Savoca Historical Ethnoanthropological Museum.

Landscape, production and environment

The landscape of the Geographical District can be described starting from the Peloritani mountains, which descends towards the Ionian Sea accompanied by the rivers that define its valleys. The highest peaks are between 12000 and 1300 m above sea level, such as Pizzo di Vernà (1287 m) at Casalvecchio Siculo and Mount Scuderi (1253 m), around which the Fiumedinisi Oriented Nature Reserve arise. The Monti Margi are the highest reliefs in the Agrò area, while Mount Kalfa overlooks Roccafiorita. Springs spring from these mountains, such as the Mancusa spring in Savoca and the Canale and Fontana springs in Roccafiorita, which feed numerous urban fountains. There are also natural shelters carved into the rock and once used as hermitages. At higher altitudes, the forested Mediterranean vegetation is sometimes interrupted by the moonscapes of the pastures. Near the towns, the agricultural landscape with its mosaic of crops becomes prevalent. The presence of mulberry trees testifies to the flourishing cultivation of silk-worms, introduced by the Saracens and developed until 1400 during the Bourbons' reign. The Geographical District is highly specialised in the production of citrus fruits such as the Limone Interdonato di Messina IGP and the Limone Verdello. The cultivation of citrus fruits, together with that of olive trees, distinguishes the landscape at lower altitudes, at the mouths of streams and close to coastal towns. The presence of water is fundamental to the area for urban and agricultural water supply and the tourist and sea-side activities of the coastal centres. The latter are pivotal centres from which to explore the valleys towards the more inland areas.

The economy based on agro-pastoral activities has been documented since ancient times: the valleys were once defined as "the granary of the Roman Empire". Numer-ous historical agroforestry fairs attract the communities of the valleys: the Fair of San Francesco da Paola and the Fair of Santa Lucia in Savoca date back to the 17th century, and the Fair of S. Pietro in Casalvecchio Siculo. The culinary tradition emphasises local raw materials, such as pork, sheep and lamb, bluefish, mustard, pulses, sheep's milk cheeses and seasonal vegetable preserves, oil and wine.

2.4 Local Planning and European Financing

A first comprehensive analysis was drawn up on the basis of the public funding received during the two programming cycles 2007–2013 and 2014–2020. The term "public fund-ing" in the context of this research means the contribution of European, national and regional funding. Details of the allocation of public funding in the case-study area, have been calculated using the source of the OpenCoesione dataset, updated at 31/08/2020 (Open Coesione).

Figure 6 shows the total amount of public funding in the area, about 3.2 billion, of which only ¼ was actually allocated. In addition, a total of private funding EUR 64.5 million are committed. As for the reading instead of the per capita financing, there is an issue related to the database of Open Cohesion: each municipality is associated with the entire financing of projects, even when the project is located in several municipalities. For example, the municipalities of Forza d'Agrò, Pagliara, Sant'Alessio Siculo, Itala, Savoca, Scaletta Zanclea, Alì Terme, Furci Siculo, Nizza di Sicilia and Roccalumera are all beneficiaries of the funding in the thematic area "Transport and infrastructure network" for the intervention "Messina-Catania itinerary: Giampilieri-Fiumefreddo doubling". For this intervention, 2.3 billion have been allocated and as a result each municipality is associated with 2.3 billion (Table 4).

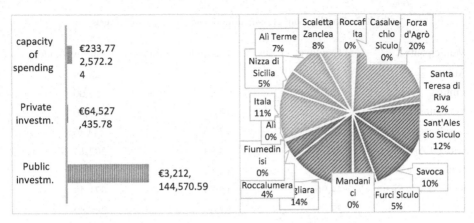

Fig. 6. Framework financing projects and financing distribution per capita

Table 1. Geo-demographic framework of the study area - ISTAT 2011–2019

Municipality	Area (km²)	Altitude (msl)	Population 2019	Pop. density 2019	Variation of pop 2019–2011
Antillo	43,6346	480	868	19,89	−124
Limina	9,9924	552	761	76,16	−139
Roccafiorita	1,1681	723	186	159,23	−42
Casalvecchio Siculo	33,6218	420	775	23,05	−132
Forza d'Agrò	11,189	420	887	79,27	9
Santa Teresa di Riva	8,1175	6	9394	1157,25	154
Sant'Alessio Siculo	6,1676	15	1532	248,39	35
Savoca	9,0755	303	1761	194,04	−5
Furci Siculo	17,9132	9	3298	184,11	−130
Mandanici	11,8536	417	569	48,00	−60
Pagliara	14,4792	200	1140	78,73	−90
Roccalumera	8,906	7	4119	462,50	14
Fiumedinisi	36,6938	200	1362	37,12	−197
Alì	15,9386	450	734	46,05	−89
Itala	10,9835	210	1535	139,76	−128
Nizza di Sicilia	13,4154	9	3641	271,40	−82
Alì Terme	6,2744	9	2431	387,45	−136
Scaletta Zanclea	4,7618	12	1972	414,13	−277

Table 2. Employment classification - Istat 2011 (8milaCensus)

Municipality	Employment rate	Unemployment rate	Turnover index
Antillo	32,79	16,57	229,79
Limina	25,03	22,90	555,00
Roccafiorita	34,63	14,46	260,00
Casalvecchio Siculo	32,25	17,23	230,36
Forza d'Agrò	38,12	24,94	302,13
Santa Teresa di Riva	39,71	15,82	423,94
Sant'Alessio Siculo	44,96	15,89	371,43
Savoca	37,69	21,57	264,89
Furci Siculo	41,34	16,18	398,64
Mandanici	31,49	19,55	341,67
Pagliara	33,61	22,86	312,73
Roccalumera	38,85	16,43	478,85
Fiumedinisi	37,56	12,26	257,47
Alì	36,30	21,39	229,17
Itala	35,23	22,74	262,20
Nizza di Sicilia	38,98	21,13	322,87
Alì Terme	36,38	15,46	349,11
Scaletta Zanclea	33,92	23,95	306,48

Table 3. Housing stock size- Istat 2011 (8milaCensus)

Municipality	Incidence of buildings in good state of conservation	Incidence of buildings in bad state of conservation	Consistency of historic houses occupied	Average age of recent housing stock
Antillo	67,68	14,64	2,08	32,95
Limina	74,79	1,32	0,00	35,33
Roccafiorita	72,32	12,43	10,19	21,70
Casalvecchio Siculo	49,10	5,20	1,57	42,50
Forza d'Agrò	84,30	1,81	4,87	29,19

(*continued*)

Table 3. (*continued*)

Municipality	Incidence of buildings in good state of conservation	Incidence of buildings in bad state of conservation	Consistency of historic houses occupied	Average age of recent housing stock
Santa Teresa di Riva	66,46	4,22	1,77	28,00
Sant'Alessio Siculo	73,74	2,26	2,38	25,72
Savoca	69,76	1,02	5,33	30,28
Furci Siculo	79,10	1,12	3,05	25,62
Mandanici	78,21	0,51	5,96	36,42
Pagliara	72,74	6,30	5,15	33,59
Roccalumera	66,21	2,14	9,06	24,79
Fiumedinisi	63,37	4,95	35,06	35,95
Alì	55,63	6,57	40,38	29,73
Itala	77,36	1,65	7,16	21,99
Nizza di Sicilia	82,57	1,59	1,14	24,88
Alì Terme	81,77	0,17	0,54	26,38
Scaletta Zanclea	48,09	7,27	4,77	30,98
Case study average	70,18	4,18	7,80	29,78
Sicily	73,8	3	5,3	31,2
Italy	83,2	1,7	10,2	30,1

Table 4. Interventions and social services of the municipalities Istat 2014

Municipal Interventions and social services - 2014			
Disabled people	259.309,00 €	*Multiuser*	18.600,00 €
Dependencies	42.514,00 €	*Household and minors*	1.081.869,00 €
Immigrants and nomads	5.750,00 €	*Poverty*	164.450,00 €
Elderly	376.363,00 €		
Total expenditure (EUR) - 2014			1.948.855,00 €

3 Conclusion

The research is in its first phase; the activities are still in progress, in particular as regards the cognitive aspects. In the continuation of the activities, particular attention will be paid to two aspects: the involvement of citizens and in particular of young people; inter-institutional dialogue and cooperation. At the same time, it will be necessary to refine the techniques to be used for the selection of strategic objectives and projects capable of pursuing them more effectively.

Note: The article is the result of the joint efforts of the authors. However, the following are to be attributed: paragraphs 1 to Francesco Calabrò; paragraphs 2 to Giuseppe Bombino; paragraphs 2.1 to Viviana Vinci; paragraphs 2.2, 2.4 to Giuseppina Cassalia; paragraphs 2.3, 3 to Lidia Errante.

References

ISPRA: Gli indicatori del CLIMA in Italia nel 2019 (2020)

IRSSAT: DESERTIFICAZIONE IN SICILIA I Comuni della Provincia di MESSINA versante ionico (2020)

Praticò, S., Di Fazio, S., Modica, G.: Multi temporal analysis of sentinel-2 imagery for mapping forestry vegetation types: a google earth engine approach. In: Bevilacqua, C., Calabrò, F., Della Spina, L. (eds.) NMP 2020. SIST, vol. 178, pp. 1650–1659. Springer, Cham (2021). https://doi.org/10.1007/978-3-030-48279-4_155

Filippone, G., Laganà, V.R., Di Gregorio, D., Nicolosi, A.: Collective and commercial catering services of the Ho.Re.Ca channel: a case study in Calabria (Italy). In: Bevilacqua, C., Calabrò, F., Della Spina, L. (eds.) NMP 2020. SIST, vol. 178, pp. 823–833. Springer, Cham (2021). https://doi.org/10.1007/978-3-030-48279-4_77

Atlante Statistico dei Comuni. http://asc.istat.it/ASC/. Accessed 20 Mar 2021

Open Coesione: www.opencoesione.gov.it. Accessed 02 Mar 2021

ISTAT (8milaCensus): http://ottomilacensus.istat.it/. Accessed 20 Mar 2021

PAI. Piano Stralcio di Bacino per l'Assetto Idrogeologico. Unità fisiografica n. 3. Capo Scaletta – Capo Schisò. http://www.sitr.regione.sicilia.it/pai/unita03.htm. Accessed 18 Mar 2021

International Workshop on Transformational Urban Mobility: Challenges and Opportunities During and Post COVID Era (FURTHER 2021)

Developing Flexible Mobility On-Demand in the Era of Mobility as a Service: An Overview of the Italian Context Before and After Pandemic

Tiziana Campisi[1](✉) ⓘ, Chiara Garau[2](✉) ⓘ, Giovanna Acampa[1] ⓘ,
Francesca Maltinti[2] ⓘ, Antonino Canale[1] ⓘ, and Mauro Coni[2] ⓘ

[1] Faculty of Engineering and Architecture, University of Enna Kore, Cittadella Universitaria, 94100 Enna, Italy
tiziana.campisi@unikore.it
[2] Department of Civil and Environmental Engineering and Architecture, University of Cagliari, 09129 Cagliari, Italy
cgarau@unica.it

Abstract. The COVID-19 pandemic required the implementation of restrictions in the transport sector, changing the movement habits of users and, at the same time, highlighting the importance of creating a flexible transport system aimed at guaranteeing an uninterrupted supply of goods and people in any event. In the last decade, the pace at which sustainable and resilient mobility strategies were developed grew significantly due to the spread of technologies (such as ITS systems) and digital platforms related to Mobility-as-a-Service (MaaS). These strategies might improve the overall efficiency of the transport system and reduce dependence on private cars in urban area. Moreover, the development of the demand responsive transport (DRT) is one of the solutions for planning end-to-end travel according to the transport needs. Actually DRT, such as the other shared modes, appears more convenient and capable to turn private car superfluous, reducing traffic congestion and noise and atmospheric pollution levels. After a review of the state of the art in literature, this paper shows the results of a descriptive and a preliminary analysis of DRT services in Italy. In particular, in the studied areas, the authors detected the type of service given and its national displacement, the category of users, the kind of stops, the fleet of vehicles and the presence of shared mobility services. Finally, the authors assessed the possibility to include these services within the Maas platforms suggesting some possible strategies for optimizing the implementation of intelligent mobility systems at Italian national level.

Keywords: Sustainable local public transport · Flexible mobility on demand · Mobility-as-a-Service (MaaS) · Shared mobility · Demand responsive transport (DRT)

1 Introduction

The current pandemic has inevitably led to rethinking new ways of life (such as smart working [1]), and new forms of travel, questioning the previous demand for mobility

© Springer Nature Switzerland AG 2021
O. Gervasi et al. (Eds.): ICCSA 2021, LNCS 12954, pp. 323–338, 2021.
https://doi.org/10.1007/978-3-030-86979-3_24

and the offer of services and infrastructures. Several studies applied on the European contexts addressed the impacts of COVID-19 on public transport, walking and other mobility choices [2–4]. With regard to local public transport (LPT), the rules on quotas within public transport and on the necessary social distancing have made all shared modes perceived as "less attractive" [5]. This was evidenced for the pandemic period (i) by the significant decline in daily use of LPT [6]; (ii) by an increase in the use of private vehicles [7], and (iii) by an overall increase in mobility on foot or by bicycle for short trips [8]. Therefore, the need to pursue new modes of transport is evident in order to be able to encourage sustainable travel, also considering that the pandemic has generated new areas with weak demand. In other words, areas with a reduced presence of transport supply that do not include only the peripheral areas but also those that, due to the economic restrictions of the transport companies, have been characterized by a reduced or absent presence of connections.

Furthermore, the pandemic has led many companies and administrations to plan mixed forms of work (in person and in smart working mode) as a stable model for future work [9]. In relation to transport sector, a correlation exists between the implementation of smart working with the reshaping of the staggered schedules of daily journeys and also with probably a possible on-site road toll system (feasible only if initially intervening on improving the infrastructure is possible). A general reduction in the demand for transport for home-work reasons could better support the current pressure on the transport network, also in light of current habits, such as the restart of the use of private vehicles to the detriment of public means. Therefore, a future for public transport assumes even more a necessary duty, to guarantee the right to mobility for all, also in view of the concept of "expanded accessibility" [10].

Considering these premises, the strategies for improving cycling and pedestrian infrastructures [11], the provision of vouchers for the purchase of micro-mobility and/or electric mobility [12–14] can reduce the use of private vehicles, especially for first and last mile travel, by leading to a reduction in congestion, to a lower environmental impact and to a constant respect for social distancing.

With the pandemic, the reduction in the number of passengers has led to the purchase of fewer season tickets and, consequently, has caused large losses for the service operators. For this reason, the busiest lines before the pandemic could be weakened to have frequencies similar to those in rural areas before the COVID-19 emergency. A solution to this problem could be the support of public transport with on demand responsive transport (DRT) services, as often happens in areas with low demand. In the hypothetical case that a public transport service is converted into a DRT service, all passengers will have to book in advance. On the one hand, the security of always finding a place on board and being able to travel with greater safety conditions exists. In addition, the possibility of DRT services also makes possible to reduce the risk and the perception of the same risk by users [15]. On the other hand, the difficulties of having all travel information from each passenger, protected by current legislation and not obliged to release all data. A more useful solution could be to monitor, through the Bluetooth and wi-fi technologies incorporated in all smartphones, the quality of the travel experience [16, 17], the number of passengers on board each vehicle and at each stop in real time, reshaping the concept of mobility in smart mobility [18, 19], within the smart cities' paradigm [20–22]. Based on these considerations, this work investigates firstly mobility as a service, (recognized in the literature as MaaS) and secondly the DRT concept. Subsequently, the literature relating to European and Italian DRT services is analysed, focusing on a first step of exploratory investigation of DRT services in Italy and activated in the last decade. Finally, the authors define a characterization of the services in order to understand their potential and possible integration within the MaaS digital platforms.

1.1 The Evolution of MaaS in the Pandemic Era

Mobility as a service (MaaS) has as its core in most Countries the shared modes of public transport and rideshare (Uber, Ola, Didi and/or taxi) and the shared mobility of cars, bicycles and micro-mobility. In the pandemic era, the word "service" connected to MaaS can have a much broader and more meaningful multisectoral definition, which can be the basis of a business case that can turn into a new commercial proposition [23]. Social distancing, until a vaccine is widely available and administered, appears to be the primary means of suppressing the spread of Covid-19. MaaS can be a way to stop a decline in the use of public transport by users for example by offering a series of incentives (discounts) for the first and last mile when using public transport. The issue of hygiene in Uber and in taxis still remains a concern for many users today. Sharing space within a vehicle (although risk levels increase) can become minimal when traveling with a group of family members and this could incentivize the use of shared mobility and the use of on-demand mobility. Mobility-as-a-Service (MaaS) combines the digitalization of services as the main enabling factor with the integration of multiple collective and individual modes of traditional and shared transport, offering increasingly flexible, personalized travel solutions to the user. This makes possible to implement mobility strategies aimed at improving the transport offer and, at the same time, a reduction in CO_2 emissions and pollution, thus supporting the advancement of the European Green Deal agenda. With this in mind, the DRT could become a turning point for public transport, because it is an important link within the intermodal transport chains that build the core of Mobility as a Service and provide more alternatives to the private car. Indeed, the DRT inclusion in the itinerary planning and booking systems offers users the possibility to choose between different travel options, taking into account travel time, fares and transport means. The possibility of planning a multimodal itinerary using a single search and a single booking system is a great advantage for the user. The flexibility and adaptability of the itinerary encourages a more rational use of one's own vehicle. The technological platforms for DRTs permit: (i) travel optimization; (ii) cashless payment systems; (iii) integration of booking and payment systems including other services (MaaS); (iv) better synchronization of the modal interchange; (v) the achievement of a wider audience of users. The DRT can also contribute to reduce journeys with individual vehicles by intercepting occasional needs and/or weak or disadvantaged users [24]. The service can use low-zero emission vehicles and the inclusion in sustainable urban mobility plans (SUMPs) can incentivize the reduction of road congestion [25, 26]. To optimize the service, some companies aim to increase the filling coefficient of vehicles and in a multimodal context can help make the LPT system more efficient [27]. The next paragraph illustrates the diffusion of the DRT service in Europe and Italy, highlighting its characteristics and the connection to other forms of mobility such as shared ones (cars and bicycles).

1.2   The Growth of the DRT Service in Europe

The on-demand transport is also known as Flexible Transport Services (FTS) [28], Dial-a-Ride [29] or Paratransit [30] and it is a service between taxi and conventional bus. Public transport can be classified as on-demand transport or DRT if the service is available to the public without any limitation to particular groups of users based on age or disability criteria or the place of work. A DRT service is generally limited to a defined operational zone, within which journeys must begin and end. Trips can be completely free or adapted to routes and timetables, varied as needed. In general, the service is provided by low-capacity road vehicles such as small buses, vans or taxis; the service responds to changes in demand by modifying its route and/or its timetable and the fare is applied based on the passenger and not the vehicle. Table 1 describes the characteristics of on-demand transport, compared with the bus transport service and also of shared taxis (another form of DRT). The latter operate along a fixed route at specific times, but can change their original route for picking up or dropping off passengers who have requested the deviation. The vehicles used for DRT services are usually small minibuses, reflecting the low number of passengers, but also allow the service to provide door-to-door service as close as possible, being able to use residential roads, such as, for example, the "door to door" and on-call bus service, called Amico Bus, of CTM, the public transport company of Cagliari [31, 32]. In some cases, taxis are hired by the DRT provider to serve their routes on demand. DRT programs can be fully or partially funded by the local transit authority.

The main features of the DRT are: (i) user-oriented (flexibility/adaptability of the route, timetables and frequency based on demand); (ii) accessibility of the service online, through specific platforms available for smartphones, apps, PCs; (iii) versatility of use, by considering the areas and users to be served (more calibrated vehicles and mileage). Exogenous factors influencing the performance of public transport are related to the characteristics of the operating environment and include car ownership rates, economic conditions, etc. [33–36]. Recently, different types of power supplies and systems are used in different parts of the world. An automated demand-responsive transport system (ADRTS) as an urban public transport service for the city of Arnhem in the Netherlands indicates operated by highly automated vehicles (AV) [37], in which driver costs and programming constraints are eliminated as well as through the comparison of systems

Table 1. Comparison of the different types of public mobility

Features	DRT	Bus	Taxi	Details
Type of vehicle	Min 9 seats	Min 18 seats	Min 1 seats	Diversification of the user and the areas to be served (such as those with low demand)
Type of service	Flexible	Fixed	Single ride	Service dynamically adaptable to the basic route, stops and passage frequencies based on requests entered by users through a digital platform
Frequency of service	Discontinuous manner	Continuous manner	Frequency depending on demand	BUS service scheduled while the DRT is booked

shared automated vehicles in a parallel transit service (PTS) and a tailored time-varying transit service (TVTS) [38]. In the past, the spread of the DRT service was common in economically less developed countries, where institutional and/or land use factors prevent conventional buses from meeting the demand [39]. In the UK and Western Europe in general, such flexible transport options are largely focused on meeting the needs of passengers with mobility problems. Since the 1970s, on-demand transport has been seen on several occasions as the solution to transport problems. Particularly when the more traditional services are not economically sustainable, despite several barriers (technological, social, market, economic and institutional ones) have so far prevented their widespread adoption [40]. However, this lack of adoption may be about to change. Indeed recently, new developments in operational and vehicle technology, coupled with significant cuts in public transport subsidy budgets, are promoting the integration of transport provision across a range of different sectors. Some studies focus on their strategic, tactical and operational results at the different levels. Over the past decade, Demand Responsive Transport (DRT) services have grown in popularity for several reasons, including: (i) the lack of traditional regular buses and taxis services; (ii) the lack of special transport services; (iii) new developments in Community transport system; (iv) the development of the Maas; (v) the new concept of a post-pandemic weak demand area. Traditional on-demand services are often criticised due to their relatively high cost of provision, their lack of flexibility in route planning and their inability to handle high demand. The potential to overcome these limitations can be realized through the introduction of telematics-based on-call services, particularly analysed by Mageean et al. [41]. They highlighted the results of the assessment of on-demand technologies and operations in urban and rural contexts across Europe. Figure 1 shows several projects launched and completed since 2012.

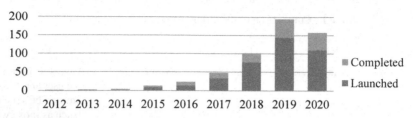

Fig. 1. On-demand ride pooling service per Year. Source: https://lukas-foljanty.medium.com/map ping-the-global-on-demand-ridepooling-market-f8318de1c030

The combination of an on-demand service and a scheduled service offers better mobility and greater service coverage. Studies conducted in the Netherlands show a performance scoreboard for on-call service and related changes in accessibility. From this study the calculation of generalized travel times of on-demand journeys and DRT's alternatives can help to identify whether the on-demand transport is used as a comple- ment or a substitute for LPT [42]. This study is a pioneer in measuring the increase in accessibility that the implementation of on-call transport has ensured to passengers of on-demand transport, compared to the LPT alternative. The results of an empirical analysis showed a reduction of more than half of users for half of the trips made using the on-demand service, compared to LPT alternatives. This reduction was most noticeable in areas with a low supply of LPT connections.

Other research provided an alternative categorization of major implementation issues, in order to support transit authorities in their effort to understand methodological steps for assessing potential transport investments of such services [43]. Other studies conducted between 2005 and 2011 in the UK showed that the DRT service was linked to "social need" in terms of people accessing the services. Particularly in 2011, the service was particularly related to the geography of the place or areas served (areas with low demand such as rural areas or suburbs). Furthermore, the importance of the environment as a target of on-demand schemes has apparently decreased in recent years, from being a "secondary" target in 2005 to being almost ignored in 2011 [44–47].

The results obtained from a survey released in the UK in 2014 highlighted an increas- ing role for stakeholders from the voluntary sector and the private sector on on-demand services. Furthermore, the survey found that the number of interested passengers is influ- enced by the size of the operation (in terms of seats offered) and by the use of smaller "car" vehicles, particularly in rural areas [48].

Several comparative studies with local public transport relating to the application of specific analysis models are found in the literature in which different methods have been used to compare on-demand transport with buses and other "traditional" transport services, from simulation based on simulation agents to agents and algorithmic approaches [30, 49] to economic and qualitative approaches [29]. Everyone focuses on different aspects of the problem. In addition to simulation methods, which often focus only on travel optimization, in favour of the operator, extensive research is also devoted to the use of analytical methods. Analytical models for various network layouts are developed to compare the performance of on-demand transport with alternative modes [50, 51]. This allows both operator and user side modelling, developing cost functions that are minimized to find the optimal values of the network design variables, balancing the cost and the cost of the user. Although many network layouts and contexts are studied, no generic analytical model is developed for the case of connecting low-demand long-distance areas with a nearby city center, in a typically call-to-call context.

With the exception of [52] that however develops generic analytical formulations to evaluate on-call services in cases of low long-distance demand by presenting the numerical results of a case study in the long-distance area of Thessaloniki, Greece.

2 Methodology

This paper focused on a descriptive and a preliminary exploitation analysis of DRT services in Italy, and was structured as follows: (i) First general assessment of the geospatial identification of the service and the presence of shared mobility in the areas examined; (ii) Second evaluation on the type of user of the service; (iii) Third evaluation on active services and available fleet. As regards the first assessment, the on-call transport services were identified and divided into the various regions and provinces, by analysing, at the same time, the presence of car and bike sharing services. These services are examined in depth in various researches, for the characterisation of users [53, 54] and also for the definition of the service [55, 56]. At the same time, the type of stop was assessed by classifying the presence of fixed stop or demand services as defined in Fig. 2.

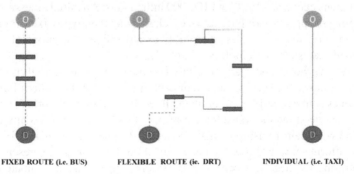

FIXED ROUTE (i.e. BUS)   FLEXIBLE ROUTE (ie. DRT)   INDIVIDUAL (i.e. TAXI)

Fig. 2. Type of stop assessed by classifying the presence of fixed stop or demand services

The DRT service is characterised by a specific collection point and a time window for collection. Some DRT systems can be defined through one or both ends of a route (e.g. an urban centre, an airport or an interchange).

DRT systems allow passengers to request travel by booking with a central dispatcher that determines available travel options based on users' location and destination. This is possible through fleet telematics technology in the form of vehicle tracking systems, planning and dispatch software, and a laptop in the vehicle. Various degrees of fixity can be applied in route planning and stopping points, so that specific destinations are served. Most of the on-call services are on a small scale, or aimed at specific categories of people characterizing the community. In the second evaluation phase, the different types of users were investigated, by classifying 7 different types for purposes mostly of the home-work or home leisure type. Finally, the type of fleet, the type of service, ie whether temporary (test pilot) or continuous, and the presence of the service on the MaaS digital platforms were researched. The data collected were then classified initially by associating a single character to each individual user or to sample (DRT service) and subsequently through a "complex" distribution with at least two characters (for example the name and surname of the user).

3 Results

DRT schemes currently are in urban and peri-urban areas, as well as in rural communities. The service is generally operated by both public transport companies and private service providers. DRT systems are offered as intermediate collective transport services for general users or as schemes for specific user groups. In Italy it is possible to identify about 25 DRT services. They are mostly located in the North of Italy (64%), then in the central regions (32%) and finally only 4% in the regions of Southern Italy, as shown in Fig. 3.

Some of these services are active starting from 2021. The coverage of the service in relation to the size of the city shows that small cities and metropolises are served by 28% of the services surveyed, while a higher percentage, 36%, covers areas with a population between 100,001–200,000 inhabitants. Finally, only 8% covers urban centers with populations between 50,000 and 100,000 inhabitants. An initial assessment is made by considering the presence of DRT services, classifying their type (fixed or on demand) and analysing the presence of shared mobility as a possible other mode of transport in the cities analysed, such as Empoli (see Table 2).

Table 3 shows the second evaluation based on the type of user, classifying 7 different types. Table 4 shows the services and their users in the Central-southern Italy area. Of the 23 services active in Italy, 87% of them allow the transport of workers and students and all except one allow the transhipment of people with disabilities. Only the Rimini service allows company transhipment. Considering the presence of these services within the Maas platforms, it was highlighted that only about 10 services are present within the digital platforms. Of these services it was considered appropriate to evaluate the type of service and fleet as well as the use as shown in Table 5.

PT nighttime

PT city-wide

PT rural

Pilot

Fig. 3. Distribution of DRT in Italy

Table 2. DRT services in Italy from 2016

Area	Region	City	Typology*	Car sharing	Bike sharing
North Italy	Lombardy	*Milan	On demand	Yes	Yes
		Vimercate (MB)	Fixed	No	Yes
		Mantua and its Province	Fixed	Yes	Yes
		Crema, Cremona and neighbouring areas	Fixed	Yes	Yes
		Pavia and neighbouring areas	Fixed	Yes	Yes
	Piedmont	Alexandria	Fixed	Yes	Yes
		Turin and its Province	Fixed	Yes	Yes
	Liguria	Genoa	Fixed	Yes	Yes
		Sarzana (SP)	Fixed	Yes	Yes

(continued)

Table 2. (*continued*)

Area	Region	City	Typology*	Car sharing	Bike sharing
	Aosta Valley	Aosta and neighbouring areas	Fixed	No	Yes
	Veneto	Padua	Fixed	Yes	Yes
Central Italy	Emilia Romagna	Parma	N.d	Yes	Yes
		Modena and its province	Fixed	Yes	Yes
		Bologna and its province	Fixed	Yes	Yes
		Ferrara	Fixed	Yes	Yes
		Reggio Emilia and neighbouring areas	Fixed	Yes	Yes
		Rimini and neighbouring areas	On demand	Yes	Yes
	Lazio	Rome	On demand	Yes	Yes
	Tuscany	Siena	N.d	Yes	Yes
		Empoli	N.d	Yes	Yes
		Florence	Fixed	Yes	Yes
		Livorno	Fixed	Yes	Yes
		Prato	Fixed	Yes	Yes
	Umbria	Perugia	Fixed	Yes	Yes
		Terni	N.d	Yes	Yes
		Narni (TR)	Fixed	No	Yes
		Castiglione del Lago (PG)	Fixed	No	Yes
Islands	Sardinia	Cagliari and neighbouring areas	On demand	Yes	Yes

*Fixed = variable route with fixed stops
On Demand = Variable route and on-demand stops
N.d. = not definited

Table 3. Type of users (North Italy)

Users	Aosta and neighbouring areas — Allo Bus e Allo Nuit	Genoa — Drinbus	Vimercate (MB) — Autoservizi Zani	Crema, (CR) and neighbouring areas — Miobus	Pavia and neighbouring areas — Miobus	Cremona and Province — Stradibus	Alessandria — Eccobus	Turin and Province — Provibus	Padoa — /	Cagliari and neighbouring areas — Amico Bus
Workers	■	■	■	■	■	■	■	■	■	■
Students	■	■	■	■	■	■	■	■	■	
Disabled people	■	■	■	■	■	■	■	■	■	■
Senior citizens	■	■	■	■	■	■	■	■	■	■
Tourists	■	■	■	■	■	■	■	■	■	
Leisure	■	■	■	■	■	■	■	■	■	
Companies										

Table 4. Type of users (Central-southern Italy)

Users	Modena and Province — Tper	Bologna and Province — Tper	Ferrara — Aladino	Reggio Emilia and neighbouring areas — Concabus	Rimini and neighbouring areas — /	Roma — Tper	Florence and neighbouring areas — Ataf Nottetempo	Livorno — CTT Nord Servizio Taxi	Prato — Pronto Bus	Perugia — Pronto Bus	Terni — Telebus	Narni (TR) — Chiama bus	Castiglione del Lago (PG) — /
Workers	■	■	■	■	■		■	■	■	■	■	■	■
Students	■	■	■	■	■		■	■	■	■	■	■	■
Disabled people	■	■	■	■	■		■	■	■	■	■	■	■
Senior citizens	■	■	■	■	■	■	■	■	■	■	■	■	■
Tourists	■	■	■	■	■	■	■	■	■	■	■	■	■
Leisure	■	■	■	■	■		■	■	■	■	■	■	■
Companies				■									

Table 5. Status of business to Government (B2G) service considering the period 05–09 2020.

North-West Italy			
	Vimercate	Pavia	Stadella Varzi
Company		Shotl (ES)	
Service Name		Miobus	
Operator	Zani viaggi	Autoguidovie	
Main Use	1	2	1 1
Fleet Size	2	1	2 1
Lauch Date	02/2019	09/2019	
End Date	01/2020		

North-Est Italy			
	Padua	Venice	Belluno
Company	Padam (IT)	MVMANT (IT)	Shotl (ES)
Service Name	Night Bus	Venice Mestre On-Demand Pilot	Prontobus
Operator	Busitalia Veneto	Radiotaxi Cooperative of Venice Mestre	Dolomitibus
Main Use	2	3	4
Fleet Size	1	1	4
Lauch Date	01/2019	01/2017	08/2020
End Date		02/2017	

Central and South Italy		
	Ravenna	Ragusa
company	Shotl (ES)	MVMANT (IT)
service name	Ravenna On-Demand Pilot	On-Demand Pilot in Ragusa
operator	TCL	/
main use	4	3
fleet size	2	1
lauch date	09/2020	04/2016
end date		04/2016

service 1=PT city wide 2= PT Night time 3= Budget city-wide 4= PT rural

4   Discussions and Conclusions

On-demand transport services usually operate with vehicles of lower capacity than traditional public transport, ensuring greater flexibility and effectiveness in the organization
of routes and transit times. This can exemplify some national recommendations on
COVID-19 infections. On-demand transport services are often used to power public
transport in areas with low passenger demand, where a regular bus service is not considered economically profitable. Examples of low demand areas are typically rural and
peri-urban areas, where poor transport system affects the social-economic development
and the determinants of the productive activities, as happens in inner areas of Sardinia
[57]. Furthermore, it can be used to provide services for particular categories of users

(e.g. people with disabilities). In this perspective, the spread of the DRT in areas that have remained without mobility services due to the pandemic could be a mitigation and resolutive action. In order to spread the possible multimodal choice and the selection of the most convenient transport service, different modes of transport must be implemented in the different urban and extra-urban contexts of Italy. At the same time, these services should relate to digital platforms for exemplifying reservations.

Unfortunately, demand mobility services are still small and some of them are just test pilots. The Government will have to encourage, in synergy with public transport companies, this mode of transport in order to achieve greater results in terms of sustainable and resilient mobility. This work therefore lays the foundations for further assessments and in particular the exploration of the characteristics of the services currently active through the dissemination of survey campaigns for the knowledge of customer satisfaction and the improvement of future services.

Acknowledgement. This study was supported by the MIUR (Ministry of Education, Universities and Research [Italy]) through a project entitled WEAKI TRANSIT: WEAK-demand areas Innovative TRANsport Shared services for Italian Towns (Project code: 20174ARRHT /CUP Code: J74I19000320008), financed with the PRIN 2017 (Re-search Projects of National Relevance) programme. We authorize the MIUR to reproduce and distribute reprints for Governmental purposes, notwithstanding any copy-right notations thereon. Any opinions, findings and conclusions or recommendations expressed in this material are those of the authors, and do not necessarily reflect the views of the MIUR.

Author Contribution. This paper is the result of the joint work of the authors. 'Abstract' and 'Results' were written jointly by all authors. Tiziana Campisi wrote 'Methodology'; Chiara Garau wrote 'Introduction'; Antonino Canale wrote 'The evolution of MaaS in the pandemic era' and 'The growth of the DRT service in Europe'. Tiziana Campisi and Chiara Garau wrote 'Discussions and Conclusions'.Tiziana Campisi funded the manuscript.

References

1. Beck, M.J., Hensher, D.A.: Insights into the impact of COVID-19 on household travel and activities in Australia-The early days under restrictions. Transp. Policy **96**, 76–93 (2020)
2. Bucsky, P.: Modal share changes due to COVID-19: The case of Budapest. Transp. Res. Interdiscip. Perspect. 8, 100141 (2020)
3. Politis, I., et al.: Mapping travel behavior changes during the COVID-19 lock-down: a socioeconomic analysis in Greece. Eur. Transp. Res. Rev. **13**(1), 1–19 (2021). https://doi.org/10.1186/s12544-021-00481-7
4. Campisi, T., Basbas, S., Al-Rashid, M.A., Tesoriere, G., Georgiadis, G.: A region-wide survey on emotional and psychological impacts of COVID-19 on public transport choices in Sicily. Italy. Trans. Transp. Sci. (2021). https://doi.org/10.5507/tots.2021.010
5. Wielechowski, M., Czech, K., Grzęda, Ł: Decline in mobility: public transport in Poland in the time of the COVID-19 Pandemic. Economies **8**(4), 78 (2020)
6. Torrisi, V., Inturri, G., Ignaccolo, M.: Introducing a mobility on demand system beyond COVID-19: evidences from users' perspective. In: AIP Conference Proceedings, vol. 2343, no. 1, p. 090007. AIP Publishing LLC (2021)

7. Beck, M.J., Hensher, D.A., Wei, E.: Slowly coming out of COVID-19 restrictions in Australia: Implications for working from home and commuting trips by car and public transport. J. Transp. Geogr. **88**, 102846 (2020)
8. Moslem, S., et al.: Best–worst method for modelling mobility choice after COVID-19: evidence from Italy. Sustainability **12**(17), 6824 (2020)
9. Bolisani, E., et al.: Working from home during COVID-19 pandemic: lessons learned and issues. Manag. Mark. Chall. Knowl. Soc. **15**(s1), 458–476 (2020)
10. Rassu N., et al.: Elderly people and local public transport - a focus on their travel behavior - the case of Cagliari. In: International Conference on Computational Science and Its Applications, pp. 690–705. Springer, Cham (2020)
11. Campisi, T., et al.: Cycling master plans in Italy: The I-BIM feasibility tool for cost and safety assessments. Sustainability **12**(11), 4723 (2020)
12. Campisi, T., Basbas, S., Skoufas, A., Akgün, N., Ticali, D., Tesoriere, G.: The impact of COVID-19 pandemic on the resilience of sustainable mobility in sicily. Sustainability **12**(21), 8829 (2020)
13. Porcu, F., Olivo, A., Maternini, G., Coni, M., Bonera, M., Barabino, B.: Assessing the risk of bus crashes in transit systems. Eur. Transp. (81) (2021). Paper n° 4. ISSN 1825-3997. https://doi.org/10.48295/ET.2021.81.4
14. Kaya, Ö., Alemdar, K.D., Campisi, T., Tortum, A., Çodur, M.K.: The development of decarbonisation strategies: a three-step methodology for the suitable analysis of current EVCS locations applied to Istanbul, Turkey. Energies **14**(10), 2756 (2021). https://doi.org/10.3390/en14102756
15. Campisi, T., Canale, A., Ticali, D., Tesoriere, G.: Innovative solutions for sustainable mobility in areas of weak demand. Some factors influencing the implementation of the DRT system in Enna (Italy). In: AIP Conference Proceedings, vol. 2343, no. 1, p. 090005. AIP Publishing LLC (2021)
16. Barabino, B., Coni, M., Olivo, A., Pungillo, G., Rassu, N.: Standing passenger comfort: a new scale for evaluating the real-time driving style of bus transit services. IEEE Trans. Intell. Transp. Syst. **20**(12), 4665–4678 (2019)
17. Coni, M., et al.: On-board comfort of different age passengers and bus-lane characteristics. In: Gervasi, O., et al. (eds.) ICCSA 2020. LNCS, vol. 12255, pp. 658–672. Springer, Cham (2020). https://doi.org/10.1007/978-3-030-58820-5_48
18. Garau, C., Masala, F., Pinna, F.: Benchmarking smart urban mobility: a study on Italian cities. In: Gervasi, O., et al. (eds.) ICCSA 2015, LNCS, pp. 612–623. Springer, Cham (2015). https://doi.org/10.1007/978-3-319-21407-8_43
19. Coni, M., Garau, C., Pinna, F.: How has Cagliari changed its citizens in smart citizens? exploring the influence of ITS technology on urban social interactions. In: Gervasi , O., et al. (eds.) Computational Science and Its Applications – ICCSA 2018, pp. 573–588. Springer, Cham (2018). https://doi.org/10.1007/978-3-319-95168-3_39
20. Pinna, F., Masala, F., Garau, C.: Urban policies and mobility trends in Italian smart cities. Sustainability **9**(4), 494 (2017)
21. Garau, C., Zamperlin, P., Balletto, G.: Reconsidering the Geddesian concepts of community and space through the paradigm of smart cities. Sustainability **8**(10), 985 (2016)
22. Garau, C., Annunziata, A.: Smart city governance and children's agency: an assessment of the green infrastructure impact on children's activities in Cagliari (Italy) with the tool "opportunities for children in urban spaces (OCUS)." Sustainability **11**(18), 4848 (2019)
23. Canale, A., Tesoriere, G., Campisi, T.: The MAAS development as a mobility solution based on the individual needs of transport users. In: AIP Conference Proceedings, vol. 2186, no. 1, p. 160005. AIP Publishing LLC (2019)

24. Campisi, T., et al.: Innovative solutions for sustainable mobility in areas of weak demand. Some factors influencing the implementation of the DRT system in Enna (Italy). In: AIP Conference Proceedings, vol. 2343, no. 1, p. 090005. AIP Publishing LLC (2021)
25. Torrisi, V., Garau, C., Ignaccolo, M., Inturri, G.: "Sustainable Urban Mobility Plans": key concepts and a critical revision on SUMPs guidelines. In: Computational Science and Its Applications – ICCSA 2020, pp. 613–628. Springer, Cham (2020). https://doi.org/10.1007/978-3-030-58820-5_45
26. Torrisi, V., Garau, C., Inturri, G., Ignaccolo, M.: Strategies and actions towards sustainability: encouraging good ITS practices in the SUMP vision. In: AIP Conference Proceedings, vol. 2343, no. 1, p. 090008. AIP Publishing LLC (2021)
27. Abdullah, M., et al.: Service quality assessment of app-based demand-responsive public transit services in Lahore, Pakistan. . Appl. Sci. **11**(4), 1911 (2021)
28. Brake, J., Nelson, J.D., Wright, S.: Demand responsive transport: towards the emergence of a new market segment. J. Transp. Geogr. **12**, 323–337 (2004)
29. Daganzo, C., Ouyang, Y.: A general model of demand-responsive transportation services: from taxi to ridesharing to dial-a-ride. Transp. Res. Part B: Methodol. 213–224 (2019). https://doi.org/10.1016/j.trb.2019.06.001
30. Charisis, A., Iliopoulou, C., Kepaptsoglou, K.: DRT route design for the first/last mile problem: model and application to Athens, Greece. Public Transport **10**(3), 499–527 (2018). https://doi.org/10.1007/s12469-018-0188-0
31. Maltinti F., et al.: Vulnerable users and public transport service: analysis on expected and perceived quality data. In: Gervasi, O., et al. (eds.) Computational Science and Its Applications – ICCSA 2020, pp. 673–689. Springer, Cham (2020). https://doi.org/10.1007/978-3-030-58820-5_49
32. CTM Homepage. https://www.ctmcagliari.it. Accessed 12 Apr 2021
33. Georgiadis, G., Politis, I., Papaioannou, P.: Come l'ambiente operativo influenza l'efficacia del trasporto pubblico? Evidence from European Urban Bus Operators. Sostenibilità **12**(12), 4919 (2020)
34. Cordera, R., Canales, C., dell'Olio, L., Ibeas, A.: Elasticità della domanda di trasporto pubblico durante le fasi recessive dei cicli economici. Transp. Politica **42**, 173–179 (2015)
35. Abdullah, M., Ali, N., Dias, C., Campisi, T., Javid, M.A.: Exploring the traveler's intentions to use public transport during the COVID-19 pandemic while complying with precautionary measures. Appl. Sci. **11**(8), 3630 (2021)
36. Abdullah, M., Ali, N., Javid, M.A., Dias, C., Campisi, T.: Public transport versus solo travel mode choices during the COVID-19 pandemic: self-reported evidence from a developing country. Transp. Eng. **5**, 100078 (2021)
37. Alonso-González, M.J., Liu, T., Cats, O., Van Oort, N., Hoogendoorn, S.: The potential of demand-responsive transport as a complement to public transport: an assessment framework and an empirical evaluation. Transp. Res. Rec. **2672**(8), 879–889 (2018)
38. Wang, S., de Almeida Correia, G.H., Lin, H.X.: Exploring the performance of different on-demand transit services provided by a fleet of shared automated vehicles: an agent-based model. J. Adv. Transp. **2019**, 1–16 (2019)
39. Cervero, R.: Paratransit in America Praeger Westport, Connecticut (1997)
40. Enoch, M, Potter, S., Parkhurst, G., Smith, M.: INTERMODE: Innovations in Demand Responsive Transport. Department for Transport and Greater Manchester Passenger Transport Executive, London (2004)
41. Mageean, J., Nelson, J.D.: The evaluation of demand responsive transport services in Europe. J. Transp. Geogr. **11**(4), 255–270 (2003)
42. Alonso-González, M.J., et al.: The potential of demand-responsive transport as a complement to public transport: an assessment framework and an empirical evaluation. Transp. Res. Rec. **2672**(8), 879–889 (2018)

43. Papanikolaou, A., Basbas, S., Mintsis, G., Taxiltaris, C.: A methodological framework for assessing the success of Demand Responsive Transport (DRT) services. Transp. Res. Procedia **24**, 393–400 (2017)
44. Laws, R.: Evaluating publicly-funded DRT schemes in England and Wales. Doctoral dissertation, Loughborough University (2009)
45. Finn, B.: Towards large-scale flexible transport services: a practical perspective from the domain of paratransit. Res. Transp. Bus. Manag. **3**, 39–49 (2012)
46. Laws, R.: DRT schemes in England and Wales and considerations for their future. In: 87th Annual Meeting of the Transportation Research Board. Paper, pp. 08-0892. National Academy of Sciences (2008)
47. Ryley, T.J., Stanley, P.A., Enoch, M.P., Zanni, A.M., Quddus, M.A.: Investigating the contribution of Demand Responsive Transport to a sustainable local public transport system. Res. Transp. Econ. **48**, 364–372 (2014)
48. Davison, L., Enoch, M., Ryley, T., Quddus, M., Wang, C.: A survey of Demand Responsive Transport in Great Britain. Transp. Policy **31**, 47–54 (2014)
49. Inturri, G., Giuffrida, N., Ignaccolo, M., Le Pira, M., Pluchino, A., Rapisarda, A.: Testing demand responsive shared transport services via agent-based simulations. In: Daniele, P., Scrimali, L. (eds.) New Trends in Emerging Complex Real Life Problems. ASS, vol. 1, pp. 313–320. Springer, Cham (2018). https://doi.org/10.1007/978-3-030-00473-6_34
50. Nguyen-Hoangab, P., Yeung, R.: What is paratransit worth? Transp. Res. Part A: Policy Pract. **44**, 841–853 (2010)
51. Mageean, J., Nelson, J.D.: The evaluation of demand responsive transport services in Eu rope. J. Transp. Geogr. **11**(4), 255–270 (2003)
52. Papanikolaou, A., Basbas, S.: Analytical models for comparing demand responsive transport with bus services in low demand interurban areas. Transp. Lett. **13**, 1–8 (2020)
53. Torrisi, V., Ignaccolo, M., Inturri, G., Tesoriere, G., Campisi, T.: Exploring the factors affecting bike-sharing demand: evidence from student perceptions, usage patterns and adoption barriers. Transp. Res. Procedia **52**, 573–580 (2021)
54. Campisi, T., Torrisi, V., Ignaccolo, M., Inturri, G., Tesoriere, G.: University propensity assessment to car sharing services using mixed survey data: the Italian case study of Enna city. Transp. Res. Procedia **47**, 433–440 (2020)
55. Campisi, T., Ignaccolo, M., Inturri, G., Tesoriere, G., Torrisi, V.: The growing urban accessibility: a model to measure the car sharing effectiveness based on parking distances. In: Gervasi, O., et al. (eds.) Computational Science and Its Applications – ICCSA 2020, pp. 629–644. Springer, Cham (2020). https://doi.org/10.1007/978-3-030-58820-5_46
56. Caggiani, L., Camporeale, R., Ottomanelli, M., Szeto, W.Y.: A modeling framework for the dynamic management of free-floating bike-sharing systems. Transp. Res. Part C: Emerg. Technol. **87**, 159–182 (2018)
57. Coni, M., Garau, C., Maltinti, F., Pinna, F.: Accessibility improvements and place-based organization in the Island of Sardinia (Italy). In: Gervasi, O., et al. (eds.) Computational Science and Its Applications – ICCSA 2020: 20th International Conference, pp. 337–352. Springer, Cham (2020). https://doi.org/10.1007/978-3-030-58820-5_26

Factors Influencing Public Transport Demand in Sicily During COVID-19 Era: A Study of Commuters' Travel and Mode Choice Behaviors

Socrates Basbas[1] , Georgios Georgiadis[2]([✉]) , Tiziana Campisi[3] ,
and Giovanni Tesoriere[3]

[1] School of Rural and Surveying Engineering, Faculty of Engineering, Aristotle University of
Thessaloniki, 54124 Thessaloniki, Greece
[2] School of Civil Engineering, Faculty of Engineering, Aristotle University of Thessaloniki,
54124 Thessaloniki, Greece
ggeorgiadis@civil.auth.gr
[3] Faculty of Engineering and Architecture, University of Enna Kore, Cittadella Universitaria,
94100 Enna, Italy

Abstract. Since the spread of the COVID-19 pandemic in March 2020, the transport system has suffered a profound reduction in demand worldwide. In order to understand which factors played a crucial role in reducing transport demand, an online questionnaire survey was conducted exploring one of the regions of Italy, i.e. Sicily, which was severely affected by the pandemic and was characterized by the greatest transport disruption among the other Italian regions. The survey was answered by 700 respondents who were frequent PT commuters before the outbreak of the pandemic. It collected sociodemographic information, highlighted the public transport demand figures before and after the lockdown period in Sicily and assessed the acceptance rates of the national recommendations which aimed to prevent contagion and encourage the use of PT. The survey data were analyzed using descriptive and cluster analysis techniques. During the examined periods, the results demonstrated three (3) clusters of PT commuters in Sicily and associated them with certain sociodemographic characteristics and acceptance rates of the national PT recommendations. Our findings lay the basis for public transport service improvements which could help local authorities to cope with such extreme conditions and perform a successful restart of operations.

Keywords: Public transport · COVID-19 · Italy · Transport demand · Travel
behavior · Transport policy · Cluster analysis

1 Introduction

European cities are increasingly confronted with transport problems. Migration from cities to the suburbs is leading to settlement structures with long distances to travel. This urban sprawl goes hand in hand with an increase of car ownership rates and commuter

© Springer Nature Switzerland AG 2021
O. Gervasi et al. (Eds.): ICCSA 2021, LNCS 12954, pp. 339–353, 2021.
https://doi.org/10.1007/978-3-030-86979-3_25

traffic. Boosting mobility is one of the main objectives of governments while reducing traffic, accidents and pollution is a common challenge for all major cities. According to the European Commission, transport congestion in and around urban areas represents a cost of around EUR 100 billion a year, or 1% of EU GDP, due to delays and pollution [1]. In addition, one in three fatal accidents occurs in urban areas. Urban mobility accounts for 40% of CO_2 emissions from road transport and up to 70% of other pollutants [1]. Another serious problem in urban areas, which unfortunately continues to worsen, is noise pollution, mainly from road traffic.

In this context, the relationship between Public Transport (PT) and the environment is a topic which is constantly under investigation worldwide towards achieving sustainable urban mobility objectives [2–5]. The EU has earmarked funds to co-finance projects to help cities implement or/and upgrade urban PT systems by means such as metro, trams and buses. In addition, PT priority measures [6, 7] have been implemented in urban areas in order to increase the attractiveness of the systems and subsequently increase the demand.

There are many factors which affect the demand for PT and quality plays an important role among them. PT agencies need to receive a feedback from passengers in order to improve the quality of delivered services [8]. This task becomes more essential in the COVID-19 era due to the restrictions imposed in the operation of the various PT systems. Intelligent Transportation Systems (ITS) can offer a lot in the bidirectional communication between PT operators and passengers that can yield significant benefits towards the fulfilment of sustainable urban mobility goals and the promoting of PT systems by increasing their attractiveness and their adaptability to continuously changing environments [9, 10]. For instance, the traditional information provided through Variable-Message Sign (VMS) screens at bus stops [11] can be complemented with the new regulations due to the COVID-19 pandemic. The use of questionnaire-based surveys also proved to be a very effective tool to investigate the impact of COVID-19 to transport systems and particularly to the perceived quality of transport services [12–15]. The impact of the COVID-19 pandemic to PT is an issue of major concern worldwide and it has been investigated in countries such as the UK, Germany, China, the Netherlands etc. [16–19].

This paper focuses on Sicily, which is one of the most affected regions in Italy from the COVID-19 pandemic. Since March 2020, there has been a collapse in the use of PT in Italy due to the COVID-19 related restrictions and measures [20, 21]. In fact, people preferred to walk or cycle for short journeys or use private transport for medium and long distances [22]. Italy, along with other European countries, has issued a series of national recommendations which aimed at reducing infection while travelling by PT and respecting social distancing. In order to adapt and sustain PT services, both during and after the pandemic, it is essential to understand the PT demand trends and classify the PT users in order to identify the criticalities related to the implementation of national recommendations. This process will enable authorities to develop short- and long-term plans of PT service improvement measures. This paper analyses sociodemographic, PT demand and perception data from a questionnaire survey that was implemented in Sicily and targeted PT commuters. The objective of this research is to shed light on the PT demand variations during the COVID-19 pandemic in Sicily and to investigate, by means of cluster analysis, whether the travel behaviour of PT commuters was influenced by their sociodemographic profiles and their opinion on the nationwide PT related recommendations.

The rest of the paper is as follows. The next section describes the COVID-19 timeline, PT characteristics and related recommendations in Sicily and Italy. Section 3 explains the questionnaire survey and the methodology we applied to analyse the collected data. Section 4 presents and discuss the results of our analysis while Sect. 5 summarizes the conclusions.

2 Background

2.1 PT Characteristics in Sicily Prior to the COVID-19 Outbreak

Before the COVID-19 pandemic, the Italian National Institute of Statistics (ISTAT) recorded that in 2019 PT buses, trolleybuses and trams were used at least once by around 13 million people, i.e. a quarter of the population aged 14 and over (24.6%). This was mainly habitual use: around 3 million people in Italy used PT every day and the same number of people used it at least a few times during the week. PT services were used mainly in metropolitan areas, in the central regions and in the North-West of Italy.

In the region of Sicily, until 2019, there were approximately 0.4 buses in circulation per 1,000 inhabitants (for a total of 2,490 buses), which is a figure that is slightly below the national average (0.7). Of these, 936 buses provide urban Local PT (LPT) services, and the rest of them are devoted to the Regional PT services (RPT). According to ISTAT and ACI data (2017), in Sicily, 12.4% of the population uses PT for commuting (i.e. work and study purposes). The number of cars and motorbikes to the total population, which is considered as an indicator of private transport that could substitute PT, is rather high, i.e. 779 per 1,000 inhabitants. The data show that LPT plays a subordinate role with respect to personal mobility, even when compared to the already low average use in southern Italy. Sicily is the Italian region with the lowest frequent use of rail transport. According to recent data provided by the ISTAT (2018), only 1.2% of workers, schoolchildren and students aged three years and over use the train on a frequent basis to travel to work, kindergartens, or schools (against a national average of 6%). Particularly low PT shares are also found in other southern Italian regions, such as Sardinia. Opposite figures are recorded in Northern Italy and in Campania (8.9%).

Overall, there is a very high level of user dissatisfaction with the PT services in Sicily. The greatest criticism pertains to the frequency of PT services, their punctuality, the availability of seats on-board, the cleanliness of the vehicles, the cost of tickets, and the availability of PT information. In the pre-pandemic phase, Sicily already showed a reduction in the use of PT, even though this negative figure is more limited for bus transport than that observed for the use of rail transport. Before the pandemic, PT was used to a greater extent by female users, both in Sicily (21.5%) and in Italy (25.5%). The spread of teleworking and the closure of schools at various COVID-19 periods from March 2020 until March 2021 have reduced the number of PT users while the fear of potential contagion has often prompted travellers to use their private cars.

2.2 The COVID-19 Pandemic Timeline in Italy

The timeline of the COVID-19 pandemic in Italy can be defined by three (3) periods:

1. The first period, which is characterised by social distancing rules and finally by the lockdown (started on 11 March and ended on 16 May 2020), aimed at reducing the possibility of encountering the new Coronavirus, which was freely circulating in the environment. The adopted measures made it possible to reduce new infections as much as possible and to relieve the pressure on the intensive care units of hospitals.
2. The second period covers the summer and autumn period of 2020 and ends in December 2020 with the discovery of the COVID-19 vaccine. The second period can be divided in two (2) phases:

   a. Phase I, during May–September 2020, in which certain mobility and other restrictions were relaxed and
   b. Phase II, during October–December 2020, in which COVID-19 infections began rising and restrictions started gradually to apply again.

3. The third period from January 2021, which is still ongoing, is associated with new waves of infection and modified forms of the new Coronavirus.

2.3 The PT Recommendations Issued by the Italian Government

In order to travel safely during the second period of the COVID-19 pandemic in Italy, a set of eight (8) recommendations for bus PT systems has been issued taking into account the "Guidelines" contained in the Annex 9 of the Prime Ministerial Decree of 26 April 2020, which pertained to personal mobility matters. The objective of these recommendations was to safeguard the health protection of PT personnel (i.e. drivers, customer care staff etc.) and PT passengers at stops/stations and on-board, in order to support the resumption of operations and therefore the mobility of people through the efficient management of critical issues related to the risks of crowding and exposure to possible sources of contagion. Table 1 lists these eight (8) recommendations.

In light of these eight (8) recommendations, local governments and transport operators in Italy have realised that planning new sustainable and resilient strategies is necessary to restore the balance between transport supply and demand [23, 24]. Specifically, the PT operators have drawn up operational plans to differentiate the flows of passengers boarding and alighting PT vehicles and to limit movements within transport hubs as well as at passenger waiting areas. They have also periodically arranged for the systematic sanitation of premises, vehicles and equipment used by travellers and/or personnel in accordance with the methods defined by the Ministry of Health and related Institutes. Disinfectant solution dispensers have been installed in PT stations and inside vehicles' cabins. Waiting areas have been equipped with staff to check body temperature or with automatic systems for this purpose. In PT buses, limitations in the maximum number of people on board have been applied, while PT agencies have also set up ad hoc signs and markers on seats to indicate those of them that cannot be used in line with the social distancing requirements. In the case of non-scheduled transport services, passengers

Table 1. National recommendations in Italy for PT systems after the COVID-19 lockdown

#	Recommendation	Location
1	Do not use PT if you have suspected symptoms of COVID-19 disease	General
2	Purchase tickets electronically, online or via app, whenever possible	PT stops and stations
3	Follow the signs and routes indicated inside stations or at stops, always keeping a distance of at least one (1) meter from other people	
4	Use the indicated vehicle access doors for boarding and alighting, always keeping a safe distance of one (1) meter from other people	On-board
5	Sit only in the permitted seats, keeping a distance from other occupants where required	
6	Avoid approaching or asking the driver for information	
7	During trip, frequently sanitize your hands and avoid touching your face	
8	Use the IMMUNI app to control the spread of the virus	General

were forbidden to occupy the seat next to the driver and no more than two passengers were allowed on the rear seats provided they were equipped with safety devices. In the absence of such devices, only one passenger was allowed. On vehicles approved for the carriage of six or more persons, not more than two passengers were permitted per row of seats, provided that they were wearing facemasks. If possible, bulkheads could be fitted. In addition, the use of a Bluetooth-based application, called IMMUNI [25] for smartphones and tablets was disseminated for the general control of the presence of "COVID-19 positive" people in the vicinity of the user.

3   Methodology

3.1   Study Area and Sample

The region of Sicily was among those most affected by the number of COVID-19 infections and deaths during the first and second period of the pandemic. It is also characterised by a medium-low infrastructure and is an island that is easily reached by plane or ferry. Sicily has been the subject of studies in the PT sector for a number of years [26, 27], and in the pandemic phase some researchers have attempted to analyse the trends between transport supply and demand in advance [28, 29]. The sample investigated, was randomly selected from the lists of frequent passengers of LPT and RPT services. All these passengers reside in the main cities of Sicily and frequently use PT to travel from/to home to/from work, i.e. they are defined as PT commuters. The survey sample consists of 700 PT commuters.

3.2 Questionnaire Survey

The implementation of an online questionnaire survey made it possible to easily acquire data from these 700 PT commuters and in particular data relating to three (3) different aspects:

1. Sociodemographic characteristics, such as gender, age, residential area, and income.
2. Trip frequency for commuting by LPT and RPT services in Sicily during three (3) distinct time periods of the COVID-19 pandemic: (a) before the COVID-19 pandemic, (b) Phase I (May–September 2020) and (c) Phase II (October–December 2020).
3. The level of PT commuters' acceptance against the national recommendations for PT systems (Table 1). The survey participants were asked to indicate their agreement or disagreement with each one of the recommendations, by answering to the following question: *"Do you agree, remain neutral or disagree with the following eight (8) national recommendations for PT systems?"*.

The questionnaire survey was carried out from October to December 2020. It was designed and uploaded on the Google platform and disseminated via Facebook and WhatsApp websites.

3.3 Data Analysis

In this study, descriptive statistics were used to estimate and compare: (a) the PT demand trends in Sicily, during the three (3) examined periods of the COVID-19 pandemic and (b) the acceptance rates of survey participants against the national PT recommendations.

In order to investigate whether the PT demand is associated with certain personal characteristics and opinions, we employed a two-step cluster analysis approach to identify homogenous groups of PT commuters. Therefore, we selected the PT trip frequency and sociodemographic variables as input variables for the clustering and we ran two (2) separate analyses to reflect Phase I and Phase II conditions respectively. Then, the acceptance rates on national PT recommendations were compared between cluster members so as to highlight any important differentiations among their opinions.

Two-step cluster analysis has been extensively used in a variety of research fields and disciplines, and allows for the simultaneous analysis of diverse data, such as demographic, psychographic, and behavioral [30]. For this study, we utilized the SPSS software [31] to perform this analysis using the log-likelihood measure. In the two-step cluster analysis, the original cases are first grouped into pre-clusters and then the standard hierarchical clustering algorithm is used to define a range of possible clustering solutions. To define the best number of clusters, the Schwarz's Bayesian information criterion is considered [32]. To validate the cluster analysis results we took into account the *silhouette measure of cohesion and separation*, which is required to be over 0.0, as well as the *importance* of each input variable in the clusters, which are determined by the respective χ^2 -tests' results that are automatically performed by the SPSS routines for all categorical variables.

4   Results and Discussion

4.1   PT Commuters' Profile and Demand Trends

The sociodemographic information, which was collected by the questionnaire survey, demonstrates the basic profile attributes of the 700 PT commuters in our sample. Female (56.3%) and male (43.7%) PT commuters are almost equally represented within our sample. The majority of the PT commuters belongs to the young age groups of 22–25 (33.57%) and 26–30 years old (39.43%). The age groups of above 36 years old have much lower representation (4.7%). The PT commuters are categorized against freelancers (14.7%), employees (59.7%) and other type of occupation (25.57%). Regarding their household monthly income, 25.1% of the respondents earns an income which is below 1,000 euros, while 31.6% of them earns between 1,001–1,500 euros. Incomes of 1,501–2,000 euros and of more than 2,000 euros are also satisfactorily represented in the sample (26.1% and 17.1% respectively). The 33.4% of the survey participants live in Cities (Ragusa, Siracusa, Caltanissetta, and Trapani), the 28.3% in towns (Enna and Agrigento), and the 19.9% of them in Metropolises (Palermo, Messina, and Catania) of Sicily. The rest of them (18.43%) resides in small towns.

Figure 1 shows the trip frequency rates, which were reported by the 700 PT commuters for the LPT services they used in Sicily, during the three (3) examined COVID-19 periods. Before the COVID-19 outbreak, almost all of the survey participants (92%) used LPT services for one or more times per day for commuting. After the end of the lockdown, in Phase I, only a small percentage of them (9.9%) continued to use LPT in the same frequency rates, while almost half of them (46.9%) abandoned LPT. In Phase II, though we observe a slight increase of the PT commuters who returned to the frequent use of LPT (14%), the percentage of those who stopped using LPT still remains high (41.6%), indicating that the return to typical PT ridership and operational conditions was not achieved. Figure 2 presents a similar trend for RPT services as well.

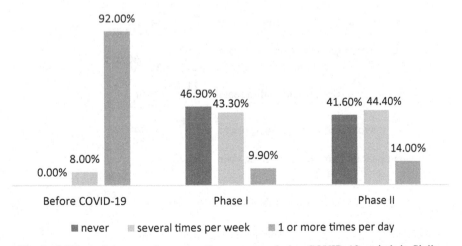

Fig. 1. LPT trip frequency for commuting purposes during COVID-19 periods in Sicily.

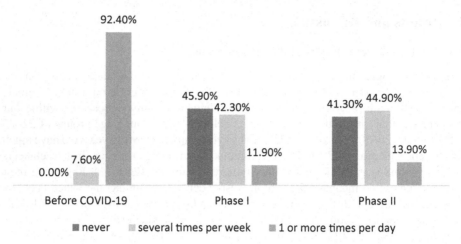

Fig. 2. RPT trip frequency for commuting purposes during COVID-19 periods in Sicily.

4.2 Acceptance Rates of National PT Recommendations

Figure 3 presents the agreement levels on the eight (8) national PT recommendations, which were expressed by the 700 PT commuters in the questionnaire survey.

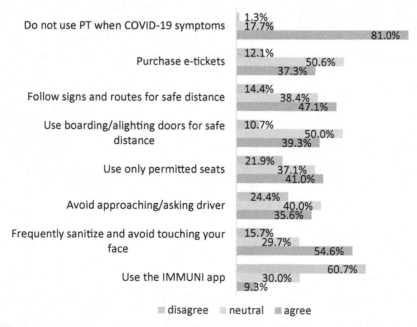

Fig. 3. Acceptance rates of recommendations when using PT among survey participants.

Among the eight (8) recommendations, the one which asks travelers to avoid using PT when they have suspected COVID-19 symptoms concentrates a very high level of agreement among participants (81%). Almost no one was found to disagree with this recommendation (1.3%). This finding demonstrates the relative importance that the PT commuters show on the personal responsibility they carry in terms of spreading the COVID-19 disease. In the same manner, high acceptance rates are also observed for the recommendations: *"During trip, frequently sanitize your hands and avoid touching your face"* (54.6%), and *"Follow the signs and routes indicated inside stations or at stops, always keeping a distance of at least one meter from other people"* (47.1%). Contrary to them, the use of IMMUNI app seems that has not attracted the attention of PT commuters, since 60.7% of them disagrees with the effectiveness of the respective advice. The rest of the recommendations gather similar acceptance levels, ranging between 35% and 41%. Interestingly, the purchasing of e-tickets and the use of the designated boarding/alighting doors are indifferent to the majority of the respondents (neutral opinions of 50.6% and 50% respectively). This probably indicates the relative difficulty to follow these two advices in practice within the PT network of Sicily.

4.3 Clustering of PT Commuters

The results of the two-step cluster analysis indicated two (2) clusters of PT commuters for Phase I. Table 2 shows their basic features. We obtained a silhouette measure of cohesion and separation which is over 0.5 and denotes a good fit of this clustering model. As explained in the Methodology Section, we tested all trip frequency and sociodemographic variables as inputs to the clustering procedure. However, only three (3) of them were found to be important and able to define homogenous groups of PT commuters. Specifically, the frequency of LPT and RPT use were the most important variables (input importance > 0.8) and thus determined the labels of the two clusters, namely Regular &

Table 2. Composition of PT commuters' clusters in Phase I.

Cluster features		1	2
Label		Regular & Frequent PT commuters	Non-PT commuters
Size		386 (55.1%)	314 (44.9%)
Ratio of largest to smallest cluster sizes		1.23	
Silhouette measure of cohesion and separation		>0.5	
Input variables	Trip frequency LPT	Several times per week (100%) & 1 or more times per day (100%)	Never (95.7%)
	Trip frequency RPT	Several times per week & 1 or more times per day (100%)	Never (97.8%)
	Age	26–30 (64.5%)	22–25 (54.0%)

Frequent PT commuters and Non-PT commuters. This fact also reconfirms the descriptive statistics results which showed that the LPT and RPT demand figures follow similar trends after the lockdown period in Sicily.

Age was a less important variable (input importance < 0.2), and highlights that the first cluster concentrated the majority (64.5%) of the 26–30 age group, while the second cluster gathered the most respondents (54%) which belonged to the 22–25 age group. No other sociodemographic variable was found to be an important factor for clustering. This is an indication that the PT mode choice for commuting in Phase I is not significantly associated or explained by the sociodemographic attributes of the travelers.

Similar findings were also obtained from the Phase II clusters and presented in Table 3. The frequency of LPT and RPT use appear again as the dominant input variables (input importance > 0.8) which characterize three (3) clusters of PT commuters, namely Frequent, Regular and Non-PT commuters. Regarding the residential area, the 49% of the town residents belong to the cluster of the Non-PT commuters and the 47.9% of the city residents to the cluster of the Regular PT commuters. However, the importance of this variable is comparatively lower (input importance < 0.2). As in Phase I, no other sociodemographic variable was found to be a critical factor for determining clusters of PT commuters.

Table 3. Composition of PT commuters' clusters in Phase II

Cluster features		1	2	3
Label		Frequent PT commuters	Regular PT commuters	Non-PT commuters
Size		101 (14.4%)	314 (44.9%)	285 (40.7%)
Ratio of largest to smallest cluster sizes		3.11		
Silhouette measure of cohesion and separation		>0.5		
Input variables	Trip frequency LPT	1 or more times per day (100%)	Several times per week (99%)	Never (97.6%)
	Trip frequency RPT	1 or more times per day (100%)	Several times per week (100%)	Never (98.6%)
	Residential area	City (15.8%)	City (47.9%)	Town (49.0%)

Table 4 shows the four (4), out of the total eight (8), national PT recommendations that had differentiated acceptance rates within the cluster members in Phase I and Phase II.

For Phase I clusters, Table 4 shows that the majority (57.5%) of the Frequent and Regular PT commuters are neutral towards the "Purchase of e-tickets" while most of the Non-PT commuters (45.2%) agree with this advice. Additionally, the "Use of permitted seats on-board" concentrates the agreement of the 45.1% of Cluster 1 members, while

38.9% of Cluster 2 members are indifferent to this advice. The same pattern also applies for the "Avoiding approaching/asking drivers" recommendation, which draws comparatively more attention within Frequent and Regular PT commuters (38.1%) compared to the Non-PT commuters (32.5%). These findings indicate the relative importance that was given to the two recommendations, i.e. "Use of permitted seats on-board" and "Avoiding approaching/asking drivers", from the commuters who resumed PT use after the end of the lockdown period in Sicily, and demonstrate two important fields where PT agencies should pay attention for successfully adapting their services in the COVID-19 era. The relatively lower agreement for the "Purchase of e-tickets" within Cluster 1 members probably highlights practical difficulties to follow this recommendation in the PT system of Sicily.

In the same manner, for Phase II clusters, Table 4 figures also show that there are differentiations among the opinions of the three (3) cluster members, regarding the recommendations on permitted seats, approaching driver, and use of boarding/alighting doors. However, these differentiations are much lower compared to the Phase I case and cannot easily demonstrate a certain opinion pattern.

Table 4. Acceptance rates of recommendations within the clusters of PT commuters

Recommendations		Phase I clusters		Phase II clusters		
		1	2	1	2	3
Purchase e-tickets	Disagree	11.7%	12.7%	10.8%	8.9%	14.7%
	Neutral	57.5%	42.0%	51.0%	50.5%	50.2%
	Agree	30.8%	45.2%	38.2%	40.6%	35.1%
Use only permitted seats	Disagree	19.2%	25.2%	19.4%	21.8%	24.6%
	Neutral	35.8%	38.9%	40.8%	37.6%	33.0%
	Agree	45.1%	36.0%	39.8%	40.6%	42.5%
Avoid approaching/asking driver	Disagree	24.6%	24.2%	26.1%	24.8%	22.5%
	Neutral	37.3%	43.3%	41.7%	38.6%	38.6%
	Agree	38.1%	32.5%	32.2%	36.6%	38.9%
Use boarding/alighting doors properly for safe distancing	Disagree	9.6%	12.1%	8.6%	9.9%	13.3%
	Neutral	53.9%	45.2%	51.9%	44.6%	49.8%
	Agree	36.5%	42.7%	39.5%	45.5%	36.8%

5   Conclusion

In this study we used questionnaire survey data to investigate the PT demand characteristics and their explanatory factors in Sicily, Italy after the end of the COVID-19 lockdown period. Our sample consisted of 700 PT users who were frequent PT commuters before the COVID-19 pandemic. Their answers were analyzed by employing descriptive statistics and cluster analysis. Empirical findings showed that the PT demand for commuting trips was reduced by half in the LPT and RPT services of Sicily during the second period of the pandemic (approximately May–December 2020). This reduction of demand was horizontal among the different groups of commuters, since the cluster analysis results showed that their sociodemographic attributes play no or little importance for explaining the frequency of LPT and RPT commuting trips. Commuters in Sicily were found to be great supporters of the national recommendations that pertained to their personal responsibilities against COVID-19 spread when using PT. The recommendations regarding the "Use of permitted seats on-board" and the "Avoiding approaching/asking bus drivers on-board" were highlighted as the most critical ones among the commuters that returned to LPT and RPT services after the end of lockdown. On the other hand, the national PT recommendations that were based on online applications, such as IMMUNI and e-ticketing, did not gather high acceptance due to (potential) practical difficulties.

Our findings highlighted the most important national PT recommendations and thus highlighted the fields where local authorities and PT agencies should focus in order to adjust the PT operations in the post lockdown phase and create attractive PT services during any pandemic or relatively extreme situation that may appear again in the future. In fact, when the restrictions will be reduced, national and local authorities will have to understand whether the mobility changes triggered by COVID-19 are positive or negative, in terms of their impact on energy use, safety and long-term health and environmental outcomes. Certainly, governments that have already designed sustainable transport policies for the post-COVID-19 period can draw on previous crisis experiences to predict likely behaviour and design policies that are fit for purpose.

Therefore, in view of the inconveniences caused by the pandemic, this study indicated that it is necessary to analyse PT using a bottom-up approach that rewards participatory planning [8, 11, 28, 33]; it is also necessary to analyse not only the characteristics of the service provided but also the psycho-social aspect of users [34] and possible mobility alternatives that allow social distancing to be respected and the service to be complementary, such as DRT and minibus services [35, 36], and shared mobility services [37, 38]. In this respect, considering the low acceptance rates of online apps in Sicily, PT agencies should continue developing attractive customer service platforms and investing in their social media strategies to promote such apps to their customers [36, 39].

The most important limitation of this study was that the sample of PT commuters did not adequately represent all demographic groups, especially the age-related ones. This is due to the inherited weaknesses of online surveys, which do not attract the attention of older people, but they are the only feasible survey tool under COVID-19 restriction measures. Further research should also explore the role of additional PT qualitative attributes in PT demand and should also cover the third period of the pandemic (i.e. from January 2021 and onwards) so as to determine a more comprehensive understanding of the PT demand under these extreme conditions.

Acknowledgments. The authors acknowledge financial support from the MIUR (Ministry of Education, Universities and Research [Italy]) through a project entitled WEAKI TRANSIT: WEAK-demand areas Innovative TRANsport Shared services for Italian Towns (Project code: 20174ARRHT/CUP Code: J74I19000320008), financed with the PRIN 2017 (Research Projects of National Relevance) program. We authorize the MIUR to reproduce and distribute reprints for Governmental purposes, notwithstanding any copyright notations thereon. Any opinions, findings, and conclusions or recommendations expressed in this material are those of the authors and do not necessarily reflect the views of the MIUR.

Author Contributions. This paper is the result of the joint work of the authors. 'Abstract', 'Introduction', 'Methodology', and 'Results' were written jointly by the authors. T.C. and G.T. discussed on the state of the art. S.B. and G.G. designed the methodological approach and discussion. Supervision and research funding; T.C., S.B., and G.T.

Funding. This research work was partially funded by the MIUR (Ministry of Education, Universities and Research [Italy]) through a project entitled WEAKI TRANSIT.

Conflicts of Interest. The authors declare no conflict of interest.

References

1. European Commission: Green Paper - Towards a new culture for urban mobility {SEC(2007) 1209} COM/2007/0551 final
2. Basbas, S., Nikolaou, K., Toskas, G.: Environmental impacts of bus traffic in the Thessaloniki Metropolitan Area. J. Environ. Prot. Ecol. **2**(3), 567–574 (2001)
3. Mahmood, M.N., Avishai (Avi), C., Farzan, G., Scott, T.: Environmental impacts of public transport systems using real-time control method. Transp. Res. Part D: Transp. Environ. **51**, 216–226 (2017)
4. Vicente, P., Sampaio, A., Reis, E.: Factors influencing passenger loyalty towards public transport services: does public transport providers' commitment to environmental sustainability matter? Case Stud. Transp. Policy **8**(2), 627–638 (2020)
5. Ma, L., Graham, D., Stettler, M.: Air quality impacts of new public transport provision: a causal analysis of the Jubilee Line Extension in London. Atmos. Environ. **245**, 118025 (2021)
6. Pettersson, F., Sørensen, C.H.: Why do cities invest in bus priority measures? Policy, polity, and politics in Stockholm and Copenhagen. Transp. Policy **98**, 178–185 (2020)
7. Goryaev, N., Myachkov, K., Larin, O.: Optimization of "green wave" mode to ensure priority of fixed-route public transport. Transp. Res. Proc. **36**, 231–236 (2018)
8. Stelzer, A., Englert, F., Hörold, S., Mayas, C.: Improving service quality in public transportation systems using automated customer feedback. Transp. Res. Part E: Logist. Transp. Rev. **89**, 259–271 (2016)
9. Torrisi, V., Garau, C., Inturri, G., Ignaccolo, M.: Strategies and actions towards sustainability: encouraging good ITS practices in the SUMP vision. In: AIP Conference Proceedings, vol. 2343, no. 1, p. 090008. AIP Publishing LLC (2021). https://doi.org/10.1063/5.0047897
10. Coni, M., Garau, C., Pinna, F.: How has Cagliari changed its citizens in smart citizens? Exploring the influence of ITS technology on urban social interactions. In: Gervasi, O., et al. (eds.) ICCSA 2018. LNCS, vol. 10962, pp. 573–588. Springer, Cham (2018). https://doi.org/10.1007/978-3-319-95168-3_39
11. Politis, I., Papaioannou, P., Basbas, S., Dimitriadis, N.: Evaluation of a bus passenger information system from the users' point of view in the city of Thessaloniki. Greece. Res. Transp. Econ. **29**(1), 249–255 (2010)

12. Campisi, T., Basbas, S., Skoufas, A., Akgün, N., Ticali, D., Tesoriere, G.: The impact of COVID-19 pandemic on the resilience of sustainable mobility in Sicily. Sustainability **12**, 8829 (2020)
13. Przybylowski, A., Stelmak, S., Suchanek, M.: Mobility behaviour in view of the impact of the COVID-19 pandemic—Public transport users in Gdansk case study. Sustainability **13**, 364 (2021)
14. Politis, I., et al.: Mapping travel behavior changes during the COVID-19 lock-down: a socioeconomic analysis in Greece. Eur. Transp. Res. Rev. **13**(1), 1–19 (2021). https://doi.org/10.1186/s12544-021-00481-7
15. Nikiforiadis, A., Ayfantopoulou, G., Stamelou, A.: Assessing the impact of COVID-19 on bike-sharing usage: the case of Thessaloniki, Greece. Sustainability **12**, 8215 (2020)
16. Eisenmann, C., Nobis, C., Kolarova, V., Lenz, B., Winkler, C.: Transport mode use during the COVID-19 lockdown period in Germany: the car became more important, public transport lost ground. Transp. Policy **103**, 60–67 (2021)
17. Dong, H., Ma, S., Jia, N., Tian, J.: Understanding public transport satisfaction in post COVID-19 pandemic. Transp. Policy **101**, 81–88 (2021)
18. Gkiotsalitis, K.: A model for modifying the public transport service patterns to account for the imposed COVID-19 capacity. Transp. Res. Interdisc. Perspect. **9**, 100336 (2021)
19. Vickerman, R.: Will COVID-19 put the public back in public transport? A UK perspective. Transp. Policy **103**, 95–102 (2021)
20. Murgante, B., Borruso, G., Balletto, G., Castiglia, P., Dettori, M.: Why Italy first? Health, geographical and planning aspects of the COVID-19 outbreak. Sustainability **12**(12), 5064 (2020)
21. Gutiérrez, A., Miravet, D., Domènech, A.: COVID-19 and urban public transport services: emerging challenges and research agenda. Cities Health 1–4 (2020). https://doi.org/10.1080/23748834.2020.1804291
22. Moslem, S., Campisi, T., Szmelter-Jarosz, A., Duleba, S., Nahiduzzaman, K.M., Tesoriere, G.: Best–worst method for modelling mobility choice after COVID-19: evidence from Italy. Sustainability **12**(17), 6824 (2020)
23. Cartenì, A., Di Francesco, L., Martino, M.: The role of transport accessibility within the spread of the Coronavirus pandemic in Italy. Saf. Sci. **133**, 104999 (2021)
24. Tuite, A.R., Ng, V., Rees, E., Fisman, D.: Estimation of COVID-19 outbreak size in Italy. The Lancet. Infect. Dis. **20**(5), 537 (2020)
25. IMMUNI Homepage. http://www.immuni.italia.it/. Accessed 21 Mar 2021
26. Franzitta, V., Curto, D., Rao, D., Viola, A.: Hydrogen production from sea wave for alternative energy vehicles for public transport in Trapani (Italy). Energies **9**(10), 850 (2016)
27. Genna, G.: The transportation system in the Sicilian touristic development. In: ERSA Conference Papers, number ersa06p652 (2006)
28. Campisi, T., Akgün, N., Ticali, D., Tesoriere, G.: Exploring public opinion on personal mobility vehicle use: a case study in Palermo, Italy. Sustainability **12**(13), 5460 (2020)
29. Campisi, T., Basbas, S., Skoufas, A., Akgün, N., Ticali, D., Tesoriere, G.: The impact of COVID-19 pandemic on the resilience of sustainable mobility in Sicily. Sustainability **12**(21), 8829 (2020)
30. Rundle-Thiele, S., Kubacki, K., Tkaczynski, A., Parkinson, J.: Using two-step cluster analysis to identify homogeneous physical activity groups. Mark. Intell. Plann. **33**(4), 522–537 (2015)
31. IBM Corp. Released 2017. IBM SPSS Statistics for Windows, Version 25.0. IBM Corp., Armonk, NY
32. Norusis, M.J.: IBM SPSS Statistics 19 Procedures Companion. Addison Wesley, TX, Boston (2011)

33. Tesoriere, G., Campisi, T.: The benefit of engage the "crowd" encouraging a bottom-up approach for shared mobility rating. In: Gervasi, O., et al. (eds.) ICCSA 2020. LNCS, vol. 12250, pp. 836–850. Springer, Cham (2020). https://doi.org/10.1007/978-3-030-58802-1_60

34. Al-Rashid, M.A., Goh, H.C., Harumain, Y.A.S., Ali, Z., Campisi, T., Mahmood, T.: Psychosocial barriers of public transport use and social exclusion among older adults: empirical evidence from Lahore, Pakistan. Int. J. Environ. Res. Public Health **18**(1), 185 (2021)

35. Akrioti, M., Basbas, S., Georgiadis, G., Nathanail, E.: Investigation of minibus public transport service characteristics in an urban area through the use of a stated and revealed preference survey. In: Nathanail, E.G., Adamos, G., Karakikes, I. (eds.) CSUM 2020. AISC, vol. 1278, pp. 11–20. Springer, Cham (2021). https://doi.org/10.1007/978-3-030-61075-3_2

36. Abdullah, M., Ali, N., Shah, S.A.H., Javid, M.A., Campisi, T.: Service quality assessment of app-based demand-responsive public transit services in Lahore, Pakistan. Appl. Sc. **11**, 1911 (2021)

37. Campisi, T., Torrisi, V., Ignaccolo, M., Inturri, G., Tesoriere, G.: University propensity assessment to car sharing services using mixed survey data: the Italian case study of Enna city. Transp. Res. Proc. **47**, 433–440 (2020)

38. Campisi, T., Ignaccolo, M., Inturri, G., Tesoriere, G., Torrisi, V.: The growing urban accessibility: a model to measure the car sharing effectiveness based on parking distances. In: Gervasi, O., et al. (eds.) ICCSA 2020. LNCS, vol. 12255, pp. 629–644. Springer, Cham (2020). https://doi.org/10.1007/978-3-030-58820-5_46

39. Georgiadis, G., Nikolaidou, A., Politis, I., Papaioannou, P.: How public transport could benefit from social media? Evidence from European agencies. In: Nathanail, E.G., Adamos, G., Karakikes, I. (eds.) CSUM 2020. AISC, vol. 1278, pp. 645–653. Springer, Cham (2021). https://doi.org/10.1007/978-3-030-61075-3_63

Standard Cost of Local Public Transport in the Post-COVID-19 Era: The Italian Case

G. Acampa[1]([⊠]), M. Grasso[1], C. M. Parisi[1], D. Ticali[1], and A. Severino[2]

[1] Faculty of Engineering and Architecture, University "Kore" of Enna, 94100 Enna, Italy
{giovanna.acampa,mariolina.grasso,dario.ticali}@unikore.it
[2] Civil Engineering and Architecture Department, University of Catania, 9531 Catania, Italy
alessandro.severino@unict.it

Abstract. Local Public Transport (LPT) plays a key role in the economic system of any country. The Covid-19 outbreak and subsequent lockdowns led to an unprecedented economic crisis in this sector. Governments had to block all unnecessary travel and keep only essential services moving, reducing public transport services (air, train, bus, metro, etc.) by more than 90%. Despite the economic aids provided by Governments, many LPT companies are facing a crisis that they are unlikely to be able to overcome. This for two reasons: skepticism of passengers in the use of public transport, and therefore reduced revenue from ticket sales, and additional costs for the vehicles' sanitization Focusing on the Italian case, and especially on Sicily, the paper aims to analyze the standard costs of the LPT road service and assess the cost increase in which companies have to incur in order to meet the guidelines imposed by Government and encourage citizens to use public transport. The paper relies on the results of a direct investigation on clients' attitudes through a questionnaire submitted to a population travelling to and from the city of Enna in the centre of Sicily.

Keywords: COVID-19 · Local public transport · Standard cost · Sustainable mobility

1 Introduction

In the last decades, the rapid growth of population and its concentration in urban areas forced a quick and continuous evolution towards sustainable urban mobility. To date, mass public transport is the only suitable solution to meet the needs of large-scale urban mobility for short and medium distance travel. According to the latest UITP report (2018), mass public transport serve more than 53 billion passenger all over the world (with an 19% increase as compared to 2012) [1]. This has had positive effects on public and private investment aimed at increasing the level of service provided.

Due to the Covid-19 outbreak, mass public transport witnessed a steep fall in users. The close proximity among passengers turns the transmission of pathogens much more likely, and public transport has become the catalyst for the COVID outbreak [2, 3].

This phenomenon forced Governments all over the world to reduce and limit the operating efficiency of passenger transport and ensure minimum level of service by

© Springer Nature Switzerland AG 2021
O. Gervasi et al. (Eds.): ICCSA 2021, LNCS 12954, pp. 354–369, 2021.
https://doi.org/10.1007/978-3-030-86979-3_26

keeping LPT only partially operating. In the first three months (from February to April 2020) the actions taken to curb the pandemia inevitably caused an economic and social crisis. Over four billion people worldwide lived in lockdown for months and the limited travel had a drastic impact on the public transport system: a significant decrease in revenues (in some cities by more than 90% less), an increase in the costs of disinfection activities and the implementation of containment measures (such as social distancing) aimed at reducing the risk of virus transmission [4]. In addition, users prefer to use the private vehicle to avoid contact with other.

The steep decrease in the use of public transport has led not only to increased use of private vehicles but also sustainable transport means (bicycles, electric micro-mobility, car sharing, etc.) [5, 6]. Having more private cars on the road certainly brought negative impacts in terms of environmental pollution, public land occupation, traffic congestion, longer travel time [7], stress for travellers and dissatisfaction of citizens [8]. On the other hand, the increase in the use of sustainable means of transport such as bicycles and electric micro-mobility drastically reduced pollution in urban areas.

In any case, the pandemia lead to the financial collapse of local public transport companies. Most commuter rail, subways, and bus hubs reported significant declines because many people avoided and are still avoiding public transportation both for fear of contagion and compliance with advisory and precautionary measures [9]. The result is an inevitable deterioration of providential services (reduction in the number of daily rides and increase in ticket prices), which may push users to prefer private to public transport. Therefore, fewer passengers translate into less money for transportation agencies and the slowdown of economic activity in large cities.

Many governments adopted specific economic support measures for the Covid-19 emergency, both for service operators and users, but it is often insufficient.

In Italy, the Legislative Decree no. 34 of May the 19th 2020 [10] provided for an initial allocation of 500 million euros for the year 2020 as a compensation for the reduction in passenger tariff revenues in the period from 23 February 2020 to 31 December 2020.

This research aims to analyse the impact of such measures once addressed the cost structure and allocation of economic resources for local public transport (LPT) by analysing the standard costs of local public transport taking into account three factors: the commercial speed (VC) of the vehicles, the amount of service offered (Km) ("bus-km service" or "seat-km service"), and the degree renewal of the fleet (Akm).

Some researchers worked on the cost structure of LPT companies focusing on the estimation of variable and total costs [11–15]. Others suggested to rely on demand indicators such as passenger-travel or passenger-kilometre and supply indicators such as vehicle-kilometre or place-kilometre [16]. Many researchers also discussed the effect of economies of scale and population density on LPT costs [12, 13, 17, 18].

Between 2014 and 2016, Avenali et al. [19, 20] carried out a research leading to the adoption in Italy of the Ministerial Decree no.157 of 28 March 2018 [21]. According their studies, commercial speed is the most important cost factor, while economies of scale have little influence and are limited to small groups of services. The results show a strong correlation between investments in the bus fleet and the costs incurred in providing the service [22]. On the basis of these studies, this paper aims to provide an overview of how standard costs have changed in the post-COVID 19 era.

The results highlight the need to reassess the allocation of economic resources to local public transport companies following the provisions of decrees such as the Italian Prime Ministerial Decree of 26 April 2020 [23] the opportunity to balance the higher costs incurred by transport companies.

2 Mobility During the COVID 19 Outbreak: Public Transport Trend – The Italian Case

The COVID 19 health emergency and the measures taken to contain the pandemia had a significant impact on the entire transport and mobility system. In Italy, two Prime Ministerial Decrees issued on March the 9th 2020 [24] banned all forms of people gathering in public or open places and suspended all non-essential commercial and catering activities, allowing mobility only for proven work needs, cases of clear necessity or travel for health reasons. In the weeks following the publication of the Decrees by the Italian Government these restrictive measures generally defined by the term "lockdown", were adopted by most European countries. Google and Moovit insight made available reports showing the impact of these restrictions imposed on the mobility system. The pre-emergency and post-emergency data were compared, taking as a baseline the start date of the survey, January the 13th 2020, until March the 1th 2021 (when this study was completed). These reports are updated daily both by Google and Moovit[1]. Google made available reports showing the evolution trend towards shops, restaurants, bars, museums, places for the purchase of essential goods, parks, means of transport, workplaces and places of residence. The analyses provided by Moovit, taking the data by Google analysis, revealed the percentage of change in demand for public transport worldwide.

For this paper, we referred to reports on the main European countries affected by the pandemia: Italy, Spain, France and Germany focusing on public road transport data. The reference period for all data analysed is from January the 13th 2020 (start date of the survey) to March the 1th 2021 (last update).

The data provided by Google highlighted the percentage change in the attendance of most popular spots for daily life, grouped in venues for retail and free time (shops, restaurants, bars, museums), for the purchase of essential goods (groceries, pharmacies), parks, transport vehicles, workplaces and residence (apartments, houses etc.). The data collected by country gives an idea of the impact of the pandemia on both the demand for non-systematic mobility (e.g. attendance in bars, restaurants, museums, shops) and systematic mobility (e.g. attendance in workplaces). A location attendance is quantified by counting users who have logged into their Google account, saved their location history and activated the "Location Reporting" function. The visitors' attendance distribution is calculated on the basis of the number of visits and the length of stay; then, the median value is taken as a daily measure of visits. With this data, it was possible to calculate the overall average variation of the displacements (Table 1).

We focused especially on the mobility trend towards public transport spots (bus stations, trains, airports, etc.). In Italy, as well as in Spain, France and Germany travels

---

[1] This application is based on the official information delivered by local administrations and public transport operators to users in order to offer the best available route of LTP in real time.

Table 1. Mobility trend according to Google.

Country	Retail and free time (bar, restaurant etc.)	Grocery and pharmacy	Parks	Public transport stations	Work places	Residence
Spain	−34%	2%	−8%	−26%	−20%	7%
Italy	−29%	1%	9%	−35%	−24%	9%
France	−34%	1%	34%	−28%	−31%	10%
Germany	−38%	0%	62%	−32%	−24%	10%

to public transport spots fell by 30% compared to the baseline [25]. Looking at the Google data, it can also be seen that the decrease in the trend of mobility towards public transport spots almost overlaps the decrease in travel to workplaces. It suggests that travel on public transport is mainly due to work needs; thus smart-working at home can only negatively impact on LPTs. As mentioned before Moovit insight analyze Google's data referring to public transport. In particular, Fig. 1 shows a comparison between the aforementioned Country within the time laps considered (January 13th 2020 to March 1th 2021) and the public transport mobility trends.

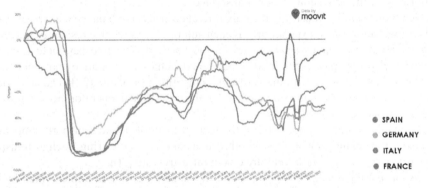

SPAIN
GERMANY
ITALY
FRANCE

Fig. 1. Moovit public transport report during Covid 19[2]

Among all the Country took under exam there is a homogeneous trend and all the mobility trends referring to public transport are under the baseline starting from the first days of March 2020 when the pandemic began.

---

[2] Source: www.moovit.com

3 Materials and Methods

3.1 Local Public Transport (LPT)

Local public transport (LPT) plays a key role in urban and suburban mobility and had significant impacts in terms of development and competitiveness of the entire national economy. Like other local public services, it contributes significantly to improving citizens' quality of life [26].

In the main EU countries, mobility produces more than twice as much income as in Italy (e.g. Germany reaches a value of € 28.1 billion). The effect is a quality offer that attracts increasing volumes of traffic. The level of infrastructure and the efficiency of the service are the elements that make the difference to achieve a competitive offer. In fact, the higher the levels of efficiency, the more local public transport is able to take away parts of demand from private transport and provide added value to the community.

3.2 Standard Cost for LPT According to Italian Law

According to the fiscal federalism approach, standard cost is a benchmark adopted by Governments to allocate economic resources to Regions. In Italy, the law on fiscal federalism no.42 of 2009 [27] sets the historical cost criterion (based on the expenditure incurred in the previous year) to quantify the economic resources to be allocated to local authorities for the provision of essential services.

Needs and standard costs are the only reference criteria to balance and review local and regional authorities' expenditure, as each authority is to receive resources matching with its needs. Resources are assessed on the basis of objective parameters and no longer in relation to past expenditure. Operators thus have an incentive to promote their efficiency, in accordance with the yardstick competition principle [28]. The authorities shall grant economic resources on the basis of the costs that an operator faces to provide an efficient service.

Standard costs are set not only for the management of public transport companies, but also for the management of many other areas of civil engineering, such as transport infrastructure [29] and wastewater treatment infrastructure [30].

As far as LPT is concerned, the use of the standard cost was implemented by the Stability Law of 2014, which called the Ministry of Transport to define (with uniform criteria at national level) the standard costs of the local and regional public transport services (LPT) and the criteria to update and implement them. In addition, the law specified that the standard cost should take into account the *"context factors"* (e.g. commercial speed, economies of scale, production technology, modernisation of rolling stock and a reasonable profit margin for the transport carrier).

The first national law that introduced in Italy the definition of standard cost (Law no. 151/1981[3]) established the National Transport Fund. It defined the standard cost as *"Economic cost of services with reference to criteria and parameters of strict and efficient management, divided by categories and modes of transport and taking into account,*

---

[3] Law no. 151 of 10 April 1981: Framework law for the ordering, restructuring and strengthening of local public transport.

through comparative analysis, the quality of the service offered and the environmental conditions in which it is carried out"[4].

Another important law in this context is the Decree no. 50 of March the 24th 2017 that contains the following principles:

- call for tenders for all local and regional transport services, including rail services;
- exceeding the 35% threshold for the share of operating costs to be covered by revenues;
- introduction of the mandatory separation of the management function from the regulatory, guidance and control function of regional and local public transport services.

In summary, there are two important legislative provisions: putting aside the criterion of "historical cost" as a parameter for the distribution of public economic resources from the State to the Regions (and from the latter to local authorities and businesses) and the call for tendering procedures to increase the competition in the offer of services. The standard cost therefore has a dual function: on the one hand, it allows a better allocation of available public resources and, on the other, it encourages an increase in the efficiency of the system through the optimization of internal management costs.

Standard Cost Model

The Ministerial Decree no.157 of 28 March 2018 (*"Definition of standard costs of local and regional public transport services and criteria for updating and application"*) completed the complex regulatory process regarding standard costs in the public transport sector.

The Ministerial Decree defines the standard cost according to a function that takes into account different production technologies (buses, tramways, subways, regional railways), demand conditions (metropolitan areas and areas with weak demand), commercial speed, modernisation of rolling stock and reasonable profit margins.

Regarding road transport service, the calculation takes into account the qualitative and quantitative characteristics of the service and explains the variability of costs through a top-down approach.

According to the regulations, the standard cost depends on the commercial speed (VC) of the vehicles, the amount of service offered (Km) ("bus-km service" or "seat-km service"), and the degree renewal of the fleet (Akm).

$$CS = f(VC; Km; Akm) \tag{1}$$

Where:

- *VC* is the commercial speed (km/h)
- *Km* is millions of bus-kilometres
- *Akm* is the degree of renewal of the fleet (€/km).

---

[4] In this law, rail services were excluded from the fund.

3.3 The Management Cost of LPT During the COVID-19 Outbreak

The Guidelines for the information of users of public transport have been subject to numerous changes during the issuance of the various Prime Ministerial Decrees containing urgent measures to deal with the epidemiological emergency from COVID-19 (frequency in October became fortnightly!), in order to adapt them to the evolution of the pandemic scenario.

Thus, from their first edition (Prime Ministerial Decree of April the 14th 2020 with the Annex No. 9) to the current version (Prime Ministerial Decree of March the 2nd 2021 with the Annex No. 14), the national legislator has varied, according to need or strategic choice, certain parameters, such as, but not limited to, the crowding index of the specific public means of transport, alongside refinements of the text and/or correction of material errors, in accordance also with the impact that the recovery of economic activities foreseen in phase 2 and above all schooling in attendance could determine, and in fact has determined, on the local transport system. And, specifically, starting from the Prime Ministerial Decree of August the 7th 2020, it has also entered into the merit of some types of public transport, such as dedicated school transport.

For local public road transport, the contagion curbing measures include:

Daily disinfection of public transport and sanitisation in relation to specific company realities.

- Separation of the driver's seat from the passengers;
- Separation of the entry and exit of passengers using the central and back doors and in respect of appropriate waiting times in order to avoid contact between those who get off and those who get on;
- Suspension of the sale and control of tickets on board;
- Checking the correct use of personal protective equipment (masks and gloves);
- Installation of hydroalcoholic dispensers for passenger use;
- Communications on board of the vehicles by affixing signs showing the correct way of behaving.

These requirements inevitably lead to additional costs for operators of public road transport services in addition to those that they have to face in normal situations.

In this research, the authors define a new standard cost (Eq. 4) for local public transport services in the post COVID-19 era as the sum of the standard cost under normal pre COVID-19 conditions and the additional costs necessary to meet the Decree of the President of the Council of Ministers indications for contagion containment.

$$CS_{post\ COVID-19} = CS + C_x \tag{2}$$

4 Results

4.1 Local Public Transport in Sicily (Italy)

Sicily is the largest island in the Mediterranean (about 25,800 km^2), the Italian region with the largest extension and is the fourth most populous region in Italy (about 5 million residents, 8.4% of total residents in Italy).

The Sicilian road system is about 30,500 km long: about 700 km of motorways, about 3,500 km of roads of State interest while the management of about 26,000 km of roads is under the responsibility of Local Authorities. Sicily is the third Italian region (after Piemonte and Lombardia) by extension of motorway network. Precisely, its extension in relation to the number of inhabitants is equal to 1.3 km^2 per 10,000 inhabitants compared to an Italian average of 1.1 km^2, and that in relation to the territorial extension is equal to 2.6 compared to the Italian average of 2.2 per 100 km^2. For most of the Sicilian territory, the extra-urban public transport system by road is the only alternative mode of transport to private cars. The total volume of journeys to 2016 amounts to 60,215,611 bus * km/year.

Sicily has 83 public road transport companies and the average volume delivered in 2016 is 725,000 buses * km. About 18% of the companies (15 out of 83) provide a higher-than-average annual volume of journeys: this confirms the current fragmentation of the service in Sicily with a large number of companies operating with marginal production volumes (less than 100,000 vehicles km/year). About the 24% of the annual kilometres of suburban services is provided by the company AST (Azienda Siciliana Trasporti) owned by the Sicilian Region, about 9% by SAIS Trasporti, 8% by SAIS Autolinee and 7% by Interbus. The three quarters of the Sicilian companies (exactly 66 companies) provide less than 1% of the total regional supply [31].

Analyzing the data provided by Moovit is it possible to calculate the percentage decrease in the use of public transport during this pandemic period.

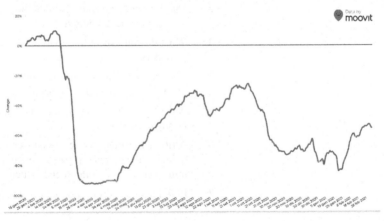

Fig. 2. Sicily public transport report during Covid 19

As can be seen from Fig. 2, the trend in Sicily is above the national average, with a decrease compared to the baseline of 45% [32].

4.2 Questionnaire Through Google Surveys

The starting point for this paper was a survey that aimed at getting a first evaluation on the approach to transport modes in the post COVID-19 period. The survey was completed online using social and fast communication methods that made it easy and straightforward to respond to the questions picking an answer out of a multiple-choice. It was administered to users mostly interested in suburban public road transport. In fact, most of the subjects investigated live in the municipalities surrounding the city of Enna and move systematically to and from larger urban centres by bus. Only a small part of the investigated users lives in large urban areas with different integrated transport modes (metro, bus, etc.). Below is the model of the questionnaire divided into 4 sections and the most significant results (Table 2).

Table 2. Questionnaire through google surveys

Section	No.	Question
Personal data	1.1	Gender
	1.2	Year
	1.3	Degree
	1.4	Recidence
Transport habits	2.1	How often do you use public transport?
	2.2	What type of public transport do you use most?
Change in transport modes in the post Covid 19 era	3.1	Awareness of the epidemia
	3.2	Do you think you'll use public transport again in the next 6 months?
	3.3	What do you expect from public service providers?
	3.4	Reduction of physical contact with personnel or mechanical obliteration machines
	3.5	Attitude towards prior allocation of seats on public transport
	3.6	Attitude towards leaving seats unoccupied reducing the number of passengers in public transport increasing the social distance
	3.7	Individual devices useful on public transport (gloves and masks)
	3.8	Frequency of visiting public places (shopping centres, cinemas, theatre)
Transport sharing	4.1	Use of shared transport vehicles
	4.2	Frequency of use of means of transport sharing

The results of the survey show that in ordinary conditions (prior to COVID-19) the interviewed users tend not to choose public transport for urban and suburban travels in the Region of Sicily and this is probably also due to the law level of the services offered.

The 35% of respondents do not use public transport and 25% rarely use it (once a week) (Fig. 3a). According to the survey, bus is the preferred public transport mode by almost 58% of respondents (Fig. 3b). This is also due to the low number of trains in Sicily.

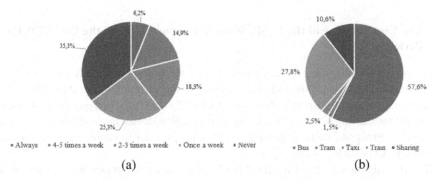

(a)   (b)

Fig. 3. (a) 2.1 Frequency of use of public transport before outbreak; (b) 2.2 Most used public transport.

As a result of the pandemia, 30% of respondents prefer not to use public transport and 63% prefer to use it only when necessary (Figs. 4a and b). This means that we should expect a reduction in the number of people using public transport in the post-COVID period and consequently in the economic income from ticket sales.

In addition, users confirm that they will use public transport only if precautionary systems are in place, consistent with measures meant to curb contagion on transport vehicles. In fact, 48% of the interviewees ask for a reduction in the number of passengers in order to keep the social distancing among passengers and 29% ask for frequent sanitization interventions on vehicles.

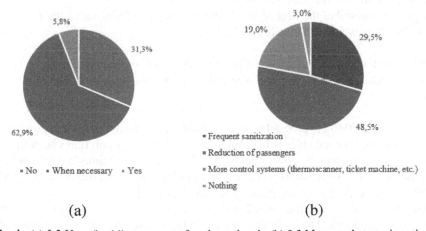

(a)   (b)

Fig. 4. (a) 3.2 Use of public transport after the outbreak; (b) 3.3 Managers' strategic actions.

In general, the results of the survey are not encouraging for local public transport operators. The paper therefore addresses the issue of standard costs of local public transport services by road and the variation of these costs caused by the COVID-19 outbreak.

4.3 The Cost Increase of the Public Road Transport in Sicily the Post COVID-19 Period

Given the methodology for the determination of the CS standard cost in public road transport, the objective of this study is to determine the variation of the standard cost for the local public road transport in Sicily post-COVID-19 $CS_{post\ COVID-19}$ (Eq. 4) where Cx represents the impact of costs relating to protection devices, sanitization, increased on-board controls and reduced passenger capacity, in order to ensure compliance with current anti-COVID legislation.

The investigation scope of the local public road transport service was chosen on the basis of the survey results, considering that most of the respondents are users of the extra-urban public road transport service in Sicily.

We then proceeded with the calculation of the CS on the basis of data provided by the main public road transport company in Sicily, AST (Azienda Siciliana Trasporti), which on its own carried out 24% of the annual trips of Sicilian suburban services[5].

According to the Ministerial Decree no.157 of March 28th 2018, the standard cost referred to the extra-urban service is:

$$CS\left(\frac{€}{bus-km}\right) = 2,77 \tag{3}$$

Where:

- Commercial speed VC = 63 km/h
- Annual kilometers km = 14.579.909 km
- Degree of renewal of the fleet A_{KM} = suburban degree of renewal of the fleet €/km = 0,35 €/km, where its value is 5.087.070 €.

As a result of the spread of the COVID-19, the value of CS increased by a certain amount C_x. The value of C_x is given by the costs for the following items per vehicle unit (bus):

- Sanitization: 150 €/g to proceed with daily sanitization and assuming that purchase of equipment and consumables is handled in house by the operator. It has been hypothesized that sanitization is carried out with a frequency of 1–2 times a day depending on the number of trips and passengers. The monthly cost would therefore be equal to 150 €/g per n. 20 days, corresponding to 3,000 €/month;
- Termoscan: one-off purchase in n.2 units for each vehicle to be installed at the two entrance/exit doors. The cost amounts to 2,000 €/cad and therefore totals 4,000

---

[5] It should be specified that AST provides a mixed service (urban and suburban). For the sake of this study, we selected data related only to the extra-urban service.

€/vehicle. Assuming an amortization time of the technology in 2 years, it is estimated a cost corresponding to about 100 €/month having foreseen the incidence of 10% monthly maintenance;

- Alternating seats (capacity reduction): considering that a bus has an average overall capacity of around 70 seats and that the average occupancy coefficient can generally be considered to be around 60% of this capacity, an average presence of around 42 users is obtained compared to the mandatory reduction to 35 in the case of alternating seats. The post COVID19 situation would therefore lead to a reduction in the number of users on average by about 10% compared to the average. Given the modest loss of the number of users and the variability in the cost of the ticket depending on the journey, given the difficulty of identifying an objective and unambiguous amount and the amount itself, this is considered negligible;
- Electronic ticketing and reserved seats: electronic ticketing is already in use by most operators but with the post COVID19 experience and the reduced availability of seats it is necessary to estimate an implementation of the service, technology and management. This higher cost can be considered negligible if offset by the resulting reduction in staff costs and therefore the transfer of man-hours to other services. Increase in costs equal to 0 €;
- Increased on-board control in order to comply with the rules: since the post COVID19 situation imposes a new behavioral regulation on users, it is necessary to proceed with the implementation of the on-board service that could be offered by the driver himself but with a waste of time and therefore with a loss of service efficiency. For this reason, it is possible to estimate an increase in staff costs of about 15% of the corresponding salary of about 600 €/month;
- Sanitizers and PPE on board (possible sale on site): in order to guarantee the minimum conditions required by the user it is necessary to install at least 2 dispensers containing sanitizing gel inside the vehicle. The supply and installation costs about 150 €/cad, to which must be added to the supply of consumables and maintenance. Based on market research and on the analysis of users' consumption, it is estimated that the cost of supply and installation is negligible because it is much lower than maintenance and recharging, which amounts to about 50 €/g, corresponding to about 1,000 €/month. The PPE provided for in the standard and/or regulation is not taken into account as it is assumed that it is already in disposable condition in order to avoid possible contacts from the outside to the inside of the vehicle. In any case, the PPE is considered to be already owned by the user and is therefore not considered to be costs attributable to the service provider;
- Driver protection and separation systems: in order to protect and safeguard the health of the driver it is necessary to isolate the area occupied by the driver from the transit of users. This intervention has a market survey estimated cost of about € 500 one-off and a total duration of about 2 years. The incidence of the cost is therefore about 15 €/month including ordinary maintenance.

The prices indicated above refer to a market analysis conducted in the territory of the Region of Sicily.

From the sum of the above costs, the C_x cost increase for the service provider amounts to approximately 4,715 €/month for each vehicle in use for extra-urban transport.

Considering that every month a single bus travels an average of 3,355 km (data extracted from the 2019 service map):

$$CS \left(\frac{€}{month}\right) = CS \left(\frac{€}{KM}\right) * Q \left(\frac{km}{month}\right) = 2{,}77 \ x \ 3355 = 9.310{,}77 \ €/month \quad (4)$$

The latter is the amount that the operator (AST) should receive as public contribution. So the total cost $CS_{post \ COVID-19}$ is equal to:

$$CS_{Post \ COVID-19} = CS \left(\frac{€}{month}\right) + C_x \left(\frac{€}{month}\right) = 9.310{,}77 + 4.715 \quad (5)$$
$$= 14.025{,}77 \ €/month$$

As a result, costs increased by 34% compared to pre-COVID-19 situation.

5 Discussion and Conclusions

The analysis of the additional costs necessary to maintain the attractiveness of the extra-urban LPT service shows that in some cases the same service becomes economically unsustainable in the post COVID-19 period.

The higher cost of the services requested by passengers must be covered by public spending because it cannot be passed on to users who would otherwise find it neither convenient nor useful to use public extra-urban road transport compared to private transport. The cost of the ticket for public transport by road has already been reduced by regional intervention aiming to guarantee a service to all interested users at a satisfactory level of quality suitable for the mode of transport in question.

The experience of COVID-19 requires a serious reflection on emergency and post emergency situations that must be organized in advance in order to avoid situations of improvisation such as those in progress, which are short-sighted healing interventions that need to be continuously corrected because they are neither scheduled nor planned. Indeed, the current situation leads to choices that neither the public administrations nor the managing authorities themselves had even slightly hypothesized.

This article, through an investigative action based on an online questionnaire, has made it possible to carry out a first preliminary analysis that will be subsequently detailed by increasing the number of users involved. The processing of the answers received from the interviewees made it possible to identify at an early stage the intentions of the systematic users of suburban public transport by road and that concern infrastructural and management interventions.

The article proposes an analysis of the standard costs of local public transport considering three factors:

– Commercial speed is a qualitative (economic) characteristic of the service, which is difficult for the provider to control. In particular, the impact of this variable on the cost can be expected to be significant and non-linear, i.e. a marginal increase in commercial speed reduces the cost to a greater extent for rather slow services than for fairly fast ones. The statistical model adopted by Boitani and Avenali [19], therefore, takes account of this possible non-linearity, assuming a functional form that with respect to commercial speed can behave as a linear function with dashes.

– Regarding the number of service vehicle-kilometres, the size of the service provided, and hence the size of the operators, can have an important influence on the ability of firms to acquire production inputs for which the conditions typical of markets in perfect competition (e.g. vehicles) cannot be found. Therefore, the size of the hero-derived service can be expected to play some role in determining the cost of the service, indicating the presence of economies or diseconomies of scale.
– The large difference in purchase costs between vehicles with different traction types, and between recently purchased vehicles and vehicles still in operation but purchased in the past (which represent a significant difference in the cost of the service) but purchased in the past (which represent an important share of those used overall in Italy), suggests that the degree of modernisation of the rolling stock may represent a driver of the cost of the service, that can be controlled by the operator providing the service.

The infrastructural actions include the installation on the means of transport of specific and dedicated technologies that on average can be activated in short notice. The management activities, on the other hand, involve an organizational change in the service management which also in this case require a longer time to be implemented. In both cases, the activities carried out by the managers of the extra-urban public road transport service include a significant communication and awareness raising action towards the user, who is alternatively forced to use private rather than public transport vehicles with the related economic, environmental and congestion impact. The interventions to be carried out by the Managers are even more complex and time-consuming if the financing has to be covered by the Public Administration, which to date (almost three months after the beginning of the pandemia) has not made it clear. The result of the current situation is therefore that the user, due to the changed approach to the health security measures expected to be carried out in public transport, tend to switch to private transport. It also points out that it is necessary to plan and schedule technological solutions and appropriate funding to provide public transport in general with all the useful and appropriate equipment to ensure a "safe" level of service for users. The specific case of the COVID-19 has led to a sudden collapse of overall mobility due to the lockdown strategy, but if such strategy would not have been chosen, the effect would have been a steep increase in the number of private vehicles on the roads putting the whole urban and suburban transport system in a critical position.

References

1. UITP - Advancing Public Transport: World Metro Figures 2018. In: UITP (2018). https://www.uitp.org/world-metro-figures-2018. Accessed 24 Apr 2020
2. Qian, X., Sun, L., Ukkusuri, S.V.: Scaling of contact networks for epidemic spreading in urban transit systems (2020). ArXiv Preprint ArXiv200203564
3. Morawska, L., Tang, J.W., Bahnfleth, W., et al.: How can airborne transmission of COVID-19 indoors be minimised? Environ. Int. **142**, 105832 (2020). https://doi.org/10.1016/j.envint.2020.105832
4. AppleMaps COVID-19 - Report sui trend di mobilità. In: Apple. https://www.apple.com/covid19/mobility. Accessed 9 Jul 2020

5. Campisi, T., Acampa, G., Marino, G., Tesoriere, G.: Cycling master plans in Italy: the I-BIM feasibility tool for cost and safety assessments. Sustainability **12**, 4723 (2020). https://doi.org/10.3390/su12114723
6. Campisi, T., Torrisi, V., Ignaccolo, M., et al.: University propensity assessment to car sharing services using mixed survey data: the Italian case study of Enna city. Transp. Res. Procedia **47**, 433–440 (2020). https://doi.org/10.1016/j.trpro.2020.03.155
7. Acampa, G., Ticali, D., Parisi, C.M.: Value of travel time: an economic assessment for transport appraisal decision-makers, Rhodes, Greece, p. 160009 (2019)
8. Acampa, G., Marino, G., Parisi, C.M.: Social network as tool for the evaluation of sustainable urban mobility in Catania (Italy). In: Bevilacqua, C., Calabrò, F., Della Spina, L. (eds.) NMP 2020. SIST, vol. 178, pp. 243–253. Springer, Cham (2021). https://doi.org/10.1007/978-3-030-48279-4_23
9. Hawkins, A.J.: Coronavirus is taking a big bite out of public transportation ridership in the US. In: The Verge (2020). https://www.theverge.com/2020/3/13/21179032/public-transportation-coronavirus-covid19-ridership-nyc-sf-la-dc. Accessed 8 Mar 2021
10. Law Decree 19 May 2020 no. 34 ("Decreto Rilancio") Italian Government. In: Gazzetta Uff. https://www.gazzettaufficiale.it/eli/id/2020/03/09/20A01558/sg. Accessed 4 Aug 2020
11. Obeng, K., Sakano, R.: Total factor productivity decomposition, input price inefficiencies, and public transit systems. Transp. Res. Part E Logist. Transp. Rev. **38**, 19–36 (2002). https://doi.org/10.1016/S1366-5545(01)00010-2
12. Fraquelli, G., Piacenza, M., Abrate, G.: Regulating public transit networks: how do urban-intercity diversification and speed-up measures affect firms' cost performance? Ann. Public Coop. Econ. **75**, 193–225 (2004). https://doi.org/10.1111/j.1467-8292.2004.00250.x
13. Cambini, C., Piacenza, M., Vannoni, D.: Restructuring public transit systems: evidence on cost properties from medium and large-sized companies. Rev. Ind. Organ. **31**, 183–203 (2007). https://doi.org/10.1007/s11151-007-9153-9
14. Ottoz, E., Di Giacomo, M.: Diversification strategies and scope economies: evidence from a sample of Italian regional bus transport providers. Appl. Econ. **44**, 2867–2880 (2012). https://doi.org/10.1080/00036846.2011.568399
15. Berechman, J.: Cost structure and production technology in transit. Reg. Sci. Urban Econ. **17**, 519–534 (1987). https://doi.org/10.1016/0166-0462(87)90014-7
16. Cambini, C., Filippini, M.: Competitive tendering and optimal size in the regional bus transportation industry: an example from Italy. Ann. Public Coop. Econ. **74**, 163–182 (2003). https://doi.org/10.1111/1467-8292.00220
17. Filippini, M., Prioni, P.: The influence of ownership on the cost of bus service provision in Switzerland - an empirical illustration. Appl. Econ. **35**, 683–690 (2003). https://doi.org/10.1080/0003684032000056788
18. Boitani, A., Nicolini, M., Scarpa, C.: Do competition and ownership matter? Evidence from local public transport in Europe. SSRN Electron. J. (2010). https://doi.org/10.2139/ssrn.1557151
19. Avenali, A., Boitani, A., Catalano, G., et al.: Un modello per la determinazione del costo standard nei servizi di trasporto pubblico locale su autobus in Italia. Econ. E Polit. Ind. 181–213 (2014). https://doi.org/10.3280/POLI2014-004009
20. Avenali, A., Boitani, A., Catalano, G., et al.: Assessing standard costs in local public bus transport: evidence from Italy. Transp. Policy **52**, 164–174 (2016). https://doi.org/10.1016/j.tranpol.2016.06.007
21. MIT - Ministero delle Infrastrutture e dei Trasporti Decreto ministeriale numero 157 del 28/03/2018. http://www.mit.gov.it/normativa/decreto-ministeriale-numero-157-del-28032018. Accessed 9 Jul 2020

22. Avenali, A., Boitani, A., Catalano, G., et al.: Assessing standard costs in local public bus transport: a hybrid cost model. Transp. Policy **62**, 48–57 (2018). https://doi.org/10.1016/j.tra npol.2017.03.011

23. Decree of the President of the Council of Minister: Decree of the President of the Council of Ministers 26 April 2020 further implementing provisions of the Decree-Law February 23, 2020, n. 6, containing urgent measures regarding the containment and management of the epidemiological emergency from COVID-19, applicable on the whole national territory (2020)

24. Decreto-Legge del 19 maggio 2020, n. 34 Misure urgenti in materia di salute, sostegno al lavoro e all'economia, nonche' di politiche sociali connesse all'emergenza epidemiologica da COVID-19. https://www.gazzettaufficiale.it/eli/id/2020/03/09/20A01558/sg. Accessed 9 Jul 2020

25. Google COVID-19 Community Mobility Report. In: COVID-19 Community Mobility Report. https://www.google.com/covid19/mobility?hl=it. Accessed 9 Jul 2020

26. Cassa Deposito e Prestiti: Luci e ombre della mobilità urbana in Italia: ripartire dal trasporto pubblico (2019)

27. Law fiscal federalism: Law fiscal federalism no. 42/2009 (2009). https://www.gazzet taufficiale.it/gunewsletter/dettaglio.jsp?service=1&datagu=2009-05-06&task=dettaglio& numgu=103&redaz=009G0053&tmstp=1241691584038. Accessed 6 Jul 2020

28. Shleifer, A.: A theory of yardstick competition. RAND J. Econ. **16**, 319–327 (1985)

29. Wang, W., Zhong, M., Hunt, J.: Analysis of the wider economic impact of a transport infrastructure project using an integrated land use transport model. Sustainability **11**, 364 (2019). https://doi.org/10.3390/su11020364

30. Acampa, G., Giustra, M.G., Parisi, C.M.: Water treatment emergency: cost evaluation tools. Sustainability **11**, 2609 (2019). https://doi.org/10.3390/su11092609

31. Regione Sicilia: Piano Integrato delle Infrastrutture e della Mobilità, p. 218 (2017)

32. Moovit Moovit Public Transit Index. https://moovitapp.com/insights/en/Moovit_Insights_ Public_Transit_Index-countries. Accessed 9 Jul 2020

COVID-19's Effects over E-commerce: A Preliminary Statistical Assessment for Some European Countries

Tiziana Campisi[1]([✉]) [iD], Antonio Russo[1] [iD], Giovanni Tesoriere[1] [iD],
Efstathios Bouhouras[2] [iD], and Socrates Basbas[2] [iD]

[1] Faculty of Engineering and Architecture, University of Enna Kore, Cittadella Universitaria,
94100 Enna, Italy
tiziana.campisi@unikore.it
[2] School of Rural and Surveying Engineering, Aristotle University of Thessaloniki,
54124 Thessaloniki, Greece

Abstract. The advent of e-commerce has surged during the recent COVID-19 pandemic period. Already in 2019, many habits of users concerning online shopping platforms have changed: the age of those buying online has risen, the average income has fallen and the contagion has reached all urban and rural areas, even the smaller towns and villages. Since March 2020, when increased restrictions were applied, an increase in shopping of various kinds in several European and non-European countries is recorded. Many operators had to modify their logistics and change their interfaces. In short, the emergency has given a huge cultural boost to e-commerce. Tens of thousands of small retailers found themselves in the position of not being able to welcome consumers into their shops or being forced to create e-shops in a very short period of time and thus they identified home delivery as an opportunity not to be missed. Remote payment was the first, but not the only, effect. The present paper analyses the correlation between online shopping habits and socio-demographic characteristics in 27 European countries. The results were obtained from a descriptive statistical evaluation and the correlation between the variables was defined by the chi-square calculation. The results lay the foundations for the definition of the change in transport demand by home-purchase motivation and allow to define some considerations on the emission patterns that characterise transport demand.

Keywords: E-commerce · Mobility and logistics · COVID-19 · Inferential statistics

1 Introduction

E-commerce has a long and rather interesting history, starting almost 40 years ago. The first experiences took place in the late '60s with the American company CompuServe, which is considered to be the first e-commerce company to be founded in 1969 [1], but it was only in 1979 that electronic shopping was introduced [2].

O. Gervasi et al. (Eds.): ICCSA 2021, LNCS 12954, pp. 370–385, 2021.
https://doi.org/10.1007/978-3-030-86979-3_27

For two decades, e-commerce remained a rather small sector. Since 1990, with the launch of World Wide Web (www), millions of people have been able to access e-commerce services on the Internet [3]. The '90s saw the founding of the current global e-commerce market leader with the establishment of the companies Amazon in 1995 [4], PayPal in 1998 [5] and Alibaba.com in 1999 [6] respectively.

In addition, Walmart launched its online shopping site in 2000, marking the entry of traditional retail players into e-commerce. The evolution of B2C (Business to Consumer i.e. direct sales to the consumer) is related to a number of factors such as the increased diffusion of the internet, which has made it possible for more people to buy goods online; the diffusion of smartphones and other mobile devices, making online buying easier, faster [7] so much and more secure so that some prefer to speak of "m-commerce" instead of "e-commerce" [8–11] or even of "u-commerce" [12] and a general optimisation in the logistics network, which has made deliveries more flexible and reduced the order-delivery lead-time allowing e-commerce platforms to modulate the offer according to the lead-time required by the user. The outbreak of COVID-19, which became a worldwide pandemic in March 2020, caused a further surge in e-commerce related retail sales [13]. A number of pandemic-related factors have made online shopping indispensable: restriction measures, blockades, social distancing and fear of contagion. These factors have also forced large segments of the population world widely who previously bought mainly at retail level to switch to online shopping.

Finally, entire sectors have had to adapt to the restrictions imposed by the pandemic, such as the food sector, which has seen online commerce as a real possibility as the last element in the supply chain [14–17], while other sectors inevitably grew up significantly during the pandemic as pharmaceutical e-commerce.

The changes imposed by the COVID-19 pandemic affected the whole world, although there were differences related to political and economic characteristics and the different ways in which blockades were implemented in different countries.

In the United States of America (USA), there has been a generalised growth in the share of e-commerce in the total retail market as well as in Canada [18], while a growth shared by the People's Republic of China [19] and India [20] are also recorded [21]. Europe has also been affected by this growth. Data predicts for around 27 European countries a growth in e-commerce sales orders of 30% in April 2020 compared to April 2019, while for the entire retail sector an overall decrease is predicted [22] as presented in Fig. 1. E-commerce has already influenced city mobility in the pre COVID-19 era, being characterised by a pervasive presence of last-mile logistics, which contributes to traffic congestion and pollution [23] and, for the same reason, has imposed heavy changes in companies' delivery methods.

In Europe, COVID-19 has strongly influenced transport modal choices [24–26] and main travel reasons [27–29]. This was mainly due to possible contagions and respect for social distancing [30, 31]. The psychosocial aspect played a role in the propensity of users to move outside their homes. This paper preliminarily investigates how the evolution of e-commerce together with COVID-19 might change the demand for transport in Europe. In addition, attention is paid to how e-commerce may affect transport [32] and logistics in urban areas. Starting from an analysis of the literature on e-commerce in the years 2015–2020, the main variables defining the demand for transport were investigated, as well

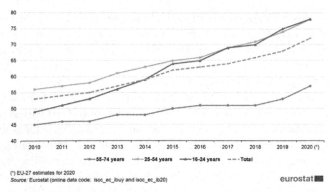

(¹) EU-27 estimates for 2020
Source: Eurostat (online data code: isoc_ec_ibuy and isoc_ec_ib20)   eurostat■

Fig. 1. Internet users who bought or ordered goods or services for private use in the previous 12 months by age group, EU-27, 2010–2020, Source: "E-Commerce statistics for individuals, Statistics Explained", Available online: https://ec.europa.eu/eurostat/statistics-explained/pdfsca che/46776.pdf

as the correlations that exist between some psychosocial variables and the propensity to use devices such as Personal Computers or tablets/smartphones and sites related to online sales. The statistical correlations between the different variables highlighted a series of useful observations for the development of more in-depth research in the field of post-pandemic mobility and logistics.

2   Methodology

2.1   Case Study Area Description

The analysis was conducted through an initial survey step by selecting the countries with the largest accessible databases of population and e-commerce data. In particular the analyzed area defined by the 27 European countries highlighted and colored in red in Fig. 2 including United Kingdom, which was member of the European Union until December 31, 2020. The choice of survey area is related to data collection and comparison.

In addition, some of these countries have suffered the first impacts of COVID-19 and applied strong travel restrictions, such as Italy, followed by France and Spain. In addition, some of these countries have experienced a strong increase in the use of online shopping during the pandemic period, along with a growth in businesses and online services. The variables defining the area under investigation were obtained from the main international databases and are described in the following paragraphs.

2.2   Variables Selection

For the preliminary statistical survey, $n =$ states were considered in a time period covering two years, i.e. $t = 2019, 2020$. The variables investigated are summarized in Table 1. The variables in the first section are related to the propensity of Internet usage and online

Fig. 2. Selection of country on Europe during period 2019–2020

Table 1. Investigated variables related to e-commerce habits and socio demographic

ID	Units	Variable descriptions	Sources	Details
1st e-commerce habits				
$NW_{i,t}$	[%] Percentage of people (Dimensionless variable)	The percentage of internet users (aged 16–74)	[33] [34]	where i = country and t = year
$NE_{i,t}$	[%] Percentage of people (Dimensionless variable)	The percentage of individuals aged 16–74 who purchased online		
2nd socio-demographic data				
$GDPpc_{i,t}$	[k$] Thousands of international dollars	Gross Domestic Product per capita	[33] [34]	
$MA_{i,t}$	[y] Years	Median Age of population		
$U_{i,t}$	[%] Percentage of people (Dimensionless variable)	Unemployment		
$E_{i,t}$	[%] Percentage of people (Dimensionless variable)	Population by educational attainment level (tertiary) and age (%) (15–64)		

shopping, while the second section shows some of the socio-demographic or economic characteristics commonly used in different studies of transport demand

Socio-demographic variables have been selected in accordance with [33, 34] and are among the most common and readily available variables to describe population. The variables have been considered as average values and the variable "median age" considers an algebraic average calculated considering the data series of 2018 and 2020. In addition, the unemployment rate was considered by analysing the fluctuation of the different periods of the year and it is obtained considering the average value of the monthly value of unemployment for the entire year *t*. The variable *Ei,t* was chosen as a socio-demographic variable in order to understand how well the working-age population can be correlated with the other variables related to e-commerce habits through a linear regression analysis.

3   Results

The statistical analysis was conducted by combining the variables "2 by 2", first with reference to the same section and then to the two different ones. For each of the pairs of variables considered, a scatter plot or scatter graph was obtained, which is a type of graph in which two variables of a data set are plotted on a Cartesian space and from which it was possible to evaluate the linear correlation coefficient *r* Nine different correlations were analysed/ considered:

1) correlation of two variables of the same section i.e. $NW_{i,t}$ and $NE_{i,t}$;
2) correlation between the propensity to e-commerce with respect to the economic parameter i.e. $NW_{i,t}$ and $GDPpc_{i,t}$;
3) correlation between the propensity to internet with respect to the economical parameter i.e. $NE_{i,t}$ and $GDPpc_{i,t}$;
4) correlation between the propensity to e-commerce with respect to the social parameter i.e. $NW_{i,t}$ and $MA_{i,t}$;
5) correlation between the propensity to internet with respect to the social parameter i.e. $NE_{i,t}$ and $MA_{i,t}$;
6) correlation between the propensity to e-commerce with respect to the labor parameter i.e. $NW_{i,t}$ and $U_{i,t}$;
7) correlation between the propensity to internet with respect to the labor parameter i.e. $NE_{i,t}$ and $MA_{i,t}$;
8) correlation to the propensity to e-commerce with respect to the educational parameter $NW_{i,t}$ and $E_{i,t}$;
9) correlation to the propensity to internet with respect to the educational parameter $NE_{i,t}$ and $E_{i,t}$;

Thus in Fig. 3, the two variables of the first section were correlated by placing $NW_{i,t}$ on x-axis and $NE_{i,t}$ on y-axis.

Among the hypotheses for the definition of the graph it results that

$$NW_{it} = NE_{it}, \forall i, t \tag{3.1}$$

This represents the bisector of the first and third quadrants, and identifies two different areas, characterised by the following relationships

$$NW_{it} < NE_{it}, \forall i, t \tag{3.2}$$

$$NW_{it} > NE_{it}, \forall i, t \tag{3.3}$$

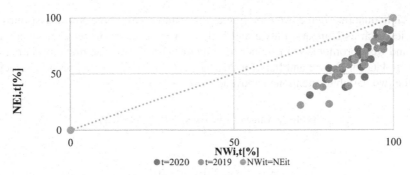

Fig. 3. Scatter plot between NW_{it} and NE_{it}

It can be noted that the points above the line represent unrealizable situations (expressed by Eq. 3.2, while the points below the line identify the domain of existence, through Eq. 3.3). Then considering the two straight lines whose equations are

$$NW_{it} = 0, 5, \forall i, t \tag{3.4}$$

$$NE_{it} = 0, 5, \forall i, t \tag{3.5}$$

They have identified four quadrants in the xy-plane, each of which is characterised by different conditions.

The upper left quadrant is a sector entirely in the non-existence domain:

$$\begin{cases} NW_{it} < 0, 5 \\ NE_{i,t} > 0, 5 \end{cases}, \forall i, t \tag{3.6}$$

The upper-right quadrant locates points (states) in which most population both connects to the internet and purchases goods online

$$\begin{cases} NW_{it} > 0, 5 \\ NE_{i,t} > 0, 5 \end{cases}, \forall i, t \tag{3.7}$$

The bottom right quadrant identifies states where the internet is widespread but e-commerce is lower

$$\begin{cases} NW_{it} > 0, 5 \\ NE_{i,t} < 0, 5 \end{cases}, \forall i, t \tag{3.8}$$

Finally, the bottom-left quadrant locates point in which less than the 50% of population uses internet and e-commerce.

$$\begin{cases} NW_{it} < 0, 5 \\ NE_{i,t} < 0, 5 \end{cases}, \forall i, t \tag{3.9}$$

The graph shows that most European countries are in the upper right quadrant. Some South East European countries such as Bulgaria, Cyprus and Greece are visible in the lower right quadrant in the two time frames 2019 and 2020. Some North East European countries such as Hungary, Latvia and Lithuania were in the lower right quadrant in 2019 and were promoted to the upper right quadrant in 2020. The first correlation used identical data for France and Italy for 2019 and 2020. The linear regression associated with the two variables mentioned above is showed in Table 2.

Table 2. Value of r between $NW_{i,t}$ and $NE_{i,t}$

	$NE_{i,t}$	
r	$t = 2019$	$t = 2020$
$NW_{i,t}$	0,92	0,88

For both years a value of **r** close to one was obtained, i.e. a significant correlation. This result is also related to the fact that a greater diffusion of internet guarantees more opportunities for online shopping; similarly, an increase in the need to shop online, which occurred during the pandemic, forces the more reluctant sections of the population to adopt internet. The slight variation in the value of r is explained by the fact that the $NW_{i,t}$ variable is close to the maximum in many countries, and therefore has lower margins of growth, while online shopping is a widespread habit but with still several possibilities of further development. The second proposed correlation is presented in Fig. 4.

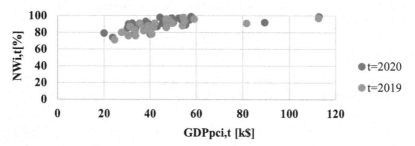

Fig. 4. Scatter plot between $NW_{i,t}$ and $GDP_{pci,t}$

The scatter plot examined shows the relationship between the number of people who had access to the internet and the gross domestic product per capita of a country.

Both sets of points, for $t = 2019$ and $t = 2020$, appear to show a linear correlation, although it is weaker than the relationship between the previous variables. The value of the variable on the x-axis is in the range 20 mo$ $<GDPCpc_{i,t}$ <60 mo$ for all countries considered. Exceptions are Ireland and Luxembourg, which show values above 80mo$, while $NW_{i,t}$ values are still high. It can be seen that the series referring to $t = 2020$ are higher than those referring to $t = 2019$, due to the already discussed increase in the number of online users, but at the same time has undergone a shift to the left at some points, due to the negative effects of the pandemic on the economy and thus on **$GDPpc$**. The third correlation is presented in Fig. 5.

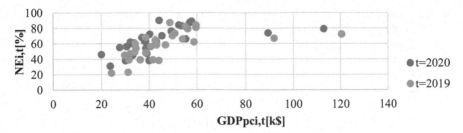

Fig. 5. Scatter plot between NE_{it} and $GDP_{pci,t}$

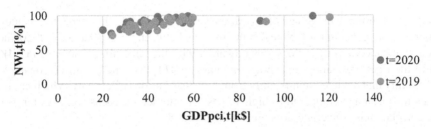

Fig. 6. Scatter plot between NW_{it} and $GDP_{pci,t}$

It can be seen that, unlike to the previous case, the values on the y-axis are more distributed, because online shopping is not yet a majority practice in all European countries, where internet is used by more than 70% of the population in all the states considered. It should also be noted that the $t = 2020$ series' values are also higher. This is due to a general increase in the value of $NE_{i,t}$, but at the same time several values have shifted to the left, due to the negative effects of the pandemic on **GDP**. The value of the linear regression is presented in Table 3.

Table 3. Value of r *between* $NW_{i,t}/NE_{i,t}$ and $GDP_{pci,t}$

	$GDP_{pci,t}$	
r	t = 2019	t = 2020
$NW_{i,t}$	0,64	0,62
$NE_{i,t}$	0,56	0,59

The identified values, are higher than 0.5 for each pair of variables considered and for each value of t, therefore they show a good linear correlation between the variables considered. Note how the correlation between $NW_{i,t}$ and $GDPpc_{i,t}$ decreases by 0.04 between $t = 2019$ and $t = 2020$, due to the fact that the series $NW_{i,t}$ are close to the maximum and therefore they present margins of lower growth, as presented in Fig. 7.

It can be seen that for both values of t, there is an inverse correlation between the two parameters. This shows that the number of people accessing internet are inversely

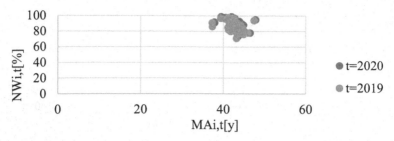

Fig. 7. Scatter plot between $NW_{i,t}$ and $MA_{i,t}$

correlated with the average age of a country's residents, while the respective values is higher for younger countries. Note that in this case, between $t = 2019$ and $t = 2020$, there was a simultaneous shift in the series upwards, with the generalised increase in $NW_{i,t}$, and to the right, indicating an average increase in $MA_{i,t}$ for the countries considered. One country that deviates significantly from this distribution is Germany, which has high values for mean age compared to high values for internet access as well. As far as the fifth correlation is concerned, it is presented in Fig. 8.

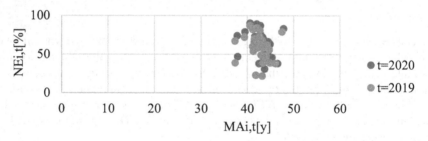

Fig. 8. Scatter plot between $NE_{i,t}$ and $MA_{i,t}$

The scatter plot shows a negative correlation between the two variables. Again, the larger magnitude of the NEi,t values is reflected in a wider distribution, covering a much wider range of y than the same range for the NWi,t value. However, the correlation seems to exist, but with less regularity: the curve is almost vertical and there are more outsiders than in the previous case.

Looking at the graph, however, the median age of a country can influence online purchases. The curve between years 2019 and 2020 presents a substantial increase in value with respect to the y-axis. Therefore, we proceeded with the evaluation of the r coefficient, obtaining the following from Table 4.

All values are negative, which means that the variables are linearly anti-correlated. However, we have proven that the correlation values between $NW_{i,t}$ and $MA_{i,t}$ are, for both t values, higher than the corresponding r values between $NE_{i,t}$ and $MA_{i,t}$, thus revealing a stronger negative link for online logins with average age. Moreover, between years 2019 and 2020, the values undergo a significant negative variation.

Table 4. Value of r between $NW_{i,t}/NE_{i,t}$ and $MA_{i,t}$

	$MA_{i,t}$	
r	$t = 2019$	$t = 2020$
$NW_{i,t}$	−0,30	−0,45
$NE_{i,t}$	−0,16	−0,28

The next step is to explore the correlation between the e-commerce propensity variables and the unemployment rate of country i. The objective is to identify whether a form of linear relationship can emerge between the state of a country's labor market and the country's e-commerce conditions, resulting Fig. 9.

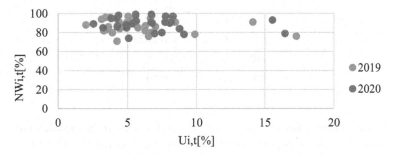

Fig. 9. Scatter plot between $NW_{i,t}$ and $U_{i,t}$

The scatter plot between $NW_{i,t}$ and $U_{i,t}$ does not seem to present a clear correlation between the two variables considered.

The variable $U_{i,t}$ has a large range, going from very low values of the order of 3.5% to very high values that exceed 15%.

Furthermore, the COVID-19 pandemic has had different effects on different countries, largely causing an increase in the percentage of unemployed, generating, in the graph under examination, a shift to the right of the series, as presented in Fig. 10.

The scatter plot between $NE_{i,t}$ and $U_{i,t}$ represented in Fig. 8 is rather similar, in terms of their characteristics, to the diagram represented in Fig. 7.

Even in this case, as for all the other $NE_{i,t}$ plots, the greater range implies a greater dispersion of the values. Compared to the previous case, Fig. 8 presents a form of negative linear correlation between the two values.

This fact could mean that higher unemployment would generate fewer online purchases, and this would be compatible with the already demonstrated positive correlation between $NE_{i,t}$ and $GDPpc_{i,t}$.

Correlation r is evaluated for the pairs considered as t varies. Results are presented in Table 5.

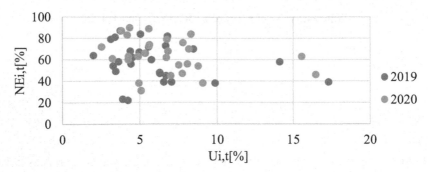

Fig. 10. Scatter plot between $NE_{i,t}$ and Ui,t

Table 5. Value of r between $NW_{i,t}/NE_{i,t}$ and $U_{i,t}$

r	$U_{i,t}$	
	$t = 2019$	$t = 2020$
$NW_{i,t}$	−0,21	−0,16
$NE_{i,t}$	−0,24	−0,29

The values of the coefficients are negative for all four cases considered; it is confirmed that $NE_{i,t}$ and $U_{i,t}$ have a negative correlation, but it is clarified that also the pair $NW_{i,t}$ and $U_{i,t}$ has a weak linear anticorrelation.

However, to confirm the considerations previously hypothesized, the values of the correlation $NW_{i,t}-U_{i,t}$ is, in absolute value, lower than the corresponding values of r for $NE_{i,t}-U_{i,t}$.

Furthermore, while for $NW_{i,t}-U_{i,t}$ there is a slight decrease in the absolute value of r, due to the fact that $NW_{i,t}$ has lower growth margins, in the case of $NE_{i,t}-U_{i,t}$ there is an increase in absolute value of r between $t = 2019$ and $t = 2020$.

The last two correlations concerned the variables in the first section of Table 1 with respect to the percentage of graduates aged 15–64, as presented Fig. 11.

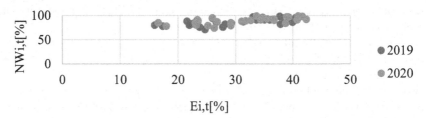

Fig. 11. Scatter plot between $NW_{i,t}$ and $E_{i,t}$

The graph presented in Fig. 11 shows a similar trend to other correlations already described with a narrow range of values for *y* and a range of high values for *x* due to the great variability of the percentage of graduates in the different European countries. The distributions, for both years, seem to show a marked positive correlation; the change between 2019 and 2020 is linked to the increase in the value of $NW_{i,t}$, which is close to reaching its maximum for the reasons described above, and to the increase in $E_{i,t}$ in most of the countries considered. Finally, the last correlation is presented in Fig. 12.

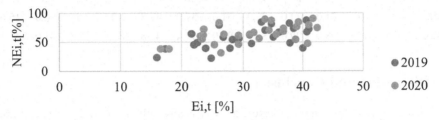

Fig. 12. Scatter plot between $NE_{i,t}$ and $E_{i,t}$

This diagram has the same characteristics as the diagrams where the variable $NE_{i,t}$ was examined. Both series considered for the two time values $t = 2019$ and $t = 2020$, have more dispersive values than in the previous case represented in Fig. 10. At the same time, however, a correlation is identified, albeit less pronounced than in the previously analysed case. These two graphs would therefore seem to present that, in countries where there is a higher percentage of university graduates in the population, the residents tend to use more online shopping and more online access. The considerations made through the calculation of r for the pairs of variables identified are verified. The results are summarised in Table 6.

Table 6. Value of r between $NW_{i,t}/NE_{i,t}$ and $E_{i,t}$

r	$E_{i,t}$	
	$t = 2019$	$t = 2020$
$NW_{i,t}$	0,67	0,63
$NE_{i,t}$	0,58	0,55

A linear correlation for the two pairs of variables considered when time varies is thus evident.

To confirm the hypotheses made previously, we note that, for each value of t, r is greater for the pair $(NW_{i,t})-(E_{i,t})$ than for the pair $(NE_{i,t})-(E_{i,t})$ confirming thus that the correlation between the behaviour of the percentage of graduates is more marked with access to the internet than with purchases on the internet. Finally, Table 7 is given as a summary of the values in 2019 and 2020 relating to the mean values (A.V.), standard deviation (S.D), maximum (Max) and minimum (Min) value of each variable analysed.

Table 7. Trends of examined variables

	$GDP_{pci,t}$		$Nw_{i,t}$		$Ne_{i,t}$		$Ma_{i,t}$		$U_{i,t}$		$E_{i,t}$	
Year	2019	2020	2019	2020	2019	2020	2019	2020	2019	2020	2019	2020
A.V	47,5	44,5	87,1	89,0	58,2	64,0	42,5	42,9	6,0	6,7	30,6	31,5
S.D	19,7	19,1	7,3	6,7	17,7	16,0	2,2	2,3	3,3	3,2	7,4	7,4
Min	24,2	20,0	71,0	74,0	22,0	31,0	37,3	37,8	2,0	2,5	16,0	16,6
Max	120,5	112,9	98,0	99,0	87,0	90,0	47,4	47,8	17,3	16,5	41,0	42,4

4   Discussion and Conclusion

The perception of shopping as a leisure activity really only arose in the '80s and '90s, when leisure time and disposable income increased rapidly following an economic boom accompanied by a large flow of credit, which defined that era, creating habits as shopping trips mainly for people living in the richest countries of Europe. Consumer spending has become an extremely important component to be analysed when examining the overall state of an economy and its future prospects.

People during the COVID-19 pandemic had to spend a lot of time at home due to the restriction measures applied resulting the implementation of new and in some cases innovative solutions such as teleworking and distance learning. Inevitably people turned to online purchasing to cover their needs, basic or not.

In Europe, e-commerce has grown significantly during recent years and some of the world's most sophisticated e-commerce markets are located in the EU-27, such as France and the Netherlands. E-commerce has passed from the stage of being a trend to a new independent market which year by year becomes stronger and larger, affecting people's mobility and retail sector's operational characteristics. The growth of B2C (Business to Consumer) also has a social and economic impact that will grow in the coming years. The current study lays the foundations for a preliminary statistical survey that considered 27 European countries and the UK in order to assess the possible correlations between variables that often characterise the demand for mobility from a socio-demographic point of view and variables related to the use of the Internet and e-commerce. Rapid spread of e-commerce has had an impact on the liveability of our cities, where the sustainable and resilient development of local communities are two of the main objectives for various governments in order to guide the purchasing sector towards an effective and efficient model and towards an overall redevelopment of the sector itself. The results of the research carried out showed a direct proportionality between the propensity to buy online and internet access, since the greater availability of the network (e.g. the recent 5G) together with the free spread of Wi-Fi services mean that an increasingly large population can use this communication channel. The COVID-19 pandemic has affected the correlation of the gross domestic product variable associated with internet and e-commerce use. The scatter plots presented on the above, a direct proportionality between certain correlations which could lead to a post-pandemic modification of travel habits and motivations, generating a reorganisation of general urban mobility, reducing home-shopping trips and also the possible relocation of new commercial areas. Local authorities will have to examine closely and through time the evolution of e-commerce, in order to design and implement new rules, aiming to integrate goods' delivery service with all other modes of transport, without ignoring at the same time the upturn in traffic already under way. Logistics operators will be called upon to be more sustainable by introducing, for example, the use of low-impact environmental-friendly vehicles. The development of e-commerce cannot disregard the definition of the right logistics' strategy, as it affects costs, consumer perception and satisfaction. The main consideration is that the major e-commerce players continue to move up the service benchmarks in B2C product delivery (e.g. home delivery).In the future, the distance between producers to consumers could become shorter, driving many countries to gear up in order to meet domestic demand. For e-commerce, the future of logistics will consist of the development of flexible and customised shipping solutions, tailored to the specific needs of individual e-shoppers and the definition of a calendar based on hourly (and no longer simply weekly or monthly) delivery times and/or shortened delivery times. Furthermore, the supply chain and the city logistic sector is expected to be modified as currently existing links might disappear or be transformed. Retail shops won't have to keep stocked products, urban consolidation centers might be upgraded as an intermediate link of the supply chain and overall last mile delivery will have to be reorganized to cover the needs of the consumers. Supply chain will have to be re-organized and even perhaps re-invented, without diverging from one of its primary targets, which is to become sustainable. Although the last years, environmental friendly vehicles were introduced as a possible solution for the last mile delivery, the last two years, drones have become for researchers the new favourite transport mode, combining sustainability, speed, low cost and reliability, as new technologies (i.e. 5G mobile networks) emerge. These new types of delivery bring new business models to the forefront which could make possible what seemed unthinkable only a few years ago. E-commerce from the beginning, was relying to the fast evolution of technology in order to grow up and increase its share. COVID-19 pandemic forced the majority of people to find solutions through new technologies, speeding up the adoption of e-commerce not only as an inevitable choice by the consumers but also as a preferable one.

References

1. Horvath, P.: CompuServe (1996). https://doi.org/10.1007/978-3-663-07679-7_3. https://en.wikipedia.org/wiki/CompuServe
2. https://www.bigcommerce.com/articles/ecommerce/#ecommerce-timeline
3. Wymbs, C.: How e-commerce is transforming and internationalizing service industries. J. Serv. Market. **14**, 463 (2000)
4. Vladimir, Z.: Electronic commerce: structures and issues. Int. J. Electron. Commer. **1**(1), 3–23 (1996)
5. Introduction to PayPal. In: Pro PayPal E-Commerce (2007). Apress. https://doi.org/10.1007/978-1-4302-0353-7_1
6. Lin, M.: Alibaba and Tencent Continued (2021). https://doi.org/10.13140/RG.2.2.13096.70406
7. Schmuck, R., Benke, M.: An overview of innovation strategies and the case of Alibaba. Procedia Manuf. **51**, 1259–1266 (2020). https://doi.org/10.1016/j.promfg.2020.10.176

8. Киш, Л.М.: Adaptation of b2c e-commerce to the conditions of the COVID-19 pandemic. East European Sci. J. **12**(64), 4+14–19 (2020)

9. Maamar, Z.: Commerce, e-commerce, and m-commerce: what comes next? Commun. ACM **46**(12), 251–257 (2003)

10. Niranjanamurthy, M., Kavyashree, N., Jagannath, S., Chahar, D.: Analysis of e-commerce and m-commerce: advantages, limitations and security issues. Int. J. Adv. Res. Comput. Commun. Eng. **2**(6), 2360–2370 (2013)

11. Tran, H.: From E-Commerce to M-Commerce. J. Textile Sci. Fashion Technol. 6 (2020). https://doi.org/10.33552/JTSFT.2020.06.000630.

12. Fong, A., Hui, S.: From E-Commerce to M-Commerce (2014)https://doi.org/10.1002/978047 0030851.ch8

13. Jelassi, T., Martínez-López, F.: Moving from Wired e-Commerce to Mobile e-Commerce and U-Commerce.In: Strategies for e-Business. Classroom Companion: Business. Springer, Cham (2020) https://doi.org/10.1007/978-3-030-48950-2_12

14. Austin, L., King, C.P., Christopher, N., Judith, B.: Measuring retail e-commerce sales (2021)

15. Sayyida, S., Hartini, S., Gunawan, S., Husin, S.: The Impact of the COVID-19 Pandemic on Retail Consumer Behavior. Aptisi Trans. Manage. (ATM) **5**, 79–88 (2021). https://doi.org/10.33050/atm.v5i1.1497.

16. Aydoğan, S.: COVID-19 and E Commerce (2020)

17. Boyaci G., Cennet, I., Salam, C., Ooi Galanakis, C.: Transformation of the food sector: security and resilience during the COVID-19 pandemic. Foods **10**, 497 (2021)https://doi.org/10.3390/foods10030497

18. Fernández R. (2020). https://www.statista.com/statistics/1115549/visited-pharmacy-web sites-during-the-coronavirus-lockdown-in-spain-january-to-march/

19. Harrisson, B., Jean, P., Dahl, B.: COVID-19 & Ecommerce In: Canada - A Performance Index From 50 Online Stores (2020)

20. Tanna, J.: E-commerce growth In: International Market (2021)

21. Vulusi, K.: E-commerce Growth in India: a study and the potential of its future (2020)

22. Alfonso, V., Boar, C., Frost, J., Gambacorta, L., Liu, J.: "E-Commerce in the pandemic and beyond", Report No 36 published by the Banks for International Settlements (2021). https://www.bis.org/publ/bisbull36.pdf

23. Impact of the Coronavirus on e-commerce, Survey Results Report, Ecommerce Europe (2021). https://www.ecommerce-europe.eu/wp-content/uploads/2021/01/Coronavirus-Sur vey-Report-January-2021.pdf

24. Hudda, N., Simon, M.C., Patton, A.P., Durant, J.L.: Reductions in traffic-related black carbon and ultrafine particle number concentrations in an urban neighborhood during the COVID-19 pandemic. Sci. Total Environ. **742**, 140931 (2020)

25. Moslem, S., Campisi, T., Szmelter-Jarosz, A., Duleba, S., Nahiduzzaman, K.M., Tesoriere, G.: Best–worst method for modelling mobility choice after COVID-19: evidence from Italy. Sustainability **12**(17), 6824 (2020)

26. Campisi, T., Basbas, S., Skoufas, A., Akgün, N., Ticali, D., Tesoriere, G.: The Impact of COVID-19 pandemic on the resilience of sustainable mobility in sicily. Sustainability **12**(21), 8829 (2020)

27. Falchetta, G., Noussan, M.: The Impact of COVID-19 on Transport Demand, Modal Choices, and Sectoral Energy Consumption in Europe (2020)

28. Chinazzi, M., et al.: The effect of travel restrictions on the spread of the 2019 novel coronavirus (COVID-19) outbreak. Science **368**(6489), 395–400 (2020)

29. Abdullah, M., Dias, C., Muley, D., Shahin, Md.: Exploring the impacts of COVID-19 on travel behavior and mode preferences. Transp. Res. Interdiscip. Perspect. **8**, 100255 (2020). ISSN 2590-1982https://doi.org/10.1016/j.trip.2020.100255

30. Drift, S., Wismans, L., Kalter, M.-J.: Changing mobility patterns in the Netherlands during COVID-19 outbreak. J. Loc. Based Serv. 1–24(2021) https://doi.org/10.1080/17489725.2021.1876259
31. Choi, W., Shim, E.: Optimal strategies for social distancing and testing to control COVID-19. J. Theor. Biol. 512, 110568 (2021). ISSN 0022-5193https://doi.org/10.1016/j.jtbi.2020.110568
32. Tirachini, A., Cats, O.: COVID-19 and public transportation: current assessment, prospects, and research needs. J. Public Transp. **22**(1), 1 (2020)
33. Basbas, S.: The Impact of E-commerce on Transport. In: WIT Transactions on Information and Communication Technologies, vol. 36. WIT Press (2006). ISSN 1743-3517 (on-line)https://doi.org/10.2495/IS060331
34. https://ec.europa.eu/eurostat/statistics-explained/index.php?title=E-commerce_statistics
35. https://ec.europa.eu/eurostat/statistics-explained/index.php?title=E-commerce_statistics_for_individuals

The Impact of COVID-19 Pandemic on the Perception of Public Transportation Users in Amman (Jordan)

Motasem Darwish[1](✉) ⓘ, Tiziana Campisi[2] ⓘ, and Ghaida Abu Rumman[3]

[1] Department of Civil Engineering, Middle East University, Amman 11831, Jordan
Mdarwish@meu.edu.jo
[2] Faculty of Engineering and Architecture, University of Enna Kore, Cittadella Universitaria, 94100 Enna, Italy
[3] Department of Civil Engineering, Isra University, Amman 11622, Jordan

Abstract. The global pandemic of COVID-19 has a significant impact on the public transportation (PT) sector and users' perception. This study aimed to assess the public transportation users' perceptions, needs, and preferences during the COVID-19 pandemic in Amman, Jordan. A cross-sectional correlation design was used to recruit 510 participants between March 2020 - October 2020. We used an online survey that included the users' sociodemographic data sheet, frequency of using PT and other traveling modes, and travelers' perception towards PT before and after the pandemic. This study indicated a dramatic decrease in using PT during the pandemic, reaching 50%, and a reduction in the frequency of PT daily usage from 16% to 4%, however, all other traveling modes experienced an increase. In addition, 50% of the participants indicated that social distancing was the most important criterion to choose the mode of traveling during the pandemic, while equally 22% of the participants considered the duration and cost before traveling as an important criterion. A significant correlation between the frequency of using PT during the pandemic and anxiety was observed. However, the frequency of using PT or walking indicated a significant correlation with education levels only before the pandemic. Besides, 50% and 40% of the participants reported that neither public transportation nor walking infrastructure conditions were appropriate, respectively. The study yielded important empirical data that can be employed in PT planning and understanding users' preferences during this pandemic and for anticipated coming waves.

Keywords: Public Transportation · COVID-19 · Amman · Travelers' perception

1 Introduction

Late 2019, a cluster of pneumonia cases with unidentifiable causes was reported in Wuhan, China, which was attributed later to the novel Coronavirus (COVID-19) [1]. On

The original version of this chapter was revised: Table 5 on Page 396 was corrected. The statement "(before the pandemic)" has been removed from the headings "Number of walking days", "Number of days using the private car", "Number of days using public transportation", "Reasons for choosing the means of traveling". The correction to this chapter is available at
https://doi.org/10.1007/978-3-030-86979-3_51

March 11, 2020, the WHO announced the novel COVID-19 virus as "a global pandemic" after the spread of the virus to more than 200 countries, and urged governments to respond promptly to contain the virus spread.

Accordingly, governments implemented various actions and measures, such as but not limited to, social distancing, closing schools and universities, forcing online education, prohibiting public gathering, closing public places (libraries, religious places, cinemas), restricting private cars usage, constraining public transportation full capacity, banning air traveling, and imposing both: partial and complete lockdown. These measures have imposed unprecedented challenges on healthcare systems, economic, industrial, aviation, and transport sectors on a global scale. During the pandemic, urban traveling and transport sectors have been hit severely due to the enforced restrictions (e.g., reduction of operation capacity, transit stations closure), which aimed to contain the virus transmission. Literature has reported that public transportation was affected the most [2, 3], in which 80% to 90% reduction rate was observed in various major cities [4].

Various studies have highlighted the need for users to walk or cycle more, especially in pandemic areas such as China or Italy [5]. Other studies have promoted the development of strategies to disseminate sustainable and resilient forms of mobility[6, 7]. Furthermore, the need to promote safe public transport use during the current and any possible future pandemics[8], and the need for sustainable and safe forms of shared mobility [9], highlighted the importance of implementing new policies. However, the pandemic also results in a shift in traveling modes, leading to increased use of private transportation than public means. Subsequently, reduced and disrupted service supply has taken place, which in turn led to limited capacity, longer waiting times, and the increasing concerns of unavoidable close contact in public transportation and stations [10]. Figure 1 shows the noticeable variation in using public transportation stations based on Google mobility reports data in 4 cities: Dubai, Amman, Manchester, and Rome [11].

The figure illustrates the percentage changes for each day compared to the median value for the corresponding day of the week over 5 weeks (January 3–February 6, 2020).

The authorities' recommendations for using public transportation during the pandemic varied across the countries based on factors such as cultural habits, the extent of transit usage, the prevalence of the pandemic, and socio-economic factors. For instance, the United Kingdom and Netherland advised the public to avoid using mass transit as possible [12, 13]. Sweden issued a similar statement and operated public transit at or near nominal levels to reduce the infection rate. The USA encouraged employers to offer incentives for using other transportation modes such as bikes, private cars, and walking [14]. New South Wales, Australia reduced the operating capacity dramatically to ensure social distancing [15].

Nonetheless, other countries adopted various adaptation techniques to ensure the availability and continuity of public transportation. In China, the government reduced the buses' capacity to 50% [16], while in South Korea, the buses and metro guidelines required travelers to wear masks at all times, besides, provided auto train operation, and avoided metro stopping at congested stations [17]. Other countries such as Taiwan requested only wearing masks and prohibited travelers from talking to each other to minimize contagious risks [18, 19]. However, in Jordan and United Arab Emirates (UAE), public transit was prohibited during the lockdown and resumed when the lockdown was eased, which took place under two compulsory conditions including: buses operate at 50% capacity, and travelers put on masks at all times [20, 21].

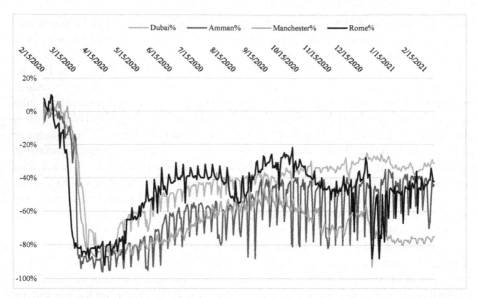

Fig. 1. The percentage changes for each day in using public transportation stations compared to the median value for the corresponding day of the week, over 5 weeks (January 3–February 6, 2020) [11].

In Jordan, the first COVID-19 case was reported on March 2, 2020, followed by several cases [22, 23]. Subsequently, the government established rules and recommendations, including coordinating public campaigns (as from March 6), borders' closure (as from March 17), school and workplace shutdown, complete lockdown, banning private car use, and inter- governorate travel. It is worth mentioning that people were allowed to move out to buy essentials on foot with a time window between 10 am and 6 pm (from March 18) [23]. The complete and strict lockdown lasted in action until late April (April 30). Afterward, the government eased the lockdown and allowed many sectors to resume work except those with large human workforces in which social distancing was difficult to maintain (i.e., schools, universities, gyms, public gatherings, church, and mosque). However, curfew remained active after 6 pm up to 6 am, and on Fridays [24]. Recently, the Jordanian government modified the curfew hours to be from 10 pm to 6 am, while the restriction on the sectors involving large gatherings remained with no change [25]. Furthermore, various actions were imposed on public transportation, such as reducing operating capacity, compulsory mask-wearing policy, social distancing (1–2 m distance), disinfecting vehicles and transportation modes, besides installing transparent barriers between the driver and the passengers in all taxis [25]. Public transportation in Jordan has encountered a wide range of challenges, such as but not limited to a lack of organizational legislation and service providers [26]. The Jordanian government has invested minimal budget in the public transportation sector compared to other sectors. For example, the government has paid more attention to security, defense, education, health, and investment domains [26, 27]. Furthermore, only

13% of the total trips in Amman, the capital and the most populated city in Jordan, are made by public transportation [26, 28]. Moreover, the government policies and regulations have fallen short in terms of supporting and promoting the use of public transportation [26]. Recent reports issued in 2017 stated that the public transportation sector was in need of complete structural reform to overcome major obstacles such as lack of subsidiary system, multiple public entities regulate the sector in Jordan, lack of professional transportation companies, besides the taxation regulations, which support individual ownership rather than large investments and companies [29]. Studies on public transportation in Jordan have concluded that the most challenging issues for public transportation in Jordan were the public sector and its related regulations, and the lack of technical and managerial capacities [26, 27, 29]. During the pandemic, few researchers have assessed the public transportation users patterns and the pandemic impact on the resilience of the transportation sector using either data sets based on aggregated and anonymized data from mobile phones such as Google mobility reports [30], and Apple Mobility reports [31], or national reports issued by local authorities [32]. In Italy, the analysis of a large-scale dataset on de-identified, geo-located smartphone users indicated a reduction of up to 50% of the total trips between Italian provinces, following the lockdown [33]. Beria and Lunkar [34], who used data provided by the "Facebook data for good" program, confirmed the reduction of internal mobility between Italian provinces and reported that there was a noticeable reduction in the number of trips that occurred in the earliest affected regions compared to central and south Italian cities. Tirachini and Cats [10], who investigated governments' response and the future research needs in terms of public transportation to adapt to the COVID-19 pandemic, reported that maintaining public transportation was the most challenging issue during pandemics, besides, the capability of transitioning to post-pandemic conditions would be a concern. Dzisi and Dei [35] indicated that public transportation was still perceived as a risky area for spreading the virus, although there was a high adherence rate from the government and operators to the safety guidelines. In Sicily (Italy), researchers reported that, during the pandemic, people showed positive opinions towards using micromobility (e,g, scooters) rather than shared public transportation[36]. In addition, investigating the ridership variation in public transportation in Sweden [37], the subway system in New York [38], bus ridership in Nashville and Chattanooga [39] confirmed a significant reduction in ridership during the pandemic, and that public health was a matter of concern in public transportations. Since March 2020, the dissemination of online surveys has made it possible to continue investigating travel habits while respecting travel restrictions imposed by some countries [9, 40]. The need to know users' travel habits during the various pandemic phases has led to several studies being carried out, investigating randomly or specific population groups. These activities make it possible to increase the democratic participation of the population in the planning activities of local authorities [41] and in improving the services offered by transport operators [42, 43]. Assessing the impact of the lockdown on population mobility is important to help characterize the changes in social dynamics that influenced the viral spread. Using travel patterns reconstructed from mobile phone trajectories, travel in France was assessed at both local and national scales [44]. In addition, studies analyzed various socio-demographic variables that have predicted public response to public transportation usages such as educational levels, income, age, workplace types, and gender [45, 46]. Although few studies investigated the pandemic impact on service users' behaviors, most of these studies took place in western communities in which generalizing the results to the Jordanian population could be difficult. Given that, we believe that the ill public transportation sector in Jordan suffers the most during the pandemic, yet, no study has investigated the impact of the pandemic on public transportation from the service users' perspectives. Hence, our study adds to the body of literature in terms of transportation sectors in the developing world. This study aims to investigate the impact of the COVID-19 pandemic and related governmental actions, such as the partial lockdown and social distancing, on the public transportation users' behavior in Amman- Jordan. Therefore, the various variables such as the mode of transportation, the frequency of usage of public transportation, and health variables were assessed using a structured questionnaire. The results of this timely study would be of importance to the authorities to improve public transportation regulations and planning guidelines in Amman, besides understanding users' preferences. In Sect. 2, we present the methods, statistical tools, and data used to explore and analyze public transportation preferences. Subsequently, the results are discussed in Sect. 3. Finally, we present our conclusions and recommendations in Sect. 4.

1.1 The Spread of Transportation Modes in Jordan Before the Pandemic

Jordan's transport systems have spread rapidly and in a heterogeneous manner, mostly favoring private transport. This is due to the fact that public transport has only in recent years been more widespread in the implementation of these services, starting from a condition of almost absence throughout the territory and reduced definition of the routes. The only public transport system consists of collective taxis (known as service taxis) and minibusses, both white in color. There are no timetables, and the buses only leave when they are full.

In general, collective taxis run on fixed routes, which are often not indicated on any 'official' chart at the stops, let alone online. Collective taxis travel only within cities, while minibusses also run short (Amman-Salt, Amman-Madaba, Amman-Irbid, etc.) and long (e.g., Amman-Aqaba) routes outside cities. The cost of collective taxis and minibusses is very low, ranging from about 0.35JD to 4JD. As of 2018, it seems that the public transport situation has improved before the spread of the pandemic. In the city of Amman, a new public bus service called Amman Bus has been introduced, covering the entire area of the capital, right up to the outlying areas. The new buses are larger and more modern than minibusses, and above all have fixed timetables and routes that can be easily consulted on a specific app. The cost of Amman Bus is slightly higher than that of minibusses, but still low. The coaches of the Jett Bus company cover most of the tourist routes in the country. Uber and Careem (Middle Eastern version of Uber) services are available throughout the country, but are much more frequent in Amman.

Finally, yellow taxis (in Amman) and green taxis (in Aqaba) are common. These are private taxis that operate in a similar fashion to taxis in Italy. They take passengers to any destinations, but are obviously much more expensive than collective taxis. The city of Amman has one of the highest rates of car ownership in Jordan (100 cars per 1,000 inhabitants), and the public transport sector has often been little used by the population. However, cuts in government subsidies on fuel prices, failure of the urban infrastructure to match growing demand, pollution, and congestion problems have revealed the need for a change in the city's management. Since 2006, the city has set up a transport planning department whose competencies cover all modes of transport, from private cars to public transport and pedestrians. In addition, a master plan called TMMP was drawn up with a time horizon of 2025, aiming at the deployment of BRT (Bus Rapid Transit) and LRT (Light Rail Transit) with a view to sustainable and resilient mobility. Unfortunately, the pandemic has reduced mobility and led people towards different mobility choices, as explained in the following paragraphs.

2 Methodology

This research aims to investigate the impact of COVID-19 on public transportation users' perceptions and preferences. Various variables representing socio-demographic, frequency of using transportation modes, and perception of transportation users and health variables were collected through a survey.

2.1 Design and Data Collection Procedure

This study used a cross-sectional correlational design, in which a standardized survey [36] was adopted to explore participants' responses toward forms of slow mobility (e.g., Scooters), public transportation (e.g., Taxis), and shared mobility (e.g., Buses) before and during the COVID-19 pandemic.

The survey was circulated online through the random selection of road users using the Google survey platform, bearing in mind that we uploaded a cover page with the survey. We explained the purpose of the study and added the researchers' details for any further questions. Also, we marked it as a required field, so each participant is required to read and sign it before he/she can start answering the survey. We also asked the participants not to write any identifying information to maintain the anonymity of the survey. We also made sure that every participant can submit only one survey, and the system denied more than one trial from the same participants.

2.2 Measurements

This study used a survey which has three sections: sociodemographic data questionnaire (gender, age, city of residence, educational levels, employment, working/education conditions, Average commuting distance), users' behaviors (walking habits and public transportation habits before and after the pandemic, respectively), and perceptions of onboard public transportation users to investigate the health and psychology response during traveling (anxiety, stress, health concerns). Tables 1, 2, and 3 show the questionnaire variables and description of each variables.

Table 1. Variables collected in the survey reflecting the socio-demographic during the COVID-19 pandemic.

Section 1: Sociodemographic variables		
Variable	Description	Value
Gender	Please specify your gender	Male: Female
Age group	Please specify your age group	18–25,26–40,41–55,56–70, Over 70
City of Residence	Are you a residence of Amman during Pandemic?	Yes: No
Education	Please specify your education	Primary School, Higher secondary, Bachelor, Master, Ph.D., Other
Employment	Please specify your employment status	Employee, Self Employed, Part-time employee, Unemployed, Student
Working/Education Condition	If you are an employee or a student, how do you work during a pandemic?	remote/online study, at office/school/shop
Average commuting distance	What is your average commuting distance in urban?	Less than 2 km,2–5 km,5–10 km, More than 10 km

2.3 Sample Size

In this research, 510 participants who lived in Amman-Jordan between March/2020 and October/2020 were recruited. The sample size was calculated based on a population of 4,500,000 [47], and to ensure reliable results. The sample size was considered appropriate for a margin of error equals 4.34%, at a significance level of a = 5% [48].

2.4 Statistical Analysis

The data were coded and entered using the Statistical Package for Social Sciences (IMB SPSS) version 21 For statistical analysis. Thereafter, the data were checked for any outliers and deviant cases to assure the data homogeneity. In addition, the Spearman correlation coefficient was applied to assess the direction and the magnitude of the relationship between the study-related variables. A p-value of < 0.5 was considered significant.

Table 2. Variables collected in the survey reflecting pre/post-pandemic travel behavior during the COVID-19 pandemic.

Section 2 Pre/ Post Pandemic traveling behavior

Variable	Description	Value
Travel pattern and Frequency	How do you prefer to travel to work/leisure before the COVID19 pandemic? How do you prefer to travel to work/leisure during the COVID19 pandemic?	1: Public transport 2: Micromobility (bicycle, scooter) 3: Walking 4: Private car
Walking	Frequency of walking per week before COVID-19 spread? (work/leisure) Frequency of walking per week during COVID-19 spread? (work/leisure)	1: Whole week (seven days) 2: 6 days 3: 5 days 4: Less than 5 days
Private car	Frequency of using private car per week before COVID-19 spread? (work/leisure) Frequency of using private car per week during COVID-19 spread? (work/leisure)	1: Whole week (seven days) 2: 6 days 3: 5 days 4: Less than 5 days
public transport	Frequency using public transport per week before COVID-19 spread? (work/leisure) Frequency using public transport during COVID-19 spread? (work/leisure)	1: Whole week (seven days) 2: 6 days 3: 5 days 4: Less than 5 days
Motivation	What is the main motivation while choosing the travel mode before the pandemic? What is the main motivation while choosing the travel mode during the pandemic?	1: Social distancing 2: Affordability 3: Travel time 4: Environmental concerns

Table 3. Variables collected in the survey reflecting public transportation users perception during the COVID-19 pandemic

Section 3 User Perception

Variable	Description	Value
Public transportation infrastructure level (conditions inside of the busses and stops)	On a scale from 1 to 5, where 1 corresponds to the best possible score and 5 to the worst, how do you evaluate the level of public transportation infrastructure in your city?	1 2 3 4 5
Health-related safety perception	What is your health-related safety perception on the availability of a healthy environment when using public transport during the COVID-19 pandemic?	1: Not safe 2: Slightly unsafe 3: Moderately safe 4: Safe 5: Very safe
Stress/anxiety	Do you feel stressed/anxious while using public transport during the COVID-19 pandemic?	1: Totally disagree 2: Disagree 3: Neutral 4: Agree 5: Totally agree
Public transportation use	If the PT infrastructure level increases in your city, do you consider using PT more during and after the pandemic?	1: Totally disagree 2: Disagree 3: Neutral 4: Agree 5: Totally agree
Walking infrastructure level	On a scale from 1 to 5, where 1 corresponds to the best possible score and 5 to the worst, how do you evaluate your city's level of walking infrastructure?	1 2 3 4 5
Walking	If the walking infrastructure level increases in your city, do you consider walking for a short distance more during and after pandemics?	1: Totally disagree 2: Disagree 3: Neutral 4: Agree 5: Totally agree
Remote working	Do you think that remote working/studying should remain after the pandemic?	1: Totally disagree 2: Disagree 3: Neutral 4: Agree 5: Totally agree

3 Results

In this research, a sample of 510 participants was recruited from the residents of Amman-Jordan during the first pandemic phase. The sample consisted of 348 (68.2%) males and 162 (31.8%) females. Data were collected using a survey circulated through Google forms and anonymous voluntary participation. The participants' age ranges from 18 t0 70, with noticeable participation from the age groups between 18–25 and 26–40, reaching up to 64% and 27%, respectively (Table 4). Furthermore, the high participation of the age group between 18–25 could be due to the age structure of Jordanian society, where 53% is under the age of 24 years [49]. Furthermore, 82% of the participants had a higher secondary certificate, and 81% worked remotely during the first wave of the COVID-19 outbreak. Additionally, 36% of the participants reported that they traveled more than 10 km/ day, while 24% traveled up to 2km/day. The results have indicated a noticeable reduction in public transportation usage during the COVID-19 pandemic. Table 5 indicates that users' preferences have changed during the first wave, where only 11% preferred public transportation for traveling mode during the pandemic compared to 20% before the pandemic. In contrast, a slight increase between 2% and 3% was noticed in relation to the usage of other modes of transportation such as cars, taxis, as well as walking.

The frequency of using public transportation declined noticeably; only 4% of the study participants used public transportation on a daily basis (7 days/week) compared to 16% before the pandemic. However, an increase from 60% to 78% in public transportation usage occurred for users who travel less than 5 days/ week.

Table 4. Frequency and percentage (%) of socio-demographic variables

Variable	Frequency (%)	Variable	Frequency (%)
Age (year)		Work conditions	
18–25, n (%)	324 (63.5%)	Virtual, n (%)	412 (80.8%)
26–40, n (%)	137(26.9%)	office, n (%)	98 (19.2%)
41–55, n (%)	42 (8.2%)	Education level	
56–70, n (%)	6 (1.4%)	Primary School	24 (4.7%)
Gender		Higher secondary	422 (82.7%)
Male, n (%)	348 (68.2%)	Bachelor	38 (7.5%)
Female, n (%)	162 (31.8%)	Master	9 (1.8%)
Employment status		Doctorate	14 (2.7%)
Freelance, n (%)	48 (9.4%)	Other	3 (0.6)
Student, n (%)	241 (47.3%)	Moving around	
Unemployed, n (%)	67 (13.1%)	<2 km, n (%)	123 (24.1%)
Fulltime work, n (%)	127 (24.9%)	2–5 km, n (%)	90 (17.6%)
Part time work, n (%)	27 (5.3%)	6–10 km, n (%)	115 (22.5%)
		>10 km, n (%)	182 (35.7%)

Similarly, for pre and post-pandemic travel behavior, the results shown in Table 5 were obtained.

Table 5. Frequency and percentage (%) of pre/post-pandemic travel behavior variables.

The means of transportation	Pre	Post
A cab, n (%)	53 (10.4%)	61(12.0%)
Private vehicle, n (%)	326 (63.9%)	345 (67.6%)
By foot, n (%)	26 (5.1%)	39 (7.6%)
Public transportation, n (%)	102 (20.0%)	56 (11.0%)
Others, n (%)	3 (0.6%)	9 (1.8%)
Number of walking days		
<5 day, n (%)	223 (43.7%)	308 (60.4%)
5 days, n (%)	99 (19.4%)	86 (16.9%)
6 days, n (%)	69 (13.5%)	65 (12.7%)
7 days, n (%)	119 (23.3%)	51 (10.0%)
Number of days using the private car		
<5 day, n (%)	164 (32.2%)	262 (51.4%)
5 days, n (%)	83 (16.3%)	84 (16.5%)
6 days, n (%)	64 (12.5%)	65 (12.7%)
7 days, n (%)	199 (39.0%)	99 (19.4%)
Number of days using public transportation		
<5 day, n (%)	306 (60.0%)	395 (77.5%)
5 days, n (%)	82 (16.1%)	49(9.6%)
6 days, n (%)	44 (8.6%)	46 (9.0%)
7 days, n (%)	78 (15.3%)	20 (3.9%)
Reasons for choosing the means of traveling		
Duration of traveling, n (%)	218 (42.7%)	115 (22.5%)
Social distancing, n (%)	59 (11.6%)	247 (48.4%)
Financial issues, n (%)	192 (37.6%)	112 (22.0%)
Environmental factors, n (%)	41 (8.0%)	36 (7.1%)

On the other hand, the results indicated that social distancing was the most important criterion to choose traveling mode during the pandemic, where almost 50% chose their travel mode based on social distancing adherence issues. However, in terms of trip duration as well as trip cost, 22% considered each criterion before traveling. Furthermore, before the pandemic, trip duration and trip cost were the most important criteria to select the traveling mode, where 43% and 37% of the participants considered these criteria respectively, while only 11% considered social distancing before choosing travel means.

A potential explanation for that is the serious consequences of COVID-19 on health. In addition, participants using their cars less than 5 days/week increased from 32% to 52% after the pandemic, with a slight increase in other categories (5 days/week and 6 days/week). However, the percentage of participants using cars every day (7days/week) reduced from 39% to 19%. This could be related to the governmental restriction on traveling during the weekends. On the other hand, a noticeable increase in participants walking habits to and from their work/ shopping locations for less than 5 days/ week, reaching up to 61% after the pandemic, compared to 43% before the pandemic. A possible explanation could be related to the restrictions that were put on transportations modes. Furthermore, the results in Table 6 indicate that 60% of users agree and totally agree that they felt anxious during their trips in public transportation. However, 60% and 80% of participants reported that they would agree and totally agree to use public transportation and walking as a travel mode if the infrastructure was improved, respectively.

This could be related to the nature of the spread of the COVID-19 virus. Keep in mind that 50% and 40% of the participants agreed (i.e., the selected value of 5), using a Likert scale from 1 to 5, that neither public transportation nor walking infrastructure statuses are appropriate, respectively. However, approximately 60% of the participants reported that public transportation lacked health conditions and selected 4 and 5 on a Likert scale (Table 7).

Table 6. Frequency and percentage (%) of public transportation user's perception during the COVID-19 pandemic.

	Totally disagree	Disagree	Neutral	Agree	Totally agree
Feeling anxious	37 (7.3%)	23 (4.5%)	136 (26.7%)	146 (28.6%)	168 (32.9%)
Using Public transportation (if infrastructure is improved)	38 (7.5%)	28 (5.5%)	129 (25.3%)	205 (40.2%)	110 (21.6%)
Walking (if infrastructure is improved)	22 (4.3%)	10 (2%)	78 (15.3%)	224 (43.9%)	176 (34.5%)

Finally, the correlation matrix (Table 8) indicated a significant relationship between PT using during the pandemic and anxiety, which agrees with the results of similar studies [50]. Moreover, the results indicated that the frequency of using PT or walking is significantly correlated to education levels only before the pandemic. These results might be attributed to the implementation of lockdown measures such as shifting the academic sector to online education. In addition, the results did not show any significant role for gender in determining the frequency of using travel mode neither before nor after the pandemic.

Table 7. Frequency and percentage (%) of public transportation user's perception during COVID-19 pandemic on Likert scale 1 to 5, where 1 corresponds to the best possible score and 5 to the worst.

	1	2	3	4	5
Public transportation Infrastructure level (Status) of appropriateness	22 (4.3%)	35 (6.9%)	88 (17.3%)	113 (22.2%)	252 (49.4%)
Walking Infrastructure level (Status) of appropriateness	29 (5.7%)	63 (12.4%)	99 (19.4%)	117 (22.9%)	202 (39.6%)
Health-related safety perception on using public transport during COVID-19 pandemic?	29 (5.7%)	46 (9%)	121 (23.7%)	116 (22.7%)	198 (38.8%)

Table 8. Correlation matrix between study-related variables

	1	2	3	4	5	6	7	8	9	10	11
1	1										
2	-0.074	1									
3	-.123**	.177**	1								
4	.097*	0.041	.866**	1							
5	0.009	-.091*	-0.045	-0.011	1						
6	-0.003	0.051	-0.085	-.094*	0.014	1					
7	0.074	0.017	-0.047	-0.02	.362**	.768**	1				
8	-0.027	-0.067	0.013	-0.01	.088*	-.160**	0.026	1			
9	-0.059	-.089*	0.021	0.02	-0.045	-.145**	-.123**	.334**	1		
10	-0.042	-0.07	-0.02	-0.014	0.008	-0.001	-0.006	.243**	.110*	1	
11	0.044	-0.065	0.039	0.035	-0.064	-0.073	-0.073	-0.036	-0.019	-.144**	1

1- Gender
2- Education Level
3- Age group
4- Employment status
5- Frequency of walking per week before COVID-19 spread? (work/leisure)
6- Frequency of walking per week during COVID-19 spread? (work/leisure)
7- Frequency of using private car per week before COVID-19 spread? (work/leisure)
8- Frequency of using private car per week during COVID-19 spread? (work/leisure)
9- Frequency using public transport per week before COVID-19 spread? (work/leisure)
10- Frequency using public transport per week during COVID-19 spread? (work/leisure)
11- Anxiety

4 Conclusion

During the COVID-19 pandemic, the transportation sector was affected dramatically, while people's mobility was reduced and challenged by the various implemented regulations. It is evident that people's use of public transport mode (i.e., busses) was reduced after the pandemic, while other traveling methods such as using private cars, taxis, or on foot have increased. Shared public transportation was the only travel mode which has a reduction of 50% in usage, while the usage of all other transportation modes was increased during the pandemic. This agrees with the user's main criterion for choosing traveling mode, which showed that considering social distancing increased from 11% before the pandemic to 50% after the pandemic.

Moreover, the results indicated a significant correlation between using PT and anxiety during the pandemic, which is mainly related to the increased risk of being infected in PT due to limited space. Furthermore, private cars are the most preferred method to travel in Amman, mostly due to the lack of proper walking and public transportation infrastructure, according to participants' perceptions. However, the percentage of travelers who travel to and from work/shopping centers on foot less than 5 days/week increased during the pandemic. This indicates the importance of improving the walking infrastructure, which would reduce the disease spread, and reduce the need to implement social distancing measures in public transportation.

Finally, people in Jordan were not sure that public transportation was safe; hence, actions are needed to regain people's confidence in public transportation safety. Current health and social distancing measures are not enough. The increasing importance of social distancing, health, and safety concerns in public transportation confirms the need for new designs and plans to reconstruct the transportation sector. Furthermore, this research uses a cross-sectional design, which precludes the cause and effect relationship. Hence, the generalizability of the results should be taken with caution. Although we believe our study yielded very important empirical data that can be used to implement future PT plans in Amman. The present work lays the foundations for further research steps: in particular, it will be possible to analyze the correlation between the parameters acquired by means of a bivariate assessment, and a second investigation step will cover the current period and provide a comparison of the data from the beginning to the end of the pandemic period.

Conflicts of Interest:.   The authors declare no conflict of interest.

References

1. World Health Organization. https://www.who.int/news/item/27-04-2020-who-timeline---cov id-19. Accessed 16 Jan 2020
2. Astroza, S., et al.: Mobility changes, teleworking, and remote communication during the COVID-19 Pandemic in Chile. Transport Findings (2020)
3. Molloy, J., Schatzmann, T., Schoeman, B., Tchervenkov, C., Hintermann, B., Axhausen, K.W.: Observed impacts of COVID-19 on travel behaviour in Switzerland based on a large GPS panel. Arbeitsberichte Verkehrs-und Raumplanung, vol. 1544 (2020)

4. Batsas, M.: Public transportation authorities and COVID-19: short to medium term impacts and interventions. International Association of Public Transport, Australia/New Zealand (2020)

5. Moslem, S., Campisi, T., Szmelter-Jarosz, A., Duleba, S., Nahiduzzaman, K.M., Tesoriere, G.: Best–worst method for modelling mobility choice after COVID-19: evidence from Italy. Sustainability **12**, 6824 (2020)

6. Moraci, F., Errigo, M.F., Fazia, C., Campisi, T., Castelli, F.: Cities under pressure: strategies and tools to face climate change and pandemic. Sustainability **12**, 7743 (2020)

7. Amekudzi-Kennedy, A., Labi, S., Woodall, B., Chester, M., Singh, P.: Reflections on pandemics, civil infrastructure and sustainable development: Five lessons from COVID-19 through the lens of transportation (2020)

8. Abdullah, M., Ali, N., Dias, C., Campisi, T., Javid, M.A.: exploring the traveler's intentions to use public transport during the COVID-19 pandemic while complying with precautionary measures. Appl. Sci. **11**, 3630 (2021)

9. Torrisi, V., Campisi, T., Inturri, G., Ignaccolo, M., Tesoriere, G.: Continue to share? An overview on italian travel behavior before and after the COVID-19 lockdown. AIP Conference Proceedings, vol. 2343, p. 090010 (2021)

10. Tirachini, A., Cats, O.: COVID-19 and public transportation: current assessment, prospects, and research needs. J. Public Transp. **22**, 1 (2020)

11. Google LLC. https://www.google.com/covid19/mobility. Accessed 10 Apr 2021

12. Department for Transport, United Kingdom. https://www.gov.uk/guidance/coronavirus-covid-19-safer-travel-guidance-for-passengers. Accessed 16 Jan 2021

13. Government of Netherland. https://www.government.nl/topics/coronavirus-covid-19. Accessed 16 Jan 2021

14. Centers for Disease Control and Prevention. https://www.cdc.gov/coronavirus/2019-ncov/community/office-buildings.html. Accessed 16 Jan 2021

15. Transport for NSW. https://transportnsw.info/covid-19. Accessed 16 Jan 2021

16. Shen, J., et al.: Prevention and control of COVID-19 in public transportation: experience from China. Environ. Pollut. **266**, 115291 (2020)

17. Park, J.: Changes in subway ridership in response to COVID-19 in Seoul, South Korea: implications for social distancing. Cureus **12**, e7668–e7668 (2020)

18. Basso, L.J., Sepúlveda, F., Silva, H.E.: Public Transport Policies after COVID-19 Confinement. Available at SSRN 3693098 (2020)

19. Acosta, M., Nestore, M.: Comparing public policy implementation in Taiwan and Vietnam in the early stages of the COVID-19 outbreak: a review. SocArXiv **2020**, 1–7 (2020)

20. Jabeen, A., Ansari, J., Ikram, A., Abbasi, S., Khan, M., Rathore, T., Safdar, M.: Comparison of actions taken by Pakistan, United Arab Emirates and Vietnam for COVID-19 prevention and control. Global Biosecurity 1, (2020)

21. Land transport regulatory commission. https://www.jordantimes.com/news/local/transport-sector-regulators-seek-adherence-public-health-measures. Accessed 16 Jan 2021

22. World Health Organization. https://www.who.int/countries/jor. Accessed 16 Jan 2021

23. Blavatnik School of Government. https://covidtracker.bsg.ox.ac.uk/. Accessed 16 Jan 2021

24. CNN. https://edition.cnn.com/2020/03/25/middleeast/jordan-lockdown-coronavirus-intl/index.html. Accessed 16 Jan 2021

25. Ministry of Health in Jordan. https://corona.moh.gov.jo/en/MediaCenter. Accessed 16 Jan 2021

26. Shbeeb, L.: A review of public transport service in Jordan: challenges and opportunities. Al-Balqa J. Res. Stud. البلقاء للبحوث والدراسات **21**, 4 (2018)

27. Imam, R.: Measuring public transport satisfaction from user surveys. Int. J. Busin. Manage. **9**, 106 (2014)

28. Makhamreha, Z., Almanasyeha, N.: Analyzing the state and pattern of urban growth and city planning in Amman using satellite images and GIS. Eur. J. Soc. Sci. **24**, 252–264 (2011)
29. CSBE: A policy study report and general review of the draft law for the regulation of the transportation of passengers of 2016. Center for the Study of the Built Environment (2017)
30. Wielechowski, M., Czech, K., Grzęda, Ł.: Decline in mobility: public transport in Poland in the time of the COVID-19 pandemic. Economies **8**, 78 (2020)
31. Hadjidemetriou, G.M., Sasidharan, M., Kouyialis, G., Parlikad, A.K.: The impact of government measures and human mobility trend on COVID-19 related deaths in the UK. Transp. Res. Interdiscip. Perspect. **6**, 100167 (2020)
32. Aloi, A., et al.: Effects of the COVID-19 lockdown on urban mobility: empirical evidence from the city of Santander (Spain). Sustainability **12**, 3870 (2020)
33. Pepe, E., Bajardi, P., Gauvin, L., Privitera, F., Lake, B., Cattuto, C., Tizzoni, M.: COVID-19 outbreak response: a first assessment of mobility changes in Italy following national lockdown. medRxiv (2020)
34. Beria, P., Lunkar, V.: Presence and mobility of the population during Covid-19 outbreak and lockdown in Italy. Sustain. Cities Soc. **65**, (2020)
35. Dzisi, E.K.J., Dei, O.A.: Adherence to social distancing and wearing of masks within public transportation during the COVID 19 pandemic. Transp. Res. Interdiscip. Perspect. **7**, 100191 (2020)
36. Campisi, T., Basbas, S., Skoufas, A., Akgün, N., Ticali, D., Tesoriere, G.: The impact of COVID-19 pandemic on the resilience of sustainable mobility in Sicily. Sustainability **12**, 8829 (2020)
37. Jenelius, E., Cebecauer, M.: Impacts of COVID-19 on public transport ridership in Sweden: analysis of ticket validations, sales and passenger counts. Transp. Res. Interdiscip. Perspect. **8**, 100242 (2020)
38. Teixeira, J.F., Lopes, M.: The link between bike sharing and subway use during the COVID-19 pandemic: the case-study of New York's Citi Bike. Transp. Res. Interdiscip. Perspect. **6**, 100166 (2020)
39. Wilbur, M., et al.: Impact of COVID-19 on Public Transit Accessibility and Ridership. arXiv preprint arXiv:2008.02413 (2020)
40. Zhang, J., Hayashi, Y., Frank, L.D.: COVID-19 and transport: Findings from a world-wide expert survey. Transp. Policy **103**, 68–85 (2021)
41. Campisi, T., Akgün, N., Ticali, D., Tesoriere, G.: Exploring public opinion on personal mobility vehicle use: a case study in Palermo Italy. Sustainability **12**, 5460 (2020)
42. Tesoriere, G., Campisi, T.: The benefit of engage the "Crowd" encouraging a bottom-up approach for shared mobility rating. In: International Conference on Computational Science and Its Applications, pp. 836–850. Springer, Cham (2020). https://doi.org/10.1007/978-3-030-58802-1_60
43. Campisi, T., Ignaccolo, M., Tesoriere, G., Inturri, G., Torrisi, V.: The evaluation of car-sharing to raise acceptance of electric vehicles: evidences from an italian survey among university students. SAE Technical Paper (2020)
44. Pullano, G., Valdano, E., Scarpa, N., Rubrichi, S., Colizza, V.: Population mobility reductions during COVID-19 epidemic in France under lockdown. MedRxiv (2020)
45. Almlöf, E., Rubensson, I., Cebecauer, M., Jenelius, E.: Who is still travelling by public transport during COVID-19? Socioeconomic factors explaining travel behaviour in stockholm based on smart card data. socioeconomic factors explaining travel behaviour in stockholm based on smart card data (September 8, 2020) (2020)
46. Bhaduri, E., Manoj, B.S., Wadud, Z., Goswami, A.K., Choudhury, C.F.: Modelling the effects of COVID-19 on travel mode choice behaviour in India. Transp. Res. Interdiscip. Perspect. **8**, 100273 (2020)

47. DFPS: Directorate of Family and Population Surveys: Estimated Population of the Kingdom by Governorate, Locality Sex and Households,2020 (2020)
48. Naing, L., Winn, T., Rusli, B.N.: Practical issues in calculating the sample size for prevalence studies. Arch. Orofac. Sci. **1**, 9–14 (2006)
49. https://www.cia.gov/the-world-factbook/countries/jordan/#people-and-society. Accessed 20 Jan 2021
50. Taubman – Ben-Ari, O., Chasson, M., Abu Sharkia, S., Weiss, E.: Distress and anxiety associated with COVID-19 among Jewish and Arab pregnant women in Israel. J. Reproduct. Infant Psychol. **38**, 340–348 (2020)

International Workshop on Geodesign in Decision Making: Meta Planning and Collaborative Design for Sustainable and Inclusive Development (GDM 2021)

Landscape Information Modelling to Improve Feedback in the Geodesign International Collaboration for Carbon Credit Enhancement in Metropolitan Regions – The Case Study of Fortaleza, Brazil

Newton Moura[(⊠)] [iD], Joana Guedes, Emiliano Cavalcante, Morganna Oliveira,
Ana Maia, Anne Castro, Eugênio Moreira[iD], Daniel Cardoso, and Vitor Sampaio[iD]

Universidade Federal do Ceará (UFC), Av. da Universidade 2890, Fortaleza, Brazil
newtonbecker@ufc.br

Abstract. Better landscape designs demand better landscape analysis and vice versa. At regional scale, this feedback demands precision and integration among multiple scales. This work prospects the potential of information modelling to improve Geodesign in decision making and collaborative design through increasing feedback. As a participant of the International Geodesign Collaboration (IGC) workshop "Trees for Metropolitan Regions", this research has been developed for the Metropolitan Region of Fortaleza (MRF), the 6th largest in Brazil, located on the Northeast coast, and aimed at increasing green areas for Carbon Credit (CC) purposes. This methodological research achieved a script for subsequently information modelling application, which will improve precision in the achievement and evaluation of pre-established goals.

Six methodological steps accomplished a selection of data for latter parametric modelling: 1. Reading enrichment and definition of the planning concept; 2. Division of the metropolitan region into Landscape Units (LU); 3. Selection of squared cut out samples for each LU; 4. Proposition of innovative solutions; 5. Design for CC increment through conservation, expansion, and creation of green areas; 6. Evaluation of CC enhancement and feedback. For the fifth step, three future scenarios have been designed, in 2035 and 2050: the traditional, the late adopter and the early adopter. Replicating designed green areas from samples to their respective LU resulted in a total CC increase of 33.19% for the traditional scenario, 44.29% for the late adopter and 87.71% for the early adopter, all for 2050, which goal has been established by the IGC at 30%. Information modelling, using the identified parameters in this work, may review, accelerate and improve these results. This improvement will be enhanced when precision of sample recognition is increased to define smaller cut out squares. With opportunities of resources for data processing and design, information modelling allows the design of samples on microscale to feedback regional planning, which leads to adaptive goals and to

Supported by International Geodesign Collaboration (IGC); Universidade Federal do Ceará (UFC); FUNCAP; UFMG (Contribution to the projects CNPq 401066/2016–9 and FAPEMIG PPM-00368–18).

© Springer Nature Switzerland AG 2021
O. Gervasi et al. (Eds.): ICCSA 2021, LNCS 12954, pp. 405–419, 2021.
https://doi.org/10.1007/978-3-030-86979-3_29

develop a valuable tool for integration among multiple scales through Landscape Information Modeling (LIM).

Keyword: Geodesign · Metropolitan region · Landscape information modelling · Carbon credit · Fortaleza

1 Introduction

Evaluations and actions on landscape have seized the opportunity of the current transformative era of science, technology and innovation (STI) [1]. Landscape has been assessed through mathematical and computational models as much as any built infrastructure, which has provided a quantifiable and technological approach [2]. Available computer aid, especially regarding information modelling, which intertwines graphic and data [3], has provided an evolving prospect to be explored in landscape planning and design. Beyond representation, accuracy and quantification, technology has enabled better inclusion, participation and understanding from multiple stakeholders, especially from the community. Landscape professionals are not working alone. They are listening better from diversity and justice.

Geodesign [4] is an ongoing method that benefits from digital technology to encourage inclusion and participation in landscape practices. As an interdisciplinary planning method that uses systems thinking, geospatial technologies, and community participation to address environmental, social, and governance issues throughout the planning process [5], Geodesign is the methodological approach that supports this research in the application of information modelling to landscape planning. Using the Metropolitan Region of Fortaleza (MRF) as a case study, which represents the complex social and environmental dynamics of a growing touristic coastal area in Brazil's Northeast, this work prospects the steps for the application of information modelling to enhance feedback between landscape analysis (input) and design (output). The theoretical and practical basis for this research evolved from a worldwide network workshop entitled "Trees for Metropolitan Regions", supported by International Geodesign Collaboration (IGC).

1.1 Geodesign for a Global Green Design

Geodesign is a co-creation method of analysis (Geo) and project (Design) through a series of landscape transformation studies. It offers multiple scenarios for collaborative negotiation and definition of the best predictable alternatives for what it defines as an early adaptive design, with preparedness for the urgent challenges of mankind, especially in the context of the urban environment, such as development, maintenance, and protection [6]. The purpose of this methodology is to support cooperation in the construction of ideas, seeking specific goals, and taking into account the diversity of views and values from different stakeholders.

The particular workshop promoted by IGC and presented in this paper targets a design on a global scale for 2050. It aims to identify suitable areas to plant one trillion trees within metropolitan regions worldwide and raise Carbon Credit (CC) by up to 30% through increasing green areas within the participant regions. For the case study of the MRF, the 6th largest in Brazil, the Geodesign Framework proposed by Steinitz [4] has been applied from the technical perspective of graduate and postgraduate students, professionals and researchers of Architecture and Urbanism and Environmental Engineering. A free digital platform for collaborative landscape analysis and proposal, developed in Brazil, the GisColab [7], was applied to accomplish the GeoDesign methodology. Considering the pandemic context of isolation, the platform supported very properly the discussions around the structuring and experimentation of an investigation process for improving studies in Geodesign, especially addressing the identified conflict of precision among multiple scales.

As a record of a methodological experimentation, the steps and procedures performed at this empirical work intend to subside the subsequent application of information modeling in planning (macro scale) and design (microscale), suitable for conservation, expansion and creation of green areas, with CC purposes at regional level. Based on theoretical approaches which support the greening of human settlements (Green Infrastructure and Nature Based Solutions), this research addresses parameters of urban sustainability that will be translated into design through application of information modeling to the landscape (Landscape Information Modelling - LIM).

1.2 Urbanization for Preservation: Green Infrastructure and Nature Based Solutions for a Sustainable Sprawl

Ecosystem services encompass a wide range of abiotic, biotic and cultural (ABC) functions and provide direct, economically and technically measurable benefits to man, classified as provision, control or culture [8]. At this work, CC is the ecosystem service addressed at metropolitan and global scale.

From ecosystem services, novel approaches have emerged to deal with numerous environmental, economic and social challenges, especially in large, growing cities. This paper focuses on green infrastructure (GI) and nature-based solutions (NBS) as premises to procedures for LIM exploration and respectively as the physical support and the techniques to enhance ecosystem services. For GI, this support consists of an interconnected green network which offers immediate and long-term solutions [9–12]. In the urban landscape, this network is a system of hubs (urban forests and parks), linear structures (such as street trees or water bodies) and stepping stone corridors (private gardens, green roofs) [12].

Inherently merged to GI, NBS are living solutions inspired by nature, that use nature and/or are supported by nature and perform a valid alternative for infrastructure development in new urbanization and infrastructure update in cities that are considering ways to rethink their time horizon and costs in maintaining them [13].

Currently, with most people in the world living in cities, the urban population is expected to continue growing [14] and, due to climate change, it is also predicted an increase in flood risk, heat stress, water shortage and air pollution [15]. Alves et al. [16] state that these environmental issues aggravate social and economic challenges and emphasize likely worst scenarios for large cities in developing countries, such as the case study of Fortaleza and its Metropolitan Region. Even with different severity, enhancement of livability, sustainability and resilience in cities is a global task, although addressed in local (neighborhood, regional, national) scale [10]. Facing these multiple threats, GI and NBS are novel approaches that can reduce vulnerability and increase resilience and environmental justice [17] as their practices promote an urban sprawl that encompasses multi-functional green. Urbanization, therefore, when based upon these more sustainable approaches, is no longer an adversary of conservation, but an ally that suits population growth and urban sprawl with preservation, expansion and creation of green areas and their potential ecosystem services.

This urbanization model demands accuracy to negotiate the (social and environmental) callings and the priorities of each place with specific goals of planning and design, such as raising CC through the increase of green, as addressed in this work. This negotiation is exactly what Geodesign promotes in a participative and collaborative fashion. In Geodesign, precision is achieved not only through accurate data, but also through better feedback between inputs (Geo) and outputs (Design). In the case study of the MRF, LIM is a promising method to improve this feedback.

1.3   Landscape Information Modelling (LIM) and Geodesign: Shared Benefits for the Global Metropolitan Green Through Parametric Modelling

According to Eastman, et al. [3], information modelling brings the asset of a single data source that comprises two main components: (i) a graphic reproduction of the geometry (model), from which we can extract the 2D technical drawings; (ii) an integrated database that stores all information, properties, relationships, and presentations.

Information modelling also incorporates dynamic processes to design and enables visualization of several different possibilities before assembling the optimal result. This dynamic emerges from parametric modeling based on the principle that each model is built with entities, whose attributes may be fixed or variable. Fixed attributes are controlled and correspond to form, materials, performance and costs [3]. Variable attributes or parameters are the rules that define the geometric behavior (lines, surfaces, volumes, and their associations) and non-geometric behavior (materials, quantitative, performance, etc.) of the fixed ones, allowing objects to be automatically adjusted according to controlling and context changing.

Towards a LIM perspective and strategy, considering the changing essence of landscape, parametric modelling is a promising tool not only to incorporate dynamism to the processes of landscape planning and design but to achieve dynamic models where interactions among landscape, society and environment may be more accurately represented by functions and algorithms. Since it shares the benefits of integration, participation and dynamics with Geodesign, parametric modelling becomes the category of LIM addressed in this research for precision in the definition of the most suitable areas for green enhancement within the MRF.

2   Methodology

General guidelines from IGC for this workshop followed the methodology from Steinitz [4], which is based on three fundamental steps called "iterations". The first "iteration" justifies the choice of the study area and "why" it is relevant: a complete study is made through models that describe the area and support the construction of proposals for alternative futures. The second "iteration" consists of a methodological review to identify possible adjustments. The third and last "iteration" aims to answer "what, where, and when".

For this research, the first "iteration" corresponded to the "Geodesign Workshop" held in March 2021, promoted by the Geoprocessing Lab of the School of Architecture of the Federal University of Minas Gerais (UFMG) in partnership with the School of Architecture and Urbanism of the Federal University of Ceará (UFC). For the second "iteration" two arrangements have been made: (i) the size of the study area (total area of approximately 7,434.91 million square kilometers and 4,137,561 inhabitants) brought to a division of the MRF into Landscape Units (LU) following the geosystems methodology that outline these units based on social and environmental homogeneity. [18]; (ii) the complexity of data - reinforced by diversity of them among the LU, and the constraint in the number of participants in the local workshop due to quarantine and pandemic aggravation in Brazil - pointed out that the steps for the application of Geodesign could benefit from information modelling to enhance precision of results. The third step consisted of the choice of smaller samples within each LU, in which the landscape design propositions were made for the early adapter future of the LU, in 2035 and 2050 at a more approximate scale (Fig. 1).

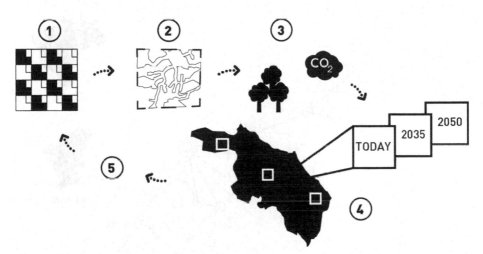

Fig. 1. Methodological diagram for LIM application to improve Geodesign feedback. 1 - Preliminary parameter for inputs. Layers used in spacial diagnosis; 2 - Proposed green areas; 3 - Giscolab platform algorithm; 4 - Percentage of carbon credit in different time scenarios; 5 - Future improvements in machine learning.

The MRF is characterized as a polarized metropolitan agglomeration, significative in the context of economic globalization. The contrast regarding development among Fortaleza and other cities of the MRF confirms the strong hierarchy present in the territory based on a center-periphery model. This condition is reinforced by the concentration of public investments in the capital. In the social sphere, the centralized model reveals itself not only as a producer of inequalities, but based on unequal relations: the exacerbated dimensions of the City of Fortaleza is product of a system that engenders the irreversible impoverishment of the population through mechanisms of dispossession. The current structure is strategic for a development based on the exportation of the territory resources, which creates a system of transference of surplus value from labor exploitation. Production, orchestrated in this way, is not aimed at local development or specialized in the needs of the region's inhabitants, but in exogenous demands [19].

Based on the approach that the current trend of urban sprawl and growth within the MRF is unsustainable and thus unsuitable to green enhancement, regional planning for the MRF examined the territory possibilities for a multi polarized economic and spatial configuration, and made it feasible with the least possible environmental impact (Fig. 2). Then a macro-scale approach was devised to address relevant issues at the micro-scale. According to Novotny; Ahern; Brown [20], this method supports understanding the formation processes and future results, making it possible to deal with information beyond human intentionality - the proposals were made according to local specificities. The following 6 steps attended the Geodesign and IGC guidelines and also incorporated adjustments from "iterations" to improve integration among multiple scales and to subsidize LIM application for precision enhancement in results.

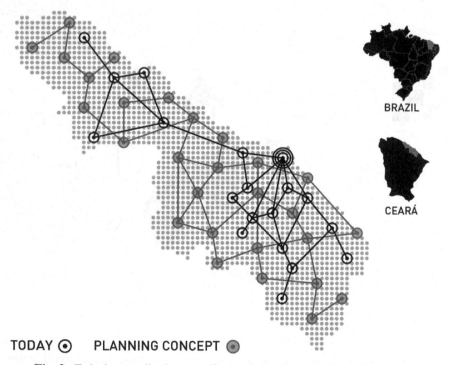

TODAY ⊙   PLANNING CONCEPT ◉

Fig. 2. Today's centralized metropolitan region and proposed planning concept

2.1 Reading Enrichment and Definition of the Planning Concept

This first step supports shared and participative comprehension of the case study region, and it consists of inserting pinned thematic annotations on a cartographic base of the MRF within the Giscolab platform. In order to elaborate these observations, the available 40 maps in the platform, organized in 10 categories (1. Vegetation/Green; 2. Agriculture; 3. Hydrography/Blue; 4. Housing; 5. Transport/Grey; 6. Institutions; 7. Industry and Commerce; 8. Energy; 9. Tourism and Recreation; 10. Carbon Credit) have been analyzed, individually and collectively. In the later, superpositions of maps granted better characterization of the area. Complementary information was also collected about the municipalities to understand their historical-economic-territorial formation and their main attributes and potentials.

2.2 Division of the Metropolitan Region into Landscape Units (LU)

The second stage was a methodological adjustment in an attempt to achieve Geodesign results within the programmed workshop period of April, 2021, Considering the extension of the case study, the complexity of data, the constraint in the number of workshop participants due to pandemic aggravation, and the lack of familiarity with other municipalities rather than Fortaleza, the region was divided into sub-areas. This resulted in the delimitation of 4 Landscape Units (LUs): 1. Coast; 2. Ridges; 3. Caatinga (Brazilian savannah); and 4. Productive macro region (Fig. 3).

This approach provides comprehension of the landscape as a mosaic of interacting systems. It also makes it possible to arrive at a more detailed analysis of the internal peculiarities of each LU, pointing out homogeneous and heterogeneous characteristics in each of them. This classification dialogues with the concept of geosystems [21].

The demarcation of the 4 LUs was based on the aerial images of the MRF available at Giscolab. These images were overlaid by layers of geographic and spatial data in order to cluster similarities and homogeneous biogeophysical aspects, as defined by MONTEZUMA et al. [22] and in accordance with Landscape Ecology principles:

"(...) set of elements from the biogeophysical support, which includes, in the first level of analysis: topographic features; hydrology; coverage and land uses, identifiable through the interpretation of satellite images, photos of overflights, and field surveys" [22]

The boundaries of the LUs were not restricted to the administrative limits of the municipalities within the MRF as an attempt to recognize the existing dynamics in the territories that behave beyond political demarcation. It also considered the elements of the urban structure, observed through the layers of data available on the Giscolab platform, such as the urban-rural relationship, population density data, land use, concentration of urban services, and branching of the road network. The 4 LUs are described below:

a) *Coast*:
   It displays two contrasting sectors, which appear to be temporal mirrors from one another. The Eastern territory is a large urban area which is widely occupied and

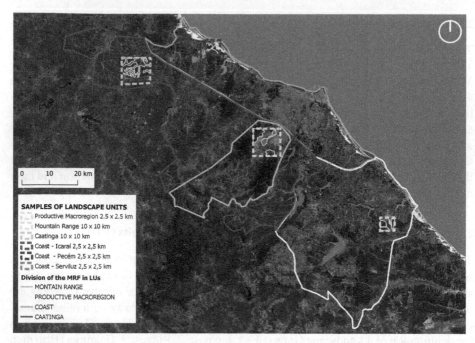

Fig. 3. Division of the Metropolitan Region of Fortaleza into Landscape Units

urbanized and concentrates most of the urban services and the higher population density (although it lacks qualified green open spaces and presents low environmental conditions). The Western portion presents a lower density and follows traditional planning, remaining a current vector of attraction for occupation.

b) *Ridges (mountain range)*

This LU has been delimited mainly based on its distinguishing topographic features. Much of this territory has steep slopes and masses of preserved vegetation. It is a region with high water provision relevance. Within them are located the springs of important water axes that flow towards the ocean and Fortaleza. Along them, landscape and territory adjusted themselves into river floodplains. There is a trend of the rapid advance of urban expansion onto this unit, with a mainly residential characteristic, expressed by many new ground divisions and real estate development.

c) *Caatinga (Brazilian savannah)*

This unit was defined by the area of occurrence of the biome of the same name in the territory, which is very well-preserved Brazilian savannah and surrounds the Ridges, expanding to the west of this LU. To the North, it plays an important role as a transition zone between the forested vegetation of the Ridges and the denser urban occupation of Fortaleza. To the West and South, this unit is still very little urbanized and is used mainly as an area for agricultural production, being shredded into large properties used for this purpose. The LU covers parts of 13 of the municipalities studied.

d) *Productive Macro Region*
   This area presents municipalities with similar characteristics related to agricultural and cattle production. Despite presenting large green patches of unoccupied soil, these are of low-quality vegetation, typical of degraded soil.

2.3 Selection of Samples for Each Landscape Unit

The methodological adjustment that divided the studied metropolitan region into LUs resulted in areas with yet large extensions to be analysed and designed during the workshop period. An additional arrangement was then made and the LUs were distributed among the workshop participants who assessed their potentials and conflicts in order to select cut out samples able to adequately represent scenarios of the region at the microscale. It was also a strategy to identify new places for decentralization, using existing urbanization processes as an opportunity for planning a sustainable growth of medium cities. This approach allowed a detailed reading of the current situation so that proposals and means of implementation could be developed for what was identified as the most critical situation at the site. Thus, the samples were proposed starting with 5×5 km area units, with multiples of this value being used when this size was insufficient to be representative.

2.4 Proposition of Innovative Solutions

The division into LUs served to identify the great heterogeneity of the MRF. Such recognition led to the selection of different proposals for each LU in the fourth stage to achieve the final objective: sustainable development. The proposals were chosen from the catalog of ideas provided by Geodesign so that they would be consistent with the local characteristics. From there, the fourth step was the graphic definition of the maps, through the creation of polygons and points, where the innovative proposals would be implemented. These proposals were organized around future scenarios for the years 2035 and 2050, using innovative urban design and planning solutions as support to achieve the desired carbon credit goals in each scenario. This design was later used to verify the influence of the innovative area on carbon credit generation in the fifth and last stage.

2.5 Design for Expansion of CC Through Conservation, Expansion, and Creation of Green Areas

The definition of a clear and specific objective made each LU to be worked according to its specificity for the same purpose, being able to promote the flexibility of the types of proposed interventions, selecting them according to their particularities (Fig. 4).

2.6 Evaluation of Carbon Credit Enhancement for Design Feedback

Giscolab provided an algorithmic script for latter parametric modelling that expressed for the participants the quantitative significance of the carbon's credit area proposed on the territory. It was possible to visualize its size in Km^2, participation in the MRF's

Synthesis of steps 2.3 , 2.4 , 2.5			
	Coast sample	Ridge sample	Caatinga sample	Productive macro region sample
2.3 Selection of samples	Due to the strong spatial contrasts 3 samples were selected for the complete depiction of the area . The Eastern sample is widely occupied and urbanized and concentrates most of the urban services and the higher population density. The Western sample has a lower density and follows traditional planning, remaining a current vector of attraction for occupation. With the exception of these two extremes, the area is mostly recognized as a touristic region because of its beaches, it was where the third sample was chosen.	The sample connects to the MRF through its water and road axes, both very capillarized. Presence of rocky formations and abundant water resources, besides being an indigenous reserve area. The growth of the urban agglomeration results in conflicts among the urban expansion area, the conservation units, and existing preservation areas.	Large area of expressive vegetation (Caatinga) with high metrics for CC and patches of agricultural land in contrast with consolidated and expansion area.	The predominant activity of land use in the LU is rural, with a large presence of agriculture and livestock. A large presence of farms in the area of agriculture and also expressive vegetation divided into two biomes: caatinga and coastal vegetation.
2.4 Proposition of innovative solutions	For 2035 and 2050, gradually create a more efficient flow structure, improving the connection with Fortaleza through a coastal corridor of railway lines and shared transportation. For new occupations and urban renewal, the adoption of self-sustainable compact neighborhoods was indicated. Linear parks and green corridors, permeable sidewalk materials, and green roofs on buildings were also proposed.	For 2035, the proposals aim to make the new urban occupations compatible, combining green areas with educational uses, ecotourism, water BMP, and restoration of riverside ecosystems. It is also proposed the exploitation of cultural traditions as economic possibilities and the creation of mixed neighborhoods, supported by more efficient public transportation and rooftop solar energy production. By 2050, it is proposed to intensify these strategies, adding more technological innovations.	For 2035 have a resilient and repair character for vegetation, the use of shared bicycles, the smart city consolidated, use of sunlight for irrigation and the presence of renewable energy. For 2050 the intensification of the proposals of 2050, solar roads, sharing taken to the local economy and sustainable neighborhoods.	It is expected that a low-density occupation pattern will continue, inserted in agricultural lands in a dispersed way, with sustainable productive sites. The denser urban core will expand along the existing roads and highways, and around the consolidated urban core to the north. As an alternative to extensive farming strategies such as food forests, carbon farmings, rewilding, and adoption of agrotourism are proposed as another income possibility for sustainable farms.
2.5 Design CC	In the consolidated area it is proposed to gradually substitute the gray infrastructure with an integrated system of green infrastructure, which would increase the urban vegetation cover along the roads, and connect parks and wetlands. In the developing area it is proposed the conservation of these connections in their natural state, besides the preservation of parks constituted by dune areas; the proposal of occupation in the territory through compact neighborhoods. In the more touristic area, it is proposed the expansion of its tourist vocation through ecotourism poles, based on the strategy of conservation of the existing green areas.	In traditional planning, this sample would suffer reduction and loss of quality of its green areas to give way to the expansion of urban patches, which would advance over forest masses and water resources. Managing conflicts through innovative proposals for 2035, it is possible to conserve and qualify the existing vegetation, adapting the urban expansion to a design that allows the maintenance of ecological services (protection and recovery of APPs, APA, and indigenous reserve). Strategies such as compact neighborhoods, permeabilization of urban soil, adoption of renewable energy, and shared transportation can enable balanced urban expansion. For 2050, new green areas are created in continuity with the 2035 proposals, improving the shape and core area of LUs.	For the traditional scenario it was proposed the consolidation of the area of urban expansion and the increase of the road network and the conservation of the vegetation close to water resources. In the 2035 scenario, in addition to the conservation of the vegetation stretches of the previous proposal, would be added links between the stretches forming a unit. In the final proposal for 2050, the quality of the CC would be taken into account with the reduction of the existing borders in the previous proposal.	It has been proposed solutions that integrate low-density urban life and expansion with agriculture and the rural identity of the place, such as food forests, agrotourism, carbon farming, and rewilding. Due to the nature of the proposals, green areas are dispersed throughout the territory, within productive lands, and promote a gradual recovery of areas that today are degraded by extensive farming. Thus, the sample would combine conservation, expansion, and creation of green areas overtime in the territory.

Fig. 4. Synthesis of steps 2.3, 2.4, 2.5.

goal, tree units and quantity of CO_2 below and above the ground. During the execution, the visualization of these numbers served as a guide for the intervention in such a way that was pursued that these areas overcome quantitatively the proportional goal for the MRF, even if it was roughly. Throughout the development of the traditional, 2035 and 2050 scenarios, it was possible to establish gradual vegetation masses, defining foremost interventions for 2035 and which ones could be added for the 2050 goal achievement.

After designing samples, the indexes informed by the platform were used to calculate the metrics impact in proportion to each landscape unit. We organized the data found into a table, through which the corresponding area in each LU was found. Hereupon, for the verification of the accomplishment of the goals from the algorithm, bigger polygons were drawn in the Giscolab platform with the corresponding area calculated on the table.

3 Results

3.1 Percentage of Carbon Credit Enhancement for the Traditional and Early Adapter Scenarios for 2035 and 2050

The traditional scenario kept the current logic of urban expansion consuming green areas - the proposal was just to maintain the existing vegetation. The results showed that the coast has the worst performance, reaching only about 1/3 of the proportional goal of the productive macroregion. On the productive macroregion and ridges LUs, the results are consequences of the low population density and urban expansion. Although similars, the indexes for coast and caatinga LUs are based on different reasons: while the coast reflects the real state exploitation; the caatinga is a consequence of the urban expansion and local type of vegetation.

In 2035, the inicial innovative proposals were adopted. The proportional goal of coast, caatinga and ridges LUs increased until similar levels of the productive macroregion - coast presented the greatest advance, almost triplicating its indexes. Observing the indexes of the productive macroregion it is seen that there was no significant advance - the goal adopted for the proposals there was to increase the quality of the existing vegetation.

Consolidation and expansion of the strategies adopted in 2035 were the approach for 2050 scenario. Advance appears in all the indexes of all the LUs: with exception of the caatinga sample, LUs almost doubled indexes.In coast LU, which comprehends the capital, the existence of areas already dense and consolidated motivated the adoption of radical strategies to recover nature, aligned with the general goal of MRF's decentralization. Analysing the caatinga and productive Macro region LUs, it is verified that even areas with good performance can be improved. The case of caatinga LU shows the difficulty faced by some biomes in reaching the established indexes (Fig. 5).

3.2 Design Parameters for Enhancement of Green Areas Thorough Conservation, Expansion or Creation

The following images represent schematic scenarios that synthesize the proposals prepared for the samples of each LU, illustrating temporally the implementation of carbon credit patches (Fig. 6).

		Coast	Hills	Caatinga	Productive Macro region
	LU area (km²)	892,59	952,37	2.210,67	1.793,26
	Sample area (km²)	75	100	100	25
Traditional	Proportional goal (%/Km²)	0,003	0,007	0,004	0,01
	Project CO2 captured ABOVE ground (MgC/Km²)	152	406,6	263,72	585,92
	Project CO2 captured BELOW ground (MgC/Km²)	80,27	214,72	139,27	309,42
	Project tree numbers (units/Km²)	10.158	27.174	17.625	39.158
2035	Proportional goal (%/Km²)	0,009	0,009	0,005	0,01
	Project CO2 captured ABOVE ground (MgC/Km²)	802,78	513,17	306,601	605,56
	Project CO2 captured BELOW ground (MgC/Km²)	423,94	271	161,91	319,79
	Project tree numbers (units/Km²)	34.925	34.296	20.491	40.471
2050	Proportional goal (%/Km²)	0,024	0,01	0,01	0,022
	Project CO2 captured ABOVE ground (MgC/Km²)	1.437,83	578,02	597,31	1.350,05
	Project CO2 captured BELOW ground (MgC/Km²)	759,31	305,25	315,43	712,95
	Project tree numbers (units/Km²)	96.094	38.630	39.919	90.227

Fig. 5. Calculation summary table

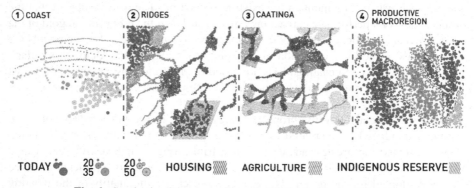

① COAST   ② RIDGES   ③ CAATINGA   ④ PRODUCTIVE MACROREGION

TODAY   20/35   20/50   HOUSING   AGRICULTURE   INDIGENOUS RESERVE

Fig. 6. Synthesis of the propositions in CC for the designed samples

3.3 Parameters for Latter Landscape Information Modelling Application

Steps for the Geodesign application resulted in the clustering of common parameters among all samples. These parameters were essential subsidies to design the green areas to be preserved, expanded or created. The analyzed mosaic of maps (Fig. 7) then consists of the script with a list of characteristics for subsequent application of an algorithm that is able to recognize data patterns for the most suitable places to green in a metropolitan region.

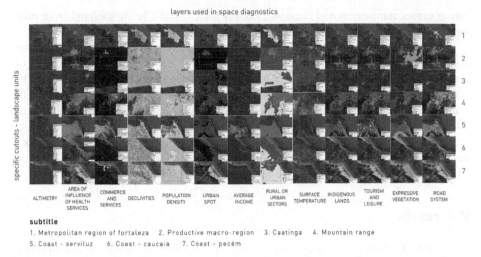

Fig. 7. Parameters for green and CC enhancement

4 Conclusions

Planning the intervention on the samples targeting the increase in 30% CC for the case study area, the MRF, represented an exercise of imagining the instant feedback from the cut out scale designs to macro effects, set off by the replication of micro strategies. Through the algorithm available by Giscolab, which helped the feedback, it was realized how the projection of the effect on interventions at design level on the regional goal achievement can be didactical for planners: observe, during the polygons tracing, the quantity and impact of the proposals makes the interscalar comprehension much more tangible.

Studying the microscale in the MRF territory reveals the perpetuation of environmental conflicts - although with much less intensity- similar to the ones already seen in Fortaleza. It has been observed the occupational pattern repeating the advance over fragile areas and the adoption of outdated strategies for the management of water and land resources. The development of new neighbourhoods shows the continuance of the functional similarity instead of multifunctional approach: the urban expansion is mostly for habitational purposes. How can the cities become less dependent on the capital if they keep adding so little diversity?

The habitational insecurity related to environmental degradation is connected with the tactics adopted by new urbanizations - if they will consider the ecosystem functions provided by nature; if they will find the specific strategy for each territory to guarantee the natural infrastructure maintenance. Planning of the CC areas on the microscale, we can see that they are not sustainable if they can't relate to local characteristics. Clearly, delimitating forests for preservation will not be sufficient as a way of resistance to the conflicts generated by the urban expansion. Which institutional, economic and social functions can add to each spatial sample, subsidizing the continuity of the green area? For this reason, the scale integration was very useful to allow the comprehension that the conservation, ampliation and creation of areas for CC can't be dissociated from other aspects of urban planning. In reality, they will be enabled or prevented by them.

This exercise of feedback between scales shows the contribution of local interventions on regional and global goals, allowing for more precise planning through incorporating the existing differences and making more manageable the difficulties in the comprehension of great territorial dynamics. The Giscolab algorithm facilitated the continuous feedback process, necessary for the selection of suitable proposals for the established goal. As a recommendation for future studies, we saw the necessity for more precision in the algorithm development so it can incorporate a greater amount of local specificities. We emphasize the possibility of using parametric modelling as a way of toll improvement, thus enhancing the feedback between Geo and Design.

References

1. Fukuda, K.: Science, technology and innovation ecosystem transformation toward society 5.0. Int. J. Product. Econ. **220** (2020). https://doi.org/10.1016/j.ijpe.2019.07.033
2. Cantrell, B.E., Holzman, J.E.: Responsive Landscapes: Strategies for Responsive Technologies in Landscape Architecture. 1st edn. Routledge, London (2015). https://doi.org/10.4324/9781315757735
3. Eastman, C., Teicholz, P., Sacks, R. Liston, K.: BIM Handbook: A Guide to Building Information Modeling for Owners, Managers, Designers, Engineers, and Contractors. 2nd edn., Wiley, New Jersey (2008). https://doi.org/10.1002/9780470261309
4. Steinitz, C.: A Framework for Geodesign: Changing Geography by Design. Esri Press, Redlands (2012)
5. Davis, J., Pijawka, D., Wentz, E.A., Hale, M.: Evaluation of community-based land use planning through Geodesign: Application to American Indian communities. Landscape Urban Plann. **203** (2020). https://doi.org/10.1016/j.landurbplan.2020.103880
6. Casagrande, P.B.: O framework geodesign aplicado ao Quadrilátero Ferrífero (Minas Gerais/Brasil): a geologia como base de planejamento de futuros alternativos para o Quadrilátero Ferrífero. Dissertation, Universidade Federal de Minas Gerais (2018)
7. Moura, A.C.M., Freitas, C.R.: Brazilian Geodesign Platform: WebGis & SDI & Geodesign as co-creation and geo-collaboration. In: Gervasi, O., et al. (eds.) ICCSA 2020. LNCS, vol. 12252, pp. 332–348. Springer, Cham (2020). https://doi.org/10.1007/978-3-030-58811-3_24
8. Millennium Ecosystem Assessment (MEA).: Ecosystems and human well-being: Wetlands and water synthesis. World Resources Institute, Washington (2005)
9. Cameron, R.W., et al.: The domestic garden – Its contribution to urban green infrastructure. Urban Forest. Urban Green. **11**(2), 129–137 (2012). https://doi.org/10.1016/j.ufug.2012.01.002
10. Badiu, D.L., Nita, A., Iojă, C.I., Niţă, M.R.: Disentangling the connections: a network analysis of approaches to urban green infrastructure. Urban Forest. Urban Green. **41**, 211–220 (2019). https://doi.org/10.1016/j.ufug.2019.04.013
11. Rolf, W., Hansen, R., Rall, E., Chapman, E., Pauleit, S.: Urban green infrastucture planning: a guide for practicioners (2017)
12. Niţă, M.R., Pătroescu, M., Badiu, D.L., Gavrilidis, A.A., Avram, M.-E.: Indicators for evaluating the role of green infrastructures in sustainable urban development in Romania. Forum Geografic **XVI**(1), 75–81 (2018). https://doi.org/10.5775/fg.2018.106.i
13. Frantzeskaki, N.: Seven lessons for planning nature-based solutions in cities. Environ. Sci. Policy **93**, 101–111 (2019). https://doi.org/10.1016/j.envsci.2018.12.033

14. United Nations, Department of Economic and Social Affairs, Population Division.: World Urbanization Prospects: The 2014 Revision. United Nations, New York (2014)
15. Field, C.B., et al. (eds.).: IPCC 2012: Managing the Risks of Extreme Events and Disasters to Advance Climate Change Adaptation. Cambridge University Press, Cambridge (2012)
16. Alves, A., Gersonius, B., Kapelan, Z., Vojinovic, Z., Sanchez, A.: Assessing the co-benefits of green-blue-grey infrastructure for sustainable urban flood risk management. J. Environ. Manage. **239**, 244–254 (2019). https://doi.org/10.1016/j.jenvman.2019.03.036
17. European Environment Agency.: Climate change, impacts and vulnerability in Europe 2012. Rosendahls-Schultz Grafisk, Copenhagen (2012)
18. Sotchava, V.B.: Por uma teoria de classificação de geossistemas da vida terrestre. Biogeografia, **14** (1978)
19. Santos, M.: O espaço dividido: os dois circuitos da economia urbana dos países subdesenvolvidos. 2nd edn. Edusp, São Paulo (2004)
20. Novotny, A., Ahern, J., Brown, P.: Water Centric Sustainable Communities. Wiley, Hoboken (2010)
21. Magalhães, D.M.: Uso de drones como suporte ao planejamento territorial: Da coleta de dados à geovisualização. Universidade Federal de Minas Gerais, Thesis (2021)
22. Montezuma, R.C.M., Tângari, V.R., Isidoro, I.A., Magalhães, A.M.: Unidades de paisagem como um método de análise territorial: integração de dimensões geo-biofísicas e arquitetônico-urbanísticas aplicada ao estudo de planície costeira no Rio de Janeiro. In: AppUrbana 2014. UFPA, Belém (2014)

Decision Making and Geodesign: A Collaborative Territorial Planning Proposal for the Metropolitan Region of Belém, Pará, Brazil

Alan Nunes Araújo[✉], Tiago Barreto de Andrade Costa[✉],
Bruno Daniel das Neves Benitez[✉], Fabricio Martins Silva[✉],
and Joabi Luiz Lima De Lima[✉]

Federal University of Pará, Belém, Brazil
alanaraujo@ufpa.br, joabi.lima@ifch.ufpa.br

Abstract. This paper is the result of a case study based on the geodesign proposal (Steinitz 2012) adapted to the metropolitan reality of Belém, Pará, Brazil. Composed of seven municipalities and with about 1.7 million inhabitants, this metropolitan region is the second most populous in the Brazilian Amazon. Paradoxically, even in the midst of high rainfall, a dense hydrographic network and an abundance of water resources, Belém shows significant vulnerability in terms of the quality and quantity of water accessed by its population. According to the Sanitation Panel, 39.8% of the population in the Metropolitan Region of Belém (MRB), does not have access to drinking water (Brasil 2018). In turn, 90.1% do not have sewage collection and treatment, further aggravating the water crisis, socioeconomic and health inequality. This reality requires more effective urban planning with regard to the vulnerabilities presented. In this scenario, geodesign represented an interesting methodological approach, primarily for highlighting the importance of the water issue in Belém and also for sketching propositional scenarios, in a collaborative way and based on Geographic Information System (GIS).

Keywords: Territorial planning · Geodesign · GISColab · Pará

1 Introduction

The metropolitan regions integrate between their cities a series of relations of dependence and centrality materialized in continuous or discontinuous flows of urban services that occupy, in turn, the same territory, requiring a shared management of these spaces and inter-municipal articulation for greater functioning and mobility, less environmental impact and conflict reduction. The Brazilian Federal Constitution, promulgated in 1988 brought the state as a major interlocutor of development policies and urban and rural planning in the country, triggering the emergence of important laws that address related issues to planning, such as the 9433 Law in the year 1997 that instituted the national

O. Gervasi et al. (Eds.): ICCSA 2021, LNCS 12954, pp. 420–436, 2021.
https://doi.org/10.1007/978-3-030-86979-3_30

Water Resources Policy until Law 10257 in 2001, that established the general guidelines of urban policy and more recently Law 13089 that institutes the Metropolis Statute.

In this context, according to Rocha et al (2016), the propagation of a discourse and actions favorable to the territorial approach to development and public policies associated with national, regional, and local levels is increasingly evident. Therefore, it is necessary that Planning, to be effective, is not incarcerated in the deterministic ideal and that has as its essence, predictability (Camargo 2009). Therefore, it is necessary, in addition to Planning, a greater ordering of the information that make up the Territory, fostering a vast field of analysis and spatial projections and forecasts.

In this respect, Geodesign fits within an innovative and important area in terms of thinking, planning, and designing the region, considering that it appears as a large set of issues and methods necessary to solve complicated and significant problems at different geographical scales (Steinitz 2012). The spatial complexity, seen until then in various phases of regional planning as obstacles, in Geodesign become an important stage within a collaborative proposal, complementing knowledge and defining priorities.

In this approach, the opinion of the actors involved in the process, that is, people who live, know and use the studied territory, gain prominence and will be fundamental to draw spatially and plan better and closer to the real from a collaborative perspective and that can assist more sustainable and democratic decision-making. The geovisualization is also relevant part of the process because it will provide a collection of spatial information that will make systems, and therefore assist in political proposition and interventions in space. Therefore, the practice of G eodesign requires collaboration between professions of environmental design, geographic sciences, information technologies and local people (Fig. 1). (Steinitz 2012).

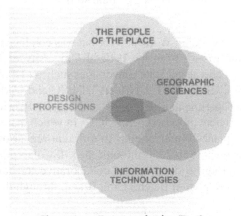

Changing Geography by Design

Fig. 1. A framework for geodesign

The Specialist responsible for planning, in this perspective, will no longer be the author of the idea, but, from listening, the decoder of the collective will and for that, it becomes essential to materialize methodologies, such as those proposed by Geodesign so that the collective establishes priorities, and the planner better meets expectations. Among the methodological scripts of Geodesign, the one proposed by Steinitz (2012) is perhaps the closest to collaborative listening (Fig. 2), as in a Workshop format it is divided into six models and which in turn will be subdivided into two phases. The first, more technical and not necessarily with consultation with society, will be responsible for the survey, treatment and organization of spatial information grouped through Systems giving shape to the Models of Representation, Process and Evaluation. Subsequently, the second stage, more practical, will take place during the participatory planning workshop, which will involve the various actors that make up the territory to be planned, forming the last three Models (Change, Impact and Decision). (Moura 2019).

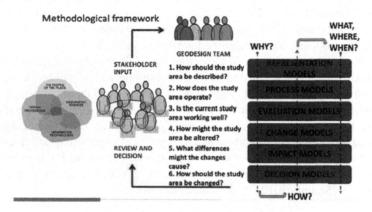

Fig. 2. Geodesign framework

This methodological proposal in Workshop format was conducted in Brazil by Professor Ana Clara Mourão Moura from the Federal University of Minas Gerais and involved several Brazilian Federal and State Universities such as (UFMG, UFRRJ, UFJF, USP, UFCE, UFPE, UFG, UFPA, UFT, UNIFAP, UDESC and UNESP of Rio Claro) as well as two planning departments (SEMA-AP and SETRAP) with the objective of composing a global experiment proposed by the IGC[1] in which, based on collaborative planning, he studied and planned interventions in different scenarios for Metropolitan Regions between the years 2035 to 2050 through the GISColab platform. The article in question intends, therefore, to describe the collaborative territorial planning proposal for the Metropolitan Region of Belém, Pará, Brazil. through the Geodesign.

2   Geographic Location

The Metropolitan Region of Belém (RMB) has an area of 1820km^2 and is composed of seven socioeconomically integrated municipalities (Belém, Ananindeua, Marituba, Benevides, Santa Bárbara do Pará, Santa Izabel do Pará and Castanhal) being the capital

---

[1] https://www.igc-geodesign.org/.

of the state of Pará, Belém, the most populous municipality and economic and financial center of the State, but geographically limited by its semi - peninsular condition surrounded by Guajará Bay and the banks of the Guamá River (Fig. 3), reverberating today, in an intense process of expansion and vertical urban to towards the other municipalities that follow the axis of the highway BR 316 (final stretch of the Belem-Brasilia highway) and it will be detailed later in this article. Ananindeua and Marituba have been expanding to a large extent with the function of sleeping cities for significant contingents working in Belém.

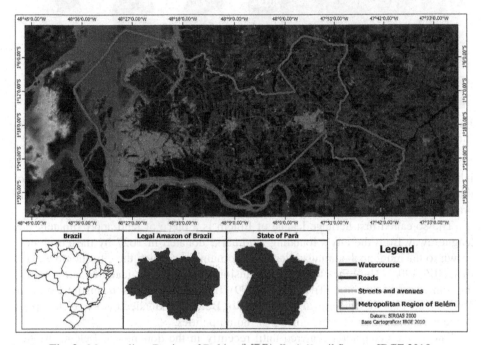

Fig. 3. Metropolitan Region of Belém (MRB), Pará, Brazil Source: IBGE 2010.

All the MRB, inserted in the Amazonian domains (Fig. 4), had, in 1985, an area of 61.32% of Forest, reducing to 51.62% in 2000 and in 2019, 46.72%. In contrast, the Farming class in 1985 occupied an area of 16.68%, growing to 23.47% in 2000, and in 2019 26.77%. This growth also followed the Non-Vegetated Area class, which in 1985 occupied 4.31%, in 2000 7.04% and in 2019 8.78%. These values justify, despite the high number of forest areas, a high tendency to change this class to others, mainly pasture or urban area, present in the Non-Vegetated Area class. These changes reflect not only the environmental impact on the Amazon ecosystem, but also on the living conditions in the "Metropolis of the Amazon".

The RMB has a population of 2,101,883 inhabitants, of which 66% constitute the 1.4 million inhabitants of Belém. RMB concentrates approximately 40% of the wealth produced in the State and 35% of the entire population of Pará (IBGE 2010). Except for Santa Bárbara, with 32% of the urban population, all other municipalities have their

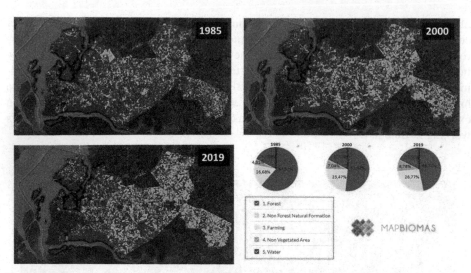

Fig. 4. Land Use and Coverage in the MRB 1985, 2000 and 2019 **Source:** Project Map-Biomas Alerta 2021

inhabitants predominantly residing in the municipal headquarters. The highest rates of this reality are concentrated in Belém, Ananindeua and Marituba and Castanhal, where practically the entire population is in the headquarters.

The so-called first heritage league of Belém is a piece of land approximately one league away from the city's founding landmark, donated in 1627 by the Portuguese crown to the municipal administration, as a domain over which the city should expand (MUNIZ, 1904). Until the 1980s, the expansion of Belém practically occurred within the framework of this limit (Trindade Jr. 1999). In fact, it is only in the institution of the 1993 master plan that the official urban space of Belém is extended to more distant parts of the municipality and towards the other municipalities.

Due to the occupation centered until recently in the domains of Belém, the first league is the area of the city that concentrates the highest population density, which is not homogeneously distributed in its interior. The largest population concentration, as can be seen in Fig. 4, is represented by the so-called "lowlands", areas located in altimetric levels more subject to flooding, which were occupied throughout the formation of the urban space of Belém, predominantly by populations of lesser power acquisitive (Trindade Jr 1999). Therefore, these areas of more floodable soil and of high population density, represent the oldest peripheries of the urban space in Belem, and this condition will multiply throughout the other municipalities of the RMB more recently, with residences on irregular street layouts and close to the channels (water courses), showing spontaneous occupations and without urban planning (Fig. 5).

The physiographic characteristic of the urban site of Belém will also dictate the socio-environmental problem that involves these lowland areas. Geomorphologically, a significant portion of the RMB's territory is located on fluvial plains, represented by tributary floodplains of Guamá and Guajará Bay, which is constituted in an estuarine region approximately 100 km from the Atlantic Ocean.

Despite the distance to the ocean, due to the peculiar characteristics of the great mouths of the Amazon basin, the urban site of Belém is affected by the tidal cycle, which enters several kilometers in the rivers of the Amazon. Thus, daily the high tide retains the outflow of the water courses that cut through the city, increasing its levels. Such a process becomes more intense at high tides (tides of the moon).

In parallel to this fluvial and geomorphological dynamics, RMB is traditionally known for its frequent and high rainfall. It rains with almost daily frequency, mainly between the months of January to April. Several of these rain events have torrential characteristics (Fig. 5).

It is in this physiographic context that the urban space of the study region is inserted. The lowlands, in turn, are the most vulnerable portions to this water dynamic, because in addition to being found in the lower elevations, they are also the areas of natural flooding of the water courses that flow into Guamá and Baía do Guajará.

In addition to this, the intense waterproofing process of urban soil, which naturally already has deficiencies in its vertical drainage, since it is formed by a hydromorphic pedology (of floodplain), further aggravates the picture of constant and frequent flooding of the lowlands (Fig. 5).

Due to these characteristics, the socio-environmental and sanitary occupation of these floodplains, requires and since the beginning of the occupation, significant technical interventions to control the tide, urban drainage, sanitary sewage, among others. Such interventions are such that until the rubber cycle, authorities, and elites, in the process of official occupation of the city of Belém, chose to avoid low-lying regions.

On the other hand, the poorest populations, immigrating from riverside regions to the RMB, largely occupied these wetlands, not only because of the greater adaptability to fluvial and rainfall variations, but mainly because these areas did not arouse the interest of the real estate sector, therefore, liable to occupy spontaneously and informally. In yet with the process of urban density and without an adequate presence of the government, new problems have emerged: sewage, garbage collection, urban accessibility, violence etc. L Evando such areas today accumulate various social disadvantages.

Fig. 5. City of Belém - Pará **Source**: Eloí Raíol 3D, Folha Uol, O liberal

Thus, in contrast to the lowlands, the regions of "firm lands", that is, with higher altimetry (greater than 4 m), with a lower demographic density, they are, therefore, in addition to less humid areas, those that shelter the populations wealthier (TRINDADE Jr, 1999). Its structure of roads and public spaces represents what was made effective by the official plans for the expansion of the urban network, set in motion throughout the various cycles of spatial production in the city of Belém (PENTEADO, 1968). In these areas, the blocks and streets have more regular formats, expressing the planning in the layout.

In the parts of the oldest occupation of the firm lands it is where the most verticalized portions are found, the result of transformations that have been occurring in the last decades (oliveira et al. 2005). The intensification of building incorporations, increasingly tall and always with non-popular standards, shows a spatial restructuring in the housing trends of the population with the highest purchasing power, located in these drier lands of the first heritage league (oliveira et al. 2005). Figure 5 highlights the referred vertical area on the "firm lands" where a significant portion of the current Belenese elite resides, and which will also be repeated in the other municipalities of the MRB.

This phase is approximately from the 1980s to the present day, mainly following the highway axes of BR-316 and Rod. Augusto Montenegro (TRINDADE Jr. and LECIONE, 1998). Figure 3 shows the population growth and expansion of the urban area from the early years of this phase to the present day. It is possible to see in more detail how the metropolitan dispersion referred to by Trindade Jr. and Lecione (1998) took place.

In this new framework of transformations, the form of expansion of the periphery with occupation of the lowlands of the first heritage league, which give rise to what Cardoso et al. (2015) called the nearby periphery, it begins to give way to another process of peripheralization, that of distant peripheries, which spread in expansion of the city, after the institutional belt and in the direction of Ananindeua.

Basically, the production of this new peripheral spatial structure, in addition to the institutional belt, was guided by the following logic: the lands immediately next to the Augusto Montenegro Highway were reserved by developers and landowners as a value reserve to be built in a second moment intended for to the more affluent social classes (Cardoso and Ventura Neto 2013). Behind these land reserves, the government has built popular housing projects since 1970 (Cardoso and Ventura Neto 2013). The interstices of these formal groups were being occupied irregularly by precarious forms of housing that today constitute the spatial expression of what Cardoso and Ventura Neto (2013) are calling distant peripheries.

We also draw attention to the southeastern portion of the expansion area. This is where most of the popular housing estates are concentrated and where, especially since the mid-2000s, there has been the installation of housing and urban equipment along the Augusto Montenegro Highway, aimed at the population with the greatest purchasing power. It is the construction of more exclusive spaces in areas previously reserved by the real estate market (Cardoso And Ventura Neto 2015). In this way islands of lesser social vulnerability are being created in the production of this expansion space in the city of Belém. In this process, the intense replacement of the areas of Native Amazon Forest by the expansion of the urban network stands out.

The fact that Belém was born with an eminently urban function of commerce and territorial dominance of the Amazon, a function that it still maintains today, bequeathed to the municipality an inexpressive rural space in its immediate surroundings, practically nonexistent. In this way, the expression of the urban transition that Brazil experienced in the last century, meant in Belém, not a demographic inversion of a rural population for an urban population, but, an exponential increase in its urban population contingent that occurred mainly due to the migration of people from other parts of the Brazilian territory.

With the expansion of the urban ax of Belém over most of its continental area, with the exception of some forests, nowadays, in addition to the predominantly urban population, its territory is also clearly covered by the urban, but with vast growth potential towards the municipality of Castanhal. This in turn, marked by nuclei of concentration of wealth, circumscribed by vast extensions of precarious areas in terms of infrastructure, housing, accessibility, public security, among others.

3 Tools and Methods

For implementation of the Workshop Geodesign on the metropolitan region of Belém, was used technology GISColab, Brazilian platform Geodesign developed by UFMG, based on the SDI standard (Spatial Data Information) and OGC to consumption data via WMS or WFS, allowing both the cases the performance increase by WPS (Web Processing Service). In this sense, on the first day of the event, a collection of official maps was made available to the Workshop participants, organized by the Geoprocessing Laboratory of the UFMG School of Architecture and Urbanism by Systems, which make up the first stage proposed by Steinitz (2012) in which the Spatial information is associated with the Models of Representation, Process and Evaluation. In turn, the second stage is actually the materialization of the Workshop and divided into 4 parts (Fig. 6):

The steps described above were developed in four virtual meetings, during the month of April 2021. Initially 9 participants were part of the team, but during the process there were withdrawals and ending on the last day with 5 participants, the same from the beginning to the end. and composed of professors from the Federal University of Pará, students and researchers who study the Metropolitan Region of Belém. Due to the small number of people, it was not necessary to divide into other groups, remaining the same in all phases involving the collaborative planning proposal of the RMB until the year 2050 added to the carbon credit planning for the same region. Thus, the meetings took place as follows:

3.1   Day 1 – Enrichment of Reading and Creation of Notes

After individual consultation of the material (videos, books, and articles) made available by Professor Ana Clara explaining all the concepts related to Geodesign, the participants were received with a succinct explanation of the Workshop proposal and later they listened together to the video that explained the phase of the Enrichment of Reading and creation of notes. At this moment, the mediator also explained about the GIS-COLAB platform and the data that would be used in this stage. Thus, the first activity

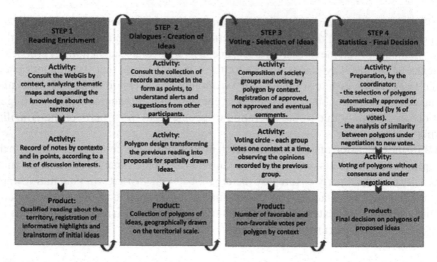

Fig. 6. Operational architecture of the Geodesign Workshop Source: Moura; Freitas, 2020

consisted of handling the platform and consulting the cartographic base, grouped by systems.

The first activity proposed was reading the platform, understanding the layers and taking notes on problems and potentialities. The meeting started with the reception of the participants and an explanation of the general aspects and objectives of the workshop. Subsequently, the participants were distributed in each of the groups, where they would be guided by a "mediator", in charge of explaining in detail the platform and the existing data and assessing whether they would be relevant to assist in the creation of the notes. It was collectively defined that data insertion was missing to aid the analysis. Thus, the participants inserted the cartographic base of the Agrarian Reform Settlements into the platform, in addition to updating school points, hospitals and the Federal Government's Minha Casa Minha Vida program.

At the end of the first moment, in a collective and collaborative way, the participants opened for discussion, pondering the systems and maps that deserved more evidence within the context of the MRB. After some time, they started to insert notes related to this spatial information (Fig. 7), however, closer to the individual experience and experience, a step not only necessary for data analysis, but also for the use of these notes in later activities that involve planning. The reference of colors and symbols was made available through a Table of Notes by the organizing team of the Workshop.

3.2   Day 2 – Creation of Proposals with the Continuation of the Existing Planning

The second day as c atom the first, had an initial explanation of the mediator, and then the team began the planning phase and propositions the years 2035 and 2050 for the Metropolitan Region of Belém, but following the traditional planning "non- adopter". In this sense, a planning without innovation and closer to the Brazilian and regional reality was followed. Thus, the participants started the annotations, inserting in the system the

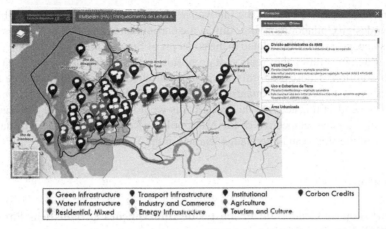

● Green Infrastructure	● Transport Infrastructure	● Institutional	● Carbon Credits
● Water Infrastructure	● Industry and Commerce	● Agriculture	
● Residential, Mixed	● Energy Infrastructure	● Tourism and Culture	

Fig. 7. Result of the first day of the workshop – GISColab platform Source: The authors, 2021.

annotations related to the creation of proposals related to various issues that involve the limitations and potential of planning the RMB.

3.3   Day 3 – Creation of Proposal with Some Innovations

The third day, with participants more accustomed to the platform and Geodesign, began with the creation of proposals for the RMB, as did the second day, however in a more innovative planning concept, the "late adopter". In this regard participants were encouraged by the mediator to establish proposal of great local and regional impact, even if a financial and technological support necessary also higher. The objective of this stage is precisely to think of the RMB for the years 2035 and 2050 with innovations and many innovations, not only in relation to changes in the territory, but also in the establishment of forest areas for the preservation, creation, and expansion of carbon credit.

The objective of this dynamic is to simulate in the period 2035–2050, what changes the territory would experience in the form of planning, adopting measures of innovation. It was hoped that two scenarios could be compared: starting from an existing reality (2021), the year 2035 arrives with traditional planning and, from the year 2035 to 2050, the planning would begin to adopt more innovative forms, being created in a different way. moderately restricted and not what would be possible to implement in fifteen years.

The creation of the proposals remained the same as in the previous dynamic, with point, line, and polygon, with the polygons representing the proposals related only to the " carbon credit" system. To assist in the innovative proposals, it was suggested to consult the existing bank of ideas on the website of IGC - International Geodesign Collaboration, 2021.

3.4   Day 4 – Creation of Proposal with Many Innovations and Voting

On the last day of the Workshop, the team met to collectively think of the RMB in an even more innovative way, "late adopter" for the year 2050. For this purpose, it was necessary once again to consult the innovative proposals suggested by IGC - International Geodesign Collaboration. In addition, the participants consulted in the days before this last stage, proposals also related to the concepts of Smart Cities, with the objective of improving and innovating the creation of proposals and more directed to the Amazonian reality. In addition to these proposals, the group continued to delimit areas for the carbon credit stock and the respective quantification for the RMB.

After the end of this activity, the participants went for an analysis of the main proposals within a new perspective of the Metropolitan Region of Belém and finally, an evaluation of the stages and knowledge learned in the Workshop.

4 Results

4.1 Workshop de Geodesign: Propostas de Intervenções Urbanísticas Para a RMB Em 2035 E 2050

The "Creation of proposals with the continuation of the existing planning" stage made it possible to think and create interventions for the RMB for the year 2035 and 2050, but in a more conservative way and without technological innovations. The result that was achieved within the collaborative planning was interesting and appropriate to the local reality. Thus, as some examples, proposals were launched for a new location of the Sanitary Landfill, considering the current sanitary and environmental standards. Proposal for the creation of highways, aiming to reduce the flow of vehicles on the main roads and streets of RMB. As it is an economically vulnerable region and in full population growth, the disorganized urban expansion generates pressure on natural areas, with water, even located in the Amazon, the most worrying element in relation to this issue, since according to the Ministry of Cities (201 7) 39.8% of the MRB population does not have access to drinking water. In turn, 90.1% do not have sewage collection and treatment, further aggravating the water crisis, socioeconomic and health inequality, and the need for effective urban planning. So, they were elaborated also proposals for the creation, expansion and technological overhaul of Water and Sewage Treatment Plants. Another recurring problem in the RMB is the flooding points, either due to the action of the tides, or even due to the high rainfall. In this sense, were propose the creation and maintenance system of dikes, formed by channels and sluices automatized the s and integrad the s tidal information and climatological to reduce points of flooding in flood urban areas. In addition, it was also proposed to create channels for draining rainwater.

Moving forward in the proposals for the respective years (2035 and 2050) but at the stage of Creation of proposal with some innovations (Fig. 8), we prepare innovative proposals, to turn the MRB into a Smart and Sustainable Region. As an example, in this phase of the Workshop, the participants proposed the installation of residential wind turbines, in which the system uses solar energy and air flows throughout the buildings and converts them into electricity. Water Retention Parks have also been proposed to take advantage of water surplus from the concentration of rainwater for domestic and commercial use. It was also proposed to create the APA of the Belém-Barcarena Islands, in that area there are large remnants of Alluvial Rainforests and açaí crops. For Tourism and Leisure, the Creation and Expansion of Ecopark s in the Amazon was proposed, where tourists can have the experience of knowing the Amazon biome in all its potential, at the same time that animals are protected and released into nature.

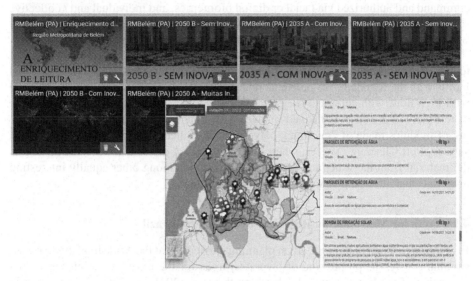

Fig. 8. Creation of proposals with the continuation of the existing planning **Source**: The authors, 2021.

The last stage of urban planning proposals for the RMB for 2035 and 2050 was the Creation of proposal with many innovations and voting (Fig. 9) in which very innovative proposals had been developed. Thus, proposals were made for innovations in air and rail transport (currently nonexistent in the RMB) such as Transportation Networks via Pipes composed of a high-speed train that would circulate through a kind of closed tunnel under the ground, interconnecting the metropolitan regions of Belém.

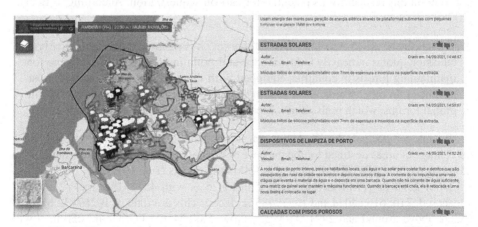

Fig. 9. Creation of proposal with many innovations **Source:** The authors, 2021.

Automated stations were also proposed, with a facial or digital biometric reader, eliminating tickets and ticket cards. They also proposed the creation of Libraries of the Future, where the physical content is only for exhibition, and the research will be done by voice command and authorized via facial or digital biometrics, and individual and / collective rooms (maximum 5 people) with highchairs. technological power. Carbon installation, with its soils managed to trap carbon and transform its APPs into carbon credit assets.

Construction of vegetated linear corridors along intra-urban channels, contributing to the decommissioning of the hydrographic network. Installation of Floating Wind Farms with the foundation of pure concrete and stuck, at the bottom of the sea or rivers with high flow, with currents. They are so flexible that they can be scaled to any size of turbine. Solar Roads, to take advantage of all potential in Northern Brazil, consisting of modules made of 7mm thick polycrystalline silicone and inserted into the road surface. Port Cleaning Devices, where the river current drives a water wheel that lifts the material from the water and deposits it in a barge, among other equally interesting proposals that allowed planning the RMB of the future.

4.2   Trees for Metropolitan Region of Belém, Pará, Brazil

In addition to the collaborative urban planning carried out at the workshop, there is also, simultaneously, the proposition of favorable areas for the creation, maintenance, and expansion of the Forest areas, also between the years 2035 and 2050, not only within the perspective of environmental conservation, but also aiming to meet the Sustainable Development Goals (SDG) United Nations Organization, which stands out for this study the mitigation of climate change from carbon sequestration.

The Amazon is a key environment for this discussion, given that despite the intense deforestation encouraged by the Brazilian state in the 20th century through the National Integration Plan and nowadays, with the dismantling of the inspection bodies and the lag of a precise and adequate environmental agenda. the global discussions, which in turn favor an exponential increase not only in deforestation, but also in the outbreaks of forest fires. Even so, the Amazon has the largest forest spot on the planet and gains notoriety in this respect for its potential for carbon sequestration. According to Becker (2005):

> What is the Kyoto Protocol if not the air market? It is an attempt to establish carbon emission quotas in heavily industrialized and polluting countries in exchange for maintaining forests in countries equipped with them. The air market is the most advanced. In other words, these real markets try to institutionalize themselves in global forums, which is also a new aspect within international law (Becker 2005).

In this perspective, the Workshop participants sought to analyze and establish a percentage of areas destined for the purpose of the carbon credit stock, according to the definitions of the SDG. Thus, it came to following results (Fig. 10):

Until 2050 they will increase CCO2 in 87.25%, with 45125155 trees: 22077054 conserved, 7168616 added and 15879485 replaced. This is a total of 10267432 MgC of CCO2 above ground and 2491283 MgC below, 5.09 MgC / PC. Until 2050 they will increase CCO2 in 73.41%, with 37956539 trees: 220770534 conserved, 0 added and

15879485 replaced. This is a total of 8636341 MgC of CCO2 above ground and 2095516 MgC below, 4.28 MgC / PC. Until 2050 they will increase CCO2 in 0%, with 4284034 trees: all of them conserving existing areas, none added, and none replaced. This is a total of 974756 MgC of CCO2 above ground and 236514 MgC below, 0.48 MgC / PC.

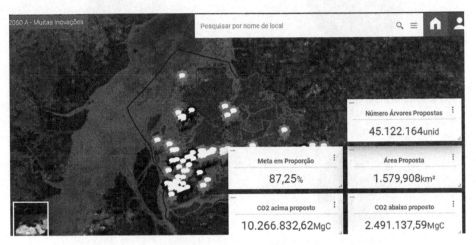

Fig. 10. Carbon credit areas – RMB **Source:** The authors, 2021.

4.3   Final Form on the GEODESIGN Brazil Workshop: Trees for Metropolitan Regions

From the work done, the participants answered a form with the objective of identifying the profile of the participants and the knowledge before and after the workshop (Fig. 11). In this regard, some of the results were that for RMB the team varied between 60% professors at the Federal University of Pará, 20% students and 20% researchers. Of these, 40% already knew about Geodesign processes, 20% did not and 40% are not sure. A relevant fact also concerns their knowledge, before the Workshop, in relation to the region. Thus, 60% already had relevant knowledge, 20% already knew the region fully and 20% are not sure about the subject. Finally, the last graph shows the importance of the workshop, not only for the knowledge of Geodesign, but also for its expansion in relation to the Metropolitan Region of Belém, with 60% being completely sure and 40% with the certainty that the Workshop enabled this expansion of knowledge.

What is your occupation?

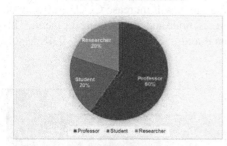

Before the workshop, I already knew the Geodesign process.

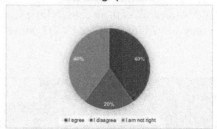

Before the workshop, I already knew the main characteristics of RMB

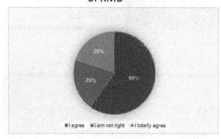

After the workshop ended, I believe that my knowledge and interest in the area of study was expanded.

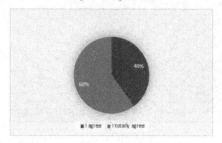

Fig. 11. Profile and Diagnosis of Workshop participants Source: The authors, 2021.

5 Closing Remarks

This article was able to achieve the proposal defined in its general objectives, which consisted of elaborating a collaborative territorial planning proposal for the Metropolitan Region of Belém, Pará, Brazil, through Geodesign. It was found that prior to the Workshop, not all the team understood Geodesign, as well as a lack of more in-depth knowledge about the Belém Metropolitan Region itself. Later, in addition to the knowledge learned, the collaborative planning proposal allowed not only the sharing of thoughts, expectations, experiences, and knowledge among the participants, but it also enabled a new perspective on regional and territorial planning through Geodesign, with information being the central issue of the process, and not just a specific and technical step when planning the space.

It is important to note that despite a process that is broadly democratic and rich in details and information, doubts, and debates about what should or should not be planned also occurred in the process. Thus, on the first day, the doubt that arose in the reading enrichment phase was precisely the need for enrichment of the information itself, since despite the Workshop starting with an official cartographic base and very well organized by the coordinating technical team of the event, more up-to-date details were missing, such as data from hospitals, schools, social housing programs for the low-income population, among others. Participants also identified some classification errors in land use and coverage, mainly with the presence of extensive agricultural areas within the urban area. Finally, the absence of cartographic bases very necessary for studies in the Amazon was also raised, such as Quilombola Territories, Areas destined to Agrarian Reform and a map, from the altimetric levels, separating the areas from 0 to 2 m of altitude and above 2 m, since despite a physical division, it is also of a social and economic order, mentioned in the work as "lowland" wetland areas and with a predominance of poorer populations and "terra firme" areas, at higher points and with predominance of the middle and upper class. In this sense, with the possibility of entering information on the GISColab platform, participants with more technical experience, updated and inserted information to bring the maps closer to reality for the following activities.

Once this process was done, the other stages of the Workshop were fundamental so that collectively, the participants realized that water is the most necessary element to plan intelligently and sustainably the territory of the Metropolitan Region of Belém. In addition to the rainforests with predominantly Amazonian landscapes, mainly on the edges of the Metropolitan Region and in the islands, the region has a percentage lower than that recommended by the SDG for access to drinking water and sewage treatment. Soon the most critical point becomes in fact the sanitary issue and the pressure of urbanization and agriculture, without planning for the forest regions, many of them recharge areas and fundamental for the water supply for the whole region, such as the Park State of Utinga, an important environmental reserve, but under great pressure from this growth. From this observation, several proposals without innovation, with innovation and with many innovations were also created based on this logic, which also influenced when planning favorable areas for carbon credit.

References

1. Steinitz, C.: A Framework for Geodesign – Changing Geography by Design. Esri Press, Redlands (2012)
2. Instituto Brasileiro de Geografia e Estatística (IBGE). Censo Brasileiro de 2010. Rio de Janeiro: IBGE (2018)
3. Rocha, G.M.; Teisserenc, P. (Org.); Vasconcellos Sobrinho, M. (Org.): Aprendizagem Terri- torial: Dinâmicas Territoriais, Participação Social e Ação Local na Amazônia. 1a. ed. Belém do Pará: NUMA - UFPA, . vol. 1 (2016)
4. Camargo, L.H.R.: ORDENAMENTO TERRITORIAL E COMPLEXIDADE: POR UMA REESTRUTURAÇÃO DO ESPAÇO SOCIAL. In: almeida, flávio gomes et. al. (Org.). ORDENAMENTO TERRITORIAL. 1ed.rio de janeiro: bertrand, pp. 21–53 (2009)
5. Moura, A.C.M.: O Geodesign como processo de co-criação de acordos coletivos para a pais- agem territorial e urbana. In: LADWIG, Nilzo Ivo; CAMPOS, Juliano Bitencourt (org.). Planejamento e gestão territorial: o papel e os instrumentos do planejamento territorial na interface entre o urbano e o rural. Criciúma (SC): UNESC, 2019. Cap. 1.
6. de Palma Muniz, J.: Patrimônios dos conselhos municipaes do Estado do Pará. Aillaud (1904)
7. Projeto MapBiomas Alerta – [versão] - Sistema de Validação e Refinamento de Alertas de Desmatamento com Imagens de Alta Resolução (2021). https://plataforma.brasil.mapbiomas. org/
8. Trindade Jr., Saint-Clair Cordeiro da. Assentamentos urbanos e metropolização na Amazônia brasileira: o caso de Belém. Encuentro de Geógrafos de América Latina, VII (1999)

436   A. N. Araújo et al.

9. Penteado, A.R.: Belém: (estudo de geografia urbana). Belém: UFPA, 1968, vol. 2 (Coleção amazônica. Série José Veríssimo). Disponível em: http://livroaberto.ufpa.br/jspui/handle/pre fix/43
10. Oliveira, J., França, C.F.D., Bordalo, C.A.L.: A verticalização em Belém-Pará, Brasil, nos últimos trinta anos: a produção de espaços segregados e as transformações socioambientais. ANAIS DO X Encontro de Geógrafos da América Latina, vol. 10, pp. 10609–10620 (2005)
11. Trindade Jr., S.-C.C.d., Lecione, S.: A cidade dispersa: os novos espaços de assentamento em Belém e a reestruturação metropolitana. 1998. Tese de Doutorado, Universidade de São Paulo, São Paulo (1998)
12. Ministério Das Cidades: Diagnóstico dos serviços de água e esgotos – 2017. Sistema Nacional de Informações sobre Saneamento 2017. Disponível em: < http://www.snis.gov.br>. Acesso abril (2021)
13. Cardoso, A.C.D., Do Vale Gomes, T., De Melo, A.C.C.: Respostas da Concepção atual de regulação urbanística aos Desafios socioambientais de Belém (PA). InSitu–Revista Científica do Programa de Mestrado Profissional em Projeto, Produção e Gestão do Espaço Urbano, vol. 1, no. 2, pp. 68–86 (2015)
14. Cardoso, A.C.D., Neto, R.d.S.V.: A evolução urbana de Belém: trajetória de ambiguidades e conflitos socioambientais. Cadernos Metrópole, vol. 15, no. 29, pp. 55–75 (2013)
15. Moura, A.C.M., Freitas, C.R.: Brazilian geodesign platform: webgis and SDI and geodesign as co-creation and geo-collaboration. In: Gervasi, O. et al. (eds). Springer Nature Switzerland, pp. 332–348 (2020)
16. PNUD - Programa das Nações Unidas para o Desenvolvimento. Disponível em: <https://www.br.undp.org/content/brazil/pt/home/sustainable-development-goals.html. Acesso abril 2021
17. Becker, B.K.: Geopolítica da Amazônia. Estudos Avançados 19(53), 71–86 (2005)

Geodesign Applied to Propositional Scenarios of Medium and Long-Term Sustainable Projects for Rio de Janeiro Metropolitan Region, Brazil

Tiago Badre Marino[1](✉) [ID], Cézar Henrique Barra Rocha[2] [ID],
Ashiley Adelaide Rosa[3] [ID], and Tiago Augusto Gonçalves Mello[4] [ID]

[1] Instituto de Agronomia, Departamento de Geociências, Universidade Federal Rural do Rio de Janeiro, BR-465, Km 7, Seropédica, Brazil
tiagomarino@ufrrj.br
[2] Faculdade de Engenharia, Universidade Federal de Juiz de Fora, R. José Lourenço Kelmer, Juíz de Fora, Brazil
barra.rocha@engenharia.ufjf.br
[3] Instituto de Geociências, Universidade Federal de Minas Gerais (IGC UFMG), Av. Pres. Antônio Carlos 6627, Belo Horizonte, Brazil
ashiley.rosa@arquitetura.ufjf.br
[4] Escola de Arquitetura, Universidade Federal de Minas Gerais (EA UFMG), R. Paraíba 697, Belo Horizonte, Brazil
tiagoaugustogm@ufmg.br

Abstract. As the world has become more connected, the scale of cities would be no different. Thus, it became necessary to expand the solutions to meet the planning expectations related to the urban environment in response to contemporary challenges. At the same time, the advent of new information and communication technologies, combined with the popularization of mobile devices, created opportunities to increase the involvement of ordinary citizens in activities of geolocalized data generation and maintenance - Volunteered Geographic Information. Parallel to this scenario of collective data generation, Geodesign framework emerges to support decision making, based on the generation of critical awareness and the co-creation of ideas. In this context, this article reports the experience of a methodological experiment developed in the scope of the project "Geodesign Brazil: Trees for Metropolitan Regions" through the case study of Rio de Janeiro Metropolitan Region, in which workshops were held using the collaborative and digital platforms GISColab and Vicon SAGA. For four weeks a group of collaborators gathered into virtual meeting platforms to apply Geodesign methodological procedures, performed into the following steps: (1) analyzing and enriching the local knowledge base with geolocalized annotations; (2) propose projects considering non-adopter, early adopter, and late adopter scenarios for 2035 and 2050; (3) evaluate their impacts over the UN Sustainable Development Goals. The study showed that inclusive and democratic methodologies supported by platforms encourage discussion, and support decisions on the importance of conscious urban and environmental planning.

The original version of this chapter was revised: The name of one of the Authors was corrected as "Cézar Henrique Barra Rocha". The correction to this chapter is available at https://doi.org/10.1007/978-3-030-86979-3_51

© Springer Nature Switzerland AG 2021, corrected publication 2021
O. Gervasi et al. (Eds.): ICCSA 2021, LNCS 12954, pp. 437–447, 2021.
https://doi.org/10.1007/978-3-030-86979-3_31

Keywords: Volunteered geographic information · Sustainable development
goals · Urban planning · Collaborative design

1   Geodesign and Volunteered Geographic Information in the Perception and Collaborative Construction of the Urban Space

As the world has become more connected, the scale of cities would be no different. Thus, it is necessary to expand expectations and develop processes that relate to the urban environment in response to contemporary challenges. Regarding the activity of urban planning, the active participation of all actors, whether users or specialists, has become essential. However, when it comes to collectivity, there are countless challenges inherent in the premise of mediating conflicts of interest. In this context, there is the proposal of Geodesign as a method to support decision making, based on the generation of critical awareness and the co-creation of ideas [1–6].

Geodesign proposes design models for and with the landscape, being the synthesis of a set of concepts and methods from the association of geosciences and design disciplines. The main objective of its application is the elaboration of collective agreements for the modification of the territory through co-creative projects and plans [1, 2, 6, 7]. The method improves traditional planning activities based on the potential of Geographic Information Systems (GIS) and geovisualization, which become a common language among those involved. Through shared codes, it is possible to collect ideas collectively for the territory, based on impact analysis and simulations on demand. Thus, Geodesign integrates scientific knowledge and social values into the design of alternative futures [5, 6].

In the last decade, the Geodesign method has gained evidence, having been applied at different scales - e.g., towns [8], water courses [9], and neighborhoods [10]; for different purposes - e.g. multidisciplinary planning [11], landscape and wildlife management [12], and propositions for climate action [13, 14]; and localities - e.g. Asia [15, 16], Europe [17, 18], Africa [19, 20], and Americas [21, 22]. This diverse applicability reiterates the potential and versatility of the methodological mark.

Considering the current world scenario of social isolation, it is important to mention that geodesign workshops can occur both in person and virtually. Other than that, the methodology can be conducted analogically and digitally. In the digital scenario there are online platforms, such as Geodesign Hub®[1] and GISColab[2] [23], that allow groups to work presential or remotely, with no limit on the number of participants involved, through a server that stores data, and organizers that conduct the co-creation or codesign dynamics.

In parallel, the advent of new information and communication technologies, combined with the popularization of mobile devices, create opportunities for increasing the generation of contextual information, originated from social participation, especially when individuals face problems and see opportunities in their own communities. Portable equipment, smartphones equipped with multimedia resources (photos, videos, audios) and GPS receivers, wireless networks and smart objects expand the limits of places and moments in which an individual can collaborate, as they allow the use of data

---

[1] Geodesign Hub® - https://www.geodesignhub.com.
[2] GISColab - http://www.giscolab.com/geodesign.

from their location and make environments increasingly interactive, changing their relationship with the urban space and opening space for the offer of innovative collaborative services [24].

In this context, the involvement of ordinary citizens in activities of generation and maintenance of geolocalized data - Volunteered Geographic Information (VGI), has become a common fact, intensely fostered, not only by non-profit initiatives, such as OpenStreetMap®, but also by the giant digital platforms, such as Google®.

In this scenario, this article reports on the experience of a methodological approach developed within the scope of the project "Geodesign Brazil: Trees for Metropolitan Regions" - a network of collaborators from all regions of the country that aims to discuss and propose ideas for their respective locations using Geodesign, in the realization of workshops and using the Brazilian platform GISColab, among other resources and specificities of each region. In the case study reported, specifically, the collaborative platform Vicon SAGA was also used.

2   The Dynamics of the Workshop in the Light of Geodesign: Processes and Procedures

In addition to the countless and increasingly simplified possibilities for building knowledge databases and voluntary participation, supported by Geodesign, a group of 10 researchers met virtually to develop a simulated model of sustainable territorial planning for the Rio de Janeiro Metropolitan Region (RJMR). It is important to point out that the majority of the group did not inhabit in the region.

The project proposals developed at the workshop were developed in two-time scenarios (i) 2035 and (ii) 2050, medium and long term, respectively; and in three variations of propositional positioning for each time scenario, being (i) non adopter; (ii) late adopter; (iii) early adopter; following the framework suggested by IGC [25].

In addition, the dynamics of the workshop developed in four meetings (Fig. 1), and in (i) the first meeting, reading enrichment was carried out; in the (ii) second moment, the non-adopter proposals for 2035 (Group A) and non-adopter proposals for 2050 (Group B) were prepared, both observing the information constructed in the reading enrichment; at (iii) the third meeting, late adopter proposals for 2035 were prepared, observing reading enrichment (Group A) and late adopter proposals for 2050, observing non-adopter proposals for 2035 (Group B); and in the last meeting (vi) the proposals for 2050 early adopter were collectively elaborated and negotiated, observing the late adopter proposals for 2035 (Group A and B), in order to also meet all the systems and variants put up for discussion in relation to the objectives of the agenda Sustainable Development Goals (SDG), established by the United Nations General Assembly in 2014 [26].

For the purposes of applying the Geodesign methodology, a fundamental factor is the need to provide a fully interactive, integrating environment, which enables the process of joint discussions and decisions, that is, collaboratively, and in the current context also remotely. Thus, meeting the methodological requirements, and operating in a free and objective manner, the web platforms Vicon SAGA[3] and GISColab were adopted jointly

---

[3] Vicon SAGA - https://viconsaga.com.br/.

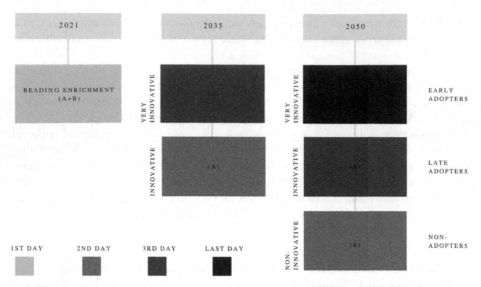

Fig. 1. Methodological development of the workshop in steps. Source: The authors.

by the work team, to support and register the products of the activities, annotations, and project proposals, respectively, as detailed below.

The study area in the reported experience, Rio de Janeiro Metropolitan Region (RJMR), also known as Grande Rio (Fig. 2), is home to approximately 13 million inhabitants [27], being the second largest metropolitan area in Brazil (after São Paulo), the third in South America and the 16th largest in the world in 2020.

In this context, considering its geographical position and due to historical, economic, legal, and political processes, the RJMR is currently considered the second pole of demographic concentration and economic activities in the country, containing a large volume of activities and flows, supply of more specialized assets and services, and a high rate of urbanization. In the state, the RJMR concentrates, on average, 90% of the state population and is overburdened regionally by the concentration of most services, reducing the political and economic strength of the interior of Rio de Janeiro [28].

Step 1: Reading Enrichment

The first methodological step consists of interpreting the collection of thematic carto-graphic databases in the study area, based on the overlap of the thematic classes of each of the maps raised, considering: (i) physical factors, such as terrain topography, geomorphology, soils; (ii) biotic, such as expressive vegetable mass and NDVI; and (iii) anthropic, such as transport, housing, industries, commerce, and education. The data collection was extracted from Brazilian institutional bases, satellite image, and OpenStreetMap® and processed by Geoprocessing Laboratory[4] staff.

From the combined interpretation of these data layers, the systems can provide, in a holistic way, intrinsic and relational information about distances, proximity, access, age,

---

[4] The Geoprocessing Lab (Geoproea) - https://geoproea.arq.ufmg.br/laboratorio.

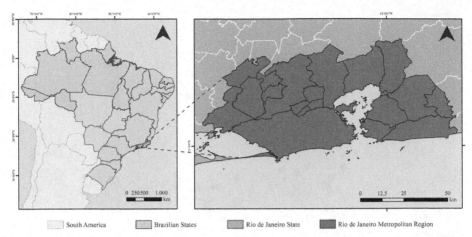

South America   Brazilian States   Rio de Janeiro State   Rio de Janeiro Metropolitan Region

Fig. 2. Study area: Rio de Janeiro Metropolitan Region, Brazil. WGS84. Source: The authors.

dependence, similarities and other characteristics of the environment [29]. Therefore, the wide and diversified thematic cartographic collection made available to the work team helps them to understand the local geodiversity, in addition to pointing out, by the combination of independent factors, areas with potentials or demands (risks).

Each contributor of the workshop had access to the Web SIG Vicon SAGA, where he or she could perform, in an agile and direct way, the geolocalized annotation of his observations regarding demands and potentials relevant to the enrichment of the current knowledge base of RJMR. At the end of the stage, 87 notes were added to the knowledge base (Fig. 3), categorized according to the following themes: agriculture (1%), trade and industry (8%), energy (9%), housing (16%), hydrography (14%), institutions (5%), transport (18%), tourism and culture (23%), and vegetation (6%).

Step 2: Elaboration of Non-adopter and Late Adopter Scenarios
In the stage of preparing non-adopter proposals for the years 2035 and 2050, the work team sought to add the demands registered based on reading enrichment, added to the examples of successful projects previously practiced by managers public services in the country. Many proposals were motivated by the main challenges and chronic problems faced by the citizens residing in RJMR (e.g., supply of energy, water, and urban mobility).

Among the project proposals prepared by the group, the following stand out: (i) industrial pollution control mechanisms; (ii) creation of ecological corridors with the objective of connecting the fragments and reducing the impact of heat islands; (iii) encouraging and making urban expansion compatible with the promotion of tourism, leisure, and culture; (iv) light rail; and (v) creation of a green belt for the preservation of Baía de Guanabara.

In the late adopter scenarios for the years 2035 and 2050, it is possible to observe a certain difficulty in preparing proposals, especially to meet the goals established for carbon credit (an increase of 30% by 2050). However, the results were satisfactory and among the proposals, the following stand out: (i) restoration of riparian ecosystems; (ii) use of navigable maritime strips for public transport; (iii) creation of optimized

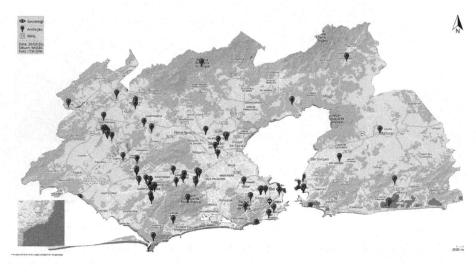

Fig. 3. Reading Enrichment: Map of Rio de Janeiro Metropolitan Region with notes from contributors regarding demands and potentials relevant to the enrichment of the current knowledge base. Source: Vicon SAGA Platform - RJMR Geodesing Project (link).

and shared workspaces; (iv) sea wave energy; and (v) conservation and expansion of expressive vegetation cover. All designs are indicated at Fig. 4, below.

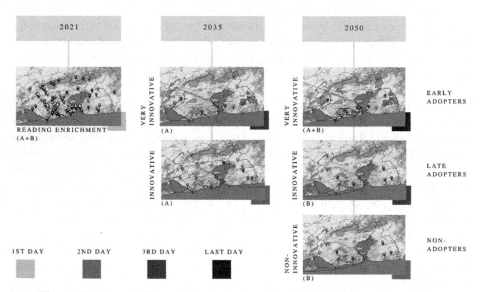

Fig. 4. Resulting medium and long-term scenarios for RJMR. Source: The authors.

Step 3: Elaboration of the Early Adopter Scenario
Finally, in the early adopter positioning, for the year 2050, the increase in participation was quite considerable in quantity and quality of the proposals, it is believed that due to the familiarity established systematically with the methodology. In this way, it is worth highlighting some interesting proposals: (i) seawater desalination complexes for the purpose of supplying this resource to the population; (ii) monitoring panel of individualized health of the population; (iii) high-speed train; (iv) sustainable community complexes; and (v) conservation, creation, and expansion of expressive vegetation cover. This stage was also marked by negotiation and mediation, using resources available on the GISColab platform, carried out to reach a common consensus on the final proposal.

3 Results and Discussion: Analysis of the Impacts of Proposed Projects Against the Sustainable Development Goals (SDGs)

After completing the proposed steps, carried out through group discussions, over the 4 meetings in Google Meet virtual rooms, the final step consists of analyzing the impact of the suggested projects within the 3 innovation scenarios for the year 2050 on the 17 objectives of the sustainable development agenda (SDGs), established by the United Nations General Assembly in 2014 [26]. The SDGs cover social and economic development issues, from poverty eradication, actions against global climate change, even the development of sustainable cities and communities.

Figure 5 presents the matrix of correlation and weighting of the impacts caused by the project proposals for the scenarios non-adopter (a), late adopter (b) and early adopter (c) for the year 2050 in relation to the SDG proposed by the UN.

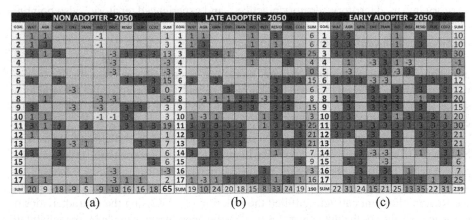

(a)   (b)   (c)

Fig. 5. Correlation matrix and weighting of the impacts caused by the project proposals for 2050 on the 17 Sustainable Development Goals proposed by the United Nations [26]. Source: Authors.

From the analysis of the impact matrices, it was found that the positive impact caused by the proposed projects on the sustainable development goals was enhanced as the innovation scenarios intensified. In other words, they were more daring.

In addition, the sums available at the ends of the matrices made it possible to verify in a direct and quantifiable way which systems (columns) were more or less contemplated. Similarly, the sum represented at the right end of the matrix, made it possible to verify the intensity of compliance with the sustainability goals (lines). For example, for the non-adopter scenario (Fig. 5a), it appears that the Water system (WAT) was the most contemplated by the proposed projects. On the other hand, in this same scenario, the Institutional system (INST), in addition to not having been favored, was severely damaged (negative sum equal to –19), given the impacts caused by the proposed projects. Under the aspect of sustainable objectives, while the goal "11 - Sustainable Cities and Communities" was the most privileged by the proposals, the goal "8 - Decent work and economic growth" was the most affected by the actions proposed in this scenario.

In this way, evaluative instruments, such as the impact matrix presented, act as a fundamental analytical resource for the process of prognosis of sustainable evolution. Therefore, it is essential that the methodology considers and enables the construction and analysis of these quantitative models. In a systematic way (in rounds, for example), it is possible to foster reflections and discussions among the community involved about the impacts (positive and negative) of the proposed projects. Thus, the group will be able to reflect and even reconsider on the feasibility of certain proposals that may negatively enhance sustainable objectives, operating as feedback mechanisms for the support system for territorial planning.

4 Conclusions

This experience showed the relevance of social relations in the territory and converge to the concept of cartography of social action presented by Ribeiro and Silva [30], who argue that "cartography must value social experience, really tracing the transformation of territory into used territory, territory practiced, and experienced territory", also pointing out that the territory should not be a category of analysis when it is disassociated from the relations that coexist there.

The importance of extracting geolocalized information lies in its various possible applications, whether public or private, in various areas of knowledge. In the case of urban planning, the growing need for knowledge and monitoring of the geographical space finds in Remote Sensing tools that allow obtaining information necessary for effective environmental management.

The practice taken corroborates with the results achieved on the activity reported by Scorza (31), in which the workshop participants showed adherence to the taxonomy and gave positive feedback regarding the proposed method. Furthermore, since most of the group does not live in the region, it is important to emphasize that the dynamic, especially the Reading Enrichment step, fulfilled the function of addressing the characteristics of the place. The use of the map layers, as well as the appointments made by the inhabitant participants – here supported by Vicon SAGA, were widely considered in the proposition phases. These findings reiterate the acceptability of the Geodesign method and highlights the improvements proposed by the Brazilian platform.

The dynamics of the workshop, as well as its processes and procedures, allowed realize the potential to be explored regarding use of digital and online tools in collaborative planning of the cities, especially in the current context of the global pandemic.

In this sense, although at first it seems like a weakness, working with a group of people in the workshop who did not belong or knew the study area, makes the reading enrichment step quite important for the exploration of georeferenced data, and as a consequence, to the formation of knowledge and critical thinking about the territory.

As for the analysis of compliance with the SDGs, although the matrices show optimistic scenarios, there is a gap in the literature to be worked on regarding the establishment of less subjective metrics to assess compliance and performance, and in this sense, a potential development of future studies.

Finally, inclusive and democratic methodologies, such as Geodesign, supported by collaborative and digital platforms, such as GISColab and Vicon SAGA adopted in the study (among many others existing in the field of VGIs), showed and supported the discussion of the importance of urban and environmental planning conscious for the guarantee of environmental resources in the medium and long term.

Acknowledgment. The authors are grateful for the collaboration of all students who participated in the workshop; for the assistance of Ana Clara Mourão Moura (UFMG), who coordinated the project "Geodesign Brasil: Trees for Metropolitan Regions"; for the support of the Geoprocessing Laboratory (Geoproea/EAUFMG) staff; the GISColab platform (CNPq Project 401066/2016–9/ FAPEMIG PPM-00368–18). The authors also thank Graduate Program in Geography (PPGGEO/IGC-UFMG) and Graduate Program in Agricultural Education (PPGEA/UFRRJ) for the financial support.

References

1. Steinitz, C.: A Framework for Geodesign: Changing Geography by Design. Esri Press, Redlands, 360 p. (2012)
2. Miller, W.: Introducing Geodesign: The Concept. ESRI Press, Redlands, 36 p. (2012)
3. Dangermond, J.: GIS: Designing our future. ArcNews Online (2009). http://www.esri.com/news/arcnews/summer09articles/gis-designing-our-future.html
4. Flaxman, M.: Geodesign: fundamental principles and routes forward. Presentation to the Geodesign Summit (2010). https://www.esri.com/videos/watch?videoid=elk067YU2s8
5. Ervin, S.: A system for geodesign. In: DLA - Digital Landscape Architecture 2011: Teaching Landscape Architecture, Proceedings. Bernburg e Dessau, Alemanha. DLA, Germany (2011). http://www.kolleg.loel.hs-anhalt.de/landschaftsinformatik/fileadmin/user_upload/_temp_/2011/Proceedings/305_ERVIN_2011May10.pdf
6. Moura, A.: O Geodesign como processo de co-criação de acordos coletivos para a paisagem territorial e urbana. In: Ladwig, N., Campos, J. (eds.) Planejamento e gestão territorial: o papel e os instrumentos do planejamento territorial na interface entre o urbano e o rural. Criciúma (SC). UNESC (2019). https://doi.org/10.18616/pgtur01
7. Lieven, C., Lüders, B., Kulus, D., Thoneick, R.: Enabling digital co-creation in urban planning and development. In: Zimmermann, A., Howlett, R.J., Jain, L.C. (eds.) Human Centred Intelligent Systems. SIST, vol. 189, pp. 415–430. Springer, Singapore (2021). https://doi.org/10.1007/978-981-15-5784-2_34
8. Davis, J., Pijawka, D., Wentz, E., Hale, M.: Evaluation of community-based land use planning through Geodesign: application to American Indian communities. Landscape Urban Plan. **203** (2020). https://doi.org/10.1016/j.landurbplan.2020.103880

9. Nyerges, T., et al.: Geodesign dynamics for sustainable urban watershed development. Sustain. Cities Soc. **25**, 13–24 (2016). https://doi.org/10.1016/j.scs.2016.04.016

10. Monteiro, L., Moura, A., Zyngier, C., Sena, I., Paula, P.: Geodesign facing the urgency of reducing poverty: the cases of Belo Horizonte. DisegnareCon **11**(20), 6.1–6.25 (2018). https://doi.org/10.20365/disegnarecon.20.2018.6

11. Rafiee, A., van der Male, P., Dias, E., Scholten, H.: Interactive 3D geodesign tool for multidisciplinary wind turbine planning. J. Environ. Manag. **205**, 107–124 (2018). https://doi.org/10.1016/j.jenvman.2017.09.042

12. Perki, R.: Geodesigning landscape linkages: coupling GIS with wildlife corridor design in conservation planning. Landscape Urban Plan. **156**, 44–58 (2016). https://doi.org/10.1016/j.landurbplan.2016.05.016

13. Wu, C., Chiang, Y.: A geodesign framework procedure for developing flood resilient city. Habitat Int. **75**, 78–89 (2018). https://doi.org/10.1016/j.habitatint.2018.04.009

14. Fragomeni, M., Bernardes, S., Shepherd, M., Rivero, R.: A collaborative approach to heat response planning: a case study to understand the integration of urban climatology and land-use planning. Urban Clim. **3** (2020). https://doi.org/10.1016/j.uclim.2020.100653

15. Huang, G., Zhou, N.: Geodesign in developing countries: the example of the master plan for Wulingyuan national scenic area, China. Landscape Urban Plan. **156**, 81–91 (2016). https://doi.org/10.1016/j.landurbplan.2016.05.014

16. Chen, Y., Dang, A., Peng, X.: Building a cultural heritage corridor based on geodesign theory and methodology. J. Urban Manag. **3**, 97–112 (2014). https://doi.org/10.1016/S2226-5856(18)30086-4

17. Campagna, M., Di Cesare, E., Cocco, C.: Integrating green-infrastructures design in strategic spatial planning with geodesign. Sustainability **12**(5), 1820 (2020). https://doi.org/10.3390/su12051820

18. Eikelboom, T., Janssen, R.: Collaborative use of geodesign tools to support decision-making on adaptation to climate change. Mitig. Adapt. Strat. Glob. Change **22**(2), 247–266 (2015). https://doi.org/10.1007/s11027-015-9633-4

19. Rekittke, J., Paar, P., Ballal, H.: Experience of a genuine geodesign act. J. Digital Landscape Archit. **4**, 196–204 (2019). https://doi.org/10.14627/537663021

20. Janssen, R., Dias, E.: A pictorial approach to geodesign: a case study for the Lower Zambezi valley. Landscape Urban Plan. **164**, 144–148 (2017). https://doi.org/10.1016/j.landurbplan.2017.03.014

21. Haddad, M., Moura, A., Cook, V., Lima, T.: The social dimensions of the iron quadrangle region: an educational experience in geodesign. Prof. Geograph. **1**, 1–17 (2021). https://doi.org/10.1080/00330124.2021.1895849

22. Hulse, D., et al.: Anticipating surprise: using agent-based alternative futures simulation modeling to identify and map surprising fires in the Willamette Valley. Oregon USA. Landscape Urban Plan. **156**, 26–43 (2016). https://doi.org/10.1016/j.landurbplan.2016.05.012

23. Moura, A.C.M., Freitas, C.R.: Brazilian Geodesign Platform: WebGis & SDI & Geodesign as Co-creation and Geo-Collaboration. In: Gervasi, O., et al. (eds.) ICCSA 2020. LNCS, vol. 12252, pp. 332–348. Springer, Cham (2020). https://doi.org/10.1007/978-3-030-58811-3_24

24. Filippo, D., Filho, J.V., Endler, M., Fuks, H.: Mobilidade e ubiquidade para colaboração. In: Pimentel, H., Fuks, M. (eds.) Sistemas Colaborativos. 1a Edição ed., p. 416 (2011)

25. IGC, the International Geodesign Collaboration group, was formed to explore scenario-driven designs for regional and local-scale study areas that address future global changes (2021). https://www.igc-geodesign.org/

26. UN. United Nations: Open Working Group proposal for Sustainable Development Goals (2014). http://undocs.org/A/68/970

27. IPEA. Instituto de Pesquisa Econômica Aplicada. Projeto de Governança Metropolitana no Brasil. Oficina 1 - Arranjos Institucionais de Gestão Metropolitana (2012). https://www.ipea.gov.br/redeipea/images/pdfs/governanca_metropolitana/projeto_g overnanca_oficina1_rj.pdf
28. Marafon, G.J., Ribeiro, M.A., Côrrea, R.S., Vasconselos, V.N.: Geografia do estado do Rio de Janeiro: da compreensão do passado aos desafios do presente. Grama Editora, Rio de Janeiro, 161 p. (2011)
29. Xavier-Da-Silva, J., Marino, T.B.: A Geografia no apoio à decisão em situações de emergência. In: XIII Encuentro de Geógrafos de América Latina, San Jose. Revista Geografia de Costa Rica. San José (2011). https://sites.google.com/a/geogroupcr.com/revista-geografia-de-costa-rica/xiii-egal-2011-costa-rica
30. Ribeiro, A., Silva, C.A.: Cartografia da Ação e a Juventude na cidade. In: Ribeiro, A.C.T., da Silva, C.A., Campos, A. (eds.) Cartografia da ação e movimentos da sociedade: desafios das experiências urbanas. Lamparina, Rio de Janeiro (2011)
31. Scorza, F.: Training Decision-Makers: GEODESIGN Workshop Paving the Way for New Urban Agenda. In: Gervasi, O., et al. (eds.) ICCSA 2020. LNCS, vol. 12252, pp. 310–316. Springer, Cham (2020). https://doi.org/10.1007/978-3-030-58811-3_22

Geodesign Using GISColab Platform: SDI Consumed by WMS and WFS & WPS Protocols in Transformative-Learning Actions in Planning

Ana Clara Mourão Moura$^{(\boxtimes)}$ [iD], Christian Rezende Freitas [iD],
Vanessa Tenuta de Freitas [iD], and Ana Isabel Anastasia de Sa [iD]

Escola de Arquitetura, Laboratório de Geoprocessamento, Universidade Federal de Minas Gerais (UFMG), Rua Paraíba 697, Belo Horizonte, Brazil
anaclara@ufmg.br, christianrezende@alomeioambiente.com.br,
vanessa.vtf@gmail.com, isabelanastasia@gmail.com

Abstract. Territorial planning is undergoing significant transformations that establish as working conditions the use of web-based geospatial technologies, the use of methods for sharing decisions and listening to citizens and the wide use of mechanisms to facilitate understanding due to geovisualization. Among these resources, the methods of planning by Geodesign stand out, which were adapted in the proposal of the web-based platform GISColab, elaborated with the purpose of favoring the shared planning by co-creation. The platform extensively applies the resources of Spatial Data Infrastructures (SDI's) through protocols established by OGC (Open Geospatial Consortium) for consumption of information via WMS (Web Map Service) or WFS (Web Feature Service), allowing in both cases the increment in performances by WPS (Web Processing Service). The article discusses the differences in information consumption and illustrates them through two case studies: Trees for Metropolitan Regions, in which the accesses to data were built by WFS and support to decisions were based on WPS; and Geodesign at Participatory Budgeting where accesses were via WMS. The conclusions indicate the importance of public data being, in fact, of public access and consumption, demonstrating the positive impact of alignment with data exchange protocols. The GISColab platform, developed according to these principles, supports participatory planning, expressively communicative and in transformative-learning actions.

Keywords: Participatory planning · Spatial data infrastructure · OGC protocols

1 Introduction - Contemporary Participatory Planning Based on Geodesign and the Emergency of GISColab

The significant development and propagation of geo-information technology made tools that respond to models of representation, analysis, simulation and proposition of territorial occurrences and conditions, much more accessible to users that need to work with spatial investigation. In truth, these tools facilitate the processes that were previously

O. Gervasi et al. (Eds.): ICCSA 2021, LNCS 12954, pp. 448–462, 2021.
https://doi.org/10.1007/978-3-030-86979-3_32

conceived as models in analogical form, when their execution came at great expense. Today they are significantly simpler due to the advent of informatics, thus favoring interesting possibilities for spatial analysis. Exploratory and investigative studies are empowered by geo-visualization resources, allowing involvement of different actors in decision-making and opinion building in shared planning through co-creation.

It has been 50 years since the ideas regarding the "ladder of citizen participation" by Arnstein [1] were first published, and they still motivate and drive urban and territorial planning activity, considering that co-creative planning is a contemporary value that helps to advances mechanisms of participation. The author points out that during the initial stage, comprised of the first two steps of the ladder, citizens are manipulated and falsely convinced of their participation, in what she defines as "therapy". During the second stage, composed of three steps, appeasement is sought as the participants are offered information and some inquiry is made, though limited to the appeasing process. On the third stage, also composed of three steps, citizens achieve some degree of power, as partnerships are suggested, some autonomy is delegated and, at last, citizens have some control over results. Among many publications developed from the initial proposal, it´s interesting to mention Rocha's [2] work, arguing for the expansion of studies on the "ladder of empowerment", understood as a contemporary variation of the participation model defended from the 1980's onward [3–6]. Based on the elements of locus, process, goals and power experience, Rocha [2] defines a new 5 step ladder, which include atomistic individual empowerment, embedded individual empowerment, mediated empowerment, social-political empowerment, and political empowerment. The development of the process starts by altering one's individual conditions until it is possible to alter the general conditions of an entire society. Since it creates an increasingly wider approach, the author emphasizes a growing pattern between each stage, so all levels need to be stimulated and worked on.

It is important to note that although both authors refer to this process as a "ladder", this does not necessarily mean one step is less important than the other, or that it should be an error or mistake that was overcome by advancing to the next one. For instance, informing citizens is part of Arnstein's [1] step 3, which does not mean it has to be abandoned, surpassed or anything along these lines. In our understanding, there are keywords and values that need to continue to exist for participation to evolve and indeed become socially beneficial as it expands planning capacity. They include the need to: inform, consult, promote partnerships, conscious delegation of tasks, favor individual improvement, mediate collective actions, and achieve political development by understanding that collective agreements are a way to maximize consensus.

One may state, as proposed by Innes [7], that the 1990's saw the emergence of a line of thought that defends interactive planning as a communicational activity, incorporating communities, political issues and public decision-making processes. To understand the context surrounding this idea, Khakee [8] presents an axial planning structure that ranges from the approaches of Rational-Comprehensive Planning; Incremental Planning, Advocacy Planning, Implementation-Oriented Planning, Strategic planning, Transactive or Participatory Planning, Negotiative Planning and Communicative Planning.

In the Rational-Comprehensive approach, the planner decomposes reality to its individual components in order to interpret them. This results in a hierarchical matrix with the actions that are limited to the political and technical spheres, which does not include citizen participation. The Incremental Approach consists of facing only the most important issues and to seek small, incremental changes, wherein community role is taken into consideration, but as information providers. The Advocacy Planning approach proposes that populations are heard through different groups that represent society, and when there are no groups capable of representing certain sectors, their interests would be defended by planners. Implementation-Oriented focuses on discussing processes in a way that guarantees that the planning is executed and is not limited to an analytical portrayal of the problems. Strategic Planning argues for the substitution of proposed solutions for a given set of commitments, and in doing so, includes the participation of the population and the search for consensus among actors in the different stages of planning. Transactive or Participatory planning suggests an association between technicians and citizens, which imposed the need for planners to have skills related to communication and social psychology, since their role would be that of a mediator for social and urban changes. Negotiative Planning is based on creating mutual agreements and commitments, which involves citizens, companies, and public authorities. At last, Communicative Planning defends each process is unique and specific to each situation, and that planners are non-neutral elements of this process, though they should commit to building consensus amongst participants [9–12].

As is the case when analyzing the ladder of participation and the ladder of empowerment, one needs to understand that even though each new form of planning emerges from criticisms to previous processes, a lot of these proposed actions and modes of planning still play a fundamental role and should not be promptly discarded. The Advocative position should be limited to how the planner acts to decode the collective will, an ability that may be developed by methodical processes for hearing and mediating, which leads us to the proposals made by Transactive Planning. The Strategic Approach can continue to exist by building consensus regarding the priorities of each proposal, which are built collectively. Negotiative Planning is based on the maximization of consensus, in which the demands and concessions are clearly defined. The focus on building consensus is still present in Communicative Planning, which clearly states there is no single path, but rather that each case is unique in its requirements, as argued by Forester [13], who describes it as a process of "Transformative Learning".

In face of the values and demands imposed by contemporary reality, one of the methods that planners can resort to is Geodesign, as it is based on the creation of workshops that bring together different social actors. Geodesign is design "with" and "for" the territory. It seeks a contextualized transformation of landscapes, respecting nature and local culture. Geodesign can provide a systematic methodological model for regional, urban and local planning, aiming towards the sustainable integration of human activities within natural environments, respecting of cultural peculiarities and allowing for a democratic decision-making process.

It is a method for the collective construction of alternative futures for a given landscape or territory, applicable in any scale and in which listening to citizens is crucial for building opinions and making decisions. It is widely supported by geovisualization platforms. The basic principle is to inform participants of the essential characteristics of the area, and to do so it is necessary to provide a set of thematic information, as well as synthesizing them into the main systems, which will become the basis for the co-creation of policies and projects.

Different authors have discussed the concepts and work models used in Geodesign [14–18]. Starting from a common conceptual base, each researcher builds their own framework, which is practically a matter of producing data and information regarding the area's current conditions, followed by participants visualizing and interpreting the information. After this stage, representatives from different sectors of society are asked to collectively build proposals for projects and policies that aim to transform the area, thus reflecting upon its alternative futures. The ideas that are formulated by each group are confronted and analyzed in terms of their impact and proposed goals, to finally achieve a final design by approximating consensuses.

Considering the classification scheme of Khakee [8], we believe the proposal of Geodesign was planned to be more associated to Transactive or Participatory planning, since the role of the conductor was expected to be that of a mediator for social and urban changes and, as the term specifies, a "mediator". But in some cases, it´s based on significant interference of the conducting agent in classifying the areas that can receive proposals, determining which impacts are positive or negative, establishing goals (targets). If the process is well conducted, the organizer will act facilitating negotiations as a mediator. But it depends on the framework and on the tools employed.

The principles of Geodesign were adopted in the GISColab web-platform, developed by the of Geoprocessing Laboratory of Architecture School, Federal University of Minas Gerais, Brazil: Prof. Ana Clara Moura and Christian Freitas. The platform is sufficiently flexible to be used according to the itineraries required for each case study. GISColab's Geodesign practices are also based on Transactive or Participatory Planning, but it goes further, due to significantly advances Communicative Planning, since the platform can be adapted to include different frameworks and provide proper support to the information required by each case study, thus favoring a fully "Transformative Learning" process.

Through GISColab, we advocate for sharing a systematic analysis of territories, but also to include citizen's views as a way to provide more information, in a process we named "Reading Enrichment", In which citizens inform themselves through a collection of data organized by specialists' knowledge, then contribute with their own information and analysis of existing conditions, not necessarily in this order, but organized according to dynamic processes. We defend widespread access to information to avoid reductionist syntheses that end up conditioning decisions, since each social group can choose their own scope and indicate it as appropriate or inappropriate for a specific condition. Therefore, information is provided in a way that is flexible enough not to be supported solely by variables, but rather in "Contexts", and allow participants to create analytical and synthetic compositions according to their own interests.

In GISColab, participants develop and register ideas that are subject to discussions in the form of "Dialogs", and there is no pre-established definition of "right or wrong", nor positive or negative impact, but rather a sum of comments that stimulate individual decision-making. This process can be associated to the principle of "Actionable Consensus", as proposed by Healy [19].

GISColab's Geodesign process can be conducted by planners according to a freely established itinerary, favoring co-design and co-creation. However, the right to make individual remarks and register a vote are guaranteed by registering them in "Dialogs" and by using the "Like or Don't Like" resource. It bears noting Friedman's [20] emphasis that the planner's goal cannot be limited to "getting to a yes", since planning is not necessarily a decision, as it can also be the starting point for building opinions and understandings regarding the territory. Planning can be a support to decision making or a support to opinion making. It is also necessary to invoke Sandercock's [21] warning that, in planning, there is always some risk regarding the ability of each social group to affect planning outcomes, though this can take place even in a local scale, when a group includes individuals who control the speaking and, ultimately, the decisions that are made. In that sense, individual participation is also promoted in our process, but in balance with group participation.

We would like to stress that GISColab planners can orchestrate the dynamics of discussion and collective idea-building according to their own judgment, freely defining their work itinerary, because the platform is quite flexible and open to the development of scripts that take specific actions. For instance, calculating goals, defining scores, creating a voting hierarchy, performance board and any other forms that support the visualization of information deemed relevant. These are done through the "Dashboards" or "Widgets", or calculations done during the integration with data bases on a web server. Hence, there is no "right" or "wrong" in how the tool will support planning because there are several possible ways to adapt it, even during a workshop, as one realizes that planning should be kept flexible, evolutionary, and dynamic.

It is our belief that Geodesign, and its application in the form of GISColab, is a relevant response to contemporary challenges, in which planners can take collective will into account and build co-designed proposals through active listening and citizen participation. Therefore, advancing a process that reduces urban planners' role as authors and amplifies their role as decoders of collective will [22].

2 Methodology - The Proposal of GISColab

According to a new line of thought within information technology, named SOA - Service Oriented Architecture [23], the constant use of the Internet in the contemporary world constitutes an infrastructure in which systems are intrinsically connected and in co-dependence. Such technologies are at the foundation of SDI - Spatial Data Infrastructure, proposed by the Mapping Science Committee of the US National Research Council in 1993, and incorporated by INSPIRE (Infrastructure for Spatial Information in Europe) in 2007 [24].

In Brazil, the intention of providing resources on spatial data infrastructure was registered on Decree 6.666 of November 27h, 2008, published by the Ministry of Planning, in which the National Spatial Data Infrastructure was officially created. It was expected that this principle would also be transplanted into state and city scales, fostering and facilitating the access and consumption of geographic information. In order to fully provide access to information, it would be necessary to take interoperable aspects into consideration, which would translate into an effort towards the standardization, sharing and integration of geospatial data.

To achieve interoperability, the OGC (Open Geospatial Consortium) developed a specification for mapping on the web, which is based on a non-proprietary system, thus allowing users to consume data regardless of the software they use [25]. Geographic data consumption uses the WMS (Web Map Service - OpenGIS Web Map Serive Interface Standard), WFS (Web Feature Service - OpenGIS Web Feature Service Interface Standard) and WMTS (Web Map Tile Service) standards and can also be incremented with WPS (Web Processing Service).

OpenGIS® Web Map Service Interface Standard (WMS) offers a simple HTTP interface for requesting images from the georeferenced map and one or more databases. A WMS request defines the geographic layer and area of interest for processing. Specifications include at least three different contents in response to the user's request: a) metadata; b) the map with the specified geographic parameters and c) information regarding some specific feature presented on the map [26].

The OpenGIS® Web Feature Service Interface Standard (WFS) also allows the exchange of geographical information through HTTP protocols in GML language. Geographic Markup Language (GML) is a standardized XML language that provides a specialized vocabulary for working with geospatial data. The GML language allows the codification of geographic characteristics beyond modeling, transportation and storing geographical data, in different vectorial and matrix formats [27].

In line with OGC proposals, the GISColab Platform can be described in terms of 4 technological components that, albeit distinct, are complementary:

(a) Geographic Base - The collection of information produced that can be stored in BDG, Shapefile for vector-type information and GeoTIFF for raster-type data.
(b) Geoserver Map Server - The map Server is responsible for converting geographical information into webservices, making the distribution of data more dynamic and guaranteeing interoperability. (Geoserver - http://geoserver.org/ - a Java-based server that allows users to visualize and edit geospatial data. Using open standards established by the OGC).
(c) Metadata Catalog - The metadata catalog Server is responsible for documenting all the information produced that will be used in decision-making and spatial analysis processes. It plays the crucial role of formalizing and registering the spatial set that was used as data for the decision making, as well as the information produced by reading and analyzing basic information. (Geonetwork - https://geonetwork-openso urce.org/ - a catalog application for managing spatially georeferenced resources. Currently, it is used in several spatial data infrastructure across the globe).
(d) WebMap/WebGIS - WebGIS is responsible for retrieval and visualization of information registered in the metadata catalog, as well as organizing information in way that provides a better context for the data and groups of data. Moreover, complementary resources were developed, which allow it to be used for Geodesign and processes of shared decision making. (Mapstore2 - https://mapstore2.readthedocs. io/en/user_docs/ - WebGIS software that is highly modular and open-sourced, developed by GeoSolutions to create, manage, and share maps/panels in a more secure manner).

3   Two Case Studies Conducted in GISColab: With WFS, WMS and WPS Support

In virtue of the limitations imposed by remote work during the 2020–2021 COVID pandemic, the Geoprocessing Laboratory from Architecture School of UFMG, had to develop and test new capacities for conducting Geodesign workshops in a completely remote mode. These challenges resulted in the expansion of the GISColab facilitation tools and the collaboration of different groups, leading to the creation of a study network.

A group consisting of 14 Brazilian universities came together in order to test a single Geodesign protocol for the subject "Trees for Metropolitan Regions", according to the guidelines defined by the IGC global group [28]. It emphasized the creation of mechanisms for characterizing, measuring and incrementing carbon sequestration, with the goal of reducing global climate change. The universities involved and their respective metropolitan areas (MA) were: Universidade Federal do Pará (Belém MA), Universidade Federal de Minas Gerais (Belo Horizonte MA), Universidade do Estado de São Paulo campus Rio Claro and Universidade de Campinas (Campinas MA), Universidade do Extremo Sul Catarinense (Carbonífera MA), Universidade do Estado de Santa Catarina (Florianópolis MA), Universidade Federal do Ceará (Fortaleza MA), Universidade Federal de Goiás (Goiânia MA), Universidade Federal do Amapá e Secretarias do Estado do Governo do Amapá (Macapá MA), Universidade Federal de Tocantins (Palmas MA), Universidade Federal de Pernambuco (Recife MA), Universidade Federal Rural do Rio de Janeiro and Universidade Federal de Juiz de Fora (Rio de Janeiro MA), Universidade do Estado de São Paulo (São Paulo MA).

Before the pandemic, a workshop associated with the subject of Participatory Budgeting was already planned, as part of Ana Isabel Anastasia de Sá doctoral work, using Belo Horizonte as a case study. The initial idea was to conduct the workshop on the university's computer labs, which would privilege in-person discussions. However, the restrictions imposed by the pandemic made the workshop much closer to what would be desirable for a shared planning that involved a broader group of social actors, facilitated by Internet access, although it is necessary to recognize the difficulties of the digital access inequalities. But the possibility for wider diffusion of information in this case is something worth highlighting. The workshop was conducted by the doctoral candidate, with support from the Geoprocessing Laboratory from Architecture School of UFMG team and the participation of academics, people from different city regions and technicians from the Belo Horizonte town administration.

The case study on the Metropolitan Regions presents is an example of a workshop in which the assembly of data and access to WebGis was based on the usage of data from the (SDI) (Spatial Data Infrastructure) platform via WFS (Web Feature Service). The process requires structuring a database of geospatial data, based on the exchange of information through HTTP protocols in GML (Geographic Markup Language), a standardized XML language that provides a vocabulary specific for working with this type of spatial data.

The case study on Participatory Budgeting is also an example of a workshop in which the WebGIS assembly provides support to the overall process, consuming data via WMS (Web Map Service) and connected the layers through a Service Catalog that seeks the URL (Uniform Resource Locator).

3.1 Brazilian Geodesign: Trees for Metropolitan Regions

The development of 12 parallel case studies encompassing Brazilian's metropolitan regions, meant it was necessary to establish a set of standard practices for the processes, thus allowing comparative studies on their performance. The Geoprocessing Laboratory from Architecture School of UFMG was put in charge of producing the entire collection of data for all the case studies, guaranteeing all work was performed under a shared, common ground. Moreover, it intended to show that the process was scalable and could be reproduced in other locations in Brazil to perform regional scale planning.

The starting point included the 10 systems proposed by the IGC-2021 group regarding that year's experiment, namely: vegetation, hydrography, habitation, transportation, institutions, industry and commerce, agriculture, energy, tourism and culture, carbon credit. The first 8 were defined by IGC-2021's project, which left two other systems open for participants to choose. Brazil chose tourism, leisure and culture, due to its national importance, and carbon credits sequestration after a specific study was conducted, to discuss the subject in terms of metropolitan regions. The first step was to define the minimum data and which analyses would provide support for understanding the 10 systems, and a list comprised of 42 maps was produced.

A total of 18 data platforms were consulted to produce theses maps or acquiring the necessary information. This is because the national SDI platform (INDE - Infraestrutura de Dados Espaciais), despite being used for most of the information layers, did not contain all necessary data for the systems included in the workshop. Three of these 18 platforms were international ones (two of them for acquiring satellite images to vegetation classification indexes and surface temperature, topographic images for the calculation of slope inclination and altimetry and one for collaborative data). It is worth noting that a lot of the available platforms have IDE characteristics, but since they do not fully attend the conditions and standards defined by the norm, they may not be classified as complete IDEs. However, for the purpose of this work, they were considered as such, given that they are storages of publicly available geospatial data. From the 15 national platforms, 13 of them were of national character, 1 of them was for a specific portion of the country and 1 was for state-level data.

None of the platforms provided WMS data consumption, or the access format did not fully adhere to OGC standards, which would mean using a link for direct consumption of the layer in the form of an entry on GISColab's Web-GIS. The main national platform in Brazil, INDE, does not provide information via WMS, but we can consume data by downloads. Minas Gerais' data infrastructure (SISEMA) does not provide WMS access but also does offer some downloads. The issue is that even though some platforms provide some sort of WMS access, we are not able to use the data as the basis for the layers used on applications if they are not completely compatible with OGC standards.

Given the inability to make a direct use of the data via WMS, we opted for the longer work involved in using it via WFS, in which we need to download and upload as we tweak the data to fit their more specific purposes. This includes standardizing captions, symbols, or the application of distribution models and spatial analysis. Therefore, the layer acquires some degree of authorship, although the origins of the data are clearly defined. Out of 42 layers, 21 were subject to a process of cropping for defining the area of analysis, projection, grouping captions to suit our goals and standardizing them. However, 21 of them were the product of spatial analysis models based on activity concentration (weighted kernel); hierarchical classification (alpha-numeric table associated with a cartographic base); definition of areas according to normative parameters (buffers); thematic creation using altimetry, slope inclination, isolation, surface temperature; algorithm application (NDVI); calculation of metrics (landscape ecology).

It should be noted that, for this case study, WPS (Web Processing Service) resources were used in widgets, which were programmed to provide a dynamic visualization of automated calculations during the workshop. The study was centered on a discussion regarding carbon sequestration and credits, and the request was that participants created proposals for conservation, creation and extension of areas for the recovery of CO_2 emissions. During this process, as participants created polygons related to these ideas, their areas were computed and the percentage increase in carbon sequestration was also computed and calculated to check if the goal of 30% of increasement was achieved, what was the number of trees that resulted from the increment in areas, the amount of CO_2 in MgC above or below surface and the size of the area in km^2. The processing stage acted as a dynamic support for decisions [29] (Fig. 1).

As part of the analyzes proposed by the IGC, there was also the analysis of the proposals created by the participants and their contribution to the SDGs. In the first case studies, the coordinators carried out this assessment after the creation of the proposals, observing and suggesting which of the SDGs each idea could contribute to, and filling in a spreadsheet with the evaluation of the contributions. During the development of the workshops, we observed that it would be more interesting for the author of the proposal to indicate, in his opinion, to which SDG his idea could contribute, and for the system to calculate and present the sum of the contributions. For this, it was programmed a dynamic layer using WPS, which searches for the data of the ideas created and presents a graph in a widget indicating on the x axis the list of the SDGs and on the y axis the quantity of ideas associated with each objective. This is a way to monitor how each objective is being met by the participants (Fig. 2).

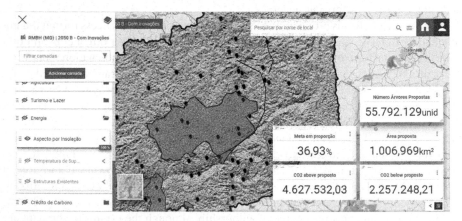

Fig. 1. Belo Horizonte M Region example: the use of WFS and WPS. Source: The authors.

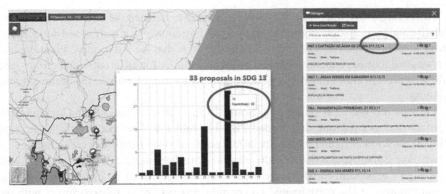

Fig. 2. Salvador M Region example: the use of WPS to SDGs' analysis. Source: The authors.

The advantage of working with WFS access is that the organizer creates the information layers and adapts them to the specific needs of the research. However, this does require special knowledge in data modeling and geoprocessing. An experienced researcher will need, on average, 36 h of work to prepare the 42 layers, 4 h to structure the server database and 4 h to set up WebGIS and geovisualization. This adds up to an average of one hour per layer. If it were possible to access the data via WMS, the stages of preparing and structuring the database on the server would be mitigated, leaving only the need to address layers via URL on WebGIS, and thus reducing average work hours to around six to ten minutes per layer once its web address has been identified.

3.2 Participatory Budgeting: Sharing Decisions in City Planning

The employment of Participatory Budgeting (PB) gained worldwide notoriety in urban planning after the second UN-Habitat meeting in Istanbul (Turkey), 1996, and became something of particular interest in Brazil after the World Social Forum held in Porto Alegre, in 2001 [30]. However, both the interest and the results produced by this practice have declined in virtue of their quality, not to mention that they became mostly consultive instruments, which are not really open to shared planning.

The current study, a simulation of a public query on resource distribution via PB using the Geodesign method and GISColab platform, had the goal of avoiding the existing pattern of previous queries in Belo Horizonte, which had a predominantly consultive nature, and sought instead to test the creation of collective ideas via digital processes.

Participatory budgeting was first implemented in Belo Horizonte in 1994. Up until 1999, PB took place annually, and became bi-annual since. The Digital Participatory Budget was implemented in 2006 and took place four times after, in the years of 2006, 2008, 2011 and 2013. The process was expected to increase general participation, including groups that would generally not take part on in-person meetings. Notwithstanding, parallel processes with in-person discussions for regional areas were kept, and digital PB was conducted in a fully on-line environment. In 2006, there was an attempt to integrate these processes, with proposals being discussed in-person and voting taking place in a broader, digital way. Leading up to 2006, around 10% of the population would participate in these votes, an amount that fell to 0.4% by 2013 [31].

According to Avritzer [32], the expectation was to balance the articulation of representative and participatory democracies by providing equal participation and deliberation power to all citizens. However, what was observed is that the Advocative Planning pattern was maintained, with the technical board accounting for different social groups, and little advance towards Transitive or Participatory Planning, let alone Communicational Planning.

Perhaps the issue, as pointed by Souza [33], is that a cautious and instrumental approach was not the one that guided PBs, but rather a view that sought to increase political consciousness and reform social and political systems through collective action. Hence, Ana Isabel Anastasia de Sá doctoral work had an interest in experimenting with Geodesign's approach, in which the method or itinerary must be clearly presented as the central axis of the participants' co-creation process. Also, to experiment with the Brazilian GISColab platform and the flexibility it provides for adopting different work itineraries.

GISColab can receive data by preparing and uploading the layers chosen by the coordinator, who will develop maps via geoprocessing and symbol application, structured as a WebGIS (Geographic Information System that is transmitted and accessed through the web). However, one of the key potentials uses of the tool is the ability to consume data via WMS, a process in which it will directly connect to an SDI (Spatial Data Infrastructure) and directly access the available maps, without the need for further preparation, but receiving the symbols as the original [34].

There are still few SDI platforms in Brazil which allow WMS access to data, but it is worth mentioning that this possibility is what truly makes SDI a public service. For studies in the Belo Horizonte municipality the local SDI, BHMaps [35], was conceived entirely within OGC standards, and based on WMS. This favors an approach in which workshop organizers define only the information layers that are considered of interest and load them up via their URL.

The reason for using a database which, in turn, uses existing layers is that we wanted to maintain a language that has already been shared by users (BHMaps is already known as Belo Horizonte's information platform). The expectation is that this would help participants understand the area and allow them to dedicate themselves to creating proposals. The visualization symbols (captions and their graphic rendering) are inherited from the original layers, which is another way of maintaining the connection to the data that users are already familiar with.

However, BHMaps has hundreds of layers organized in 29 main themes, which could lead to a sort of information maze if they were entirely consumed. Hence, the organizer had to make a strategic choice regarding the most relevant layers, 69 in total, with users being allowed to include new layers as they deemed necessary.

The maps were organized according to the main themes that impact PB decisions, or that are generally dealt with in PB proposals, namely: social welfare, culture and tourism, education, sports and leisure, habitation, environment, public squares, mobility and transportation, health, demographics, land division, urban legislation, soil usage and occupation, infrastructure, urban cleaning, slope inclinations, economic activity, free access to internet, and risk (Fig. 3).

Fig. 3. Participatory budgeting in Belo Horizonte: the use of WMS. Source: The authors.

GISColab's Geodesign process followed the stages of "Reading Enrichment", in which participants inform themselves and register information through map layers, including the area conditions, registering alerts on potential uses, vulnerabilities, specific characteristics of the territory that they would like to highlight for consideration in proposals. The second stage, the "Idea Proposition", comprises participants' coming up with their own ideas, though it is possible to exchange thoughts with the remaining participants through videoconferencing, so ideas can emerge from either individual citizens or as a collective effort by a group. On the third stage all ideas are commented on, in the "Dialogs" process, so that they can be subject to questioning, gain support, have further information added to them or receive requests for additional information. In the final stage, the "Voting", they voted on each idea and a hierarchy is set according to the amount of "likes" received and the limits imposed by financial resources, given that they are also scored based on their cost range.

4 Results and Conclusions

The first consideration advanced by this paper regards the role of Geodesign, developed through the GISColab platform, as a methodological support for the development of participatory planning according to contemporary values. There are various publications regarding the processes of Geodesign, in which authors present their work structures as itineraries, mostly through standard scripts that are portrayed as applicable to different case studies. The studies that are made possible by using GISColab do not start from a pre-fixated protocol, but rather have the necessary flexibility to allow for adaptations even during the workshop, in virtue of the specific needs of each group, territory, set of goals. However, that requires the planner not to act as an author of the project, but rather as someone who decodifies the collective will [22]. To do so, it is worth noting the approach Khakee [8] classified as Transactive or Participatory planning, in which the orchestrator needs to have communicational skills and be able to achieve a sort of psychological pairing with participants, to know the right moment to propose specific resources and procedures.

The work itinerary that was most tested in GISColab and adopted in the two case studies portrayed in this paper, albeit with some occasional differences and adaptations made to better serve different purposes, was the one that initiates with "Reading Enrichment", with the goal of informing participants and collecting their information regarding the territory. This stage is followed by "Idea Proposition", which can take place in synchronous or asynchronous processes, and in which dynamic tools provide a significant support by offering participants feedback on quantitative data, goals, percentages, comparisons. In that sense, such support is in line with the principles of the planning typology defined by Khakee [8] as Strategic planning, since a few sets of expectations or principles can be established to create agreements.

In the case study Trees for Metropolitan Regions, an expectation for increments in carbon sequestration was established, expanding areas with robust vegetation by 30% until 2050, a value that is supported by bibliographic reference. This was achieved by implementing dynamic calculations that would compute the performance of each proposal and present partial results on widgets. In the Participatory Budgeting case study, the mechanisms used were voting and score calculation, based on the costs of each proposal and the limits of the budget, which were used to create a hierarchy.

Once the ideas are proposed, the "Dialogs" mechanism has been widely used. In it, participants can comment, question, complement or defend the ideas that are portrayed, so that they are not left in isolation, but rather interpreted as part of a context and eventually, even be improved through collective co-design. Therefore, this stage of the planning can be classified, according to Khakee's [8] model, as Communicative, because it is a way to articulate and favor the achievement of maximum consensus, with ample hearing and the right to individual manifestations.

At last, since the platform is open to WPS programming, it can receive additional data that is deemed relevant by participants via WMS or WFS, at any given stage. Thus, participants can take control over the set of information and perform individual judgments regarding which areas they consider apt or inapt for intervention, areas that are or are not in need of new uses, or if it is indicated for new ideas or not. In such sense, it allows for a type of planning that Forester [13] classified as "Transformative-Learning".

Finally, a discussion is due regarding consumption expectations and the use of geospatial information in web-based platforms that support planning. For participants to use information that is already publicly available, we highlight the importance of SDI platforms that adopt WMS standards plus OGC precepts. However, there is the risk that this kind of spatial data usage creates an exponential demand in data server infrastructure, since the more useful the platform, the more other platforms will be connected to it. From a planning point of view, the interest and the growth in use are incredibly positive factors, since they remove data from a state of stale information and place them as the basis from processes that transform society. The issue of scalability, though, is something to be reckoned with. The technology to solve this problem is already available, for instance by employing WMTS (Web Map Tile Service), which facilitates map consumption by pre-rendering the layers that will be visualized in a faster and optimized manner.

This does not mean that the importance of WFS geospatial data consumption should be understated, since they allow the planner to work with the geovisualization of information to favor strategies and create alerts for participants. Nonetheless, one must need to be prepared to face significant demands of time and expert knowledge regarding geoprocessing to prepare the layers that will serve as foundation for the workshop.

In both cases, between the consumption of spatial data via WMS, WFS or WMTS, the potential of WPS must be noted when it comes to the production of dynamic data that fulfills the strategic goals of information consumption in decision making processes. Some keywords will define the development of tools that support planning, and Geodesign specifically: scalability, flexibility, geovisualization.

Acknowledgments. The authors thank CNPq support through the project 401066/2016–9 and FAPEMIG PPM-00368–18.

References

1. Arnstein, S.: A ladder of citizen participation. Am. Plan. Assoc. **35**(4), 216–224 (1969)
2. Rocha, E.: A ladder of empowerment. J. Plan. Educ. Res. **17**, 31–44 (1997). https://doi.org/10.1177/0739456X9701700104
3. Rappoport, J.: In praise of paradox: a social policy of empowerment of prevention. Am. J. Commun. Psychol. **9**(1), 1–26 (1981)
4. Forester, J.: Planning in the face of power. University of California Press, Berkeley (1989)
5. Zimmerman, M.A.: Taking aim on empowerment research. On the distinction between individual and psychological conceptions. Am. J. Commun. Psychol. **18**(1), 169–177 (1990)
6. Friedman, J.: Empowerment: the Politics of Alternatives Development. Blackwell, Cambridge (1992)
7. Innes, J.: Planning theory's emerging paradigm: communicative action and interactive practice. J. Plan. Educ. Res. **14**(3), 183–189 (1995)
8. Khakee, A.: Evaluation and planning: inseparable concepts. Town Plan. Rev. **69**(4), 359–374 (1998)
9. Pressman, J., Wildavsky, A.: Implementation. University of California Press, Berkeley (1973)
10. Kinyashi, G.F.: Towards Genuine Participation for the Poor: Critical analysis of Village Travel and Transport Project (VTTP). Morogoro, Tanzania (2006)
11. Oliveira, J.A.P.: Desafios do planejamento em políticas públicas: diferentes visões e práticas. Revista de Administração Pública **40**(2), 273–287 (2006)
12. Stumptener, A.: E-learning-module: the basics of watershed management. Freie Universität Berlin (2020). https://www.geo.fu-berlin.de/en/v/geolearning/watershed_management/introduction_wm/natural_resource_management_planning/how_to_plan/planning_models/index.html. Accessed 17 May 2019
13. Forester, J.: The Deliberative Practitioner: Encouraging Participatory Planning Processes. MIT Press (1999)
14. Dangermond, J.: GIS: Designing our future. ArcNews, Summer (2009). http://dx.doi.org/10.11606/gtp.v14i1.148381
15. Ervin, S.: A system for Geodesign. Keynote: 27 May 2011, pp. 158–167 (2011). http://www.kolleg.loel.hs-anhalt.de/landschaftsinformatik/fileadmin/user_upload/_temp_/2012/Proceedings/Buhmann_2012_19_Ervin_Keynote_2011.pdf. Accessed 27 Jan 2018

16. Flaxman, M. Geodesign: fundamental principles and routes forward. Talk at GeoDesign Summit (2010). https://www.esri.com/videos/watch?videoid=elk067YU2s8. Accessed 17 Jan 17 2019

17. Miller, W. R. Introducing Geodesign: The Concept. Esri Press, Redlands, 35 p (2012). https://www.esri.com/library/whitepapers/pdfs/introducing-geodesign.pdf. Accessed 27 Nov 2018

18. Steinitz, C.: A Framework for Geodesign: Changing Geography by Design. ESRI Press, Redlands (2012)

19. Healey, P.: Collaborative Planning: Shaping in Fragmented Societies. Macmillan International Higher Education (1997)

20. Friedmann, J.: The uses of planning theory: a bibliographic essay. J. Plan. Educ. Res. 28(2), 247–257 (2008)

21. Sandercock, L.: Towards Cosmopolis. Planning for Multicultural Cities. Wiley, London (1998)

22. Moura, A.C.M.O.: Geodesign como processo de cocriação de acordos coletivos para a paisagem territorial e urbana. In: Ladwig, N.I., Campos, J.B. (eds.) Planejamento e gestão territorial: o papel e os instrumentos do Planejamento Territorial na Interface entre o Urbano e o Rural. Criciúma - SC: UNESC (2019). http://repositorio.unesc.net/handle/1/7018

23. Oliveira, P.A., Davis Junior, C.A., Oliveira, P.F.A.: Proposição de infra estrutura de dados espaciais (SDI) local, baseada em arquitetura orientada por serviços. In: X Brazilian Syposium on GeoInformatics, 2008, Rio de Janeiro (RJ). Proceedings of the X Brazilian Symposium on GeoInformatics. Porto Alegre (RS): SBC Sociedade Brasileira de Computação (2008)

24. Craglia, M., Campagna, M.: Advanced Regional Spatial Data Infrastructures in Europe. European Commission; Joint Research Centre; Institute for Environment and Sustainability (2009)

25. Belussi, A., Catania, B., Clementini, E., Ferrari, E. (eds.): Spatial Data on the Web: Modeling and Management. Springer, Heidelberg (2007)

26. Percivall, G. (ed.): OpenGIS® Reference Model. Document number OGC 03-040 Version: 0.1.3. Open Geospatial Consortium, Inc. (2003)

27. GeoConnections: Mapping the future together online. GeoConnections Canada (2010). http://www.geoconnections.org

28. IGC: the International Geodesign Collaboration group, was formed to explore scenario-driven designs for regional and local-scale study areas that address future global changes. https://www.igc-geodesign.org/

29. Moura, A.C.M., Freitas, C.R.: Scalability in the application of geodesign in Brazil: expanding the use of the Brazilian Geodesign platform to metropolitan regions in transformative-learning planning. Sustainability 13(12) 6508, 1–18. (2021). https://doi.org/10.3390/su13126508

30. Sampaio, R.C.: Orçamentos Participativos Digitais: um mapeamento mundial das experiências já realizadas e suas contribuições para e-participação e e-democracia. UFBA, Salvador (2014)

31. Coleman, S., Sampaio, R.C.: Sustaining a democratic innovation: a study of three e-participatory budgets in Belo Horizonte. Inf. Commun. Soc. 20(5), 754–769 (2017)

32. Avritzer, L.: O Orçamento Participativo e a Teoria Democrática: um balanço crítico, pp. 13–60. A inovação democrática no Brasil. Cortez, São Paulo (2003)

33. Souza, C.: Construção e Consolidação de Instituições Democráticas: papel do orçamento participativo. São Paulo em Perspectiva 15(4), 84–97 (2001)

34. Moura, Ana Clara Mourão; Freitas, Christian Rezende. Brazilian Geodesign Platform: WebGis & SDI & Geodesign as Co-creation and Geo-Collaboration. Lecture Notes in Computer Science. 1ed.: Springer International Publishing, v. 12252, pp. 332–348 (2020). Available in: https://doi.org/10.1007/978-3-030-58811-3_24

35. BHMaps: SDI from Belo Horizonte Town Office. http://bhmap.pbh.gov.br/v2/mapa/ide bhgeo#zoom=4&lat=7796893.0925&lon=609250.9075&baselayer=base

Geodesign Brazil: Trees for the Metropolitan Area of São Paulo

Adriana Afonso Sandre[1]($\boxtimes$) (iD), Amanda Lombardo Fruehauf[2] (iD),
Augusto Akio Lucchezi Miyahara[3] (iD), Ashley Adelaide Rosa[4] (iD),
Cíntia Miua Maruyama[5] (iD), Giuliano Maselli Locoselli[6] (iD),
Leticia Figueiredo Candido[6] (iD), Magda Adelaide Lombardo[2] (iD),
Matheus Aguiar Coelho[7] (iD), Rafael Pollastrini Murolo[8] (iD),
Riciane Maria Reis Pombo[9], Taícia Helena Negrin Marques[10] (iD),
and Paulo Renato Mesquita Pellegrino[8] (iD)

[1] Faculdade de Arquitetura e Urbanismo, Universidade de São Paulo (FAU USP), Rua do Lago, 876, and Guajava Projeto, Pesquisa e Desenvolvimento, Rua Mantiqueira 126, São Paulo, Brazil
adriana.sandre@usp.br

[2] Escola Superior de Agricultura Luiz de Queiroz, Universidade de São Paulo (ESALQ USP), Av. Pádua Dias 11, Piracicaba, Brazil
amandalombardo@usp.br

[3] Instituto de Biociências, Universidade de São Paulo, Rua Do Matão, trav. 14, São Paulo 321, Brazil
augusto.miyahara@usp.br

[4] Instituto de Geociências, Universidade Federal de Minas Gerais (IGC UFMG), Av. Pres. Antônio Carlos 6627, Belo Horizonte, Brazil
ashiley.rosa@arquitetura.ufjf.br

[5] Centro de Estudos do Mar, Universidade Federal do Paraná, Av. Beira Mar, Pontal do Sul, Brazil

[6] Instituto de Botânica, Secretaria de Infraestrutura e Meio Ambiente, Av. Miguel Stéfano 3687, São Paulo, Brazil

[7] Escuela Técnica Superior de Arquitectura, Universidade da Coruña, Campus da Zapateira 15071, Coruña, Spain

[8] Faculdade de Arquitetura e Urbanismo, Universidade de São Paulo (FAU USP), Rua Do Lago, São Paulo 876, Brazil
prmpelle@usp.br

[9] Guajava Projeto, Pesquisa e Desenvolvimento, Rua Mantiqueira 126, Sao Paulo, Brazil

[10] Departamento de Ordenamiento Territorial y Construcción, Facultad de Ingeneria Agrícola, Universidad Nacional Agraria la Molina, Av. La Molina s/n, Lima, Peru
thnegrin@lamolina.edu.pe

Abstract. Trees are central in the Nature-based Solutions for promoting simultaneously quality of life and biodiversity while providing mitigation and adaptive ecosystem services in the cities. Based on the Geodesign framework using the GIS-Colab Platform, the impact of decision-making scenarios on tree-cover changes, as well as the consequences it will have for carbon sequestration, was evaluated for 2020, 2035 and 2050 in the Metropolitan Area of São Paulo (MASP). This metropolitan area is one of the largest urban conglomerates in the world with more than 22 million people. It lies on the Atlantic Rainforest Biome, a tropical moist

© Springer Nature Switzerland AG 2021
O. Gervasi et al. (Eds.): ICCSA 2021, LNCS 12954, pp. 463–475, 2021.
https://doi.org/10.1007/978-3-030-86979-3_33

broadleaf forest regarded as a world hotspot of biodiversity. First, a diagnostic of the current conditions was elaborated using available layers of geospatial data from the MASP. Then the future tree cover was discussed according to three scenarios: i) the non-adopters that represent the business as usual; ii) the late-adopters that develop innovative actions from 2035; and iii) early-adopters that undertake innovative interventions of urban greening from 2020. The vegetation cover was estimated to be reduced by 4% considering the current non-adopter scenario by 2050. On the other hand, vegetation cover has the potential to increase 30% in 2050, once there is an early adoption of innovative interventions, promoting various ecosystem services and co-benefits that support the quality of life and the biodiversity in the MASP, while fostering the carbon credit in the city through vegetation carbon sink. This article points to possible pathways required to attain desired afforestation goals in the MASP following the Geodesign framework. This framework proved to be effective even though it was based only on remote meetings, imposed by the social distancing during the pandemic of COVID-19.

Keywords: Urban trees · Carbon credit · Geodesign framework · Early-adopter

1 Introduction

Cities are renowned for their direct and indirect negative impacts on the global biogeochemical cycles and on the resilience of the world's natural environments. As major drivers of global environmental changes, cities are now seen as the main source of solutions, helping to support mitigation and adaptation plans to climate change based on global agreements like The Paris Agreement [1], and strategies for a sustainable world such as the Sustainable Development Goals [2]. Urban forests can be defined in its broad sense as the set of all forest fragments, parks, gardens and street trees [3]. The role of urban forests on CO_2 sequestration largely depends on the protection of the natural capital of cities and the availability of open spaces for afforestation. As in many cities worldwide, transport is the main source of carbon dioxide in the metropolitan areas of Brazil. The infrastructure that supports urban mobility, together with housing, also competes for the available open spaces for greening in the urban fabric. Therefore, integrated multi-sectorial approaches are essential for any actions promoting the protection of the urban forest and the afforestation of the available spaces to promote urban carbon sink.

Integrating mobility, housing and green infrastructure in urban planning to mitigate atmospheric carbon dioxide, especially in the large metropolitan areas, will inevitably lead to other positive impacts of urban forests. Ecosystem services, such as: reduction of air pollution, shading and stabilization of temperature and noise reduction [4–6] would foster the quality of life in the cities by improving mental and physical health. In addition, the improvement of the urban environment by planting trees also reflects on the way people live and move, increasing the efficiency of the urban activities. Both urban afforestation and high efficiency of the urban activities may reduce the environmental impacts and massive carbon footprint of the cities.

The balance between urban CO_2 sources and sinks depends on the historical processes of land-use change and occupation of the cities that are based on the dynamics and impacts of decision making. The Metropolitan Area of São Paulo (MASP) is an example of one of the largest urban conglomerates in the world that face problems created by unplanned growth during the last decades. This area hosts more than 22 million inhabitants distributed along 39 municipalities. Out of the total 8051 km^2 [8] of the MASP, almost 56% is covered by trees [9]. Tree cover, however, is rather unequal and it is mostly concentrated on two main protection areas in the continuous green belt across the north (Serra da Cantareira), and south (Serra do Mar) of the MASP borders that provide many ecosystem services to the cities including water supply.

This study presents the results of a co-design process, based on Steinitz's Geodesign Framework [10], conducted by a multidisciplinary group of experts. The main objective was to evaluate the deforestation and afforestation trends on the MASP′s urban forests by 2050 under three different decision-making scenarios, I) non-adopters, II) late-adopters, III) early adopters. These scenarios are then discussed in the light of carbon sink and credits of carbon. The research presented here is part of the "Geodesign Brazil: Trees for Metropolitan Regions", a study that is being conducted in nine different metropolitan areas of the country.

2 Material and Methods

With the aim to increase the vegetation cover and carbon sink in at the MASP, a group of 13 researchers of various fields, worked remotely during synchronous workshop sessions using the GISColab platform.[1] This platform was developed by the Geoprocessing Laboratory of the School of Architecture of the Federal University of Minas Gerais. It uses the Geodesign framework but in a flexible approach that is adapted to the Brazilian context. The combination of Geodesign framework and GISColab platform allows the co-design of ideas and plans for large regions and are specially suitable for remote work during the pandemic.

The co-design workshops took place in four thematic meetings (Fig. 1), namely: (i) reading enrichment, which consists of obtaining and evaluating georeferenced data to characterize the current scenario of vegetation cover; (ii) development of non-adopter scenarios (2035–2050) according to the business as usual; (iii) development of late-adopter scenarios (2050) built upon the non-adopter scenario up to 2035, and the late adoption of innovations; and finally, (iv) development of early-adopter scenarios (2035–2050) that adopt innovative actions right from the beginning.

Initially, the available database on the GISColab platform was analyzed by the participants, who identified the most relevant data layers to the MASP and then estimated and established goals for the changes in the number of street trees; water reservoirs; detention ponds; green detention reservoirs; informal settlements; urban sprawl; natural and planted forest areas; and urban Heat Islands for the three scenarios (Table 1).

For all scenarios, the values of increasing or decreasing percentage of green cover related to 2020/21 were estimated to 2035 and 2050. Linear trends from historical

---

[1] The Brazilian Geodesign platform - GISColab has the premise of supporting and connecting Spatial Data Infrastructure (SDI), WebGis, and Geodesign in order to provide integrated and georeferenced information on the territory, enabling a wide availability of data to support the discussions and negotiations on the adopted spatial profile [11]. Available at: http://www.gis colab.com/geodesign/#/.

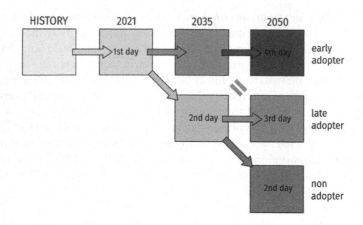

Fig. 1. Geodesign workshops workflow. Source: Authors. Adapted from IGC, 2021.

datasets starting in 1985 up to the present were used for the extrapolations. The number of detention ponds proposed by the Master Plan for the Macrodrainage of the Alto Tietê Basin [12] was evaluated, considering not only the construction rate and the typology, but whether they would be made by concrete or integrate the Green Infrastructure. In addition, future urban sprawl was extrapolated by analyzing the census datasets [13] that also includes the distribution and growth of slums and urban settlement areas, and changes in natural and planted forests available on MapBiomas (MapBiomas/IBGE)[2]. For street trees, data from the Municipal Plan for Urban Trees [14] were used, including data on tree fall, replacement of senescent individuals, and planting. Finally, the goals for the afforestation of the MASP were discussed and defined by the present group of researchers during the workshop.

2.1 Reading Enrichment

The workshop took place remotely to cope with the social distancing protocols of the COVID-19 pandemic, which allowed the participation of researchers from various institutions with different backgrounds. This early step was essential to promote an appropriate collaboration, following the Geodesign framework [10]. The team first discussed national and international reference cases, in different contexts and scales, and then proposed guidelines, general strategies and public policies to guide the development of the workshop. Overall, they aimed at conserving the protected areas and existing vegetation, increasing the vegetation cover in urban, peri-urban and rural areas, and restoring mainly riparian forests. Two examples of these strategies can be mentioned: I) the support to plant trees through public policies and environmental compensation plans mainly for the construction industry, and II) the creation and implementation of an afforestation plan

---

[2] The Expressive Vegetation Map in GISColab was based on Vegetable Cover Maps of Brazilian Biomes developed by GeoPrea Laboratory (EAU/UFMG). Available at: http://mapas.mma.gov.br/mapas/aplic/probio/datadownload.htm?/mosaicos_vegetacao/.

for streets and highways, with recommendations of appropriate techniques and species for each context.

The metropolitan structuring axes were identified, which serve as the basis for planning the MASP urban area growth, with special attention to the green areas. Areas for conservation were identified, such as the natural forests from the São Paulo Green Belt Biosphere Reserve (UNESCO) that includes remnants of the Atlantic Rainforest such as Cantareira State Park and the Capivari Monos Permanent Protection Area. The Green Belt is currently threatened by the urban sprawl of the MASP with a high pressure on the native forests and water resources. In summary, the reading enrichment allowed filling the gaps in the database, while evaluating the past trends and understanding the current dynamics of the city for the landscape prognosis in future scenarios.

2.2 Non-adopter (2035 and 2050)

The non-adopter scenarios for 2035 and 2050 were discussed based on four pillars, (i) the current legal instruments concerning the cities' master plans, urban forests, green areas, protected areas and open spaces; (ii) the current trends in tree planting and survival rates; (iii) the pressure for land development from the construction industry and real estate market; and (iv) the illegal activities that take place especially in the Green Belt at the borders of the MASP.

Most cities in the MASP updated their master plans recently or are in the process of establishing new plans. These plans regulate the land use across the city, defining the maximum verticalization, economic activities and minimum percentage of green and open spaces in the cities' districts, to name a few. Therefore, such mechanisms have the potential to protect some of the cities' green spaces, but not all of them, according to the percentages of development area allowed in each district. In addition, laws and regulations already define extensive protected areas in the MASP including remnants of the Atlantic Rainforest, such as State and Municipal Parks, Ecological Stations, which are unlikely to change soon.

Some of the mentioned plans also established goals for tree planting in the cities, so that thousands of trees are being planted yearly in the MASP. There are also groups of activists regularly planting trees in the city [15]. However, there is still a huge backlog of poorly managed trees that are prone to fail especially during the summer, or the wet season. More than 2,000 mature trees fall only in the city of São Paulo every year [16]. In addition, there is a high mortality rate in the new plantation programs in the cities. Although the number of individuals is likely to increase in 2035 and 2050, the ecosystem services balance such as carbon sink is likely to be negative with the significant reduction of the mature tree cover over the cities.

Tree cover may also be threatened by the current pressures from the construction industry and real estate market [17]. Especially for the largest cities of the MASP, the available space for construction of new buildings is becoming increasingly rare, threatening the few non-protected green areas in the city, some of them still baring significant native fauna and flora. The current laws and regulations are not sufficient to keep these areas under protection as many compensatory mechanisms are available allowing the development of these private lands.

Finally, public areas in the green belt are currently endangered by the activities of organized crime. Extensive areas of native vegetation around the main water reservoirs of the MASP are being converted into informal settlements [17, 18]. Although they are considered Permanent Protected Areas, the expansion of forest conversion is at a rate far superior to that of State oversight. The municipalities of the MASP have adopted the strategy of promoting the urbanization of the informal settlements and not the reallocation of these vulnerable families that is usually adopted in many other cities worldwide [19]. As a result, large areas of Native Atlantic Rainforest will be permanently lost affecting the water security of more than 20 million people [20, 21].

The water supply system is already threatened by the combination of recurrent unfavorable climate conditions and increasing water demand in the MASP. The increasingly frequent climate extremes such as the drought caused by an unusual mid-troposphere blocking during the summer of 2014 [22] potentially affects the water supply in the cities of the MASP. For instance, by the end of 2014, the Cantareira system, the main potable water reservoir of MASP, had a negative 2% total volume compared to normal levels. Such unfavorable climate conditions observed in the last years are consistently decreasing the volume of water in the main reservoirs [23], which is likely to continue to decrease in the upcoming years [24].

Following the trend described before, street afforestation is expected to increase by 18% in 2050, which is not sufficient to replace the ecosystem services lost by the senescence, removal and fall of mature trees. A 5% increase in informal settlements is also projected together with an increase of 34% in urban sprawl and a consequently reduction of natural forest areas by 4%. Planted forests are expected to increase by 78% (Eucalyptus, Pine) negatively impacting the urban and peri-urban biodiversity. Regarding the impacts on the recharge of water reservoirs due to the expansion of impervious cover, a drastic reduction in reservoirs of 76% is expected in the MASP. The construction of detention ponds on urban areas, must increase by 146%, competing for available open space which could be partially or totally used for planting trees. Green detention reservoirs and recovery wetlands to be built, would show a decrease of 1%. Regarding the Urban Heat Island, it is predicted an average of 22 °C of surface temperature in the central area of São Paulo city (the warmest area in the MASP), related to its surrounded rural and natural areas.

2.3 Late-Adopter (2035 and 2050)

Similar trends to the non-adopter scenario described above are expected up to 2035 in the late adopters scenario. It is only after 2035 that a significant change is expected in the actions from policy makers and society regarding the main environmental, social, and economic issues in the city. These issues are then tackled by the implementation of innovative solutions that must account for the possible negative impacts of the non-adopter approach on the urban green infrastructure.

Thus, the measures necessary for the qualification of the urban environment by 2050 start upon an already vulnerable environment and may be less effective compared to the current needs of the MASP. Three approaches guided the innovative action to start in 2035, namely: I) protecting, II) expanding and III) creating a green infrastructure. These approaches relied on the control of urban sprawl, qualification of the existing land cover, promotion of green and blue infrastructure.

To achieve the objective to increase the tree cover in the MASP, these actions should be considered simultaneously to offer a real change in the development of the city from 2035 until 2050. We identified the main points to control the reduction of pre-existing green areas and promote the afforestation of new areas. First, there is a need of controlling the urban sprawl of the metropolitan area of São Paulo, including the optimization of the existing urban land occupation. Central areas that have a large accumulation of vacant buildings offer most opportunities for change.

The requalification of the existing occupation of the urban landscape must rely on the implementation, monitoring, continuous revision and sectorial articulation of different public policies, such as: (i) public policies, with focus on encouraging the protection of green areas with financial incentives, based on the payment for ecosystem services, while including innovative solutions such as: green roof, cisterns, green wall with climbing plants; and (ii) elaboration of new housing policies that consider the synergy between conservation of green buffer zones and the sustainability of local economic activities, by a green-economy concept.

These policies should provide structure for urban redevelopment projects through urban design with Green Infrastructure principles, in a wide participatory and inclusive manner, by maintaining the population in the site, but within a secure and eco-friendly condition.

In addition, one must also consider the relationship between trees and urban water that lead to a gradual change from a conventional "gray" monofunctional infrastructure, into a system of multifunctional green infrastructure. The following actions were considered: (i) the transformation of the existing edges of the Flood Storage Reservoirs System. These areas present the potential to be reforestated, while planning areas of permanence and social interaction. (ii) development of plans focused on the water quality of the reservoirs, considering the concept of regeneration in urban design of the respective water basins; (iii) environmental program for reforestation of existing urban watersheds, altogether with related public housing policies; and (iv) restoration of the riparian forests of the Pinheiros and Tietê River.

Finally, the reconfiguration of the urban forest was also discussed. This concept considers the complete system of open spaces in the metropolitan area, the protected and natural reservoirs, public parks, squares, streets, and private free spaces.

The main condition to protect the existing green assets, besides the topics already discussed here, focused on better management practices of urban trees and vegetation: (i) improving the urban aerial electrical distribution system, that currently present serious conflicts with the existing street-trees; (ii) elaboration of a specific master plan for trees management, introducing processes of optimization, such as the concept of reverse logistics to consider the pruning tree residues applications in civil construction, urban furniture, fertilization, etc.; and (iii) development of a master plan for planting new trees, considering the different existing biomes and innovative solutions.

To increase tree-coverage within the urban built area, different actions were brought to discussion considering the 2050 scenario, that were based on previous experiences, such as the Sacramento "Green City", in the U.S.A., examples from Singapore, and the revision of local experiences in Brazil such as Maringá city. They include: (i) public policies that encourage urban planting and afforestation, considering its ecosystem services; (ii) redesign of existing streets with based on Green Infrastructure principles associated with the creation of sustainable and safe urban mobility; and (iii) optimization of parking spots as the main strategy for making additional space feasible for permeable areas, afforestation, and the implementation of green-blue infrastructural components and urban farming infrastructures.

Thus, the 2035 late-adopter scenario most of the items analyzed (see Table 1) considered 50% less changes related to the 2050 non-adopter scenario. For example, the impact on drinking water reservoirs in the late-adopter 2035 scenario corresponds to a reduction of 38% in relation to 2020. By 2050, the late-adopter scenario is expected to lead to positive changes. This was reflected in almost all the items evaluated, like increasing the number of street trees by 30%, reducing water availability by only 10%, decreasing the number of detention ponds on forests to 83%, while increasing green detention reservoirs by 10%. A drastic reduction of 0.5% of informal settlements is also predicted, and a limited increase of urban sprawl of 9%, while increasing afforestation by 45%. There is still an expected increase in the Urban Heat Island - UHI but limited to 10 °C.

2.4 Early Adopters (2035 and 2050)

The proposed measures in the early-adopter scenario relied on the most innovative public policies, many not yet developed or practiced in the city of São Paulo. The scenarios considered the application of green infrastructure technology to promote the conservation and expansion of forest fragments and green areas. In addition, a great effort for creating new urban forests is fostered by different activities.

These activities include planting street trees, planting trees in the parking spots, in at least 2 parking spaces every 100m. In each parking spot, there is room for planting up to 16 trees, which would be associated with bio-retention structures. According to these plans, the scenarios developed showed a significant increase in the vegetation cover of the MASP compared to the levels of 2020, and consequently reaching the established goal of 30% increase in vegetation cover, resulting in a more sustainable urban development under the aspects analyzed, as described in Table 1.

The early-adopters scenario of 2035 considered similar rates that the late-adopter 2050 for issues such as, number of trees on the roads, urban sprawl evolution and urban heat islands, while more significant positive changes were predicted for the other items. By 2035, it is expected a 10% increase in water reservoir volume, a 4% reduction in detention ponds built on forests, and an increase of 35% in green detention reservoirs. It is also expected a total control of the growth in informal settlements, a 15% increase in natural forests and a 10% increase in planted forests, and a 10 °C increase in surface temperature due to UHI. By 2050 the scenario is rather optimistic, with 50% more street trees, 25% more water availability, 8% less detention ponds built on forests and 70% more green detention reservoirs.

It is also expected a significant reduction in informal settlements, a controlled urban sprawl around 4% increase, 30% more natural forests and 15% more planted forests, and only a 5 °C rise in surface temperature due to UHI (see Table 11 for the complete data). The predicted lower impact of UHI in early-adopter scenario by 2050 assumes of a greener city [25]. Urban environmental planning actions outlined within green infrastructure strategies would leverage the preservation of forests, planting of trees, and construction of green detention reservoirs (Fig. 2).

Table 1. Predicted changes of the Metropolitan Region of São Paulo (total area 7 946,84 km^2) according to the early, late and non-adopters' approach. The increased percentage is related to the 2020/21 and the references for Early adopters are based on goals for the Design decisions. The year 2035 is similar for late and non-adopter.

	CURRENT	EARLY		LATE		NON	REFERENCES
	2020	2035	2050	2035	2050	2050	
Number of street trees based on the balance between planted and fallen plus removed trees.	652,146	30%	50%	9%	30%	18%	[16, 26]
Impacts on the recharge of water reservoirs due to expansion of impervious cover	1.132. 610.000m³	10%	25%	- 38%	-10%	-76%	[23, 27]
Detention ponds over urban forests to be built.	48 un.	-4%	-8%	73%	83%	146%	[26, 12]
Green detention reservoirs and recovery wetlands to be built.	0 un.	35%	70%	1%	10%	1%	[26, 11]
Increase/Reduction in informal settlements	88,34 km²	0%	-5%	2,5%	0,5%	5%	[13, 24, 28]
Urban sprawl evolution	2.038,69 km²	8%	4%	17%	9%	34%	
Increase/Reduction in Natural forest areas due to urban sprawl/reduction	3.581,85km²	15%	30%	-2%	-2,5%	-4%	MapBiomas platform Growth compared with 1985-2019 period
Increase in Planted Forest (Eucalyptus, Pinus and Araucaria) areas due to urban sprawl/reduction	260,92 km²	10%	15%	40%	45%	78%	
Increase in the Urban Heat Islands: average of the surface temperature of central area of SP less rural areas	15°C	10 °C	5 °C	18 °C	10 °C	22°C	[29]

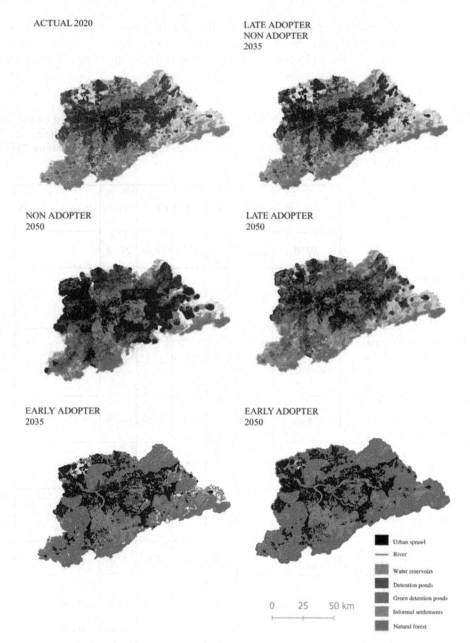

Fig. 2. Spatial distribution of the most relevant layers of the Metropolitan Region of São Paulo for the actual scenario (2020) and the prediction changes for 2035 and 2050 according to the early, late and non-adopters' approach described in Table 1

3   Conclusion

Using the Geodesign principles and framework, supported by the GISColab Platform, allowed the group to list the main problems related to the green infrastructure in the MASP, and create three theoretical scenarios, I) non-adopters, II) late-adopters and III) early-adopters, for 2035 and 2050. The scenarios based on the business as usual from the non-adopter approach point to a significant reduction in the recharge of water reservoirs and the natural forest areas. There is one exception related to the total number of street trees that are likely to increase, which may not reflect on the ecosystem services they provide as the number of old growth trees are expected to decrease sharply. These changes in the overall vegetation cover are expected to sustain the current environmental degradation by increasing the Urban Heat Islands and reducing the water supply.

Similar trends are expected in the scenarios of the late adopters up to 2035, when changes in planning and management of the urban green infrastructure take place. This scenario then assumes innovative technologies, based on green infrastructure, among others that lead to more favorable predictions compared to the non-adopter scenario. In the early adopters, such innovative technologies are implemented by 2020 resulting in a significant increase in the number of trees and carbon biomass in the MASP.

The experience of working with the GISColab platform made it possible to bring together several researchers from different areas to collaborate in the elaboration of different scenarios for tree cover and carbon sink across the MASP for 2035 and 2050. This was only possible based on a successful remote work, which would otherwise be much more difficult to carry out in the current moment of the coronavirus pandemic.

Acknowledgments. The authors would like to thank Ana Clara Moura (UFMG) who coordinated the project "Geodesign Brasil: Trees for Metropolitan Regions"; for the support of the Geoprocessing Laboratory (Geoproea/EAUFMG) staff; and the GISColab platform (CNPq Project 401066/2016–9/ FAPEMIG PPM-00368–18). The authors also thank FAPESP for the financial support (FAPESP 2019/08783–0, 2020/09251–0, 2020/14163–2).

References

1. United Nations: Paris Agreement. United Nations Framework Convention on Climate Change, Paris (2015)
2. United Nations: Transforming our world: the 2030 Agenda for Sustainable Development. United Nations Framework Convention on Climate Change (2015)
3. Konijnendjik, C.C.: A decade of urban forestry in Europe. Forest Policy Econ. **5**(2), 173–186 (2003). https://doi.org/10.1016/S1389-9341(03)00023-6
4. Kaplan, S.: The restorative benefits of nature: toward an integrative framework. J. Environ. Psychol. **15**, 169–182 (1995). https://doi.org/10.1016/0272-4944(95)90001-2
5. Mascaró, L., Mascaró, J.J.: Ambiência Urbana. 3. ed. +4 Editora, Porto Alegre (2009)
6. McPherson, E.G., Simpson, J.R., Peper, P.J., Xiao, Q.: Benefit-cost analysis of Modesto's Municipal urban forest. J. Arboric. **25**(5), 235–248 (1999)
7. Moreira, T.C.L., et al.: Green spaces, land cover, street trees and hypertension in the Megacity of São Paulo. Int. J. Environ. Res. Public Health **17**(3), 725 (2020). https://doi.org/10.3390/ijerph17030725

8. Emplasa, Empresa Paulista de Planejamento Metropolitano S/A (2010). http://www.metada dos.idesp.sp.gov.br/catalogo/srv/por/catalog.search#/metadata/5ffa3008-8fb8-4180-a56b-f5f3e0d3fa5a. Accessed on 25 April 2021
9. Wagner, F.H., Hirye, M.C.M. Tree Cover for the Year 2010 of the Metropolitan Region of São Paulo, Brazil. Data 2019 4(4), 145 (2019). https://doi.org/10.3390/data4040145
10. Steinitz, C.: A framework for Geodesign: changing geography by design. ESRI Press, Redlands (2012)
11. Moura, A.C.M., Freitas, C.R.: Brazilian geodesign platform: WebGis & SDI & geodesign as co-creation and geo-collaboration. In: Gervasi, O., et al. (eds.) ICCSA 2020. LNCS, vol. 12252, pp. 332–348. Springer, Cham (2020). https://doi.org/10.1007/978-3-030-58811-3_24
12. São Paulo (Prefeitura): Plano Diretor de Macrodrenagem da Bacia do Alto Tietê. Departamento de Águas e Energia Elétrica (2013)
13. Instituto Brasileiro de Geografia e Estatística: Censo Brasileiro de 2010. IBGE, Rio de Janeiro (2012)
14. São Paulo (Prefeitura): Plano Municipal de Arborização Urbana. Secretaria do Verde e Meio Ambiente (2020)
15. Silva, E.M.F., et al.: Um novo ecossistema: florestas urbanas construídas pelo Estado e pelos ativistas. Estudos Avançados 33(97), 81–101 (2019). https://doi.org/10.1590/s0103-4014.2019.3397.005
16. Locosselli, G.M., Miyahara, A.A.L., Cerqueira, P., Buckeridge, M.S.: Climate drivers of tree fall on the streets of São Paulo, Brazil. Trees 1–9 (2021). https://doi.org/10.1007/s00468-021-02145-4
17. Torres, H., Alves, H., Oliveira, M.A.: São Paulo peri-urban dynamics: some social causes and environmental consequences. Environ. Urban. 19(1), 207–223 (2007). https://doi.org/10.1177/0956247807076784
18. Walker, A.P.P., Alacrón, M.A.: The competing social and environmental functions of private urban land: the case of an informal land occupation in São Paulo's South Periphery. Sustainability 10(11), 4160 (2018). https://doi.org/10.3390/su10114160
19. Gonçalves, J.M., Gama, J.M.R.F.: A systematization of policies and programs focused on informal urban settlements: reviewing the cases of São Paulo, Luanda and Instambul. J. Urban. 13(4), 466–488 (2020). https://doi.org/10.1080/17549175.2020.1753228
20. Brito, F.M., Miralgia, S.G.E.K., Semensatto Jr., D.L.: Ecosystem services of the Guarapiranga Reservoir watershed (São Paulo, Brazil): value of water supply and implications for management strategies. Int. J. Urban Sustain. Develop. 10(1), 49–59. Taylor & Francis, London (2018). https://doi.org/10.1080/19463138.2018.1442336
21. Young, A.F.: Urban expansion and environmental risk in the São Paulo Metropolitan Area. Climate Res. 57, 73–80 (2013)
22. Marengo, J.A., Alves, L.M., Ambrizzi, T., Young, A., Barreto, N.J.C., Ramos, A.M.: Trends in extreme rainfall and hydrogeometereological disasters in the Metropolitan Area of São Paulo: a review. Ann. N. Y. Acad. Sci (2020). https://doi.org/10.1111/nyas.14307
23. SABESP, Companhia de Saneamento Básico do Estado de São Paulo: Portal dos mananciais. http://mananciais.sabesp.com.br/Situacao. Accessed on 29 April 2021
24. Pasternak, S., D'Ottaviano, C.: Favelas no Brasil e em São Paulo: avanços nas análises a partir da Leitura Territorial do Censo de 2010. Cad. Metrop. 18(35), São Paulo (2016). https://doi.org/10.1590/2236-9996.2016-3504
25. Lombardo, M.A.: Ilha de calor nas metrópoles. 1. ed. Hucitec, São Paulo (1985)
26. São Paulo (Prefeitura), Fundação Centro Tecnológico de Hidráulica (Org.): Caderno de bacia hidrográfica: córrego Jaguaré. SIURB/FCTH, São Paulo (2016)
27. Tundisi, J.G.: Ciclo hidrológico e gerenciamento integrado. Cienc. Cult. 55(4), São Paulo, 31–33 (2003). https://doi.org/10.1177/0956247807076784

28. Pasternak, S., Bogus, L.M.: Favelas na Macrometrópole Paulista. XXII SIIU - Seminário Internacional de Investigação em Urbanismo. São Paulo e Lisboa (2020). https://dx.doi.org/https://doi.org/10.5821/SIIU.10116

29. Lombardo, M.A.: O uso de geotecnologias na análise das mudanças climáticas na metrópole de São Paulo. Revista Geográfica de América Central **2**, 1–19 (2011)

The Potential of Geodesign for the Optimization of Land Use in the Perspective of Sustainability: Case Study of the Metropolitan Region of Campinas

Andréia Medinilha Pancher[1]([✉]) [iD], Ana Isabel de Sá[2] [iD], Marcelo Costa[1] [iD],
and Tiago Oyan Aguiar[1] [iD]

[1] Institute of Geosciences and Exact Sciences, Paulista State University (Unesp), Avenida 24A,
Rio Claro 1515, Brazil
{am.pancher,marcelo.costa1998,tiago.oyan}@unesp.br
[2] Federal Institute of Education, Science and Technology of Minas Gerais (IFMG), Rua Érico
Veríssimo, Santa Luzia/MG, Santa LuziaBairro Londrina 317, Brazil
ana.sa@ifmg.edu.br

Abstract. The main objective of this article is to present and discuss the experience of a Geodesign workshop aimed at the Metropolitan Region of Campinas,
SP. It was intended to debate the potential of the Geodesign method to reflect
on the characteristics of the territory and propose alternatives for the proper use
and occupation of land in the region from the perspective of sustainability. The
workshop offered support for the participants to co-create alternatives for the sustainable planning of the territory and to develop the potential of the area. Its main
characteristic was the elaboration of proposals based on the sustainability triad:
Environmental, Economic and Social. The results showed that the methodology
favors the preparation of proposals for adequate land use, allowing for an evolutionary process of co-creation of ideas, as the activities were developed in an
evolutionary way, that is, the proposals were created for the 2035 and 2050 scenarios, no innovations, few innovations and many innovations. After the preparation
and presentation of the proposals, the groups analyzed them for the 2050 scenario,
showing that this step is essential for the critical analysis of the ideas, allowing to
verify which systems were fully contemplated, which were moderately covered
and which were not adequately covered. Thus, it is suggested that the evaluation
stage precedes the adequacy and finalization of the proposals.

Keywords: Geodesign · Metropolitan regions · Territorial planning · Co-creation

1   Introduction

In Brazil, the urbanization process intensified from the 1960s onwards, generating a
rural exodus, that is, the population leaving the countryside for urban areas. Most of
the population started to live in cities, generating its rapid growth. Based on data from

the National Household Sample Survey (PNAD) [1], 84.72% of the Brazilian population lives in urban areas, and 15.28% in rural areas. This intense urbanization process triggered the phenomenon of metropolization, that is, cities grew beyond their limits, forming large metropolitan centers. The country comprises 74 metropolitan regions, which constitute complex territories, demanding effective planning methodologies.

This article presents the experience of the Geodesign workshop aimed at the collective development of proposals for the Metropolitan Region of Campinas (São Paulo, Brazil), in March 2021, with students from the "Urban Environmental Quality Analysis: support of geotechnologies for integration of thematic data", given by Professor Andréia Medinilha Pancher at UNESP. Two students from the postgraduate program in Geosciences at UNICAMP also participated.

This experiment was part of a group of workshops in 12 of the 74 metropolitan regions of the country, coordinated by professor Ana Clara Moura, from UFMG, all using the geodesign method and the Brazilian geodesign platform GISCoLab, created with the support of CNPq (project 401066/2016–9 and FAPEMIG PPM-00368–18) [2]. Each Metropolitan Region had its local coordination – in this case, Professor Andréia Pancher, from UNESP. In each case, certain aspects and approaches related to specific territories and stakeholder groups were emphasized. In the case of Campinas, it was decided to use the tripod of sustainability as a base, guiding the practice based on the potential contributions of the proposals to social, environmental and economic issues.

Geodesign was adopted as a methodology, an alternative for the collective solution of conflicts that settle in the territory. According to Steinitz [3], this method is based on and covers a set of questions and methods necessary to solve complex design problems, in varied geographical scales, ranging from a neighborhood to a city, a landscape or a watershed.

Geodesign is adequate for the exercise on screen, since it is based on the knowledge of the characteristics of a territory for the elaboration of proposals compatible with not only economic, but also social and environmental development. In this way, the method makes it possible to conduct collaborative practices that favor the broad participation of actors involved in the territory, including from researchers, planners, to the community that lives in the areas of interest.

2 Methodology

The workshop presented in this paper adopted geodesign as a method, a concept created by a group of researchers from the Harvard Computer Graphics Lab, from the beginning of the 21st century [4].

It starts from the principle of associating GIS systems with spatial analysis techniques, based on the production of visualizations, simulations and models of physical-territorial reality. In other words, the geographic dimension, geo, is allied to the purposeful nature of design practices [5]. In general, cartographic bases with different information about the territory to receive interventions are used, organized in superimposed layers, as a background for the collective exercise of deliberation on territorial transformations – co-design or co-creation.

In order to explain geodesign, Goodchild [5] emphasizes the distinction between Design with a capital "D" and a lower "d". The design with a lowercase "d" would be a simplistic or even naive approach, anchored in the search for an "optimal solution" based on the combination of the initial objectives with the existing variables and restrictions. It would almost be an automation of the decision-making process based exclusively on technical parameters, enabling one to always arrive at a single result.

Design with a capital "D", on the other hand, would be the set of practices that take into account the conflicts between the actors involved in decision making, their biases, and the dialogue necessary to achieve a result - which may not always be the more appropriate based on technical parameters, but that reflects the possible consensus within a given group and its interests. In this sense, the GIS technological framework is used to support and improve the negotiation processes and the political nature inherent to territorial planning, and not to eliminate them, as is the objective of proposals such as SDSS (Spatial Decision Support Systems). For this, it is necessary to repeatedly return to the beginning of each stage of representation and design (feedback loops, or iterations), enabling the verification of the proposed decisions [5].

Based on these assumptions, Steinitz [3] proposes a framework for geodesign: a methodological framework in which six questions must be asked (explicitly or implicitly) by the working group, at least three times, constituting iterations that feedback and generate different models of the territory until the negotiation of a final proposal (Fig. 1).

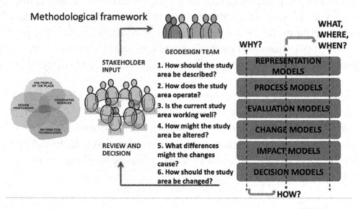

Fig. 1. Geodesign framework proposed by Steinitz [3].

Throughout this process, six models are generated – representation, process, evaluation, change, impact and decision – through which the process must move in search of a final collective agreement. In the following topics, it will be presented how these models were approached in the workshop in question, as well as the necessary adaptations to adapt the methodological framework to the analyzed context. The summary of the methodological steps of this work is shown in Fig. 2.

The main tool used to support the process was the GISCoLab platform [2]. GISCoLab was developed in partnership with GEOPROEA researchers, between 2015 and 2018, based on a series of case studies on Geodesign and co-creation of ideas for the territory. The analysis of the results of these experiences led the group to propose the development of a Brazilian platform, seeking to circumvent identified critical aspects, such as the risk

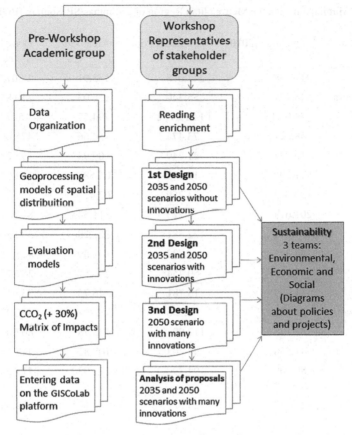

Fig. 2. Main steps in methodological framework. Source: The authors.

of inducing consensus or the low openness to participation in the initial stages of the processes.

Next, the characterization of the study area and the construction of working models for the MRC workshop will be addressed.

2.1 Area Characterization

The area of analysis was the metropolitan region of Campinas (MRC), created in 2000 through Complementary Law n° 870, of 19/06/2000. According to an estimate by the Brazilian Institute of Geography and Statistics (IBGE) [6], the MRC is formed by 20 municipalities, housing 3,304,338 inhabitants, with 2,725,293 people living in urban areas and only 71,844 in rural areas. The total land area is 3,644.9km², therefore, the demographic density is 767.40 inhab./km². (Table 1).

According to the data in Table 1, it is evident that the MRC is densely occupied, especially the urban area. It is a dynamic region, both economically and technologically, encompassing important research and teaching centers. The intense development of this

Table 1. Municipalities in the Metropolitan Region of Campinas/SP. Source: IBGE [6, 7].

Municipalities	Population (2010)	Estimated Pop. (2020)	Area (km^2)	Dem. Density (inhab./km^2)
Americana	210.638	242.018	133,91	1.807,29
Artur Nogueira	44.177	55.340	178,03	310,85
Campinas	1.080.113	1.213.792	794,57	1.527,61
Cosmópolis	58.827	73.474	154,66	475,05
Eng. Coelho	15.721	21.249	109,94	193,28
Holambra	11.299	15.272	65,58	232,89
Hortolândia	192.692	234.259	62,42	3.752,95
Indaiatuba	201.619	256.223	311,545	822,43
Itatiba	101.471	122.581	322,28	380,36
Jaguariúna	44.311	58.722	141,39	415,32
Monte Mor	48.949	60.754	240,57	252,54
Morungaba	11.769	13.781	146,75	93,91
Nova Odessa	51.242	60.956	73,79	826,07
Paulínia	82.146	112.003	138,78	807,05
Pedreira	41.558	48.463	108,82	445,35
Sta Bárbara D'Oeste	180.009	194.390	271,030	717,23
Sto Antonio de Posse	20.650	23.529	154,133	152,66
Sumaré	241.311	286.211	153,46	1.865,05
Valinhos	106.793	131.210	148,54	883,33
Vinhedo	63.611	80.111	81,60	981,75
Total	**2.808.906**	**3.304.338**	**3.792**	**871,40**

region caused the rapid occupation of the territory, without adequate planning. As a result, serious damage to natural resources was unleashed in this territory, demanding more effective land use and occupation strategies. The study area can be better understood in Fig. 3.

2.2 Preparatory Stage of the Workshop

To carry out a particular spatial analysis, with a view to proposing changes for the proper use and occupation of land, it is necessary to know the characteristics of the territory considered. Therefore, it is necessary to establish the analysis of thematic data of the study area, which was selected based on the most relevant themes to meet the expectations of the discussion.

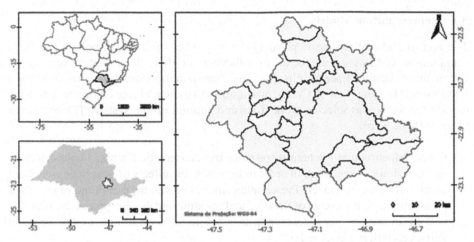

Fig. 3. Study area - metropolitan region of campinas (MRC). Source: The authors.

Thus, in the first preparatory stage, the academic group from the Federal University of Minas Gerais developed the Representation Models, comprising 43 layers of cartographic and thematic data of the main characteristics of the study area, obtained from various official databases. For this stage, 15 days of work were required in the geoprocessing laboratory LABGEO/UFMG. Then, the information layers were inserted into the GISCoLab platform. This platform was created by Christian Resende Freitas and Ana Clara Mourão Moura (UFMG); it is characterized by being dynamic and interactive, allowing the stages of the workshop to be organized in contexts.

In the second stage, the data layers were transformed into Process Models, allowing to analyze the spatial distribution of occurrences and phenomena, as well as the influence of each variable on the RMC, showing the functioning of the study area. Using geoprocessing methods, hypsometry and slope models were generated; of land use and land cover, through the digital classification of orbital images; of the vegetation quality index, by calculating the NDVI (Normalized Difference Vegetation Index); water supply, sanitary sewage, health and school service buffers, accessibility and capillarity of the transport network, concentration of commerce and services, in addition to the percentage of distribution of young people, average income estimate, population density, relative information to agriculture, energy (insolation, surface temperature), tourism and leisure, and carbon credit (core area metrics, by form factor and connectivity). These layers of geographic information served as the basis for the group's work.

3 Development and Analysis

After the previous elaboration of the cartographic and thematic data, the representation, process and impact models were organized, as well as the workshop, which are detailed in the following items.

3.1 Representation Models

The natural and anthropogenic physical characteristics of the metropolitan region of Campinas served as the basis for the establishment of 10 systems: Water, Agriculture, Green Infrastructure, Energy Infrastructure, Transport Infrastructure, Trade/Industry, Institutions, Housing, Carbon Credit, in addition to a system of free choice, which in the case of this study was selected as the Tourism/Culture/Leisure System. The objectives of the systems were:

a) Green Infrastructure - where to propose the conservation areas, implementation or expansion of vegetation, in order to minimize the effects of heat in densely built areas, restore the Permanent Preservation Areas, improve the conditions of protected areas, minimize the events of flooding and flooding and erosive processes, from the analysis of the existing vegetation distribution in the form of biomes, conservation units, vegetation quality index.

b) Hydrography – which springs and water courses require proposals for the recovery of the green, for the protection of water sources and ecological potential.

c) Housing - selection of the most suitable areas for the implementation of new housing, considering the most appropriate characteristics of the relief (hypsometry and slope), taking into account the urban expansion area, as well as the legislation regarding APPs and conservation units.

d) Transport – which sectors require improvements or expansion of road, rail and urban transport routes, considering accessibility and capillarity.

e) Institutions – in which areas there is a demand for health services, schools, taking into account the characteristics of the population (% of children, young people and the elderly) and the areas of influence of these services.

f) Trade/Industry – which areas can be expanded and which are suitable for expanding commerce and industry, based on information on average income and population density.

g) Agriculture – which areas are suitable for agricultural activity or for expanding existing ones, based on information on land use and occupation, altimetry, soils, insolation, road infrastructure.

h) Energy – which sectors are potential for the installation of new energy generators, considering the production of sustainable energy, such as solar (analyzing the conditions of insolation and surface temperature).

i) Carbon Credit – propose the conservation, expansion or creation of vegetation, with a view to increasing the carbon credit, considering the surface temperature, the characteristics of the existing vegetation (core area, shape, connectivity,).

j) Tourism/Culture and Leisure – identify favorable areas, using favorable aspects, such as archaeological sites, caves, museums, technology centers, theaters, cinemas, for exploration or increased visitation activities.

Below, some images of the representation model are shown, covering the Environmental axis: Land Use and Coverage and Conservation Units; Social: Practiced Urban Patch and Health and Education Equipment; and, Economic: Transport (Highways, Railways and Urban Roads) and Income, which deal with some characteristics of the MRC.

The elaboration of the models was based on satellite images (Sentinel 2A, from the Copernicus Program), through classification according to Land Use; as well as data provided by the public administration (urban stain, health and education equipment, income, administrative limits and Conservation Units for sustainable use and permanent protection) (Fig. 4).

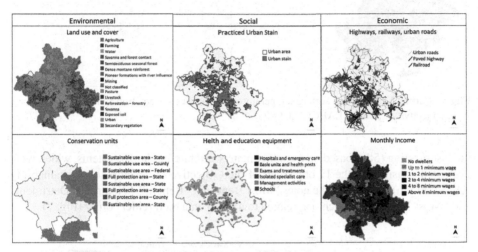

Fig. 4. Some thematic cartographic data produced, considering the sustainability triad. Source: LABGEO/UFMG.

3.2 Processes Models

The process models allow us to understand the functioning of the area, through the classification of the data elaborated, based on the interest of each System. In this model, there is a combination of data and the production of new information by the participants, presenting an analytical dimension.

Thus, the collection of thematic data from the RMC was distributed among the 10 systems. For each System, thematic maps were processed based on specific sustainability demands. From this collection, the maps referring to the Carbon Credit System stand out, involving the calculation of the surface temperature (from the mildest to the highest); the estimate of the most expressive vegetation; core area metrics, ranging from bad (no core area) to good (best core area dimension); metrics by form factor (perimeter/area), from bad (greater complexity) to good (less complexity); connectivity metrics (low to high); plus a summary of metrics (from bad to good). The processing of these data allowed the generation of representative maps of areas with conserved vegetation, areas that deserve attention in terms of restoration actions, and areas lacking green (Fig. 5).

3.3 Impact Models

The evaluation of the impact of the proposals was carried out predominantly in a qualitative way and consisted of a judgment. In the case of this study, this step was carried out in

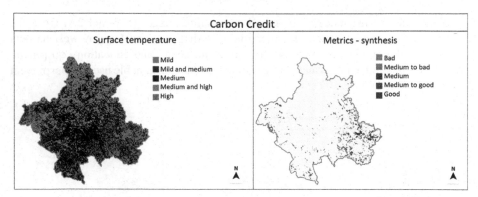

Fig. 5. Carbon Credit Maps: surface temperature and metrics - vegetation synthesis (core, shape and connectivity). Source: LABGEO/UFMG.

the last meeting (5th), based on a conflict matrix containing the 10 systems, which were evaluated considering the 17 objectives of the Objective of development sustainability (ODS) (Fig. 6), attributing the notes "Most Benefit", "Benefit", "Neutral", "Detriment" and "Most Detriment", each one related to a color in a hierarchical order (Fig. 7).

Sustainable Development Goals	AGUA WAT	AGRIC AGR	VEGET GRN	ENERG ENE	TRANS TRAN	COMIN IND	INSTI INST	HABIT RESID	TUR	CC02 CC02	SOMA sum
1. No Poverty	1	3		1	-1	1	3	1			4
2. Zero Hunger	3				-1	3		3			-3
3. Good Health and Well-being	3	3	3	3	3	1	3	3	3		4
4. Quality Education	1	3	1	3	-1		3			1	-1
5. Gender Equality	0		0	3		1	-1		0		-8
6. Clean Water and Sanitation	3	-1	1	3	-3	-3	0		1		-4
7. Affordabel and Clean Energy	1		1	3	3	3	0	3	1	1	10
8. Decent Work and Economic Growth	3	3		1	1	3	3	3			8
9. Industry, Innovation and Infrastructure	3			1	3	3	1		3		10
10. Reduced Inequality	3					-1	3	0			0
11. Sustainable Cities and Communities	3	3		1	3	3	0	3	3		10
12. Responsible Consumption and Production	3	3	3	3	-1	0		0			5
13. Climate Action	3		3	3	-1		0				8
14. Life Below Water	3	3	1	-3	-3	3	0	0		1	-12
15. Life on Land	3		3	-3	-3	3	1	1	3		-12
16. Peace and Justice Strong Institutions	3	0	0	0	0		3	0	0	0	0
17. Partnerships to achieve the Goal	3	3		1			3	3	3		6

EARLY ADOPTER - MUITAS INOVAÇÕES - 2050

Scale of Evaluation		
Most benefit	3	#7030A0
Benefit		#CC66FF
Neutral	0	#BFBFBF
Detriment	-1	#FFFF00
Most Detriment	-3	#FF9933

Fig. 6. Matrix SDG - Sustainable Development Goals. Source: International Geodesign Collaboration (IGC). https://www.igc-geodesign.org/project-workflow (2021). Adapted by the workshop collaborators).

Through this matrix, after the preparation of the proposals, it is possible to qualify the extent to which the proposals reached the sustainability goals, rating them from -3 to 3, with -3 and -1 being the proposals that did not reach the goals, 1 are the proposals that achieved the objectives to some extent and 3 are the ones that best achieved the objectives.

Most Benefit	Benefit	Neutral	Detriment	Most Detriment
3	1	0	-1	-3

Fig. 7. Matrix SDG rating scale. Source: International Geodesign Collaboration (IGC). https://www.igc-geodesign.org/project-workflow (2021).

Thus, each axis of the sustainability triad analyzed and qualified the proposals of the other two groups, considering the systems linked to them. Thus, the Environmental axis analyzed the proposals of the Economic and Social axes, the Economic axis analyzed the ideas of the Environmental and Social axes and the Social axis evaluated the proposals of the Environmental and Economic axes. In addition, each group analyzed their own proposals.

3.4 The Workshop: Co-creation of Ideas

With the Representation, Process and Impact Models prepared, it was possible to start the workshop. The workshop was organized in 5 meetings of 4 h each, totaling 20 h of activities, within the scope of the Urban Environmental Quality Analysis discipline: integration of thematic data, from the graduate program at UNESP in Rio Claro. From a total of 12 participants, there were 10 PPGG students and 2 UNICAMP graduate students. Due to the COVID-19 pandemic, the event was held entirely through the Google Meet platform. Andréia Medinilha Pancher (UNESP) led the workshop, with the support of Ana Isabel de Sá (IFMG) and Ana Clara Mourão Moura (UFMG).

Participants were divided into 3 groups and were instructed to prepare and defend proposals based on the tripod of sustainability: Environmental, Economic and Social. Each group created a google meet room to work within their axes. Participants were instructed to draw policy and project diagrams for the 10 systems: Vegetation, Hydrography, Housing, Transport, Institutions, Trade/Industry, Agriculture, Energy, Tourism/Culture/Leisure and Carbon Credit, considering the vulnerabilities and potential of the area.

In the 1st meeting, all participants performed the reading enrichment, a stage that allowed knowledge of the 43 layers of data, organized in GISCoLab, as well as the overlapping of layers, for the integrated analysis of information. It is noteworthy that at this stage, it is possible to enter additional information through notes. In the case of the metropolitan region of Campinas, from the integrated analysis of thematic cartographic data, vulnerable areas were identified, considering the environmental, economic and social points of view. Thus, the weaknesses of the Permanent Preservation Areas, due to urban occupation, were discussed; the importance of preserving conservation units, to expand the vegetation area and, consequently, contribute to carbon credits. In addition, the issue of expanding the housing and transport supply (collective transport and the use of smarts) was discussed, adopting more sustainable models.

At the 2nd meeting, employees were separated into three groups: Environmental, Economic and Social, choosing which group they would like to participate in. However, they were also able to give their opinion on the other topics. Next, they were instructed to prepare the proposals without innovations, that is, without looking for new things, projection in the traditional, taking into account the 2035 and 2050 scenarios. For the preparation of the proposals, project diagrams were drawn (which can be realized in the short term) and policies (intentions, which can be implemented in the long term) using GISCoLab's design resources. It is noteworthy that for almost all systems, dots and lines were used for the preparation of proposals. However, for the Carbon Credit System the ideas were designed using polygons. In the first part, the three groups, gathered in different virtual rooms, made proposals without innovations for the 2035 scenario. In the second part, the groups made proposals without innovations for the 2050 scenario. To allow the development of the 2050 scenario, some actions had to be proposed in the 2035 scenario, receiving adjustments and selecting the most interesting annotations.

At the 3rd meeting, the groups made proposals with innovations. In the first part of the meeting, all participants made proposals with innovations for the 2035 scenario, based on enriching reading. For all the workshops, a 30% increase in vegetation was defined as a goal, adding to the proposals of the 2035 and 2050 scenarios. For that, it was necessary to propose an increase in carbon credit through the conservation of areas with robust fragments and that they need maintenance and investment to maintain themselves properly; expansion in areas with fragments, but in need of improvement in their conditions; and, creation of green areas, where there is no vegetation, but which are able to be implemented. In the 2nd part of the meeting, all participants made proposals with innovations for the 2050 scenario, based on the 2035 proposals. The groups were able to use ideas from existing innovations on the International Geodesign Collaboration (IGC) event website (igc-geodesign) (igc-geodesign.org/global-systems-research), as well as had the opportunity to suggest their own ideas, based on their research or professional experiences.

At the 4th meeting, participants created ideas with many innovations for the 2050 scenario, being able to continue the 2035 proposals. In addition, they were able to extract ideas from the IGC website for the 2050 scenario, adapting them to the Brazilian reality, in specific, the Metropolitan Region of Campinas (Fig. 8).

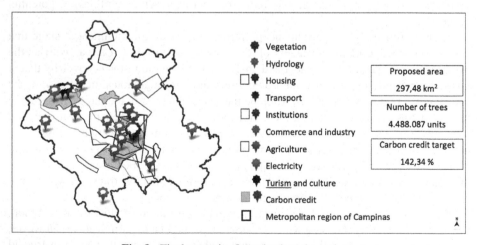

Fig. 8. Final scenario. Organization: the authors.

Once the diagram design step was completed, everyone voted on the proposals created for all systems, using the Like and Don't Like feature, available on the GISCoLab platform. In addition to voting, participants were able to add comments to each proposal, in order to clarify the reasons for voting against or even proposing adjustments or changes to the location of the approved proposals.

During the activities, analyzing the development from the 1st to the 4th meeting, an evolution in the preparation of proposals was evidenced, from 43 proposals without innovations to 47 proposals with many innovations, highlighting that many ideas built in the scenarios with innovations were taken advantage of, continued and improved.

The proposal analysis stage (5th meeting) proved to be fundamental, as it allowed everyone to know all the ideas developed by the three groups, as well as making a critical analysis of the weaknesses and potential of collective creation. Taking into account the scenario without innovations, with innovations and even with many innovations, the groups showed that the collective construction of ideas occurred in an evolutionary way, allowing for the expansion of proposals and better achieving sustainability goals.

In addition to the positive aspects identified by the groups, the weaknesses of some themes were also highlighted. With regard to gender equality, the social group noted that no proposals were made to address the vulnerability of specific social groups. Also, ideas were developed for the modernization of housing, in order to alleviate physical and natural problems, such as thermal comfort, issues related to slope, etc., however, there was a lack of proposals for the construction of new housing for the part of the population that is not assisted.

The Economic group also made a critical analysis of the proposals. Regarding the goals for reducing poverty, hunger, gender equality, that is, social aspects, the group also identified weaknesses. For example, innovations in the means of transport (vehicles powered by solar or electric energy) were proposed, but the issue of harassment that occurs in public transport towards women was not considered. As a solution, they could propose the separation of public transport, serving only women. It should be noted that social proposals like these would require a broad debate in society. For the scenario without innovations, it was evident that the adoption of traditional, non-innovative proposals resulted in ideas that were not linked to the three axes: Environmental, Economic and Social, that is, without establishing inter-relations. In this sense, the economic group gave great importance to agricultural issues, such as the proposal for urban gardens, but the impact that such actions may have on animals living in areas where gardens will be implemented were not considered.

In the analysis of the proposals by the Environmental group, based on the scenario with innovations, positive effects on health, well-being and gains in the issues of poverty and hunger were highlighted, through actions related to the implementation or improvement of infrastructure (sanitation, for example), climate, reflecting in improvements in water quality, in the expansion of carbon credits, among others.

Regarding the proposals for the vegetation system, the environmental group highlighted the recovery of riparian forests along the drainage network and, mainly, around the springs; suggested the interconnection between conservation areas, through the establishment of flora and fauna corridors. Also, urban afforestation on sidewalks, as well as the implementation of Environmental Protection Areas and Areas of Relevant Eco-logical Interest (ARIE), which can be some massive forests existing in cities or even isolated trees. In addition, green roofs were proposed, the transformation of urban voids into urban gardens. These proposals directly reflect on the volume and quality of water and on the Carbon Credit. For the water system, the group proposed the reduction of charges for its use for those who implement the collection and use of rainwater and for industries that develop technologies for the reduction and rational use of water. In urban areas, integration of vegetation with buildings and water retention in public, residen-tial and commercial buildings. Also, the elimination of areas of diffuse contamination, which contaminate underground water tables, in addition to greater control of polluting sources. In rural areas, the implementation of drip and digital irrigation.

The economic group presented proposals for the use of photovoltaic panels in 50% of homes in the MRC; expansion of the use of solar energy on highways, providing the neediest population living in the surrounding area with energy generated at a reduced cost. In addition, the generation of energy from natural waterfalls in rivers, without the construction of reservoirs; this type of power generation involves low investment. Also, implementation of Power to Gas plants (electrolysis and hydrogen process) throughout the region. In addition to these ways of generating energy being sustainable, it would allow the metropolitan region of Campinas to be self-sufficient in the production of electricity. Another proposal of the group was related to family and organic agriculture, which includes ecological pest control, with support from the government. Thus, green roofs were suggested for the implementation of urban and community gardens. Another proposal was the creation of a family farming program, with credit lines.

With regard to industry and commerce, encouragement of innovation for all industries in the MRC and implementation of intelligent infrastructure in the streets of central busi-nesses, integrating tenants and customers through a quality virtual connection. Include small traders in the Magnetic Levitation Transport (MAGLEV) system, paying lower rents and allocating stations. For transport, the group proposed expanding MAGLEV and creating new stations to serve more municipalities in the MRC.

The Social group proposed the implementation of smart windows in all constructions. In the health area, the idea was to implement virtual care, through the direct connection of the patient with doctors and databases and remote examinations (reduction in waiting time, travel and transport costs). In relation to the transport system, the idea was to increase tax incentives to electrify 100% of the public and private vehicle fleet, as well as for mass transport and the consolidation of urban cycle paths. Also, the use of the solar highway.

For tourism, the consolidation of Glampings in natural areas with replicable struc-tures inspired by nature, brings the idea of natural design, encouraging environmental tourism and conservation of the area. In addition, the creation of self-sufficient stadiums in water collection and treatment, solar energy production, and sewage treatment, with multiple entertainment functions. For rectified and channeled urban rivers or streams, remove the concrete or pavement that are covering the waterways, restoring them to their original condition, allowing the creation of parks close to these areas and the expansion of systems leisure activities for the population. For the water supply network, insert sensors in all public and private buildings and in the water transport network, connecting them to an online central.

For the housing system, it was proposed to replace concrete with materials that contribute to lowering the temperatures of cities. Another idea was the implementation of green streets in the urban perimeter with the objective of increasing the vegetation, constituting a necessary measure to meet the carbon credit and improve the quality of life of the population of the MRC, which lacks urban green. For transport, it was suggested the expansion of tax incentives to electrify 100% of the public and private vehicle fleet, encourage mass transport and consolidation of urban cycle paths.

Given the above, the evaluation process served to analyze the proposals together, reflecting on the possibilities of adaptations, adjustments and adjustments, allowing for the improvement of ideas, making them more effective and coherent with the reality studied.

4 Conclusions and Discussions

The results obtained at the workshop demonstrated the potential of the Geodesign methodology for territorial assessment and planning, allowing the analysis of a large volume of thematic data from the MRC, in an interrelated way, enabling the elaboration of proposals to mitigate vulnerabilities and take advantage of potentialities of the area.

It is a methodology that favors and encourages teamwork, allowing for the enrichment, complementarity and integration of proposals. Through the dialogues established in the meetings, all participants had moments of speech, enriching the elaboration of proposals with different academic and professional experiences, favoring critical analysis.

In addition, during the meetings there was an evolution of the proposals, allowing for surpassing the established target of 30% of carbon credit. For the 2050 scenario with innovations, there was an increase of 96.54% of CCO_2, which can be explained by the low vegetation index in the MRC, which led the group to create more proposals for this System.

The evaluation stage of the proposals proved to be fundamental, as it served to think about possibilities for adaptations/adaptations, allowing for the improvement of ideas, making them more effective in alleviating the problems of vulnerabilities and making better use of the potential of the analyzed area. Thus, it is suggested that this evaluation step be carried out before the closing of the proposals.

The groups made proposals within their axes, but many have an interface with the other axes as well, evidencing the existing integration to achieve sustainability. It should be noted that several innovative proposals for the 2050 scenario can only be implemented if they are started in the 2035 scenario, as they require time to develop, mature and consolidate, as is the case with the implementation of vegetation.

The Geodesign methodology offers the opportunity for everyone involved to present their ideas and to listen to the proposals of others, favoring teamwork, generating an enrichment of ideas, expanding the possibilities for actions, enhancing the adequate planning of the territory.

An important aspect highlighted by the environmental group is that this work dynamic, of co-creation of ideas, allows the integration of knowledge between professionals from different areas, resulting in collective proposals, therefore broader and more complete, taking advantage of the experiences of all involved.

Furthermore, it is important to point out that Geodesign allowed an evaluation of territorial data and the elaboration of proposals in a democratic way. The GISCoLab platform is a very important contribution tool for collaborators to enter information in order to create a critical/analytical scenario in relation to the data that were initially fed by the organizers.

Acknowledgments. The authors thank CNPq support through the project 401066/2016-9, FAPEMIG PPM-00368-18 and LABGEO/UFMG, for the creation of the GISCoLab and for preparing the databases. Also thank the Graduate Programs in Geography at UNESP and UNICAMP, as well as the organization of the event.

References

1. Instituto Brasileiro de Geografia e Estatística – IBGE. Conheça o Brasil – População: População Rural e Urbana. Disponível em: https://educa.ibge.gov.br/jovens/conheca-o-brasil/populacao/18313-populacao-rural-e-urbana.html. Acesso em: 26 abr 2021
2. Freitas, C.R.: Tecnologias de Geoinformação no Planejamento Territorial: novas formas de produção, compartilhamento e uso de dados espaciais 2020. Tese – Universidade Federal de Minas Gerais – UFMG, Programa de Pós-Graduação em Arquitetura e Urbanismo Belo Horizonte (2020)
3. Steinitz, C.: A Framework for Geodesign: Changing Geography by Design. ESRI Press, Redlands (2012)
4. Batty, M.: Planning support systems and the new logic of computation. Regional Dev. Dialogue. [s.l.], pp. 1–17 (1995)
5. Goodchild, M.F.: Towards geodesign: repurposing cartography and GIS? Cartogr. Perspect. **66**, 7–22 (2010)
6. Instituto Brasileiro de Geografia e Estatística – IBGE. Disponível em: https://cidades.ibge.gov.br › brasil › sp. Acesso em: 14 mai. 2021.
7. Instituto Brasileiro de Geografia e Estatística – IBGE: Estimativas da população.. Disponível em: https://www.ibge.gov.br/estatisticas/sociais/populacao/9103-estimatives-de-populavao.html?=&t=downloads. Acesso em: 14 mai. 2021

Using Geodesign to Plan the Future of Macapa Metropolitan Region, State of Amapa, Brazil: A Support to Expanding Collaborative Technical Performance

Gustavo Adolfo Tinoco Martínez[1]([⊠]), Fabiana Carmo de Vargas Vieira[1],
Caroline Cristiane Rocha[1], Ana Corina Maia Palheta[2], and Sara Heloiza Alberto Neri[2]

[1] Universidade Federal de Minas Gerais, Av. Presidente Antônio Carlos,
Belo Horizonte 6627, Brazil
[2] Secretaria de Meio Ambiente do Estado do Amapá – SEMA, Av. Mendonça Furtado, 53,
Macapá, Brazil

Abstract. The experience is part of a broader one, Geodesign Brazil: Trees for metropolitan regions, composed of a set of workshops that were held in twelve Brazilian metropolitan areas, that in Amapa was conducted by technicians of two planning state departments. The workshop aimed to develop dialogs and proposals for alternative futures to the metropolitan region, targeting the years of 2035 and 2050. The goal was to discuss ten main topics: vegetation, hydrography, housing, transportation, institutions, trade and industry, agriculture, energy, tourism and culture, and carbon credit. The GISColab platform was used as a tool for registering opinions, alerts, ideas and voting of designs for each scenario. The workshop was developed over four stages: reading enrichment and note creation; creation of proposals with that continued the existing planning; creation of proposals with some innovations; creation of proposals with many innovations and a final voting. The experience pointed to an active participation of the actors in the discussion process, but a limitation in changing from analysis to proposals, mainly accepting innovative ideas, a fact possibly related to the wide technical experience of the participants in public agencies, who acted during the meetings in the same way that they do in their professional practices: discussing the difficulties and consequences of implementing innovations. However, as a result, when comparing the first designs to the last ones, it was possible to observe improvements in performance and an adherence to a new way of planning.

Keywords: Collaborative planning · Geodesign · GISColab · Amapa

1 Introduction

There are several challenges to overcoming the distance between what is proposed in urban planning and its actual effects in urban landscape. One of them is the distance that separates technical knowledge and the empirical knowledge, borne out of inhabitants' everyday lives. Understanding the information produced by technicians is a task that

© Springer Nature Switzerland AG 2021
O. Gervasi et al. (Eds.): ICCSA 2021, LNCS 12954, pp. 491–506, 2021.
https://doi.org/10.1007/978-3-030-86979-3_35

requires abstract thought and codification, and empirical knowledge is often disregarded. Therefore, citizen participation in the decisions that define urban space are becoming ever smaller.

Despite significant advances in laws and planning within Brazilian cities, particularly after the Statute of Cities, from 2001, citizen participation is still incipient, and so-called democratic processes simply fulfill bureaucratic guidelines without including citizens in collective decisions.

In Geodesign, information is considered the bedrock for everything else. Data production would be the moment in which citizens could provide information and the transformation of that data would bring about a debate regarding the needs and potential uses of urban spaces. The careful consideration of the data contributes to a better understanding of the collective values and culture, as they relate to different social groups. The planning scale for geodesign is somewhere in between that of geoscience and architecture. In geodesign, change and sustainability are sought through a combination of factors, such as quantity, cost, and quality.

Moura and Santana [1] argue that there is a new role for technicians. They are no longer to act in a purely authorial fashion, but rather as those who decode the collective will, which, in turn, requires carefully listening to the communities involved. Geodesign then emerges as a methodology that provides support to shared creation and decision-making processes. It seeks to build a collective planning that stems from the information regarding the territory, resorting to the potentialities of Geographic Information Systems. In other words, a geodesign process can use data distribution models in territories, so that relevant layers can be combined and used for debate, which later allows to construct syntheses regarding a given field of study [2].

According to Moura [2], geodesign has shown itself as a method supported by geoinformation technology and sharing of data, information and knowledge on the territory, which ultimately results in a co-built agreement, a portrait of citizen values. It offers the possibility of building a collaborative form of planning, in which different social agents can contribute to decision-making. Aside from that, it is also a way towards overcoming public hearings, that simply fulfill a norm and do not promote citizen power [3].

The proposal of the International Geodesign Collaboration (IGC[1]), a geodesign study network coordinated by Carl Steinitz, is to create a framework for optimizing co-creation processes. According to Steinitz [4], the stages of geodesign are comprised of six models: Representation, Processes and Evaluation - which should be priorly developed by technicians - and Change, Impact and Decision - developed during a participatory planning workshop.

Moura and Freitas [5] argue that the form of geodesign proposed by Steinitz [4] has faced challenges in the context of Brazil, particularly regarding the languages, modes and expression, visualization of information and access to final and partial products. The changes that were made in the framework resulted in the Brazilian platform Gis-Colab, developed by the aforementioned authors. The platform focuses on developing a methodology that is comprised of four stages: 1) Reading enrichment and annotation; 2) proposal creation; 3) dialogs and negotiation; and 4) final voting.

---

[1] https://www.igc-geodesign.org/.

Through the GisColab platform, and Geodesign's concepts of participation and collaboration, and as part of an international experiment - Geodesign Brazil: Trees for metropolitan regions[2]- a workshop was conducted regarding the Macapá Metropolitan Area (MMA) in Amapá State, Brazil. The goal of this paper is to describe the experience derived from said workshop, remarking the challenges and possibilities offered by digital platforms in regional-scale urban planning. For the workshop, the platform was connected to a database with a collection of maps built by the Geoprocessing Lab at the School of Architecture at UFMG using data collected in the INDE platform (National Spatial Data Infrastructure).

In these cases, the workshops are of academic nature and, therefore, do not intend to build proposals that will actually take place. The proposed exercise is to investigate on-line participation methods use as planning tools and provide, through dialog and negotiation, the experience of collectively planning a metropolitan area for the years of 2035 and 2050. The recently-created MMA has a unique landscape and culture, considering it is located in the far-northern area of the country, within the Equator Line and in the vicinity of Amazon River's delta. Thus, we expect that the results of the different spatial analyses, tables and charts that were built using a questionnaire at the end of the workshop, can express the relationship between citizens and their territory.

2   Case Study MACAPÁ Metropolitan Area

Macapá Metropolitan Area, located in the state of Amapá, with a total area of 22.339,46 km^2 accounts for 14,94% of state's total territory (see Fig. 1). According to IBGE data 2020, the estimated population of Macapá is 512.902, 123.092 for Santana and 22.053 in the city of Mazagão. The population of the three cities that form MMA accounts for 76% of the total population of Amapá.

MMA is located on the left bank of the mouth of the Amazon River, which potentially favors ports designed for exporting, and also attractive for services and commerce. Its cultural and landscape values contribute to tourism - for both business as well as ecotourism -, given that aside from the mouth of the Amazon River, the city of Macapá is also crossed by the Equator Line (see Fig. 2) and is strongly influenced by the Marajoara islands, in the neighboring state of Pará.

Amapá's climate is equatorial (warm and humid), with two well defined seasons. A rainy winter, that lasts from January to June, and a dry summer, that lasts the remainder of the year. Its vegetation cover is diversified, including Cerrado (savanna), Firm Ground Forests (typical of the Amazon Forest) and Floodplain Forests, with mangrove vegetation in its shores (see Fig. 3). The Firm Ground Forest, located in northern Mazagão, is preserved as part of a conservation unit named Amapá State Forest or FLOTA/AP, created in 2006 with the goal of achieving sustainable use of forest resources in the state

---

[2] The experiment was a joint effort by twelve Brazilian metropolitan areas, through ten federal universities (UFMG, UFRRJ, UFJF, USP, UFCF, UFPE, UFG, UFPA, UFT, UNIFAP), two state universities (UDESC and UNESP at Rio Claro) and two offices related to the secretary of planning (SEMA and STRAP). The common goal was to discuss proposals for different scenarios, in the years of 2035 and 2050. The goal was to be part of the IGC's global project.

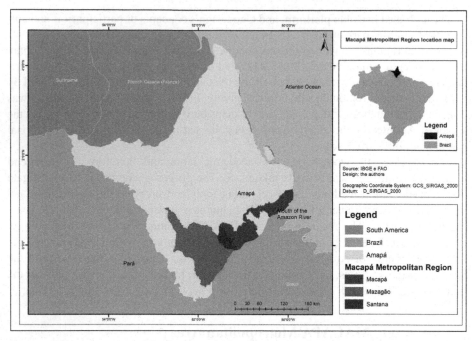

Fig. 1. Macapá metropolitan area map.

of Amapá. The area is destined for the exploitation of both wood/lumber-related and non-related products in a sustainable fashion. To the south, human occupation encompasses most of the metropolitan area, but the cities of Macapá and Santana are much more connected than the other parts of MMA.

The Accessibility and Capillarity map shows how the low-density of pathways is widespread in the region. Macapá bears a high density, in line with its status as the capital city of Amapá state (see Fig. 4).

The occupation of Amapá's territory took place during the Second World War and during the post-War period. According to Porto [6], the 1940's saw the beginning of iron extraction in the Vila Nova River, with Hanna Corporation in 1945, and manganese in the Serra do Navio region in 1957–1997 by Indústria de Comércio e Mineração (ICOMI). The cities of Santana and Serra do Navio were built alongside the mining infrastructure (railroad, port, road and a hydroelectric plant), propelled by ICOMI and heavily influencing the urbanization of Amapá.

Brazil, worrisome of invasions and foreign exploitation of its natural resources, worked towards incorporating the area through public projects for highways, under the slogan of "integrar para não entregar", that is "integrate to not give away". On Fig. 5, we can see this take place between the decades of 1950 and 1970, when Macapá, Santana and Mazagão had a population leap from 25.666 inhabitants (1950) to twice as much in 1960, reaching almost 100.000 people in the 1970's. However, in the remainder of Amapá state, growth remained stagnate. From 1991 onwards the population of the cities that would form the metropolitan area grows by an extra 100.000 inhabitants, which is

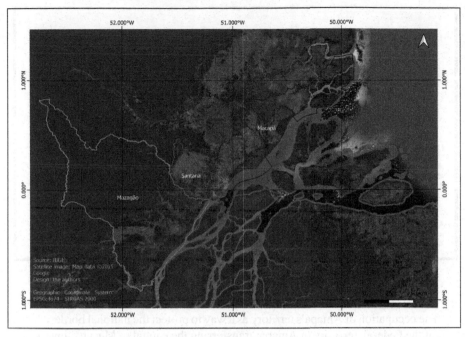

Fig. 2. The mouth of the Amazon river and Macapá metropolitan area.

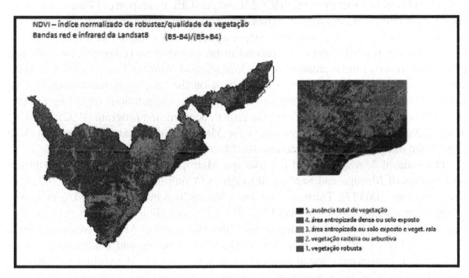

Fig. 3. Normalized difference vegetation index/vegetation quality.

visible over the next decades, due to migratory influxes. According to Porto [6], this is due to the following factors:

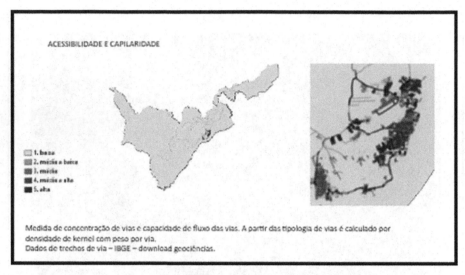

Fig. 4. Accessibility and capillarity

"The occupation of Amapá's territory as a way to protect the national border; the creation of the Federal Territory of Amapá; transferring the capital to Macapá; investments in mining in Amapá's territory (gold, manganese) and the Macapá area; establishment of mining and wood-timber industries (ICOMI and AMCEL); creation of Companies towns (Serra do Navio; Vila Amazonas); expansion of the agricultural frontier; local political actions (elections for city councilors, congresspeople and senators; new municipalities being created); Amapá statehood; creation of protected areas (conservation units and indigenous reservations); creation of the Macapá and Santana Free Commerce Area; hopes for new investments (bridges being built on the Oiapoque and Matapi rivers); paving of the BR-156 highway; the new mining cycle; expectations regarding the creation of the Macapá Free Trade Zone; the growth acceleration program (PAC); stimulus to agricultural businesses; the creation of the Macapá and Santana Metropolitan Area (2003); the integration of Magazão into the Macapá Metropolitan Area (2016)".

The state of Macapá created the Macapá Metropolitan Area (MMA), comprised of the cities of Macapá and Santana, through the Complimentary Law N. ° 0.021, in February 26th, 2003 [7]. Thirteen years later, Mazagão is included in MMA, under the Complimentary Law N. ° 95, of May 17th, 2016 [8]. According to AMAPÁ [9] "the lines of common interest between the three cities of the Metropolitan Area are basic sanitation, urban mobility, health, law enforcement, education, housing and integrated planning for sustainable economic, social and territorial development." According to Porto [6], Mazagão received stimulus to conclude its infrastructure building, particularly the bridge of Matapi river, which allows for greater connectivity, flux and fluidity between the cities of the metropolitan area. However, it is possible to note the cities that form MMA hold a somewhat timid conurbation between Macapá and Santana.

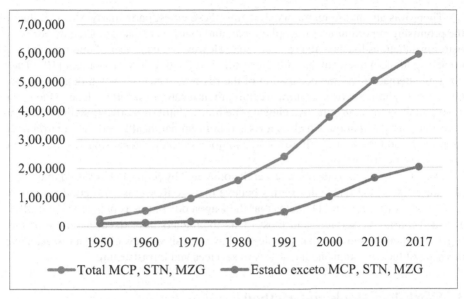

Fig. 5. Population of Macapá, Santana and Magazão [6].

The ressaca (see Fig. 6) was defined by the Environmental Law N. ° 948/48 of the City of Macapá, as: "Water accumulation bays, influenced by the behavior of tides, rivers and rain drainages". Neri [10] describes the ressaca as the following:

"Ressaca is a regional expression used to designate an ecosystem that is typical of Amapá's shores. They are areas that fit into Quaternary terrains, which behave as natural water reservoirs, characterized as a complex and unique ecosystem that is subject to the regime of the tides, as part of an intricate set of canals and streams (igarapés 2), and the seasonal rain cycle, therefore presenting a flood season (January to June) and a drought season (August to December)".

Fig. 6. Ressacas in their natural state, in the city of Macapá, and Occupations.

There was an intense migratory flow into these cities, particularly Macapá, due to the promising opportunities for employment, and many were also attracted by access to better installations like hospitals and schools. However, the number of unemployed was greater than the work available, which resulted in many informal workers [10]. Their housing alternative was the occupation of the ressacas, because even though there was no access to public services or infrastructure, their location was often close to the urban center, making them an attractive choice. The houses built over stilts (palafitas) have no access to basic sanitation, which is a risk to both human health and the environment. Moreover, fish farms (pisciculture) pose a major risk to the fauna, since exotic fish are bred as a source of income.

Despite all these adversities, a research conducted by Souza [11] showed that 100% of inhabitants of the Lagoa dos Índios believe that the Ressacas offer good conditions for living. However, Neri [11] notes that the Lagoa dos Índios is unique since it offers access to all public services and most of its inhabitants have fixed-income jobs (see Fig. 6). Although it poses a risk, people still have a positive view of life in ressaca areas in virtue of their location and the access to services and infrastructure.

3   Workshop: Tools and Methods

In virtue of the IGC's global project, a total of ten key topics were chosen for discussion, in the form of systems that were evaluated during the collaborative process: vegetation, hydrography, housing, transportation, institutions, commerce and industry, agriculture, energy and carbon credit. The geospatial data that best described each system were gathered according to their availability in municipal, state and federal databases.

The data was processed and organized into a collection of maps, and then exported to the GisColab platform. This process was in charge of the coordinators of the experiment, at the Geoprocessing Lab at Minas Gerais Federal University's School of Architecture. (Geoproea - UFMG). The data was retrieved from platforms belonging to public institutions and freely available for download, followed by an upload to the platform using WFS (web feature service), since direct access via WMS (web map service) is not supported by these platforms and the data would require further processing to fit within the goals of the study.

The workshop was conducted over the course of four virtual sessions in March 2021. There 18 people attending, mostly university and public service personnel, a lot them working as technicians for public offices dedicated to territorial planning. Participants were divided into two work groups, "Group A" and "Group B", which worked with different time horizons. The former would develop scenarios for the year of 2035, whereas the latter would focus on proposals for the year of 2050.

A series of videos explaining how to use the platform and the goals for each day of the workshop were presented to help participants access the platform, share information and create proposals. The videos were quite relevant for participants who were not familiar with the functionalities of GisColab. They were presented at the start of each session.

3.1 Day 1 – Reading Enrichment and Note Creation

The first stage of the workshop involved understanding the platform and its layers, after which notes were taken regarding problems and potentialities. The session started by welcoming participants and explaining the general aspects, as well as the goals, of the workshop. Participants were then divided into each group, where they would be guided by a "mediator", who explained the platform and the available data, as well as provided support in the creation of the notes.

Once participants were distributed in online chatrooms, they were explained how the GisColab platform works with special regard to how the spatial data for each system could be visualized and how the color scheme for the captions was organized. Participants were encouraged to access the platform from their own computers and read each one of the layers, to then provide their opinion regarding their usefulness for creating notes.

Once the reading part was done, the workshop proceeded with the discussion regarding the aspects of the area that were worth highlighting and which were not yet provided in terms of data. Said process resulted in the creation of specific notes about the area, which could be later retrieved, during the proposal creation stage. These notes were characterized as observations, problems, potentialities, and alerts regarding the Macapá Metropolitan Area, according to each participant's views.

The notes made by each participant were included in the platform by the mediator, with captions adhering to the color scheme and symbols that corresponded to each of the ten previously defined systems. Participants were informed of the possibility to include new notes over the course of the week, between the first and second encounter, as a way to further advance discussions on the region (see Fig. 7).

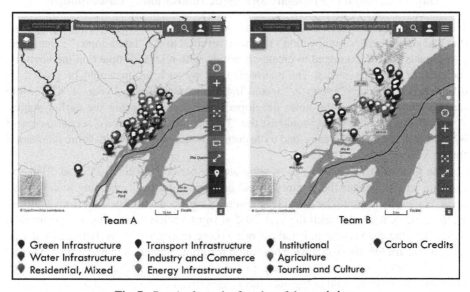

Fig. 7. Results from the first day of the workshop.

3.2 Day 2 – Creation of Proposals – Without Innovations, "Non-Adopter"

Following the methodological procedure proposed by the IGC and adopted by the international groups, the second session aimed to evaluate the scenarios that would be produced when applying traditional planning, without innovative interventions on the territory - a stage defined as the "non-adopter". For the years of 2035 and 2050, planning was to follow traditional political actions, with a future scenario designed according to Brazil's reality and resulting from traditional planning paradigms already used in the country's territorial planning.

This stage started with participants reading the notes that were created in the previous encounter, by both groups, followed by spatial identification. Afterwards, they received an explanation regarding the necessary procedures for building their proposals within the platform. The proposals were created based on three basic geometric shapes: points, lines, closed polylines and polygons. The designs followed the standard colors for each system, defined by the IGC's research team. Proposals regarding carbon credit were only allowed to use polygons, the other systems used open and closed polylines, to avoid the visual complexity of overlapping polygons.

Participants would check the sets of layers per system, use overlaps and transparencies between them, pick the themes they deemed most important for collective analysis and then design their ideas. The location of the proposals would result from this spatial analysis, but also based on the oral contributions by participants, who would add more information based on their expert knowledge. The debates were quite good and served as supports for the decisions.

3.3 Day 3 – Creation of Proposals with Some Innovations, "Late-Adopter"

The third session proposed a new scenario, where MMA would implement proposals that had some degree of innovation - the stage referred to the "late-adopter". Therefore, participants were encouraged to create proposals with relevant impact on the territory, for each of the ten systems. The approach used by each group would be guided by different perspectives: "group A" would build proposals for the year of 2035 using reading enrichment and the notes developed by the group during the earlier stages; "group B", on the other hand, would use the "2035 with no innovations" scenario created by "group A" as their reference, and try to come up with proposals with some innovation for the year of 2050.

The goal of this dynamic was to simulate the period between 2035 and 2050 and evaluate which changes the territory would undergo in terms of planning with innovations. Hopefully, it would be possible to compare two scenarios: Starting from a current reality (2021), it would reach the year 2035 using traditional planning and, from then until 2050, the proposal would start adopting more innovative ideas, but at a moderate pace and restricting those that were not suited for implementation in under fifteen years.

Their ideas were drawn according to the same, previous, dynamic, using points, lines, closed polylines and polygons, with standardized colors per system. Once again, polygons were only used to represent proposals related to the "carbon credit" system.

Aside from debating proposals using each participant's knowledge of the territory, they were also presented with access to a preexisting database with ideas provided by the IGC website and named "*Assumptions*"[3]. These ideas could be used by participants if they were deemed feasible for implementation in the MMA. The proposals that were adopted would be highlighted so that they could be referenced back to the database using the same code presented on the website.

3.4 Day 4 – Creation of Proposal with Many Innovations and Voting, "Early-Adopter"

The last session had the goal of creating a scenario in which both groups would build plans with several innovations, which would have a major impact on the territory if they were implemented - the "early-adopter". The "Assumptions" database was used once more to aid participants in the creation of their proposals, as well as the same representation scheme.

Before finishing their proposals for the creation, conservation and expansion of areas with robust vegetation to contribute to carbon sequestering, groups were able to use a platform plug-in that would show the percentage of the area necessary to achieve a minimum value defined by carbon credit directives (30% of the MMA).

At last, the final two stages were dedicated to commenting and voting. Participants in "group A" would discuss the context and scenario provided by "group B", and "group B" would do the same based on the work provided by "group A". The goal of this was to consolidate the ideas that were most well-structured, using the questions made in comments, although participants expressed that there was little time available for the task.

After reading the proposals and the comments for each proposal, participants would then vote on them. This stage was also conducted within GisColab and, in each proposal, participants from the evaluating group had the chance to issue a positive or negative vote through the "like" and "don't like" resources. They could also annex, if deemed necessary, comments regarding the proposals in the form of warnings, or suggesting spatial-technical modifications as a requisite for approving the proposal. The voting was individual, and each participant had the right to cast one vote per proposal.

4 Results

Based on the study conducted, we hereby present our evaluation of the discussions between participants, who presented their stances based on their knowledge of the MMA over the course of these encounters. Most participants had institutional ties to public planning offices. This relates to their knowledge on the subject, acquired from their everyday technical work, which played a fundamental role in the decision-making processes. Yet, when questioned on their knowledge of the main characteristics of the MMA, 41% replied that they did not know them, perhaps due to the large territorial extension of the MMA and empty areas that they may have never visited before (see Fig. 8). Over the course of the workshop, it was possible to notice that the cities that form the MMA are not quite connected, which likely explains why part of its population has a challenging time with knowing the full scope of the region.

---

[3] https://www.igc-geodesign.org/global-systems-research.

Regarding the data used, some degree of appropriation by participants was noted when they faced the need for additional spatial information, so they uploaded it themselves (a process that was facilitated by the platform's interface, which supports alternative information sources). Regarding the available spatial information, the less relevant data, or that were least considered in the "reading enrichment" stage were those regarding "airfields", "insolation per aspect", "youth percentage" and "ducts".

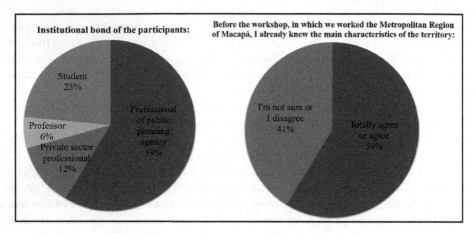

Fig. 8. Charts used for analyzing participants' profiles.

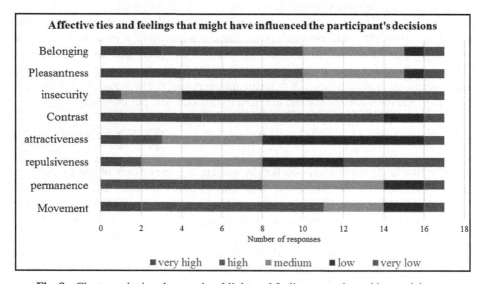

Fig. 9. Charts analyzing the emotional links and feelings experienced by participants.

Regarding the influence of their emotional links to the area, positive or negative, on the decision-making process, participants were asked to express eight possible feelings that they experienced during the workshop (see Fig. 9). According to their replies, it was possible to note participants would experience feelings of significant "contrast" regarding the area. On the other hand, in what touches the realm of belonging and pleasantness, ten participants replied they were "very high" and "high", a fact that is possibly related to their experiences with the local population, and who even work in their own city offices.

Regarding the use of the platform, it was notable that most participants understood the process of geodesign (82%) and there was an increase in the number of people who replied they had knowledge of the method (see Fig. 10). Regarding how easy they considered each stage of the workshop, it is possible to note an increase in those who marked that was quite easy between the first and final stages, which may be explained by: 1) The participants' knowledge of geographical information systems and geospatial software usage in their day-to-day activities; 2) the explanations on how to use the platform; and 3) the presence of mediators in each group and the video explanation on how to use the platform, during the start of each encounter (see Fig. 11).

When asked if they contributed with notes and proposals in each stage of the work-shop, it's possible to note a significant amount of them (over 80% in each encounter) made a proposal regarding the area of study and according to the proposed themes. This demonstrates they were able to appropriate the platform during the event, in terms of reading enrichment as well as of proposals made for the metropolitan area (see Fig. 12).

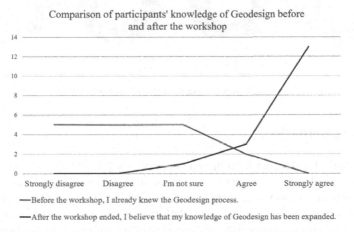

Fig. 10. Charts analyzing participants' comprehension of the Geodesign process.

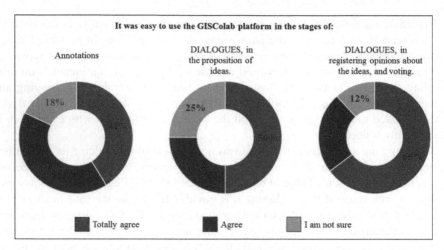

Fig. 11. Charts analyzing their opinions on the use of the platform.

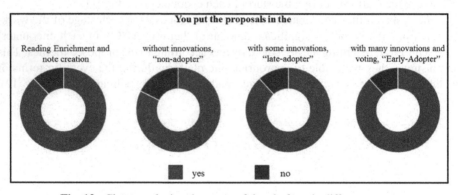

Fig. 12. Charts analyzing the usage of the platform in different stages.

5   Closing Remarks

Since the goal of geodesign is to provide support for populations to make decisions based on a critical understanding of the potentialities and problems of their territories, it is important to stay alert regarding how those involved in these processes deal with spatial representation (the use of a digital platform). The search for a common language and shared assumptions can often be obstructed using complicated digital tools or highly technical discourse with no political consciousness. We should ask ourselves: how can the proposals developed by collective participation surpass the model of just hearings [3], to be part of public policies (which take place in a large period) or projects (implementation/transformation over a shorter period)? This is something to be sought after in processes like the one hereby presented.

Therefore, it is important to pay attention to particularities. For instance, even if the noting stage involves a dynamic that assumes the mapping of specificities, once citizens are invited to speak about their place of use (housing, work) and appropriation, their ideas tend to remain generic. This is interesting to note, because it reveals how challenging it is to achieve actual, legitimate participation in planning. Another issue we noted is the difficulty in thinking in terms of a Metropolitan Region, and the possibilities for integrating different municipalities. How can geodesign collaborate on integrating the scales?

In the proposition stage it is important to discuss local potentialities. In several moments, talking about issues is more effective. Knowledge regarding the area discussed (through technical data and empirical knowledge by local inhabitants) is essential to think strategically and propose actions that will not only solve something in the area, but also optimize what is considered positive.

Another approach that should be taken is the assessment of the extent to which the proposed future scenarios contribute to the Sustainable Development Goals proposed by the UN for the 2030, Agenda 2015. The Geodesign process can assist in proposing ideas considering the goal of the 17 objectives, and analysis of the results of the case study demonstrated that the proposed scenarios show an increase from Non-Adopter to Early-Adopter, with emphasis on water themes, transport, parks, urban and organic agriculture, but there are few proposals to eradicate poverty. People should be encouraged to think of a better city that also includes the UN Sustainable Development Goals.

At last, it is important to note that the logic of using three different stages (no innovations, some innovation and several innovations), defined by the IGC international group, was not well-received by the group. They had not yet worked in this manner and did not see a lot of sense in stimulating innovations within their local reality because basic issues of everyday life should be solved first to plan for innovations.

During the experiment, they behaved in the same manner they do when performing their daily activities as state workers, who need to fulfill requirements, evaluate the impact and the feasibility of the proposals before registering them, also accounting for the different areas of expertise represented in the workshop. Hence, mediators noted a certain hesitancy in coming up with bolder propositions, particularly when they involved innovations (Late-adopter and Early-adopter), but the overall experience was seen as positive and as a possible way to provide support to opinion-building processes in the public sector, as well as an interesting tool for decision-making.

Acknowledgments. The authors thank CNPq support through the project 401066/2016-9 and FAPEMIG PPM-00368-18. We thank the pos-graduation programs the support for participation in the event (Arquitetura e Urbanismo, Geografia, Análise e Modelagem de Sistemas Ambientais).

References

1. Moura, A.C.M., Santana, S.: From authorial drawings to the parametric modeling of territorial occupation: representation and modeling influences in the process of designing the urban space. Rev. Brasileira. Cartogr. **66**(7), 1451–1463 (2014)
2. Moura, A.C.M.: O Geodesign como processo de co-criação de acordos coletivos para a paisagem territorial e urbana. In: Ladwig, N.I., Campos, J.B., (org.). Planejamento e gestão territorial: o papel e os instrumentos do planejamento territorial na interface entre o urbano e o rural. Criciúma (SC). UNESC, Cap. 1 (2019)

3. Arnstein, S.R.: A ladder of citizen participation. J. Am. Plan. Assoc. **35**(4), 216–224 (1969)
4. Steinitz, C.: A framework for Geodesign – changing geography by design. ESRI Press, Redlands (2012)
5. Moura, A.C.M., Freitas, C.R.: Brazilian geodesign platform webgis and SDI and geodesign as cocreation and geocollaboration. In: Gervasi, O. (ed.) Computational Science and Its Applications ICCSA 2020. Lecture Notes in Computer Science, pp. 332–348. Springer, Cham (2020). https://doi.org/10.1007/978-3-030-58811-3_24
6. Porto, J.L.R.: The construction of Amapá urban-metropolitan condition. ISSN 1980–5772 e ISSN 2177–4307 ACTA Geográfica, Boa Vista, v.12, n.29, mai./ago. De, pp. 145–159 (2018)
7. ALAP – ASSEMBLEIA LEGISLATIVA DO ESTADO DO AMAPÁ: Lei Complementar n° 0021, de 26 de fevereiro de 2003. Institui a Região Metropolitana do Município de Macapá, Estado do Amapá, e dá outras providências (2003)
8. ALAP – ASSEMBLEIA LEGISLATIVA DO ESTADO DO AMAPÁ: Lei Complementar n° 95, de 17 de maio de 2016. Dá nova redação ao Parágrafo único do art. 1° da Lei Complementar n° 0021, de 26 de fevereiro de 2003, que inclui o Município de Mazagão à Região Metropolitana de Macapá AP (2003)
9. AMAPÁ (Estado): Governo do Estado oficializa criação da Região Metropolitana de Macapá. Amapá, 09 de abril de (2018). Disponível em: https://portal.ap.gov.br/noticia/0904/governo-do-estado-oficializa-criacao-da-regiao-metropolitana-de-macapacessadoem. acessado em 05 Apr 2021
10. NERI, Sara Heloiza, A.: A Utilização das ferramentas de Geoprocessamento para identificação de comunidades expostas a hepatite A nas áreas de ressacas dos municípios de Macapá e Santana/AP. Tese (Engenharia Civil), Programa de Pós-Graduação de Engenharia, Universidade Federal do Rio de Janeiro, Rio de Janeiro, p.189 (2015)
11. Souza, J.S.A.: Qualidade de vida urbana em áreas úmidas: Ressacas de Macapá e Santana - AP. Tese M.Sc., CDS/UNB, Brasília/DF, Brasil (2003)

Asynchronous Mode in the Webgis: A Challenge to Ensure Greater Popular Participation

Patricia PortoCarreiro[1]([✉]), Patricia Vieira Trinta[2], and Thiago Lima e Lima[3]

[1] CEA/UFPE, Recife-PE and PPG-ACPS/UFMG, Belo Horizonte, MG, Brazil
ppc@ufpe.br
[2] Centro Universitário Estácio São Luís, São Luís, MA, Brazil
[3] GEOPROEA/EA/UFMG, Belo Horizonte, MG, Brazil

Abstract. The covid-19 pandemic has resumed old discussions about the virtual environments´ different functionalities needed to subsidize online activities synchronously (in real-time) or asynchronyously (not in real-time). This article discusses the inclusion of features in the webgis to ensure that their activities can be promoted in a totally asynchronous way, especially when they aim at popular participation. The discussion was developed within the Geodesign Brazil project, which promoted 12 similar workshops, between March and April 2021, each in a metropolitan region of Brazilian capitals. The project focused on the use of Geodesign supported by Giscolab (Brazilian online platform for Geodesign) to identify problems and create territorial proposals on 10 themes (water infrastructure, agriculture, green infrastructure, energy infrastructure, transport infrastructure, industry and commerce, institutional, residential, tourism and culture, carbon storage). Specifically, this article reports the experience that took place in the Recife metropolitan region's workshop, capital of Pernambuco, state of Northeast Brazil. Since it was decided to apply asynchronous dynamics, adjustments and additions of resources were necessary to make it viable, mostly to ensure users' interest, participation and linkage to the project. The asynchronous mode in webgis is a challenge, as it requires resources for greater clarity in the definition of activities; forms of feedback and personification of users' paths and to incentivize the users to complete the activities proposed.

Keywords: Geographic information system · Participatory planning · Geodesign

1 Introduction: The Collaborative Design and the Popular Participation in Post-pandemic City Planning

In addition to climate change, which may be reaching the point of no return, the COVID-19 pandemic has come to ratify how human activities directly affect the quality of the environment and are responsible for the degradation of biodiversity and, thus, for the vulnerability of our planet.

Modern cities have developed through the growing financialization of the economy, which has led to a concentration of wealth and an increase in social inequalities; high

© Springer Nature Switzerland AG 2021
O. Gervasi et al. (Eds.): ICCSA 2021, LNCS 12954, pp. 507–520, 2021.
https://doi.org/10.1007/978-3-030-86979-3_36

urban population density and great need for mobility of people and products [1]. And so, they have become gateways to disease, as evidenced by the current pandemic. However, the consequent and compulsory home confinement of humanity caused a change in values and a change in consumption patterns and, mainly, highlighted the essential human needs to: (1) enjoy open spaces and (2) have access to basic products, reinforcing the intrinsic relationship of the rural with the urban world.

Furthermore, emergency moments, as economic crisis in 2008, as in the current health crisis, lead to the emergence of citizenship initiatives to support and care for the most fragile. Such crises often exerted political pressure and promoted legislative changes, adding value and social innovation, showing alternatives for sociability in cities and offering us the possibility of rethinking and redesigning cities, as there is an urgent need to change our way of life.

Digital technologies have been pointing out possibilities of how the city can be appre-hended, modeled and managed through the participation of its citizens in the processes of collective socio-spatial decision-making in order to (re)invent it successively; and this is the path in which this article is inserted. For, the covid-19 pandemic resumed old discussions about the different functionalities of digital environments necessary to subsidize online activities synchronously (in real time) or asynchronously (not in real time).

The asynchronous mode in webgis is a challenge, as it requires resources for greater clarity in the definition of activities; forms of feedback and personification of users' paths and promotion of incentives to users to carry out activities. This article specifically discusses the inclusion of resources in webgis to ensure that activities can be promoted in a completely asynchronous manner, especially when they aim at popular participation. Although digital technologies contribute, we also have to find out what their impact on our lives is, in terms of better sociability and, consequently, in combating the emergence of climate and biodiversity.

2 GEODESIGN: The Urban Planning Complexity and the Importance of the Citizen Collaboration and Participation

According to Moura and Freitas [2], Geodesign is product of the evolution of studies that uses geoinformation technologies that prefer representations of spatial reality, focusing on participatory and shared planning by improving communication between different actors in the collective spatial decision-making processes.

Seen as a meta methodology for spatial design processes, in this research, because it adapts to different contexts, scales and proposals, it systematizes the multidisciplinary work of the planning process from the reading and characterization of the area to the development of the proposal, generating models with geographic information and impact simulations supported by digital technologies, which assist in decision making for the preparation of analyzes and spatial projects from the global to the architectural scale [3, 4].

In "The Geodesign framework", Steinitz [5] presents an integrated approach where the design process is divided into stages according to the scale of the intervention and the dimension of the proposal. As it is a set of methods developed to solve problems at different geographical scales, it is necessary to follow the steps, "Iterations of Geodesign", from a generic methodology that systematizes the spatial process and, for that, it presents the necessary tools and how to apply them (see Fig. 1).

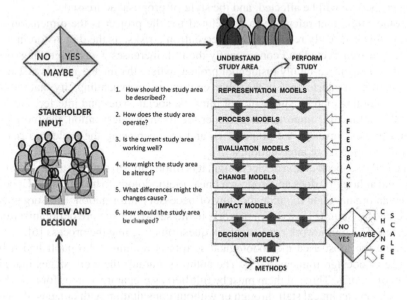

Fig. 1. The team and the Geodesign framework. Source: Steinitz, 2012.

For Steinitz [5], a proposal guided by Geodesign means to develop a project through cooperative work that unite knowledge from different areas of activity between scientists, designers and from the first moment, involving the local population. For this, the team involved in the project must be formed by: (1) designers, (2) digital technologies professionals, (3) geography scientists and (4) local people.

These four agents provide information to the design process organized by "Geodesign Iterations" where answering questions generates answers such as information for the construction of models to describe the area, what can be changed, how to change and what it can cause [6].

These professionals work cooperatively to develop the project. However, the process is not simple or linear and therefore must be coordinated. The difference of Geodesign is the proposal for systematization and awareness of the stages of the design process.

The structure presented by Geodesign is the same for any intervention, which allows the proposal to be adapted to reality and the level of deepening of the answers to the framework questions [6].

The Geodesign application follows a framework and in order to use this framework, the following parameters must be analyzed and defined: (1) The study area delimitation; (2) The level of detail and in-depth of the information; (3) The nature of the intervention; and (4) Who are those affected. Next, it is necessary to know the geography of the area, its physical and social characteristics, the natural environment and understanding of cultural issues [5].

To filter the process information, it is necessary to define the scale of intervention (local, regional or global), in this process it represents the level of information and details necessary for the project, and, in addition, they are related to the level of the intervention, how many people will be affected, and the style of proposal addressed.

Another important reference to be defined for the project is the dimension of the proposal, this is directly related to the intervention's risks, as the dimension increases, more people are affected and consequently the risk increases. Geodesign interventions can vary from a single-family residential project, where the intervention is restricted to the lot, with little interference in the urban context, to an expanding city that requires a study of natural resources, simulation of impacts, social issues and interferes in a large group. Given this, it is important to consider the form of intervention, the more people involved the less invasive the proposal is, and by decreasing the scale and risks, the proposals become more interventionist [5].

Due to the scope of action of Geodesign, it is impossible to develop a step-by-step for its use, and although it does not propose a linear methodology to be followed, Geodesign presents an organization to guide the flow of necessary information. This organization is presented by Steinitz [5] as a Framework, in the sense of structure or organization, for Geodesign. This framework consists of six questions to guide the process [6].

Among the most used methodological scripts is Steinitz, who published it in the book The Geodesign framework [5]. The author separates the work stages into six, in the form of models. Three of them must be fulfilled as preparatory steps for a workshop, prepared by the technical staff through or without consultation with citizens, depending on the expertise of those involved and the knowledge about the challenges of the case study (Representation Models, Processes and Evaluation). After the preparation steps are over, three more steps are elaborated, which take place during a participatory planning workshop to which the different interest groups in the case study are invited (Models of Change, Impact and Decision) [7].

In addition to the questions, models are presented that help in their respective answers, each question in the framework is answered by a model, also presented in the book. The models offer different information on a specific stage of the project. This framework is repeated three times in a cyclic manner during the process, each of these repetitions making up an iteration.

Iterations, as in algebra, are processes used to solve problems through successive repetition operations. The process consists of repeating the framework questions three times. At the end of each iteration, the product of each one is related to the design process [6].

3 GISCOLAB: Webgis, Planning Support System (PSS) and Metaplanning for Citizen Collaboration and Participation

The inclusion of citizen participation in the spatial decision-making process, mainly for urban planning, both to guarantee their participation and their effective collaboration, has largely been made possible by the evolution of GIS. Initially, such computational systems were seen as a geographic database, where georeferenced information was arranged in contextualized layers (thematic maps) and could be manipulated and interpreted to obtain analyzes and to support proposals for a spatial area as a result of a consultation.

However, assuming a consensual urban proposal as a result is also assuming it as a shared spatial decision-making process with the inclusion of new actors and new points of view and management of the planning process itself. For that, they need to be supported by several functionalities that are being added to the GIS, generating extensions such as, for example, webgis, PPS and metaplanning.

In this sense, it can be said that the advent of GIS has expanded from the production and consumption of data to the support of information construction and the inclusion of new actors. In parallel to GIS development the recognition of different stakeholders in a planning process started to have the support of a PSS (Planning Support System), based on clear definition of actors, tasks, responsibilities, flow of use and production of geographic data. The PSS is designed to address complex planning problems by associating **three general components according to a systemic planning approach: GIS, models and visualization instruments** [2].

With environmental issues on the agenda, especially those related to climate and biodiversity, territorial issues become urgent and, consequently, the spatial decision-making process as well. Thus, laws that require citizens to be consulted on territorial issues of collective interest are being regulated for different planning scales. In the Brazilian legislation, it was from the Federal Constitution of 1984, called citizen's constitution, that the defense of this inclusion of new actors and collective decisions in the planning began. Principles related to regional and urban planning were inserted in the City Statute, law 10.257 of 2001, which defines that citizen participation and shared decisions in planning are mandatory.

Because the planning process is highly dependent on the spatial, normative, sociocultural context, of the scale and of the technical competence, the replication of PSS in con-texts other than those that were initially designed is discouraged. The PSS should not be reused, except when there is a restructuring of its architecture according to the context of the new process [8].

Thus, a tool is needed to guide the creation of a metaproject (project of the planning process) of the project's path, with a defined time, but at the same time flexible, to guarantee the understanding on the part of all the participants in the phases of work. In addition to this, it is necessary that information and supports are explained before the process to create an open, shared and common knowledge base.

It is suggested that Geodesign can be seen as this tool, a metamethodology, to support the creation of metaprojects, as it favors the creation of different representations of the spatial reality that interact and create a common understanding of planning issues. In addition to improving the visualization of information and communication between different actors for participatory and shared planning.

According to Moura and Freitas [2], the evolution of the idea of Geodesign is structured in the areas of geovisualization, geo-collaboration, citizen participation, web platform and production of information. Based on the extensive practical experience and data obtained in 35 workshops using the Geodesign's traditional framework, the authors built a Brazilian platform for Geodesign, o GiscoLAB, to provide integrated and geo-referenced information, enabling a wide availability of data for subsidize collaborative initiatives in urban planning.

Such an undertaking wants to provide a tool with resources such as SDI (Spatial Data Infrastructure) and WebGis, enabling an open architecture to dialogue with other systems and to support functionalities with a focus on co-creation and geo-collaboration [2] (see Fig. 2).

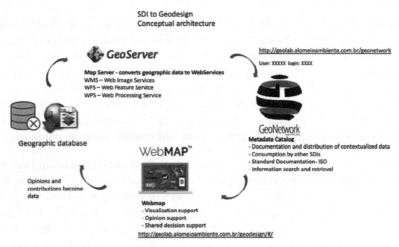

Fig. 2. Giscolab´s the conceptual architecture. Source: Moura and Freitas (2020)

Based on this understanding, the GISCOLAB was used in this estudoa for discussions over the territory. He has performed as a powerful tool of co-creation and geo-collaboration, but this research is to investigate whether its functions are suitable for application in asynchronous mode.

4   Geodesign Brasil Project: RM-Recife

The Used Framework
The thirteen workshops from the research "GEODESIGN BRASIL: TREES FOR METROPOLITAN REGIONS", included the one reported in this article, followed the guidelines of the Geodesign Framework by Carl Steinitz. However, the "evaluation models" were not used, based on experiences reported by the Geoprocessing Laboratory from the School of Architecture in the Federal University of Minas Gerais, Brazil. The "evaluation models" were criticized in workshops inserted in the Brazilian context by participants who were active and would prefer to produce their own judgment about the territory. Moreover, some of the workshop's participants adopted a passive posture, and didn't reflect about how the data presented operated in the study region [2]. Considering that, a collection of 40 maps was prepared as "process models" to give support to the participants, so they could have information about the studied place.

For this research's workshops, it was considered the requirements by IGC 2021. They have required 10 systems, 8 of them being fixed and 2 of them being flexible. All of them following a color scheme for further visual comparison (see Fig. 3). The flexible systems chosen by this research were carbon sequestration, because of the emphasis in this subject on the event's premise, and tourism/leisure, because of the relevance of the theme in the Brazilian socioeconomic context.

Another expectation of IGC 2021 is to start the workshop from a 2021 current scenario to propose a planning for 2035 and 2050. For this to happen, there were placed three scenarios where the participants, divided in Group A and B during all the experience, would work following a workshop schedule (see Fig. 4).

The participants' proposals should contemplate the 10 systems, but always giving priority to projects that could be associated with carbon credit. Moreover, at the end of the workshop, an increase the area of robust vegetation by 30% by 2050, as a contribution to carbon sequestration, was expected. In this way, the project contribution to the "Trillion Trees Initiative" and to project and global Carbon Storage could be evaluated [9].

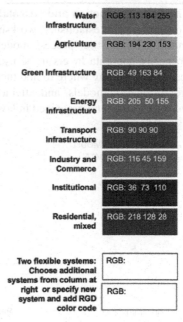

Fig. 3. Geodesign systems and colors by IGC 2021

IGC Requirements

The proposals produced by the participants should take into account the Seventeen Sustainable Development Goals (SDGs) proposed by ONU for further assessment. Moreover, they must have considered the Global Assumptions and Innovations, a list of innovations that would occur by the year of 2050 identified by a group of experts [9].

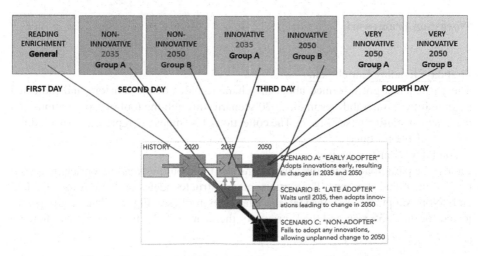

Fig. 4. Geodesign workshop schedule and groups, by the authors.

The Data Production and Giscolab Platform

Considering the established workshop systems, a technical team decided which data would compose the "process models" used as support for the geodesign workshops. Primarily, the data layers to be used for each system were chosen and posteriorly a research regarding where to find them was conducted. The downloaded data originated "representation models" and, after a series of treatment on ArGIS, the "process models" were generated and organized in layers within the 10 systems (see Fig. 5).

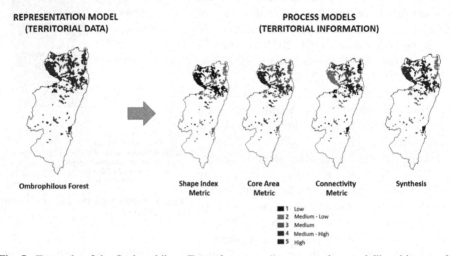

Fig. 5. Example of the Ombrophilous Forest layer as a "representation model" and its transformation in "process model", which is interpreted and displayed as Landscape Metrics used in this research (shape index, core area, connectivity and synthesis), by the authors.

The participants used a login and password made available by the workshop mediators to access the project in your metropolitan region. Once inside the project, the participant accessed the "Context" where they would work that day, following the schedule (see Fig. 6).

Workshop Framework

First day: Reading Enrichment

The participants got informed about the characteristics of the territory and indicated potentialities, vulnerabilities in the 2020 scenario through the tool of "Annotations" on the Giscolab platform (see Fig. 7). The collection of 40 maps of "representation models" were available for query.

Second day: Non-Innovative

Firstly, the participants read the annotations available on the "reading enrichment context" of the A and B groups. The participants constructed ideas for "Late Adopter" 2035 and "Non-Adopter" 2050, through the Dialogues tool (see Fig. 8). The A group projected for the 2035 year and the B group for the year of 2050. It was necessary that the

Fig. 6. Giscolab interface after the participant's login, by the authors.

Fig. 7. Insertion of an annotation in the Giscolab platform, by the authors.

participants followed a temporal logic, thus the A group thought about proposals that necessarily should be initiated in 2035, so they could have a chance to be achieved until 2050. Successively, the B group needed to continue the ideas stablished in 2035, so a mismatch among the proposal didn't happen.

Third day: Innovative

A and B groups constructed ideas for "Early Adopter" 2035 and "Late-Adopter" 2050, respectively, through the Dialogues tool, following the temporal logic exposed in the second stage of the workshop. In this day, the participants used the Global Assumptions and Innovations provided by IGC 2021. The use of this list was not obligatory. They also had the target to increase of 30% of CCO2 until 2050, using the tool Widgets that calculates the percentage reached, number of trees and the sequestration of CO2 above and below ground.

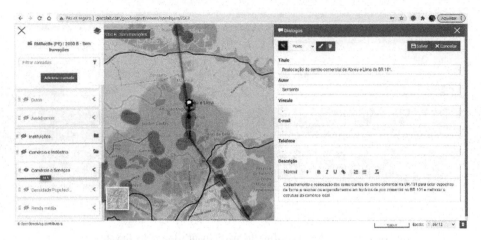

Fig. 8. Insertion of a dialog in the Giscolab platform, by the authors.

According to [10], the problem of the balance of carbon sequestration could be resolved until 2050, if the increment of 30% of robust vegetation of the world happens. This publication brings a quantitative of trees that exists in the world and from this data, a calculation of tree units to be planted in every of the 13 metropolitan regions, this goa in km^2 and also the proportion regarding the 30% to be reached. Beyond that, according to maps made available by [11], was made a calculation of the sequestration of CO2 above and below ground (see Table 1).

Table 1. Data regarding carbon sequestration from the Recife's metropolitan region, by the authors.

Total Trees	6447092
Area/km²	453,25
Area/ha	45325,22
Trees/km²	14224,1412
Trees/ha	142,2407216
Target of 30% Increase in Trees	1934127,6
30% in km²	135,975
CO² Above Ground	1206635
CO2 Below Ground	379849
30% CO2 Above Ground	361990,5
30% CO2 Below Ground	113954,7

Fourth day: Very innovative.
In this stage, A and B groups constructed ideas for "Early-Adopter" 2050, following the temporal logic exposed in the second stage of the workshop, through the "Dialogues" tool. The used of the Global Assumptions and Innovations and Widgets regarding carbon sequestration remained.

For this last stage of the workshop, the construction of ideas for all the 10 systems should be guaranteed. Besides, the minimum reach of 30% of carbon credit expansion, area expansion, number of trees and CO2 levels below and above ground had to be reached. The design proposals from A and B groups were integrated in one final design through comments and voting on the "Dialogues" tool.

Questionnaire.
After the completion of the workshop activities, a questionnaire produced on Google Docs was sent in order to outline the participants' profile. Among the required information are name; studied metropolitan region; knowledge, potential and vulnerabilities of geodesign; knowledge and interest in the territory; opinion on the difficulty of the methodological process and the Giscolab platform; between others.

5   Asynchronous Mode: The RM-Recife Case Study

Synchronicity is the quality or state of being synchronic, of what occurs at the same time, simultaneously [12]. It means making something happen at the same time. In virtual environments, synchronous and asynchronous modes refer to two possible types of online interactions. In the first, the activities (learning, communication, work, fun,…) are carried out with the participants running them online, but at the same time. In the second mode, each participant will perform them at a different time. Both options have their advantages and disadvantages and some things in common, but require different features to be supported by digital environments.

The main benefit of the synchronous mode is that there is real interaction with other people, even if virtually, allowing exchanges and feedbacks (knowledge, experiences, points of view, …) between the participants, in addition to the activities taking place on a scheduled basis. The main benefit of the asynchronous mode, on the other hand, is that participants can perform activities at their own pace and schedule, with a reduction in the need for people to travel, greater range of participants and less infrastructure. Both can be used in a complementary way, there is no better way, but the most suitable for certain activities and for a socio-cultural reality.

In our case, the Geodesign workshop at RM-Recife, was initially designed to be synchronous like all the other 12, the option for asynchronous mode occurred abruptly, one week before the start of activities, to meet the various requests from interested parties who claimed clash of hours with other online activities and greater convenience in being able to program.

So, this research was born, under the largest of Geodesign Brazil, as an answer to the need to make the conditions for its realization flexible within an extremely complex context, the pandemic peak of the 2nd wave of COVID-19 in March 2021. And still, taking advantage to verify the robustness of the Giscolab tool, as well as the applicability of Geodesign in cases of building a spatial proposal with the participation of a community in a media city.

Thus, the central objective of the RM-Recife experiment became, in addition to collaborating with Geodesign Brazil, to assess the challenges of the asynchronous mode in the spatial decision-making process by checking the suitability of Geodesign and Giscolab. Specifically, it would also be like keeping people interested throughout the course of this process.

Thus, all stages of the workshop were carried out asynchronously. To make this possible, a YouTube channel IGC 2021 _ RM-Recife[1] was created first where participants were provided with a series of tutorial videos that explained each step and exemplified how they would be implemented in Giscolab (see Fig. 9).

Fig. 9. YouTube channel with explanatory videos by Prof. Ana Clara Mourão from EA / UFMG.

In addition, two WhatsApp groups, A and B, were set up, according to the research dynamics of Geodesign Brasil, for communication between participants and mediators, making it possible to clarify doubts about the process, share ideas and even report errors that happened on the Giscolab platform.

In the first stage, there was a certain inertia of the participants, after viewing the explanatory videos, in the execution of activities in Giscolab, so tutorials in PDF were made, exclusive for RM-Recife, with a step by step to be done by clarifying and exemplifying in greater detail the execution of activities at Giscolab. The repercussion of these tutorials caused some participants to follow their paths and complete the workshop.

With the asynchronous mode, although the number of participants doubled (30 people registered in all), only 8 participated and 5 concluded the workshop. Among those enrolled we had people linked to architecture and urbanism, geography, cartography, water resources management and the environment.

---

[1] The Youtube Channel IGC 2021 _ RM-Recife can be found in the following link: https://www.youtube.com/playlist?list=PLW17cGAXz6HpyI_QpxvhVSmX3YS5NYtxc.

The group of participants who concluded declared that the main difficulty was to apprehend the complexity of the project on a regional scale and to be confident in their own decision-making. They justified such difficulties by declaring:

a) The importance of different profiles for the construction of a coherent spatial proposal;
b) The difficulty of spatializing georeferenced information;
c) The difficulty of crossing data that requires special knowledge and spatial reasoning;
d) The difficulty of constructing complementary views, because there remains a specific and personal view.

In short, once it was decided by the asynchronous dynamics, adjustments and additions of resources, described above, were necessary to make it feasible. The asynchronous mode proved to be a challenge, as it requires resources before the implementation of activities in Giscolab for greater clarity in the definition of activities; forms of feedback and personification of users' paths and promotion of incentives for users to carry out and conclude activities.

In Giscolab, the asynchronous mode that seemed to bring ease due to the flexibility of time and work pace of each participant, initially proved to be an obstacle to the proper functioning of the workshop itself, since spatial decision-making guided by Geodesign requires a shared build. Because it is believed that it is necessary to build a vision that composes the various interests first in the formulation of the spatial problems of the studied area and, as this decision process matures, it results in consensual solutions.

It was evident that it is not possible to build shared knowledge through the various visions and knowledge of the various participants without necessarily having interaction between people, even without being in the same physical space. It is fundamental to the shared decision-making process that Geodesign proposes to synchronicity.

6   Conclusions and Discussions: Challenges to Expand Collaboration and Popular Participation in Urban Planning

The IGC 2021 _ RM-Recife workshop was not designed to take place in asynchronous mode, but to reach a larger number of participants and test the Geodesign metamethodology and the Giscolab webgis tool, this dynamic was tested.

Initially, in this embryonic research, the asynchronous mode seems to be incompatible with the dynamics proposed by Geodesign, although its implementation in Giscolab is viable. You can add internal communication features (chats, bulletin board,...), version management (who did what and when) and improve the tool's support for asynchronous mode. However, in relation to Geodesign, its core is the construction of knowledge shared by the contribution of several specialized views that complement each other and that respond to the necessary complexity to a response of making a spatial decision. In other words, the process needs to be collaborative so that the product reflects the scalar and dimensional complexity, to guarantee greater popular participation in collaborative territorial projects.

Finally, the asynchronous mode requires more studies to be adopted with Geodesign. However, it is worth expanding the discussion about which steps or processes in Geodesign can be asynchronous, or should all steps be synchronous.

Acknowledgments. The authors thank CNPq support through the project 401066/2016-9 and FAPEMIG PPM-00368-18 and the key software used GISColab of the GEOPROEA/EA/UFMG & Christian Freitas. Finally, CEA/UFPE and PPG-ACPS/UFMG for the support to taking part in the conference.

References

1. UN-HABITAT: Planning Sustainable Cities: Global Report on Human Settlements (2009). http://unhabitat.org/books/global-report-on-human-settlements-2009-planning-sustainable-cities/. Accessed 09 May 2017
2. Gervasi, O., et al. (eds.): ICCSA 2020. LNCS, vol. 12251. Springer, Cham (2020). https://doi.org/10.1007/978-3-030-58808-3
3. Hoeven, F., Nijhuis, S., Zlatanova, S., Dias, E., Spek, S.: Geo-design: Avanços na conexão entre tecnologia de informação geográfica, planejamento urbano e arquitetura de paisagem. Pesquisa em Série de Urbanismo (RiUS), vol. 4, ISSN 1875–0192 (impresso), E-ISSN 1879–8217 (online) Delft: TU Delft Open (2016)
4. Flaxman, M., Steinitz, C., Faris, M., Canfield, T., Vargas-Moreno, J.C.: Alternative Futures for the Telluride Region. Telluride Foundation, Colorado (2010)
5. Steinitz, C.: A Framework for Geodesign: Changing Geography by Design. ESRI Press, Redlands (2012)
6. Lee, D.J., Dias, E., Scholten, H.J. (eds.): Geodesign by Integrating Design and Geospatial Sciences. Springer International Publishing, Cham (2014)
7. Moura, A.C.M.: O Geodesign como processo de co-criação de acordos coletivos para a paisagem territorial e urbana. In: Ladwig, N.I., Campos, J.B. (org.). Planejamento e gestão territorial: o papel e os instrumentos do planejamento territorial na interface entre o urbano e o rural. Cap. 1, UNESC, Criciúma - SC (2019)
8. Campagna, M.: Sistemas de Suporte ao Planejamento (Planning Support Systems): Retrospectivas e Prospectivas. In: Moura, A.C.M. (Org.). Tecnologias de Geoinformação para representar e planejar o território urbano. 1ed.Rio de Janeiro: Interciência, vol. 1, pp. 219–258 (2016)
9. IGC: Projects workflow: How will IGC studies be carried out? (2021). https://www.igc-geodesign.org/project-workflow. Accessed 20 June 2021
10. Crowther, T.W., et al.: Mapping tree density at a global scale. Nature **525**(7568), 201–205 (2015)
11. Spawn, S.A., Gibbs, H.K.: Global Aboveground and Belowground Biomass Carbon Density Maps for the Year 2010. ORNL DAAC, Oak Ridge (2020)
12. Sincronicidade. In: DICIO. Dicionário Online de Português. https://www.dicio.com.br/sincronicide/. Accessed 08 May 2021

11th International Workshop on Future Computing System Technologies and Applications (FiSTA 2021)

Deep Fake Recognition in Tweets Using Text Augmentation, Word Embeddings and Deep Learning

Senait G. Tesfagergish[1], Robertas Damaševičius[1（✉）], and Jurgita Kapočiūtė-Dzikienė[2]

[1] Kaunas University of Technology, 51368 Kaunas, Lithuania
robertas.damasevicius@ktu.lt
[2] Vytautas Magnus University, 44404 Kaunas, Lithuania

Abstract. Spreading of automatically generated clickbaits, fake news, and fake reviews undermines the veracity of the internet as a credible source of information. We investigate the problem of recognizing automatically generated short texts by exploring different Deep Learning models. To improve the classification results, we use text augmentation techniques and classifier hyperparameter optimization. For word embedding and vectorization we use Glove and RoBERTa. We compare the performance of dense neural network, convolutional neural network, gated recurrent network, and hierarchical attention network. The experiments on the TweepFake dataset achieved an 89.7% accuracy.

Keywords: Deep fake · Fake news detection · Text classification · Natural language processing · Social media analytics · Deep learning

1 Introduction

High-quality texts generated Artificial Intelligence (AI)- algorithms (aka deep fakes) have swarmed social networks and messaging services and started to influence real-world events. For example, bots on social media use auto-generated messages to subvert the democratic voting process, promote violence, and defy the values of democratic countries [1]. A recent but rapidly spreading phenomenon of "fake news", i.e., viral social media posts viral posts that are made to look like real news reports [2], have overshadowed the political discourse on major recent political events such as Brexit [3] and US Presidential elections of 2016 [4]. Other controversial and widely discussed topics of interest such as vaccination [5] and most recently, the COVID-19 pandemic [6] have gone beyond misinformation and may have caused literal deaths. The phenomenon of "fake news" has been aggravated by computer-aided tools such as generative chatbots [7] and news headline generators [8]. In particular, auto-generated clickbait, i.e., social media posts or online articles aimed at increasing the network traffic to the actual article or user page [9]. Another example is that of fake reviews, which aim to improve or disrupt the popularity of some product on review aggregators or e-commerce websites [10] can cause tangible financial damage both to product producers as well as consumers, which follow the

© Springer Nature Switzerland AG 2021
O. Gervasi et al. (Eds.): ICCSA 2021, LNCS 12954, pp. 523–538, 2021.
https://doi.org/10.1007/978-3-030-86979-3_37

advice of distorted consumer recommenders [11]. Finding fake reviews may involve solving related problems such as intent detection [12], phishing detection [13], topic propagation [14], and topic recommendation [15]. These tools employ natural language processing (NLP) techniques and AI methods such as chatbots [16], artificial neural networks (ANN), supervised learning, and deep learning techniques such as generative adversarial networks (GAN) [17] to create realistic texts that can promote disinformation and sow discord among the society. The latter has caused considerable debate on the dark side of AI and its future trends and threats to our political institutions and social development [18, 19]. The complexity of this effort requires multidisciplinary effort from the research community [20] as it deals with multifaceted aspects of technology, social structures, and psychology.

Recent efforts of recognizing fake content on the internet have focused on supervised learning techniques [21]. Both traditional machine learning techniques such as Support Vector Machine (SVM), Decision Trees (DT), Random Forest (RF) and Hidden Markov Models (HMM) as well as move recent deep learning models such as Recurrent Neural Networks (RNN) and Convolutional Neural Networks (CNN) are applied [22]. Specifically, Ren and Ji [23] suggested a gated recurrent NN to recognize deceptive spam. They employed word embeddings that are learned using the continuous bag-of-words (CBOW) approach to obtain global semantic representation that can alleviate the problem of scarce data. Hajek et al. [24] adopted n-grams, a Skip-Gram Word2Vec model to create word embeddings from a consumer review corpus, which is combined with and various lexicon-based emotion features. For classification, they used a hybrid "Network in Network" architecture that allowed them to capture the complex features in the high-dimensional representation space. Zheng et al. [25] suggested a clickbait convolution-al neural network (CBCNN) that used pre-trained Word2Vec to capture the semantics of the clickbait headlines and used various kernels to find the characteristics of the headlines. Ajao et al. [26] used unidirectional Long Short-Term Memory (LSTM) with Convolutional Neural Network (CNN) model for classification of fake vs genuine tweets. The initial unidirectional LSTM layer is used to keep information from the previous context, without storing the context information. Asghar et al. [27] used the Bidirectional LSTM-CNN model to classify tweets into rumors and non-rumors, achieving 86.12% accuracy. In this model, CNN layer receives input from BiLSTM with contextual information, thus improving over the Ajao et al. [26] approach. Fang et al. [28] built a model for determining the authenticity of the news based only on their content by using a combination of CNN with a self multi-head attention mechanism. Ghanem et al. [29] suggested an LSTM neural network model that is emotionally enriched to recognize false news and clickbait. Jwa et al. [30] apply the Bidirectional Encoder Representations from Transformers (BERT) model to identify fake news by checking the relationship between headline and the main body of news. Kaliyar et al. [31] propose a deep CNN (FNDNet) for fake news detection. The network learns the features for fake news classification via multiple layers of the network achieving an accuracy of 98.36%. Liu & Wu et al. [32] proposed a deep neural network to detect fake news early using a custom feature extractor, a position-aware attention mechanism, and a multi-region mean-pooling mechanism to perform feature aggregation. Umer et al. [33] proposed a hybrid model that combines CNN with LSTM, in combination with dimensionality reduction using

Principal Component Analysis (PCA) and Chi-Square. The approach achieved 97.8% accuracy on the fake news challenge dataset.

In the context of small data [34], i.e., the unavailability of sufficient data for efficient training of neural networks, especially deep network architectures with a large number of trainable parameters, the problem is especially relevant in under-resourced languages, for which there are a limited amount of texts or only small corpora available. The problem in the NLP domain may be solved through a variety of techniques such as using pre-trained networks and applying transfer learning [35] or increasing dataset size via data augmentation [36]. In the latter cases, the size of the dataset can be increased by creating new samples via thesaurus substitution, wod2vec substitution, and addition of meaningless words [37], by masking and replacing words in original samples [38], replacing high-frequency words with low-frequency words source [39], replacing the word with a word sampled from the frequency distribution of the dictionary [40], using a bi-directional language transformation model to generate a replacement word [41], or using a soft probability distribution to change the word representation [42].

Summarizing, the classical machine learning methods require tedious feature engineering by experts to assure high performance. Deep learning solves this problem by using word embedding and deep neural networks, but are not very good if the semantics of words changes over time.

The novelty and contribution of this paper are as follows: We developed a deep learning model to detect the fake tweets generated by bots by combining the advantages of CNN and the hierarchical attention network. The best model obtained high performance in fake news detection and achieved an accuracy rate of 89.7% on the TweepFake [43] benchmark dataset. We compare the performance of classical machine learning and deep learning methods applied to this problem. Our results showed that the proposed classifier can achieve better performance when comparing the accuracy with previous works.

2 Methods

2.1 Problem Definition

We address the problem of classifying tweets into artificially generated (i.e., created by a bot) and human-created. To discriminate between the tweets, the task is treated as a binary classification problem. We define the training dataset as $D = \{d_1, d_2, d_3, \ldots d_n\} \in \mathcal{R}^{zxm}$, while each row $d_i \in R_n$ is a data sample and each column $C_i \in \mathcal{R}^z$ is a label for train dataset $y \in \{0, 1\}$, if 1, then it is fake (generated), else it is real (created by a human). We aim to develop and analyze deep learning models, which can learn from available data to accurately classify fake and real tweets.

2.2 Text Preprocessing

Before translating the text into a vector form, it goes through a pre-processing process. The pre-processing process consists of several parts: filtering (removing punctuation marks, hyphens and extra spaces), replacing upper cases with lower cases, spelling correction, stopword removal and stemming (replacing a word with its semantic base).

For spelling correction, we use Python 3 Spelling Corrector. For stopword removal, we remove 421 stopwords for English text included in the Fox [44] list. Tokenization is performed by using whitespaces and non-alphanumerical characters as delimiters. We follow the following set of heuristic rules as suggested in [45]:

(1) replace characters ! " # $ % & *< = > ? @ \ | ~ with spaces;
(2) remove any of " . : ; " if followed by a space:,
(3) remove the brackets ( ) [ ] ;
(4) remove the quotation marks;
(5) remove apostrophes and slashes if followed by space.

After tokenization, we use stemming to further normalize the morphological variants of the base word. In this paper, we use the S stemmer [46], which removes only a few common word endings, and it is less aggressive as other stemmer.

2.3 Dataset Augmentation

Data augmentation is advantageous for low-resource NLP tasks [47]. We used the techniques described in [48] as follows: (1) random replacement of words in tweets with their synonyms; (2) random insertion of synonyms of words (using wordnet) in a tweet. (3) random swap of words in the tweet. (4) random deletion for each word in the tweet with a probability p. The preliminary checking ensures that the word can be replaced, word for replacement is not a determiner and it does have synonyms.

2.4 Vector Representation

Feature selection is very important for document classification problems [49]. We used GloVe [50], a model that combines the features of a singular decomposition and methods Word2Vec. The first step is to construct a co-occurrence matrix X from the training dataset. The meaning of X_{ij} indicates how often the word j occurs in the context of the word i. To quantify the semantic similarity between words i and j the ratio of the probabilities of their joint occurrence in the context is used, where w_i, w_j are word vectors, $\tilde{\hat{w}}_k$ is a context vector.

$$F\left(w_i, w_j, \widehat{w}_k\right) = \frac{P_{ik}}{P_{jk}} = \frac{X_{ik}/\sum_m X_{im}}{X_{jk}/\sum_n X_{jn}} \tag{1}$$

The semantic proximity of the vectors obtained is determined by their scalar product. The GloVe model learns vectors in such a way that their scalar product approached the logarithm of the probability of the appearance of words in the training set. To reduce the weight of the joint occurrences of words that are rare (carry less information) or do not occur at all, as well as reduce weight for too frequent joint appearances. We adopt a weighted least squares regression model as target learning function (loss function) (1), where w_i is the vector of the main words, $\widehat{w}_j$ is the context vector, b_i and $\hat{b}_j$ are scalar values of deviations for the main word and context word, respectively, V is the size of the dictionary:

$$J = \sum_{i,j=1}^{V} f(X_{ij}) \left(w_i^T \hat{w}_j + b_i + \hat{b}_j - log X_{ij} \right)^2 \tag{2}$$

Here $f()$ is the weight function.

Another vector representation we use is a Robustly Optimized BERT Pretraining Approach (RoBERTa) [51], which uses BERT-based dynamic masking, a transformer model to masks and predict tokens, which extracts contextual features of texts.

2.5 Dense Neural Network

A dense neural network is a network made of regular deeply connected layers. It is a common and frequently used neural network type. The architecture is such that all the neurons, in one layer are linked to the neurons in the next layer.

Let the output of the dense neural network be known $y(t)$ at the input $X(t)$, where $X(t)$ is a vector with components $(x_1, x_2, \ldots, x_n)$, t is the number of the sequence value, $t = \overline{1, T}$ (T is predetermined). To find model parameters $w = (w_0, w_1, \ldots w_m)$ and $V_k = (V_{1k}, V_{2k}, \ldots V_{nk})$, h_k, $k = \overline{1, m}$ such that the model output $F(X, V, w)$ and the real output of the MLP $y(t)$ would be as close as possible. The relationship between the input and output of a two-layer perceptron is established by the following relationships:

$$Z_k = \sigma(V_{1k}x_1 + V_{2k}x_2 + \ldots V_{nk}x_n - h_k), k = \overline{1, m} \tag{3}$$

$$y = \sigma(w_1 Z_1 + w_2 Z_2 + \ldots w_m Z_m + w_0) \tag{4}$$

Here we used the three-layer network architecture as shown in Fig. 1, with 768 neurons in the input layer (corresponding to the number of RoBERTa features) and 10 neurons in the intermediary layer. Network training occurs by applying a gradient descent algorithm (such as error backpropagation) similar to a single-layer perceptron.

2.6 Convolutional Network

A convolutional neural network is usually an alternation of convolutional layers, subsidizing layers, and with fully connected output layers. All these layers can be placed in any order. In the convolutional layer, neurons that use the same weights are put into feature maps, and each neuron is linked with a portion of the neurons of the previous layer. When calculating the network, each neuron performs a convolution of a certain area of the previous layer. A layer in which each neuron is connected to all neurons at the previous level, with each connection having its weight. Unlike fully connected, in the convolutional layer a neuron is connected only with some neurons of the previous level, that is, the convolutional layer is similar to the convolution operation, where only a small weight matrix (convolution kernel) is used. Layers of this type perform dimensionality reduction. the method of selecting the maximum element is used - the entire feature map is divided into cells, from which the maximum value is selected. The dropout layer is a

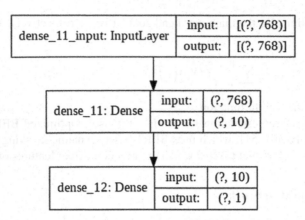

Fig. 1. Schematic representation of the densely connected neural network

way to combat overfitting in neural networks. Dropout regulation consists of changing the structure of the network: each neuron is ejected with a certain probability p.

The architecture we used is presented in Fig. 2. The model has one embedding layer, one convolutional layer, global max pooling, and a dropout layer.

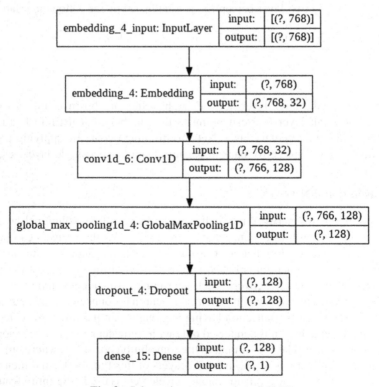

Fig. 2. Schematic representation of CNN

2.7 Recurrent Neural Network and Gated Recurrent Unit

The Recurrent Neural Network (RNN), with the help of the hidden layer h, the model can save information about the previous input signals, and at the end of the data sequence, carry out the sentiment classification. The extensions of RNN are the GRU (Gated Recurrent Unit) [52] and LSTM (Long-Short Term Memory) [53] models. In them, unlike the usual RNN, each neuron is a memory cell, the contents of which can be updated or discarded.

The memory cells GRU and LSTM are shown schematically in Fig. 3. In the GRU network, the OUT value is determined by the activation of the reset r and update z filters. LSTM uses a more complex computation scheme, applying three filters: input filter i, forget filter f, and output filter o. A controlled recurrent neuron contains one gate less than a long short-term memory cell. The update gate determines the amount of information obtained from the past state. The reset gate works like the forget valve in the long short-term memory cell. As GRU only has two a reset gate and an update gate, its training speed is faster than other RNNs.

Based on previous output h_{t-1} and current input x_t, a reset gate is used to determine which part of information should be reset, Eq. (5), while an update gate is used to refresh the output of the GRU h_t, Eq. (8). The hidden layer is calculated according to Eq. (7). The latest output can be calculated according to Eq. (8). The gates z_t and r_t, and parameters, W_z, W_r and W, of GRU are updated in the training process.

$$z_t = \sigma(W_z \bullet [h_{t-1}, x_t]), \tag{5}$$

$$r_t = \sigma(W_r \bullet [h_{t-1}, x_t]), \tag{6}$$

$$h_t{}' = \tanh(W \bullet [r_t * h_{t-1}, x_t]), \tag{7}$$

$$h_t = (1 - z_t) * h_{t-1} + z_t * h_t{}'. \tag{8}$$

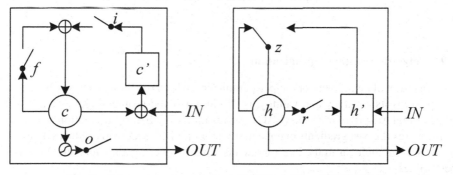

Fig. 3. Schematic representation of LSTM (left) and GRU (right)

2.8 Hierarchical Attention Network

The hierarchical attention network (HAN) model [54] aims to capture two basic insights a hierarchical structure of a text on different levels (words form sentences, sentences form a message), as well as document representation. The model uses a word encoder, i.e., a bidirectional GRU, along with a word attention mechanism to encode each sentence into a vector representation. These sentence representations are passed through a sentence encoder with a sentence attention mechanism resulting in a document vector representation. This final representation is passed to a fully connected (FC) layer with the activation function for prediction as follows (Fig. 4):

$$x_{it} = W_e w_{it}, \tag{9}$$

$$\overrightarrow{h}_{it} = \overrightarrow{GRU}(x_{it}), \tag{10}$$

$$\overleftarrow{h}_{it} = \overleftarrow{GRU}(x_{it}). \tag{11}$$

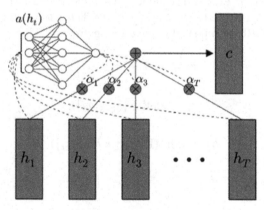

Fig. 4. Hierarchical attention network

2.9 Network Training Optimization

Optimization of neural network hyper-parameters, which rule how the network operates and governs its accuracy and validity, is still an unsolved problem. Here we adopt the Exponential Adaptive Gradients (EAG) optimization [55]. EAG optimization (Algorithm 1) measures the past gradients exponentially more and consecutively reduces adaptivity of the second moment to the latest gradients when network parameters are close to the best values.

3 Dataset and Results

3.1 Dataset and Exploratory Analysis

We used TweepFake [43], a Twitter deep fake dataset available from Kaggle (https://www.kaggle.com/mtesconi/twitter-deep-fake-text). The dataset is balanced and contains 25,836 tweets (half human and half bots generated, 23647 in the training dataset, and 2922 in the testing dataset), which were randomly extracted from the human and corresponding imitating bot account pairs. The bots use various NLP generation techniques, i.e., Markov Chains, RNN, GPT-2, and LSTM. Both bot and human-created texts have a similar distribution of the number of words (Fig. 5), while humans tend to use longer words (Fig. 6). On the other hand, bots use more stop words than humans as indicated by the stop word ratio (Fig. 7). The figures show histograms with corresponding probability distributed functions (PDFs) approximated using kernel density estimation. Since PDFs are approximated, their tails in some cases exceed the minimum and maximum values in the dataset.

Algorithm 1. Exponential Adaptive Gradients

Input: $x \in F, \{\alpha_t\}_{t=1}^{T}, (\beta_1, \beta_2) = (0.9, 10^{-4})$

Output: x_{t+1}

Initialize $m_0 = 0, v_0 = 0$

FOR $t = 1$ to T DO

$\quad g_t = \nabla f_t(x_t)$

$\quad m_t = \beta_1 \cdot m_{t-1} + (1-\beta_1) \cdot g_t$

$\quad v_t = (1+\beta_2)v_{t-1} + \beta_2 \cdot g_t^2$

$\quad \hat{v}_t = v_t / [(1+\beta_2)^t - 1]$

$\quad V_t = diag(\hat{v}_t)$

$\quad x_{t+1} = \prod_{F, \sqrt{V_t}} (x_t - \alpha_t m_t / \sqrt{V_t})$

ENDFOR

3.2 Evaluation of Performance

The true labels are compared against the predicted labels and the true positive (TP), false positive (FP), true negative (TN), and false-negative (FN) values are calculated. Recall, Precision, Accuracy, Error Rate, and F-score are calculated as follows:

$$FPR = \frac{\sum_{i=1}^{m} [a(x_i) = +1][y_i = -1]}{\sum_{i=1}^{m} [y_i = -1]} \tag{12}$$

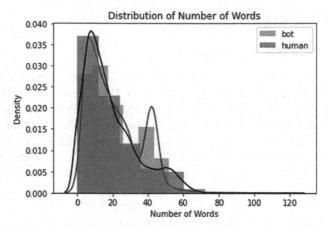

Fig. 5. Distribution of the number of words in the training dataset

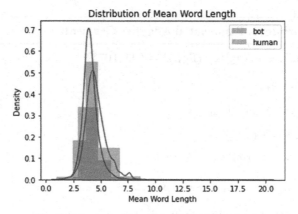

Fig. 6. Mean word length in the training dataset

$$TPR = \frac{\sum_{i=1}^{m}[a(x_i) = +1][y_i = +1]}{\sum_{i=1}^{m}[y_i = +1]} \tag{13}$$

$$FNR = \frac{\sum_{i=1}^{m}[a(x_i) = -1][y_i = +1]}{\sum_{i=1}^{m}[y_i = +1]} \tag{14}$$

Here $a(x)$ is classifier with inputs $X^m = (x_1, \ldots, x_m)$, and $(y_1, \ldots, y_m)$ are outputs. Precision, Recall and Accuracy are calculated as follows:

$$Precision = \frac{TPR}{TPR + FPR} \tag{15}$$

$$Recall = \frac{TPR}{TPR + FNR} \tag{16}$$

$$Accuracy = \frac{\sum_{i}^{p} N_i}{T} \tag{17}$$

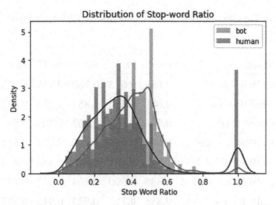

Fig. 7. Stop word ratio in the training dataset

Here FPR is False Positive Rate, TPR is True Positive Rate, FNR is False Negative Rate, N_i is the sum of correctly classified data samples, and T is the total number of data samples. The F1 measure is a harmonic mean between precision and recall:

$$F1 = 2 \cdot \frac{Precision \cdot Recall}{Precision + Recall} \tag{18}$$

If the classifier allows you to estimate the probability of an object belonging to the desired class, then a qualitative assessment of the curve, constructed for different values of this probability, we also assume AUC.

3.3 Settings

We have implemented our model using Python on Google Colab environment. For text augmentation, we use EDA [48], which adopted yje techniques described in Sect. 2.3. For embedding, we use Glove and RoBERTa. To obtain word embeddings, we use Flair [56], in which we have selected a language model enabling fine-tuning on BERT, and the training the GRU RNN along with the classification layer included language model fine-tuning. To tune the hyper-parameters of our deep learning network, we used Hyperopt [57]. We tuned learning rate, batch size, the number of convolutional and fully connected (FC) layers, the size of the kernels and number of filters in CNN, and the number of the neurons in the FC layers, and the number of LSTM cells. To mitigate the effect of overfitting, we used the early stopping approach.

3.4 Results

To compare, as baselines we use simple classical machine learning models: term frequency–inverse document frequency (TF-IDF) with logistic regression (LR) classifier and a bag-of-words (BoW) with logistic regression. We also implemented a simple dense neural network, with only 2 layers. The results are presented in Table 1.

Table 1. Summary of the classification performance using 10-fold cross-validation. Best values are boldened.

Model	F1	Pr	Re	AUC	Acc
BoW + LR	0.686	0.613	0.780	0.759	0.673
TF-IDF + LR	0.681	0.568	0.853	0.753	0.635
Glove + DN	0.703	0.599	0.862	0.789	0.691
RoBERTa + DN	0.801	0.645	0.832	0.821	0.811
RoBERTA + CNN	0.816	0.657	0.845	0.834	0.820
RoBERTa + LSTM	0.835	0.690	0.864	0.852	0.854
RoBERTa + HAN	**0.855**	**0.71**	**0.923**	**0.913**	**0.897**

Classification performance of the best deep network model is given in Fig. 8.

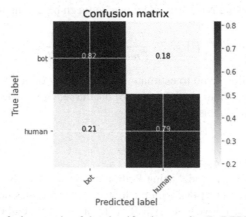

Fig. 8. Confusion matrix of the classification results (RoBERTa + HAN)

We compare our results with those of Fagni et al. [43], which is as far as we know the only work that has reported the results on this dataset. They also used BERT-type transformers (BERT, DISTILBERT, ROBERTA) and XLNET, however, they did not employ text augmentation. The comparison of results is presented in Table 2. Surprisingly, Fagni et al. [43] achieved better precision, whereas we achieved higher recal.. By using the text augmentation technique combined with RoBERTa, we were able to achieve similar results in terms of accuracy (89.7%), which underlines the importance of text augmentation for text classification using short texts and small datasets.

Table 2. Comparison of the proposed model performance with the results achieved by Fagni et al. [43]. Best values are boldened.

Model	F1	Pr	Re	Acc
BERT [43]	0.892	0.884	0.892	0.891
DISTILBERT [43]	0.888	0.882	0.888	0.887
ROBERTA [43]	**0.897**	0.891	0.897	0.896
XLNET [43]	0.882	**0.922**	0.882	0.877
RoBERTA + HAN (proposed)	0.855	0.71	**0.923**	**0.897**

4 Conclusions

In this paper we have addressed the problem of recognizing automatically generated tweets by exploring different neural network models. To improve the classification results, we used the text augmentation techniques. To obtain features from the text we used word embedding and vectorization. We compared the performance of dense neural network, convolutional neural network, gated recurrent network, and hierarchical attention network on the TweepFake dataset. The best results were achieved by RoBERTA + HAN architecture, which reached an accuracy of 89.7%.

Acknowledgment. Future work will aim on the improvement of discussed architectures specifically focusing on the problem of the small dataset.

References

1. Paterson, T., Hanley, L.: Political warfare in the digital age: cyber subversion, information operations and 'deep fakes.' Aust. J. Int. Aff. **74**(4), 439–454 (2020)
2. Tandoc, E.C., Lim, Z.W., Ling, R.: Defining "Fake news": a typology of scholarly definitions. Digit. Journal. **6**(2), 137–153 (2018)
3. Bastos, M.T., Mercea, D.: The brexit botnet and user-generated hyperpartisan news. Soc. Sci. Comput. Rev. **37**(1), 38–54 (2019)
4. Assibong, P.A., Wogu, I.A.P., Sholarin, M.A., Misra, S., Damasevičius, R., Sharma, N.: The politics of artificial intelligence behaviour and human rights violation issues in the 2016 US presidential elections: An appraisal. In: Sharma, N., Chakrabarti, A., Balas, V.E. (eds.) Data Management, Analytics and Innovation. AISC, vol. 1016, pp. 295–309. Springer, Singapore (2020). https://doi.org/10.1007/978-981-13-9364-8_22
5. Wang, Y., McKee, M., Torbica, A., Stuckler, D.: Systematic literature review on the spread of health-related misinformation on social media. Soc. Sci. Med. **240**, 112552 (2019)
6. Shimizu, K.: 2019-nCoV, fake news, and racism. Lancet **395**(10225), 685–686 (2020)
7. Kapočiute-Dzikiene, J.: A domain-specific generative chatbot trained from little data. Appl. Sci. **10**(7), 2221 (2020)
8. Dandekar, A., Zen, R.A.M., Bressan, S.: Generating fake but realistic headlines using deep neural networks. In: Benslimane, D., Damiani, E., Grosky, W.I., Hameurlain, A., Sheth, A., Wagner, R.R. (eds.) DEXA 2017. LNCS, vol. 10439, pp. 427–440. Springer, Cham (2017). https://doi.org/10.1007/978-3-319-64471-4_34

9. Chakraborty, A., Paranjape, B., Kakarla, S., Ganguly, N.: Stop clickbait: detecting and preventing clickbaits in online news media. IEEE/ACM Int. Conf. Adv. Soc. Netw. Anal. Mining, ASONAM **2016**, 9–16 (2016)

10. Malbon, J.: Taking fake online consumer reviews seriously. J. Consumer Policy **36**(2), 139–157 (2013)

11. Ji, Z., Pi, H., Wei, W., Xiong, B., Wozniak, M., Damasevicius, R.: Recommendation based on review texts and social communities: a hybrid model. Access **7**, 40416–40427 (2019)

12. Kapočiūtė-Dzikienė, J., Balodis, K., Skadiņš, R.: Intent detection problem solving via automatic DNN hyperparameter optimization. Appl. Sci. **10**(21), 1–21 (2020)

13. Wei, W., Ke, Q., Nowak, J., Korytkowski, M., Scherer, R., Woźniak, M.: Accurate and fast URL phishing detector: a convolutional neural network approach. Comput. Netw. **178**, 107275 (2020). https://doi.org/10.1016/j.comnet.2020.107275

14. Zhang, B., Wei, W., Wang, W., Li, Y., Cui, H., Si, Q.: Modeling topic propagation on heterogeneous online social networks. In: 2018 IEEE 18th International Conference on Software Quality, Reliability, and Security Companion, QRS-C 2018, pp. 641–642 (2018)

15. Lin, J., et al.: Attention-based high-order feature interactions to enhance the recommender system for web-based knowledge-sharing service. In: Huang, Z., Beek, W., Wang, H., Zhou, R., Zhang, Y. (eds.) WISE 2020. LNCS, vol. 12342, pp. 461–473. Springer, Cham (2020). https://doi.org/10.1007/978-3-030-62005-9_33

16. Omoregbe, N.A.I., Ndaman, I.O., Misra, S., Abayomi-Alli, O.O., Damaševičius, R.: text messaging-based medical diagnosis using natural language processing and fuzzy logic. J. Healthcare Eng. **2020**, 1–14 (2020)

17. Li, C., Su, Y., Liu, W.: Text-to-text generative adversarial networks. International Joint Conference on Neural Networks (IJCNN), Rio de Janeiro, Brazil, pp. 1–7 (2018)

18. Wogu, I.A., Misra, S., Assibong, P., Adewumi, A., Damasevicius, R., Maskeliunas, R.: A critical review of the politics of artificial intelligent machines, alienation and the existential risk threat to America's labour force. In: Gervasi, O., et al. (eds.) ICCSA 2018. LNCS, vol. 10963, pp. 217–232. Springer, Cham (2018). https://doi.org/10.1007/978-3-319-95171-3_18

19. Wogu, I.A.P., Misra, S., Roland-Otaru, C.O., Udoh, O.D., Awogu-Maduagwu, E., Damasevicius, R.: Human rights' issues and media/communication theories in the wake of artificial intelligence technologies: The fate of electorates in twenty-first-century american politics. In: Advances in Electrical and Computer Technologies, pp. 319-333 (2020)

20. Lazer, D.M.J., et al.: The science of fake news: addressing fake news requires a multidisciplinary effort. Science **359**(6380), 1094–1096 (2018)

21. Reis, J.C.S., Correia, A., Murai, F., Veloso, A., Benevenuto, F., Cambria, E.: Supervised learning for fake news detection. IEEE Intell. Syst. **34**(2), 76–81 (2019)

22. Bondielli, A., Marcelloni, F.: A survey on fake news and rumour detection techniques. Inf. Sci. **497**, 38–55 (2019)

23. Ren, Y., Ji, D.: Neural networks for deceptive opinion spam detection: an empirical study. Inf. Sci. **385**, 213–224 (2017)

24. Hajek, P., Barushka, A., Munk, M.: Fake consumer review detection using deep neural networks integrating word embeddings and emotion mining. Neural Comput. Appl. **32**(23), 17259–17274 (2020). https://doi.org/10.1007/s00521-020-04757-2

25. Zheng, H., Chen, J., Yao, X., Sangaiah, A.K., Jiang, Y., Zhao, C.: Clickbait convolutional neural network. Symmetry **10**(5), 138 (2018)

26. Ajao, O., Bhowmik, D., Zargari, S.: Fake news identification on twitter with hybrid CNN and rnn models. In: 9th International Conference on Social Media and Society, pp. 226–230 (2018)

27. Asghar, M.Z., Habib, A., Habib, A., Khan, A., Ali, R., Khattak, A.: Exploring deep neural networks for rumor detection. J. Ambient. Intell. Humaniz. Comput. **12**(4), 4315–4333 (2019). https://doi.org/10.1007/s12652-019-01527-4

28. Fang, Y., Gao, J., Huang, C., Peng, H., Wu, R.: Self multi-head attention-based convolutional neural networks for fake news detection. PLoS ONE **14**(9), e0222713 (2019)
29. Ghanem, B., Rosso, P., Rangel, F.: An emotional analysis of false information in social media and news articles. ACM Trans. Internet Technol. **20**(2), 19 (2020)
30. Jwa, H., Oh, D., Park, K., Kang, J.M., Lim, H.: exBAKE: Automatic fake news detection model based on bidirectional encoder representations from transformers (BERT). Appl. Sci. **9**(19), 4062 (2019)
31. Kaliyar, R.K., Goswami, A., Narang, P., Sinha, S.: FNDNet – A deep convolutional neural network for fake news detection. Cogn. Syst. Res. **61**, 32–44 (2020)
32. Liu, Y., Wu, Y.B.: FNED: A deep network for fake news early detection on social media. ACM Trans. Inf. Syst. **38**(3), 25 (2020)
33. Umer, M., Imtiaz, Z., Ullah, S., Mehmood, A., Choi, G.S., On, B.: Fake news stance detection using deep learning architecture (CNN-LSTM). Access **8**, 156695–156706 (2020)
34. Yao, H., Jia, X., Kumar, V., Li, Z.: Learning with small data. ACM SIGKDD International Conference on Knowledge Discovery and Data Mining, pp. 3539–3540 (2020)
35. Molina, M.Á., Asencio-Cortés, G., Riquelme, J.C., Martínez-Álvarez, F.: A preliminary study on deep transfer learning applied to image classification for small datasets. In: 15th International Conference on Soft Computing Models in Industrial and Environmental Applications (SOCO 2020), pp. 741–750 (2021)
36. Moreno-Barea, F.J., Jerez, J.M., Franco, L.: Improving classification accuracy using da-ta augmentation on small data sets. Expert Syst. Appl. **161**, 113696 (2020)
37. Sun, X., He, J.: A novel approach to generate a large scale of supervised data for short text sentiment analysis. Multimedia Tools Appl. **79**(9–10), 5439–5459 (2018). https://doi.org/10.1007/s11042-018-5748-4
38. Park, D., Ahn, C.W.: Self-supervised contextual data augmentation for natural language processing. Symmetry **11**(11), 1393 (2019)
39. Fadaee, M., Bisazza, A., Monz, C.: Data augmentation for low-resource neural machine translation. arXiv:1705.00440 (2017)
40. Xie, Z., Wang, S.I., Li, J., Lévy, D., Nie, A., Jurafsky, D., Ng, A.Y.: Data noising as smoothing in neural network language models. arXiv:1703.02573 (2017)
41. Kobayashi, S.: Contextual augmentation: Data augmentation by words with paradigmatic relations. arXiv:1805.06201 (2018)
42. Gao, F., et al.: Soft contextual data augmentation for neural machine translation. In: Proceedings of the 57th Annual Meeting of the Association for Computational Linguistics, pp. 5539–5544 (2019).
43. Fagni, T., Falchi, F., Gambini, M., Martella, A., Tesconi, M.: TweepFake: About detecting deepfake tweets. PLOS ONE **16**(5), e0251415 (2021)
44. Fox, C.: A stop list for general text. ACM SIGIR forum **24**(1–2), 19–21 (1989)
45. Jiang, J., Zhai, C.: An empirical study of tokenization strategies for biomedical information retrieval. Inf. Retrieval **10**, 341–363 (2007)
46. Harman, D.: How effective is suffixing? J. Am. Soc. Inf. Sci. **42**(1), 7–15 (1991)
47. Li, Y., Li, X., Yang, Y., Dong, R.: A diverse data augmentation strategy for low-resource neural machine translation. Information **11**(5), 255 (2020)
48. Wei, J.W., Zou, K.: EDA: Easy data augmentation techniques for boosting performance on text classification tasks. In: Proceedings of the 2019 Conference on Empirical Methods in Natural Language Processing and the 9th International Joint Conference on Natural Language Processing (EMNLP-IJCNLP), pp. 6382–6388 (2019)
49. Nasir, I.M., et al.: Pearson correlation-based feature selection for document classification using balanced training. Sensors **20**(23), 6793 (2020)
50. Pennington, J., Socher, R., Manning, C.: Glove: global vectors for word representation. Conference on Empirical Methods in Natural Language Processing, pp. 1532–1543 (2014)

51. Liu, Y., et al.: RoBERTa: A Robustly Optimized BERT Pretraining Approach. arXiv:1907. 11692 (2019)
52. Cho, K., et al.: Learning Phrase Representations using RNN Encoder-Decoder for Statistical Machine Translation. arXiv:1406.1078 (2014)
53. Hochreiter, S., Schmidhuber, J.: Long short-term memory. Neural Comput. **9**(8), 1735–1780 (1997)
54. Bahdanau, D., Cho, K., Bengio, Y.: Neural machine translation by jointly learning to align and translate. arXiv:1409.0473 (2014).
55. Ragab, M.G., et al.: A novel one-dimensional cnn with exponential adaptive gradients for air pollution index prediction. Sustainability **12**, 10090 (2020)
56. Akbik, A., Bergmann, T., Blythe, D., Rasul, K., Schweter, S., Vollgraf, R.: FLAIR: an Easy-to-Use Framework for State-of-the-Art NLP. In: Proceedings of the 2019 Conference of the North American Chapter of the Association for Computational Linguistics: Human Language Technologies, NAACL-HLT 2019, pp. 54–59 (2019)
57. Bergstra, J., Komer, B., Eliasmith, C., Yamins, D., Cox, D.D.: Hyperopt: a python library for model selection and hyperparameter optimization. Comput. Sci. Discov. **8**(1), 014008 (2015)

Development of an RL-Based Mechanism to Augment Computation Offloading in Edge Computing

Shintaro Ide$^{(\boxtimes)}$ and Bernady O. Apduhan$^{(\boxtimes)}$

Graduate School of Information Science, Kyushu Sangyo University, Fukuoka, Japan
k20gjk01@st.kyusan-u.ac.jp, bob@is.kyusan-u.ac.jp

Abstract. The explosive growth of data generated by the widespread use of IoT devices and the increasing realizations of IoT applications that require real-time responses have made it difficult for traditional cloud computing or edge computing to keep up with the tasks processing demands and/or near real-time response requirements of applications. We employ the strategy of computation offloading to nearby edge nodes to meet these requirements on time. In this research, we developed an efficient offload broker mechanism using deep reinforcement learning to perform optimal task allocation and computation offloading on this platform. Experiments show that the model learns the policies for offloading tasks to the optimal nodes appropriately. These promising results will enlighten more computation offloading issues to improve the efficiency of the model and its deployment in edge computing environment.

Keywords: Edge computing · Computation offloading · Reinforcement learning

1 Introduction

With the increasing realization of IoT (Internet of Things) applications, large amount of data is being generated every day [1]. One such example is the video data taken from the many surveillance cameras installed throughout a city. In the event of an unexpected incident or accident, these camera images are reviewed, verified, and presented as evidence. However, due to the large amount of generated video data, the old data is often discarded without being utilized. To this, by using edge computing and AI technologies, we envisioned to utilize this data and investigate its potential for the prevention and countermeasures against untoward incidents and accidents.

Edge computing [2] is an evolving technology wherein the data is processed at the edge servers which are close to the data source. It has the potential to significantly reduce the processing dependency on cloud data centers to process and support the near real-time responses required by applications. Edge computing complements cloud computing. However, the computing power of edge servers are limited compared to servers at data centers. Due to this limited computing power of edge servers, there is the risk of losing real-time performance when edge servers are processing compute-intensive applications.

© Springer Nature Switzerland AG 2021
O. Gervasi et al. (Eds.): ICCSA 2021, LNCS 12954, pp. 539–548, 2021.
https://doi.org/10.1007/978-3-030-86979-3_38

In this research, we study an efficient computation offloading [3, 4] strategy and develop a computation offloading mechanism (a.k.a, offloading broker) to support the near real-time processing requirements of applications in an edge computing environment. Likewise, this study includes a scheme to orchestrate the computation offloading in part or as a whole to nearby edge servers on demand.

2 Related Work

Zihan, et al. [5] developed a cooperative computing system consisting of MEC (Edge Cloud), MCC (Central Cloud), and local computing (mobile devices) as a test environment to study effective offloading decisions and resource allocation in the limited computing power environment of Mobile Edge Computing (MEC). Based on the proposed system, a Q-Learning based offloading policy was designed to pre-schedule the computational resources for each task and make optimal offloading decisions and resource allocation. The authors built a MEC environment considering mobility as a test environment for optimal task offloading. Whereas, in our study, we constructed and experimented with an environment that considers non-mobile edge devices such as surveillance cameras and sensor devices.

Whereas, Hossain [6] et al., proposed an RL-based scheme for Industrial IoT (IIoT) environment using edge computing. They proposed an RL-based scheme for IIoT, which is a research area with many topics such as computational complexity, latency minimization, task offloading, storage management, and power consumption. The authors found an optimal task offloading policy using Q-Learning, a popular reinforcement learning algorithm, in an IIoT environment where each device has computational power. In our study, we also used a reinforcement learning algorithm for task offloading, but the difference is that each device does not have computational power and the generated tasks must be offloaded.

3 System Organization and Experiment Environment

As shown in Fig. 1, we consider a local edge computing (LEC) system consisting of edge servers $E = \{0, 1, ... N\}$, offload broker server, and edge devices $e = \{1, 2, ... n\}$. In this system, an edge device, which is the data source, first sends a request to process a task to its edge server. In this case, each edge device is preset to its nearest edge server. (Here, the edge device selects the closest one from the location information of the surrounding edge servers).

The edge server (a.k.a. client edge server) that receives the task processing request determines whether or not the task can be handled by its own task processing capacity. If the task can be handled, it executes the task and returns the result to the edge device. If the task cannot be handled, it makes a query to the offload broker server. The offload broker server periodically obtains and maintain a record of the processing capacity, available network bandwidth, and location information of all edge servers within its domain. Along with these parameters, the offload broker server scans the record and apply an efficient edge server selection algorithm based on the client server requirements. With the selection result, the offload broker server will then inform the client edge server of the most suitable node which can carry out the efficient processing of the tasks to be offloaded. The task offloading and computation then takes place.

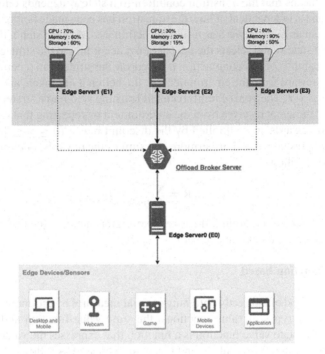

Fig. 1. Local edge computing system

4   Computation Offloading Broker

In this section, we proposed a dynamic computation offloading broker for efficient computation offloading and to minimize the processing delay.

4.1   The Computation Model and Deep Reinforcement Learning

In order to realize the proposed method, we developed a Computation Offloading Broker using DDPG (Deep Deterministic Policy Gradient), which is one of the deep reinforcement learning algorithms.

Deep reinforcement learning is a type of machine learning method that combines reinforcement learning, in which the system itself learns autonomously through trial and error, and neural networks. In reinforcement learning, the agent that actually performs the action learns to maximize the reward in a given environment. In addition, reinforcement learning is modeled by a Markov Decision Process (MDP), which is defined as follows,

$$P(s_t|s_{t-1}, s_{t-2}, \ldots, s_0) = P(s_t|s_{t-1}) \tag{1}$$

MDP means that the transition condition to a state s_t depends only on the previous state s_{t-1} and is independent of how the transition has been made before. Let us denote the environment as E, the reward as r, and the action as a. At each step t, the agent observes the current state s_t and selects the next action a according to the strategy π. The strategy is the probability of selecting action a based on the strategy in a certain state. Then, it receives a reward from the environment for the action it has taken, and transitions to the next state $st + 1$. The goal of reinforcement learning is to find a strategy that maximizes the reward the agent receives from the environment by repeating this sequence of events. The future rewards are multiplied by the discount rate γ ($0 \leq \gamma \leq 1$) to express them in terms of present value. Furthermore, the sum of the rewards, or cumulative reward, is expressed as follows,

$$R = \sum_{t=0}^{\infty} \gamma^t r_{t+1} \tag{2}$$

In reinforcement learning, there are two major methods for finding a strategy that maximizes such a cumulative reward.

- **Value function based**

It is a method of indirectly obtaining optimal measures by estimating a value function. There are two types of value functions: the state value function and the action value function. The state value function is a function that expresses the value in a certain state when a certain measure is taken, and it can be expressed as follows.

$$V^{\pi}(s) = E\left[\sum_{i=1} \gamma^{i-1} r_{t+i}|s\right] \tag{3}$$

The action value function is a function that expresses the value of a certain action in a certain state when a certain measure is being taken, and the same equation can be obtained as follows. The action value function is also called the Q-value.

$$Q^{\pi}(s, a) = E\left[\sum_{i=1} \gamma^{i-1} r_{t+i}|s, a\right] \tag{4}$$

The above two value functions are interconnected, and the action a based on the strategy π that maximizes the action value function $Q^{\pi}(s, a)$ is the factor that ultimately maximizes the state value function $V^{\pi}(s)$.

$$\pi^*(s) = \arg max_{a \in A(s)} Q^*(s, a) \tag{5}$$

- **Policy function based**

It refers to the method of directly obtaining measures and improving the current measures without going through a value function. A typical approach is the measure gradient method. The policy gradient method is an approach in which the measures are functions represented by a certain parameter θ, and the measures are learned directly by learning that parameter. Assuming that the measure model is $\pi_\theta(s, a)$, the learning of the parameter θ can be expressed as follows

$$\theta \leftarrow \theta + \delta \nabla_\theta J(\theta) \tag{6}$$

Here, δ means the learning rate. The effect of a change in the parameter θ on the objective function can be expressed by the measure gradient theorem as follows

$$\nabla_\theta J(\theta) = E_s\left[\sum_a Q^\pi(s, a)\nabla_\theta(a|s; \theta)\right] = E_{(s,a)}\left[Q^{\pi_\theta}(s, a)\nabla_\theta log\pi_\theta(a|s)\right] \tag{7}$$

4.2 Actor-Critic

Actor-Critic is a policy-based reinforcement learning algorithm [7]. It is an approach that directly improves the actor that decides the behavior, while simultaneously learning the criterion that evaluates the strategy. In general, the use of Actor-Critic is less susceptible to blurring of rewards and enables fast and stable learning. Figure 2 below shows the architecture of Actor-Critic.

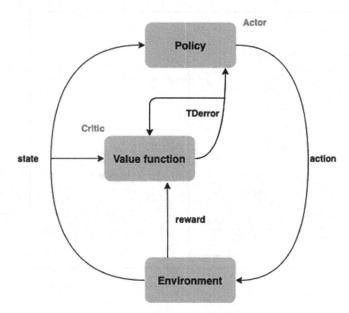

Fig. 2. The actor-critic architecture

4.3 Deep Deterministic Policy Gradient (DDPG)

DDPG is an algorithm that combines the decisive measure gradient method and DQN in the framework of Actor-Critic. In DQN, $Q(s,a)$ of each state is calculated by measures, and the action that maximizes the Q value is selected and acted upon. However, this method has the disadvantage that it can only handle discrete actions. On the other hand, DDPG does not seek the action that maximizes the Q-value, but rather parameterizes the measures and directly outputs the action, which corresponds to a continuous action space [8, 9].

Definitions of Parameters Using RL

To model this problem using RL, we define the Agent, State, Action, and Reward as follows.

- **Agent:** Edge devices that perform real-time critical tasks n.
- **State:** The agent state S_n, consists of the computational resources available at each edge server and the location information of each edge device.
- **Action:** $A_t \in [0, 1]$ where $A_t = 0$, edge device n is not offloaded and its task is processed, and when $A_t = 1$, the edge device offloads its task to the optimal edge server according to the current policy.
- **Reward:** Total number of tasks processed at each time step t.

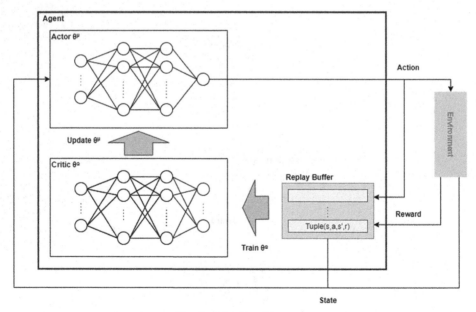

Fig. 3. DDPG architecture

In this study, the behavioral space of the offloading decision and computational offloading process in the edge computing environment is modeled using DDPG as a continuous behavioral space. The architecture of DDPG is shown in Fig. 3. First, we initialize the memory for the current state, transition state, reward function, and replay buffer. The replay buffer is a method that stores some of the experience in the environment in a buffer rather than directly. This makes it possible to utilize not only the most recent experience but also the past experience during learning. Next, a soft update is performed to prevent overestimation of the state. After that, the Actor network makes the offloading decision according to the current strategy, and the Critic network evaluates it. If the specified episode has not been reached, the same process is repeated again.

The process is summarized in the flow chart below Fig. 4.

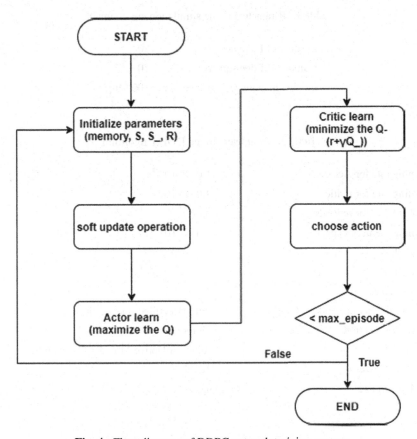

Fig. 4. Flow diagram of DDPG network training process

5 Simulation Results and Observations

In this section, we perform simulations to evaluate the proposed method using deep reinforcement learning. DDPG is implemented using Tensorflow [10].

5.1 Simulation Setting

In order to implement the Local Edge Computing (LEC) System in a virtual simulation environment, we set some parameters. The parameters in the simulation environment are summarized in Table 1, and the parameters for the DDPG algorithm are summarized in Table 2.

Table 1. Parameters in the simulation environment

Number of Edge devices	50
Number of Edge servers	10
Bandwidth between Edge servers	100 Mbps

Table 2. Parameters in the DDPG algorithm

Learning rate for Actor	1.0×10^{-4}
Learning rate for Critic	2.0×10^{-4}
Discount rate for rewards	0.99
Learning memory capacity	1.0×10^{4}
Actor's Layer	4
Critic's Layer	4
Hidden Layer	2
Activation function (Hidden Layer)	Relu (Rectified linear unit)
Activation function (Output Layer)	Sigmoid
Optimization function	Adam(Adaptive Moment Estimation)
Mini Batch Size	32
Soft Update rate	0.01

5.2 Simulation Results

The results of the simulation with the above parameters are shown in Fig. 5 below. Here, the x-axis is the number of episodes and the y-axis is the reward obtained in each episode.

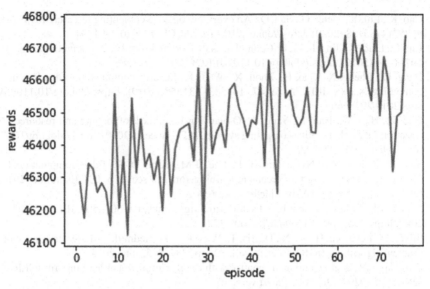

Fig. 5. Simulation results

5.3 Discussion of Results

From Fig. 5, we can see that the value of the reward earned by the agent increases as the episode progresses. Here, the reward value means the total value of tasks processed within one episode. This can be considered that the learning model is able to offload the requested tasks to the appropriate edge server properly. The variation in the value of the reward can be attributed to the fact that the epsilon-greedy method (which takes random actions with a certain probability and discovers unknown gradients) is employed in the learning process of the model.

6 Conclusion and Future Work

In this paper, we considered strategies to deal with the rapidly increasing task processing demands from edge devices and proposed a dynamic computational offloading method using deep reinforcement learning. We employed the DDPG algorithm to minimize the task processing speed per unit time, and confirmed that the agent learns a policy to offload the task to the most appropriate node.

In the future, we will compare our proposed method with existing methods in order to evaluate its efficiency and provide us insights on related vital issues. We also aim to improve the simulation system to be closer to the real-world edge computing environment.

References

1. IDC Corporate, IoT Growth Demands Rethink of Long-Term Storage Strategies, 27 July 2020. https://www.idc.com/getdoc.jsp?containerId=prAP46737220

2. Cao, K., Liu, Y., Meng, G., Sun, Q.: An overview on edge computing research. IEEE Access **8**, 85714–85728 (2020). https://doi.org/10.1109/ACCESS.2020.2991734
3. Lin, L., Liao, X., Jin, H., Li, P.: Computation offloading toward edge computing. Proc. IEEE **107**, 1–24 (2019). https://doi.org/10.1109/JPROC.2019.2922285
4. Jiang, C., Cheng, X., Gao, H., Zhou, X., Wan, J.: Towards computation offloading in edge computing: survey. IEEE Access **7**, 131543–131558 (2019). https://doi.org/10.1109/ACCESS.2019.2938660
5. Gao, Z., Hao, W., Han, Z., Yang, S.: Q-learning-based task offloading and resources optimization for a collaborative computing system. IEEE Access (2020). https://doi.org/10.1109/ICCC49849.2020.9238925
6. Sajjad Hossain, Md., Nwakanma, C.I., Lee, J.M., Kim, D.-S.: Edge computational task offloading scheme using reinforcement learning for IIoT scenario. ICT Express **6**, 291–299 (2020). https://doi.org/10.1016/j.icte.2020.06.002
7. Awate, Y.P.: Policy-gradient based actor-critic algorithms, pp. 505–509. IEEE Xplore, May 2009. https://doi.org/10.1109/GCIS.2009.372
8. Silver, D., Lever, G., Heess, N., Degris, T., Wierstra, D., Riedmiller, M.: Deterministic policy gradient algorithms. In: ICML 2014, vol. 32, pp. 387–395, June 2014
9. Lillicrap, T.P., et al.: Continuous control with deep reinforcement learning. In: ICLR 2016, arXiv:1509.02971, Jul 2019 (latest version)
10. Tensorflow: The Python Deep Learning library https://www.tensorflow.org/

An Initial Assessment of a Chatbot for Rumination-Focused Cognitive Behavioral Therapy (RFCBT) in College Students

Alana Lucia Souza Oliveira[1]([✉])[iD], Leonardo Nogueira Matos[1][iD],
Methanias Colaço Junior[1][iD], and Zenith Nara Costa Delabrida[2][iD]

[1] Post-Graduate Program of Computer Science, Federal University of Sergipe,
São Cristovão, SE, Brazil
{alanalso,leonardo}@dcomp.ufs.br
[2] Psychology Department, Federal University of Sergipe, São Cristovão, SE, Brazil
zenith@ufs.br

Abstract. Context: According to the WHO, suicide is the 2nd leading cause of death for young people aged 15 to 28, which often may have been the result of a depressive or anxiety disorder. **Objective:** To construct and evaluated a Chatbot that dialogues with college young people, with the purpose of disseminating mental health and ameliorate both depressive and anxious symptoms. **Method:** Our Chatbot is based on Rumination-focused Cognitive Behavioral Therapy (RFCBT), which focuses on observing the interaction between thought feelings and actions. For evaluation, an experiment that reached 105 young people was carried out. The bot's dialogues were constructed from psychological literature on RFCBT and tests were performed based on the PHQ-4 protocol and rumination tests. It is worth mentioning that the whole experiment was analyzed and authorized by the Ethics Committee. **Results:** The experiment results statistical significance was confirmed and obtained through T-test, for the rumination tests, and Wilcoxon Test, for the PHQ-4, obtaining p-values lower than 0.05. **Conclusion:** It has been shown that there was a change in symptoms after the use of Chatbot, as a result of mitigating the symptoms of evaluated mental disorders.

Keywords: Chatbot · Psychology · Well-being · Depression · Rumination · Experimentation

1 Introduction

In recent years, development and interest in Chatbot technology have increased. Companies such as Facebook, Microsoft and Amazon have exploited this technology with the creation of some chatbots. Microsoft, with Cortana, and Apple, with

© Springer Nature Switzerland AG 2021
O. Gervasi et al. (Eds.): ICCSA 2021, LNCS 12954, pp. 549–564, 2021.
https://doi.org/10.1007/978-3-030-86979-3_39

SIRI, for example, which act as personal assistants in a human-machine relationship. This interest in developing chatbots, capable of autonomous conversation and with learning ability, has been strongly driven by the large availability of bots development platforms in large social networking sites.

Thus, having these platforms as great tools to reach people through social messaging networks, and, in parallel, the growth in the development of mental health interventions offered on the Internet, as well as applications to complement existing mental health treatments [1], chatbots become a natural expansion line for these interventions. If implemented to work in social networks of text exchanges, such as WhatsApp, Facebook and Telegram, they become a more natural way for individuals to get involved with technology and have easier access to health treatments, since they are the environments most used for exchanging messages today. In this sense, the ability of technology to act on men's mental health problems has already been evaluated and evidenced [2], with demonstrations that a well-designed health-related conversation agent can establish a therapeutic relationship.

In addition to these observations, Stanford University has constructed the Woebot [3], a conversation agent that aims to evaluate the feasibility of a conversation interface and applies a technique called CBT (Cognitive Behavioral Therapy) through an automated chatbot, to facilitate engagement and reduction of depression or anxiety symptoms. Considering the great result that Woebot was able to validate in the intervention among university students, an opportunity to explore these techniques for young university students in Brazil, using the Portuguese language, is observed. This concern is justified by the severity of mental health disorders, therefore, according to the WHO (World Health Organization) [4], in 2012, there were 2,898 suicides of 13 to 29 year old, the age group comprising the university phase. Thus, the present work intends to go further on what has already been done by Woebot, since the choice of working with other therapy, the Rumination-focused Cognitive Behavioral Therapy (RFCBT), has demonstrated the primary target for decreasing and/or preventing depressive thoughts and actions is to focus on Rumination.

In this context, this project main goal was to develop a chatbot for Facebook Messenger platform. A chatbot that is able to help, mainly, young university students with the knowledge of Behavioral Cognitive Therapy focused on Rumination. The purpose is to offer this university population, a support tool for the knowledge of a treatment possibility for students' mental health. Moreover, the bot also aims to increase self-awareness of students own mental health, with daily dialogues that make the user to have a continuous learning conversation with the bot.

The chatbot, named Rumi, was used in an experiment with academic students, to evaluate the use and efficiency of a chatbot in the dissemination of mental health and the RFCBT. The results indicated that there were differences between the two applied psychological questionnaires, the PHQ-4 and the Rumination test, in favor of the use of Rumi. In other words, there was a significantly decrease in users feelings like anxiety, depression and rumination.

The remainder of this paper is organized as follows. Section 2 presents the theoretical base. Section 3 talks over the created chatbot. Section 4 describes related work. Section 5 presents the Methodology used for building chatbot. Section 6 details the experimental evaluation of the approach. Section 7 discusses the obtained results. Section 8 goes over the threats to the validity of the study. Finally, Sect. 9 presents the conclusions and discussion for future works.

2   Background

This section presents the theoretical background used in chatbot and the basis of this paper data analysis. At first it is talked about the Rumination-focused Cognitive Behavioral Therapy (RFCBT) is discussed and secondly it goes over the psychological tests applied for evaluation, PHQ-4 and the Rumination tests.

2.1   RFCBT

The Rumination-focused Cognitive Behavioral Therapy (RFCBT) is a variant of Behavioral Cognitive Therapy (CBT), developed by Watkins et al. (2007) [5]. The term that differentiates it, "Rumination", is defined by Watkins (2016) [6] "as recurring and repetitive thinking about symptoms (fatigue, low mood), feelings, problems, disturbing events and negative aspects about oneself, usually focusing on their causes, meaning and implications". For Nolen-Hoeksema, Mcbride and Larson (1997) [7], apud Watkins (2016) [6], rumination is like "the passive and repeatedly focusing of the symptoms of distress and the circumstances surrounding these symptoms".

To its creators, "although RFCBT is still grounded within the core principles and techniques of CBT for depression [8], this involves several additional new elements". In practice, RFBCT uses functional analysis to help patients realize that their negative rumination can be useful and guide them on how to switch to the most effective style of thinking. Functional analysis focuses on the variability of: (a) rumination (e.g., differences between useful and useless thinking about problems); (b) associated behaviors (for example, procrastination) and (c) behaviors against rumination, such as effective involvement in tasks. This detailed functional context analysis is then used to help patients to: (a) recognize the warning signs for rumination; (b) develop alternatives, strategies and contingency plans (for example, relaxation, assertiveness); and (c) changing environmental and behavioral standards (for example, changing the balance of routine tasks and obligations to do self-realising activities) [5].

In addition, Watkins et al. (2007) [5] present experiential imaging exercises and behavioral experiments as facilitators of a shift to a more useful style of thinking. Patients use targeted images to vividly recreate previous states when a more useful style of thinking was active, such as memories of being completely absorbed in an activity or experiences of being compassionate to themselves. Such exercises provide a direct counterpoint to rumination and can be used in contingency plans. These adaptations mean that RFCBT differs from standard

CBT to depression, which focuses on modifying the content of thoughts, by having a greater emphasis on directly modifying the thought process.

In [6], the adaptation of RFCBT to internet is introduced, with several justifications for the development of a variant of RFCBT that can be implemented remotely, are: accessibility, availability, convenience and coverage for psychological treatments. Depression, according to the author, is the greatest challenge among the world's health problems, being highly prevalent, chronic and dissonant. For this reason, traditional face to face therapy will never be widely available enough to reduce the major problem of depression. It is worth noting that the online version is not yet with free access and that the chatbots are an alternative to the north and feedback of an online version.

2.2 PHQ-4

The PHQ-4 test [9]) is an ultra-brief tool, valid for detecting anxiety and depression disorders. This is a 4-item self-report health questionnaire, with two questions from a 2-item depression scale (PHQ-2) and two questions from a 2-item anxiety scale (GAD-2), as a way to identify aspects of depression and anxiety. The test is validated in United States, but its validation in Brazil is still required. To start the adaptation process to Brazil, the applied test was translated. Default answers are scored as follows: "Not once" = 0, "Several days" = 1, "More than half the days" = 2, and "Almost every day" = 3. The sum of the questions is the variation between 0 and 12 points, thus, operative disorders are classified as normal, when scored from 0 to 2, mild, from 3 to 5, moderate, from 6 to 8, and severe, from 9 to 12. The test had in the following format:

- How many times in the last week have you felt uncomfortable, nervous or restless?
- How often in the last week have you been bothered by not being able to stop or control the concern?
- How many times in the last week have you felt upset because of the little interest or pleasure in doing things?
- How many times in the last week have you felt down, depressed or hopeless?

For each of the questions, these were the alternative answers: several days, more than half the days or almost every day.

2.3 Rumination Test

In view of the RFCBT, author Watkins (2016) [6] created a Rumination test that should be performed every 7 days, to check the effectiveness of the Therapy and to know how the current mental state of the patient/client under analysis is. In this work, as it was an experience outside an office and far from a psychologist/psychiatrist, the therapy itself was not applied and the original test was remodeled to a leaner version, as well as being adapted to the chatbot interface.

Thus, the participants answered the following questions from the rumination test, in scale format, during the dialogue with the bot:

- Last week, what percentage of time did you spend thinking repeatedly, insisting or worrying about negative thoughts about a disturbing issue, event, or problem?
- What percentage of your time did you use to control and stop negative thoughts so they do not interfere with your plans or prevent you from doing what you wanted last week?
- How much of your time did you spend avoiding or procrastinating doing things last week?
- How much avoiding things interfered with or prevented you from doing what you wanted last week?

For each of the questions, these were the alternative answers: 0%, 10%, 20%, 30%, 40%, 50%, 60%, 70%, 80%, 90% or 100%.

3   Rumi

This section introduces Rumi, the chatbot created to be part of the experiment. The term "Rumi" comes from rumination, which is the aspect worked on in the therapy. It has been built through Chatfuel tool and its dialogues have been based on the therapy framework proposed in [6], which proposes 12 themes for each day of dialogue, but that were distributed in 15 days. Such dialogue has been built with the help and supervision of a psychologist.

The daily dialogues are based on following themes: Initial presentation of what therapy is. An initial explanation of what it works for and a presentation of Rumi communication platform and application of the PHQ-4 and the Rumination test; Introduction of Rumination as a habit, and as habit it can be changed; Introduction of the term Procrastination and Avoidance and how these affect in everyday life; SMART(Specific, Measurable, Achievable, Relevant, and Time-bound) Goals; Self-monitoring on symptoms such as Rumination and how to detect them.; "If-Then" method; Reapplication of the initial Rumination test; Self-love; Functional Analysis of Thoughts; Realignment in relation to the SMART methodology; Concrete and Abstract thoughts; Meditation; Self-esteem; Relapse prevention and a review of everything that has been presented during the last days and Farewell; and the application of the web-adapted PHQ-4 test and of the adaptation of the Rumination test.

Furthermore, in more worrying cases, through natural language processing provided by the Chatfuel tool, participants were encouraged to call 188 (Life Valuation Center number in Brazil) and 192 numbers, for emergencies and also to contact a specialist.

With the construction of Rumi, it was published and ran through a Facebook page with the URL = https://www.facebook.com/rumibot.bot/, for use and interaction with users.

4   Related Works

This section consists of work that is in line with this paper goal of using chatbot technology to help its user's mental health.

4.1   Woebot

Woebot is a chatbot created to work for the mental health of young university students through the use of psychology techniques. It was implemented by a research group at Stanford University in the United States. In the Woebot website [10], Woebot is defined as "a chatbot that helps monitor mood and learn about yourself. Based on a therapeutic framework known as Cognitive Behavioral Therapy, Woebot asks people how they are feeling and what is happening with their lives in the form of brief daily conversations". Woebot also talks to people about mental health and well-being, sending videos and other useful tools, depending on the mood and needs of the person at that time. It is the analogy to a self-help book able to learn about the person and become more specific to their needs over time.

In terms of technology, there is natural language processing in conjunction with the CBT technique, with interactions with the user that begin with a general investigation of the user's context (e.g., "What is happening in your world right now?") and your mood (for example, "How are you feeling?"), with responses provided as images of words or emojis, to represent that moment [3]. After collecting mood data, participants are presented with basic concepts related to CBT by a brief video link or by brief "word games", designed to facilitate teaching about cognitive distortions. In the initial process included by the authors, there is an introduction to the bot, noting that although the bot looks like a person, it is closer to "choosing its own self-help book" and therefore not fully able to understand what the user's needs are. The bot also briefly explains CBT and notifies the user that although a psychologist is "watching things" (for example, monitoring), this does not happen in real time and therefore the service should not be used as a substitute for a therapy [3]. In addition, in more worrisome cases, participants are encouraged to call 911 (emergency number in the United States).

As an assessment, Woebot was used as an intervention to decrease symptoms of depression in students. Two groups of university students participated in the research for two weeks [3]. Some tests were applied to evaluate the effectiveness of two interventions: using chat to read and read a self-help book. The tests included questionnaires scientifically evaluated and recommended for their effectiveness in psychology. The results evaluated the symptoms of depression by means of a covariance analysis between the tests applied in the groups. It was found that the group that received the chat intervention had a much greater improvement in the symptoms of depression than the self-help book group, demonstrating that even the short-term intervention had some effect, which suggests a great possibility to use the chatbot for this emerging area of mental health.

The bot works through English language interactions and a fee is charged after 15 days of free use. In addition, Woebot can be accessed via Facebook (https://www.facebook.com/HiWoebot/) or via an application on Android or IOS.

4.2 Owlie

According to its authors, Owlie is a chatbot that was created "to make available to the public as many new therapy tools as possible" [11]. This bot uses practical experiences in the field of psychology, with evidence based medicine (EBM) therapies scientifically evaluated, applying a rule-based decision and technology algorithm (word matching).

Owlie has three main characteristics: empathetic listening, tools/exercises, and therapeutic education. In this context, emotional crisis management is one of its main functions, helping users take responsibility for their own recovery and move towards a better quality of life. Currently, he also works 24 h a day, through his Facebook page (https://www.facebook.com/owlielechatbot), however, Owlie only talks to people through the French language.

5 Methodology

All tasks and methodological phases are described in the Table 1. The initial phase was called "Before the Experiment", the experiment phase has the same name and the analysis of the experiment was called only "Analysis". The experiment and its self-contained methodology, as well as its execution, will be detailed in the next section.

6 Experiment

This section describes an experimental evaluation of our approach. The presented experimental process follows the guidelines of Wohlin et al. (2012) [12]. This section focuses on the experiment definition and planning. The following section present the obtained experimental results.

6.1 Goal Section

The main objective of our study is to investigate the possibility of using chatbot technology to disseminate mental health through daily dialogues, increasing self-knowledge regarding participants' mental health and reducing symptoms such as rumination, anxiety and depression. The goal is formalized using the GQM Goal model proposed by Basili and Weiss (1984) [13] and presented by Solingen and Berghout (1999) [14]: **Analyze**, through a controlled experiment, one chatbot tool with cognitive behavioral therapy focused on Rumination, **in order** to evaluate, **with respect to** verify the possibility of use, effectiveness and quality of the mental health dissemination, **from the point of view** of psychologists, programmers and university students, **in the context** of University.

Table 1. Complete methodology procedure

	Performed tasks	Goals
Before	Meta-analysis research about chatbots and apps designed to aid mental health	This research was aimed at providing greater familiarity with the problem in order to make it more explicit and to provide the main hypothesis of using technology as a way to positively assist in prevention, treatment or help with mental health
	Descriptive Research about target population	Description of characteristics of young people and their mental health in Brazilian universities
	Chatbot and Dialog Development	Chatbot development using software development techniques and building dialogs that were used based on RFCBT
	Field research	Exploratory research in which, in addition to bibliographic and/or documentary research, data collection was performed in the target population and in order to understand aspects
	Experimental Method	Planning and elaboration of the experimental method for test a hypothesis of causality, wich is explained in more detail in the Sect. 6
Experiment	Recruitment of Participants for the Experiment	Potential participants were recruited from a Facebook post, targeting a Federal University of Sergipe (UFS) community. Social media of UFS students
	Execution of the experiment	The experiment was open for 30 days to capture participants. Which in 15 days occurred the interaction of the chatbot participant
	Daily Dialogues	Application of the dialogues that are presented in the Sect. 3 for 15 days, and 2.2 and 2.3 was performed for data analysis
	Rumination Test application	At the 1st, 7th and 15th daily dialogues, were applied an adaptation of the rumination test presented in the Sect. 2.3
	PHQ-4 Test application	At the 1st and 15th of the dialogs with chatbot were applied the tests PHQ-4 presented in the Sect. 2.2
	Data Collection	During each daily dialogues, at the end of each dialogue day, the messages between the participants was stored in a database
Analysis	Quantitative data analysis	Its objective is to measure and allow hypothesis testing, as the results are more concrete compared to the tests that are applied to the PHQ-4 and Rumination-Test
	Qualitative data analysis	It aims to extract and analyze from participants their opinions on the use of chatbot and psychoeducation through a questionnaire

6.2　Planning

This subsection details all experimental design.

Context Selection. The experiment targeted academic students.

Hypothesis Formulation. The question we are trying to explore is this: Does applying chatbot in therapy dialogues, help in spreading mental health and therapy? To evaluate this question, the average of the PHQ-4 and Empathy Rumination questionnaires will be used. For this question, formally, the hypothesis that we are trying to confirm is:

Null Hypothesis $H0^R$: Rumination level, according to Rumination test, after interaction, is the same. $H0^R$: μBefore Chatbot(Levels) $=$ μAfter Chatbot(Levels).

Alternative Hypothesis $H1^R$: Rumination level, according to Rumination test, after interaction, is different. $H1^R$: μBefore Chatbot(Levels) $\neq$ μAfter Chatbot(Levels).

Null Hypothesis $H0^{AD}$**:** The levels of anxiety and depression, according to the grades of the questions in the questionnaire, in the PHQ-4 test, after the interaction, are the same. $H0^{AD}$: μBefore Chatbot(Grades) = μAfter Chatbot(Grades).

Alternative Hypothesis $H1^{AD}$**:** The levels of anxiety and depression, according to the grades of the questions in the questionnaire, in the PHQ-4 test, after the interaction, are different. $H1^{AD}$: μBefore Chatbot(Grades) $\neq$ μAfter Chatbot(Grades).

Thus, to investigate which of the hypothesis are refuted, the following dependent, independent and intervening variables will be considered:

- **Independent variables:** Chatbot Development Tool; Rumi; Questionnaires; and the RFCBT protocol.
- **Dependent variables:** Dialogues, from which were derived: Anxiety and Depression levels (Questionnaire PHQ-4 - applied every 7 days); Rumination Level (Rumination Questionnaire applied every 15 days); and final questionnaire about overall chatbot experience.
- **Intervening variables:** Communication between participants; Previous anxiety and depression; Variation of the daily mood in the 15 days of use; Lack of experience.

Participant and Artifact Selection. After defining hypotheses and variables to be analyzed, the participants and objects selecting process has started. Potential participants were recruited from a Facebook post, targeting a university community. Social media like WhatsApp, Instagram and even groups of study and interaction of students, to voluntarily participate in such an experimental evaluation, were used. All participants accepted the terms and conditions for participating in the experiment before starting the dialogue. Such terms have been validated by the ethics committee. 236 people have shown interest in participating in the experiment and 105 people have participated by the end of the experiment, 63 women and 42 men aged 18 to 28, inclusion criteria age for the experiment. The experiment and its dissemination lasted a month, in which each participant spent 15 days talking to the bot. For legal reasons, participants names are not disclosed in this work.

Instrumentation. The instrumentation process is initially done with the environment setup for the experiment and data collection planning. That was done in an automated way through the Chatfuel (chatbot development tool), Integromat (integration tool) and Excel Online. In short, here are the resources used: Facebook Messenger environment, for dialogue with participants; For the development of Rumi, was used Chatfuel; Integromat and Excel Online were used to capture the data; PHQ-4; and Rumination Test.

Experimental Design. The entire project and its experimental design have been evaluated and approved by the Ethics Committee, the number of the Ethical Evaluation Presentation Certificate (CAAE) is 90842818.4.0000.5546.

Entrants were sorted by gender and Facebook IDs only. The privacy and anonymity were preserved in the project. All evaluated participants signed the Informed Consent Form. In summary, the experiment was divided into the two parts below.

Daily Dialogues: On the 1st and 15th day the PHQ-4 tests will be applied. On the 1st, 7th and 15th day, an adaptation of the rumination test presented in the Sect. 2.2 and 2.3 will be performed for data analysis. After the conclusion of the dialogues, still on the same platform, participants will be sent an opinion questionnaire about what was presented by the bot. It will be reported later in the Results section.

Data collection: At the end of each day of dialogue, the messages between the parties will be stored in a database. The analysis of the collected data will be presented in the next section of this article.

6.3   Operation

This subsection describes the experiment operation process.

Preparation. The following preparation steps were carried out.

Summon up of participants: The volunteers were summoned through the social network that would be used. Later they signed the terms of conditions and ethics for the experiment. Dialogue with the Bot: The conversation has been held daily for 15 days. The bot automatically called the participant to the conversation every day at the same time that the participant had started the conversation on the first day. The tests were also carried out within the dialogue itself. At the first moment, the participants took PHQ-4 and rumination tests already dialoguing with the bot. 15 days after, the participants retook the tests to evaluate the dialog experiment impact on those. Doubts with the experiment: An email and telephone number were made available for participants to ask questions about the experiment.

6.4   Execution

After carrying out the previous steps, the experiment occurred from August 6th, 2018 at 7:00 p.m. until September 3rd, 2018 at 7:00 p.m., in a 4-week period of data collection, and was started according to the design presented above.

A 236 total people have started the conversation with chatbot and accepted the Free and Informed Consent Term, but only 105 people have concluded within the stipulated deadline. In order to answer the research questions, the following dependent variables were analyzed: PHQ-4 and Rumination tests. Applied at the first and last days of the use of the bot.

6.5   Data Validation

For the experiment, a factor (the approach used for dissemination of mental health) and two treatments have been considered: before and after the use of

Rumi. In this context, for both moments, PHQ-4 questionnaire and rumination test results were collected. For support in analysis, interpretation and validation, four types of statistical tests were used, Kolmogorov-Smirnov and Shapiro-Wilk tests were used to verify sample normality. For the Rumination Test, our sample was normal for both normality tests, so it was used the parametric Test-T. Unlike Rumination test, PHQ-4 test was not validated for normality, so nonparametric Wilcoxon Related-Samples test was used. These statistical tests were used to compare the differences of the grade means of the applications of the psychological tests before and after the interaction with the bot. In addition, all statistical tests were done from IBM SPSS Statistics 20 software.

7 Results and Discussion

Primarily, a correspondence between questionnaires and answers analysis was carried out, those who did not complete the experiment and those who were not in the age range of 18 to 28 years old were removed. After the content analysis, the score of each participant was calculated by analyzing their responses values in the tests, at the beginning and at the end of the experiment. Moreover, a detection and treatment process of outliers was performed, in order to reduce their impacts on the data set [15].

Then, it was defined a significance level of 0.05 throughout the experiment and the Kolmogorov-Smirnov and Shapiro-Wilk tests were applied for analysis of the normal distribution. For both treatments, the 1st and 2nd application of psychological tests, the values of the p-value were similar, in the contexts of each type of psychological test. Since the p-values for the rumination tests results were greater than 0.05 ($p > 0.05$), the data distribution is assumed to be normal. In the case of the PHQ-4 test results sample, the calculated p-values were less than 0.05, i.e., the hypothesis of normality of the data was rejected.

From the next section, according to the situation of the normality of the data, each psychological test will be analyzed individually, to verify the statistical significance of the results achieved after the use of the bot.

7.1 Rumination Test

This scale was applied 3 times over the 15 days. It was firstly applied at the initial conversation, the second time on the 7th day and the third time on the 15th, and last, day of dialogue with the Rumi. General averages from 1st and 15th days were analyzed. For each of the questions, the percentages of the answers are transformed into a scale of 0 to 10, so, since there are 4 questions, the final grade goes from 0 to 40. So, the averages varied from 0 to 40 for the answers, among which 40 shows a lot of Rumination feeling and 0 matches absence of Rumination. When analyzing the results and removing outliers, 99 responses were analyzed, the meaning of the responses is shown in Fig. 1.

Due to data normality, the hypothesis test applied in this context was the T-test. From this, it has been verified, on Rumination test evaluation, that there

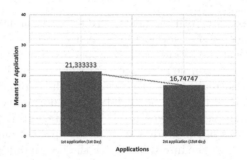

Fig. 1. Applications of rumination test

was a statistically significant difference between the first the last day of experiment, with the average having decreased from 21.333 to 16.747. The significance was found due to the Sig. obtained (p-value) of 0.000, which is less than the level of significance adopted, as shown in Fig. 2.

Paired Samples Test

| | | | | Paired Differences | | | | | |
| | | Mean | Std. Deviation | Std. Error Mean | 95% Confidence Interval of the Difference | | t | df | Sig. (2-tailed) |
					Lower	Upper			
Pair 1	Rumination_1 - Rumination_2	4,586	9,657	,971	2,660	6,512	4,725	98	,000

Fig. 2. Applications of rumination test

That demonstrates that for one on rumination symptoms, averages decrease considerably. Therefore, the null hypothesis $H0^R$ was rejected.

7.2   PHQ-4 Test

As suggested in [9], PHQ-4 should be applied every 15 days. Thus, the test was applied at the first contact with the bot and at the 15th day, and last, of the dialogue. When analyzing the results and removing the outliers and storage errors, 97 responses were analyzed.

Due to the non-normality of the PHQ-4 questionnaire data, previously pointed, the hypothesis test applied in this context will be the Wilcoxon nonparametric test, as shown in Fig. 3. In this case, it is needed to define a new null hypothesis: $H0^{AD}$: The levels of anxiety and depression, according to the distribution of the grades of the questions in the questionnaire, in the PHQ-4 test, after the interaction, are the same.

The results indicated that the performance with the use of Rumi, in favor of mental health, was higher. In other words, the overall average grade decreased from 6 to 4. In addition, according to the statistical results, the Sig. obtained (p-value) of 0.000 is less than the level of significance adopted. Therefore, the null hypothesis $H0^{AD}$ was rejected, that is, statistically, anxiety and depression

Related-Samples Wilcoxon Signed Rank Test Summary

Total N	97
Test Statistic	1051,500
Standard Error	252,178
Standardized Test Statistic	-4,130
Asymptotic Sig.(2-sided test)	,000

Fig. 3. Wilcoxon test

levels, according to PHQ-4 test, do not have same distribution of the grades of the questionnaire questions, after interaction.

8 Threats of Validity

The threats to validity for the present study were:

- **Construct validity:** The choice of subject for conversation and use of chatbot are the possible threats. The first is related to the possibility of choosing an unpleasant or unfamiliar issue to the interlocutors. To mitigate this threat, it has been chosen to address the issue in relation to the environment in which the participants live, the university and their daily lives. The second one can be caused by lack of experience in chatting with a bot through Messenger. To mitigate this, during the experiment and dialogue, the bot itself signaled ways and alternatives that the participant should do to instruct them in dialogue and self-knowledge.
- **Internal validity:** The main threats can be: response time, a sensitive subject for conversation, tiredness, current state of mental health of the participant, and demand characterization. As the tool have predefined dialogues, the response time threat could be caused by a question not being answered within 24 h, because the next day the bot starts another different dialog, leaving unanswered questions. In order to mitigate this threat, during the course of an experiment, issues that have already been extensively dealt on other days have been taken up several times. The second threat may be caused by choosing an unpleasant subject or one that brings bad feelings about something to the participant. In order to mitigate this, playful interactions with images, stories, and videos that softened the impact of the subject were chose, bringing a theoretical subject to practice. In the case of the threat of fatigue and lack of time of the participant, due to the long time of interaction, the dialogues required no more than 10 min of interaction a day. Moreover, if a participant missed a day interaction with the bot, he didn't lost the experiment. The penultimate threat is related to the possible mental state of the participant at the day of the conversation, since the interlocutors were not pre-clinicated. To mitigate this, every day, before the experiment, the Rumibot asked how the person was and whether she was interested in continuing

the conversation, regardless of their response and daily mood. Finally, in order not to influence our study, participants were not aware of factor, metrics or research hypothesis, they only knew that it was a dialog based on psychology.

– **External validity:** Due to the fact that the summons occurred through social networks, the experiment was able to reach people outside the academic scope and outside the explicit age range. Another factor was the time available for the application of the experiment. Data collection for the experiment remained opened for a month, since the experiment lasts 15 days for each participant. In this way, the experiment was able to reach more participants and these could complete the 15 days of the experiment. Lastly, more experiments will be needed to generalize the conclusions presented, however, the results allow us to draw insights to guide future investigations.

9   Conclusions

More and more people are using chatbot services to communicate with businesses and that has expanded to health care. The facilitated access to chatbot, brought by social networks, can be used as an aid in the dissemination of therapies knowledge such as the RFCBT. The need to work on mental health at universities and the lack of access to this kind of service by people are some of the reasons that magnifies the importance of admitting this new tool.

The search for mental health has been considered an urgent need worldwide, in this sense, the World Health Organization (WHO) has created a comprehensive mental health action plan 2013–2020 [16]. The plan considers that the creation of new actions concerning mental health situation of people would encourage all countries to work on this problem. Faced with this reality, according to the United Nations website in [18], WHO analyzed and estimated the costs of treatment and their results in health in 36 low, middle and high-income countries over a 15 year period (between 2016 and 2030). The research has shown that low levels of recognition and access to care for depression and anxiety cause a global economic loss of \$1 trillion a year. For that reason, this project aligns itself to solve both access to treatments and aid in the prevention and treatment of mental disorders issues.

The development of Rumi was conducted on the Chatfuel tool in combination with Integromat and Google Sheets. It has been designed to work within Facebook messenger. The bot's dialogue structure was constructed from the ideologies presented in [5], along with empathic expressions, instructional videos, and predefined learning scripts. Its development has brought some of its key requirements for easy handling, interaction, feasibility and scalability in relation to the university environment. Rumibot also provides a way of self-knowledge and disseminates therapy knowledge in a clear, intuitive and fun way, facilitating the population self-monitoring.

With the completion of the Rumi development, a final evaluation on how was the use of chatbot for this purpose experience was given to the users. The Rumination and PHQ-4 tests of depression and anxiety, which measure the current mental state of the population, were analyzed together with the Rumi dialogue, to see if these aspects would be changed for the better or for the worse. Both tests have had positive results. Rumination test has decreased its average, and the distribution of grades of the PHQ-4 questions, after interaction, also was different. In this context, we highlight the change in all aspects, rumination, depression and anxiety, which also contributes so that Rumi may help to alleviate some of the symptoms of these disorders. Therefore, chatbot technology can function as an aid tool on knowledge of behavioral cognitive therapy focused on Rumination.

9.1 Future Works

From the observations made in the user satisfaction questionnaire, applied by Rumi, it was evidenced as the need to seek improvements in some aspects of the chatbot. As a result, future work will be guided to meet the following improvements: Add new dialogs, using new theories of psychology and/or using new standardized psychiatry questionnaires that seek to assist in the prevention of suicide; And also add psychological profile detection aspects, to increase harmony, education and politeness, so that responses to the interlocutor are more empathetic. The above mentioned enhancements to Rumi are in progress, completing planned activities of this research project.

References

1. Bakker, D., Kazantzis, N., Rickwood, D., Rickard, N.: Mental health smartphone apps: review and evidence-based recommendations for future developments. JMIR Mental Health 3(1), e4984 (2016)
2. Miner, A.S., Milstein, A., Schueller, S., Hegde, R., Mangurian, C., Linos, E.: Smartphone-based conversational agents and responses to questions about mental health, interpersonal violence, and physical health. JAMA Inter. Med. 176(5), 619–625 (2016)
3. Fitzpatrick, K.K., Darcy, A., Vierhile, M.: Delivering cognitive behavior therapy to young adults with symptoms of depression and anxiety using a fully automated conversational agent (Woebot): a randomized controlled trial. JMIR Mental Health 4(2), e7785 (2017)
4. Pereira, A., Cardoso, F.: Ideação suicida na população universitária: Uma revisão da literatura (2015)
5. Watkins, E., et al.: Rumination-focused cognitive behaviour therapy for residual depression: a case series. Behav. Res. Ther. 45(9), 2144–2154 (2007)
6. Watkins, E.R.: Rumination-Focused Cognitive-behavioral Therapy for Depression. Guilford Publications, New York (2016)
7. Nolen-Hoeksema, S., McBride, A., Larson, J.: Rumination and psychological distress among bereaved partners. J. Pers. Soc. Psychol. 72(4), 855 (1997)
8. Beck, J.S.: Cognitive Behavior Therapy: Basics and Beyond. Guilford Press, New York (2011)
9. Kroenke, K., Spitzer, R.L., Williams, J.B.W., Lowe, B.: An ultra-brief screening scale for anxiety and depression: the PHQ-4. Psychosomatics 50(6), 613–621 (2009)

10. Woebot (2017). https://woebot.io/
11. Falala-Séchet, C., Antoine, L., Thiriez, I., Bungener, C.: Owlie: a chatbot that provides emotional support for coping with psychological difficulties. In: Proceedings of the 19th ACM International Conference on Intelligent Virtual Agents, pp. 236–237. ACM (2019)
12. Wohlin, C., Runeson, P., Host, M., Ohlsson, M.C., Regnell, B., Wesslen, A.: Experimentation in Software Engineering. Springer, Heidelberg (2012). https://doi.org/10.1007/978-3-642-29044-2
13. Basili, V.R., Weiss, D.M.: A methodology for collecting valid software engineering data. IEEE Trans. Softw. Eng. **6**, 728–738 (1984)
14. Van Solingen, D.M., Berghout, E.W.: The Goal/Question/Metric Method: A Practical Guide for Quality Improvement of Software Development. McGraw-Hill, New York (1999)
15. Bramer, M.: Data for data mining. In: Principles of Data Mining. UTCS, pp. 9–19. Springer, London (2016). https://doi.org/10.1007/978-1-4471-7307-6_2
16. Watts, S., et al.: CBT for depression: a pilot RCT comparing mobile phone vs computer. BMC Psychiatry **13**(1), 49 (2013)
17. Brown, L.: The conditional level of student's t test. Ann. Math. Stat. **38**(4), 1068–1071 (1967)
18. ONU Brasil: Investimento em saúde mental cresce em ritmo insuficiente, denuncia OMS (2018). https://nacoesunidas.org/investimento-em-saude-mental-cresce-em-ritmo-insuficiente-denuncia-oms/

Price Forecasting with Deep Learning in Business to Consumer Markets

Emre Eğriboz[1][(✉)] and Mehmet S. Aktaş[2]

[1] Information Technologies Institute, Informatics and Information Security Research Center, TÜBİTAK, Kocaeli, Turkey
emre.egriboz@tubitak.gov.tr
[2] Computer Engineering Department, Yildiz Technical University, Istanbul, Turkey
aktas@yildiz.edu.tr

Abstract. Price forecasting is a challenging and essential problem studied in different markets. Many researchers and institutions, academically and professionally, develop future price forecasting techniques. This study proposes a data collection and processing pipeline to forecast the next day's price of a product in business to consumer (B2C) markets using the price data obtained from web crawlers, preprocessing steps, the deep features produced by the autoencoder, and the technical indicators. For this purpose, we use web crawlers to collect different airline companies' ticket prices daily and create a price index. We apply the discrete wavelet transform (DWT) preprocessing method to denoise the price index data, calculate some technical indicators analytically, and extract the deep features of the price data via three different autoencoders, linear, stacked linear, and long short term memory (LSTM). An LSTM forecaster generates forecasts using deep and calculated features. Finally, we measure the effects of autoencoder types, and mentioned features on the forecasting performance. Our study shows that using LSTM autoencoder on denoised time series price data with technical indicators in B2C markets yields promising results.

Keywords: Deep learning · Feature extraction · Time series · Business to consumer market

1   Introduction

In the business-to-consumer (B2C) trade model, businesses market their services or products to many buyers. This commercial model can be carried out either face-to-face or online with the dramatic increase in e-commerce sales opportunities recently. Positive developments in e-commerce show that this shopping model has become widespread in recent years and will reach more consumers in the coming years [1]. The volume of e-commerce in Turkey increased by 64% in the first half of 2020 compared to the same period of the previous year and reached 91 billion 700 million Turkish Liras [2]. E-commerce is becoming more

© Springer Nature Switzerland AG 2021
O. Gervasi et al. (Eds.): ICCSA 2021, LNCS 12954, pp. 565–580, 2021.
https://doi.org/10.1007/978-3-030-86979-3_40

and more common among individuals of different ages. The proportion of e-commerce users over the age of 65 increased from 6% to 10% during the COVID-19 pandemic [3]. In such an environment, forecasting the price of a product in the next period has direct or indirect effects. It is an important research subject in terms of direct reasons such as purchasing decision, choice of the seller, procurement, price determination, and indirect reasons such as strategic planning from sales volume information [4–8].

In the field of tourism, which is an example of B2C with many service buyers and few sellers, price depends on many variables' effects such as demand, exchange rate, inflation, season, or supply [9,10].

Machine learning algorithms are often used to forecast the value of the following time period on price data [11]. The methods used in the deep learning approach, an expert in feature extraction and a sub-branch of machine learning, have achieved more successful results than classical machine learning methods in recent years [10]. Price forecasting studies with deep learning are generally used in consumer to consumer (C2C) or markets where stock movements are determinant [12]. We observe that there is a lack of studies in the literature on price forecasting in B2C markets. Furthermore, there exists studies that analyze user-system interaction data [13–23]. These studies mainly focus on data lineage of the user' s interactions for various reasons such as debugging data and transformations, auditing, evaluating the quality and trust in data. We also observe that there is lack of studies on analyzing the user-system interactions in tourism sector for the purpose of price forecasting.

In the tourism sector, where high capital is required in its establishment and management, it is necessary for businesses to forecast the future price of a product or service with deep learning supported solutions [10,24].

We perform data collection, data preprocessing, data processing, data analysis, and analysis result evaluation within the scope of this research to meet the forecasting requirement. A prototype application developed runs to demonstrate the performance of the proposed approach with different settings. This application includes experiments based on 158 days with price data from three different airline companies in Turkey. The results obtained from the methodology proposed within the scope of this study show that deep feature extraction with the LSTM autoencoder and technical indicators effectively reduces the forecasting loss in B2C markets. These results obtained confirm the proposed methodology.

Other parts of the article have been arranged as follows. Firstly, in Sect. 2, the requirements to start the study and the research questions arising from these requirements are introduced. Section 3 includes a literature review where related works are discussed. The methodology we propose for answering research questions is introduced in Sect. 4. The details of the data set used, the details of the experimental design, and the experimental results are included in Sect. 5, while the technical information about the prototype application is presented in Sect. 6. In the 7th Section, the answers given in the article to the research questions of the experimental study are presented collectively. Finally, in Sect. 8, some results are reported, and directions for future works are given.

2   Research Questions

Forecasting the future price of a product or service in B2C markets is very important, especially in sectors such as tourism, where demand forecasting is strategically vital for organizations. After the price data obtained, their noise should be removed by preprocessing studies. Technical indicators calculated used to forecast prices in stock markets of similar interest are useful auxiliary features for forecasting the price of a product in the future period. In addition to these features, the use of deep features that can be obtained from price data with deep learning methods for price forecasting in B2C markets can be beneficial for getting more accurate results. Therefore, the data should be prepared for processing by taking analytical methods and feature extraction methods as examples in similar studies. Finally, a deep learning model should be trained to create a price forecasting model, and then the trained model should be tested.

In line with these requirements, answers to the following research questions are sought in this study.

1. In B2C markets, can the historical price data and deep learning algorithms be used for forecasting the price of the next period of a product or service?
2. Which preprocessing methods can be used on price data?
3. Which deep learning methods can be used to extract features using price data?
4. Are technical indicators that can be calculated from price data useful in forecasting the next step ahead of price in B2C markets?

3   Literature Review

Discrete wavelet transform (DWT) method is used to transform a discrete time series signal into discrete meaningful components called wavelets that make up it [25]. It is frequently used as a preprocessing function to remove noise in the field of signal processing. A.J. Conejo et al. used the DWT method as a noise suppressor on electricity price data in their studies [26].

Autoencoder is an unsupervised deep learning approach used to learn domain data patterns and represent them with an artificial neural network model. The stacked autoencoder (SAE) is a derivative of autoencoders created by sequentially linking the encoded outputs. W. Bao et al. used stacked autoencoders on stock price data to reduce forecast loss [12]. L. Wang et al. used stacked autoencoders and their variants in short-term electricity price forecasting to reduce forecast loss [27]. The autoencoder and its derivative techniques improve the experimental performance in the studies by processing the domain data to make it more qualified.

Deep learning, a sub-branch of machine learning study area, learns by extracting high-level features using layers of artificial neural networks one or more times. Long short-term memory (LSTM) is a deep learning architecture with specialized recurrent neural networks (RNNs) for processing sequential data, thanks to feedback links [28]. J. Cao et al. got successful forecasting results using LSTM in their financial time series price data forecasting studies [29]. S. Bouktif et al. achieved successful forecasting results using LSTM in their study of electricity load forecasting using France metropolitan's electricity consumption data [30].

The common feature of these studies and our study, time series price data, shows that the DWT and autoencoder methods are useful in our research. Inspired by these studies, we use different autoencoder kinds in our study. In addition, the successful results obtained in the forecast of time series data in previous studies using LSTM show that the forecasting infrastructure in our study can be performed using LSTM.

4   Proposed Methodology

In tourism markets, since the service's sale is possible over the internet, it is possible to access price data from the sellers' reservation sites easily. Automatic web crawler scripts collect the data set used in this research on a daily basis by querying the price of the next day in the ticket sales system of three different airline companies. The collected data are included in the training of the LSTM forecaster model after passing through preprocessing, technical indicator calculation, DWT, and autoencoder, respectively, in the data processing workflow. The proposed data collection and processing workflow architecture is illustrated in Fig. 1.

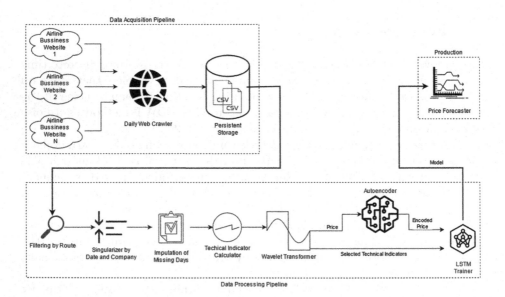

Fig. 1. Proposed data collection and processing architecture.

4.1 Daily Web Crawling

The company website where the reservation can be made online supplies the final price determined for the customer's purchase. However, during the data collection phase, this job should be done automatically on a daily basis, specific to the designated departure and landing locations and for the next day. It is very practical to use web crawlers to automate this job. The data collected, stored daily in comma-separated files (CSV), includes the cities of departure and landing airports, ticket prices, and date information.

4.2 Preprocessing

Collected data is read batch-wise from files and pass through some preprocessing steps. The first step in preprocessing is to filter the batch data based on their departure and landing location. Then, the collected data are averaged according to the date and company criteria to ensure that they are singularized from the date and the airline company criteria. In this way, only one price record per day remains from each company. Preprocessing continues with the imputation of the missing days, if any, by an average of the same day of the previous and next week and creating the daily price index. The daily price index creation process is the sum of the average ticket price of all companies on that day. Since our study is similar to the various previous studies about using price data, we apply the discrete wavelet transform to the tourism price data at the last step of the preprocessing.

4.3 Technical Indicator Calculation

It is possible to calculate some well-known technical indicators using the price index data introduced in the preprocessing section. We accept the index price we calculated as the close price for that day and using this close price, the technical indicators whose abbreviations are given in Table 1 are calculated. Please note that only the close price is used to calculate these technical indicators.

Table 1. Abbreviations of technical indicators used.

Indicator name	Description
MACD	Moving Average Convergence Divergence
BOLL	Bollinger Bands index
EMA20	Exponential Moving Average for 20 days
MA5	Moving Average for 5 days
MA10	Moving Average for 10 days
ROC	Rate of Change

4.4   Discrete Wavelet Transform

Discrete wavelet transform smooths out the outliers in the time-dependent price data and reduces the data's noise. S. Mallat proposed the wavelet representation method to decompose a multilevel signal of content at a specific resolution [31]. In this method, discrete approximations considered to belong to the main signal are calculated by passing through low pass and high pass filters. The low pass filter gives the low-frequency component (ϕ), the high pass filter gives the high-frequency component (ψ). Equation (1) and (2) formulate decomposed mother and father wavelets at the J level [32]. Generally, the father wavelet refers to a low-frequency component or approximate coefficients, and also the main wavelet refers to high-frequency components or detailed coefficients.

$$\phi_{j,k} = 2^{-j/2}\phi(\frac{t - 2^j k}{2^j}), \quad \psi_{j,k} = 2^{-j/2}\psi(\frac{t - 2^j k}{2^j}) \tag{1}$$

$$\int \phi(t)dt = 1, \quad \int \psi(t)dt = 0 \tag{2}$$

A time dependent $f(t)$ function is defined and projected onto low-frequency and high-frequency wavelets, as in Eq. (3).

$$s_{J,k} = \int \phi_{J,k}(t)f(t)dt, \quad d_{j,k} = \int \psi_{j,k}(t)f(t)dt$$
$$where \; j = \{1, 2, ..., J\}, \quad s = 2^j, \quad k = \{1, 2, ...\} \tag{3}$$

The sequence $\{S_j, D_j, D_{j-1}, ..., D_1\}$, which stands for $f(t)$, which is the sum of approximate coefficients (S_j) and detailed coefficients (D_j), is expressed as in Eq. (4).

$$f(t) = \sum_k s_{J,k}\phi_{J,k}(t) + \sum_k d_{J,k}\psi_{J,k}(t) + \sum_k d_{J-1,k}\psi_{J-1,k}(t) + ... + \sum_k d_{1,k}\psi_{1,k}(t) \tag{4}$$

Finally, with the resulting equation $f(t)$, wavelet transform is applied on time series data.

4.5   Autoencoder

Machine learning algorithms are classified as supervised and unsupervised. While unsupervised algorithms do not need labels while working, supervised algorithms work with ground truth and increase model performance in this way. Deep learning architectures are learning structures obtained by connecting different types of layers one after another in various numbers and shapes. Autoencoders are unsupervised deep learning architectures typically used to extract features or remove noise by learning domain data. An example autoencoder constructed with an encoder and a decoder is illustrated in Fig. 2.

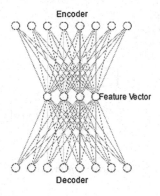

Fig. 2. An example autoencoder consists of an encoder and a decoder layer.

Autoencoder architectures vary depending on the problem and the data they are used. Autoencoder in different architectures is used in the feature extraction of price data in different markets. W. Bao et al. used the stacked autoencoder architecture to reduce the noise in the data in their study of estimating financial time series [12]. In the study, the stacked autoencoder removed the noise of the time series data and extracted the deep features. This study shows that the data in time series format is feature engineered by a stacked autoencoder built with feed-forward linear layers. The stacked autoencoder for the study is illustrated in Fig. 3.

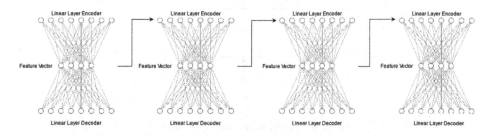

Fig. 3. A stacked autoencoder consists of 4 feed-forward linear autoencoders.

LSTM is an excellent feature extractor for time series data. In the literature, we see that this type of autoencoder is often used for the machine translation problem; however, there is a lack of its use with time series price data. We propose the sequence-to-sequence method formed by LSTM units as a feature extractor and noise suppressor. Note, LSTM is frequently used with time series data as a forecaster. The autoencoder we recommend is illustrated in Fig. 4.

From RNN to LSTM. Recurrent neural networks, unlike feed-forward networks, contain memory cells that hold the state information corresponding to

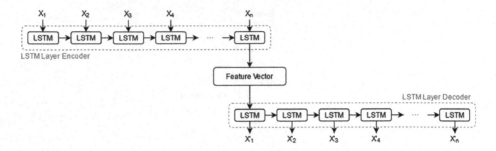

Fig. 4. An LSTM autoencoder with unrolled units.

the previous iteration. In addition to input data, state information is provided as input to the cell, providing a loop within the network. The architecture of an RNN cell is illustrated in Fig. 5. x_t in the figure represents the input vector at time t; s_t and s_{t-1} represents the state vector calculated from the input vector at t and $t-1$; W and U expressions express the weights of the input vector. The formula s_t is given in Eq. (5). The activation function f, which is used to limit the output to a certain range; there may be special functions such as tanh, sigmoid, ReLu [33].

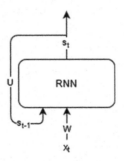

Fig. 5. Architecture of RNN unit.

$$s_t = f(Wx_t + Us_{t-1}) \tag{5}$$

LSTM is a special variant of RNN that solved the vanishing gradient problem. An LSTM unit contains the RNN memory as well as the input gate that controls the update of the cell state, the output gate that controls the value to be sent to the next cell, and the forget gate that checks the previous state of the cell in the cell [28,33]. The architecture of an LSTM cell is shown in Fig. 6.

The f_t, g_t, q_t expressions given in Eq. (6) indicate the values for the forget gate, input gate, and output gate, respectively. X_t is the input vector at time t; h_{t-1} is the output vector at time $t-1$; The U and W vectors represent the

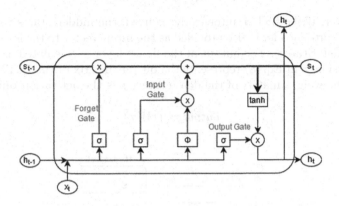

Fig. 6. Architecture of an LSTM unit.

input and recurring weights held for the respective gate. The activation function σ is the sigmoid function that returns the output between 0 and 1.

$$f_t = \sigma(U_f X_t + W_f h_{t-1}),$$
$$g_t = \sigma(U_g X_t + W_g h_{t-1}),$$
$$q_t = \sigma(U_o X_t + W_o h_{t-1}) \tag{6}$$

The expression s_t given in Eq. (7) gives the state value for the LSTM cell; The expression h_t refers to the output vector at the time t. U and W vectors are input and recurring weights retained for the LSTM cell; ϕ represents the input activation function (usually sigmoid or tanh) [28,33].

$$s_t = f_t s_{t-1} + g_t \phi(U X_t + W h_{t-1}),$$
$$h_t = tanh(s_t) q_t \tag{7}$$

4.6   LSTM Forecaster

In general, our problem is regression-based as we try to forecast the next day's ticket sale price. The autoencoder section explains how the autoencoder extracts deep features of the price data in a period. We use the LSTM forecaster to forecast the next day's price using deep encoded features and calculated technical indicators.

An LSTM forecaster usually consists of a layer containing a certain number of LSTM units and a dense layer that will produce the result attached to it; this architecture is shown in Fig. 7. The matrix used as inputs to the LSTM forecaster is the windowed data, which data can be raw or obtained from an autoencoder's encoder layer. If the LSTM autoencoder is used, the hidden states vector of the units of the autoencoder is also provided as the input vector to the forecaster (See Fig. 7: Hidden States). The output of the dense layer is calculated as in Eq. (8). The expression x in Eq. (8) represents the output matrix of the LSTM layer; W indicates the weight matrix of the dense layer; f is the activation function.

$$output = f(Wx) \tag{8}$$

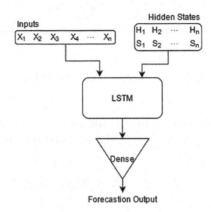

Fig. 7. An LSTM forecaster takes the windowed input matrix and the extra hidden states matrix as inputs.

5   Evaluation

This section shares the details of the data set used, the design of the experimental setup, and the experimental results.

5.1   Data Set

Web crawlers collect the training and test data set daily for domestic flight ticket prices in TRY currency between 27.07.2020 and 31.12.2020 (158 days). We filter the route as flights from the most populous city of Turkey, Istanbul, to Ankara, capital of Turkey and the second-most populous city. The route has a total of 4544 flight records from Istanbul to Ankara. Since the daily price index is created for the route after preprocessing, the data set is reduced to a total of 158 records.

5.2   Experimental Design

We set up two different experimental setups to answer research questions. The first experiment compares the performance of wavelet transform and autoencoders. The second experiment measures the contribution of the calculated technical indicators. Daubechies (db4) wavelet transform function is applied with 1 level decomposition to the data in preprocessing phase. Window size for all experiments is determined as five days by trial and error. In all experiments, the sigmoid function is used as the activation function, and Adam, a special stochastic gradient descent (SGD) function, is used as the optimizer. The LSTM forecaster layer is the same for all experiments. The LSTM layer contains 100 hidden units and then connects to the dense layer to produce the forecasting result. The first 67% portion (105 days) of the 158 days data is used for training and the last 33% portion (53 days) for the test.

In the first experiment, using and not using the wavelet transform run as separate configurations. There are four different configurations for the autoencoder; single layer linear autoencoder (Single AE), stacked linear autoencoder (SAE), LSTM autoencoder (LSTM AE), and forecasting without autoencoder. Thus, the first experiment results in eight different combinations. The SAE is obtained by connecting four consecutive single layer linear autoencoders.

The second experiment investigates which of the calculated technical indicators are appropriate to use together with the price data. All subsets of technical indicators run as separate configurations to determine the technical indicators that will provide the best benefit when used with price data. The second experiment produces a possible result of $2^6 = 64$, considering six different technical indicators and one fixed feature. Since we search the technical indicators that will provide the most benefit in our study, we share the best result of the group with n and the technical indicators belonging to the group.

The encoded feature vector size of single layer, stacked, and LSTM autoencoders is determined as 16 by trial and error.

Performance Metric. The performances of the implemented forecaster models are measured in terms of root mean square error (RMSE) and mean absolute error (MAE) metric, which are frequently used in regression problems.

5.3   Experimental Results

In the configurations introduced in the experimental design section, measurements are made with test data according to the metrics specified in the performance metric subsection.

In the first experiment, the LSTM autoencoder performed better than other autoencoders in the RMSE metric, and it seems beneficial to apply DWT regardless of the autoencoder used. Evaluation results of the Experiment 1 are presented in Table 2.

The second experiment shows that the most successful model is generated according to the RMSE metric when the technical indicators MACD, BOLL, MA5, MA10 are used in the group of 5 combinations. It is possible to make a similar observation in the MAE metric. The striking point here is observed when the second most successful model is examined. The second most successful model is created using the EMA20 and ROC technical indicators, which are the complete exclusions of the indicators used in the most successful model.

Table 2. Evaluation results of Experiment 1.

	RMSE		MAE	
	With DWT	Without DWT	With DWT	Without DWT
LSTM AE	0.0769	0.1285	0.0596	0.1032
SAE	0.0880	0.1191	0.0631	0.0916
Single AE	0.0815	0.1204	0.0586	0.0839
No AE	0.0782	0.1242	0.0566	0.0853

Table 3. LSTM AE encoded evaluation results of Experiment 2.

Feature count	RMSE		MAE	
	Features	Loss Value	Features	Loss Value
1	[close]	0.0769	[close]	0.0596
2	[close,roc]	0.0734	[close,ma10]	0.0562
3	[close,ema20,roc]	0.0698	[close,ema20,roc]	0.0521
4	[close,macd,boll,ema20]	0.0716	[close,ema20,ma10,roc]	0.0539
5	[close,macd,boll,ma5,ma10]	0.0684	[close,macd,boll,ma5,ma10]	0.0522
6	[close,macd,boll,ema20,ma5,ma10]	0.0756	[close,macd,boll,ema20,ma5,ma10]	0.0553
7	[close,macd,boll,ema20,ma5,ma10,roc]	0.0797	[close,macd,boll,ema20,ma5,ma10,roc]	0.0553

Hence, it is possible to say that the use of technical indicators achieves the highest benefit when divided into two groups. The first group consists of MACD, BOLL, MA5, and MA10 indicators, while the second group consists of EMA20 and ROC indicators; of course, the close price is included in both groups. Evaluation results of the Experiment 2 are presented in Table 3.

6   Prototype Application

The web crawler application used to collect data runs with Python 3.8.5 using the Scrapy 2.3 package. Web crawler application collects ticket prices, together with search keys and date information, from the online ticket search portal for Pegasus, Turkish Airlines, and Atlas Jet companies. The departure and landing cities are used as the search key, and the day after the web crawler is running, as the departure date.

The data processing application is implemented in Ubuntu 16.04 operating system and Python 3.6.9 using the Keras 2.4.3 application infrastructure with TensorFlow 2.2.

The system used works with "Intel (R) Xeon (R) Gold 6138 CPU @ 2.00 GHz" processor, 504 GB memory, and 4 * "Tesla V100-SXM2-16GB" graphics processors.

7   Experimental Study

This section gives the answers to the questions in the research questions section with the literature review results and the proposed methodology implementation's results.

Similar studies in the literature review section confirm that deep learning can make price forecasting to next step ahead on time series data of a product or service. Since the answer to the first research question is positive, studies are continued, and answers to other questions are sought.

The second research question, the selection of the preprocessing method, is introduced in the proposed methodology section, and its effect on the result is presented in the experimental results section. Accordingly, the positive contribution of the DWT, which is the preprocessing method for removing the noise and smoothing in the data, is shown in the experimental results section.

The third research question, in which deep learning methods can be used for feature extraction of price data, is answered as linear, stacked linear, and LSTM autoencoders. We show their performances comparatively in the experimental results section.

The answer to the last question, which is investigating the benefit of technical indicators in B2C markets, is presented in the experimental results section with the comparison table made with the subsets of all technical indicators. It is beneficial to use subsets of technical indicators for price forecasting in B2C markets.

Please note that the validity of the proposed techniques and all results obtained depends on the data. Different implementations or different data may produce different results.

8   Conclusion and Future Work

Forecasting the next step ahead of price in different kinds of markets is being more critical. It is strategically important to forecast the next price in B2C markets dominated by competitive service providers, as well as in C2C markets where consumer transactions are determinant. Eventually, various preprocessing steps should be applied, and the domain data features should be extracted to reduce the forecasting error. The problem of extracting deep and calculated features and using them with different combinations at different stages to minimize the forecasting error is always open to improvement.

We investigate the benefits of the DWT preprocessing method and the use of calculated technical indicators in B2C markets. We also test the effect of the LSTM autoencoder in the feature extraction phase on the time series price data. Our benchmarking results for forecasting airfare prices in the B2C market show that applying DWT in preprocessing, and using a subset of technical indicators, and using LSTM autoencoder for feature extraction succeed the forecaster to better results than not applying DWT, or not using technical indicators, or using other autoencoder types. The best model is obtained using moving average convergence divergence, Bollinger bands, moving average in 5 and 10 days technical indicators.

In future studies, by extracting price types such as open, high, and low from the raw data, various technical indicators to be calculated can be added to the process. In addition, different feature extractors such as convolutional neural network (CNN) can be used. Finally, even the feature extraction phase can be done using candlestick charts created by new price types extracted.

Acknowledgments. This study is carried out using the data center and web crawler facilities of Cloud Computing and Big Data Research Laboratory (B3LAB) of TÜBİTAK BİLGEM.

References

1. He, P., Zhang, S., He, C.: Impacts of logistics resource sharing on b2c e-commerce companies and customers. Electron. Commer. Res. Appl. **34**, 100820 (2019). https://doi.org/10.1016/j.elerap.2018.100820. https://www.sciencedirect.com/science/article/pii/S1567422318300863
2. 2020 yılı İlk 6 ay e-ticaret verileri açklandı (2020). https://www.eticaret.gov.tr/haberler/10040/detay
3. e-ticaret platformlarında 65 yaş üstü kullanıcı oranı yüzde 6'dan yüzde 10'a çıktı (2021). https://www.aa.com.tr/tr/ekonomi/e-ticaret-platformlarinda-65-yas-ustu-kullanici-orani-yuzde-6dan-yuzde-10a-cikti/2182333
4. Zhao, K., Wang, C.: Sales forecast in e-commerce using convolutional neural network (2017)
5. Hsieh, P.-H.: A study of models for forecasting e-commerce sales during a price war in the medical product industry. In: Nah, F.F.-H., Siau, K. (eds.) HCII 2019. LNCS, vol. 11588, pp. 3–21. Springer, Cham (2019). https://doi.org/10.1007/978-3-030-22335-9_1
6. Yan, R., Ghose, S.: Forecast information and traditional retailer performance in a dual-channel competitive market. J. Bus. Res. **63**(1), 77–83 (2010). https://doi.org/10.1016/j.jbusres.2009.02.017. https://www.sciencedirect.com/science/article/pii/S0148296309000460
7. Bandara, K., Shi, P., Bergmeir, C., Hewamalage, H., Tran, Q., Seaman, B.: Sales demand forecast in e-commerce using a long short-term memory neural network methodology. In: Gedeon, T., Wong, K.W., Lee, M. (eds.) ICONIP 2019. LNCS, vol. 11955, pp. 462–474. Springer, Cham (2019). https://doi.org/10.1007/978-3-030-36718-3_39
8. Gürbüz, A., Aktaş, M.S.: Prediction of purchase intention on the e-commerce clickstream data. In: 2019 27th Signal Processing and Communications Applications Conference (SIU), pp. 1–4 (2019). https://doi.org/10.1109/SIU.2019.8806311
9. Fronzetti Colladon, A., Guardabascio, B., Innarella, R.: Using social network and semantic analysis to analyze online travel forums and forecast tourism demand. Decis. Supp. Syst. **123**, 113075 (2019). https://doi.org/10.1016/j.dss.2019.113075. https://www.sciencedirect.com/science/article/pii/S0167923619301046

10. Law, R., Li, G., Fong, D.K.C., Han, X.: Tourism demand forecasting: a deep learning approach. Ann. Tour. Res. **75**, 410–423 (2019). https://doi.org/10.1016/j.annals.2019.01.014, https://www.sciencedirect.com/science/article/pii/S0160738319300143

11. Tseng, K.K., Lin, R.F.Y., Zhou, H., Kurniajaya, K.J., Li, Q.: Price prediction of e-commerce products through internet sentiment analysis. Electron. Commer. Res. **18**(1), 65–88 (2018). https://doi.org/10.1007/s10660-017-9272-9

12. Bao, W., Yue, J., Rao, Y.: A deep learning framework for financial time series using stacked autoencoders and long-short term memory. PloS ONE **12**(7), e0180944 (2017)

13. Aktas, M., Astekin, M.: Provenance aware run-time verification of things for self-healing internet of things applications. Concurr. Comput. Pract. Exp. (2019). https://doi.org/10.1002/cpe.4263

14. Tufek, A., Aktas, M.S.: On the provenance extraction techniques from large scale log files: a case study for the numerical weather prediction models. In: Balis, B., et al. (eds.) Euro-Par 2020. LNCS, vol. 12480, pp. 249–260. Springer, Cham (2021). https://doi.org/10.1007/978-3-030-71593-9_20

15. Tas, Y., Baeth, M., Aktas, M.: An approach to standalone provenance systems for big social provenance data. In: 2016 12th International Conference on Semantics, Knowledge and Grids (SKG), pp. 9–16 (2016)

16. Riveni, M., Nguyen, T., Aktas, M., Dustdar, S.: Application of provenance in social computing: a case study. Concurr. Comput.: Pract. Exp. **31**(3), e4894 (2019)

17. Baeth, M., Aktas, M.: An approach to custom privacy policy violation detection problems using big social provenance data. Concurr. Comput.: Pract. Exp. **30**(21), e4690 (2018)

18. Baeth, M., Aktas, M.: Detecting misinformation in social networks using provenance data. Concurr. Comput.: Pract. Exp. **31**(3), e4793 (2019)

19. Jensen, S., Plale, B., Aktas, M., Luo, Y., Chen, P., Conover, H.: Provenance capture and use in a satellite data processing pipeline. IEEE Trans. Geosci. Remote Sens. **51**(11), 5090–5097 (2013). https://doi.org/10.1109/TGRS.2013.2266929

20. Tufek, A., Gurbuz, A., Ekuklu, O.F., Aktas, M.S.: Provenance collection platform for the weather research and forecasting model. In: 2018 14th International Conference on Semantics, Knowledge and Grids (SKG), SKG '18, 14th International Conference on Semantics, Knowledge and Grids (SKG), Guangzhou, China, IEEE, pp. 17–24 (2018). https://doi.org/10.1109/SKG.2018.00009

21. Yazıcı, I., Karabulut, E., Aktas, M.: A data provenance visualization approach. In: The 14th International Conference on Semantics, Knowledge and Grids (2018)

22. Uygun, Y., Oguz, R., Olmezogullari, E., Aktas, M.: On the large-scale graph data processing for user interface testing in big data science projects. In: IEEE BigData 2020, pp. 2049–2056. IEEE (2020)

23. Olmezogullari, E., Aktas, M.: Representation of click-stream data sequences for learning user navigational behavior by using embeddings. In: In: IEEE BigData 2020, pp. 3173–3179. IEEE (2020)

24. Li, Y., Cao, H.: Prediction for tourism flow based on LSTM neural network. Procedia Comput. Sci. **129**, 277–283 (2018)

25. Chaovalit, P., Gangopadhyay, A., Karabatis, G., Chen, Z.: Discrete wavelet transform-based time series analysis and mining. ACM Comput. Surv. **43**(2), 1–37 (2011). https://doi.org/10.1145/1883612.1883613

26. Conejo, A.J., Plazas, M.A., Espinola, R., Molina, A.B.: Day-ahead electricity price forecasting using the wavelet transform and arima models. IEEE Trans. Power Syst. **20**(2), 1035–1042 (2005). https://doi.org/10.1109/TPWRS.2005.846054

27. Wang, L., Zhang, Z., Chen, J.: Short-term electricity price forecasting with stacked denoising autoencoders. IEEE Trans. Power Syst. **32**(4), 2673–2681 (2017). https://doi.org/10.1109/TPWRS.2016.2628873
28. Goodfellow, I., Bengio, Y., Courville, A., Bengio, Y.: Deep Learning, vol. 1. MIT Press, Cambridge (2016)
29. Cao, J., Li, Z., Li, J.: Financial time series forecasting model based on CEEMDAN and LSTM. Physica A **519**, 127–139 (2019)
30. Bouktif, S., Fiaz, A., Ouni, A., Serhani, M.A.: Optimal deep learning LSTM model for electric load forecasting using feature selection and genetic algorithm: comparison with machine learning approaches. Energies **11**(7), 1636 (2018)
31. Mallat, S.G.: A theory for multiresolution signal decomposition: the wavelet representation. IEEE Trans. Pattern Anal. Mach. Intell. **11**(7), 674–693 (1989)
32. Ramsey, J.B., Lampart, C.: The decomposition of economic relationships by time scale using wavelets: expenditure and income. Stud. Nonlinear Dyn. Econ. **3**(1) (1998)
33. Chollet, F., et al.: Deep Learning with Python, vol. 361. Manning, New York (2018)

Modeling and Verification of Contactless Mobile Banking System in E-Banking Using SPIN

Tej Narayan Thakur[✉] ⓘ and Noriaki Yoshiura ⓘ

Department of Information and Computer Sciences, Saitama
University, Saitama 338-8570, Japan
yoshiura@fmx.ics.saitama-u.ac.jp

Abstract. During this prevailing generation of the digital world, mobile users are multiplying globally by leaps and bounds. A mobile banking system is an electronic channel for Electronic Banking (E-Banking) all over the world. The utility of mobile banking systems has become one of the innovations to transform financial institutions from the traditional to the digital world with all the banking services. However, financial institutions do not provide enhanced banking services and electronic cheques using the mobile banking system globally. This paper proposes a new contactless mobile banking system (C-MBS) that integrates enhanced banking services with novel functions like electronic cheques, registration of the user, and cancellation of the user account included in the model. This paper develops an extended finite state machine model with parameters, variables, and constraints for C-MBS. This paper also develops a verification model of C-MBS with system properties specified utilizing process meta language (PROMELA) and security properties applying linear temporal logic (LTL). A simple promela interpreter (SPIN) is employed to verify the verification model of C-MBS. SPIN verification results confirm that the proposed C-MBS model is free from deadlocks and errors. Hence, the financial institutions can implement this model as a secure enhanced mobile banking system in E-banking. Banking users can use the enhanced banking services remotely using C-MBS on mobile and will play a significant role towards a cashless society in the digital world.

Keywords: Mobile banking system · Security · Temporal logic · SPIN · Verification

1 Introduction

Electronic Banking (E-banking) provides banking services and products through electronic channels such as mobile banking systems, Internet banking systems, ATM, telephone banking systems, etc. E-banking has many advantages along with real-time and all-time access and has been expanding globally. There are many channels for using E-banking, and the mobile banking system is becoming the most-used channel for the utilization of E-banking. Banking users do log in into the online banking (Internet banking) using the internet to get the banking services. Similarly, banking users download bank applications on their mobile and log in into the mobile banking system using the app

© Springer Nature Switzerland AG 2021
O. Gervasi et al. (Eds.): ICCSA 2021, LNCS 12954, pp. 581–597, 2021.
https://doi.org/10.1007/978-3-030-86979-3_41

to get the banking services. During this prevailing generation of the digital world, mobile users are multiplying globally by leaps and bounds. The use of mobile banking systems has become one of the innovations to transform financial institutions from traditional to the digital world with required banking services. A global pandemic (COVID-19) has created a very difficult situation, and customers would like to access all of the banking services remotely. Banking customers use mobile banking systems just for balance inquiry, mobile recharge, utility payment (such as electricity bill payment, water bill payment, etc.), small amount fund transfer in many countries. The mobile banking system is still not utilized for providing enhanced banking services (such as fund transfer, third-party payment, lending, etc.) globally. Banking customers do not use the mobile banking system because of not having enhanced banking services and security problems.

Digital 2021 global overview report [30] shows that there are approximately 5.22 billion unique mobile phone users among 7.83 billion population globally, but mobile banking users in 2019 is 1.8 billion only (Juniper research report 2020). It is a well-known fact that the number of banking customers is large, and the number of mobile banking users is low in many countries. Therefore, there is a need for complete automation and a secure mobile banking system to increase mobile banking users in E-banking.

Some research in E-banking is modeling and verification of payment systems [1], retail banking system [2], and Internet payment system [3]. The authors of [1] presented modeling and verification of Automated Teller Machine (ATM) for the interbank payment system. The authors of [2] accomplished modeling and verification of a retail banking system. Zhang, Ma, Shi, and Zhu [3] employed the model checking method to verify the security and reliability of Internet payment systems. The authors of [4] focused on modeling and verification of a new mobile payment system. Shaikh, And, and Devane [5] focused on modeling and verification of payment protocol, and the authors of [6] emphasized modeling and verification of extensible authentication protocol. Ciurea [7] developed a model of mobile application in a collaborative banking system. Aithal [8] compared a mobile banking with an ideal banking system. Bojjagani and Sastry [9] proposed a mobile banking model with an end-to-end SMS-based application system. Anwarul Islam and Salma [10] developed a model of mobile banking for banking facilities to rural people. However, the authors have not incorporated enhanced banking services in [7–10], and users have limited banking operations facilities in the proposed model of the mobile banking system. The authors of [11] performed a review of enhancements in the mobile payment system, Istrate [12] developed a cardless withdrawal system for the mobile banking system, and the authors of [13] developed a model for the mobile banking payment system. The authors of [14] developed a model for an Internet banking system, and Uddin and Akhi [15] developed a model for an electronic payment system. The developed mobile banking models [11–15] do not include all of the enhanced banking services for the end-users.

The authors presented security challenges for mobile banking systems [16], vulnerabilities in E-banking [17], enhanced security model for the mobile banking system in Tanzania [18], and a case study of Croatian banks using biometrics in the mobile banking system [19]. The authors of [20, 21] focused on practices, challenges, and security issues of the mobile banking system in India. The authors of [22–25] studied technology adoptions for the mobile banking system, and [26, 27] reviewed user satisfaction using the mobile banking system. The authors of [28] emphasized the blockchain based electronic cheque (e-cheque) clearance framework that allows the drawer to download the e-cheque as a valid e-cheque. The authors of [29] used a third party for the trust in e-cheque in the electronic payment system. However, the proposed e-cheque is not secure because the e-cheques are available in pdf form and the risk increases when the banking user downloads the pdf and uploads the pdf using the online banking system.

Some of the earlier researchers have developed models for ATM [1], retail banking system [2], and Internet payment system [3]. Some researchers have developed different models for mobile banking systems [7–15]. Some researchers have emphasized security issues [16–21] on the model of the mobile banking system. However, the adoptions for mobile banking system [22–25] and user's satisfaction using mobile banking system [26, 27] show that there is still a need for improvement in the model of the mobile banking system. Banking users download the e-cheque in pdf manually and upload the pdf [28, 29] using the online banking system. However, cybercriminals impersonate different attacks during the download and upload of the e-cheque in the online banking system. Unfortunately, earlier researchers have not incorporated the enhanced banking services and have not included automatic e-cheque in the proposed model of the mobile banking system. To overcome this gap, the paper proposes a new contactless mobile banking system (C-MBS) that consists of enhanced banking functionalities and a novel concept of a secure mobile banking based e-cheque system for banking operations.

C-MBS consists of the following modules for managing the users and providing banking services using the mobile banking system.

- Registration
- Fund transfer
- Third-party payment
- Digital lending
- e-cheque issuing
- e-cheque clearing
- Cancellation

This research aims to build an enhanced mobile banking system in which banking customers can request for registration in the mobile banking system and can use the enhanced banking services using C-MBS. C-MBS can cancel the users based on the passiveness of the users in the mobile banking system. The proposed system is developed to be considered by the banks. The system behaviors of the model are specified in a process meta language (PROMELA) and security properties are specified using linear temporal logic (LTL). This paper uses SPIN to formally verify the proposed C-MBS model of the mobile banking system. The rest of the paper is further structured as follows: Sect. 2 describes the related works. Section 3 describes the new model of a contactless mobile banking system, Sect. 4 presents the results and discussion, and Sect. 5 describes conclusions and future work.

2 Related Work

The utility of E-Banking has been expanding for digital payment in the financial world, and researchers have been working to provide better solutions for secured enhanced functionalities in E-Banking. Researchers have focused on the modeling and verification of ATM, retail banking system, Internet banking system, etc. in E-banking. Authors of [1–3] presented the modeling and verification of electronic channels in E-banking. Obaid, Kazmi, and Qasim [1] presented modeling and verification of 1-link Automated Teller Machine (ATM) for the interbank payment system. Transactional properties of 1-link ATM are specified and verified using SPIN, but security properties are not specified and verified in the system to minimize the attacks in the E-banking system. The paper recommended the mobile banking system for future research. Shi, Ma, Yang, and Zhang [2] accomplished model checking and verification of the retail banking system through an ATM using SPIN and recommended the mobile banking system as future research. Zhang, Ma, Shi, and Zhu [3] employed the model checking method to verify the security and reliability of Internet payment systems. Ahamad, Udgata, and Sastry [4] proposed formal verification of a novel payment instrument in the name of mobile traveler's check (MTC) for mobile commerce applications. Shaikh, And, and Devane [5] focused on formal verification of payment protocol using AVISPA (automated validation of internet security protocols and applications), and Hegde, H K, and Singh [6] emphasized on modeling and verification of extensible authentication protocol using PROMELA and SPIN. Ciurea [7] presented a classification of mobile applications with an accent on collaborative mobile applications. Aithal [8] compared a model of the mobile banking system with an ideal banking system that can have significant performance in specified conditions. Bojjagani and Sastry [9] proposed a model to address the security of SMS (Short Message Service) using elliptic curve cryptography and the proposed model provides end-to-end SMS communication for the banking users. Anwarul Islam and Salma [10] described mobile banking operations and banking facilities to rural people in Bangladesh.

Dahlberg, Guo, and Ondrus [11] reviewed enhancements in mobile payment research after a previous literature review (Dahlberg et al. 2008b) and pointed out that the researchers have continued to focus on the same topics for mobile payment systems. Istrate [12] developed a model of a cardless withdrawal system for mobile banking applications for payments and money transfer. Yang, Liu, and Chiu [13] developed a model for a mobile banking payment system in which customers use electronic money instead of cash. Alanazi, Alnaqeib, Hmood, Zaidan, and Nabhani [14] used unified modeling language (UML) diagrams and developed architectures for the Internet banking system. Uddin and Akhi [15] described a model of the E-wallet system as an electronic payment system to replace the existing physical wallet, with its notes, coins, plastic cards, ATM cards, and loyalty cards in Bangladesh.

Islam [16] reviewed the security challenges of mobile banking and payment system. Brar, Sharma, and Khurmi [17] studied various security aspects including vulnerabilities in E-banking. Nyamtiga, Sam, and Laizer [18] focused on an SMS-based enhanced security model with security features to enhance data protection across mobile networks for the mobile banking systems in Tanzania. Avdic [19] explained the use of biometrics in mobile banking security using a case study of Croatian banks. Gupta, Kumar, and

Bharadwaj [20] proposed a web-based application with all related information in a centralized database that provides a banking facility through which all payments can be done at a single place using a mobile banking system. Goyal, Pandey, and Batra [21] developed a classification framework for mobile banking research.

Alalwan, Dwivedi, and Rana [22] investigated the factors influencing behavioral intention and adoption of mobile banking by customers of Jordanian banks. The results showed that behavioral intention is significantly and positively influenced by performance expectancy, effort expectancy, hedonic motivation, price value, and trust. Al-Jabri and Sohail [23] investigated many factors that may help the bankers to design suitable mobile services that can be adoptable by banking customers in Saudi Arabia. Raja, Umer, and Shah [24] found the new determinants of ease of use for mobile banking adoption in Pakistan. Safeena, Date, Kammani, and Hundewale [25] determined the consumer's perspective on mobile banking adoption in India. Bharti [26] focused on the roadmap for the proper implementation and adoption of the mobile banking system for banking users. Asfour and Haddad [27] studied the mobile banking important dimensions such as reliability, flexibility, privacy, accessibility, ease of navigation, efficiency, safety, etc., and measured the impact of mobile banking on enhancing customer satisfaction in Jordan. Singh, Kumar, and Vardhan [28] proposed a blockchain based e-cheque clearance framework that allows the banking users to download the e-cheque and used it for upload as and when required or print the pdf version of the e-cheque. Yahid, Nobakht, and Shahbahrami [29] focused on the trust in e-cheque in electronic payments using a third party as a guarantor for the security of the e-cheque.

Our paper proposes a new contactless mobile banking system (C-MBS) with enhanced banking functionalities and a novel concept of a secure e-cheque for banking customers. Banks and financial institutions can implement this model for providing enhanced banking services and a secure e-cheque facility to the banking users using mobile for E-Banking globally.

3   Formal Modeling of C-MBS

The formal modeling methods provide a mechanism for eliminating problems in the early phases of the software development life cycle. There are different phases in the software development life cycle, and the software must be tested before the implementation in the real world. Software testing using test cases detects errors in the late phases of software development and costs more for fixing the errors. Model-checking and formal verification detects the bugs during the design phase of software development and helps in designing the bug-free system. The proposed model includes enhanced banking services along with e-cheque issuing and e-check clearing using the mobile banking system. Formal modeling of C-MBS consists of an extended finite state machine (EFSM) model and PROMELA model of C-MBS. Notations used in formal modeling of C-MBS are in Table 1.

Table 1. Notations used in formal modeling of C-MBS

Notation	Description	Notation	Description
reg	Registration	pmtAmt	Payment amount
par	Parameter	acBal	Account balance
usrOTP	One time password from user	crRat	Credit rating
mbsOTP	One time password from mobile banking system	minRat	Minimum rating
auth	Authentication	loanAmt	Loan amount
authoriz	Authorization	appLoanAmt	Approved loan amount
usrDOB	Date of birth from user	mbsDOB	Date of birth registered in mobile banking system
MBS	Mobile Banking System	CBS	Core Banking System

3.1 EFSM Model of C-MBS

In a conventional finite state machine (FSM), a transition is associated with a set of input boolean conditions and a set of output boolean functions. EFSM performs a state transition when a given set of conditions are satisfied. EFSM model provides a powerful model for the derivation of functional tests for software systems and protocols. EFSM model of C-MBS presents the complete life cycle of the mobile banking system including registration and cancellation of the banking users in C-MBS as in Fig. 1.

A banking user installs mobile banking applications on their mobile devices and requests for registration in C-MBS. C-MBS verifies the registration parameters such as mobile number, account number, date of birth (dob) etc. and sends OTP to the banking user. MBS verifies the OTP and registers the user in the C-MBS. The banking user requests authentication and access rights for authorization in the mobile banking system. After approval from the C-MBS, the banking user can log in into the C-MBS and perform the required banking operations using the C-MBS. Generally, banking users use the mobile banking system for statements, fund transfers, and third-party payments such as utility payment, merchant payment, QR (quick response) code payment, etc. in developing countries. The EFSM model introduces enhanced banking services such as digital lending, e-cheque issuing, and e-cheque clearing in the C-MBS that are not in practice in many countries. Banking users can request a loan using the C-MBS, and banks can approve the loan and credit in the customer account. Banking users do not have to visit the bank physically multiple times to get a loan from the bank.

There are limitations in the physical cheque, and therefore, it is necessary to switch from the physical cheque to an e-cheque in this era of digital banking. Banks manage digital certificates for the banking users for the security of the e-cheque. Banking users provide the cheque details such as payer name, account number, payee name, amount, date of payment, discount rate, etc. They sign the e-cheque digitally using a private key and request to issue the e-cheque using C-MBS as in Fig. 2. MBS sends the digitally signed e-cheque to the CBS for verification of the cheque. CBS verifies the digital

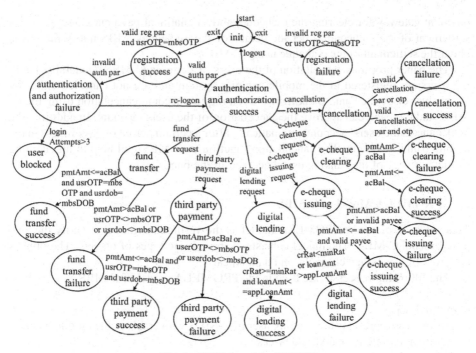

Fig. 1. EFSM model of C-MBS.

certificates and informs the MBS about the validity of the e-cheque. MBS notifies the payer about the issue of the e-check and sends it to the payee using the mobile banking system.

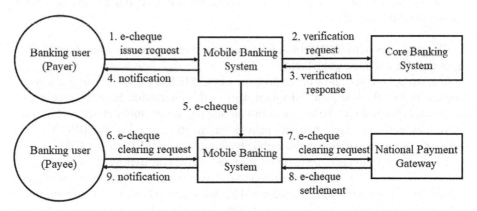

Fig. 2. e-cheque process using C-MBS

The payee does not need to download the e-cheque, and therefore, such an e-cheque mechanism is safer than the earlier pdf downloadable e-cheque. The payee request for clearing of the e-cheque using the mobile banking system. MBS requests a national payment gateway for clearing the e-cheque, and the national payment gateway makes settlement of the e-cheque as per the details of the e-cheques. MBS notify the payee about the settlement of the e-cheque using C-MBS.

The paper proposes cancellation of the users' account in C-MBS. Generally, banking users are registered in the mobile banking system and are not canceled either by themselves or by the bank. Banking users can request account cancelation using the C-MBS, and the bank can approve the cancellation of the users' account. In addition, the bank cancels the users' account automatically after a certain period of passiveness in the mobile banking system. The cancellation function in C-MBS will help in maintaining the data privacy of the banking users' account in the banks.

3.2 PROMELA Model of C-MBS

This paper develops the PROMELA model as the verification model to verify the proposed model C-MBS. The model consists of three basic types of objects. The objects are processes, message channels, and data types.

The following processes are used in the PROMELA model of C-MBS.

- mobileUser
  The process represents the banking user in C-MBS who employs the mobile banking system in mobile for banking services.
- mobileBankingSystem
  The process represents the mobile banking software which communicates with the banking users and the bank and offers banking services on their mobile.
- coreBankingSystem
  The process represents the banking application software with the bank.
- nationalPaymentGateway
  The process represents the private or government-owned centralized payment settlement system in the nation.

The processes in the PROMELA model communicate using message channels. This paper uses the channels as in Table 2.

The simple message flow of the processes in C-MBS is presented using a sequence diagram in Fig. 3. A sequence diagram depicts the interaction between processes in sequential order. It shows the flow of events among the agents (mobileUser, mobileBankingSystem, coreBankingSystem and nationalPaymentGateway) of C-MBS. A mobile user requests for registration in the mobile banking system (MBS) using C-MBS. MBS verifies the registration parameters of the user and verifies the user by sending a one-time password (OTP). After successful registration of the user, C-MBS provides interfaces to the user for the setting of authentication and authorization parameters. User requests for authentication in the system with received login credentials. MBS authenticates the users in the system after validating the authentication and authorization policies enforced for the user. MBS does not permit users to log in if they enter the wrong passwords more than three times.

Upon successful login in the MBS, the user can request for fund transfer with the required parameters. MBS forwards the request for fund transfer to the core banking

Table 2. Channel descriptions for C-MBS PROMELA model

Channel Name	Channel objective
mobileUser_mobileBankingSystem	Messages from mobileUser to mobileBankingSystem
mobileBankingSystem_mobileUser	Messages from mobileBankingSystem to mobileUser
mobileBankingSystem_ coreBankingSystem	Messages from mobileBankingSystem to coreBankingSystem
coreBankingSystem_mobileBankingSystem	Messages from coreBankingSystem to mobileBankingSystem
mobileBankingSystem_nationalPaymentGateway	Messages from mobileBankingSystem to nationalPaymentGateway
nationalPaymentGateway_mobileBankingSystem	Messages from nationalPaymentGateway to mobileBankingSystem

system (CBS). CBS approves the transaction if the transfer amount is less than or equal to the account balance and security parameters are verified. When the user requests third-party payment, MBS forwards the request to CBS and the national payment gateway. They check the constraints for the transaction and approves or disapproves of the transaction based on the parameters of the transaction. When the user requests MBS for digital lending, MBS forwards the request to CBS and grants the loan according to the credit rating of the customer. When user requests for an e-cheque issue to MBS, MBS forwards the request to CBS. CBS checks all the parameters required for e-cheque, issues e-cheque, and sends to the payee using a mobile banking system. Users do not need to download the e-cheque and just request for clearing of e-cheque using C-MBS. The settlement of the e-cheque payment is finalized by the national payment gateway.

4   Results and Discussion

This paper verifies the safety properties and temporal properties of C-MBS using SPIN for proper implementation of the model in the real world. We specified the following security properties using linear temporal logic (LTL) in the verification model of C-MBS.

LTL definition1 (LTL1)
[]((usrDob==mbsDob)&&(userMobileNo==mbsMobileNo)&&(userOTP==mbsOTP))
Authentication parameters such as dob, mobileNo and OTP received from mobile users must be the same as registered in the database of C-MBS during the system lifetime.

590   T. N. Thakur and N. Yoshiura

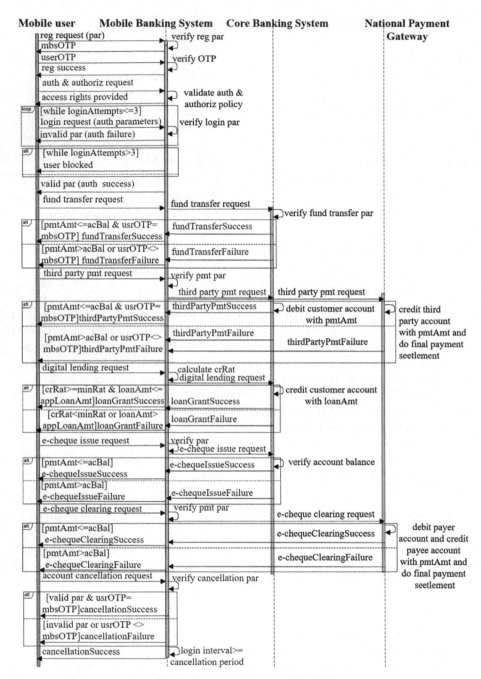

Fig. 3. Sequence diagram of C-MBS

LTL definition2 (LTL2)

[]((registrationSuccess==true)->(mobileUserDataVerification==true))

Registration of mobile users in C-MBS can be successful only when banking user data are valid.

LTL definition3 (LTL3)

[] ((userBlocked==true)->(loginSuccess==false))

Banking user login cannot be succeeded when the users are blocked in the system.

LTL definition4 (LTL4)

[] ((passwordExpired==true)->(loginSuccess==false))

If banking users' password become expired after certain allocated period of time, then user login cannot be succeeded in the system.

LTL definition5 (LTL5)

[]((IdExpired==true)->(loginSuccess==false))

Banking user login cannot be succeeded when the user's id is expired in the system.

LTL definition6 (LTL6)

[]((authenticationSuccess==true)->(registrationSuccess==true))

Authentication can be successful only if registration is also successful.

LTL definition7 (LTL7)

[]((authenticationSuccess==true)->(authorizationSuccess==true))

Authentication can be successful only if authorization is also successful.

LTL definition8 (LTL8)

[]((fundTransferSuccess==true)->(authenticationSuccess==true))

Fund transfer can be successful only if authentication of the user is also successful.

LTL definition9 (LTL9)

[]((fundTransferSuccess==true)->((loginSuccess==true)&&(authorizationSuccess==true)))

Fund transfer can be successful only if login is successful and authorization for the transaction is successful.

LTL definition10 (LTL10)

[]((((transferAmount>accountBalance)||(transferAmount>dailyLimit))->(fundTransferSuccess==false))

Fund transfer cannot be successful if either transfer amount is greater than the available account balance or transfer amount is greater than the daily limit set for the transaction.

LTLdefinition11 (LTL11)
[](((transferAmount>accountBalance)||(transferAmount>dailyLimit))->(thirdPartyPaymentSuccess==false))
Third party payment cannot be successful if either transfer amount is greater than the available account balance or transfer amount is greater than the daily limit set for the transaction.

LTLdefinition12 (LTL12)
[]((transferAmount>=0)&&(paymentAmount>=0)&&(accountBalance>=0))
Transfer amount, payment amount and account balance should always be greater than or equal to 0.

LTL definition13 (LTL13)
[](((creditRating>=minimumRating)&&(loanAmount<=approvedLoanAmount))->(digitalLendingSuccess==true))
Digital lending can be successful only if credit rating of the banking customer is equal to or above the minimum rating and loan amount is less than or equal to the approved loan amount.

LTL definition14 (LTL14)
[](((registrationSuccess==true)||(fundTransferSuccess==true))->(mbsOTP==userOTP))
Registration or fund transfer can be successful only if OTP sent from C-MBS to the user and received from the user to C-MBS remains the same.

LTL definition15 (LTL15)
[]((thirdPartyPaymentSuccess==true)->(nationalPaymentGatewayOnline==true))
Third party payment can be successful only if the national payment gateway is online.

LTL definition16 (LTL16)
[]((loginInterval>=userCancellationPeriod)->(cancellationSuccess==true))
Banking user's account cancellation from C-MBS can be successful if the login interval period is greater than or equal to the user account cancellation period set in the system.

LTL definition17 (LTL17)
[]((eChequePaymentSuccess==true)->(nationalPaymentGatewayOnline==true))
e-cheque payment can be successful only if the national payment gateway is online.

LTL definition18 (LTL18)
[]((fundTransferSuccess==true)->((authorizationSuccess==true)&&(mbsOTP==userOTP)))
Fund transfer can be successful only if authorization is successful and OTP sent from C-MBS to the user and received from the user to C-MBS remains the same.

LTL definition19 (LTL19)
[]((transferAmount<=accountBalance)&&(transferAmount<=dailyLimit))
The transfer amount must be always less than or equal to the account balance and less than or equal to the daily limit set for the transaction.

LTL definition20 (LTL20)
[](~(transferAmount<0)&&(~(accountBalance<0))&&(~(loanAmount
<0))&&(~(approvedLoanAmount<0))&&(~(paymentAmount
<0))&&(~(fromAccountBalance<0)))
Transfer amount, account balance, loan amount, approved loan amount, payment amount and account balance cannot be less than 0 during the system lifetime.

This paper verifies the safety properties and LTL properties of the proposed model C-MBS. We accomplished experiments using SPIN Version 6.4.9 running on a computer with the following specifications: Intel® Core(TM) i5–6500 CPU@3.20 GHz, RAM 16 GB, and windows10 64bit. We set advanced parameters in the SPIN environment for optimal results during the verification. We set physical memory available as 1024 (in Mbytes), maximum search depths (steps) as 100000, estimated state space size as 1000, search mode as depth-first search (partial order reduction), and storage mode as bitstate/supertrace for the verification.

Table 3. Verification results for safety properties

No. of users	Time (Seconds)	Memory (Mbytes)	Transitions	States stored	Depth	Verification status
1	4.99	6.772	12758522	612456	11659	Verified
3	7.51	7.846	12873553	616772	11469	Verified
5	10.2	11.264	13227429	620255	14375	Verified
10	57.7	16.315	13459389	619507	14106	Verified
20	108	24.136	13976019	620819	13048	Verified

After setting the parameters, we ran SPIN to verify the safety properties of C-MBS for up to 20 users. SPIN checked the state space for deadlocks and assertion violations during the verification of safety properties in C-MBS. The SPIN verification results for safety properties are in Table 3.

Table 3 shows the results obtained from SPIN demonstrating the elapsed time, total memory usage, number of states transitioned, states stored, depth reached, and verification status for safety properties for various users. The SPIN verification results show that there is an increase in the memory requirement and verification time with the increase in the number of users during the verification of the C-MBS model. The verification results show that there is no deadlocks or error in the design of the C-MBS model.

After that, we ran SPIN in the same computing environment to verify the LTL properties for 20 users. SPIN checked the statespace for never claim and assertion violations

Table 4. Verification results for LTL properties

LTL properties	Time (Seconds)	Memory (Mbytes)	Transitions	States stored	Depth	Verification status
LTL1	5.30	6.869	12780646	612189	20637	Verified
LTL2	5.35	6.869	12776991	612348	20504	Verified
LTL3	5.36	7.846	12728746	612790	27710	Verified
LTL4	5.28	7.553	12577602	612141	25968	Verified
LTL5	5.21	7.358	12412751	612309	24462	Verified
LTL6	5.23	8.139	12395190	612778	30396	Verified
LTL7	5.37	6.967	12780583	612409	21723	Verified
LTL8	5.39	8.334	12388721	612754	31557	Verified
LTL9	5.50	6.967	12725493	612239	21657	Verified
LTL10	5.12	9.409	12113245	611408	40379	Verified
LTL11	5.35	7.358	12792229	612491	24084	Verified
LTL12	5.34	7.455	12788075	612163	25109	Verified
LTL13	5.36	7.065	12673574	613144	21893	Verified
LTL14	5.27	8.041	12508195	611731	29198	Verified
LTL15	5.33	6.967	12680220	612835	21771	Verified
LTL16	5.36	6.967	12778965	612643	20976	Verified
LTL17	5.31	7.162	12679934	612184	22718	Verified
LTL18	5.21	9.116	12257835	612894	37689	Verified
LTL19	5.18	8.041	12238896	612744	29563	Verified
LTL20	5.29	6.577	12727399	611718	18187	Verified

in each run of LTL properties. The SPIN verification result for LTL properties is in Table 4. Table 4 depicts the results obtained from SPIN showing the elapsed time, total memory usage, states transitioned, states stored, and verification status for LTL properties in the C-MBS model. The SPIN verification results show that the memory requirement and verification time have not been increased significantly with the increase in the number of users during the verification of LTL properties in the C-MBS.

Table 3 shows the results after SPIN checked for the existence of deadlocks and assertion violations by generating the execution paths during the verification of the C-MBS model. Similarly, Table 4 shows the results after SPIN checked for temporal properties of the C-MBS model to conform during the system lifetime. The results of these experiments show that there is no error in the design of the C-MBS. SPIN did not generate any counterexample during the verification of the C-MBS. Hence, banks and financial institutions can implement this verified model for providing enhanced banking services to the banking users using mobile. The C-MBS model will increase the banking users to use the enhanced banking services remotely and will play a significant role in the transformation towards a cashless society in the digital world.

5 Conclusion and Future Work

In this prevailing generation of the digital world, digital products are driving our daily lives, and one of the beautiful digital products for everybody is the mobile device. Mobile users are redoubling by leaps and bounds universally. Mobile banking is an electronic channel for Electronic Banking (E-Banking) all over the world. Mobile banking users have not been increased yet significantly in proportional to the increase in the number of mobile users. Banking customers do not employ the mobile banking system because of not full automation and security problems. Therefore, this paper developed a new contactless mobile banking system (C-MBS) that includes enhanced banking services with novel functions like e-cheque, registration of the user, and cancellation of the users' account included in the model. This paper incorporated enhanced banking services such as registration of the user, fund transfer, third party payment, digital lending, e-cheque issuing, e-cheque clearing, and cancellation of the user account by using the EFSM model and PROMELA model of C-MBS. Security properties are specified using LTL, and system properties are specified using the PROMELA model of C-MBS. We used SPIN to verify the safety and LTL properties in the PROMELA model of C-MBS. SPIN verified the safety properties and the LTL properties within the C-MBS model. We observed from our experimental SPIN results that C-MBS does not have any deadlocks or errors within the model. Hence, banks and financial institutions can implement this verified C-MBS model for a secure enhanced mobile banking system that can play a significant role in making the cashless payment society in the world of E-Banking.

In future research, we will design a new mobile banking model that mitigates different attacks like man in the middle (MITM) attack, SQL injection attack, man in the browser (MITB) attack, replay attack, and other probable attacks in the banking systems. Likewise, we will extend our research in modeling and verification of digital banking and omnichannel banking in E-Banking.

References

1. Obaid, I., Kazmi, S., Qasim, A.: Modeling and verification of payment system in E-banking. Int. J. Adv. Comput. Sci. Appl. **8**(8), 195–201 (2017). https://doi.org/10.14569/IJACSA.2017.080825
2. Shi, H., Ma, W., Yang, M., Zhang, X.: A case study of model checking retail banking system with SPIN. J. Comput. **7**(10), 2503–2510 (2012). https://doi.org/10.4304/jcp.7.10.2503-2510
3. Zhang, W., Ma, W., Shi, H., Zhu, F.: Model checking and verification of the Internet payment system with spin. J. Softw. **7**(9),1941–1949 (2012). https://doi.org/10.4304/jsw.7.9.1941-1949
4. Ahamad, S.S., Udgata, S.K., Sastry, V.N.: A new mobile payment system with formal verification. Int. J. Internet Technol. Secur. Trans. **4**(1), 71–103 (2012). https://doi.org/10.1504/IJITST.2012.045153
5. Shaikh, R., And, A., Devane, S.: Formal verification of payment protocol using AVISPA. Int. J. Inf. **3**(3), 326–337 (2010). https://doi.org/10.20533/iji.1742.4712.2010.0035

6. Hegde, M.S., Jnanamurthy, H.K., J., Singh, S.: Modeling and verification of extensible authentication protocol using SPIN model checker. Int. J. Netw. Secur. Appl. **4**(6), 81–98 (2012). https://doi.org/10.5121/ijnsa.2012.4606
7. Ciurea, C.: The development of a mobile application in a collaborative banking system. Inf. Econ. **14**(3), 86–97 (2010)
8. Aithal, P.S.: A comparison of ideal banking model with mobile banking system. Int. J. Curr. Res. Mod. Educ. **1**(2), 206–224 (2016). https://doi.org/10.5281/zenodo.198708
9. Bojjagani, S., Sastry, V.N.: A secure end-to-end SMS-based mobile banking protocol. Int. J. Commun. Syst. **30**(15), 1–19 (2017). https://doi.org/10.1002/dac.3302
10. Anwarul Islam, K.M., Salma, U.: Mobile banking operations and banking facilities to rural people in Bangladesh. Int. J. Finan. Bank. Res. **2**(4), 147–162 (2016). https://doi.org/10.11648/j.ijfbr.20160204.14
11. Dahlberg, T., Guo, J., Ondrus, J.: A critical review of mobile payment research. Elsevier Electron. Commerce Res. Appl. **14**(5), 265–284 (2015). https://doi.org/10.1016/j.elerap.2015.07.006
12. Istrate, C.M.: Cardless withdrawal system for mobile banking applications. J. Mobile, Embed. Distrib. Syst. **6**(1), 11–16 (2014)
13. Yang, F., Liu, Z., Chiu, S.: Mobile banking payment system. J. Wireless Mobile Netw. Ubiquitous Comput. Depend. Appl. **2**(3), 85–95 (2011)
14. Alanazi, H.O., Alnaqeib, R., Hmood, A.K., Zaidan, M.A., Al-Nabhani, Y.: On the module of the Internet banking system. J. Comput. **2**(5), 133–143 (2010)
15. Uddin, M.S., Akhi, A.: E-wallet system for Bangladesh an electronic payment system. Int. J. Model. Optim. **4**(3), 216–219 (2014). https://doi.org/10.7763/ijmo.2014.V4.376
16. Islam, M.S.: Systematic literature review: security challenges of mobile banking and payment system. Int. J. u- and e- Serv. Sci. Technol. **7**(6), 107–116 (2014). https://doi.org/10.14257/ijunesst.2014.7.6.10
17. Brar, T., Sharma, D., Khurmi, S.: Vulnerabilities in e-banking: a study of various security aspects in e-banking. International Journal of Computing & Business Research, Proceedings of 'I-Society. pp. 2229–6166 (2012).
18. Nyamtiga, B.W., Sam, A., Laizer, L.S.: Enhanced security model for mobile banking systems in Tanzania. Int. J. Technol. Enhance. Emerg. Eng. Res. **1**(4), 4–20 (2013)
19. Avdic, A.: Use of biometrics in mobile banking security: case study of Croatian banks. Int. J. Comput. Sci. Netw. Secur. **19**(10), 83–89 (2019)
20. Gupta, R., Kumar, R.P., Bharadwaj, A.: Mobile banking system in India: practices, challenges and security issues. Int. J. Comput. Trends Technol. **43**(1), 24–48 (2017). https://doi.org/10.14445/22312803/ijctt-v43P106
21. Goyal, V., Pandey, U.S., Batra, S.: Mobile Banking in India: practices, challenges and security issues. Int. J. Adv. Trends Comput. Sci. Eng. **1**(2), 56–66 (2012)
22. Alalwan, A.A., Dwivedi, Y.K., Rana, N.P.: Factors influencing adoption of mobile banking by Jordanian bank customers: Extending UTAUT2 with trust. Elsevier Int. J. Inf. Manage. **37**(3), 99–110 (2017). https://doi.org/10.1016/j.ijinfomgt.2017.01.002
23. Al-Jabri, I.M., Sohail, M.S.: Mobile banking adoption: application of diffusion of innovation theory. J. Electron. Commer. Res. **13**(4), 379–391 (2012)
24. Raja, S.A., Umer, A., Shah, N.: New determinants of ease of use and perceived usefulness for mobile banking adoption. Int. J. Electron. Cust. Relationship Manage. **11**(1), 44–65 (2017). https://doi.org/10.1504/ijecrm.2017.086751
25. Safeena, R., Date, H., Kammani, A., Hundewale, N.: Technology adoption and Indian consumers: study on Mobile Banking. Int. J. Comput. Theory Eng. **4**(6), 1020–1024 (2012). https://doi.org/10.7763/ijcte.2012.v4.630
26. Bharti. M.: Impact of dimensions of mobile banking on user satisfaction. J. Internet Bank. Comm. **21**(1), 1–22 (2016)

27. Asfour, H.K., Haddad, S.I.: The impact of mobile banking on enhancing customers' e-satisfaction: an empirical study on commercial banks in Jordan. Int. Bus. Res. **7**(10), 145–169 (2014). https://doi.org/10.5539/ibr.v7n10p145
28. Singh, N., Kumar, T., Vardhan, M.: Blockchain based e-cheque clearing framework. Scalable Comput.: Pract. Exper. **20**(3), 511–525 (2019). https://doi.org/10.12694/scpe.v20i3.1506
29. Yahid, B., Nobakht, M., Shahbahrami, A.: Trust in e-cheque in electronic payments. New Mark. Res. J. **4**, 19–28 (2014)
30. Digital 2021 global overview report. https://datareportal.com/reports/digital-2021-global-overview-report. Accessed on 15 June 2021

International Workshop on Geographical Analysis, Urban Modeling, Spatial Statistics (GEOG-AND-MOD 2021)

Earthquake Prediction Based on Combined Seismic and GPS Monitoring Data

V. G. Gitis[ID], A. B. Derendyaev[✉][ID], and K. N. Petrov[ID]

The Institute for Information Transmission Problems, Moscow, Russia
gitis@iitp.ru

Abstract. This article presents the results of applying the method of the minimum area of alarm to the complex forecasting of earthquakes based on data of different types. Point fields of earthquake epicenters and time series of displacements of the earth's surface, measured using GPS, were used for the prediction. Testing was carried out for earthquakes with a hypocenter depth of up to 60 km for two regions with different seismotectonics: Japan, the forecast time interval from 2016 to 2020, magnitudes $m \geq 6$; California, the forecast time interval from 2013 to 2020, magnitude $m \geq 5.5$. Testing has shown the effectiveness of systematic earthquake forecasting using seismological and space geodesy data in combination.

Keywords: GPS time series · Grid-based spatio-temporal fields · Earthquake prediction · Machine learning · Method of minimum area of alarm

1 Introduction

Field observations show that anomalous changes are observed in a number of natural processes before a strong earthquake. They can relate to the characteristics of the seismic regime, the values of deformations of the earth's surface, the chemical composition of fluids, the level of groundwater, the transit time of seismic waves, variations of electric and geomagnetic fields. These phenomena are often localized near the source of a future earthquake [11,14,18,20,26,27] and can be used as precursors of earthquakes. At the same time, it is known that with an increase in the energy of the expected earthquake, the distance from the epicenter to the area of manifestation of precursors increases and can be more than 15 km [4,10], which introduces additional uncertainty in the assessment of the location of the expected earthquake.

Many aspects of earthquake prediction have been studied. They include the study of rock failure and earthquake precursor phenomena, the study of mathematical models for earthquake prediction, machine learning methods, and the

This research was partially funded by Russian Foundation for Basic Research grant number 20-07-00445.

O. Gervasi et al. (Eds.): ICCSA 2021, LNCS 12954, pp. 601–612, 2021.
https://doi.org/10.1007/978-3-030-86979-3_42

testing of earthquake prediction algorithms [12,16,23–25,29,30]. At the same time, a number of works have stated that earthquakes cannot be predicted [6,9,15].

Systematic earthquake prediction consists of the regular calculation of a limited warning zone, in which an earthquake with a magnitude above a certain threshold is expected for a certain time. The effectiveness of the forecast largely depends on the quality of the initial data and methods of their processing. We get the broadest access to regularly updated seismological monitoring data. Therefore, as a rule, in many articles, only seismological data are used. Currently, data from monitoring the displacement of the earth's surface, obtained using a global positioning system (GPS), is published in real-time for a number of seismically active regions.

In this article, we consider the results of a systematic forecast obtained with the combined use of seismological and geodynamic data. For the systematic prediction of earthquakes, we have developed a new method of machine learning, called the method of the minimum area of alarm [8]. The article is divided into three sections. In Sect. 2, we shortly describe the main elements of the forecast method. Section 3 presents the results of modeling the forecast of strong earthquakes in Japan and California, obtained on the basis of combining seismic and geodetic data.

2   Basis of a Forecasting Method

The considered approach to the systematic forecasting of earthquakes is based on the machine learning method, which we called the method of the minimum area of alarm. This method is described in [7,8]. The idea of the method is as follows.

Let there be a set of objects. An object is described by a set of its properties, expressed in numerical form (a vector of features). The values of the properties of objects, close to the maximum possible, have a low probability. Among the set of objects, there are anomalous objects (precedents). They differ from other objects in that the values of some of their properties are close to the maximum. It seems natural to classify an object as anomalous if the corresponding feature vector is greater than or equal componentwise to one of the vectors corresponding to the precedent. However, the description of the properties of objects is usually incomplete. Therefore, some precedents lack properties that are close to their maximum values. For such precedents, the number of objects classified by them as anomalous can be quite large, and the objects themselves are likely to be erroneously classified as anomalous.

The task is to find the largest number of precedents, provided that the number of objects classified by them as anomalous does not exceed the specified number. The algorithm of the minimum area of alarm is non-parametric. It refers to machine learning algorithms for one-class classification [2,13,17]. The idea of the algorithm is as follows. At the first step, for each precedent, a set of anomalous objects classified by it is built. Next, the maximum number of precedents is selected for which the cardinality of the union of these sets does not exceed a predetermined number N^*. The decision rule classifies objects only according to the selected precedents. For the rest of the precedents, new distinctive properties should be sought and added to the feature space. The amount of computations of the algorithm is significantly reduced if not the maximum number of precedents is selected, but a close one.

With a systematic forecast of earthquakes, it is required to regularly indicate on the map the alarm zone, in which the epicenter of the target earthquake is expected. A demo version of the systematic earthquake prediction system since 2018 is available on the website https://distcomp.ru/geo/prognosis/ (accessed on 15 March 2021). At each step Δt, new initial data are loaded from the seismological and geodynamic monitoring servers, they are used to calculate the spatial and spatio-temporal grid-based fields, the sample of target earthquake epicenters is supplemented, and then training is performed with all downloaded data from the beginning of training until the moment of forecasting t. As a result of training, an alarm zone with size $S^*(t)$ is calculated, in which the epicenter of the target earthquake is expected in the interval $(t, t + \Delta t)$.

A target earthquake is predicted if its epicenter falls within the calculated alarm zone. The larger the product $S^*(t)\Delta t$, the more successful the forecast. At the same time, it is obvious that the size of this region of space-time must be reasonably limited. Indicators of forecast quality are the assessment of the probability of a successful forecast of events (*forecast probability*), equal to $U = Q^*/Q$ and the *alarm volume* equal to $V = L^*/L$, where Q^* and Q are the number of predicted and all target earthquakes, $L^* = \Delta t \Sigma_{n=1}^{N} S^*(t_n)$ is the size of the spatio-temporal area of alarm, N is the number of forecast intervals, $L = NS\Delta t$ is the size of the entire analysis spatio-temporal area, S is the size of the analysis zone. As a result of training, it is desirable to obtain a solution that provides the maximum probability of a successful prediction for a given value of the alarm area. It can be seen that the alarm volume V is equal to the probability of detecting target events by random areas of size $L^* = VL$.

3   Modeling

3.1   GPS Data Preprocessing

We analyzed the time series of daily horizontal displacements of the earth's surface at the intervals 01.01.2009–26.07.2020 for Japan and 01.01.2008–14.11.2020 for California. The data obtained from the Nevada Geodetic Laboratory (NGL), http://geodesy.unr.edu/about.php (accessed on 15 March 2021) [3]. There are 1420 and 1803 GPS receiving stations in Japan and California, respectively. The analysis areas contain 1229 and 1204 stations. Networks of GPS receiving stations, areas of analysis, and epicenters of target earthquakes are shown in Fig. 1. Stations evenly cover the analysis area. The average minimum distance between stations is 12.8 km for Japan and 9.38 km for California, with standard deviations of 5.4 and 5.74 km.

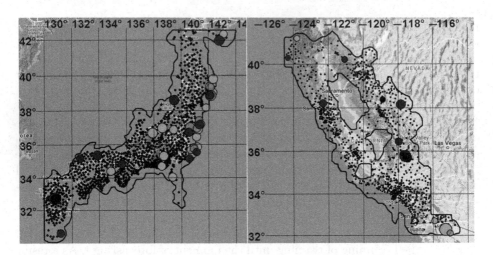

Fig. 1. Areas of analysis, Global Positioning System (GPS) ground receiving stations, and the epicenters of target earthquakes. Left: Japan, epicenters of target earthquakes with magnitude $m \geq 6.0$ in the interval 01.01.2011–26.07.2020; Right: California, epicenters of target earthquakes with magnitude $m \geq 5.5$, in the interval 23.12.2009–14.11.2020. The epicenters of the target earthquakes for which the forecast was tested are highlighted in red. (Color figure online)

The calculation of the feature fields used for earthquake prediction based on GPS data is performed in two stages. The purpose of the first stage is to extract a useful signal from the time series of coordinates of the receiving stations. The purpose of the second stage is to calculate spatio-temporal fields of forecast features.

Time Series of Earth's Surface Displacement Velocities
The initial data are daily time series of coordinates $x(t)$ and $y(t)$ of GPS ground receiving stations in the W–E and N–S directions in the intervals 01.01.2009–26.07.2020 for Japan and 01.01.2008–14.11.2020 for California. The daily horizontal velocities of the earth's surface displacements $g_x(t)$ and $g_y(t)$ are determined by two coordinates of the GPS receiving station, spaced in time by the interval T_0: $g_x(t) = (x(t) - x(t - T_0))/T_0$, $g_y(t) = (y(t) - y(t - T_0))/T_0$. There are discontinuities (gaps) in the time series. In our case, for each coordinate, there were 23682 gaps and 168218 days of missed measurements for Japan, and 29977 gaps and 357067 days of missed measurements for California. Since the displacement rate estimates are ahead of the time of the values of the first station coordinates $x(t - T_0)$ and $y(t - T_0)$ by T_0 days, each gap in the time series of station coordinates increases the number of missing values in the time series of velocities by T_0 days. With a large number of gaps, the number of missing velocity values can significantly exceed the number of missing coordinate values. To limit the number of missed velocity values, we linearly interpolate the coordinate values in the gaps less than or equal to T_0. For the gaps that more than T_0 days,

we end the calculation of the speed at the last value of the station coordinate before the start of the rupture and re-estimate the rates, starting from the first value of the station coordinate after the rupture.

To calculate the daily rates, we selected the interval $T_0 = 30$ days. For this interval, the station movement values are comparable to the noise value of daily measurements. For 30 days intervals, there are 23119 gaps in each coordinate of the Japan area, which is 97.62% of all gaps in the time series and 50537 blanks in measurements (30.04%). For California, there are 27990 measurement gaps (93.37%) and 88387 measurement gaps (24.75%) over a 30-day period for each coordinate. At the same time, the number of missing speed values in each of the W–E and N–S directions increased for Japan by $(23682-23119) \times 30 = 16890$ (10.04%), and for California by $(29977-27990) \times 30 = 59610$ (16.69%).

The first stage is completed by calculating the spatio-temporal fields of the rate components $\mathbf{V}_x$ and $\mathbf{V}_y$ in the W–E and N–S directions. The fields were presented in the grid $\Delta x \times \Delta y \times \Delta t = 0.1° \times 0.075° \times 1$ day. The calculation of the fields was carried out using an interpolation technique known as inverse distance weighting. During interpolation, the gaps in the values of the time series were not filled, but they were taken into account as the absence of the receiving station. The values of the fields $\mathbf{V}_x$ and $\mathbf{V}_y$ at the grid points for each time slice of the field of the velocity component W–E were calculated by the formula:

$$V_{xn}(t) = \frac{\sum_{k=1}^{K} g_{xk}^{(t)}/r_k^p}{\sum_{k=1}^{K} 1/r_k^p}, \tag{1}$$

where $V_{xn}(t)$ is the value of the field of the W–E strain rate component at the grid node n at the moment t, K is the maximum number of stations closest to the node n in the circle of radius R_{max}, the values of which were used for interpolation, $g_{xk}(t)$ is the value of the W–E strain rate component for the station k, $k = 1,\ldots,K$, at the time t, $r_k \leq R_{max}$ is the distance from the k-th station to the grid node n, and p is the degree that determines the dependence of the station weight on its distance to the grid node. The interpolation parameters were $K = 5$, $R_{max} = 50$ km, and $p = 1$. If $r_k = 0$, then $V_{xn}(t) = g_{xk}(t)$. The calculations of the field of the N–S strain rate components were similar.

Spatio-temporal Fields of Features

We assume that strong earthquakes are preceded by spatio-temporal anomalous changes in the regime of various deformations of the earth's surface. Therefore, we are looking for fields containing information about the anomalous values of the change in the deformation mode. The basis of the considered fields of features is the following invariants of the strain-rate fields.

– $\mathbf{F}_1$ is the field of divergence of the strain rates:

$$\mathrm{div}V_n = \frac{\partial V_{xn}}{\partial x} + \frac{\partial V_{yn}}{\partial y} \tag{2}$$

The maximum and minimum values of the divergence field refer to places where there is a relative contraction or expansion of the size of a small horizontal area.

– $\mathbf{F}_2$ is the field of rotor of the strain rates:

$$\mathrm{rot}V_n = \frac{\partial V_{xn}}{\partial y} - \frac{\partial V_{yn}}{\partial x} \tag{3}$$

The field values determine the direction and intensity of the field twisting around the vertical axis.

– $\mathbf{F}_3$ is the field of shear of the strain rates:

$$\mathrm{sh}V_n = \frac{1}{2}\sqrt{\left(\frac{\partial V_{xn}}{\partial x} - \frac{\partial V_{yn}}{\partial y}\right)^2 + \left(\frac{\partial V_{xn}}{\partial y} + \frac{\partial V_{yn}}{\partial x}\right)^2} \tag{4}$$

The fields of features $\mathbf{F}_4$, $\mathbf{F}_5$, and $\mathbf{F}_6$ represent changes in the fields of the strain rate invariants over time. They are equal to the ratios of the mean values of the invariants in two consecutive intervals to the standard deviation of this difference. The values of the fields are converted into the grid $\Delta x \times \Delta y \times \Delta t = 0.1° \times 0.075° \times 30$ days.

– $\mathbf{F}_4$ is the field of the temporal variations in the divergence strain rate.

The value of the field $f_{4n}(t)$ at time t is equal to the ratio of the difference $(\overline{\mathrm{div}_{2n}} - \overline{\mathrm{div}_{1n}})$ between the mean values of the divergence in two consecutive intervals, namely, T_1 and T_2, to the standard deviation of this difference $\sigma_n(\mathrm{div})$, $T_1 = T_2 = 361$ days.

$$f_{4n}(t) = (\overline{\mathrm{div}_{2n}} - \overline{\mathrm{div}_{1n}})/\sigma_n(\mathrm{div}), \tag{5}$$

where $\overline{\mathrm{div}_{2n}}$ is calculated from the values of field $\mathbf{F}_1$ at the interval $(t - T_2, t)$, $\overline{\mathrm{div}_1}(t - T_2)$ is calculated at the interval $(t - T_2 - T_1, t - T_2)$.

– $\mathbf{F}_5$ is the field of the temporal variations in the rotor rate.

The values of field $f_5(t)$ are calculated similarly to the values of field $\mathbf{F}_4$,

$$f_{5n}(t) = (\overline{\mathrm{rot}_{2n}} - \overline{\mathrm{rot}_{1n}})/\sigma_n(\mathrm{rot}). \tag{6}$$

– $\mathbf{F}_6$ is the field of the temporal variations in the shear deformation rate.

The values of field $f_6(t)$ are calculated similarly to the values of field $\mathbf{F}_4$,

$$f_{6n}(t) = (\overline{\mathrm{sh}_{2n}} - \overline{\mathrm{sh}_{1n}})/\sigma_n(\mathrm{sh}), \tag{7}$$

Fields $\mathbf{F}_7$, $\mathbf{F}_8$, and $\mathbf{F}_9$ represent spatial correlations of strain rate changes in a sliding window of 75×75 km^2. With this window size, the correlation coefficients are estimated in approximately 70–80 grid points of the fields.

– $\mathbf{F}_7$ is the field of spatial correlations in fields $\mathbf{F}_4$ and $\mathbf{F}_5$.
– $\mathbf{F}_8$ is the field of spatial correlations in fields $\mathbf{F}_4$ and $\mathbf{F}_6$.
– $\mathbf{F}_9$ is the field of spatial correlations in fields $\mathbf{F}_5$ and $\mathbf{F}_6$.

Correlation fields F_7, F_8, and F_9 carry information about the spatial relationship between the values of the change in the rate of different pairs of deformation types. The minimum or maximum fields of the correlation fields combine this information.

To combine information on the spatial relationship between the values of the change in the rate of different pairs of deformation types, you can use the field of maximum or minimum values of the correlation fields F_7, F_8, and F_9. This operation can be interpreted in terms of fuzzy logic [28]. For Japan, the most successful prediction of target earthquakes was obtained using the F_{10} field:

– F_{10} is the field of minimum values of the fields F_7 and F_9:

$$f_{10n} = \min(f_{7n}, f_{9n}) \tag{8}$$

The best forecast of target earthquakes according to GPS data for California was obtained from the F_4 and F_6 fields.

3.2 Seismological Data Preprocessing

Seismological data for Japan and California taken from the Japan Meteorological Agency earthquake catalogs [21, 22] and the National Earthquake Information Center (NEIC) [1] at intervals 02.06.2002–26.07.2020 and 01.01.1995–20.12.2020. They are represented by earthquakes with a magnitude $m \geq 2.0$ and a hypocenter depth $H \leq 160$ km.

– S_1 is the 3D field of the density of earthquake epicenters.
– S_2 is the 3D field of the mean earthquake magnitude.
– S_3 is the 3D field of the negative temporal anomalies of the density of earthquake epicenters.
– S_4 is the 3D field of the positive temporal anomalies of the density of earthquake epicenters.
– S_5 is the 3D field of the negative temporal anomalies of the mean earthquake magnitude.
– S_6 is the 3D field of the positive temporal anomalies of the mean earthquake magnitude.
– S_7 is the 2D field of the density of earthquake epicenters: Kernel smoothing with the parameter $R = 50$ km in the interval from the beginning of the analysis to the start of training.
– S_8 is the 3D field of quantiles of the background density of earthquake epicenters, calculated using the interval from the beginning of the analysis to the start of training, which corresponds to the density values of earthquake epicenters at the current time.

The estimation of 3D fields S_1 and S_2 was performed with the method of local kernel regression. The kernel function for the q-th earthquake has the form $K_q = [ch^2(r_q/R)^2 ch^2(t_q/T)]^{-1}$, where $r_q < R\epsilon$ and $t_q < T\epsilon$ are the distance and time interval between the q-th epicenter of the earthquake and the node of the

3D grid of the field, $\epsilon = 2$, $R = 50$ km, $T = 100$ days for $\mathbf{S}_1$ and R $= 100$ km, and T $= 730$ days for $\mathbf{S}_2$. The field $\mathbf{S}_7$ was calculated with the kernel function $K_q = [cosh^2(r_q/R)^2]^{-1}$. The parameters for evaluating the fields, the radii R, and the interval T were chosen empirically, considering the step of the network of fields and the approximate number of events in the evaluation window. To calculate the fields $\mathbf{S}_3$, $\mathbf{S}_4$, $\mathbf{S}_5$, and $\mathbf{S}_6$, Student's t-test was used. This t-statistic was determined for each grid node as the ratio of the difference in the average values of the current interval T_2 and the background interval T_1 to the standard deviation of this difference. Positive values of the t-statistic correspond to an increase in the value on the test interval.

We also analyzed fields similar to the fields $\mathbf{S}_3$, $\mathbf{S}_4$, $\mathbf{S}_5$, and $\mathbf{S}_6$, but with different values of the T_2 and T_1 intervals.

When predicting from seismological data, the following three fields turned out to be the most informative.

- $\mathbf{S}_9 = \mathbf{S}_1/(\mathbf{S}_8 + 0.001)$ is the field of ratios of the density values of the earthquake epicenters s_{1n} to the values of the quantiles of the density of the epicenters calculated on the interval from the beginning of the analysis to the start of training, which corresponds to the density values of earthquake epicenters at the current time ($s_{8n} + 0.001$).
- $\mathbf{S}_{10}$ is the field of negative anomalies of Student's t-statistic of the density of earthquake epicenters with the intervals $T_1 = 1095$ and $T_2 = 365$ days.
- $\mathbf{S}_{11}$ is the field of negative anomalies of Student's t-statistic of the mean earthquake magnitude with the intervals $T_1 = 1095$ and $T_2 = 730$ days.

For Japan, the most informative were the fields $\mathbf{S}_9$ and $\mathbf{S}_{10}$. Both of them previously proved to be the most effective in predicting earthquakes and their magnitudes in Kamchatka and the Aegean region. The anomalous values of the $\mathbf{S}_9$ field correspond to areas of the seismic process in which the density values of earthquake epicenters are quite high but significantly less than the average values of the density of epicenters in the interval from the beginning of the analysis to the start of training. The anomalous values of the $\mathbf{S}_{10}$ field correspond to the spatio-temporal regions of the seismic process, in which the average values of the density of earthquake epicenters in the T_2 interval are significantly lower than the average field values in the T_1 interval. These changes highlight anomalous areas in which a quiescence sets in after the activation of the seismic process. The time series of the $\mathbf{S}_{10}$ field simulates the preparation of strong earthquakes proposed by the AUF model proposed in [7]. For California, the most informative were the fields $\mathbf{S}_9$ and $\mathbf{S}_{11}$.

3.3 Earthquake Forecast

The training intervals start for Japan and California on 01.01.2011 and 23.12.2009 and end before the next forecast, starting on 20.11.2015 and 19.01.2013. Testing intervals are 20.11.2015–10.09.2020 for Japan and 19.01.2013–14.11.2020 for California. The areas of analysis at the testing intervals contain 14 epicenters of target earthquakes in Japan with a magnitude of

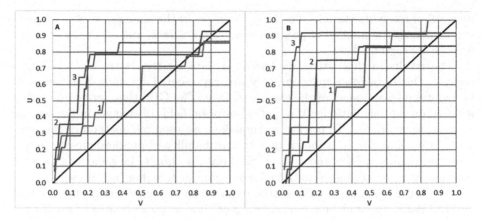

Fig. 2. Dependences $U(V)$ of the probability of a successful earthquake prediction U on the alarm volume V obtained with the different fields for Japan (A) and California (B). (1) field S_7 for both regions; (2) fields S_9 and S_{10} for Japan, S_9 and S_{11} for California; (3) fields S_9, S_{10} and F_{10} for Japan, S_9, S_{11}, F_4 and F_6 for California.

$m \geq 6.0$ and 12 epicenters of target earthquakes in California with a magnitude of $m \geq 5.5$.

In the method of the minimum area of alarm, alarm zones are constructed from a combination of spatio-temporal alarm cylinders. The parameters of the learning algorithm are the radius of the cylinders in spatial coordinates and the element of the cylinder in time. The larger the radius, the higher the alarm volume V. The larger the element, the slower the alarm zone changes. The alarm cylinder parameters are the radius $R = 16$ km and its element $T = 91$ days for Japan and $R = 18$ km and its element $T = 61$ days for California. The best forecast of target earthquakes according to GPS data for Japan was obtained from the F_{10} field, and for California from the F_4 and F_6 fields.

Figure 2 shows the dependences $U(V)$ for Japan (A) and California (B). The results for Japan obtained using 2D field S_7 of the density of earthquake epicenters (line 1), seismological fields S_9, S_{10} (line 2), and the fields S_9, S_{10} with the field F_{12} (line 3). The result of forecasting earthquakes in California obtained using field S_7, fields S_9 and S_{11}, and fields S_9, S_{11}, with the fields F_4 and F_6.

4   Conclusion

A number of seismically active regions are equipped with a rather dense network of GPS receiving stations that track the movements of the earth's surface. In our study, we tried to get answers to two questions: (1) Is space geodesy data effective for systematic earthquake prediction? and (2) Is the earthquake forecast improved if seismological data with the addition of space geodesy data? Obviously, the answers to these questions depend on the spatial density of the network of receiving stations, on the parameters of the time series of GPS measurements, on the method of preprocessing of GPS data, and on the method for forecasting earthquakes.

The results in this article are based on data for the Japan and California regions. Our data from space geodesy are represented by daily time series of horizontal displacements of the earth's surface. The GPS time series processing is based on the calculation of the spatio-temporal fields of changes in the seismic strain rate invariants. To predict earthquakes, we used our method of the minimum area of alarm. It is shown that the probability of predicting earthquakes based on combined GPS and seismological data is almost the same as a forecast based only on seismological data in Japan and much higher in California.

A number of transformations were required to calculate feature fields based on GPS data. These include interpolation of time series at relatively small time intervals of discontinuity in the operation of GPS receiving stations, calculation of time series of the components of the velocities of horizontal displacements of stations, calculation of spatio-temporal fields of components of the velocities of the earth's surface deformations, calculation of fields of invariants of velocities and fields of variation of invariants of velocities in time, calculation of spatial correlation fields, calculation of minimum and maximum values of correlations, etc. A number of parameters were used in the algorithms for calculating these transformations: the time interval for estimating the daily displacement rates, the sizes of the spatial and temporal smoothing windows and the windows for estimating the spatial correlation coefficients, as well as the time intervals for calculating the field of invariants of the strain rates. The GPS fields for Japan and California were calculated with the same parameters. The choice of transformation parameters, as well as the choice of the feature fields themselves, requires special studies. In this work, such studies were not carried out. The types of transformations of the initial data into the fields of features and transformation parameters were selected based on qualitative considerations about the methods of cleaning signals from noise, recovering missing values, and disclosing information about the spatio-temporal properties of geodynamic processes.

The method of the minimum area of alarm is universal for various types of initial data since, for forecasting, all data is converted into uniform spatial, and spatio-temporal grid-based fields. The most informative for predicting earthquakes were the fields reflecting the change in the rates of various types of deformations of the earth's surface, the change in the characteristics of the seismic regime and the spatial correlation of these processes. The modeling of the earthquake prediction in the regions under study showed that these fields' anomalous values distinguish the spatio-temporal regions preceding the appearance of the epicenters of strong earthquakes. This is the similarity of the most informative feature fields selected for forecasting in the regions of Japan and California. It should be noted that these regions differ significantly in seismotectonic and geodynamic regimes [5,19]. This testifies in favor of the universality of the proposed methods of our data preprocessing.

References

1. Barnhart, W.D., Hayes, G.P., Wald, D.J.: Global earthquake response with imaging geodesy: recent examples from the USGS NEIC. Remote Sens. **11**(11), 1357 (2019)
2. Bishop, C.M.: Pattern Recognition and Machine Learning. Springer, Heidelberg (2006)
3. Blewitt, G., Hammond, W.C., Kreemer, C.: Harnessing the GPS data explosion for interdisciplinary science. Eos **99**(10.1029) (2018)
4. Dobrovolsky, I., Zubkov, S., Miachkin, V.: Estimation of the size of earthquake preparation zones. Pure Appl. Geophys. **117**(5), 1025–1044 (1979)
5. Garagash, I., Bondur, V., Gokhberg, M., Steblov, G.: Three-year experience of the fortnight forecast of seismicity in Southern California on the basis of geomechanical model and the seismic data. In: AGU Fall Meeting Abstracts, vol. 2011, pp. NH23A-1535 (2011)
6. Geller, R.J., Jackson, D.D., Kagan, Y.Y., Mulargia, F.: Earthquakes cannot be predicted. Science **275**(5306), 1616 (1997)
7. Gitis, V., Derendyaev, A.: The method of the minimum area of alarm for earthquake magnitude prediction. Front. Earth Sci. **8**, 482 (2020)
8. Gitis, V.G., Derendyaev, A.B.: Machine learning methods for seismic hazards forecast. Geosciences **9**(7), 308 (2019)
9. Gufeld, I.L., Matveeva, M.I., Novoselov, O.N.: Why we cannot predict strong earthquakes in the earth's crust. Geodyn. Tectonophys. **2**(4), 378–415 (2015)
10. Guomin, Z., Zhaocheng, Z.: The study of multidisciplinary earthquake prediction in China. J. Earthq. Predction Res. **1**(1), 71–85 (1992)
11. Kanamori, H.: The nature of seismicity patterns before large earthquakes (1981)
12. Keilis-Borok, V., Soloviev, A.A.: Nonlinear Dynamics of the Lithosphere and Earthquake Prediction. Springer, Heidelberg (2013)
13. Khan, S.S., Madden, M.G.: A survey of recent trends in one class classification. In: Coyle, L., Freyne, J. (eds.) AICS 2009. LNCS (LNAI), vol. 6206, pp. 188–197. Springer, Heidelberg (2010). https://doi.org/10.1007/978-3-642-17080-5_21
14. King, C.Y.: Gas geochemistry applied to earthquake prediction: an overview. J. Geophys. Res. Solid Earth **91**(B12), 12269–12281 (1986)
15. Koronovsky, N., Naimark, A.: Earthquake prediction: is it a practicable scientific perspective or a challenge to science? Mosc. Univ. Geol. Bull. **64**(1), 10–20 (2009)
16. Kossobokov, V.: User manual for M8. In: Healy, J.H., Keilis-Borok, V.I., Lee, W.H.K. (eds.) Algorithms for Earthquake Statistics and Prediction, vol. 6, pp. 167–222 (1997)
17. Kotsiantis, S.B., Zaharakis, I., Pintelas, P.: Supervised machine learning: a review of classification techniques. Emerg. Artif. Intell. Appl. Comput. Eng. **160**(1), 3–24 (2007)
18. Lighthill, J.: A Critical Review of VAN: Earthquake Prediction from Seismic Electrical Signals. World Scientific (1996)
19. Lobkovsky, L., Vladimirova, I., Gabsatarov, Y.V., Steblov, G.: Seismotectonic deformations related to the 2011 Tohoku earthquake at different stages of the seismic cycle, based on satellite geodetic observations. Doklady Earth Sci. **481**, 1060–1065 (2018)
20. Mogi, K.: Two kinds of seismic gaps. Pure Appl. Geophys. **117**(6), 1172–1186 (1979)
21. Obara, K., Kasahara, K., Hori, S., Okada, Y.: A densely distributed high-sensitivity seismograph network in Japan: Hi-net by national research institute for earth science and disasterprevention. Rev. Sci. Instrum. **76**(2), 021301 (2005)

22. Okada, Y., et al.: Recent progress of seismic observation networks in Japan-Hi-net, F-net, K-net and KiK-net. Earth Planets Space **56**(8), xv–xxviii (2004)
23. Rhoades, D.A.: Application of the EEPAS model to forecasting earthquakes of moderate magnitude in southern California. Seismol. Res. Lett. **78**(1), 110–115 (2007)
24. Rhoades, D.A.: Mixture models for improved earthquake forecasting with short-to-medium time horizons. Bull. Seismol. Soc. Am. **103**(4), 2203–2215 (2013)
25. Shebalin, P.N., Narteau, C., Zechar, J.D., Holschneider, M.: Combining earthquake forecasts using differential probability gains. Earth Planets Space **66**(1), 1–14 (2014). https://doi.org/10.1186/1880-5981-66-37
26. Sobolev, G.: Principles of earthquake prediction (1993)
27. Sobolev, G., Ponomarev, A.: Earthquake Physics and Precursors. Publishing House Nauka, Moscow (2003)
28. Zadeh, L.A.: Fuzzy logic. Computer **21**(4), 83–93 (1988)
29. Zavyalov, A.: Intermediate Term Earthquake Prediction. Nauka, Moscow (2006)
30. Zhang, L.Y., Mao, X.B., Lu, A.H.: Experimental study of the mechanical properties of rocks at high temperature. Sci. China Ser. E **52**(3), 641–646 (2009)

Survey of a Peruvian Archaeological Site Using LiDAR and Photogrammetry: A Contribution to the Study of the Chachapoya

Giovanni Righetti[1], Stefano Serafini[1], Fabian Brondi Rueda[2], Warren B. Church[3], and Gabriele Garnero[4(✉)]

[1] MEDS BV, Ir. M. Schefferlaan 55, 7556 CR Hengelo, The Netherlands
[2] Instituto Geográfico Nacional, Lima, Perú
[3] Department of Earth and Space Sciences, Columbus State University, Columbus, GA, USA
[4] Interuniversity Department of Regional and Urban Studies and Planning, Politecnico e Università degli Studi di Torino, Turin, Italy
gabriele.garnero@unito.it

Abstract. In November of 2019, the company MEDS BV, based in the Netherlands but mainly active in the Americas, initiated experimental aerial remote sensing with airborne LiDAR imagery in the context of a private-public sector collaboration to enable identification of undocumented archaeological sites concealed beneath the high Andean tropical cloud forests in northern Peru's Amazonas Region. Remote sensing fieldwork and post-processing application of Deep Learning methods by MEDS BV specialists, and subsequent analysis of DTM images by archaeologists yielded a remarkably detailed picture of a forest-covered, previously unstudied sector at the extensive archaeological complex of Kuelap called Imperio. At 3000 m above sea level, the Kuelap site complex consists of at least 12 sectors and two cliff cemeteries sprawling 900 hectares along a ridge top above the western banks of the Utcubamba River valley. Kuelap's centerpiece and featured tourist attraction called "La Fortaleza" is a large settlement built atop a massive walled platform a long, prominent ridgetop. The Kuelap complex was probably the most populous locality in the Utcubamba River valley and is attributed to peoples that the Inka and Spaniards called "Chachapoya." Early Spanish settlers left no known written descriptions of the site, nor useful descriptions regarding the region's inhabitants. Consequently — and despite extensive archaeological studies — important questions concerning the political, economic, and religious roles of Kuelap in the region remain unresolved.

The project reported here has primary and secondary objectives, both resulting from multiple stages of data gathering, processing, analysis, and interpretation. The primary goal was to capture high-resolution, three-dimensional georeferenced imagery of archaeological remains hidden beneath the region's dense tropical montane forests and provide sufficient data for a rich preliminary description. This work responds to the urgent need to identify, characterize, and protect such cultural heritage from looting and destructive activities that accompany population growth and deforestation. The second objective emerged as an unexpected bonus, only because of the extraordinary success of the first. Successful imaging of surface details at Imperio provided an extraordinary opportunity to reevaluate previous interpretations of the site, and to offer an alternative novel hypothesis

© Springer Nature Switzerland AG 2021
O. Gervasi et al. (Eds.): ICCSA 2021, LNCS 12954, pp. 613–628, 2021.
https://doi.org/10.1007/978-3-030-86979-3_43

regarding Imperio's history of occupation and particularly the site's special functions. The imagery enabled identification of subtle surface features that we suggest could be overlooked and inadvertently destroyed during conventional ground-level mapping and documentation activities in such complex, overgrown terrain. Many such features are functional elements of a planned drainage system that warrants further study for long-term conservation planning.

Keywords: Kuelap · 3D model · Deep learning

1 Introduction

Aerial remote sensing with UAVs (Unmanned Aerial Vehicles) equipped with LiDAR (Light Detection and Ranging) technology has become an increasingly effective means of identifying, mapping, and analyzing surface features on archaeological sites and landscapes lying hidden beneath tropical forests in Middle America from southern Mexico through Honduras [1–4].

More recently, archaeologists have begun to deploy LiDAR aerial remote sensing in the South American tropical lowlands and Ecuadorian Andes to analyze human-modified landscapes at various scales [5–7].

Airborne LiDAR survey is still new to the Peruvian Central Andes where scientific archaeological research beginning near the end of the 19th century in unforested, and deforested regions has produced a robust archaeological record from sites near contemporary population centers. Airborne LiDAR doubtlessly has much to contribute to archaeology across the greater Andes.

However, the technology has the potential to make especially significant contributions to the archaeological record where tropical montane forests cloak undocumented and understudied sites on the eastern Andean slopes above the Amazon lowlands (Fig. 1).

Many large, abandoned settlements and monumental sites of stone masonry rarely mentioned in colonial documents remain undocumented in Peru's northern "culture area" of Chachapoyas. Kuelap's monumental core, La Fortaleza was first described in 1843 and published in 1891 [8]. This and other abandoned Chachapoya settlements and cliff tombs were familiar to local inhabitants, and subsequently visited by 19th century foreign travelers like Middendorf, Raimondi and Werthemann [9–11] a few decades earlier than more famous Inka sites such as Machu Picchu, Choquequirao, and "lost" Vilcabamba in the Andean montane forests east of Cusco.

Development of archaeology in Chachapoyas proceeded sporadically during the 20th century because infrastructure and services facilitating access to sites and sustained fieldwork were slow to penetrate the region [12, 13]. This is changing as a slow, seemly inexorable process of colonizing the eastern slope Montane and Premontane Life Zones [14, 15] between approximately 3,500 and 400 m continues to accelerate [16]. The demographic push has led to deforesting and increased looting of exposed sites before they can be documented and protected by authorities while many sites still lie hidden beneath forest canopies and Chachapoyas archaeology remains understudied and lagging far behind progress in other regions. Today the region's extraordinary archaeology and natural beauty make it a growing, popular adventure-tourism destination, and

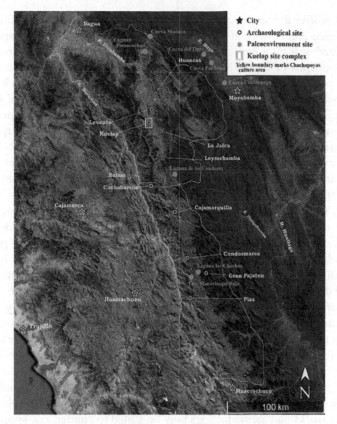

Fig. 1. Map of Chachapoyas culture area with location of Kuelap site complex.

Peru's Ministry of Culture has developed an initiative to identify, investigate, and conserve archaeological sites in and around the Chachapoyas forests. A recent evaluation by Sarmiento and colleagues [17] emphasizes the urgent need of more science-based research in the Chachapoyas cloud forests. Historical research, recent biogeographical and paleoecological studies portray a long and complex history of dynamic relationships between Tropandean forested and non-forested environments, and human inhabitants that responded to sudden and/or prolonged climate changes in interactive ways still poorly understood. Current demographic studies of populations based upon genotypes by bioarchaeologists seem likewise to reflect historical complexity. Many ancient sites and anthropic landscapes remain hidden beneath forest regrowth today. Simply put, our understanding of the Chachapoyas past is biased because of relatively frequent shifts in human demography and forest ecosystems on the Andean slopes. To locate, investigate and protect Chachapoyas cultural heritage, archaeologists have just begun using LiDAR-equipped drones to image archaeological remains. Our research represents one of Peru's first LiDAR remote sensing initiatives centered around the archaeological tourist destination of Kuelap, a sprawling site complex featuring an enormous walled settlement built on the crest of a ridgetop at 3,000 m now accessible by cable cars.

Here we proffer the results of our recent efforts to image ground surface morphology and surface architecture at Imperio, one of several smaller Chachapoya sites at Kuelap covered still by a dense remnant of humid tropical montane forest one kilometer east-southeast of Kuelap's La Fortaleza monument at 2760 m above mean sea level, UTM coordinates 18M, 177600.0 m E, 9289368.0 m S (Fig. 2). The research involved a public-private sector collaboration between Peru's Ministry of Culture and the National Geographical Institute, and MEDS BV in Amsterdam which performed the service. Two university-based archaeologists collaborated during the interpretive stage as unremunerated academic researchers.

Our presentation follows in four parts. First, we supply background information on the Kuelap archaeological complex which consists of several components or "sites" covering a large ridgetop, and specifically on the site of "Imperio" where we focused our research. We summarize previous investigations by other researchers and summarize what is known and what remains unknown about the Kuelap complex while situating it within our sketchy archaeological and ethnohistorical knowledge of the late pre-Hispanic and early Colonial Period Chachapoyas region. Second, we describe the methods and materials utilized for both the data-gathering stage, and the subsequent image analysis. Third, using the processed imagery we characterize the archaeological surface remains and their distributions in the context of Imperio's anthropogeomorphology.

The fourth stage of this presentation was not originally a part of our project prospectus. Through the course of study, it became clear that Imperio is a complex, composite "artifact," a selected landform molded and sculpted. All sites are artifacts in a manner of speaking, but Imperio experienced a use-life during which it passed through stages of remodeling and repurposing to assume symbolic functions. Subsequently, the 2019 LiDAR imagery captured one moment in a long post-abandonment stage. Numerous theoretical frameworks and methodologies may be suited to similar, site-specific imagery this kind of experimental research involves layers of interpretation that require ground-truthing. For that reason, we chose to foreground basic descriptive information that we gleaned from Imperio's imagery. However, because our initial interpretations revealed intra-site patterning that is distinctive and atypical in the Chachapoyas region, we are compelled to offer additional inferences regarding the site's chronological stages of construction and re-modeling (use-life).

This fourth step in the presentation can be considered our best attempt to interpret Imperio as a whole, as more than the sum of its parts. Unless one entertains the possibility that Imperio served functions that were symbolic rather than simply quotidian, one is left to conclude that the distributions visible on the surface show little evidence of the planned organization that we believe originally underlaid its construction and continued usage. Hence, this fourth interpretive stage reinforces our most basic interpretations of some surface features. Predominant among these are traces of buildings dismantled, ostensibly to utilize scavenged construction materials for activities necessary to repurpose the site. Low walls (or "berms") and ditches that we identified are integral parts of the Imperio as a functioning whole of great symbolic significance as we will demonstrate. Accordingly, we offer preliminary interpretations of Imperio's chronology and potential function(s), both utilitarian and symbolic. We have sufficient confidence in our basic identifications of Imperio's surface features to endeavor higher levels of inference, and we did aim to stop short of unwarranted speculation. Virtually all of our interpretations can be addressed as hypotheses with fieldwork on the ground. We included this last interpretive section in our presentation because the patterning inferred from our descriptive analysis warrants a reevaluation of Imperio's functions on the landscape. A reinterpretation of Imperio as more significant than a small agrarian settlement as first thought enables a fuller understanding of the Kuelap site complex as a whole.

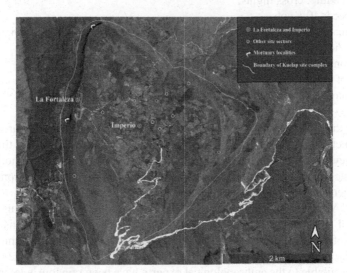

Fig. 2. Map of Kuelap site complex with locations of La Fortaleza, Imperio, and estimated boundary of site complex.

2   Materials and Methods

The research reported here was conducted with the primary objective of verifying and defining the best technology with which to identify possible settlements under the montane forest of the "Amazonas" region. For the drone flights, MEDS technicians had to size the instrumentation to be used based on:

- altitude above mean sea level,
- vegetation density,
- horological characteristics, and
- weather conditions.

To reach our goal of obtaining the highest possible number of 3D points on the ground, we planned to use:

- LiDAR instrument (accuracy 1.5 cm) equipped with high precision GNSS/IMU (planimetric positioning 5 cm, altimetric 10 cm, angular 0.015° in roll and pitch, 0.035° in the yaw).

- flight plans and acquisition parameters studied to reduce the shadow cones to a minimum.

Our parameters included:

- Flight altitude: variable from 60 to 100 m above ground level,
- Flight schedule: cross flights,
- Flight speed: 10 Knots,
- PulseRate: variable from 400 to 820 kHz based on the morphological characteristics,
- Field of View (FOV): 180°,
- Revolutions per second: 60–200 scans/s,
- Density of points detected: between 300 and 400 pt/m^2, and
- GSD photogrammetric shots: 2–5 cm.

Among the difficulties faced during the drone survey of the "Imperio" area was wind and other meteorological variability. Timing was everything, and the best time to carry out the surveys was between 11:00 AM and 2:00 PM. Due to the area's geomorphological characteristics and the altitude, the performance of the GNSS receiver was compromised, so that longer times than usual were needed for ground acquisitions.

The LIDAR data filtering and classification processes were carried out using macros in analytical software created by MEDS called ATLAS (www.theatlasgis.com). The parameters of this software development have taken into account: high humidity, dense and multilayered vegetation, and the reduced size of the objects to be searched. The data made available to the anthropological experts have been previously interpreted and extracted thanks to the use of specific developed neural networks.

Pursuing data analysis objectives, an automatic survey analysis software was implemented proceeding in four distinct phases:

- Identification of the training set,
- Learning,
- Recognition testing, and
- Application for real relief.

The selection criterion sought to include the most heterogeneous cases emphasizing visibility and the presence or absence of vegetation.

For each building identified, we determined:

- the shape (rectangular or circular),
- the centroid, and
- the approximate size (larger diameter/smaller diameter for circular or elliptical buildings, length of sides for rectangular buildings).

All of the selected buildings have a diameter less than 15 m, and this measure has been used as a sample size for software together with a search area of 30 × 30 m. Then the software started looking for buildings of the aforementioned size, and the overlap used was 50% to ensure the entirety of the sample. For each building (either for training or verification), the software generated:

- LiDAR sections centered on the building, and
- Alternated the data model, by inserting spatial transactions and rotations and altered the set of points with random noise.

Such alterations amplified to a total of 125 variants for each building, bringing the total set of samples to 10500.

The buildings identified were divided into two groups:

- the first (70%) for training neural networks, and
- the second (remaining 30%) for the verification.

The deep learning software, based on TensorFlow, was implemented in C++. The LiDAR sections were used by the recognition algorithm that provided the dimensions and orientation for each sample; based on the identification of the section with longer and shorter length for each building under study. All the data has been uploaded to the MEDS' AtlasGIS, to verify the truthfulness of obtained results through an "images comparison" technique (Fig. 3).

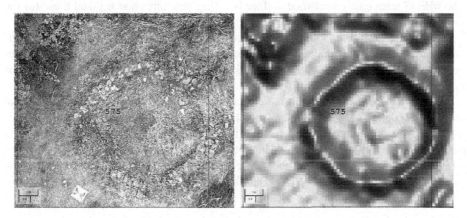

Fig. 3. Circular stone building viewed in orthophoto and DTM

3 Methodology of Image Analysis

Our methodology for experimental descriptive analysis of Imperio relied on identically georeferenced orthophotographic and Digital Terrain Model (DTM) imagery with 2 cm and 15 cm resolution, respectively. The bulk of the imagery analysis conducted by the team utilized The AtlasGIS software program which features multiple tools for visualizing and measuring site features in three dimensions yet is easier to use for relatively simple analysis than ESRI's ArcGIS.

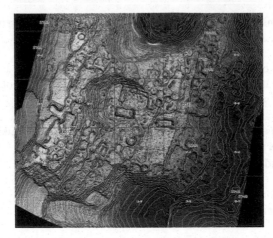

Fig. 4. Contour line overlays at 5 m and 1 m intervals shown with 50 m-grid

A color ramp overlay was created for the DTM to highlight topography and changes in elevation. Three sets of contour lines were generated as layers using 5 m, 1 m, and 0.5 m intervals (Fig. 4). The 0.5 m contour interval was useful for quickly identifying low walls that we refer to as "berms," as well as low or poorly preserved wall foundations. The MEDS team easily identified surface building structures and utilized these for the Deep Learning process.

Additional analysis enabled unusually good recognition of surface drainage patterns and more subtle features that will await ground-truthing. This process facilitated subsequent archaeological identification of buildings, free-standing walls, ditches, and berms in three-dimensions.

This is experimental research rather than one of the many kinds of archaeological projects listed in the legal document Decreto Supremo N° 003–2014-MC that provides guidelines for more conventional cultural resource documentation. Our research, and hence our report, is a non-invasive view of Imperio created to sketch general characteristics of the site's surface morphology, especially landform, cultural remains on the surface, and their relationships to one another as one small but complex component of a very large Kuelap "cultural landscape."

4   Results

The configuration of the site's constructed area is constrained by basin-shaped, eroded sinkholes, that are typical of the region's karst bedrock geology. Such concavities pock the otherwise smooth surface of the eastern slope of La Barreta, and are generally not visible with Google Earth satellite imagery, or even at ground-level where forest patches may conceal the depth of some sinks. The characteristics of karst geomorphology played a significant role in determining locations for pre-Hispanic settlements, tombs, and shrines. The configuration of the natural landform upon which Imperio was constructed undoubtedly met specific criteria identified by its builders as we hope to demonstrate in paragraphs to follow. Our LiDAR imagery facilitated creation of a polygon with an area of 3.62 hectares conforming to both the constructed area and the complex terrain. The landform viewed beneath the forest vaguely approximates symmetry along an axis trending WNW and ESE. Although we offer detailed measurements at the 10-cm level (and occasionally at the one-centimeter level) in the following paragraphs with care, readers should keep in mind that no LiDAR sensor will produce a point cloud of sufficient density and homogeneity to replicate ground topography in a forested landscape with impeccable precision, although we can expect methodological improvements after additional ground-truthing.

4.1 Infrastructure and Structures

Here we offer a list of surface elements, features, and structures that we have identified up to the present before we enter into subsequent, more complex levels of description. These were in turn divided into two categories. We have termed the smallest objects of our attention identified in the imagery as "elements" that may or may not be parts of "features" that we tentatively assigned to the first of the two major catteries, "infrastructure." These tend to be constructions on the surface including terraces, berms, drains, borrow pits, and so forth. The term "structure" is reserved for features interpreted as above-ground buildings. These three terms are used heuristically and were chosen only because they were useful to us for analysis and are useful for the description to follow. Problems with such terms arise when one risks identifying a ditch that appears to be a built drainage channel constrained by a terrace or building wall on one side and a berm on the other, and a channel eroded by surface runoff that can be traced across the site.

We identified three categories of "structures" at Imperio, but only after thorough analysis of the constructed area did we feel confident in our identifications which were usually distinguished as circular buildings and their foundations that represent the most common late pre-Hispanic form of house, or family dwelling in the Chachapoyas region. We also easily identified rectangular buildings that were uncommon in the region until the Inka conquest sometime after 1470 CE (Christian Era). Inka attribution of five of these structures can be offered with confidence because they articulate with one another to form a patio group seen frequently across the Inka empire and called a kancha in the Inka Quechua language. More puzzling at first were surface cuts, and flat circular "footprints" where we conclude that circular stone buildings (and at least one rectangular structure) were dismantled to repurpose construction materials. In sum, the three-dimensional LiDAR imagery of Imperio's constructed area allowed us to identify the remains of eight rectangular buildings and 82 circular constructions with confidence. This alone is a remarkable achievement given the dense forest cover and more than doubles the number of 40 circular constructions previously counted at the site.

Using the LiDAR imagery and the general arrangement of terraces, we determined that Imperio can be visually divided into Upper, Middle and Lower Zones for descriptive purposes. Within each of the three zones, one or more terraces extends roughly north-south across the promontory, but the central sinkhole occupies much of the Middle Zone. To distinguish each of the three zones at a more demonstrably objective level, we conducted a cursory search for meaningful statistical evidence with which to isolate and evaluate surface features. The site's small size, evidence of periodic reorganization, renovation, and the lack of better chronological control undermines our confidence in such efforts. Nevertheless, we felt that the tripartite division was visually distinctive. We hesitate to offer infer a great deal of chronological significance to the zones, although the Upper Zone shows more evidence of building dismantling. This is indicative of a relative chronology. Numerous avenues for additional research can be pursued using the LiDAR imagery, but these remain beyond the purview of this presentation.

A detailed hydrological study of Imperio's water management system and dendritic drainage pattern can begin with the three-dimensional LiDAR imagery before undertaking more extensive ground-level fieldwork. Because we are dealing with an aspect of the site's development that was crucial for habitation and use, we offer preliminary observations pertinent to the terraced system by referring to the whole as "surface infrastructure," before describing the remains of architectural living spaces built atop the surface.

4.2 Site Anthropogeomorphology

At the top of the landform visible near the WNW edge of our image (in the Upper Zone), an actively cultivated area at 2780 m elevation can be identified on both the orthophoto and the DTM image. From there, Imperio extends 220 m down a peninsular ridge trending east-southeast. Eroded sinkholes flanking the ridge on both north and south sides narrow the landform, thus rendering its prominent ridge-like appearance.

The constructed area within the image drops 40 vertical meters with an averaged gradient of 18%.

The awkward term "anthropogeomorphological" aptly describes the landform because the entire ridge surface was modified. Artificial terraces create an irregular series of "steps" descending eastward, and most or all of these are sufficiently intact to detect with our LiDAR and over one meter-high. Stone terrace facades are mentioned in all site descriptions. Space constraints would have precluded use of these terraces for cultivation on a significant scale (Fig. 5).

Fig. 5. Cultivated area at west edge of site imaged as orthophoto and DTM.

The sinkhole concavities on the promontory flanks cut deeply into the northern and southern sides nearly halfway down, constricting the site surface to 115 m at its narrowest point. The corresponding slopes on the north and south sides fall away precipitously 21 m on the north side with a 60% gradient, and 11m on the south with a gradient of 50%. Below the midsection, the promontory expands to 189 m at its widest point 55 m above the bottom which roughly corresponds to the eastern edge of the image.

Situated slightly north of the narrow midsection, the dominant and most visually striking feature on the ramp-like promontory is a wide, flat-bottomed sinkhole. This

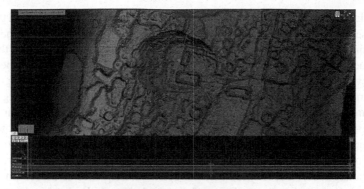

Fig. 6. The Central Sinkhole.

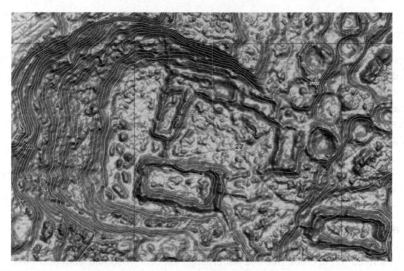

Fig. 7. Patio group or rectangular buildings within sink.

feature here referred to simply as the "central sinkhole" clearly served as the focal point of Imperio's constructed area. On the promontory surface, the concavity's diameter stretches 54 m, and the steepest wall at the northern rim falls 8.4 m with a gradient of 60%. At the cavity's western edge, the wall slopes more gently with a gradient of 22%. Arrayed on the "floor" of the sinkhole sits an orthogonal group of five rectangular buildings surrounding a patio and connected to one another by low walls (Figs. 6, 7). Because the central sinkhole appears as a "notch" in the hillside, it is crescent-shaped and open to the east where the walls of the sink meet the slope.

The appearance also recalls the shape of an amphitheater, but we eschew this descriptive term to avoid unintended interpretation of the landform's function(s).

The patio group does not occupy the entire bottom but was constructed at the sink-hole's opening and protrudes eastward onto a narrow terrace. The eastern side of the crescent formation is 31 m wide but for the purpose of access, the northern half of this width is blocked by one of the buildings. The narrow terrace extending beyond the access supports several circular buildings to the north and south. The maximum diameter of the level bottom measures north-south reaches 35 m. The entire oblong bottom of the central sink, including the constructed area, spreads over 1,677 m^2 and would have been intentionally leveled and the narrow terrace constructed, prior to erecting the patio group. The narrow terrace at the sinkhole opening ends 1.5 m above a broad terrace large enough to have functioned as a plaza for gatherings of people. The largest rectangular structure at Imperio labeled Building A sits in front of the access to the central sinkhole and the patio group. This terrace extends nearly 35 m south of Building A but narrows where constructions cluster toward the northern end. Below this terrace, and in front of the sinkhole, a large recessed, terraced corridor splits the sequence of descending terraces into northern and southern parts that can be roughly matched using bands of the color ramp, the 1-m contour lines, and surface elevation points.

4.3 Additional Aspects

Further in-depth analyses are underway which will develop aspects relating to the following

- Infrastructure: terraces, berms, and drains
- Circular constructions and indigenous community
- Rectangular constructions and the patio group

The limitations of the present document do not allow these arguments to be explored in depth.

5 Discussion: Interpreting Imperio Through Time

We are inclined to conclude that the patterning just described and visible on the surface of Imperio represents a conflation of Imperio's two most substantial occupations prior to abandonment, beginning with the Inka occupation at Kuelap and ending after a period of Spanish colonial occupation of unknown duration. The landform was also likely inhabited long before the Inka conquest. However, isolating evidence pre-dating major landscape modifications attributable to the Inka as attested by large stone terraces was not possible with our imagery, and may be difficult with ground-level investigations. The location was probably chosen as a construction site for the same compelling reasons related to its geomorphology and utility as a source of water during three successive occupations by three cultures arriving in succession.

In terms of Imperio's chronology, we hypothesize that the location was gradually, perhaps sporadically, occupied prior to Inka conquest. Presuming that the central sinkhole had always disgorged and perhaps pooled large quantities of water, the high ground of the Upper Zone would have been a preferred location to camp or reside. Earliest habitations may be among those cannibalized, but without visual evidence from the LiDAR imagery our suggestions are speculative. Some residents of a rustic hamlet may have managed access to water for irrigation on behalf of kin groups. Some may have cared for a shrine that might have existed and required maintenance. The earliest dated evidence for settlement on La Barreta by approximately AD 400 are reported from excavations at La Fortaleza, and the monument's stone walls may have been under construction by AD 900. We suggest that occupation and some construction at Imperio may have begun at about the same time, but we have no data to support the hypothesis.

Some archaeologists have posed water supply as a significant unanswered problem when considering the substantial needs of an estimated 3,000 inhabitants in La Fortaleza, the needs for agriculture, and for watering camelid herds. In reply to such questions, Ruiz has described the abundance of springs and seeps on and around La Barreta. Some seeps and springs known today by area residents would have functioned in the past. We think it likely that Imperio was already in use as a source of water for agriculture and drinking, and the bottom surface of the central sinkhole was conditioned to retain and impound water as local needs increased. Another peripheral archaeological site at Kuelap known as El Lirio also reportedly has a spring. Such places where water emanated from the ground were and often still are considered sacred by Andean peoples. On the sacred landscape of La Barreta, the water source within the central sinkhole was probably considered a pakarina, a sacred place of origin or emergence for one or more of the local kin groups, and as a source of life in the most universal sense.

6   Conclusion: LiDAR in Tropandean Cloudforests

We have squeezed many inferences from the LiDAR imagery at our disposal for this study… some critics may say too many. To generate our interpretations, we used the few descriptions of Imperio at our disposal, most of which were understandably cursory given the thick vegetation. Our experimentation with airborne LiDAR imagery convinced us that the resulting imagery is extremely valuable, especially for aerial prospecting when long-distance flights become feasible with technological advances. Perhaps the greatest value of this LiDAR technology is its ability to penetrate dense tropical forest to identify the presence or absence of archaeological settlements. We also see great value in the use of LiDAR for research conducted to support conservation planning where site locations are known. Furthermore, we propose that LiDAR imagery is capable of providing an excellent tool to aid preliminary analysis of forested sites like Imperio, and to venture hypotheses regarding complex architecture when is unexpectedly encountered as it was in this case. Without full imagery of the broader landscape including the site's cultural and environmental contexts, it is obvious that our interpretations await evaluation through appropriate ground-level fieldwork.

The use of LiDAR technology is hardly necessary in all terrains and environments to identify or analyze every kind of small or large archaeological site. Tropical montane forests of in the Andes, and especially on the eastern slopes pose special challenges for archaeological reconnaissance, and the presence of stone architecture constructed on monumental scales provide an extraordinary "testing ground" appropriate to truly challenge and evaluate LiDAR's capabilities. What we presently understand of site densities on the eastern slopes indicates that the Vilcabamba region east of Cusco, and the forested stretches of territory within the more biogeographically diverse areas of Amazonas, San Martin, and La Libertad Regions contain many monumental archaeological sites in areas remaining to be examined by archaeologists. These sites are threatened by farming and herding societies pushing eastward in search of unclaimed land parcels and perhaps more humid climates. These are not the only eastern slope regions with stone settlements beneath forests, but to all indications, their site densities are unmatched. Logically, the forested landscapes of eastern Cusco and the northeastern Peruvian Andes are ideal proving grounds for the development of LiDAR technology in Peru.

While the use of LiDAR imagery at a site like Imperio has advantages over ground survey to quickly observe spatial relationships, and to estimate structural dimensions, architectural and masonry details, and most preservation issues should be assessed by ground survey and ground-level visual observations. Using the LiDAR imagery, we found at first that the spatial organization of constructions appeared to be extremely complex but the site structure became easier to comprehend after we began to recognize the berms and channels serving as drainage infrastructure. While conducting ground-level fieldwork within tangled forests, one becomes quickly disoriented. Simply orienting oneself to conduct ground-level mapping requires cutting of vegetation, and potentially destructive "cleaning" of architectural features may follow. Furthermore, archaeologists and support crews wielding machetes and piling brush may fail to recognize relatively subtle spatial patterns before detailed three-dimensional surface mapping is completed. The activities involved in the arduous process of creating such a detailed map might inadvertently trample and further erode traces of drainage systems like Imperio's which appears to have been carefully planned by the site's builders. For these reasons, we conclude that this LiDAR imagery was an invaluable tool with which to begin study of Imperio.

We are in complete agreement with the consensus among archaeologists that the methodologies of LiDAR imaging and surface documentation complement one another, and together enable more robust descriptions needed to study and protect ancient sites and landscapes... especially in such terrain. In fact, the archaeological ground reconnaissance organized and led by archaeologist Lic. Constante Luján Bazan enabled verification of the image findings that gave us sufficient confidence to proceed. The archaeological team on the ground was also able to document such details as the traces of plaster and decorations on the church wall surfaces.

It was never the goal of this project, or even this publication, to answer the question, "What was Imperio?" Further inquiry is needed to provide plausible answers. However, we retrieved imagery attesting to the complexity of Imperio's chronology of construction, and the site's functions. We do propose that the site was more socially, economically, and politically significant than a rural agricultural hamlet as previously suggested. Somewhat miraculously, we feel that we say this with confidence although we have not touched the site surface, but present only hypotheses for others to pursue or ignore. We hope that our preliminary interpretations serve to provoke additional investigations at other archaeological sites on La Barreta and elsewhere. Perhaps this work will help confirm Ruiz's observation that the entire Kuelap settlement complex has almost twice as many habitations as we have been led to believe in literature, and on guided tours. Reevaluating La Fortaleza within an enlarged context will certainly enhance our understanding of Kuelap as a multi-functional site complex, and not just a fortress as was once commonly believed. Hopefully, a fuller analysis of the complex, combined with surface archaeological procedures, will provide a sorely needed step towards resolving controversies surrounding the site's ancient functions and meanings within the greater Chachapoyas region.

As LiDAR technology shows increasing potential for effective remote sensing, concerns regarding ethics and data access are moving to the foreground. We also regard these as very important concerns. On La Barreta, competing land claims create social friction. However, this publication was designed as a report on research and development of a particular technology. Clearly there will be questions about who should have access to the data, and we imagine that the Ministry of Culture will initiate these kinds of conversations along with other Peruvian institutions and stakeholders such as local communities. The use of LiDAR imagery can also contribute to ethical and sustainable tourism development by supporting design of scientifically correct 3D reconstructions that may be displayed on immersive Virtual, Augmented and Mixed Reality tools. Depending upon future development planning, Kuelap could be toured virtually by individuals with physical disabilities, or by others unable to undertake the rigorous trip to this high-altitude site, a visit that does require some physical stamina. As we prepared this publication during a global pandemic crisis, the advantages of such technologies became immediately obvious.

More information on the use of deep learning to discover lost cities can be found on https://www.youtube.com/watch?v=aCZwM-9nE_4&ab_channel=MEDSAM STERDAM.

Acknowledgments. Arturo Ruiz Estrada, Dr. Clinton Barineau (confirmed hydrological aspects), Lic. Constante Luján Bazán, Instituto Geográfico Nacional del Perú, Ministerio de Cultura del Perú.

References

1. Chase, A.F., Chase, D.Z.: Detection of Maya ruins by LiDAR: applications, case study, and issues. In: Masini, N., Soldovieri, F. (eds.) Sensing the Past. GE, vol. 16, pp. 455–468. Springer, Cham (2017). https://doi.org/10.1007/978-3-319-50518-3_22
2. Fisher, C.T., Cohen, A.S., Fernández-Diaz, J.C., Leisz, S.J.: The application of airborne mapping LiDAR for the documentation of ancient cities and regions in tropical regions. Quatern. Int. **448**, 129–138 (2017)
3. Inomata, T., Pinzón, F., Ranchos, J.L., Haraguchi, T., Nasu, H., Fernandez-Diaz, J.C., et al.: Archaeological application of airborne LiDAR with Object-Based vegetation classification and visualization techniques at the Lowland Maya site of Ceibal, Guatemala. Remote Sens. **9**(6), 563 (2017)
4. McAnany, P.A.: Large-scale early Maya sites in Mexico revealed by lidar mapping technology. Nature **582**(7813), 490–492 (2020)
5. Iriarte, J., et al.: Geometry by design: contribution of lidar to the understanding of settlement patterns of the mound villages in SW Amazonia. J. Comput. Appl. Archaeol. **3**(1), 151–169 (2020). https://doi.org/10.5334/jcaa.45
6. Castro-Priego, M., Olmo-Enciso, L., Labrada-Ochoa, M.O., Jijón-Porras, J.A., García-Campoverde, J.A.: Agrarian spaces, pre-Hispanic settlement and LiDAR technology in the central coast of Ecuador. Virtual Archaeology Review (2021)

7. Khan, S., Aragão, L., Iriarte, J.: A UAV–lidar system to map Amazonian rainforest and its ancient landscape transformations. Int. J. Remote Sens. **38**(8–10), 2313–2330 (2017)
8. Nieto JCaMB: Torre de Babel en el Perú. Boletín de la Sociedad Geográfica de Lima. 1891 [1843] **1**(10–12), 440–448 (1891)
9. Raimondi, A.: Imprenta Nacional, El Peru. Lima (1874)
10. Middendorf, E.W.: Peru Beobachtungen und Studien über das Land und seine Bewohner. Berlin (1895)
11. Werthemannn, A.: Ruinas de la fortaleza de Cuelap. Boletín de la Sociedad Geográfica de Lima. **2**(4–6), 147–158 (1892)
12. Church, W., Guengerich, A.: Introducción: La (re) construcción de Chachapoyas a través de la historia y la historiografía. In: Guengerich, A., Church, W., (eds.) ¿Qué fue Chachapoyas? Aproximaciones interdisciplinarias en el estudio de los Andes Nororientales del Perú Boletín de Arqueología PUCP. 23, p. 5-38. PUCP, Lima (2018)
13. Schjellerup, I.R.: Incas and Spaniards in the Conquest of the Chachapoyas. Archaeological and Ethnohistorical Research in the North-eastern Andes of Peru [Ph.D.]. Gothenburg (1997)
14. Naturales) PONdEdR. Mapa ecológico del Perú: guía explicativa. Lima: Republica del Peru, Oficina Nacional de Evaluación de Recursos Naturales (ONERN) (1976)
15. Young, K.R., León, B.: Peru's humid eastern montane forests: An overview of their physical settings, biological diversity, human use and settlement, and conservation needs: Centre for Research on the Cultural and Biological Diversity of Andean Rainforests (DIVA) (1999)
16. Schjellerup, I., La Ceja de Montaña, a disappearing landscape: interdisciplinary studies from North-eastern Peru, Aarhus Universitetsforlag (2009)
17. Sarmiento, F.O., Bush, M., Church, W., VanValkenburgh, P., Oliva, M., Delgado, E., et al.: Mountain science poised to help ecotourism in Peruvian cloud forests. Past Global Changes Magazine. **28**(1), 22–23 (2020)

Estimation of Hourly Salinity Concentrations Using an Artificial Neural Network

Vladimir J. Alarcon[1]([⊠]) [iD], Anna C. Linhoss[2], Christopher R. Kelble[3],
Paul F. Mickle[4], Joseph Bishop[3], and Emily Milton[3]

[1] Civil Engineering Department, Universidad Diego Portales, 441 Ejercito Av., Santiago, Chile
vladimir.alarcon@udp.cl
[2] Department of Biosystems Engineering, Auburn University, 3101 Shelby Center, Auburn, AL 36849, USA
alinhoss@auburn.edu
[3] NOAA Atlantic Oceanographic and Meteorological Laboratory, 4301 Rickenbacker Causeway, Miami, FL 33149, USA
{chris.kelble,joe.bishop,emily.milton}@noaa.gov
[4] Northern Gulf Institute, Mississippi State University, 2 Research Blvd., Starkville, MS 39759, USA

Abstract. Estimating salinity concentrations in coastal waters allows characterization of the spatial and temporal dynamics of the freshwater/saltwater interface. In Southeast Florida (USA) the saltwater interface is monitored and evaluated for potential impacts to public supply wellfields and biological communities. In this research, a closed-loop autoregressive neural network with exogenous inputs was developed to estimate salinity concentrations at a coastal water quality station (BISCC4) in Biscayne Bay, Florida. The neural network (ANN) is shown to successfully simulate hourly salinity concentrations for years 2015 through 2019. A statistical comparison of simulated concentrations versus observed data demonstrates that the ANN simulates salinity concentration values and trends within acceptable margin of errors ($R^2 = 0.59$, K-G = 0.64, NSE = 0.33, d = 0.86, PBIAS = 1.5%, RSR = 0.82). In its current form, the ANN model performs better in simulating salinity concentrations and trends, than an existing hydrodynamic model. These results have the potential to be applied to other coastal locations in Biscayne Bay where freshwater inputs from inland streams and canals are affecting salinity concentrations.

Keywords: Biscayne Bay · Salinity · Neural network · Southeast Florida · Prediction

1 Introduction

Salinity is a critical response variable that integrates hydrologic and coastal dynamics including sea level, tides, winds, precipitation, and streamflow [1]. The position and temporal dynamics of the freshwater–saltwater interface for larger coastal rivers results from the interaction of three principal forces: streamflow, mean tidal water levels, and

© Springer Nature Switzerland AG 2021
O. Gervasi et al. (Eds.): ICCSA 2021, LNCS 12954, pp. 629–640, 2021.
https://doi.org/10.1007/978-3-030-86979-3_44

tidal range [2]. The position of the freshwater interface determines the composition of freshwater and saltwater aquatic communities as well as the freshwater availability for water intakes [1]. Estimating salinity concentrations in coastal waters allows characterizing the spatial location of the freshwater/saltwater interface which has implications for biological communities and for urban settlements. For example, in Southeast Florida (USA) the saltwater interface is mapped as part of the water use permitting review process and to monitor for potential impacts to public supply wellfields [3].

Salinity in estuarine systems is influenced by climate and weather. The climate in Southeast Florida is characterized by hot and humid rainy summer, and mild winters. The annual average minimum, mean, and maximum temperatures in the area are 15 °C, 26 °C, and 32 °C, respectively, and the total annual precipitation average is 1507 mm. The total annual average potential evapotranspiration (ETP) loss in the area ranges from 1220 mm to 1320 mm per year [4]. Stalker et al. [5] estimated a freshwater input ratio canal/precipitation/groundwater of 37%:53%:10% in the wet season, and 40%:55%:5% in the dry season, with an error of ±25%. Approximately 75% of the total precipitation falls in the wet season, generating substantial run-off. Furthermore, discharge from regional groundwater circulation and controlled release from upstream canals provide a considerable volume of freshwater input to the water balance in the area [4]. Moreover, Biscayne Bay drains the Everglades (an extensive wetland located in Southeast Florida). This wetland is critical for water storage and recharge of the Biscayne aquifer, and is the principal source of freshwater for South Florida [6].

A recent modeling study on the hydrodynamic regime and salinity spatial distribution in Biscayne Bay (Southeast Florida, USA) was able to replicate salinity concentration values and seasonal trends occurring within the bay [7]. In this study, salinity estimations were poorest for locations close to the coast, especially during the wet season. A non-linear effect produced by freshwater inputs, which cannot be quantitatively described by mechanistic approaches, seems to be substantially affecting salinity concentrations.

The artificial neural network (ANN) method has been successfully applied to model non-linear processes. Special configurations of ANN have been successfully used to predict flow and sediment concentration time-series for rivers around the world [8, 9]. The most common models are artificial neural networks with dynamic architecture (DANN), autoregressive neural networks (ARNN), non-linear autoregressive exogeneous neural networks (NARX), and hybrid configurations that combine ANN with other modeling approaches. There are various ANN configurations that reported using artificial neural networks to predict salinity. Shahid et al. [10] used feed-forward back propagation ANN models to estimate salinity in the Grant Line Canal (California) using electrical conductivity, temperature, and pH as data inputs. Lin et al. [11] used an Elman neural network (ENN) to predict salinity intrusion at the Pearl River Delta. Zhou et al. [12] developed a hybrid model coupling the techniques of wavelet transform (WT) and artificial neural network (ANN) for forecasting estuarine salinity in the Pearl River Estuary, China. The WT-ANN was able to forecast 1 to 3 days of salinity concentrations. Rath et al. [13] developed an empirical model of salinity in the San Francisco Bay-Delta estuary using a Bayesian artificial neural network (ANN) model.

However, in most of these previous ANN applications the validation period of the model output corresponded to within-year or seasonal events. There are no ANN model applications that simulate continuous hourly salinity estimations at multiyear temporal scales.

This research presents an autoregressive neural network (with exogenous inputs) developed to forecast salinity concentrations in the coastal waters at Biscayne Bay (Florida, USA). Details are presented on input data selection, model calibration/training (optimization of model parameters), and model validation. Moreover, the developed ANN is assessed to determine if it can be used for forecasting hourly salinity concentrations for 5 continuous years.

2 Methods

2.1 Study Area

Biscayne Bay is a coastal water body located in southeast Florida (adjacent to the Miami metropolitan area) covering an area of approximately $700\ km^2$ (Fig. 1). The water depth in the bay ranges between 1.8 m and 4 m, except in dredged areas where depths can exceed 12 m [14]. The Biscayne Bay area includes the largest marine national park in the U.S. national park system: Biscayne National Park, an important part of the recreational, social, economic, and cultural life of Southeast Florida [15].

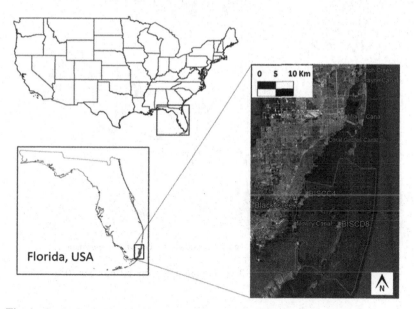

Fig. 1. Study area. Biscayne Bay and location of main streams draining to the bay.

Figure 1 shows the main canals that drain waters into Biscayne Bay including: Arch Creek, Biscayne Canal, Little River, Miami Canal, Coral Gables Canal, Snapper Creek, Black Creek, Princeton Canal, and Mowry Canal. Over a century of water management had led to no natural rivers or creeks draining into Biscayne Bay. Two water quality stations that collect salinity concentrations (BISCD8 and BISCC4) are also shown. Hourly salinity concentration data collected at those stations were used in this research.

2.2 Neural Network Development

The Nonlinear Autoregressive Exogenous Neural Network Model is a dynamical neural architecture commonly used for nonlinear dynamical systems. When applied to time-series prediction, this network configuration is designed as a feedforward time-delayed neural network, provided with feedback connections which enclose at least two layers of the network, and can use past values of predicted or true (measured) time-series [16]. In this research, salinity is forecasted using a nonlinear autoregressive exogenous neural network. Details on model development are presented in the following sections.

Input Data
The neural network was developed using hourly salinity from BISCD8 and BISCC4 water quality stations, and hourly flow from a gauge station located near the outfall of Black Creek to Biscayne Bay. Figure 2 illustrates the relationship among the observed data at those water quality stations.

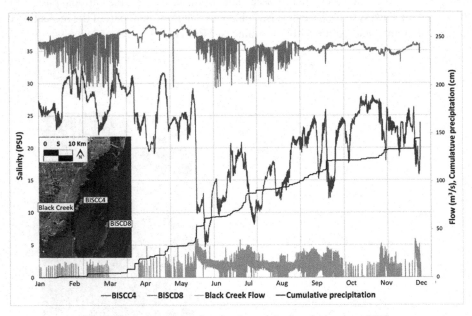

Fig. 2. Hourly salinity, flow, and precipitation during year 2013.

Figure 2 shows hourly salinity (BISCC4 and BISCD8 stations) and flow data (Black Creek) for year 2013. Cumulative precipitation in the Biscayne Area is also shown. The difference between salinity concentrations at BISCC4 and BISCD8 is striking. While BISCD8, which is closer to the ocean, recorded salinity values between 30 and 38 PSU, observed salinity at the coastal station (BISCC4) ranges between 5 and 35 PSU. The influence of freshwater inputs from rivers and canals (e.g., Black Creek, the closest stream to BISCC4), and precipitation, is evident because some of the lowest salinity values at BISCC4 occur after storm events and high flows observed at Black Creek.

However, there are decreases in salinity that do not co-occur with precipitation or flow events. At some degree, those minimum concentrations guard a relationship to salinities observed at BISCD8. This lack of flow and precipitation during periods when salinity decreases significantly suggests groundwater inputs may also play an important role in the salinity trends observed at BISCC4.

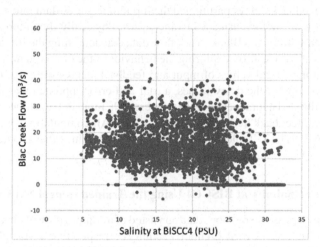

Fig. 3. Non-linear relationship between Black Creek flow and Salinity at BISCC4. Low salinity concentrations at BISCC4 are observed either for low or high flows at Black Creek.

Having identified the non-linear trend in salinity concentrations at BISCC4 (Fig. 3), an artificial neural network (ANN) was developed to capture this non-linear trend.

Neural Network Training
Observed hourly data (salinity at BISCC4 and BISCD8, and flow data at Black Creek), for years 2012 through 2019 were used for the development of the ANN. In order to explore the effect of training data size to achieve a successful prediction of salinity at station BISCC4, the number of years for training and prediction was varied. Table 1 details the process.

Table 1. Training data size

Model Rrn	Number of years used for training		
	Salinity BISCD8	Salinity BISCC4	Black Creek Flow
1	2012–2014	2012–2014	2012–2014
2	2012–2013	2012–2013	2012–2013
Final	2013–2014	2013–2014	2013–2014

Initially, observed hourly salinity data (collected at BISCC4 and BISCD8 stations), and flow data collected at Black Creek, from years 2012 through 2014, were used for training the neural net. Several combinations of yearly datasets were tested until optimal statistical indicators of fit between simulated and observed daily SST concentrations data were achieved. The final training data set corresponded to years 2013 through 2014 (Table 1) with respective input delay, k, and feedback delay, r, which are discussed below.

Input and feedback delays partitioned the input time-series data into subsets, during the computation of the forecasted SST time-series. Physically they represented the set of past BISCD8 salinity and Black Creek flow data that determine the forecasted salinity concentrations at BISCC4. By exploring the behavior of the observed data through time (Fig. 2), initial numerical values of input and feedback delays were determined. From the initial estimation of the delay values, a trial-and-error approach was followed until obtaining a calibrated neural network. In this research, input delays (k) were varied from 1:15 to 1:80 and feedback delays (r) from 1:1 to 1:6. All computations were performed using MATLAB R2017. Table 2 shows the parameter values that produced a trained network.

2.3   Forecasting Salinity at BISCC4 Using the Trained Neural Network

For the prediction phase, exogenous data consisted of a combination of observed data and predicted data. To forecast BISCC4 hourly salinity corresponding to year 2015, the ANN used observed hourly salinity and flow at stations BISCD8, BISCC4, and Black Creek, for years 2013 and 2014. The BISCC4 salinity forecasted for year 2016 was estimated using BISCD8 observed salinity and observed Black Creek flow data. However, the 2015-predicted BISCC4 salinity data was used as exogenous input. The forecast of BISCC4 salinity for years 2017–2019 was performed using BISCC4 ANN-predicted salinities. Table 2 summarizes the strategy.

Table 2.   Forecasting strategy.

Run	Exogenous input data			Predicted output
	Observed Salinity BISCD8	Observed Black Creek Flow	BISCC4	Salinity BISCC4
1	2013–2014	2013–2014	Observed 2013–2014	2015
2	2014–2015	2014–2015	Observed 2014–Predicted 2015	2016
3	2015–2016	2015–2016	Predicted 2015–Predicted 2016	2017
5	2016–2017	2016–2017	Predicted 2016–Predicted 2017	2018
6	2017–2018	2017–2018	Predicted 2017–Predicted 2018	2019

As explained in Table 2, the neural network model developed in this research is able to perform predictions of BISCC4 salinity making full use of previously predicted salinity concentrations for that station.

The measurement of how well predicted salinities matched observations was performed using several statistical indicators (Table 3). The goodness of fit was statistically assessed by the computation of the correlation coefficient (R), coefficient of determination (R^2), Nash Sutcliffe coefficient (NSE), Kling-Gupta efficiency (K-G), and Willmott's index of agreement (d). The statistical error was evaluated by the root-mean-squared-error to standard deviation ratio (RSR), and the bias of predicted salinity concentrations with respect to observed data was determined by the percent bias coefficient (PBIAS). These indicators are used for assessing ANN output [8] and are also widely used to assess hydrological and water quality modeled output [17–19]. Table 3 also shows the acceptability ranges recommended by the cited literature.

Table 3. Statistical indicators of fit and acceptability ranges.

Indicators of Fit	Formulae	Range
Root-mean-squared-error to standard deviation ratio, $RSR = \frac{RMSE}{STDEV_{Obs}}$	$\dfrac{\sqrt{\sum_{i=1}^{n}(Y_i^{Obs}-Y_i^{Sim}).^2}}{\sqrt{\sum_{i=1}^{n}(Y_i^{Obs}-Y_i^{Mean}).^2}}$	<0.79
Percent bias, $PBIAS$	$\dfrac{\sum_{i=1}^{n}\left(Y_i^{Obs}-Y_i^{Sim}\right)*100}{\sum_{i=1}^{n}\left(Y_i^{Obs}\right).}$	<±18%
Correlation coefficient, R	$\sqrt{\dfrac{\sum_{i=1}^{n}(Y_i^{Sim}-Y_i^{Mean}).2}{\sum_{i=1}^{n}(Y_i^{Obs}-Y_i^{Mean}).2}}$	>0.71
Coefficient of determination	R^2	>0.50
Nash–Sutcliffe efficiency, NS	$1-\dfrac{\sum_{i=1}^{n}\left(Y_i^{Obs}-Y_i^{Sim}\right).2}{\sum_{i=1}^{n}\left(Y_i^{Obs}-Y_i^{Mean}\right).2}$	>0.50
Kling-Gupta efficiency, K-G	$1-\sqrt{\left(\dfrac{Y_{Sim}^{Mean}}{Y_{Obs}^{Mean}}-1\right)^2+\left(\dfrac{STDEV_{Sim}}{STDEV_{Obs}}-1\right)^2+(R-1)^2}$	>0.50
Willmott's index of agreement, d	$1-\dfrac{\sum_{i=1}^{n}\left(Y_i^{Obs}-Y_i^{Sim}\right).2}{\sum_{i=1}^{n}\left(\left|Y_i^{Sim}-Y_{Obs}^{Mean}\right|+\left|Y_i^{Obs}-Y_{Obs}^{Mean}\right|\right).2}$	>0.65

Y_i^{Obs} = Observed SST concentration

Y_i^{Sim} = Simulated SST concentration

Y_{Obs}^{Mean} = Mean of observed SST concentration

Y_{Sim}^{Mean} = Mean of simulated SST concentration

n = Total number of daily SST concentrations

3 Results

3.1 Training Phase

Table 4 summarizes the main neural network parameters calculated from the training phase. The parameter values shown in the table were selected from sensitivity analysis, where each parameter was varied until the network produced predictions of salinity concentrations for BISCC4 that matched observed concentrations.

Table 4. Artificial neural network parameters and features.

Feature	Adopted value
Number of layers	3 (input, hidden, output)
Number of nodes in hidden layer	1
Architecture	Closed loop
Number of iterations	100
Input delays	1:40
Feedback delays	1:1
Train ratio	70/100
Value ratio	15/100
Test ratio	15/100
Training algorithm	Bayesian regularization

As shown in Table 4, a closed-loop network architecture was adopted. This type of artificial neural network feeds back the actual output data, therefore it is a real-time configuration [20]. However, the network was trained under an open loop configuration in which it uses *a priori* target information to simulate output feedback.

Figure 4 shows the results for the training phase. As detailed above, observed data for years 2013 and 2014 were used. The training targets were salinity concentrations for BISCC4. The simulated concentrations for BISCC4 (training outputs) were calculated using observed Black Creek flow data and observed salinity data at BISCD8.

As illustrated in Fig. 4, the trained network captures observed BISCC4 salinity concentration values and trends very well for years 2013 and 2014 ($R > 0.99$, $R^2 > 0.99$). Nevertheless, the actual test of a trained ANN is in the prediction phase, where it is used to estimate future targets based on past information.

3.2 Forecasting/Prediction Phase

The trained network was used to predict hourly salinity concentrations at BISCC4, for years 2015 through 2019. Figure 5 shows the forecasting results achieved using the trained neural network. In addition to showing the observed and ANN-predicted salinity concentrations, the figure shows the predictions performed by the hydrodynamic model.

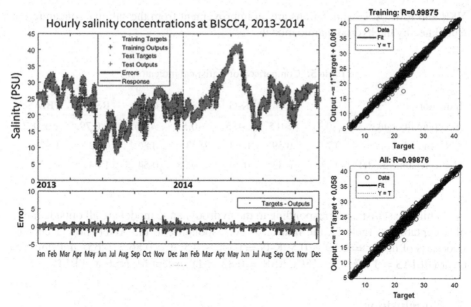

Fig. 4. Training phase results for years 2013 and 2014. Simulated and observed hourly salinity concentrations at BISCC4 are compared.

Clearly, the ANN captures the salinity temporal dynamics better than the hydrodynamic model. The goodness of fit of predicted concentrations to observed concentrations was measured by the indicators described in Table 3.

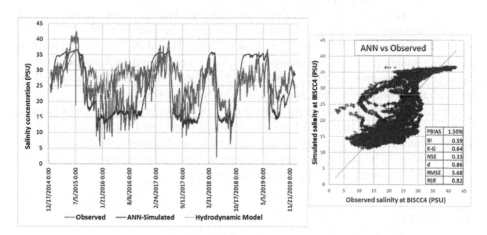

Fig. 5. Predicted hourly salinity concentrations at BISCC4 for years 2015–2019.

As evidenced in Fig. 5 and Table 5, the ANN developed in this research simulates hourly salinity concentration values and trends (for years 2015 through 2019) well. All statistical indicators are within their ranges of acceptability with the exception of

NSE and RSR. ANN simulations are an improvement from the salinity concentrations calculated by the hydrodynamic model.

Table 5. Comparison of statistical indicators.

Indicator	R	R^2	K-G	NSE	d	RSR	PBIAS
Acceptability range	>0.71	>0.5	>0.5	>0.5	>0.65	<0.79	<±18%
ANN model	0.77	0.59	0.64	0.33	0.86	0.82	1.5%
Hydrodynamic model	0.65	0.43	0.33	−0.08	0.54	1.04	−22.2%

While the statistics corresponding to the hydrodynamic model are all outside ranges of acceptability (Table 5), the indicators corresponding to the ANN show acceptable goodness of fit ($R^2 = 0.59 > 0.5$; K-G = 0.64 > 0.5; d = 0.86 > 0.65) and statistical error (PBIAS = 1.5% < ± 18%; RSR = 0.82 < 1), except for NSE and RSR.

4 Conclusions

In this research, a closed-loop autoregressive neural network (with exogenous inputs) successfully simulated hourly salinity concentrations for 5-years, 2015 through 2019, at a coastal water quality station (BISCC4) in Biscayne Bay, Florida, USA. Training of the network was performed using observed salinity concentrations for BISCC4, observed Black Creek flow data (a nearby stream), and observed salinity data at BISCD8 (a water quality station located 10 km away from BISCC4).

Statistical indicators of goodness of fit show that the ANN developed in this research correctly simulates salinity concentration values and trends ($R^2 = 0.59$, K-G = 0.64, NSE = 0.33, d = 0.86, PBIAS = 1.5%, RSR = 0.82). The ANN could be improved in capturing salinity peaks and minimums to achieve better NSE and RSR indicator values. However, in its current form the ANN model performs better in simulating salinity concentrations and trends, than an existing hydrodynamic model.

The results presented in this paper have the potential to be applied to other coastal locations in Biscayne Bay and elsewhere in which important freshwater inputs from inland streams are likely affecting salinity concentrations. Moreover, the developed neural network could be used to estimate groundwater flows contributions, in combination with simulations from an existing hydrodynamic model.

References

1. Conrads, P.A., Darby, L.S.: Development of a coastal drought index using salinity data. Bull. Am. Meteor. Soc. **98**, 753–766 (2017). https://doi.org/10.1175/BAMS-D-15-00171.1
2. Conrads, P.A., Roehl Jr., E.A.: Analysis of salinity intrusion in the Waccamaw River and the Atlantic Intracoastal Waterway near Myrtle Beach, South Carolina, 1995–2002. USGS Scientific Investigations Rep. 2007–5110, 41 pp (2007)

3. Shaw, J E., Zamorano, M.: Saltwater Interface Monitoring and Mapping Program. Water Resources Division, South Florida Water Management District (2020). https://www.sfwmd.gov/sites/default/files/documents/ws-58_swi_mapping_report_final.pdf

4. Abiy, A.Z., Melesse, A.M., Abtew, W., Whitman, D.: Rainfall trend and variability in Southeast Florida: Implications for freshwater availability in the Everglades. PLoS ONE **14**(2), e0212008 (2019). https://doi.org/10.1371/journal.pone.0212008

5. Stalker, J., Price, R., Swart, P.: Determining spatial and temporal inputs of freshwater, including submarine groundwater discharge, to a subtropical estuary using geochemical tracers, Biscayne Bay. South Florida. Estuaries and Coasts **32**, 694–708 (2009). https://doi.org/10.1007/s12237-009-9155-y

6. Lorenz, J.J.: A review of the effects of altered hydrology and salinity on vertebrate fauna and their habitats in Northeastern Florida Bay. Wetlands **34**(1), 189–200 (2013). https://doi.org/10.1007/s13157-013-0377-1

7. Alarcon, V.J., Linhoss, A., Kelble, C., Sanchez, G., Mardonez, F., et al.: Tidally forced saltwater intrusion into the Coral Gables Canal. Florida, USA (2021). (In process)

8. Alarcon, V.J.: Hindcasting and forecasting total suspended sediment concentrations using a NARX neural network. Sustainability **13**, 363 (2021). https://doi.org/10.3390/su13010363

9. Afan, H.A., El-Shafie, A., Mohtar, W.H.M.W., Yaseen, Z.M.: Past, present and prospect of an Artificial Intelligence (AI) based model for sediment transport prediction. J. Hydrol. **541**, 902–913 (2016). https://doi.org/10.1016/j.jhydrol.2016.07.048

10. Shahid, E.S., Salari, M., Rastegar, M., Sheibani, S.N., Ehteshami, M.: Artificial neural network and mathematical approach for estimation of surface water quality parameters (Case study: California, USA). Desalin. Water Treat. **213**, 75–83 (2021). https://doi.org/10.5004/dwt.2021.26709

11. Lin, K., Lu, P., Xu, C.-Y., Yu, X., Lan, T., Chen, X.: Modeling saltwater intrusion using an integrated Bayesian model averaging method in the Pearl River Delta. J. Hydroinf. **21**(6), 1147–1162 (2021). https://doi.org/10.2166/hydro.2019.073

12. Zhou, F., Liu, B., Duan, K.: Coupling wavelet transform and artificial neural network for forecasting estuarine salinity. J. Hydrol. **588**, art. no. 125127 (2020). https://doi.org/10.1016/j.jhydrol.2020.125127

13. Rath, J.S., Hutton, P.H., Chen, L., Roy, S.B.: A hybrid empirical-Bayesian artificial neural network model of salinity in the San Francisco Bay-Delta estuary. Environ. Model. Softw. **93**, 193–208 (2017). https://doi.org/10.1016/j.envsoft.2017.03.022

14. Caccia, V., Boyer, J.: Spatial patterning of water quality in Biscayne Bay, Florida as a function of land use and water management. Mar. Pollut. Bull. **50**, 1416–1429 (2005). https://doi.org/10.1016/j.marpolbul.2005.08.002

15. USGS.: Changing Salinity Patterns in Biscayne Bay, Florida. Prepared in cooperation with South Florida Water Management District and Biscayne National Park (2004). https://doi.org/10.3133/fs20043108

16. Boussaada, Z., Curea, O., Remaci, A., Camblong, H., Mrabet, N.B.: A Nonlinear Autoregressive Exogenous (NARX) Neural network model for the prediction of the daily direct solar radiation. Energies **11**, 620 (2018). https://doi.org/10.3390/en11030620

17. Moriasi, D.N., Arnold, J.G., Van Liew, M.W., Bingner, R.L., Harmel, R.D., Veith, T.L.: Model evaluation guidelines for systematic quantification of accuracy in watershed simulations. Trans. ASABE **50**, 885–900 (2007). https://doi.org/10.13031/2013.23153

18. Ang, R., Oeurng, C.: Simulating streamflow in an ungauged catchment of Tonlesap Lake Basin in Cambodia using Soil and Water Assessment Tool (SWAT) model. Water Sci. **32**, 89–101 (2018). https://doi.org/10.1016/j.wsj.2017.12.002

19. Knoben, W.J.M., Freer, J.E., Woods, R.A.: Technical note: Inherent benchmark or not? Comparing Nash-Sutcliffe and Kling-Gupta efficiency scores. Hydrol. Earth Syst. Sci. **23**, 4323–4331 (2019). https://doi.org/10.5194/hess-23-4323-2019
20. Hussein, A.A.: Derivation and comparison of open-loop and closed-loop neural network battery state-of-charge estimators. Energy Procedia **75**, 1856–1861 (2015). https://doi.org/10.1016/j.egypro.2015.07.163

Tracing and Modeling of the COVID-19 Pandemic Infections in Poland Using Spatial Interactions Models

Piotr A. Werner$^{(\boxtimes)}$ (iD)

Faculty of Geography and Regional Studies, University of Warsaw, Krakowskie.Przedmiescie 30, 00-927 Warsaw, Poland
peter@uw.edu.pl

Abstract. The nexus of factors influencing the dissemination of the SARS-CoV-2 virus is so complex that identification of (some) determining factors of COVID-19 spatial diffusion is significantly hampered. COVID-19 characterize of specific dynamics and enormous volume of morbidity. The aim of the study is construction of the model of spatial dissemination of COVID-19 in Poland, identification of the main outbreak places and spatial heterogeneity of pandemic based on the spatial set of first twelve months morbidity data (in 2020 and 2021). The target (prototypical) model is intended rather as the supporting tool than replacement of the well-known and used SIR or SEIR (Susceptible – Exposed – Infected - Recovered) models in epidemiology. It also assumed that the target model could be used as a priori estimation tool of the spatial locations of infections outbreaks as well as evaluation of future volume of infections due to changing numbers of exposed and recovered persons related also to, newly, introduced and continuation coronavirus (COVID-19) vaccinations. One of the expected advantages of the construed model is its spatial aspect i.e. it will enable to evaluate the potential spatial differentiation of infected number of people within the set of observed spatial units i.e. counties in Poland.

Keywords: COVID-19 · Infections · Spatial interactions · Modeling · Poland

1 Introduction

Situation related to spread of pandemic, coronavirus SARS-COV-2, has been a global challenge, touching virtually every aspect of social life in every country of the world. Looking for the solutions of the current state aimed limiting spatial extent of pandemic and its medical, healthcare, social, economic and demographic consequences in social and individual scale, engaged numerous of specialists, based also on past plagues lessons [1] and exhaustive scientific research virtually in every domain of human life. "The spread of infectious disease is inherently a spatial process; therefore, geospatial data, technologies, and analytical methods play a critical role in understanding and responding to the coronavirus disease 2019 (COVID-19) pandemic" [2]. Policy makers, scientists and journalists agree that one of the key issues of effective combat against global pandemic

© Springer Nature Switzerland AG 2021
O. Gervasi et al. (Eds.): ICCSA 2021, LNCS 12954, pp. 641–657, 2021.
https://doi.org/10.1007/978-3-030-86979-3_45

is tracing statistics, i.e., observations of the number, intensity, and spatial variation of disease status (infections). Construed spatial global, national and regional models of pandemic aim at [3]: (*) discussing a GIS technology for simulating disease outbreaks, (**) examining the relationship between numerous and different potential key variables (environmental, socio-economic, demographic etc.), (***) identifying and monitoring the spatial and temporal patterns and trends, and (****) recording and geocoding data (sometimes including symptoms, travel history, and dates of onset, admission and confirmation) to produce useful information able to support the emergency surveillance.

The nexus of factors influencing the dissemination of the SARS-CoV-2 pandemic is so complex that identification of (some) determining factors of COVID-19 spatial diffusion is significantly hampered. It shall be deemed, that COVID-19 characterize of specific dynamics and is far more transmissible [4]. Recent studies proved some specific characters of the diffusion processes in the early stages of virus outbreak among different areas (e.g. in Italy and in China) at the regional and international level [5], also correlated to individual regional physical conditions as well as social and demographic characteristics (e.g. in Spain) [6].

The aim of the study is construction of the model of spatial dissemination of COVID-19 in Poland, identification of the main outbreak places and spatial heterogeneity of pandemic based on the spatial set of first year morbidity data in 2020 in Poland. The target (prototypical) model in its core is intended rather as the supporting tool than replacement of the well-known and used SIR or SEIR[1] models in epidemiology. It also assumed that the target model could be used as *a priori* estimation tool of the spatial locations of infections outbreaks as well as evaluation of future volume of infections due to changing numbers of exposed and recovered persons related also to, newly, introduced and continuation coronavirus (COVID-19) vaccinations. One of the expected advantages of the construed model is its spatial aspect i.e. it will enable to evaluate the potential spatial differentiation of infected number of people within the set of observed spatial units (counties in Poland).

1.1 COVID-19 Disease Description and Pandemic Tracking

Usually three categories groups of characteristics of risk are enumerated: individual risk, natural environment (climatic) risk, social and demographic risk as the factors shaping the volume, intensity and spatial dispersion of diseases (epidemic). Individual risk is related to personal human physical and psychological characteristics in context of possible infection. Spatial natural conditions (e.g. temperature and humidity) are recognized as primary factors of environmental risk. The last category is related, inter alia, to mobility of people and number as well as density of population. Especially for COVID-19 pandemic which has been initially perceived as similar to epidemics in the near past (SARS, MERS) and sometimes to seasonal influenza [7–9]. However, at present, the possible seasonality of COVID-19 occurrence is not yet explained [10]. On the other side recent national analysis of the relationship between density of population and the COVID-19 infection and mortality rates for 913 metropolitan counties in the United States suggests unrelation of density to the infection rate and negativel relation

---

[1] Susceptible – Exposed – Infected – Recovered.

to the mortality rate, possibly due to greater adherence to social distancing policies and practices in denser areas and better quality of health care [11].

COVID-19 pandemic, despite the similarities to above mentioned diseases and epidemics, features the global scale, enormous dynamics and higher infection rate. There were also enormous number of particular social, economic and political global, national and local factors, which, in context of very hard-organized efforts within the national healthcare system, introduced lockdown[2] of economy and limited mobility of people shaped the spatial spread of COVID-19 pandemic. These all above-mentioned risks and factors made very difficult precisely to reflect the main determinants of current spatial trends of COVID-19 infections. Moreover, " there is much to suggest that the relatively low mortality associated with COVID-19 is the result of the introduction of severe restrictions on social life and a far-reaching freeze on the economy in Poland at a very early stage of the epidemic of this disease." [10].

Due to enormous efforts of national and local authorities related to lock-down, multiplicity and diversity of factors influencing the spread of COVID-19 as well as the psychological conditions of individuals' behavior, the complex nature of spatial aspects COVID-19 spread is much more difficult to model simultaneously in different spatial locations than at the general, i.e. at national scale. The obtained spatial model will be only the approximation at each level (global, national, regional and local).

2 Pandemic COVID-19 in Poland in 2020

From the geographical point of view, there are several spatial factors influencing spread of COVID-19, which modify local transmission based on social contacts (through droplets transmission). These are natural conditions: climate, relief and hydrography, as well as settlement structure, density of population, human (social) development level (hygiene, awareness of epidemic), and life styles i.e. mobility of population [12]. Finally yet importantly, the key element is organization of national and local healthcare system. However, due to different social and psychological phenomena and natural disruptive events, some recognized, theoretical diffusion models of infectious diseases overworked within the framework of medical geography could differ from the empirical data because of their complex nature.

Source of number of registered infections, recoveries and deaths are three sets of data collected by Polish Ministry of Health. The first data set involve data from March to May, the second one from March to September and the third data set are continuous reports, which have been published daily since the last week of November. The cumulative numbers of infections (stacked) by counties in Poland from 11 week to 41 week 2020 are presented on chart and map (Fig. 1, Fig. 2). These figures provide the some spatial regularities of COVID-19 diffusion during the observed time. There are also visible general time fluctuations and spatial trends, which undoubtedly confirm the efforts of local and national authorities to introduce lock-down strategy and dissemination of DDM (distance, disinfection, masks) rules.

There are obvious outbreaks that spread epidemic into neighborhood as well as main, greatest cities touched (in some locations not the cities itself but surrounding suburban

---

[2] i.e. a state of isolation or restricted access instituted as a security measure.

areas). Concerns about the predicted (at the end of October) forthcoming 'second wave' of epidemic had been confirmed. During one, the 48th week 2020 there were greater number of infections than in the whole time before (presented on chart and map, Fig. 3 and Fig. 4). The largest number of infections concentrated in main populated cities and their surrounding counties. All capitals of voivodships as well as main (secondary) towns, capital of counties, characterize larger number of infections than peripherals.

3 Theoretical Foundations, Methods and Operationalization of Spatial Study in the Context of Pandemics

The literature of epidemic research present numerous methods and models concerning morbidity and spatial aspects of diseases. The specialists have looked for outbreaks, i.e. places of the first appearance as well as models of spatial dynamics and dissemination of diseases. The frequent approaches used cellular automata and multi-agent simulations ([multi] agent-based modeling), which appropriately reflect direct contacts of people as well as neural nets [13]. Approaches to spatial epidemiology involve some methods using GIS (geographic information systems) as well as analytical and mapping techniques like geocoding, distance estimation, assessment of residential mobility and commuting, spatial and space-time clustering and more sophisticated applications like Bayesian approaches to disease mapping, spatial regression models (including geographically weighted regression) using also Web-based mapping aimed dissemination of scientific studies results [14]. There are also non-spatial approaches (threads) of scientific studies of epidemics that aim "to understand the causes of a disease, then to predict its course, and finally to develop ways of controlling it, including comparisons of different possible approaches. The first step is obtaining and analyzing observed data." [15].

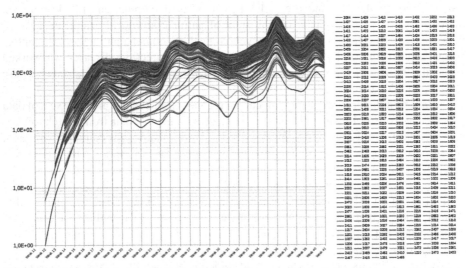

Fig. 1. Stacked, cumulative number of infections by counties in Poland by weeks (since 11 to 41 week 2020) and by counties; data source: Ministry of Health, Poland (counties identified by statistical numbers, four-digit TERYT string).

Researches concentrate on mathematical modelling for the spread of diseases using classic approaches, starting from Kermack - McKendrick epidemic (compartmental) model, and newer network models as well as the family of stochastic models, because the spread of infection is a random process [15–17].

It is used mainly for assess epidemic within geographic boundaries as entirety, treating it as the spatial homogenic unit without insight into its diversity. There must be appropriate number of different models construed for the set of different regions. The factors determining or influencing the spread of infection in different regions may differ and sometimes depend on specific set of complex conditions. There are set of different global and national models to be used to forecast the volume of infections [18–20].

The Interdisciplinary Centre for Mathematical and Computational Modelling UW (ICM UW) epidemiological model was used within the framework of proposed approach to trace the COVID-19 pandemic at the national level in Poland [20]. The results of simulation of ICM epidemiological model obtained at the national level were used, in turn, to assess the estimated number of infected population at the regional (county) level using spatial interaction models approach.

3.1 Spatial Interaction Models as a Tool for Tracing Epidemic at the Regional Level

Due to the defined above conditions of infections, which are the direct results of number of contacts of people, the proposed methodology use methods of spatial interactions modeling. A spatial interaction formula in a setting calibrated for diffusion can give the probability of contact from any location at any point in time, but this locus of greatest intensity of contact and change moves outwards from origins over time. Information requirements for the spatial interaction model calibrated for a diffusion problem include [18]: numbers and susceptibility of the population; spatial distribution of the population; and rate at which knowledge or opportunities to interact declines with distance.

Stewart [21] defined potential as a measure of the influence of population (mass - m) at some point on the Earth's surface within the distance d from this point. The term is derived from social physics, and the concept is closely connected to that of the gravity model, in that it relates mass (population) to distance. This formula defined the beginning classical approach to potential models [22]. Whereas the gravity model deals with separate relationships between pairs of points, population potential encompasses the influence of all other points on a particular one [23]. Corresponding gravity model as well as its variants became also predictors in infectious disease epidemiology [24]. A new look, based on statistical mechanics, was formulated by Wilson [25], who formulated and elucidated a family of spatial interaction models in the context of urban and regional systems, concerning, inter alia, demographic accounts and projections models, migration estimation and forecasting [26, 27]. Suitability of use a variant of spatial interaction model as a 'model of epidemics in spatially disaggregated system with interactions' has been directly confirmed by Sir Alan Wilson himself in the recently published preprint [28]. The new appeared abstract has reassured us that the research thread of using at least two of the spatial interactions models family is reasonable and may be the base of the prediction of spatial differentiation dynamics of COVID-19 spread.

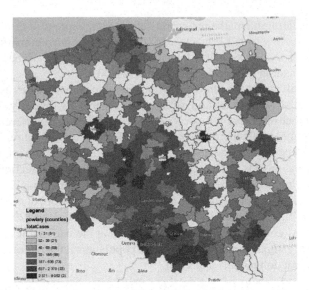

Fig. 2. Total number of infections by counties in Poland (since 11 to 42 week 2020); source Ministry of Health, Poland.

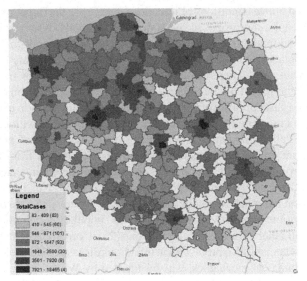

Fig. 3. Total number of infections by counties in Poland (since 48 to 52 week 2020); source Ministry of Health, Poland.

The roots of idea of use of population potential model as the measure of number of contacts between people are also derived from the earlier works related to spatial diffusion of cellular telephony [29–32] as well as taking into account 'first law of geography' [33]. Spatial interactions represent flows of activity between locations in geographical space [34]. These may be flows of people, represented by population potential values. Population potential is a measure of nearness, or accessibility, of a certain aggregation of people to a given point. The family of spatial interactions models are well suited in the context of studies of direct contacts of people, which might result the infection of disease. In fact, the gravity model of two settlement points (characterized by appropriate number of people: m and n and omitting distance) is direct mathematical model of two separate groups of people welcoming themselves. Alan Wilson [35] introduced into the spatial interaction modelling the concept of probability of such contacts taking into account also the spatial dimension (distance or its functional measure, e.g. time) as well as the evaluation of the entropy of the studied system.

The starting point is an interaction matrix analogous to contingency table (graph notation) capturing the combinations of all pairs of distant sites (places) under consideration, and whose elements are the volumes of the interaction between the ith and j^{th} source and destination points, and the origin *([O])* and destination *([D])* boundary vectors (rows and columns sums). The operationalization consisted in estimating two additional (edge) balancing vectors (A and B). This way the interaction matrix represent graph of all centroids (and edges connecting them) of counties in Poland. The main problem lies only how to treat cells on the diagonal i.e. when $i = j$, evaluation of the distances of contacts inside the county itself. Assumed finally, that the distance for contacts introduced into the model in these cases will be the radius of a circle of area equal to county area.

The general formula of population gravity between two certain points is described as $T_{ij} = f(O_i, D_j, d_{ij})$, where: *T – volume of interactions (contacts); O – origin point representing push factor (e.g. emissiveness); D – destination point representing pull factor (e.g. attraction); d – distance O-D representing spatial separation (e.g. Euclidean or road distance, time or cost function); i,j – table subscripts of points (regions).* The fifth element is matrix of distances between points (or regions, not presented in tab. 1). Summing up the individual gravity volumes for all other points or regions (including origin itself) gives the population potential for origin (or destination).

Operationalization of the above relationships using an entropy-maximizing framework seeks to reconstruct flows ([interactions, contacts]) between the set of origins and destinations by finding the most probable configurations. This is common optimization problem and including information about the total ([contacts]) inflows and outflows as well as parameters of modelling: distance decay function (d_{ij}^{β}, β – power exponent), origin *(A)* and destination *(B)* balancing factors ensuring the total (in- and out-flows) are preserved in the predicted flows. Final formulas for each of the model involving also independent variables influencing emissiveness *(V)* and attractiveness *(W)* take forms [36]:

$$\text{Unconstrained gravity model}: T_{ij} = V_i^{\mu} W_j^{\alpha} / d_{ij}^{\beta} \tag{1}$$

$$\text{Destination constrained model}: T_{ij} = B_j D_j V_j^{\mu} / d_{ij}^{\beta} \tag{2}$$

where: $B\_j = 1/(\sum\_i(V\_i^{\mu})/(d\_ij^{\beta}))$.

3.2 Operationalization in the Context of Pandemics

Looking for the real world independent variables, which influence the number of infected population, verified that the best results obtained using population number of counties, assuming that flows of spatial interactions models are represented by number of infected, which is the direct result of the number of social contacts. This way the population potential model is close to mathematical model counting the number of 'handshakes' taking into account distance measure. Two of above presented models seems adequate to apply in COVID-19 tracing. The unconstrained gravity model (1), when the only known is total number of infected people and the destination (attraction) constrained model (2), which make possible prediction of share of fixed (revealed) amount of infections at destinations that come from particular origins [26]. Two way of verification of forecast of number of infections within the counties is possible. Using collected data at national and county levels, and verifying the results using destination constrained spatial interaction model at the county level as well as unconstrained gravity model at the national level. The input in the beginning is the number of susceptible people. Later it will be possible to use updated numbers of susceptible subtracting the number of recovered (and vaccinated or planning vaccinations).

Having the collected data of number of infected and recovered (and failed) people it is possible to make the detailed calibrated local analysis of modeling spatial differentiation of infections at the county level using Python PySal SpInt library. The operationalization allows for any spatial resolution, temporal resolution, and demographic stratification. Unconstrained models are best purposed in an exploratory role, since the lack of balancing factors can result in predictions of more inflow or outflow than possible for a location [37].

4 Tracing the Pandemic COVID-19 in Poland

The record of tracing COVID-19 in Poland at the national level is presented in Fig. 4 and Fig. 6.

The data concerning infected population are only the fraction of the whole population infected. It is related to fact, that large number of infected people (especially youths) passes the disease asymptomatically and only the registered fraction of tested population is disclosed statistically. The vaccination against COVID-19 started in Poland since 27 Dec 2020. The complete collected data sets in Poland in 2020 can be treated as the state of outbreak of epidemic to the end of 2020. Only physicians and medical staff were vaccine since January 2021. The reproduction number [Rt] of outbreak over time shows differentiation (Fig. 5).

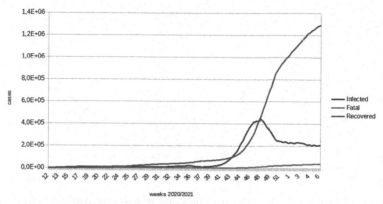

Fig. 4. Poland, COVID-19: Cases over time with monotonic increasing complemented recovered data (as Feb 07 2021, results of application: [18]).

4.1 Modeling and Simulation Infection by Counties

Preprocessing Phase

Spatial interaction models described above need calibration i.e. obtain accurate estimates of model's parameters in order to forecast interactions in system under study. As mentioned, two of them: unconstrained gravity (1) and destination (attraction) constrained (2) were chosen to simulate number of infections by counties in Poland. Preprocessing model calibration involved tracing and simulated past data of infections by counties for random as well as specific weeks during the last year and aimed confirmation that there is significant correlation between population of counties (treated as independent variable in context of possible contacts and explanation variables) and number of infections in these counties. Next, the set of parameters of spatial interactions models interpreted and compared to collected data modelling. Assumed that some of them describe the same processes and may explain similar relationships.

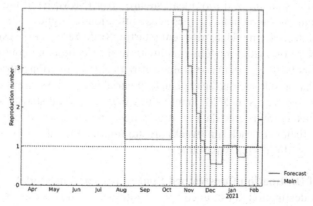

Fig. 5. Poland COVID-19: reproduction number over time (as Feb 13 2021, application forecast results [18]).

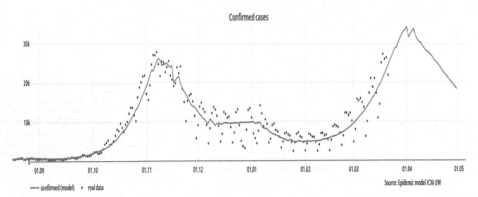

Fig. 6. Chart of identified cases of Covid-19 infection from 03/16/2020 with a prediction until 04/30/2021. Chart prepared based on the forecast from 03/19/2021 [20]

Spatial interaction models are calibrated via generalized linear modeling framework using flexibility and extendibility of regression framework, taking logarithm of both sides and obtaining Poisson log-linear model [36]. The input for model calibration were officially registered past data of infections by counties [38]. The regression made possible later to assess the regression model parameters: intercept (k, ensure the total number of infections is conserved for certain time), balancing factors (μ, origin propulsiveness or emissiveness parameter and α, destination attractiveness parameter) as well as exponential distance-decay parameter β, coefficient for the distance variable describing the diminishing effect of space [36, 37].

Modeling Spatial Differentiation of COVID-19 Infections
Spatial interaction models fit statistics utilize replacement of coefficient of determination (pseudo R^2) based on the likelihood function and its counterpart, adjusted coefficient of determination (adjusted pseudo R^2) which can be interpreted similarly – maximum value close to 1 denote better model fit [36]. Model complexity is assessed using Akaike information criterion (AIC), derived for information theory. Lower values of AIC signalizes better model fit as evaluation of the volume of information lost [39]. Statistical parameter usually utilized is standardized root mean square error (SRMSE) of the observed and simulated volume of interactions (in these case infections). Higher value of SRMSE is the indicator of decrease model assessment (starting from zero as the best fit) [36].

The procedure of spatial modeling simulation of infections by counties in Poland was repeated for above chosen unconstrained gravity and destination (attraction) models using the population statistics as the explanatory variables for the sequence of randomly, and specific chosen weeks in 2020. Input values were empirical statistical data of population and collected registered data of infections aggregated weekly by counties. The results of fit statistics for each run (week) are summarized in table (Table 1) and small charts in last row of this table (sparklines).

Verification of Destination Constrained Spatial Interaction Model
Verification of destination constrained spatial interaction model was evaluated during sixth and seven week of 2021 (1 Feb – 7 Feb) using acquired empirical aggregated data of COVID-19 infections by counties.

Table 1. Spatial interactions models fit statistics (* spatial verification; ** spatial prediction – later completed and verified).

model week No 2020/ 2021	Unconstrained gravity model				Destination (attraction) constrained model			
	pseudo R^2	adj. pseudo R^2	AIC	SRMSE	pseudo R^2	adj. pseudo R^2	AIC	SRMSE
15 [2020]	0.21	0. 208	557871.6	2.69	0.74	0.74	182944.1	1.067
20	0.20	0.197	1.72e+06	2.14	0.82	0.82	3.89e+05	0.74
30	0.16	0.164	3.15e+06	3.66	0.88	0.88	4.44e+05	1.28
40	0.50	0.50	3.41e+06	2.08	0.89	0.89	7.31e+05	1.28
50	0.78	0.78	205945.5	26.42	0.85	0.848	140473.2	20.68
1 [2021]	0.77	0.77	178070.68	28.05	0.85	0.85	118350.50	22.97
5	0.78	0.776	107080.50	26.92	0.85	0.847	73356.91	21.15
6*	0.78	0.778	103959.48	27.32	0.85	0.847	71851.31	21.05
7**	0.77	0,774	112247.09	28.04	0.85	0.846	76803.60	21.47
Chart /sparklin es/								

The general formula of destination-constrained model (2) took form for the sixth and seventh week of 2021 (Eq. 3, 4):

$$T_{ij} = exp(-9.6409 + 0.6234ln(V_i) - 0.1243 - (-0.1102)ln(d_{ij})) \qquad (3)$$

$$T_{ij} = exp(-9.7187 + 0.6363ln(V_i) - 0.1220 - (-0.1101)ln(d_{ij})) \qquad (4)$$

where: T_{ij}– modelled number of infections, V_i– population of county i, d_{ij}– distance between county i and j; for the county itself the distance taken into account was the radius of a circle of area equal to county area.

The calculated adjusted coefficient of determination (R^2) was equal 0.85 (may be interpreted as 85% of real number of infections). Total number of infected is the sum of all interactions between the each pair of counties. Evaluated modeled spatial differentiation of number of infections and residuals of regression are presented on maps (Fig. 7A and 7B). Assumption of proper assessment is based also on the observed trends of model fit statistics (see Table 2). Calculated distance decay parameter β equal -0.11 reveals that in given county the average increase of infections will be 10.4% with the growth of certain population (treated as explanatory variable, i.e. contacts) per unit of distance (per 1 km). Maps on Figs. 7A (and 7B, 7C, 7D) prove that the model presents gap and underestimate number of infected. It is expected from the parameters of model fit statistics, especially adjusted coefficient of determination (85%). Taking into account for modelling (for above chosen unconstrained gravity and destination constrained spatial interaction models) different time intervals i.e. aggregated data of infections between

10th and 42nd week of 2020 and population of counties as explanatory variables the model fit statistics were similar (Table 2).

These models fit statistics for different time intervals prove that outbreak of COVID-19 pandemic targeted over time the most populated area. These values are more reliable comparing them to data concerning one-week intervals.

Modelled values of number of infections by counties let then estimate the numbers of failed (deceased) based on e.g. general parameters of previously collected pandemic data and at last calculate the number of recovered, subtracting from the number of susceptible the volume of failed cases. It seems that longer time interval is taken into account the more responsible inferring about the general trends can be drawled from models.

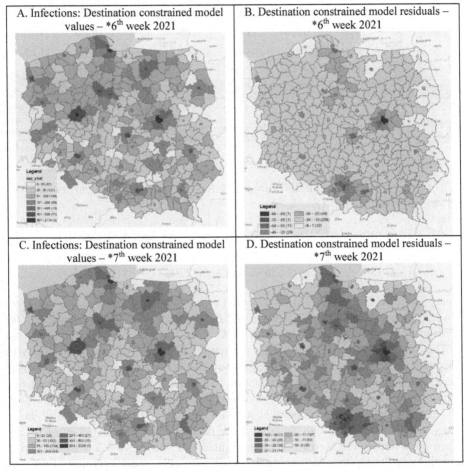

Fig. 7. Destination constrained model: COVID-19 infections in Poland by counties; sixth week 2021 - map of modeled values (A) and residuals (B, modelled - real value); seventh week 2021 - map of modeled values (C) and residuals (D)

Table 2. Spatial interactions models fit statistics (for different time intervals in early stages of outbreak)

model	Unconstrained gravity model				Destination (attraction) constrained model			
week No 2020	pseudo R^2	adj. pseudo R^2	AIC	SRMSE	pseudo R^2	adj. pseudo R^2	AIC	SRMSE
10–22/sum/	0.122	0.122	1.75e+07	2.203	0.609	0.609	7.777e+06	2.018
10–42/sum/	0.484	0.484	3.23e+07	1.607	0.947	0.947	3.33e+06	0.822
1–7 [2021] /sum/	0.779	0.779	925496.67	27.18	0.851	0.851	624561.11	21.49

4.2 Modeling COVID-19 Based on Spatial Interactions

Verification of chosen spatial interactions models for aggregated data of infections by counties in sixth week 2021 (8 Feb - 14 Feb 2021) was made based on empirical acquired. This time it was not possible to use destination-constrained model due to unknown spatial differentiation of infections by counties. The only input value was the (past) total number of infections and use the unconstrained gravity model.

The approaches of use unconstrained gravity model aimed detailed simulation of spatial differentiation of infected by counties during seven weeks of 2021. First, application of the model; second construction of new model with aggregated data since the beginning of the 2021 year. These models reflect (seventh) one-week and seven weeks modeling.

Unconstrained gravity models took different forms for one week (sixth and seventh weeks of 2021, Eq. 4 and 5) and for seven weeks (Eq. 6). The results of modelling are presented on maps (Fig. 8A, 8B, 8C).

$$T_{ij} = exp(-9.6409 + 0.6226 \; ln \; (V_i) + 0.6226 \; ln \; (W_j) - (-0.1102) \; ln \; (d_{ij})) \quad (5)$$

$$T_{ij} = exp(-9.7187 + 0.6281 \; ln \; (V_i) + 0.6281 \; ln \; (W_j) - (-0.1101) \; ln \; (d_{ij})) \quad (6)$$

$$T_{ij} = exp(-6.8791 + 0.6023 \; ln \; (V_i) + 0.6023 \; ln \; (W_j) - (-0.1153) \; ln \; (d_{ij})) \quad (7)$$

where: T_{ij} – modelled number of infections, V_i – population of county i, W_j – population of county j, d_{ij} – distance between county i and j; for the county itself the distance taken into account was the radius of a circle of area equal to county area.

Application of unconstrained gravity model for seventh week 2021 may be treated as revealing current level of infections. The cumulative number of modeled infection cases, using number of population of counties as explanatory variables within the unconstrained gravity model shows significantly higher values. It is much more than officially reported data (based on reported COVID-19 tests and treatments). "Analysis by the Interdisciplinary Centre for Mathematical and Computational Modeling University of

Warsaw (ICM UW) shows that the actual numbers of daily coronavirus infections in recent days may be about ten times higher than the numbers of confirmed infections reported by the government. That is, 20,000 confirmed infections could mean as many as ca. 200,000 actual infections that day." [20, 40]. That is why the model under research has been calibrated proportionally to the estimated values obtained using external data from SIR model [18], retaining the spatial differentiation provided by unconstrained gravity model. The predicted total number of infections in Poland showed over 40 thousands infections (42206 cases, Fig. 8D) during the studied seventh week. However, again the SIR-F model used also the data from the Ministry of Health, taken from the Report published on coronavirus infections Sars-CoV-2 [18, 19]. Much less reliable is map

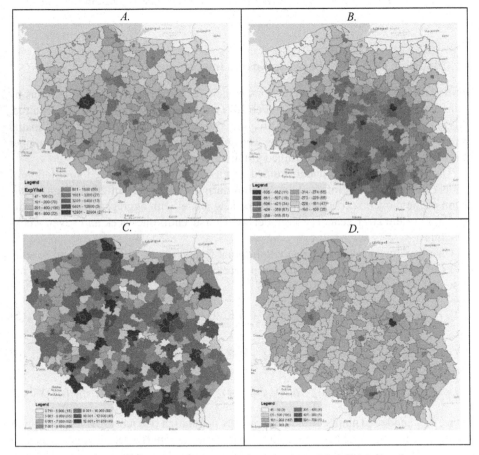

Fig. 8. Modeling of COVID-19 infected cases in Poland; A. Modeled infected cases – seven weeks 2021; aggregated unconstrained gravity model; B. Residuals of infected cases – seven weeks 2021; aggregated unconstrained gravity model; C. Modeling of infected cases – based on seven weeks 2021; aggregated unconstrained gravity and calibrated using data from external SIR models; D. Modeling of infected cases – seventh week of 2021; aggregated unconstrained gravity and calibrated using data from external SIR models

simulating infected cases for the seven weeks (Eq. 6, Fig. 8A, 8B) because the model is based on assumption that the situation of outbreak was not changing rapidly like in the past weeks. Estimated number of infected cases reached over one and half million people (modelled total value of infected cases equal for seven weeks using unconstrained gravity model, Fig. 8C).

Discussion and Conclusions

Both spatial interaction and SIR-F model were evaluated for constant explanatory variables i.e. the number of possible contacts were evaluated using as the constants the officially published number of inhabitants (by counties and total in Poland) and only changing parameters estimated during modelling were the distance-decay parameters, limiting the possible number of infected cases. The modelling just aimed verification of the matter of distance. That is why no data of predicted failed cases (deceased) were evaluated. The promising results of modeling with both models lead us to consider introducing as variables the number of recovered cases and vaccinations, which can be successively subtracted from the initial explanatory variables, i.e. the total population and population by counties. Unfortunately, up to now only total number of people vaccinated in Poland is available (starting since the beginning of 2021). A demographic stratification of contacts can be introduced into the gravity model described earlier taking age cohorts (young, working age, post-working age, or more specifically) - the interacting masses then change, but the distances remain the same.

As dependent variables, one can choose, for example, the average number of infected per week, the maximum number of infected per week instead of (as before) the sums. The input parameters can also be manipulated: either by changing the distance function or by changing the exponent of the power of the distance estimated in the models (e.g. as the mean, minimum or maximum) from a number of time periods under study, assuming a constant maximum (potential) density of contacts as interacting masses.

The number of contacts can be modified by subtotaling the number of deaths and vaccinations. Visitors (in tourist areas) and foreign visitors to the area can be added as components of the sum of contacts. Simulated results can be aggregated, e.g., to provinces and for the whole country. The paper presents the intermediate results of the ongoing research in recent state.

Acknowledgment. *This research was partially funded by IDUB against COVID-19 project granted by Warsaw University of Technology under the program Excellence Initiative: Research University (IDUB).*

References

1. Past plagues offer lessons for society after the coronavirus pandemic. https://www.sci encenews.org/article/coronavirus-covid-19-ancient-plagues-pandemics-lessons-society. Accessed on 20 Jan 2021
2. Smith, C.D., Mennis, J.: Incorporating geographic information science and technology in response to the COVID-19 pandemic. Prev. Chronic. Dis. **17** (2020). https://doi.org/10.5888/pcd17.200246.

3. Dangermond, J., Vito, C.D., Pesaresi, C.: Using GIS in the Time of the COVID-19 Crisis, casting a glance at the future. A joint discussion. J-READING - J. Res. Didactics Geography. **1**, 195–205 (2020).

4. Petersen, E., et al.: Comparing SARS-CoV-2 with SARS-CoV and influenza pandemics. Lancet. Infect. Dis **20**, e238–e244 (2020). https://doi.org/10.1016/S1473-3099(20)30484-9

5. Murgante, B., Borruso, G., Balletto, G., Castiglia, P., Dettori, M.: Why Italy first? health, geographical and planning as-pects of the COVID-19 Outbreak. Sustainability. **12**, 5064 (2020). https://doi.org/10.3390/su12125064

6. Paez, A., Lopez, F.A., Menezes, T., Cavalcanti, R., da Rocha Pitta, M.G.: A spatio-temporal analysis of the environmental correlates of COVID-19 incidence in Spain. Geograph. Anal. **53**(3), 397–421 (2020)

7. Confalonieri, U., et al.: Human health. Climate change 2007: impacts, adaptation and vulnerability: contribution of Working Group II to the fourth assessment report of the Intergovernmental Panel on Climate Change (2007)

8. Kimura, Y., et al.: Geodemographics profiling of influenza A and B virus infections in community neighborhoods in Japan. BMC Infect. Dis. **11**, 1–12 (2011)

9. Merler, S., Ajelli, M.: The role of population heterogeneity and human mobility in the spread of pandemic influenza. Proc. Royal Soc. B: Biol. Sci. **277**, 557–565 (2010)

10. Duszyński, J., et al.: Zrozumieć COVID-19. Opracowanie zespołu ds. COVID-19 przy Prezesie PAN (2020)

11. Hamidi, S., Sabouri, S., Ewing, R.: Does density aggravate the COVID-19 pandemic?: early findings and lessons for planners. J. Am. Plann. Assoc. **86**, 495–509 (2020). https://doi.org/10.1080/01944363.2020.1777891

12. Śleszyński, P.: Prawidłowości przebiegu dyfuzji przestrzennej rejestrowanych zakażeń koronawirusem SARS-COV-2 w Polsce w pierwszych 100 dniach epidemii. Czasopismo Geograficzne**91**, 5–19 (2020)

13. Iwańczak, B.: Zróżnicowanie przestrzenne zagrożenia grypą w Polsce. Prace i Studia Geograficzne **57**, 127–144 (2015)

14. Kirby, R.S., Delmelle, E., Eberth, J.M.: Advances in spatial epidemiology and geographic information systems. Ann. Epidemiol. **27**, 1–9 (2017). https://doi.org/10.1016/j.annepidem.2016.12.001

15. Brauer, F.: Mathematical epidemiology: past, present, and future. Infectious Disease Modelling. **2**, 113–127 (2017). https://doi.org/10.1016/j.idm.2017.02.001

16. Kiss, I.Z., Miller, J.C., Simon, P.L.: Mathematics of Epidemics on Networks, vol. 598. Springer, Cham (2017). https://doi.org/10.1007/978-3-319-50806-1

17. Pourbohloul, B., Miller, J.: Network Theory and the Spread of Communicable Diseases (2021)

18. CovsirPhy Development Team: CovsirPhy, Python package for COVID-19 analysis with SIR-derived ODE models. https://github.com/lisphilar/covid19-sir. Accessed on 04 Feb 2021

19. Guidotti, E., Ardia, D.: COVID-19 Data Hub. JOSS. **5**, 2376 (2020). https://doi.org/10.21105/joss.02376.

20. ICM UW Model description – COVID. https://covid-19.icm.edu.pl/en/model-description/. Accessed on 12 Feb 2021

21. Stewart, J.Q.: Empirical mathematical rules concerning the distribution and equilibrium of population. Geogr. Rev. **37**, 461–485 (1947)

22. Pomianowski, W.: Transportation network structure and spatial accessibility. Dynamic graph approach (2018)

23. Johnston, R.: The Dictionary of Human Geography. Wiley-Blackwell, Oxford (1985)

24. Yan, X.-Y., Zhou, T.: Destination choice game: a spatial interaction theory on human mobility. Sci. Rep. **9**, 9466 (2019). https://doi.org/10.1038/s41598-019-46026-w

25. Wilson, A.G.: Entropy in Urban and Regional Modelling. Pion, London (1970)

26. O'Kelly, M.E.: Spatial interaction models. In: International Encyclopedia of Human Geography. pp. 365–368. Elsevier (2009). https://doi.org/10.1016/B978-008044910-4.00529-0.
27. Rees, P., Dennett, A.: Alan Wilson – contributions to research on population and migration. Interdisc. Sci. Rev. **44**, 249–271 (2019). https://doi.org/10.1080/03080188.2019.1670428
28. Wilson, A.: Epidemic models with geography. https://arxiv.org/abs/2005.07673v1 (2020)
29. Werner, P.: Simulating of accessibility of ICT infrastructure in Poland using geographical potential models. In: Proceedings of the 16th International Conference on System Science. pp. 261–269. Wroclaw University of Technology (2007)
30. Werner, P.: Symulacja Monte Carlo rozwoju sieci teleinformatycznych, radiokomunikacji i radiodyfuzji w Polsce (na podstawie modeli potencjału geograficznego). Archiwum Fotogrametrii, Kartografii i Teledetekcji. vol. 13 (2003)
31. Werner, P.: Geograficzne uwarunkowania rozwoju infrastruktury spoleczenstwa informacyjnego w Polsce. Uniwersytet Warszawski, Wydz. Geografii i Studiów Regionalnych, Warszawa (2003)
32. Werner, P.: Konstrukcja i interpretacja modeli potencjału geograficznego w badaniach sieci teleinformatycznych. In: Problemy interpretacji wyników metod badawczych stosowanych w geografii społeczno-ekonomicznej i gospodarce przestrzennej: praca zbiorowa. Bogucki Wydaw. Naukowe (2003)
33. Tobler, W.R.: Cellular geography. In: Gale, S. and Olsson, G. (eds.) Philosophy in Geography. pp. 379–386. Springer Netherlands, Dordrecht (1979). https://doi.org/10.1007/978-94-009-9394-5_18.
34. Batty, M.: Fifty years of urban modeling: Macro-statics to micro-dynamics. In: The dynamics of complex urban systems. pp. 1–20. Springer (2008). https://doi.org/10.1007/978-3-7908-1937-3_1
35. Wilson, A.G.: Complex spatial systems: the modelling foundations of urban and regional analysis. Pearson Education (2000)
36. Oshan, T.M.: A primer for working with the Spatial Interaction modeling (SpInt) module in the python spatial analysis library (PySAL). REGION. **3**, 11 (2016). https://doi.org/10.18335/region.v3i2.175.
37. Fotheringham, A.S., O'Kelly, M.E.: Spatial interaction models: formulations and applications. Kluwer Academic Publishers, Dordrecht, Boston (1989)
38. Raport zakażeń koronawirusem (SARS-CoV-2) - Koronawirus: informacje i zalecenia - Portal Gov.pl. https://www.gov.pl/web/koronawirus/wykaz-zarazen-koronawirusem-sars-cov-2. Accessed on 07 Feb 2021
39. Akaike, H.: A new look at the statistical model identification. IEEE Trans. Automat. Contr. **19**, 716–723 (1974). https://doi.org/10.1109/TAC.1974.1100705
40. 20 tys. zakażeń dziennie? Eksperci mówią, że tę liczbę należy pomnożyć przez 10. https://biqdata.wyborcza.pl/biqdata/7,159116,26507630,20-tys-zakazen-dziennie-eksperci-mowia-ze-te-liczbe-nalezy.html. Accessed on 12 Feb 2021

On Sustainability of Urban Italian Mobility

Gabriella Schoier[✉], Giuseppe Borruso, and Beatrice Dedemo

DEAMS – Department of Economic, Business, Mathematic and Statistical Sciences "Bruno de Finetti", University of Trieste, Tigor, 22, 34100 Trieste, Italy
{gabriella.schoier,giuseppe.borruso}@deams.units.it

Abstract. The aim of this paper is to analyze the problem of the sustainability of the urban transport in Italian provinces. After defining what we mean for sustainable mobility we individuate some indicators to obtain a measure of it.

The methodology used in this paper is the Multiple Factor Analysis (MFA). This method is applied to tables in which a set of individuals is described by a set of variables and the variables are organized into groups. We have applied the MFA to the choosen indicators for Italian cities in the year 2019. This method of analysis allows to identify two main dimensions that describe more than 58% of the variability of sustainability of transports in Italian cities.

Keywords: Spatial data mining · MFA · FactoMineR · Big data

1 Introduction

Nowadays public and private organizations collect a great amount of data i.e. big data to which machine-learning techniques are performed [15].

This is the case of data regarding the urban transport sustainability recognized as a crucial economical social and political objective [10]. For obtaining this result it is necessary to define the notion of urban sustainable mobility and to choose appropriate indicators.

Big data analytics could provide opportunities to develop new knowledge to reshape our understanding of different fields and to support decision making. This is the case of urban transport sustainability recognized as a crucial economical and political goal. In order to achieve this goal it is necessary to define the notion of urban sustainable mobility and to choose appropriate indicators enabling its measurement.

The aim of this paper is to analyze urban transport mobilities at province level in Italy before the Covid- 19 crises on the base of some indicators in particular the MFA procedure has been considered. In general the Multiple Factor Analysis MFA is applied to tables in which a set of individuals (one individual = one row) is described by a set of variables (one variable = one column); within the active variables, it can account for a group structure defined by the user. Such data tables are called *individuals × variables organised into groups* [4]. In this analysis the *R* language and in particular the FactorMineR package has been used [8, 13].

O. Gervasi et al. (Eds.): ICCSA 2021, LNCS 12954, pp. 658–669, 2021.
https://doi.org/10.1007/978-3-030-86979-3_46

2 The Methodology: The Multiple Factor Analysis

In different fields of Quantitative Sciences such as Statistics, Economics and Geographical Planning there is the necessity of simultaneously consider quantitative and qualitative variables as active elements of different factorial analysis (see e.g. [2, 7, 9, 10, 14]).

MFA (see e.g. [11–13]) can be used to solve the problem of variables partition in subspaces. It refers to a Principle Component Analysis (PCA) that can analyze both quantitative and qualitative data [4]. In more details MFA is applied to tables in which a set of individuals (one individual = one row) is described by a set of variables (one variable = one column). It fundamental idea lies in the fact that within the active variables, it can account for a group structure defined by the user. Such data tables are called *individuals × variables organised into groups* [4].

In order to describe the MFA algorithm, one can consider it as a "mixture" between a PCA for quantitative variables and a Multiple Correspondence Analysis (MCA) for the qualitative variables.

MFA procedures compute a PCA of each data table and normalize them by dividing all elements by the first singular value obtained. All the normalized data tables are aggregated into a new table that is analyzed via a non-normalized PCA. This new PCA is obtained by decomposing the variance of the "compromise" into a set of new orthogonal variables (i.e., the principal components are also often called dimensions, axes, factors, or even latent variables) ordered by the amount of variance that each component explains.

The coordinates of the observations on the components are called *factor scores*; these can be used to plot maps of the observations in which the observations themselves are represented as points such that the distances in the map best reflect the similarities between them. The positions of the observations are called *partial factor scores* and can be + represented as points on a map [1].

In other words, the heart of MFA is a PCA in which the weights are assigned to the variables used in the analysis. More precisely, the same weight is associated to each variable of the group of the PCA on the group j ($j = 1,..., J$). The importance of the dimension represented by the principal component is given by its eigenvalue, which indicates how much of the total inertia (i.e., variance) of the data is explained by this component.

This shows that the inertia of *a group* represents the individuals' variability both from the point of view of their deviation from the centre of gravity and from of the between-individuals distances. Thus, the maximum axial inertia of each group of variables is equal to one.

The influence of the groups of variables in the global analysis must be balanced and the structure of each group must also be respected. The weight assigned to each variable presents a simple direct interpretation.

It allows to consider MFA as a particular Generalized Canonical Analysis. For each group of variables, MFA analysis associates a set, that is, a "cloud" of individuals and a representation of these clouds.

This representation can be obtained in different ways: as a projection of a cloud of points, as a canonical variable or using, another idea, such as that proposed by Pages et al. [13]. According to this last proposal the structure of the variables in the J groups ($j = 1,...,J$) and the use of a weighting of MFA given by the reciprocal of the first eigenvalue are taken into account. This prescaling entails that when a PCA is performed on the merged prescaled data sets, the resulting components will reflect a structure common to the data set.

Given the transition formula of the space of variables into the space of individuals, as written by Pages et al. [12], and taking into account the structure of variables in J groups and the weighting of MFA ($\frac{1}{\lambda_1^j}$ if x_k belongs to group j), the $F_s(i)$, that is, the score of the individual i on the axis (of rank) s is given by:

$$F_s(i) = \frac{1}{\sqrt{\lambda_s}} \sum_{j=1}^{J} \frac{1}{\lambda_1^j} \sum_{k=1}^{K_j} x_{ik} G_s(k)$$

where:

K_j is the number of variables in group j,
$G_s(k)$ is the score of the individual i on the axis (of rank) s,
λ_s is the s eigenvalue associated to axis s,
λ_1^j is the first eigenvalue of group j,
x_{ik} is the general term of the data table (row i, column k).

This relationship is fundamental for interpreting the position of individuals with respect to the variables. We must note that on the graphical displays derived from MFA, each individual appears as a centroid of its partial representations. (see [12]).

In the next paragraph, practical and theoretical notions referring to the object of this study have been considered.

3   The Application

3.1   The Data and the Variables

The study of sustainable mobility plays an important role in the socio-economic field and it is of great importance for the politicians and the economists.

To obtain this purpose it is essential to define the notion of sustainable mobility and to measure it.

Numerous definitions of sustainable mobility have been proposed, the most famous one has been introduced in the Brundland report according to which: "Sustainable transport meets the mobility needs of the present without compromising the ability of future generations to meet these needs." [16].

The European Conference of Ministers of Transport [3] further specified the main features that a sustainable mobility system should meet, that is:

a) allowing the basic access and development needs of individuals, companies and society to be met safely and in a manner consistent with human and ecosystem health, and promotes equity within and between successive generations;
b) being affordable, operating fairly and efficiently, offering a choice of transport mode, and supporting a competitive economy, as well as balanced regional development;

c) limiting emissions and waste within the planet's ability to absorb them, using renewable resources at or below their rates of generation, and using non-renewable resources at or below the rates of development of renewable substitutes, while minimizing the impact on the use of land and the generation of noise.

To measure the environmental sustainability of the urban mobility requires taking into account both the environmental, the economic and the social aspect. The selection process should be made explicitly and has to follow, according to the COST action 356, ten criteria: validity, reliability, sensitivity, measurability, data availability, ethical concerns, transparency, interpretability, target relevance, and actionability [6].

Because of these guidelines 13 indicators (reported in Table 1) have been selected and have been measured with respect to Italian provincial towns.

Table 1. Indicators for Sustainable mobility of Italian cities

Economy	Environment	Society
Wellness	Gasoline_Fuel	Fatal_Acccident
Salary	Disel_Fuel	Pedestrians_Deads
Employment	Low_Emission	Population
	E-Charging_Stations	Vehicles
	PM10	
	Urban_Green	

As regards the economic aspects, three indicators have been selected: Wellness, Salary, Employment.

The environmental indicators chosen are five: Gasoline_fuel, Disel_fuel, Low_Emission, E-Charging_Stations, PM_{10}, Urban_Green.

The indicators used to measure the social dimension of the Italian urban transport systems are: FatalAcccident, PedestriansDeads, Population, Vehicles.

The data font is the Italian National Institute of Statistics (Istat) [5]. As some variables are not available for all the provincial towns[1] we have not considered them.

At the provincial level, the most up-to-date available data refer to the year 2019, unless the economic variables - well and salary - which refer respectively to the years 2016 and 2017, but they have been include in the analysis as they have been considered fundamental characteristics for our purpose. The variables considered in this study are the following:

1. "City": province
2. "Position": geographic positioning (North East, North West, Centre, South and Islands)

---

[1] These cities have not be considered: Monza e della Brianza, Andria, Barletta, Trani, Sud Sardegna.

3. " FatalAccident": fatality accident rate
4. "Dead_Pedestrians": pedestrians died in accidents
5. "Population": popolation density
6. "Vehicles": vehicle density per km^2
7. "Employment": employment rate 20–64 years
8. "Wellness": wellness 2016
9. "Salary": salary 2017
10. "Gasoline": % petrol/gasoline vehicles
11. "Diesel": % diesel-fuelled vehicles
12. "LowEmission": % low emission vehicles
13. "E.charging_Stations": density of electric car charging columns
14. "PM10": maximum number of days in excess of the human health protection limit foreseen for PM10 in 2019
15. "Urban_Green": urban green density

The considered variables describe the main economic, social and environmental characteristics of the cities.

In the following Table 2 we present some descriptive characteristics of the variables.

Table 2. Some Descriptive Statistics for the chosen Indicators

Economy	Mean	Median	Standard Deviation
Wellness	17565	18355	3548.30
Salary	19131	19067	3626.77
Employment	63.80	68.85	11.11
Environment			
Gasoline_Fuel	48.00	46.90	6.66
Disel_Fuel	42.20	40.90	5.74
Low_Emission	9.798	9.200	5.20
E-Charging_Stations	2.068	0.520	4.59
PM10	21.56	12.00	23.33
Urban_Green	17.99	13.77	15.36
Society			
Fatal_Acccident	2.319	2.140	0.96
Pedestrians_Deads	16.33	14.29	10.99
Population	252.27	171.70	334.99
Vehicles	3538	3421	1220.44

3.2   The Results of the Application of the MFA

The MFA methodology permits to identify the dimensions (factors) useful for this analysis on urban mobility.

The aim of this analysis is to summarize the variables in at least two dimensions so as to be able to visualize in a two-dimensional graph which are the cities with similar characteristics and those with substantial differences.

The variables have been structured into six macro thematic groups:

1. "Label": contains the two categorical variables

   a. "City"
   b. "Position";

2. "Accident": groups accident data

   a. "FatalAccident"
   b. "Pedestrians_Deads"

3. "Population_vehicles": describes the population and rate of vehicles in circulation

   a. "Population"
   b. "Vehicles"

4. "Economic": individuates the economy of the cities

   a. "Well"
   b. "Salary"
   c. "Employment"

5. "Car": describes the composition of vehicles in circulation in the province

   a. "Gasoline"
   b. "Diesel"
   c. "LowEmission "

6. "Green": describes pollution and urban green

   a. "PM10"
   b. "Urban_Green"
   c. "E.charging_Stations"

The scree plot reported in Fig. 1 suggests to choose two or three dimensions (55,% of total variance).

If we consider the eigenvalues greater than one the first two dimensions that explain the 58.78% of the total variance have to be chosen (see Table 3).

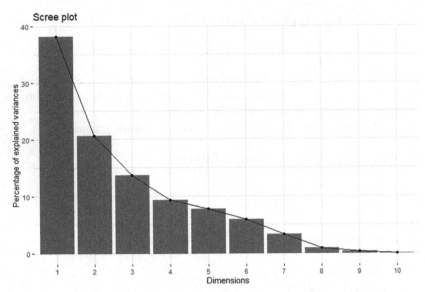

Fig. 1. Screeplot.

Table 3. Eigenvalues of the first six factors (dimensions)

	Eigenvalue	Percent	Cumulative Percent
Dimension 1	2.1728747	38.213986	38.21399
Dimension 2	1.1695242	20.568227	58.78221
Dimension 3	0.7787722	13.696137	72.47835
Dimension 4	0.5262350	9.254808	81.73316
Dimension 5	0.4417858	7.769612	89.50277
Dimension 6	0.3371337	5.929114	95.43188

The MFA analysis allows us to identify the useful dimensions (factors).

Through the two suggested dimensions we can present the result of the analysis using a Cartesian plane.

The first dimension represents the dimension that describes the economic part and the composition of the vehicles in circulation in the provinces.

The second dimension represents the social and environmental part of the provinces.

In Fig. 2 and Fig. 3 the contribution of the quantitative variables and the correlations between the variables and the two identified dimensions can be observed.

When a variable is well represented (in the sense that its variability is well explained in the factorial dimension, i.e. that much of the variability is expressed in that factor) then its image on the factorial plane approaches the circumference and the colors visually help to understand this fact. The more a variable forms a small angle with the factorial

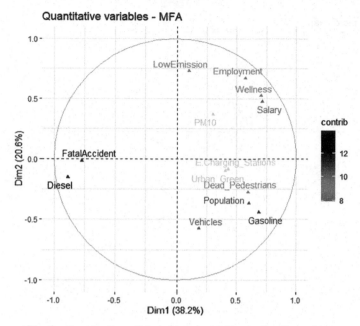

Fig. 2. Contribution of quantitative variables to the dimensions.

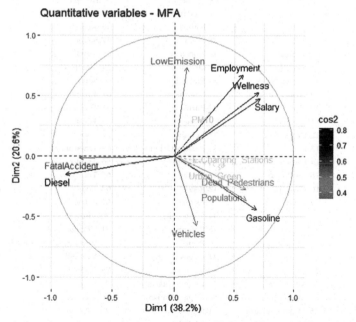

Fig. 3. Correlations between quantitative variables and dimensions. Quality of representation (cos2)

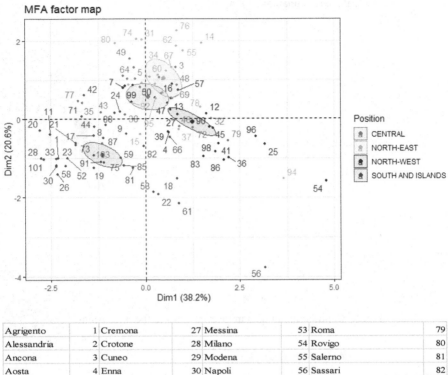

Agrigento	1	Cremona	27	Messina	53	Roma	79
Alessandria	2	Crotone	28	Milano	54	Rovigo	80
Ancona	3	Cuneo	29	Modena	55	Salerno	81
Aosta	4	Enna	30	Napoli	56	Sassari	82
Arezzo	5	Ferrara	31	Novara	57	Savona	83
Ascoli Piceno	6	Firenze	32	Nuoro	58	Siena	84
Asti	7	Foggia	33	Oristano	59	Siracusa	85
Avellino	8	Forlì-Cesena	34	Padova	60	Sondrio	86
Bari	9	Frosinone	35	Palermo	61	Taranto	87
Belluno	10	Genova	36	Parma	62	Teramo	88
Benevento	11	Gorizia	37	Pavia	63	Terni	89
Bergamo	12	Grosseto	38	Perugia	64	Torino	90
Biella	13	Imperia	39	Pesaro-Urbino	65	Trapani	91
Bologna	14	Isernia	40	Pescara	66	Trento	92
Bolzano	15	La Spezia	41	Piacenza	67	Treviso	93
Brescia	16	L'Aquila	42	Pisa	68	Trieste	94
Brindisi	17	Latina	43	Pistoia	69	Udine	95
Cagliari	18	Lecce	44	Pordenone	70	Varese	96
Caltanissetta	19	Lecco	45	Potenza	71	Venezia	97
Campobasso	20	Livorno	46	Prato	72	Verbano-Cusio-Ossola	98
Caserta	21	Lodi	47	Ragusa	73	Vercelli	99
Catania	22	Lucca	48	Ravenna	74	Verona	100
Catanzaro	23	Macerata	49	Reggio Calabria	75	Vibo Valentia	101
Chieti	24	Mantova	50	Reggio Emilia	76	Vicenza	102
Como	25	Massa-Carrara	51	Rieti	77	Viterbo	103
Cosenza	26	Matera	52	Rimini	78		

Fig. 4. Individual Factor Map for the Italian provinces

dimension, the more it is correlated with the factor and determines the interpretation of the axis.

By fixing the attention on the horizontal axis (dimension 1) we can see, on the right, the variables positively correlated with dimension 1 and on the left those negatively correlated. As one can see the first dimension explains the 38.2% of variance.

On the other axis (the vertical one) we can read, above the variables positively correlated with the dimension 2 and down the variables negatively correlated. The dimension 2 explains the 20.6% of the variance.

Figure 4 shows the similarity among the statistical units. Provinces with similar structures are therefore closer to each other and the points, which represent them, are near.

As one can see for example Milano (54) and Napoli (56) are in an "anomalous" position compared to the others:

- Milano has values in the first dimension higher than all other provinces.
- Napoli has low values in the second dimension, while average values for the first dimension. Naples is the province with a very high population density and vehicles, but its economic characteristics are on average compared to the provinces in Italy.

Based on the values of the variables they take in the two dimensions the provinces are divided in four groups:

The first quadrant groups the provinces with lower values than the average in the two dimensions.

The second quadrant presents the provinces with higher values than the average for the first dimension, while lower in the second dimension.

The third quadrant, on the other hand, contains all the provinces with higher values than the average in the two dimensions.

The fourth quadrant finally groups all the provinces with higher values in the first dimension, while lower in the second.

The provinces of the North East are positioned around the main diagonal of the third quadrant, because on average they have higher density and economic values than the provinces of the rest of Italy.

Only Trieste (94) has an anomalous position compared to the others of the North East, as it has a higher density of population and vehicles than the average.

The provinces of the North West, unlike those of the North East, are positioned on average in the forth quadrant, thus indicating lower values than the average density of population and vehicles. Asti (7) is the only province to be "abnormal" compared to the others in the North West, as it has lower values of percentage of diesel and population density.

The provinces of the South and Islands are positioned on average in the first quadrant, indicating lower value as regards economy indicators than the Italian average. It can be noted that Palermo (61) and Cagliari (18) have higher values in the first dimension than the others, indicating that they are the provinces with higher economic values compared to the other provinces of the Islands, but on average compared to all provinces of Italy.

The provinces of the South have similar values in the first dimension to the provinces of the Islands, but have more variability in the second dimension.

The provinces are also called, in the graph, mid-points, because they lie at the "center of gravity" of the thematic groups previously identified.

4 Conclusions

The aim of this paper is to analyze urban transport mobilities at province level in Italy before the Covid-19 crises on the base of some indicators in particular the MFA procedure has been considered.

After analyzing the concept of sustainable urban mobility in order to promote more sustainable urban transport systems it is important to be able to measure it. In order to do this even if there is no general agreement both on the concept of sustainable transport and on which indexes should be used to measure it appropriately, we propose a solution based on 15 indicators of urban transport sustainability referring to Italian provincial towns.

The data have been analyzed using a multivariate statistical procedure that is the Multiple Factor Analysis (MFA).

One of the advantage of MFA for analyzing a complex phenomenon as urban sustainability is that it allows us to catch the aspect of the direction and magnitude relative to the set of variables represented in the various dimensions regarding units such as in this case Italian provinces. Sustainable mobility defined through the indicators illustrated shows two main dimensions that describe more than 50% of its variability among the various Italian cities.

References

1. Abdi, H., Williams, L.J., Valentin, D.: Multiple factor analysis: principal component analysis for multitable and multiblock data sets. WIREs Comput. Stat. **2013**(5), 149–179 (2013). https://doi.org/10.1002/wics.1246
2. Bolasco, S.: Analisi Multidimensionale dei Dati. Metodi, strategie e criteri d'interpretazione, Carrocci editore, Roma (2005)
3. ECMT: Strategy for Integrating Environment and Sustainable Development into the Transport Policy. In: Adopted by the Ministers responsible for Transport and Communications at the 2340th meeting of the European Union' Council of Ministers, Luxembourg, 4–5 April 2001 (2001)
4. Escofier, B., Pages, J.: Analyses Factorielles Simples et Multiples: Objectifs, Methodes et Interpretation, 3rd edn. Dunod, Paris (1998)
5. ISTAT: dati-censimentopopolazione.istat.it/ (2018). Accessed 20 Oct 201
6. Joumard, R., Gudmundsson, H.: Indicators of environmental sustainability in transport. An interdisciplinary approach to methods. INRETS, Lyon, France (2010)
7. Jan, A.K.: Data clustering. 50 years beyond K-means. Pattern Recogn. Lett. **31**, 651–666 (2010)
8. Lê, S., Josse, J., Husson, F.: FactoMineR: an R package for multivariate analysis. J. Stat. Softw. **25**, 1–18 (2008)
9. Mayer-Schonberger, V., Cukier, K.: Big Data: A Revolution That Will Transform How We Live, Work, and Think. Mariner Books, Boston (2013)
10. Monte, A., Schoier, G., Danielis, R., Rotaris, L.: Sustainability of transport in Italian cities: an intertemporal comparison. RIEDS **LXXIII/2019**(1), 17–28 (2019)

11. Monte, A., Schoier, G.: A multivariate statistical analysis of equitable and sustainable well-being over time. Soc. Indic. Res. (2020)
12. Pages, J., Husson, F.: Multiple factor analysis with confidence ellipses: a methodology to study the relationships between sensory and instrumental data. J. Chemometr. **19**, 138–144 (2005)
13. Pages, J.: Multiple Factor Analysis by Example Using R. Chapman and Hall/CRC, London (2014)
14. Schoier, G., Borruso, G.: A methodology for dealing with spatial big data. Int. J. Bus. Intell. Data Min. **12**(1), 1–13 (2017)
15. Software Testing Help: Data Mining Vs Machine Learning Vs Artificial Intelligence Vs Deep Learning (2019). http://www.intelligenzaartificiale.it/data-mining/. Accessed March 2020
16. Zietsman, J., Rilett, L.R.: Sustainable transportation: Conceptualization and performance measures. (No. SWUTC/02/167403-1). Southwest University Transportation Center, Texas Transportation Institute, College Station, Texas: Texas A & M University (2002)

A Remote Sensing and Geo-Statistical Approaches to Mapping Burn Areas in Apulia Region (Southern Italy)

Valentina Santarsiero[1,2]([✉]), Gabriele Nolè[1], Antonio Lanorte[1], Biagio Tucci[1], Francesco Vito Ronco[3], Vito Augusto Capurso[3], and Beniamino Murgante[2]

[1] IMAA-CNR, C.da Santa Loja, Zona Industriale, Tito Scalo, 85050 Potenza, Italy
{valentina.santarsiero,gabriele.nole,antonio.lanorte,
biagio.tucci}@imaa.cnr.it
[2] School of Engineering, University of Basilicata, Viale dell'Ateneo Lucano 10,
85100 Potenza, Italy
{valentina.santarsiero,beniamino.murgante}@unibas.it
[3] Protezione Civile Puglia, via delle Magnolie, 6, Modugno, 700026 Bari, Italy
{f.ronco,v.capurso}@regione.puglia.it

Abstract. Fires represents one of the main causes of environmental degradation and have an important negative impact on the landscape. Fires, in fact, strongly influenced ecological processes and compromise the ecosystems. Measurements of the post-fire damage levels over burned areas are important to quantify fire's impact on landscapes. Remote sensing and geo-statistical approaches are useful tools for the monitoring and analysis of burned areas on a regional scale, because provides reliable and rapid diagnosis of burned areas. Spatial autocorrelation statistics, such as Moran's I and Getis–Ord Local Gi index, were also used to measure and analyze dependency degree among spectral features of burned areas. This approach improves characterization of a burnt area and improves the estimate of the severity of the fire. This paper provides an application of fire severity studies describing post-fire spectral responses of fire affected vegetation to obtain a burned area map. The aim of this work is to implement a procedure, using ESA Sentinel 2 data and spatial autocorrelation statistics in a GIS open-source environment, a graphical model that analyzes the change detection of the potential burned area, as case of study Northern part of Apulia Region (Italy) was used. The burned area was delineated using the spectral indices calculated using Sentinel two images in the period July–August 2020 and using also the land use map of the area.

Keywords: Fire perimeter · Burn severity · ΔNBR index

1 Introduction

Every year forest fire affects wide areas in the world and cause devastating damage at global scales. Forest fires represents an environmental problem that generates negative impacts on forest ecosystems and alter the structure of vegetation [3, 19]. Fire

© Springer Nature Switzerland AG 2021
O. Gervasi et al. (Eds.): ICCSA 2021, LNCS 12954, pp. 670–681, 2021.
https://doi.org/10.1007/978-3-030-86979-3_47

is considered as a major cause of biodiversity reduction, soil fertility loss, gaseous pollutants emission, and other environmental impacts. Fire danger estimation is very important in order to quantify the impact on landscape [31] and play an important role in the framework programs for mitigation, provides information about the degree of degradation.

The fire hazard estimation provides a valid support to policy makers for the design of strategies relating to fire prevention policies and monitoring of fire areas.

Burn severity is a qualitative indicator of the effects of fire on the vegetation ad forest floor. Assessing and mapping the burn severity is important to quantify and monitoring the fire effects, to evaluate post-fire dynamics and to estimate the ability of vegetation to recover after fire (generally indicated as fire-resilience) [19]. The accurate quantitative and qualitative estimation of burn-area are crucial to analyze the impact of fire on forest [1], (Landsat-8 and Sentinel-2 based Forest fire burn area mapping using machine learning algorithms on GEE cloud platform over Uttarakhand, Western Himalaya 2020).

Remote sensing technologies can provide useful data for fire management, from risk estimation [26], fire detection to post fire monitoring [19] including burn area. Burn severity and forest fire can be identified using methods generally based on the spectral reflectance properties of healthy and burnt vegetation. Thermal differences of burning pixel and background pixel are also widely used for fire detection [11]. Several vegetation indexes were used, such as NBR (Normalized Burn Difference) SAVI (Soil Adjusted Vegetation Index), NDVI (Normalized Vegetation Index). Maps obtained by between pre and post fire indexes measure biomass loss [32]. Such assessments are generally performed on perimeter fire maps, mainly using fixed threshold values to classify and map the different levels of the severity of the burb. However, many authors suggest that these fixed threshold values are generally not suitable for all type of landscape and vegetation [17, 18]. In order to overcome these limitations, many authors have proposed a new approach based on geo-statistical analyzes applied to satellite data, both to estimate the perimeter of the burned area and to evaluate the different degree of severity of the burn.

The use of solid geo-statistical analysis for processing satellite data is relatively recent, although in recent decades, geo-statistics has been integrated with remote sensing in the processing of images [5].

To date, the availability of spatial data is increasing along with the techniques and methods adopted in geographic analysis. this allows an accurate analysis of the natural phenomena that occur in the territory with the aim of fully understanding the dynamics that act in the development of the territory and in the changes of land cover, with a quantitative and modeling approach [6, 20, 23, 25].

The aim of this work is to implement an automatic procedure (tool) capable, starting from satellite image processing, to outline quickly (i.e. as soon as possible temporally close to the event) the fires and to calculate indices of severity that allow the first order impacts to be mapped (therefore immediately after the event).

The performances obtained using satellite data were carried out for fires that occurred during the fire season in the year 2020 in the northern part of Apulia region (southern

Italy). This study area was selected, first, because it is highly representative of Mediterranean ecosystems and, second, because it is an interesting test case for wildfire occurrences within the Mediterranean basin. Apulia Region is one of the Italia Regions affected every year by incendiary phenomenon, in fact the Regional Civil Protection have been estimated in 2019 about 600 fire events, of which around 450 involved wooded area [24]. The project "MESARIP satellite methodologies for the assessment of the risk of fires in the Puglia Region", in collaboration between the CNR IMAA and the Civil Protection Puglia, aims to provide tools and methodologies useful for the prevention, forecast and management of emergencies related to risk forest fires and interface also with the use of satellite technologies. The activities included in the project include that of estimating and studying fire severity and burned areas. This paper proposes a procedure that analyze and detect the change detection of the potential burned areas using ESA Sentinel 2 data and geo-statistical approaches in a GIS opensource environment. In order to implement the detection of burned areas a graphical model has been developed. The graphical modeler has been developed using QGIS opensource software and allows you to create complex models using a simple and easy-to-use interface [24, 27].

2   Material and Methods

2.1   Remote Sensing and Fire Severity Assessment

Multi-spectral and multi-temporal satellite data with medium and high spatial resolution are very appropriate to evaluate the fire severity and burned area.

In present work, to estimate more precise and accurate burn area, images of ESA (European Space Agency) Sentinel-2A and 2B satellite have been used [4] to compute burn map to assess burned areas and fire severity using geostatistical analyses. Sentinel 2 data have been composed by 12 bandwidths (see Table 1) used in different studies of vegetation and in fire severity [8]. The higher frequency and resolution of Sentinel 2 imagery offers potential improvements in accuracy issues for application in broad-scale fire severity mapping, relative to other moderate resolution sensors such as Landsat TM (30 m resolution). The higher frequency and resolution of Sentinel 2 imagery offers improvements in accuracy issues for creation in broad-scale fire severity mapping. Fire severity was stimulated using sentinel bands 2 most sensitive to changes in the post-fire reflectance value [14, 25].

After fire events the spectral behavior of vegetation changes and this increase reflectance in mid-infrared and reduce surface reflectance in near-infrared.

The Normalized Burn Ratio (NBR) index is computed on the basis of the two burn sensitive bands, infrared (NIR) and shortwave infrared (SWIR). For this reason, it is one of the best indexes to detect a burn area. The NBR index have been estimated using Sentinel 2 A and 2 B bands most sensitive to changes in the post-fire reflectance value (Band 8a and Band 12) (see formula 1).

$$NBR = (Band\ 8A - Band\ 12)/(Band\ 8A + Band\ 12) \tag{1}$$

Maps obtained by difference between NBR pre and post fire indexes (the ΔNBR index in formula 2) provide a measure of change which then can be used to estimate fire

Table 1. Sentinel 2 band set overview.

Satellite	Bands	Range wavelength (nm)	Resolution (m)
Sentinel	Band 1 –Coastal aereosol	443	60
	Band 2 – Blue	490	10
	Band 3 – Green	560	10
	Band 4 – Red	665	10
	Band 5 – Vegetation Red Edge	705	20
	Band 6 – Vegetation Red Edge	740	20
	Band 7 – Vegetation Red Edge	783	20
	Band 8 – NIR	842	10
	Band 8a –Vegetation Red Edge	865	20
	Band 9 – Water vapour	945	60
	Band 10 – SWIR – Cirrus	1375.3	60
	Band 11 – SWIR	1610.0	20
	Band 12 – SWIR	2190.0	20

severity, in fact the difference in pre and post burn NBR index could reflect the surface change and characterize burn severity degree.

$$\Delta NBR = NBR\ pre - NBR\ post \tag{2}$$

In order to assess fire severity degree, ΔNBR values was categorized. As it is known that ΔNBR ranges values are basically site-specific, fixed thresholds were not applied but [22] classification approach was adopted. In this work we selected six classes of ΔNBR: unburned; very low, low, moderate, high and very high [10, 19].

The ΔNBR index is used to produce the map of the severity of the fire on the ground. For this study, the time span analyzed was July–August 2020, where the date of July 20 was chosen as the pre fire images and the image of August 21, 2020 as the post fire image. the need to use cloud-free images.

2.2 Spatial Autocorrelation Statistics

The first law of geography "Everything is related to everything else, but near things are more related than distant things", theorized by [30], represents the cornerstone of spatial autocorrelation [6, 19].

Considering the occurrences of a space variable (etc. fire events), spatial autocorrelation measures the degree of dependence between events, while considering their similarity and their long-distance relationships. Time series data, like satellite images, can provide useful data sets to examine changes in homogeneity over time, as well as to measure the strength of the relationship between values of the same variables over a given time window [25].

The integration between satellite images and geostatistical analyzes with satellite data is a lot innovative for map and image processing. In the study of spatial variables, that is, with values that represent the variable in territorial areas, the topic of spatial autocorrelation is essential to verify whether the presence of a particular intensity of a phenomenon in a given area implies the presence of the same phenomenon in the contiguous areas.

Local indicators of spatial autocorrelation have achieved us in locating clustered pixels, by measuring the amount of elements within the "fixed neighborhood" file they are homogeneous. Among the first statistics for local spatial autocorrelation was suggested by Getis and Ord in 1992 [9], and subsequently elaborated in Ord and Getis in 1995 [9]. The index is derived from a point pattern analysis logic. In its first formulation, the statistic consisted of a ratio of the number of observations within a given one-point interval to the total count points. Statistical analysis is applied to values at nearby locations (as defined by space weights) [19]. In this paper Getis-Ord Local Gi [9, 15] have been used according with the subsequent formula (3):

$$G_i(d) = \frac{\sum_{i=1}^{n} w_i(d) x_i x_i \sum_{i=1}^{n} w_i(d)}{S(i) \sqrt{\frac{\left[(N-1) \sum_{i=1}^{n} w_i(d) - \left(\sum_{i=1}^{n} w_i(d) \right)^2 \right]}{N-2}}} \tag{3}$$

The interpretation of the Getis - Ord statistics is very simple: a value greater than the average suggests a High-High cluster or hotspot, while a less than average value indicates a Low-Low cluster or a cold spot.

Geostatistical analysis tools are available in different software, such as GIS and those of image processing. In this work, tools from packages were used QGIS software.

In the application of autocorrelation method, it is important to define the nature of the events that we investigate and the geometric relationships that exist. In the context of processing images, the spatial event is associated with a pixel and spatial autocorrelation statistics they are usually calculated considering the geographic coordinates of its centroid. The intensity, on the other hand, should be chosen by rigorously considering the empirical nature of the case study. The conceptualization of geometric relationships in the case of elaboration of images is very simple because the distance between the events is always the same or a multiple of the pixel size. The application of spatial autocorrelation statistics to remotely sensed images allow us to obtain a new raster that contains in each pixel a number that expresses how much it is autocorrelated to another pixel [24, 27].

3   Discussion and Results

The study area (see Fig. 1) was carried out in the northern part of Apulia Region (South of Italy) in Foggia Prefecture, which present an increasing of number of fire events, generally occurred in the period June–September 2020. The area is characterized by grasslands, coniferous and oak woods, and agricultural land. Climate is a typically Mediterranean climate with mild and slightly rainy winters alternating with hot and dry summers [27].

Specifically, Sentinel 2 remote sensing data used in this paper were downloaded from the THEIA website [29]. The sets of spectral bands available on the THEIA website are atmospheric corrected TOA (top of atmosphere) by means of the MAJA (Multi-sensor Atmospheric Correction and Cloud Screening) algorithm [12, 13]. The spatial coverage

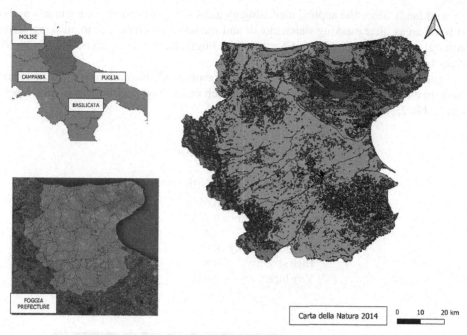

Fig. 1. Study area.

of the study area (see Fig. 1) provided by the swath of the satellite determined the extension of the study area. The ΔNBR index is used to produce the map of the severity of the fire on the ground. For this study, the time span analyzed was July - August 2020, where the date of July 20 was chosen as the pre fire images and the image of August 21, 2020 as the post fire image. The choice of these two dates is linked to the need to use images that are as clean as possible from the presence of the cloud. After calculating the ΔNBR index, we proceeded to mask it from clouds, water and shadows, in order to correct all the pixels that could have created false positives.

This kind of correction aims to eliminate the distortion of the pixels related to the presence of clouds and shadows. For the pixels with cloud cover, the clouds and shadows have been masked by operating respectively on the blue band (band 2) and on NIR (band 8), using the threshold value that best corrected the pixels affected by the presence of clouds and of shadows.

Subsequently we proceeded with the masking of all the pixels affected by the presence of water and all wetlands (sea, lakes, rivers, etc.). The index was used for this purpose NDWI (Normalized Difference Water Index) (Eq. 4):

$$NDWI = (Band\ 3 - Band\ 8)/(Band\ 3 + Band\ 8) \qquad (4)$$

The main difficulty is to reliably discriminate events identifiable as fires from fakes positive. These can often be traced back to spectral response of dry vegetation or even rapids land cover changes in agricultural areas (typically from soil with vegetation to plowed land). Since the applied methodology aims to identify burnt areas outside agricultural areas, after masking water, clouds and shadows, we proceeded to masking agricultural areas, using the Nature Charter of the Puglia Region [16] whose latest update dates back to 2013.

The ΔNBR index has been classified finding empirically its minimum and maximum value in the burned area [21]. Range between such values have been split in equal classes (see Table 2, see Fig. 2).

Table 2. ΔNBR RANGE.

Severity level	ΔNBR range
Unburned	0.05–0.1
Very low severity	0.1–0.3
Low severity	0.4
Moderate severity	0.5
High severity	0.8
Very high	>0.8

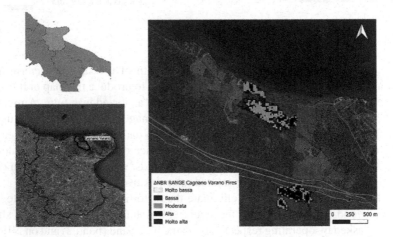

Fig. 2. Example of ΔNBR range map in Cagnano Varano municipalities.

In order to exclude false positives not otherwise identifiable, to the map of the ΔNBR obtained and corrected as described above, an analysis was subsequently applied local spatial statistics (Getis and Ord's interpretation) aimed at identifying clusters of similar or dissimilar values. The application of spatial autocorrelation statistics to remotely sensed images allow us to obtain a new raster that contains in each pixel a number that expresses how much it is autocorrelated to another pixel.

A model, called Fire Area Detection Model, (see Fig. 3) for the determination of fire severity was subsequently implemented in QGIS, which involves identifying the areas covered by the fire starting from the use of the binary map obtained from the application of spatial autocorrelation methods to the ΔNBR map and from the ΔNBR map obtained from the masking procedure.

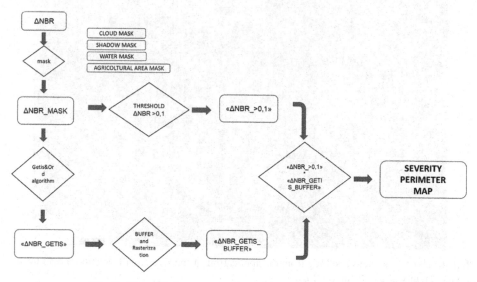

Fig. 3. Simplified representation of the applied methodology.

By applying the methodology described, it was possible to identify that, in the analyzed area, the burnt areas occupy a total one of surface of about 5 km^2 (Fig. 4).

The application of this model allows a quick and easy identification and perimeter of the burned areas.

A comparison with the true and false color images and also with the pre and post fire NBR images clearly suggests that the identified areas are correctly classified as a burnt area connected to a fire (see Fig. 5 and Fig. 6).

The output products they consist of the maps relating to the pre and post event NBR indices, in the ΔNBR for the estimation of the severity of the focus and of images in RGB composition and False Colors which are also useful for discriminating the burned areas.

The definition of the Fire Area Detection model for estimating the fire severity and perimeter of the areas traveled by fire predicts as input data the satellite data of the images relating to the days immediately before and after the fire and vector data that will be used by mask to clip the satellite image in the area of interest. The use of Sentinel 2 images with high spatial resolution and the masking of agricultural areas limited the overestimation of burnt areas. In addition, the joint use of NBR and ΔNBR spectral indices and statistical analyzes made it possible to accurately detect the burned areas.

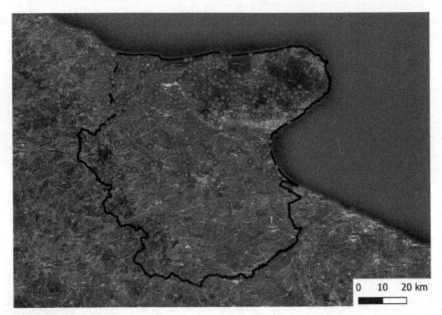

Fig. 4. Hot Spots Areas resulting from the application of the Fire Area Detection model for the period 21 July 2020/20 August 2020.

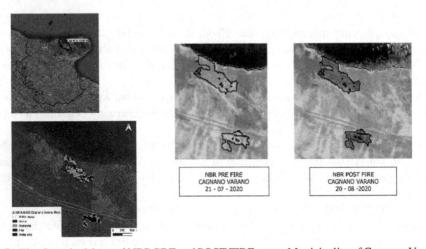

Fig. 5. Fire Severity Map and NBR PRE and POST FIRE maps, Municipality of Cagnano Varano.

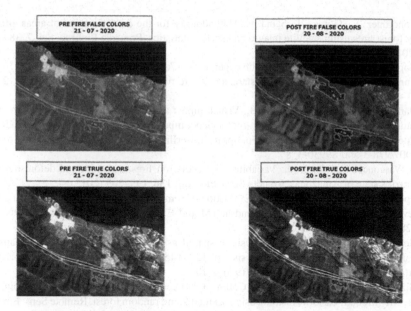

Fig. 6. Combinations in true and false colors before and after the fire, of the burned area of Cagnano Varano Municipality.

4 Conclusions

Fire severity refers to the effects of a fire on the environment, typically focusing on the loss of vegetation and including soil impacts. The accurate quantitative and qualitative estimation of burn areas are crucial to analyze the impact of fire, for monitoring fire effects, evaluating post fire dynamics as the ability of vegetation to recover after the fire event.

The availability of satellite high resolution imagery provides the opportunity to obtain useful information for fire management, from risk evaluation to post-fire damage estimation.

By combining the use of geographic information systems, remote sensing and geo-statistical analysis, the model proposed in this study provides a reliable estimate of the perimeter and mapping of burnt areas in the investigated area.

This study can be useful to spatial planning authorities as a tool for assessing and monitoring of burned areas, representing a useful tool for land management.

References

1. Atkinson, P.M., Lewis, P.: Geostatistical classification for remote sensing: an introduction. Comput. Geosci. **26.4**, 361–371 (2000)
2. Bar, S., Parida, B.R., Pandey, A.C.: Landsat-8 and Sentinel-2 based Forest fire burn area mapping using machine learning algorithms on GEE cloud platform over Uttarakhand, Western Himalaya. Remote Sens. Appl.: Soc. Environ. **18**, 100324 (2020). https://doi.org/10.1016/j.rsase.2020.100324

3. Bohórquez, L., Gómez, I., Santa, F.: Methodology for the discrimination of areas affected by forest fires using satellite images and spatial statistics. Procedia Environ. Sci. **7**, 389–394 (2011)
4. Copernicus homepage. https://scihub.copernicus.eu/dhus/#/home
5. Curran, P.J., Atkinson, P.M.: Geostatistics and remote sensing. Prog. Phys. Geogr. **22**(1), 61–78 (1998)
6. Danese, M., Nolè, G., Murgante, B.: Visual impact assessment in urban planning. In: Murgante, B., Borruso, G., Lapucci, A. (eds.) Geocomputation and Urban Planning. Studies in Computational Intelligence, vol. 176. Springer, Berlin, Heidelberg (2009). https://doi.org/10.1007/978-3-540-89930-3_8
7. de Vasconcelos, S.S., et al.: Variability of vegetation fires with rain and deforestation in Brazil's state of Amazonas. Remote Sens. Environ. **136**, 199–209 (2013)
8. Epting, J., Verbyla, D., Sorbel, B.: Evaluation of remotely sensed indices for assessing burn severity in interior Alaska using Landsat TM and ETM+. Remote Sens. Environ. **96**(3–4), 328–339 (2005)
9. Getis, A., Keith Ord, J.: The analysis of spatial association by use of distance statistics. Perspectives on Spatial Data Analysis, pp. 127–145. Springer, Berlin, Heidelberg (2010). https://doi.org/10.1007/978-3-642-01976-0_10
10. Gibson, R., Danaher, T., Hehir, W., Collins, L.: A remote sensing approach to mapping fire severity in south-eastern Australia using sentinel 2 and random forest. Remote Sens. Environ. **240**, 111702 (2020). https://doi.org/10.1016/j.rse.2020.111702
11. Giglio, L., Boschetti, L., Roy, D.P., Humber, M.L., Justice, C.O.: The Collection 6 MODIS burned area mapping algorithm and product. Remote Sens. Environ. **217**, 72–85 (2018)
12. Hagolle, O., et al. "A multi-temporal and multi-spectral method to estimate aerosol optical thickness over land, for the atmospheric correction of FormoSat-2, LandSat, VENμS and Sentinel-2 images. Remote Sens. **7**.3, 2668–2691 (2015)
13. Hagolle, O., Huc, M., Villa Pascual, D., Dedieu, G.: A multi-temporal method for cloud detection, applied to FORMOSAT-2, VENμS, LANDSAT and SENTINEL-2 images. Remote Sens. Environ. **114**(8), 1747–1755 (2010). https://doi.org/10.1016/j.rse.2010.03.002
14. Hall, R.J., Freeburn, J.T., de Groot, W.J., Pritchard, J.M., Lynham, T.J., Landry, R.: Remote sensing of burn severity: experience from western Canada boreal fires. Int. J. Wildland Fire **17**(4), 476 (2008). https://doi.org/10.1071/WF08013
15. Illian, J., et al.: Statistical Analysis and Modelling of Spatial Point Patterns. vol. 70. John Wiley & Sons (2008)
16. ISPRA homepage. http://cartanatura.isprambiente.it/Database/RiferimentiCartografici.php
17. Key, C.H.: Ecological and sampling constraints on defining landscape fire severity. Fire Ecol. **2**(2), 34–59 (2006)
18. Key, C.: Glacier Field Station Center. Evaluate sensitivities of burn-severity mapping algorithms for different ecosystems and fire histories in the United States (2006)
19. Lanorte, A., et al.: Multiscale mapping of burn area and severity using multisensor satellite data and spatial autocorrelation analysis. Int. J. Appl. Earth Observ. Geoinf. **20**, 42–51 (2013)
20. Casas, G.L., Scorza, F., Murgante, B.: New urban agenda and open challenges for urban and regional planning. In: Calabrò, F., Spina, L.D., Bevilacqua, C. (eds.) ISHT 2018. SIST, vol. 100, pp. 282–288. Springer, Cham (2019). https://doi.org/10.1007/978-3-319-92099-3_33
21. Miller, J.D., Thode, A.E.: Quantifying burn severity in a heterogeneous landscape with a relative version of the delta Normalized Burn Ratio (dNBR). Remote Sens. Environ. **109**, 66–80 (2007)
22. Miller, J.D., et al.: Calibration and validation of the relative differenced Normalized Burn Ratio (RdNBR) to three measures of fire severity in the Sierra Nevada and Klamath Mountains, California, USA." Remote Sens. Environ. **113**.3, 645–656 (2009)

23. Murgante, B., et al.: A spatial rough set for locating the periurban fringe. SAGEO (2007)
24. Nolè, G., et al.: Model of Post Fire Erosion Assessment Using RUSLE Method, GIS Tools and ESA Sentinel DATA. In: Gervasi, O., et al. (eds.) ICCSA 2020. LNCS, vol. 12253, pp. 505–516. Springer, Cham (2020). https://doi.org/10.1007/978-3-030-58814-4_36
25. Nolè, G., Lasaponara, R., Lanorte, A., Murgante, B.: Quantifying Urban Sprawl with spatial autocorrelation techniques using multi-temporal satellite data. Int. J. Agric. Environ. Inf. Syst. 5(2), 19–37 (2014). https://doi.org/10.4018/IJAEIS.2014040102
26. Rauste, Y., et al. "Satellite-based forest fire detection for fire control in boreal forests. Int. J. Remote Sens. 18.12, 2641–2656 (1997)
27. Santarsiero, V., et al..: Assessment of Post Fire Soil Erosion with ESA Sentinel-2 Data and RUSLE Method in Apulia Region (Southern Italy). In: Gervasi, O., et al. (eds.) ICCSA 2020. LNCS, vol. 12252, pp. 590–603. Springer, Cham (2020). https://doi.org/10.1007/978-3-030-58811-3_43
28. Telesca, L., Amatulli, G., Lasaponara, R., Lovallo, M., Santulli, A.: Time-scaling properties in forest-fire sequences observed in Gargano area (southern Italy). Ecol. Model. 185(2–4), 531–544 (2005). https://doi.org/10.1016/j.ecolmodel.2005.01.009
29. Theia homepage. https://theia.cnes.fr/atdistrib/rocket/#/home
30. Tobler, W.R.: A computer movie simulating urban growth in the Detroit region. Econ. Geogr. 46(sup1), 234–240 (1970)
31. van Wagtendonk, J.W., Root, R.R., Key, C.H.: Comparison of AVIRIS and Landsat ETM+ detection capabilities for burn severity. Remote Sens. Environ. 92(3), 397–408 (2004). https://doi.org/10.1016/j.rse.2003.12.015
32. Xiao, X., Braswell, B., Zhang, Q., Boles, S., Frolking, S., Moore, B.: Sensitivity of vegetation indices to atmospheric aerosols: continental-scale observations in Northern Asia. Remote Sens. Environ. 84(3), 385–392 (2003). https://doi.org/10.1016/S0034-4257(02)00129-3

Soil Erosion and Land Degradation in Rural Environment: A Preliminary GIS and Remote-Sensed Approach

Giuseppe Cillis[1](✉), Gabriele Nolè[1](✉), Antonio Lanorte[1](✉),
Valentina Santarsiero[1,2](✉), Biagio Tucci[1](✉), Francesco Scorza[2](✉),
and Beniamino Murgante[2](✉)

[1] IMAA-CNR, C.da Santa Loja, Zona Industriale, Tito Scalo, Potenza, Italy
{giuseppe.cillis,gabriele.nole,antonio.lanorte,
valentina.santarsiero,biagio.tucci}@imaa.cnr.it
[2] School of Engineering, University of Basilicata, Viale dell'Ateneo Lucano 10,
85100 Potenza, Italy
{valentina.santarsiero,francesco.scorza,
beniamino.murgante}@unibas.it

Abstract. The processes of land transformation related to soil erosion and land degradation are complex phenomena that require an approach as detailed and multidisciplinary as possible. In some Mediterranean inland areas, these issues seem to be very connected to the dynamics of transformation and abandonment of agricultural areas. In order to carry out this preliminary investigation for the assessment of dynamics and relationships between processes and land cover, an approach based on GIS and remote sensing has been applied. The study started with implementation of the Revised Universal Soil Loss Equation (RUSLE) model to calculate soil erosion on a monthly and annual basis. The resulting data were then processed through a Getis-Ord local autocorrelation index in order to produce a persistent erosion map. All datasets created were correlated with the cover classes that need more attention, i.e., arable land and post-cultivation vegetation area. All the techniques and methodologies, have been applied in a rural area of the Basilicata Region (South Italy) using exclusively a Free and Open Source Software (FoSS) GIS approach as it guarantees the possibility to perform a series of complex analyses in a simple and effective way so that they can be implemented in environmental monitoring actions and plans.

Keywords: Land degradation · RUSLE · FoSS GIS

1 Introduction

Nowadays, land degradation is one of the problems causes major consequences from an environmental point of view. In fact, this phenomenon triggers a series of related processes involving the alteration of water flows, loss of fertile soil, loss of natural habitats, ecosystem services and rural landscapes [9, 14, 20, 26]. In general terms, land degradation is a process driven by a combination of phenomena such as: aridity, soil erosion, land morphology and orography, vegetation cover, anthropogenic and climate factors [7].

One of these phenomena is soil erosion, which is due in particular, but not exclusively, to the intensity of rainfall. When short and intense rainfall affects soils without vegetation cover, runoff removes the surface layer rich in organic matter from the soil. Arid, semi-arid, and sub-humid areas with sunny exposures are generally at greater risk because they are often affected by short but intense rainfall, which instead of mitigating the effects of low rainfall, triggers erosion processes [17].

The causes of these processes are multiple but, especially in the inland areas of the Mediterranean regions, some dynamics related to agriculture have particularly influenced the degradation [1]. Specifically, agricultural overexploitation with unsustainable practices and land abandonment, are leading to alterations at the ecological level that need contextual analysis to assess medium and long-term effects. In fact, some agricultural practices, which are oriented to an over-exploitation of soils, to an excess of mechanized processing and to the use of chemistry [2], are leading to a reduction of soil quality and subsequent degradation.

The other phenomenon, i.e., the abandonment of agricultural activities and more generally of the territory, is at the attention of the scientific community as it can produce environmental and landscape impacts, as well as socioeconomic [13]. Obviously, over-exploitation and abandonment can have, in some particular territorial contexts, a close relationship. In fact, some areas may be abandoned precisely because of the problems following the excessive agricultural exploitation occurred in the past [25].

That said, the link between abandonment, soil erosion and land degradation needs in-depth methodological and technical investigation because the factors, dynamics and correlations are very varied and often divergent.

Starting from a study area located in Southern Italy (Basilicata Region) and suffering from problems of agricultural abandonment [22], land degradation [3] and soil consumption [27], GIS and remote sensing techniques were used to perform a preliminary investigation to assess the relationship between land degradation and soil erosion. After an initial statistical survey, arable land and areas with post-crop vegetation potentially susceptible to land degradation were mapped based on erosion rates estimated using RUSLE methodology and clustered using autocorrelation techniques.

Several indices of local spatial autocorrelation exist, but the one suggested by Ord and Getis [19], was used in this study. It is derived from a method of spatial autocorrelation. It is developed from a logic of point cluster analysis. In its first version, the index accounted for a relation between the number of remarks within a specified point range and the total sum of points. In a more generalized version, the index (as expressed by spatial weights) is applied to values at neighboring positions. This type of spatial clustering of soil erosion data allows us to obtain a new raster that contains in each pixel a number expressing how much it is autocorrelated to another pixel so it's possible define a persistent erosion map of the study area for the period considered.

Through the use of a Free and Open Source Software (FoSS) approach and open data freely available online, it was possible to set up a preliminary analysis in a single work environment thanks to the possibility of integrating different types of datasets and data processing techniques. The increasing efficiency of FoSS GIS analysis techniques and the interoperability of different data represent a strong point both for the researcher and for the planner who wants to realize plans and strategies coherent with the rural environmental needs and problems. In fact, this work is part of the "MEV-CSU" project (University of Basilicata, CNR-IMAA and FARBAS) whose objective is to implement new advanced methodologies for the evaluation of land consumption related to the development processes of the settlement system, relational and natural environment of the Basilicata Region.

2 Materials and Methods

The analyses and computations were performed in an area of approximately 1554 km^2 within the Basilicata Region, including 17 municipalities included in the MEV CSU project. As shown in Fig. 1, the actual area does not include the real perimeter of all municipalities but, in this first phase of work, it has been cropped on the basis of the satellite image swath used. The area is characterized by a typical Mediterranean climate, with a pronounced bi-seasonal regime with hot and dry summers and cold-humid winters. Natural risks and anthropogenic activities make this area an interesting context of study because the combination of anthropogenic activities and anthropic activities and natural risks contribute to the establishment of degradation phenomena.

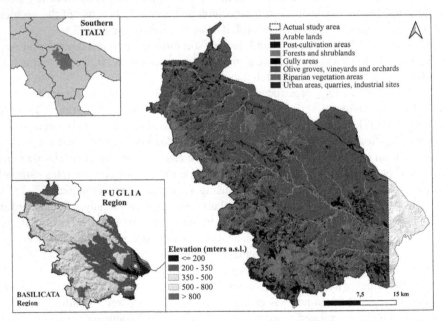

Fig. 1. Localization of study area and distribution of arable land and areas with post-cultivation vegetation.

These two categories were obtained from the Nature Map 2013 in open data format [17] aggregating some specific CORINE Biotopes classes. This dataset, although not recently processed, was chosen instead of other open data available online after comparison and verification through photo-interpretation on current orthophotos. Mapping operation shows that arable land covers 65% of the territory and that areas with post-cultivation vegetation cover only 9%.

2.1 Monthly and Annual Erosion: RUSLE Model

The first part of work involved implementation methodologies useful for estimating and mapping areas with high erosion rates. All spatial operations were performed with QGIS 3.16 software and plugins and integrated modules of GRASS GIS and SAGA GIS; instead geostatistical operations at-through R.

One of the most widely used empirical models for soil erosion assessment is the RUSLE (Revised Universal Soil Loss Equation). The model was calculated using the following equation [23]:

$$A = R \times K \times LS \times C \times P \tag{1}$$

Where:

A = annual soil loss (Mg $\cdot$ ha $-1 \cdot$ year -1);

R = precipitation erosion factor (MJ $\cdot$ mm $\cdot$ ha $-1 \cdot$ h $-1 \cdot$ year -1);

K = soil erodibility factor (Mg $\cdot$ h $\cdot$ MJ $-1 \cdot$ mm -1);

LS = slope length factor and slope slope (dimensionless);

C = crop and cover management factor (dimensionless);

P = cultivation or anti-erosion (dimensionless) practice factor.

The RUSLE is based on five variables related to precipitation regime, soil properties, topography, crop cover and management, and conservation cropping practices. The result is an estimate of the amount of soil lost due to surface erosion and erosion of the rill (canalization). The parameters calculation used in previous papers [12] has been updated and modified to make the estimate more accurate.

R-factor equation is based on the rainfall intensity developed for Basilicata in the work of Capolongo [6]; in which only the daily rainfall contributions with values greater than 10 are added up.

$$R = 0.1087 * \left[\text{daily cumulated rainfall}^{(1.86)} \right]$$

The soil erodibility K-factor is the rate of soil loss per unit of the precipitation erosion index (t $-$ ha $-$ h $-$ ha $-1 -$ MJ $-1 -$ mm -1). The calculation was based on the methodology proposed by [29]:

$$K = \left[\frac{2.1 * 10^{-4} * (12 - M) * \left[(Si + fS) * (100 - C) \right]^{1.14} + 3.25 * (A - 2) + 2.5 * (P - 3)}{100} \right] \tag{3}$$

M represents the organic matter expressed as a percentage (%) present in the soil, Si is the percentage of silt from 0.002–0.05 mm, fS the content of very fine sand with diameter 0.05–0.1 mm, and C the percentage of clay with diameter <0.002 mm.

The K values thus obtained, were multiplied by the factor 0.1313 in order to be expressed in the unit of the International System. For the definition of the factor on the area of investigation the parameters were derived from the Pedological Map of the Basilicata Region and from the Basilicata region soils database [28, 29].

The formula proposed by Mitasova [15] was used to calculate the topographic LS-factor relative to a point r:

$$LS : (\mu + 1) * \left[\frac{a(r)}{a_0} \right]^{\mu} * x * \left[\frac{sin(b(r))}{b_0} \right]^{n} \tag{4}$$

a(r) represents the product of flow accumulation and pixel resolution (in meters) and represents the unit drained area; a_0 has a value of 22.1 m and represents the standard length defined for the calculation for USLE; b(r) is the slope in radians; b_0 has a value of 9% and represents the standard slope defined for the calculation for USLE; n was chosen to be the value 1.2 based on the work of Terranova et al. [29]. The μ value is value was calculated using formula (5) where β is the ratio of erosion type caused by flow to erosion caused by precipitation impact on soil and is equal to 0.5.

$$\mu = \frac{\beta}{\beta + 1} \tag{5}$$

The LS product factor is dimensionless and it was assumed to be constant over the entire period of observation.

The C-factor is dimensionless and is calculated to consider the impacts of vegetation cover on erosion. There are several approaches to calculation in the literature as C can vary depending on the different parameters being considered. In this work, the equation defined by Kuo et al. [11] was used:

$$C = -a * SAVI + 1 \tag{6}$$

In the Eq. (6), a is land cover management factor and is assumed as a value of 1.18. The *SAVI* index (Soil-Adjusted Vegetation Index) has been elaborated starting from the Sentinel-2A images. In particular, it has been used the reprocessed images of the THEIA system [31] which allows to download images already atmospherically and topographically corrected. The value of C can vary from 0 (complete vegetation cover) to 1 (no vegetation cover or bare soil).

The last factor (P) considers the effects of agricultural practices carried out to mitigate the erosion effect of rainfall. The P factor is dimensionless and values range from 0 (presence of agricultural practices for erosion mitigation) to 1 (absence of agricultural practices for erosion mitigation). The P-factor was derived from a dataset freely available online [8, 21].

All parameters calculated (Fig. 2) were resampled to spatial resolution of Sentinel-2A (10 m) and summed to get the actual value of RUSLE expressed in Mg * ha -1 * year -1.

The RUSLE values were calculated for the following months: October, November, and December 2019 and March, April, May, June, July, August, and September 2020. For the monthly RUSLEs a specific model has been implemented by Graphical Modeler of QGIS to realize a batch processing in order to calculate the different parameters in a semi-automated way. Finally, the monthly values were summed to have an annual RUSLE value. The months of January and February 2020 were not included in the calculation of RUSLE because cloudless satellite imagery is not available for C calculation.

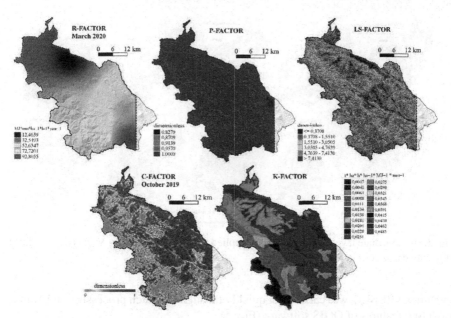

Fig. 2. The factors used to calculate RUSLE. For R and C factors, only one monthly processing each has been reported as an example.

2.2 Persistent Erosion Map

The integration of satellite imagery and geostatistical analysis is an innovative approach for analysis and mapping based on factors influenced by the spatial and geographic component. Specifically, the issue of spatial autocorrelation is fundamental to assess whether a phenomenon particularly intense in a specific area, implies the presence of the same also in contiguous areas [18]. In the present work, the autocorrelation indexes were also applied to the RUSLE model to produce a persistent erosion map.

Exploiting the potential from the R package *spdep* [4, 30], it was possible to apply several indices to the monthly RUSLE values. After several attempts, the choice fell on the G_i local autocorrelation index proposed by Ord and Getis [19].

Statistical interpretation of the index allows values to be clustered on the basis of a hot spot (pixel values greater than the mean) or cold spot (values less than the mean [23]. The index was applied individually to each month (Fig. 3) highlighting only pixels with positive autocorrelation and then subsequently cumulated into a final raster. This allowed the elaboration of a map that highlights the areas with a persistent erosion rate based on hot spot clusters.

3 Results and Discussion

The use of a FoSS and open data approach made it possible to simplify and speed up spatial analysis without losing accuracy. In addition, the possibility to integrate QGIS with R has also allowed to carry out complete geostatistical surveys reducing the work-flow to a minimum. In fact, the amount of calculations and operations of the monthly

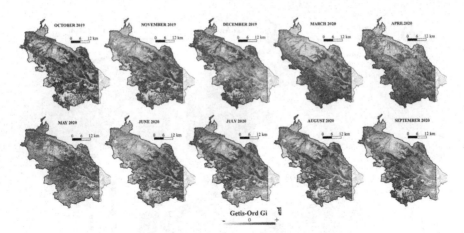

Fig. 3. Intermediate layers of Getis-Ord G_i applied to monthly RUSLEs. Values express positive or negative autocorrelation.

and annual RUSLE, was carried out quickly through the batch processing and graphical modeling features of QGIS software (Fig. 4).

The aim of this work was to relate erosion data to land cover, in order to evaluate how this process may influence degradation phenomena and the relationship between the abandonment of agricultural activities. The preliminary investigation was based on zonal statistics of average monthly and annual RUSLE values with respect to areas with arable land and post-cultivation vegetation. The data are shown in Table 1.

The analysis on annual values shows an erosion rate with same order of magnitude in two classes but with a slightly higher value in areas with post-crop vegetation. This small difference is extremely important to investigate because, generally [5] high values are noted in arable crops as they have long periods of the year with bare soil. The reason could be that the areas with post-cultivation vegetation, present a type of cover (expressed by the C-factor) and the morphological context that could influence the erosion.

From the evaluation of the arable land classes, it can be seen that the month in which the highest values are present is November 2019. This is due both to the amount of rain fallen and to the fact that November is the month in which the arable land lacks vegetative cover as it is the transition period between the end of the agricultural year and the start of sowing for the following one. for the purposes of estimating land degradation as a function of erosion, it is more useful to investigate arable land in March because in November, since there is no vegetation cover, erosion is determined, with the same erosivity of rain, only by stationary factors (R * K * LS). This is also called "Natural Potential" which does not consider the influence of vegetation. Considering that theoretically high values are unexpected, the areas in which they emerge could be indicated as those subject to a greater susceptibility to land degradation and therefore to be analysed in more detail.

On the other hand, considering the areas of post-cultivation vegetation, it can be seen that the months of greatest interest are, also in this case, November and March. November has slightly lower values than arable land, even if there is a difference in land cover in

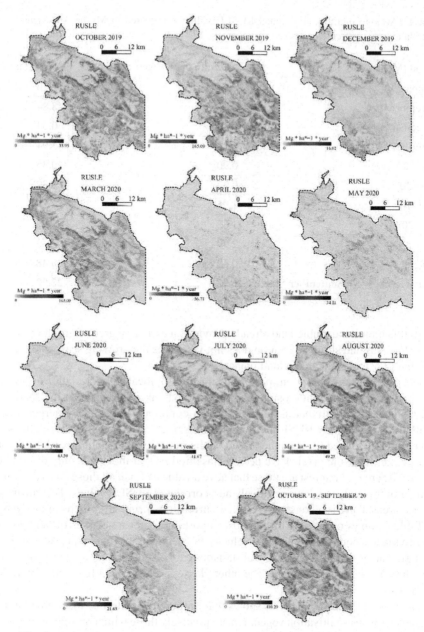

Fig. 4. Maps of monthly and annual RUSLEs expressed in Mg-ha −1 -year −1.

the two classes in this month. The reasons may be different but need a more detailed investigation as different factors could be involved, linked both to morphological and physical aspects and to different stages of abandonment. In March, on the other hand, the average value in the abandoned areas is almost double, presumably due to the fact

Table 1. Average monthly and annual RUSLE values (expressed in Mg-ha -1 -year -1) for arable lands and post-cultivation vegetation areas.

Period [Month/Year]	Post-cultivation vegetation areas	Arable lands
October '19	1.81	2.10
November '19	8.81	8.84
December '19	0.42	0.34
March '20	7.22	3.94
April '20	0.90	0.35
May '20	0.37	0.39
June '20	1.95	2.19
July '20	1.85	1.96
August '20	2.29	2.33
September '20	0.62	0.48
Year [October '19–September '20]	**26.23**	**22.92**

that in this month the arable land already provides a certain degree of ground cover and the herbaceous and shrub vegetation does not yet, since the growing season begins later than that of cereals and arable land in general.

The geostatistical operations performed through G_i local autocorrelation allowed for the creation of a persistent erosion map (Fig. 5) that takes into account the spatial and geographic relationship that may exist between contiguous areas that emerge from the calculations of monthly RUSLEs. The pixels highlighted in the map are spatially and geographically related to each other based on the intensity of the monthly RUSLE value. In this raster map, the pixels have been reclassified so that they have only discrete 0–1 values. The areas of interest are those that have a value of 1, i.e. all those areas that during all the months analyzed, have positively autocorrelated RUSLE values. This means that in these areas, there is a constant erosion contribution during all months of analysis.

Table 2 shows only some of the most important aggregate classes of land cover in order to make a comparison with the values recorded in arable land and post-cultivation vegetation areas. In addition, the zonal statistics carried out directly on QGIS allowed an immediate tabulation of the data. The other classes were derived from the Nature Map [10] as well.

The spatial statistical analysis shows that, in percentage terms, the arable land and the areas with post-cultivation vegetation are precisely those which present higher values of vegetation than the others, and that especially the latter represents more than 61%.

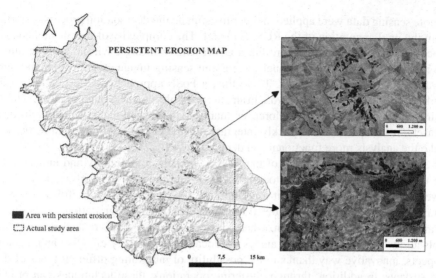

Fig. 5. In red, areas with persistent erosion estimated between October 2019 and September 2020. On the right, two details on two areas overlaid on the 2017 orthophoto.

Table 2. Table captions should be placed above the tables.

Land cover classes	Hectares (ha) in persistent erosion	% of total persistently eroded area
Arable lands	493.947	22.480
Post-cultivation vegetation area	1343.107	61.125
Olive groves, vineyards and orchards	143.895	6.549
Forests and shrublands	29.568	1.346
Riparian vegetation areas	18.518	0.843
Gully areas	149.48	6.803
Urban areas, quarries, industrial sites	18.795	0.855
Total	2197.310	100

4   Conclusion

Land degradation, defined as the loss of soil's capacity to provide ecosystem services, is a complex phenomenon that requires a multi-disciplinary approach since there are many factors that contribute to its determination. For the purpose of the objective of this study, water-related soil erosion was considered as a parameter closely related to land degradation. To do this, spatial analysis techniques based on the integration of remote sensing data were applied in order to estimate the degradation processes starting from the implementation of the RUSLE model. The complexity of the phenomena and processes analyzed cannot ignore the use of a GIS working environment that allows the integration of basic spatial analysis, remote sensing image classification and more advanced geostatistical analysis. To do this, a FoSS approach was tested so that the workflow could be reduced and work in an interoperable way with other software without losing computational capacity. Moreover, thanks to the ease of management of different datasets, it was possible to quickly integrate other types of ancillary data in order to make the analysis more functional and detailed.

Specifically, the application of the RUSLE model on a monthly and annual basis, the use of the index of local autocorrelation Gi and the analysis with respect to land cover, has allowed to implement a preliminary GIS methodology useful to elaborate data necessary to enter more in detail the dynamics of land degradation. In the inland rural areas of the Mediterranean, where processes are very different, the use of GIS tools allow to carry out detailed analysis at local scale in a very effective and, in some respects, innovative way thanks to the possibility of integrating different types of data and surveys. In addition, through clustering operations, these techniques can provide useful information for spatial decision support systems (sDSS) to identify areas that are more vulnerable and need further analysis and monitoring.

References

1. Bajocco, S., Smiraglia, D., Scaglione, M., Raparelli, E., Salvati, L.: Exploring the role of land degradation on agricultural land use change dynamics. Sci. Total Environ. **636**, 1373–1381 (2018). https://doi.org/10.1016/j.scitotenv.2018.04.412
2. Basso, F., Pisante, M., Basso, B.: Soil erosion and land degradation, In: Geeson, N.A., Brandt, C.J., Thornes, J.B., (eds.) Mediterranean Desertification, a Mosaic of Processes and Responses. John Wiley & Sons, Ltd (2002)
3. Basso, B., et al.: Evaluating responses to land degradation mitigation measures in Southern Italy. Int J Environ Res. **6**(2), 367–380 (2012)
4. Bivand, R.S., Wong, D.W.S.: Comparing implementations of global and local indicators of spatial association. TEST **27**(3), 716–748 (2018). https://doi.org/10.1007/s11749-018-0599-x
5. Borrelli, P., Robinson, D.A., Fleischer, L.R., et al.: An assessment of the global impact of 21st century land use change on soil erosion. Nat. Commun. **8**, 2013 (2017). https://doi.org/10.1038/s41467-017-02142-7
6. Capolongo, D., Pennetta, L., Piccarreta, M., Fallacara, G., Boenzi, F.: Spatial and temporal variations in soil erosion and deposition due to land-levelling in a semi-arid area of Basilicata (Southern Italy). Earth Surf. Proces. Landforms: J. British Geomorph. Res. Group **33**(3), 364–379 (2008)
7. D'Odorico, P., Bhattachan, A., Davis, K.F., Ravi, S., Runyan, C.W.: Global desertification: drivers and feedbacks. Adv. Water Resour **51**, 326–344 (2013)
8. ESDAC.   https://esdac.jrc.ec.europa.eu/content/support-practices-factor-p-factor-eu. Accessed on 15 Jan 2021
9. González Díaz, J.A., Celaya, R., Fernández García, F., Osoro, K., Rosa García, R.: Dynamics of rural landscapes in marginal areas of northern Spain: past, present, and future. Land Degrad Dev. **30**, 141–150 (2019). https://doi.org/10.1002/ldr.3201
10. ISPRA. https://www.isprambiente.gov.it/it/servizi/sistema-carta-della-natura. Accessed on 14 Jan 2021

11. Kuo, K.T., Sekiyama, A., Mihara, M.: Determining C factor of universal soil loss equation (USLE) based on remote sensing. Int. J. Environ. Rural Dev. **7**(2), 154–161 (2016)
12. Lanorte, A., et al.: Integrated approach of RUSLE, GIS and ESA Sentinel-2 satellite data for post-fire soil erosion assessment in Basilicata region (Southern Italy). Geomat. Natl. Hazards Risk **10**(1), 1563–1595 (2018). https://doi.org/10.1080/19475705.2019.1578271
13. Lasanta, T., Sánchez-Navarrete, P., Medrano-Moreno, L.M., Khorchani, M., Nadal-Romero, E.: Soil quality and soil organic carbon storage in abandoned agricultural lands: Effects of revegetation processes in a Mediterranean mid-mountain area. Land Degrad Dev. **31**, 2830–2845 (2020)
14. Las Casas, G., Scorza, F., Murgante, B.: New Urban Agenda and open challenges for urban and regional planning. In: Calabrò, F., Della Spina, L., Bevilacqua, C. (eds.) New Metropolitan Perspectives. ISHT 2018. Smart Innovation, Systems and Technologies, vol. 100. Springer, Cham (2019). https://doi.org/10.1007/978-3-319-92099-3_33
15. Mitasova, H., Hofierka, J., Zlocha, M., Iverson, L.R.: Modelling topographic po-tential for erosion and deposition using GIS. Int. J. Geogr. Inf. Syst. **10**(5), 629–641 (1996)
16. Mohamadi, M.A., Kavian, A.: Effects of rainfall patterns on runoff and soil erosion in field plots Int. Soil Water Conservat. Res. **3**(4), 273–281 (2015). https://doi.org/10.1016/j.iswcr.2015.10.001
17. Nature Map. https://www.isprambiente.gov.it/it/servizi/sistema-carta-della-natura. Accessed on 10 Jan 2021
18. Nolè, G., Lasaponara, R., Lanorte, A., Murgante, B.: Quantifying Urban Sprawl with spatial autocorrelation techniques using multi-temporal satellite data. Int. J. Agric. Environ. Inf. Syst. **5**(2), 19–37 (2014). https://doi.org/10.4018/IJAEIS.2014040102
19. Ord, J.K., Getis, A.: Local spatial autocorrelation statistics: distributional issues and an application. Geogr. Anal. **27**, 286–306 (1995)
20. Pacheco, F.A.L., Sanches Fernandes, L.F., Valle Junior, R.F., Valera, C.A., Pissarra, T.C.T.: Land degradation: multiple environmental consequences and routes to neutrality. Curr. Opin. Environ. Sci. Heal. **5**, 79–86 (2018). https://doi.org/10.1016/j.coesh.2018.07.002
21. Panagos, P., Borrelli, P., Meusburger, K., van der Zanden, E.H., Poesen, J., Alewell, C.: Modelling the effect of support practices (P-factor) on the reduction of soil. Environ. Sci. Policy **51** (2015). https://doi.org/10.1016/j.envsci.2015.03.012(2015)
22. Picuno, P., Cillis, G.,Statuto, D.: Investigating the time evolution of a rural landscape: How historical maps may provide environmental information when processed using a GIS. Ecol. Eng. **139** (2019). https://doi.org/10.1016/j.ecoleng.2019.08.010
23. Peeters, A., et al.: Getis–Ord's hot- and cold-spot statistics as a basis for multivariate spatial clustering of orchard tree data. Comput. Electron. Agric. **111**, 140–150 (2015). https://doi.org/10.1016/j.compag.2014.12.011
24. Renard, K.G., Foster, G.R., Weesies, G.A., Porter, J.P.: RUSLE: revised uni-versal soil loss equation. J. Soil Water Conserv. **46**(1), 30–33 (1991)
25. Rodrigo-Comino, J., Martínez-Hernández, C., Iserloh, T., Cerdà, A.: The contrasted impact of land abandonment on soil erosion in mediterranean agriculture fields. Pedosphere (2017). https://doi.org/10.1016/S1002-0160(17)60441-7
26. Scorza, F., Casas, G.B.L., Murgante, B.: That's ReDO: Ontologies and regional development planning. In: Murgante, B., et al. (eds.) Computational Science and Its Applications – ICCSA 2012. ICCSA 2012. Lecture Notes in Computer Science, vol. 7334. Springer, Berlin, Heidelberg (2012). https://doi.org/10.1007/978-3-642-31075-1_48
27. Santarsiero, V., Nolè, G., Lanorte, A., Tucci, B., Baldantoni, P., Murgante, B.: Evolution of soil consumption in the municipality of melfi (Southern Italy) in relation to renewable energy. In: Misra, S., et al. (eds.) ICCSA 2019. LNCS, vol. 11621, pp. 675–682. Springer, Cham (2019). https://doi.org/10.1007/978-3-030-24302-9_48

28. Soils database - Basilicata Region. http://www.basilicatanet.it/suoli/carta2.htm. Accessed on 02 March 2021
29. Spdep. https://cran.r-project.org/package=spdep. Accessed on 14 Feb 2021
30. Terranova, O., Antronico, L., Coscarelli, R., Iaquinta, P.: Soil erosion risk scenarios in the Mediterranean environment using RUSLE and GIS: an application model for Calabria (southern Italy). Geomorphology **112**(3–4), 228–245 (2009)
31. THEIA Homepage. https://theia.cnes.fr/atdistrib/rocket/#/home. Accessed on 20 March 2021

A Remote Sensing Methodology to Assess the Abandoned Arable Land Using NDVI Index in Basilicata Region

Valentina Santarsiero[1,2](✉), Gabriele Nolè[1], Antonio Lanorte[1], Biagio Tucci[1], Giuseppe Cillis[1], Francesco Scorza[2], and Beniamino Murgante[2]

[1] IMAA-CNR, C.da Santa Loja, Zona Industriale, Tito Scalo, Potenza, Italy
{valentina.santarsiero,gabriele.nole,antonio.lanorte,
biagio.tucci,giuseppe.cillis}@imaa.cnr.it
[2] School of Engineering, University of Basilicata, Viale dell'Ateneo Lucano 10,
85100 Potenza, Italy
{valentina.santarsiero,francesco.scorza,
beniamino.murgante}@unibas.it

Abstract. European Commission in 2009 assessed that in the period 2015–2030 about 11% of agricultural land in the EU are under high potential risk of abandonment due to factors, which has strong and known environmental and socio-economic consequences. The diverse impacts of abandonment need to be addressed via a broader set of policy instruments to alleviate the negative effects or even - reverse the trends in the early stages of the process. The clear identification of abandoned agricultural land is fundamental for a correct mapping for the future management and monitoring of the territories. In this context, this study proposes an innovative method for the detection and mapping of abandoned arable land through the use of remote sensing techniques and geo-statistical analysis. The combined use of Sentinel 2 images and the Landsat constellation, the use of NDVI index and change detection analysis made it possible to identify the change in agricultural use and/or abandonment of land in the eastern part of the Basilicata region in the period 1990–2020. (Italy). All process has been developed integrating Remote Sensing and Geographic Information System (GIS), using open-source software.

Keywords: Abandoned land · Time series · Geographic information system

1 Introduction

Most of the European territory is used for agricultural purposes, agriculture plays an important role in the conservation of the EU environmental resource [6, 7, 21]. It interacts with and contributes to the maintenance of a wide range of valuable habitats. Appropriate land management practices and agricultural practices guarantee the protection of ecosystems [1].

© Springer Nature Switzerland AG 2021
O. Gervasi et al. (Eds.): ICCSA 2021, LNCS 12954, pp. 695–703, 2021.
https://doi.org/10.1007/978-3-030-86979-3_49

In the majority of EU Member States, agricultural land is expected to decrease not only due to land-use changes in favor of urban expansion and afforestation but also to land abandonment processes [11]. Agricultural land abandonment represents the largest land-use change process in Europe [20].

The abandonment of agricultural activities and, more generally, of the territory is under the attention of the international scientific community, as it can generate environmental and landscape impacts, as well as negative socio-economic impacts [9, 13].

Environmental and social problems related to abandonment include: (1) the reduction of landscape heterogeneity (often associated with increased fire risk); (2) soil erosion and desertification; (3) the reduction of water stocks; (4) biodiversity loss [1]. The effects on the territory are very different in relation to the territorial contexts and therefore it differs according to the climatic, ecological, biological, pedological, geological and topographical differences of the territories. The causes and extent of agricultural land abandonment also differ from region to region. In fact, in the internal marginal areas of Southern Italy, starting from the 1970s/1980s, there has been a constant and exponential abandonment which is causing a change in the ecological and pedological balance of the territory. In these areas, following an increase in cereal cultivation favored by the Agrarian Reforms for the South and an increase in mechanization, there was an increase in the agricultural area also used in the most marginal areas and little devoted to cereal cultivation. In the following decades, with the changes in socio-economic conditions, due to the crisis in the agricultural sector, which made ceariculture economically unfavorable, and following agrarian reforms linked to the community agricultural policy (i. And the "set-aside"), we witnessed a a slow and progressive abandonment of agricultural cultivation [8, 23].

Among the consequences of environmental degradation linked to agricultural abandonment there is the phenomenon of land degradation, and in the specific case, of soil erosion. In fact, the abandonment of cultivated areas can cause alterations at the pedological level, which combined with anthropic factors, climatic morphology and orography of the territory, leads to surface erosion phenomena of the soils.

This paper discusses the historical analysis of abandoned agricultural land in Basilicata Region (south Italy), providing the dynamics of changes of abandoned agricultural land and the distribution of such land across the area.

The methods used to study and evaluate the abandonment and/or change of use of agricultural land in literature are common, the most common are the application of spatial analysis through GIS, remote sensing and direct measurements on soils through sampling and laboratory investigations. The remote sensing technique is more flexible because it allows in a short time observe large areas using a series of spectral indices. The remote sensed data represents a great help to support the planner in order to study the phenomenon and monitor it. Spatial data bases to refer to are, for example, those on vegetation cover and land use maps.

Several studies have shown that Basilicata is particularly affected by the phenomenon of abandonment of agricultural soils with the consequent risk of erosion and land degradation. An estimate of the abandoned land on a municipal and regional scale is of fundamental importance to identify the characterization of the surface of soils, its variations over time and the identification of the area's most susceptible to decay. A useful tool for studying the response of vegetation to changes climate is the analysis of historical series deriving from satellite images. In many studies [10, 19, 24] is done use of multi-time series to highlight positive and/or negative anomalies of the vegetation. In this work, the analyzes conducted concern the application of techniques of remote sensing and spatial analysis for estimating historical changes in agricultural land use.

This work was based on the integration of remote sensing techniques and Information Systems Geographical (GIS) with FoSS (Free and Open-Source Software) technologies and open datasets e freely available. The use of new technologies and the integration of the different datasets of territorial data, offer the opportunity to study and monitor the evolution of the territory a large temporal and spatial scale. The increasing efficiency of analysis techniques and the interoperability of the various data, represent a strength for the planner in terms of definition of plans and strategies consistent with real needs and environmental problems [15, 18, 22].

2 Material and Methods

2.1 Dataset and Instruments

The reference satellite data is Landsat, used for the calculation of the series historical data of NDVI (Normalized Difference Vegetation Index), which can be downloaded for free (after registration) from the site [5]. Landsat is a constellation of remote sensing satellites observing the Earth, represent a basic point for the historical analysis of phenomena terrestrial. The Landsat database has remotely sensed images from 1972 to present, one maximum spatial resolution of 30 m and up to 11 spectral bands.

The land cover classification has been based on two open datasets usable. The first concerns the Corinne Land Cover 2018 (CLC) provided by the Copernicus program through the Land Monitoring Service [12]. The second is the 2013 Nature Charter in scale 1:50.000 in format freely available from the ISPRA website [14].

2.2 Study Area

The study area concerns a territorial context of the Basilicata Region particularly vulnerable to the phenomenon due to the combination of anthropogenic and natural factors. The analyzes and processing were performed in an area of approximately 1550 km^2 within the Basilicata Region (Fig. 1), comprising the territory of 17 municipalities.

Analyzing the Corine Land Cover II level 2018 [corinne] land cover map with respect to the overall study area (Table 1 and Fig. 2), it can be seen that the area is mainly occupied by agricultural areas of different type. In fact, considering the arable land, the heterogeneous agricultural areas, the permanent crops (vineyards, olive groves, orchards and wood arboriculture) and stable meadows, agricultural activity is of little interest more than 80% of the entire study area. Instead, the natural areas (wooded, shrub and grassland areas) they occupy almost 18%. The study area can ideally be divided into two areas: the west part, in correspondence with the areas with a more complex and diversified morphology, it is the most heterogeneous from a land cover point of view.

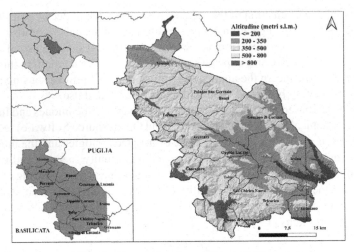

Fig. 1. Overall framing of the study area.

The remaining part, however, in the light of different morphological and geological characteristics, is represented almost exclusively by arable land and natural areas are linked to a few areas and to the impluvium areas.

3   Discussion and Results

The aim of this work is to evaluate and identify the areas subject to the phenomenon of crop abandonment and/or agricultural transition in the period 1990–2020. A first step in identifying areas subject to agricultural transition and/or crop abandonment involved the use of the normalized difference vegetation index (NDVI). NDVI is an indicator that provides crop health status based on leaves reflectance [2, 3].

This type of index is known as the most accurate indicator of ground-level biomass, as it reflects green density and photosynthetic activity [16, 17]. The NDVI vegetation index takes into account the ratio of the reflectance of the leaves to various wavelength and provides us with the health of the crop. The higher the index, the more the crop it is in optimal state. Values can be around in a range from −1 to +1 [4] (Eq. 1)

$$\text{NDVI} = \frac{NIR - RED}{NIR + RED} \tag{1}$$

The NDVI index has been extensively employed in multi-temporal approaches [2, 16, 23] because a single image of the date it is not always sufficient to differentiate crops on the basis of their spectral signatures.

The methodology herein applied, involved the use of LANDSAT 4/5 TM and LAND-SAT 8 OLI available from 1990 to 2020 (1990, 1992, 1993, 1994, 1999, 2000, 2001, 2004, 2005, 2009, 2011, 2014, 2017, 2019, 2020). To create a realistic phenological curve, it has been assumed that arable crops have an annual cyclicality, where we find a maximum of NDVI values in the spring periods (March and April) and a minimum in

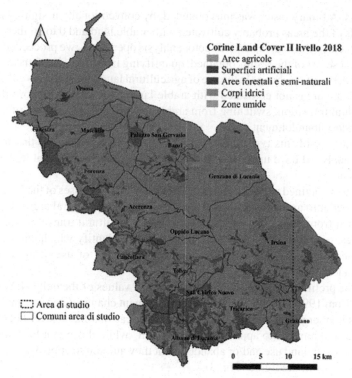

Fig. 2. Land cover map based on Corine Land Cover II level 2018 [12]

Table 1. Land cover based on Corine Land Cover I Level expressed in hectares (ha) and percentage (%) compared to the overall study area [12].

CLC 2018	Hectares	Km^2	%
Agricultural areas	126618.57	1266.18	81.45
Artificial areas	1244.04	12.44	0.80
Forest and semi-natural areas	27140.09	271.40	17.46
Water	377.29	377	0.24
Wetlands	78.99	0.79	0.05

the autumn months (October and November). In the absence of snow, the Earth's surface NDVI rarely drops to zero, as woody vegetation and soil maintain positive NDVI throughout the year. The negative and zero values are typically caused by cloud contamination, by bodies water or missing data. After calculating the NDVI difference for each year (spring - autumn), the next step was to discriminate the images related to each single year, through change detection analysis, the values of the value of the difference of NDVI of probable arable land areas (equal to NDVI values greater than 0.5) from all other values. A binary raster was thus obtained, by conventionally assigning the value 1 to the pixels of the areas probably cultivated with arable land and 0 to all the other areas.

Subsequently, through raster and vector analysis operations, we proceeded to analyze the historical series of the results obtained, quantifying in terms of km 2 the areas that do not have underwent no change in the use of agricultural land (areas always cultivated with arable land and areas not cultivated with arable land) and, above all, those that present an agricultural transition, switching from arable farming to another type of agricultural land use and/or abandonment.

The objective of this type of analysis was to be able to identify the areas that in the period analyzed have undergone a probable change in agricultural land use and/or abandonment.

The results obtained were subsequently crossed with the classes of the Nature Charter (2013) divided into agricultural areas (Fig. 17) and non-agricultural areas (Fig. 18). The data obtained from the overlay of the maps of the agricultural transition areas, divided in 3 decades, with the CNAT they made it possible to identify which classes are farms discriminated by CNAT that have been subject to change of use of agricultural land and/or abandonment.

From the preliminary investigation based on the values of the delta NDVI (dNDVI) calculated from 1990 to 2020, and from the subsequent change detection analysis on the time series it emerged that since 1990 to date the areas that have never been cultivated with arable land amount to approximately 595 km^2 while those that have undergone a possible change in land use and/or abandonment they amount to approximately 430 km^2 as can be seen from the figure (Fig. 3).

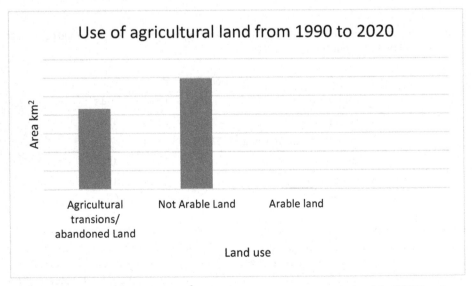

Fig. 3. Agricultural land use in km^2 resulting from the history analysis of the NDVI series.

The areas indicated as "Agricultural Transitions" indicate areas that during the thirty years 1990–2020 have undergone agricultural abandonment and/or change in land use passing from cultivation to arable land to another type of cultivation.

The Fig. 4 summarizes year by year the amount in km^2 of these areas in the years analyzed. It is clear that the years in which there has been a greater transition of agricultural land use and/or abandonment are those relating to the second and third decade.

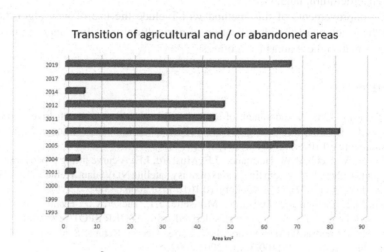

Fig. 4. Diagram in km^2 of the transition e/o abandoned area in the period 1990–2020.

It is more difficult to discriminate and evaluate abandonment from 2010 to today, as these areas may be subject to vegetative rest and/or crop rotation, and therefore need of further evaluation analyzes.

4 Conclusions

The entire procedure was carried out with QGIS e related plugins. In this work, the tools used are all open source and analytics spatial studies carried out concerned the simultaneous use of different types of free of data charge. This allows to adopt the same techniques in other territorial contexts. Landsat satellite images proved to be a particularly suitable tool for the purposes of this study provide similar information on land cover as they ensure coverage continuous and global even very distant in the past (when, very often, they represent the only source of information available).

The obtained NDVI time series data dataset provide high quality data for the mapping of the phenomenon of abandonment of arable land.

Considering the need to investigate these areas more in depth, it was carried out a study that can provide guidance for the development of an identification method of any abandoned agricultural land on a large spatial scale and managing to discriminate age of any abandonment and/or agricultural transition.

The abandonment of agricultural land, therefore, is one of the most important manifestations of change of use of cultivated land, and it is a complex phenomenon that requires a multidisciplinary approach to study its causes and consequences. Agricultural land they are typically abandoned due to a combination of economic aspects and factors natural that cause the area to rest for long periods of time.

The abandonment of agricultural land has both positive and negative effects on the environment depending on many factors such as location, frequency, subsequent management, geographical environment surrounding, and hydrological conditions of abandoned agricultural land.

Future improvements of this method will include the use of new algorithms for improve the accuracy of the identification of agricultural transition and/ or abandoned area, to distinguish these areas from others.

References

1. Rey Benayas, J.M.: Abandonment of agricultural land: an overview of drivers and consequences. CAB Rev.: Perspect. Agric. Veterinary Sci. Nutrition Natl. Resourc. **2**(057),(2007). https://doi.org/10.1079/PAVSNNR20072057
2. Bradley, B.A., Jacob, R.W., Hermance, J.F., Mustard, J.F.: A curve fitting procedure to derive inter-annual phenologies from time series of noisy satellite NDVI data. Remote Sens. Environ. **106**(2), 137–145 (2007). https://doi.org/10.1016/j.rse.2006.08.002
3. Brown, M.E., Pinzon, J.E., Didan, K., Morisette, J.T., Tucker, C.J.: Evaluation of the consistency of long-term NDVI time series derived from AVHRR,SPOT-vegetation, SeaWiFS, MODIS, and Landsat ETM+ sensors. IEEE Trans. Geosci. Remote Sens. **44**(7), 1787–1793 (2006). https://doi.org/10.1109/TGRS.2005.860205
4. de Jong, R., de Bruin, S., de Wit, A., Schaepman, M.E., Dent, D.L.: Analysis of monotonic greening and browning trends from global NDVI time-series. Remote Sens. Environ. **115**(2), 692–702 (2011). https://doi.org/10.1016/j.rse.2010.10.011
5. Earth explorer USGS home page. https://earthexplorer.usgs.gov/
6. European Commission (EC): Development of Agri-Environmental Indicatorsfor Monitoring the Integration of Environmental Concerns into the CommonAgricultural Policy. SEC (2006), vol. 1136. Commission of the European Communities, Brussels (2006)
7. European Commission: EU Agricultural Outlook: Prospects for EU agricultural markets and income 2016–2026 (2016b)
8. Falcucci, A., Maiorano, L., Boitani, L.: Changes in land-use/land-cover patterns in Italy and their implications for biodiversity conservation. Landscape Ecol. **22**(4), 617–631 (2007)
9. Food and Agriculture Organization of the United Nations (FAO): WorldAgriculture: Towards 2015/2030 an FAO Perspective. Chapter 12: Agricultureand the Environment: Changing Pressures, Solutions and Trade-offs. Earthscan, London (2003)
10. Filizzola, C., et al.: On the use of temporal vegetation indices in support of eligibility controls for EU aids in agriculture. Int. J. Remote Sens. **39**(14), 4572–4598 (2018). https://doi.org/10.1080/01431161.2017.1395973
11. Gellrich, M., Zimmermann, N.E.: Investigating the regional-scale pattern of agricultural land abandonment in the Swiss mountains: a spatial statistical modelling approach. Landsc. Urban Plan. **79**(1), 65–76 (2007)
12. Ispra/Snpa home page. https://www.isprambiente.gov.it/it/servizi/sistema-carta-della-natura
13. Khorchani, M., et al.: Effects of active and passive land use management after cropland abandonment on water and vegetation dynamics in the Central Spanish Pyrenees. Sci. Total Environ. **717**, 137160 (2020). https://doi.org/10.1016/j.scitotenv.2020.137160
14. Land Copernicus Home page. https://land.copernicus.eu/pan-european/corine-land-cover/clc 2018

15. Casas, G.L., Scorza, F., Murgante, B.: New urban agenda and open challenges for urban and regional planning. In: Calabrò, F., Spina, L.D., Bevilacqua, C. (eds.) ISHT 2018. SIST, vol. 100, pp. 282–288. Springer, Cham (2019). https://doi.org/10.1007/978-3-319-92099-3_33
16. Martínez, B., Gilabert, M.A.: Vegetation dynamics from NDVI time series analysis using the wavelet transform. Remote Sens. Environ. **113**(9), 1823–1842 (2009). https://doi.org/10.1016/j.rse.2009.04.016
17. Mohammed, I., Marshall, M., de Bie, K., Estes, L., Nelson, A.: A blended census and multiscale remote sensing approach to probabilistic cropland mapping in complex landscapes. ISPRS J. Photogramm. Remote. Sens. **161**, 233–245 (2020)
18. Murgante, B., Borruso, G., Balletto, G., Castiglia, P., Dettori, M.: Why Italy first? health, geographical and planning aspects of the COVID-19 outbreak. Sustainability **12**(12), 5064 (2020). https://doi.org/10.3390/su12125064
19. Nolè, G., Lasaponara, R., Lanorte, A., Murgante, B.: Quantifying Urban Sprawl with spatial autocorrelation techniques using multi-temporal satellite data. Int. J. Agric. Environ. Inf. Syst. **5**(2), 19–37 (2014). https://doi.org/10.4018/IJAEIS.2014040102
20. Castillo, C.P., Aliaga, E.C., Lavalle, C., Llario, J.C.M.: An assessment and spatial modelling of agricultural land abandonment in Spain (2015–2030). Sustainability **12**(2), 560 (2020). https://doi.org/10.3390/su12020560
21. REG.CEE 1272/88
22. Scorza, F., Las, G.B., Casas, B.M.: That's ReDO: ontologies and regional development planning. In: Murgante, B., et al. (eds.) Computational Science and Its Applications – ICCSA 2012, pp. 640–652. Springer Berlin Heidelberg, Berlin, Heidelberg (2012). https://doi.org/10.1007/978-3-642-31075-1_48
23. Statuto, D., Cillis, G., Picuno, P.: Using historical maps within a GIS to analyze two centuries of rural landscape changes in Southern Italy. Land **6**(3), 65 (2017)
24. Suziedelyte Visockiene, J., Tumeliene, E., Maliene, V.: Analysis and identification of abandoned agricultural land using remote sensing methodology. Land Use Policy **82**, 709–715 (2019). https://doi.org/10.1016/j.landusepol.2019.01.013

Assessment and Monitoring of Soil Erosion Risk and Land Degradation in Arable Land Combining Remote Sensing Methodologies and RUSLE Factors

Biagio Tucci[1]([⊠]), Gabriele Nolè[1]([⊠]), Antonio Lanorte[1]([⊠]),
Valentina Santarsiero[1,2]([⊠]), Giuseppe Cillis[1]([⊠]), Francesco Scorza[2]([⊠]),
and Beniamino Murgante[2]([⊠])

[1] IMAA-CNR, C.da Santa Loja, Zona Industriale, Tito Scalo, 85050 Potenza, Italy
{biagio.tucci,gabriele.nole,antonio.lanorte,
giuseppe.cillis}@imaa.cnr.it
[2] School of Engineering, University of Basilicata, Viale dell'Ateneo Lucano 10,
85100 Potenza, Italy
{valentina.santarsiero,francesco.scorza}@imaa.cnr.it,
{valentina.santarsiero,beniamino.murgante}@unibas.it

Abstract. Soil degradation is a phenomenon that describes the degradation of soil quality due to which agricultural land in particular is unproductive as a consequence of the loss of ability to produce crops and biomass. The causes are many but, especially in the inland areas of the Mediterranean regions, some dynamics related to agriculture have particularly influenced the grading process. Specifically, agricultural over exploitation with unsustainable practices and land abandonment are causing ecological alterations that require contextual analysis to assess the medium and long-term effects. The aim of this work is to investigate the role of some factors that make up the RUSLE index have in the detection and monitoring of potentially degraded areas.In particular, the areas cultivated with arable crops were chosen as the area to be analyzed, because the average annual rate of soil erosion (A factor in RUSLE equation) is high despite the presence of vegetation cover and shown evident problems due to the phenomenon of degradation. In order to identify the potential degraded areas, two factor of RUSLE index have been correlated: C factor that describes the vegetation cover of the soil and A factor which represent the amount of potential soil erosion. All methodologies have been applied in a rural area in the northern part of Basilicata Region (Italy) using GIS and remote sensing approaches, as allows the possibility to perform a series of a complex studies and can be efficiently implemented in environmental monitoring plans.

Keywords: Land degradation · Remote sensing · QGIS · RUSLE method · C-factor

© Springer Nature Switzerland AG 2021
O. Gervasi et al. (Eds.): ICCSA 2021, LNCS 12954, pp. 704–716, 2021.
https://doi.org/10.1007/978-3-030-86979-3_50

1   Introduction

The issue of environmental protection and sustainable development has been brought to the attention of the scientific community in recent decades with the aim of studying its management dynamics, defining the processes for achieving specific targets to preserve the global ecosystem. Due to a constant and increasing anthropic activity [1], the intensive production and exploitation of natural resources, also linked to the phenomena caused by climate change, we are observing an ever-diminishing capacity of the soil to satisfy the needs of the community [2].

Based on these considerations, we wanted to focus the study on one of the most widespread phenomena globally, land-degradation defined as a reduction or loss, in arid, semi-arid and dry sub humid areas, of biological or economic productivity. and the complexity of rainfed farmland, irrigated farmland or range, pasture, forest and woodland resulting from land uses or a process, or combination, of processes, including processes arising from human activities and housing models [3, 4].

In Italy 10% of the national territory is at risk of land degradation and in particular in Basilicata region the percentage of the territory affected by the phenomenon is 24.4% among the highest at national level preceded only by Sicily. To address the land degradation problem, Italy has defined a "LND Land Degradation Neutral-ty" program which provides for the balancing of the recovered soil with the degraded one [5, 6].

Soil degradation processes consist in the loss of the biophysical properties of the soil determined mainly by factors such as erosion and salinization [7].

The causes are many but, especially in the inland areas of the Mediterranean regions [5], some dynamics related to agriculture have particularly influenced the degradation processes. Specifically, agricultural over exploitation with unsustainable practices, the land abandonment, are causing ecological alterations that need analysis to evaluate the medium- and long-term effects. Indeed, some agricultural practices, which are oriented to an overexploitation of the land, to an excess of mechanized processing and the use of chemistry [8] are leading to a reduction of soil quality and subsequent degradation (erosion caused by water and wind, compaction, decrease of soil organic carbon and soil biodiversity; salinization, sodification and contamination of the soil by heavy metals and pesticides, or by excess of nitrates and phosphates). The other phenomenon, namely the abandonment of agricultural activities and more in general of the territory, is to the attention of the scientific community as it can produce environmental and landscape impacts, as well as socio-economic impacts [9]. The effects can be very variable in relation to territorial contexts and therefore they are dependent on climatic, ecological, biological, pedological and topographical factors.

The present work was developed starting from implementation of RUSLE method [10], using Remote Sensing techniques and Geographic Information Systems (GIS). Once the monthly erosion rate A was calculated, the Getis spatial autocorrelation index [11] was used in order to obtain a persistent/non persistent binary map consisting of 0 and 1, where 0 stands for non-persistent erosion and 1 for persistent erosion persistent/permanent erosion respect the entire observed period. Spatial autocorrelation measures the degree of dependence between events, considering at the same time the similarity and their distant relationships. Self-correlation indicators measure whether and to what extent a data set is autocorrelated across the study region. In the presence of positive spatial autocorrelation, similar values of the variable are spatially grouped, while in the presence of negative spatial autocorrelation, the dissimilar values of the variable are spatially grouped; the absence of spatial autocorrelation indicates a random distribution of values in space.

One of the most important factors of the RUSLE and of greatest scientific interest is represented by C Cover-management factor [12] which measures the type of management of the agricultural activity that is carried out on that soil and can take values ranging from 0 to 1 where 0 indicates good cover and agricultural management practice while 1 indicates a condition of poor management and a condition of non-vegetated soil. It is in fact the vegetation cover that plays a fundamental role in determining the degree of vulnerability of a particular area. Through the C factor compared with the persistent/n erosion rate, it is therefore possible to determine which agricultural areas are potentially degrading. In these areas there are phenomena of altered photosynthetic activity due to organic loss or climate change or incorrect management of arable land [13]. The aim of this work is to provide a tool for analyzing the phenomenon of land degradation on a large scale with a good accuracy.

2 Study Area

The analyzes and calculations were carried out in an area of approximately 1554 km^2 within the Basilicata Region (Fig. 1) including the municipalities of Tricarico, Ginestra, Irsina, Acerenza, Cancellara, Albano di Lucania, Forenza, Maschito, Oppido Lucano, San Chirico Nuovo, Grassano, Palazzo San Gervasio, Tolve, Genzano di Lucania, Venosa and Banzi. The area is characterized by a typically Mediterranean climate, with a pronounced bi-seasonal regime with hot and dry summers and humid and cold winters. Natural risks and anthropogenic activities make this area an interesting study context because the combination of human activities and natural risks contribute to the establishment of degradation phenomena.

For a more complete and detailed analysis of the characteristics of the biotypes of the study area, the Natural Habitats Map of Italy (CNAT 2013) was used because, compared to the Corine Land Cover map [14], it presents more detail in the description of land use [15]. Given the greater level of detail and accuracy, CNAT was chosen as a reference for spatial and statistical analysis (Fig. 2).

As CNAT indicates, agricultural land use classes are prevalent in the study area. In particular, just over 65% is represented by arable land including the classes "Extensive and intensive arable land" (in a higher percentage) and "Extensive crops and complex agricultural systems". The difference between the two classes refers to the structural and ecological characteristics. In fact, in continuity with what is expressed previously, the extensive crops class refers to highly fragmented cereal systems with small edges of hedges, thickets, stable meadows, etc., typical of the most morphologically heterogeneous areas. In fact, it is possible to identify them in the eastern and southern part of the study area. In particular, the southern area has less coverage of arable land and a considerable variability in terms of land cover.

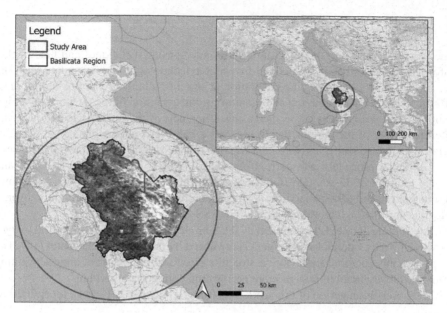

Fig. 1. Study Area

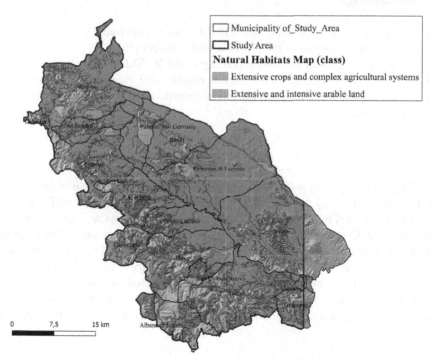

Fig. 2. Natural Habitats Map 2013 of Study Area (only arable land classes)

3 Dataset

The work was based on the integration of remote sensing techniques and Geographic Information Systems (GIS) with open-free source technologies and open data sets. The use of new technologies and the integration of the different datasets of territorial data, offer the possibility of studying and monitoring the evolution of the territory on a high temporal and spatial scale. The increasing efficiency of the analysis techniques, the interoperability of the various data represents a valid tool for the planner in terms of defining plans and strategies consistent with the real needs and environmental problems.

The entire procedure was carried out with QGIS [16] open source software and related plugins. QGIS is a GIS (Geographic Information System) software that allows you to analyze and edit spatial data, it supports both vector and raster data; moreover, it integrates processing algorithms such as GRASS GIS and SAGA GIS.

The starting dataset is represented by the Sentinel 2 medium-high resolution images provided by the Copernicus Mission [17] reworked by the THEIA data center [15]. The purpose of this scientific and technical structure is to facilitate the use of images resulting from spatial observation through more performing correction algorithms.

The observation period of this work runs from September 2019 to October 2020.

4 Methodology

Soil erosion was estimated using the RUSLE model (Revised Universal Soil Loss Equation) [10] developed from the previous USLE model [19].

The estimate of annual soil loss according to the RUSLE model (Eq. 1) is a function of five variables relating to the rainfall regime, soil characteristics, topography, crop coverage and management and conservation cultivation practices, according to the following formula:

$$A = R * K * LS * C * P \tag{1}$$

where,

A [Mg * ha-1* y − 1] is the annual average soil loss, R [MJ mm h − 1ha − 1yr − 1] is the rainfall intensity factor, K [Mg h MJ − 1mm − 1] is the soil erodibility factor, L (dimension-less) is the slope length factor, S [dimensionless] the slope steepness are calculated from [20]. Factor, C (dimensionless) is the land cover factor, and P (dimensionless) is the soil conservation or prevention practice factors [21]. Once the annual erosion rate was calculated, the problem of studying degrade phenomena was tackled through the correlation between the factor C and the eorsion rate A.

Analyzing the trend of the R factor (Fig. 3) it is highlighted that during the whole time period the average values on the study area were recorded in November 2019 and in March 2020.

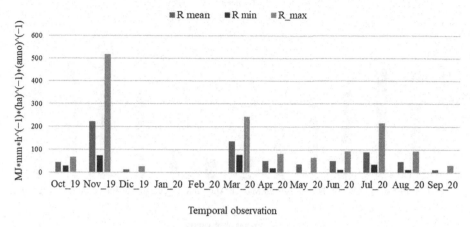

Fig. 3. R factor

By analyzing the graph of (Fig. 4), however, the average value of A in the month of March is very high. This means that despite the vegetation cover, the soil is significantly eroded by rain.

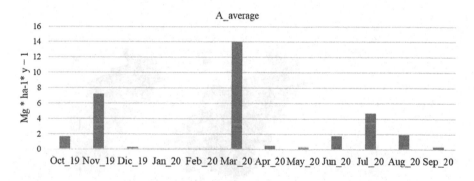

Fig. 4. A average

Finally, the trend of the C factor is also reported (Fig. 5), which shows a very low value of C which corresponds to a discrete vegetation cover.

It was therefore decided on the basis of the analysis of the monthly averages of the R, A and C factors to understand if there was a very strong relationship between them in reference to the month of March 2020 where the values show a high erosion compared to a coverage of the soil already advanced.

The methodology starts from the concept that in order to highlight if there is a proportionality between the erosion value of A and the factor C, this must be verified by trying to keep the other factors contributing to the final erosion value in a certain range.

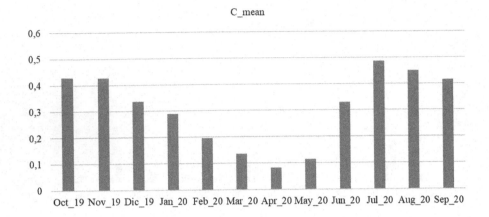

Temporal observation

Fig. 5. C_average

To do this, it was decided to use the slope and the rainfall erosivity map divided into classes and to analyze the values of A in a range set by the classes for both slope and erosivity [22]. The following Fig. 6, shows the input maps of the proposed methodology.

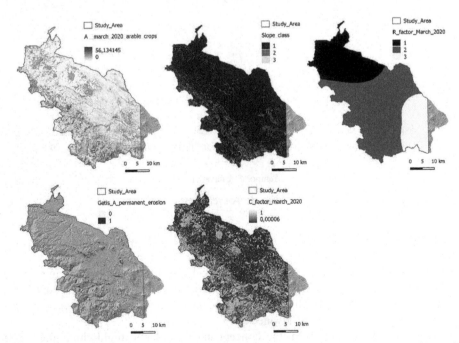

Fig. 6. Input map: erosion A in the upper left, the slope in 3 classes in the upper center, the erosion factor R in 3 classes on the right, the permanent erosion of Getis in the lower left and finally the factor C

The block diagram (Fig. 7) shows the methodology developed for the identification of potentially degraded areas. Arable land covered by vegetation is certainly more protected from erosion because the leaf surface present interposes a physical barrier to the impact of rain and the effect of debris sliding downstream [23]. Identifying the cultivated agricultural areas in which the erosion phenomenon is high, especially in the periods of growth of the vegetation, implies that that area could over time show problems caused by a not very luxuriant vegetation and an increasingly scarce growth and therefore decide to abandon that land or use it for another use For this reason, by isolating the C factor from the other factors and linking it to A in the periods of maximum vegetative activity, it is possible to obtain degraded areas as they show a high rate of erosion despite the soil being covered by vegetation.

Subsequently, the combination of all possible couples was elaborated, obtaining 9 layers of the erosion value A which fall into the same class for S slope and R erosivity. Referred to March 2020. Since the goal is to search for the correlation between A and the factor C was chosen to compare them through the linear regression analysis tool by means of which the residual map for each pair regr [A_ (i, j), C] was obtained.

In the following Table 1 the value of the correlation coefficient R has been reported for each comparison, which has moderate values only for some pairs.

The residual maps A_res (i, j) quantifies the error pixel by pixel ε calculated on the difference between the estimated value of A and real A.

$$Y = AX + B + \epsilon \qquad (2)$$

The direct proportionality (2) is given by the points closest to the regression line and therefore by the points where the value of the residuals ε is small in absolute value. Having chosen the most correlated layers R > 0.25, it was assumed to set a threshold on the choice of residuals and therefore on the error since the coefficient R is not very high. To select the values of A in which the error ε can be considered minimum, a threshold was defined (3)

$$\epsilon = |Yreal - Yest| < 2 \qquad (3)$$

around the regression line by selecting only the pixels of A most correlated with C. Finally, a threshold value greater than o equal to 5 [Mg * ha-1- * y − 1] has been chosen. The last step was to compare the map thus obtained with the permanent erosion map A, the result of which represents those agricultural areas in degradation.

5 Result and Discussion

The use of software that can implement very complex calculation procedures allows to obtain very accurate processing with few hardware resources available. All this in order to be able to monitor areas at risk of degradation in the shortest possible time.

Thanks to the interoperability of the available datasets, it is possible to aggregate multiple sources and expand the potential of remote sensing techniques for safeguarding the soil resource.

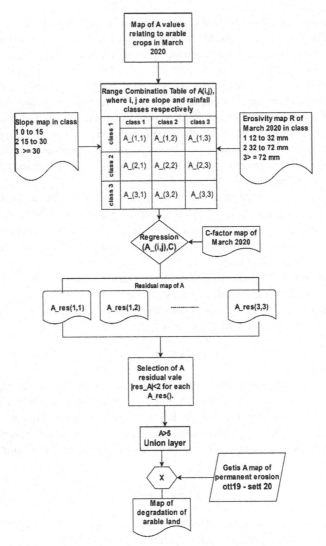

Fig. 7. Flow chart methodology

In this context, the proposed methodology aims to be able to give an innovative approach in the study of the phenomenon of land degradation. The first step in defining the methodology is the calculation of erosion A.

In fact, starting from this data and analyzing the factors that make up the RUSLE, a raster map was developed that identifies those agricultural areas potentially in degradation and showing conditions of poor productivity. The Fig. 8 shows the study area on the left, while details on some municipalities affected by the degradation phenomenon have been reported on the right by submitting the most recent orthophoto.

The following Table 2 shows for each municipality of the study area the estimated surface of the degraded area, the average value of potential erosion A relative to the

Table 1. R coefficient

regr(A_(i,j),C)	R
regr(A_(1,1),C)	−0.061179
regr(A_(1,2),C)	−0.182321
regr(A_(1,3),C)	**−0.265939**
regr(A_(2,1),C)	−0.18986
regr(A_(2,2),C)	**−0.314881**
regr(A_(2,3),C)	**−0.464801**
regr(A_(3,1),C)	0.060026
regr(A_(3,2),C)	**−0.367359**
regr(A_(3,3),C)	**−0.466316**

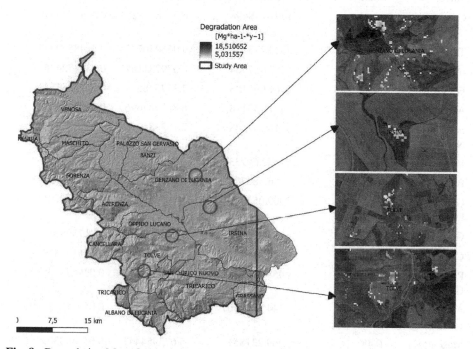

Fig. 8. Degradation Map. On the left side the Study area - In the right, particular of degradation area detected in red in the ortophoto (2017)

month of March 2020 and finally the ratio between the identified degraded area. by the algorithm and the cultivated area for each municipality. The municipality with the highest degraded surface is Tolve with 70.32 (ha) with a degraded area and agricultural area ratio of approximately 1%, followed by Genzano di Lucania with approximately 64 (ha). If the data of Genzano di Lucania may be obvious due to the very large crops land area, in the case of the municipality of Tolve the phenomenon already seems to have a greater weight.

Compared to the data of the relationship between degraded area and crops land area, an interesting fact to note refers to the municipality of San Chirico Nuovo which shows the highest percentage 1.48% compared to all the municipalities in the study area to which particular attention should be paid.

The surface of the degraded areas is approximately 250 hectares, totaling 0.25% of the entire area intended for arable land.

Table 2. Surfaces of the degraded areas -Summarize

Municipality	Degradation of arable land (ha)	Arable lands area (ha)	RUSLE (A) Average	Degradation Area/Arable land (%)
Tolve	70.32	7255.937701	7.367268234	0.9691373176
Genzano di Lucania	63.48	17918.38498	6.952897228	0.3542729999
Tricarico	36.2	8520.473156	9.066046735	0.4248590347
Irsina*	19.48	14953.27964	8.579731184	0.130272425
Forenza	14.72	6461.095185	7.3275489	0.2278251531
Acerenza	13	4497.243118	6.867987696	0.2890659824
San Chirico Nuovo	12.52	841.4932548	7.653385216	1.487831296
Venosa	6.44	11430.60733	5.785923422	0.05633996352
Banzi	3.08	6786.586724	6.46151887	0.04538363872
Oppido Lucano	2.68	3909.054331	6.709750104	0.06855878105
Ginestra	2.24	536.6577852	5.937695989	0.417398212
Cancellara	2.12	2205.97083	7.614363337	0.09610281202
Palazzo San Gervasio	1.68	4584.127325	6.926314922	0.03664819672
Albano di Lucania	0.76	1445.747507	7.738875188	0.05256796199
Maschito	0.48	3569.221851	5.673954447	0.01344830946
Grassano*	0	1231.173906	0	0
TOTAL	**249,2**	**96147.05462**	**0**	**0.259186307**

*. the data relating to the two municipalities is partial

6   Conclusion

Large-scale satellite monitoring and the availability of open data offers innovative support for the development of environmental monitoring methodologies thanks to which it is now possible to address the phenomenon of soil degradation with more in-depth analyzes. In this work, attention has been focused on the phenomenon of erosion because it is both a consequence and a cause of the phenomenon of soil degradation.

This kind of approach is not tied to any particular software or data but can be easily replicated with new generation images of greater detail.

Finally, it could be useful to investigate the land degradation phenomenon with respect to the other factors that determine potential erosion A.

References

1. Santarsiero, V., Nolè, G., Lanorte, A., Tucci, B., Baldantoni, P., Murgante, B.: Evolution of soil consumption in the municipality of Melfi (Southern Italy) in Relation to Renewable Energy. In: Misra, S., et al. (eds.) ICCSA 2019. LNCS, vol. 11621, pp. 675–682. Springer, Cham (2019). https://doi.org/10.1007/978-3-030-24302-9_48
2. Biancalani, R., Nachtergaele, F., Petri, M., Bunning, S.: Land degradation assessment in drylands methodology and results (2013)
3. United Nations: Convention to Combat Desertification in those Countries Experiencing Serious Drought and/or Desertification, Particularly in Africa. Int. Leg. Mater. **33** (1994). https://doi.org/10.1017/s0020782900026711
4. Hamdy, A., Aly, A.: Land degradation, agriculture productivity and food security. In: Fifth International Scientific Agricultural Symposium, pp. 708–717 (2014)
5. Munafò, M. (a cura di): Consumo di suolo, dinamiche territoriali e servizi ecosistemici. Edizione 2020 (2020). 978-88-448-0964-5
6. Assennato, F., et al.: Land degradation assessment for sustainable soil management. Ital. J. Agron. **15**, 299–305 (2020). https://doi.org/10.4081/ija.2020.1770
7. Matano, A.-S., et al.: Effects of land use change on land degradation reflected by soil properties along Mara River, Kenya and Tanzania. Open J. Soil Sci. **05**, 20–38 (2015). https://doi.org/10.4236/ojss.2015.51003
8. Basso, F., Pisante, M., Basso, B.: Soil erosion and land degradation. In: Presented at the Mediterranean Desertification, a Mosaic of Processes and Responses (2002)
9. Lasanta, T., Sánchez-Navarrete, P., Medrano-Moreno, L., Khorchani, M., Nadal-Romero, E.: Soil quality and soil organic carbon storage in abandoned agricultural lands: Effects of revegetation processes in a Mediterranean mid-mountain area. L. Degrad. Dev. **31** (2020). https://doi.org/10.1002/ldr.3655
10. Yorder, D.C, Foster, G.R., Renard, K.G.: Predicting soil erosion by water: a guide to conservation planning with the Revised Universal Soil Loss Equation (RUSLE). In: Agricultural Handbook No. 703. p. 404 (1997)
11. Lanorte, A., Danese, M., Lasaponara, R., Murgante, B.: Multiscale mapping of burn area and severity using multisensor satellite data and spatial autocorrelation analysis. Int. J. Appl. Earth Obs. Geoinf. **20**, 42–51 (2012). https://doi.org/10.1016/j.jag.2011.09.005
12. Panagos, P., Borrelli, P., Meusburger, K., Alewell, C., Lugato, E., Montanarella, L.: Estimating the soil erosion cover-management factor at the European scale. Land Use Policy **48**, 38–50 (2015). https://doi.org/10.1016/j.landusepol.2015.05.021

13. Imbrenda, V., DEmilio, M., Lanfredi, M., Simoniello, T., Ragosta, M., Macchiato, M.: Integrated indicators for the estimation of vulnerability to land degradation. In: Soil Processes and Current Trends in Quality Assessment (2013). https://doi.org/10.5772/52870
14. Copernicus Land Monitoring: CLC 2018—Copernicus Land Monitoring Service
15. Carta della Natura—Italiano, https://www.isprambiente.gov.it/it/servizi/sistema-carta-della-natura. Accessed on 03 May 2021
16. Welcome to the QGIS project!. https://qgis.org/en/site/. Accessed on 03 May 2021
17. Sentinel-2 - Data Products - Sentinel Handbook – Sentinel. https://sentinel.esa.int/web/sentinel/missions/sentinel-2/data-products. Accessed on 03 May 2021
18. Theia Data and Services Center – Theia. https://www.theia-land.fr/en/theia-data-and-services-center/. Accessed on 04 May 2021
19. Wischmeier, W.H., et Smith, D.D.: Predicting rainfall erosion losses - A guide to conservation planning. U.S. Department of Agriculture, Washington D.C., Agriculture Handbook 537, p. 58 (1978)
20. Lazzari, M., Gioia, D., Piccarreta, M., Danese, M., Lanorte, A.: Sediment yield and erosion rate estimation in the mountain catchments of the Camastra artificial reservoir (Southern Italy): A comparison between different empirical methods. CATENA 127, 323–339 (2015). https://doi.org/10.1016/j.catena.2014.11.021
21. Panagos, P., Borrelli, P., Meusburger, K., van der Zanden, E.H., Poesen, J., Alewell, C.: Modelling the effect of support practices (P-factor) on the reduction of soil erosion by water at European scale. Environ. Sci. Policy. 51, 23–34 (2015). https://doi.org/10.1016/j.envsci.2015.03.012
22. Gayen, A., Saha, S., Pourghasemi, H.R.: Soil erosion Assessment using RUSLE model and its Validation by FR probability model. Geocarto Int. 35 (2019). https://doi.org/10.1080/10106049.2019.1581272.
23. Alexandridis, T.K., Sotiropoulou, A.M., Bilas, G., Karapetsas, N., Silleos, N.G.: the effects of seasonality in estimating the C-factor of soil erosion studies. L. Degrad. Dev. 26, 596–603 (2015). https://doi.org/10.1002/ldr.2223

Correction to: Computational Science and Its Applications – ICCSA 2021

Osvaldo Gervasi, Beniamino Murgante, Sanjay Misra,
Chiara Garau, Ivan Blečić, David Taniar,
Bernady O. Apduhan, Ana Maria A. C. Rocha,
Eufemia Tarantino, and Carmelo Maria Torre

Correction to:
O. Gervasi et al. (Eds.): *Computational Science*
and Its Applications – ICCSA 2021, **LNCS 12954,**
https://doi.org/10.1007/978-3-030-86979-3

In the originally published version, in the article "The Impact of COVID-19 Pandemic on the Perception of Public Transportation Users in Amman (Jordan)" (DOI: https://doi.org/10.1007/978-3-030-86979-3_28) in Table 5, which is at Page 396 of the published book, the statement "(before the pandemic)" was added in the headings by mistake. The statement has been removed. The correct headings are "Number of walking days", "Number of days using the private car", "Number of days using public transportation", "Reasons for choosing the means of traveling".

In the originally published version of chapter 31, the name of one of the Authors was incorrect. The Author's name has been corrected as "Cézar Henrique Barra Rocha".

The updated version of these chapters can be found at
https://doi.org/10.1007/978-3-030-86979-3_28
https://doi.org/10.1007/978-3-030-86979-3_31

Author Index

Printed in the United States
by Baker & Taylor Publisher Services